Essentials of Economics in Context

Essentials of Economics in Context is specifically designed to meet the requirements of a one-semester introductory economics course that provides coverage of both microeconomic and macroeconomic foundations. It addresses current economic challenges, paying specific attention to issues of inequality, globalization, unpaid work, technology, financialization, and the environment, making the text a genuinely twenty-first century introduction to economics.

Aspects of history, institutions, gender, ethics, and ecology are integrated throughout the text, and economic analysis is presented within broader themes of human well-being, and social and environmental sustainability. Theoretical expositions in the text are kept close to reality by integrating numerous real-world examples and by presenting the material in the recognized accessible and engaging style of this experienced author team.

Key features of *Essentials of Economics in Context* include:

- an inclusive approach to economics, where the economy is analyzed within its social and environmental context
- an innovative chapter examining data on various economic indicators
- focus on goals of human well-being, stability, and sustainability, and inclusion of core and public purpose spheres, instead of solely focusing on market activities
- a wealth of online materials such as slides, test banks, and answers to exercises in the book

This text is the ideal resource for one-semester introductory economics courses globally.

Neva Goodwin is Distinguished Fellow at the Economics in Context Initiative at the Global Development Policy Center at Boston University, USA.

Jonathan M. Harris is Senior Research Associate at the Global Development and Environment Institute at Tufts University, USA.

Pratistha Joshi Rajkarnikar is Associate Director at the Economics in Context Initiative at the Global Development Policy Center at Boston University, USA.

Brian Roach is Director of the Theory and Education Program at the Tufts University Global Development and Environment Institute, and a lecturer at Tufts and Brandeis Universities, USA.

Tim B. Thornton is Senior Research Fellow at the Economics in Context Initiative at the Boston University Global Development Policy Center, USA, and Director of the School of Political Economy, Australia.

Essentials of Economics in Context

Neva Goodwin,
Jonathan M. Harris,
Pratistha Joshi Rajkarnikar,
Brian Roach and
Tim B. Thornton

Routledge
Taylor & Francis Group

NEW YORK AND LONDON

First published 2021
by Routledge
52 Vanderbilt Avenue, New York, NY 10017

and by Routledge
2 Park Square, Milton Park, Abingdon, Oxon, OX14 4RN

Routledge is an imprint of the Taylor & Francis Group, an informa business

Library of Congress Cataloging-in-Publication Data
A catalog record for this book has been requested

ISBN: 978-0-367-24561-0 (hbk)
ISBN: 978-0-367-24547-4 (pbk)
ISBN: 978-0-429-28308-6 (ebk)

Typeset in Bembo
by Apex CoVantage, LLC

Visit the companion website: http://www.bu.edu/eci/essentials

Contents

CONTENTS

Figures

Tables

Boxes

Preface

For students taking a one-semester introductory economics course, *Essentials of Economics in Context* lays out the key concepts of economics in a manner that is thorough, up to date, and highly readable. Whether students take this class simply to gain some understanding of how economics can be useful to them or go on to further studies in economics or business, this book will equip them with the tools and the critical understanding that they need to succeed. It introduces students both to the standard topics taught in most introductory courses and to a broader set of topics to deepen comprehension of the economic realities of the twenty-first century.

The study of economics should not be highly abstract but closely related to real-world events. *Essentials of Economics in Context* addresses this challenge by keeping the theoretical exposition close to experience. The authors believe that students will achieve a deeper understanding of economic theory if they can relate it to contemporary issues of interest and importance.

This textbook is written to encourage engaged and critical thinking about topics in economics. While demonstrating the uses of economic theory, it also provides a variety of viewpoints. Woven throughout the book are themes of great importance in everyday life as well as for an understanding of the economy. There is discussion of standard neoclassical market theory and related topics, but the text also integrates broader themes of social and environmental well-being and sustainability, with specific attention to issues of inequality, globalization, unpaid work, technology, and the environment, as well as the financialization of the economy. These elements are not add-ons but are integrated within discussions of historical, institutional, political, and social factors that affect, and are affected by, the economy.

The microeconomic and macroeconomic subject matter in *Essentials of Economics in Context* summarizes and simplifies material from the two-semester text *Principles of Economics in Context* (2nd ed.) and the single-semester texts *Macroeconomics in Context* (3rd ed.) and *Microeconomics in Context* (4th ed.), also published by Routledge.

On pages xxxi–xxxiv, you will find several possible course plans based on different emphases (such as ecological, global, and human development). We hope that this will help in planning the course that will best suit the needs of instructors and students.

CONTENT AND ORGANIZATION

Some of the innovative features of this text are apparent in even a quick scan of the table of contents, the sample course outlines on pp. xxxi–xxxiv and the data presentations in Chapter 0. Although this textbook takes a broader and more contextual approach to economic activities, it fits these within a familiar overall organizational strategy.

- **Part I, "The Context for Economic Analysis,"** presents the themes of the book and the major actors in the economy. It begins with the innovative "Chapter 0," which provides background information and statistics on some key economic, ecological, and socioeconomic indicators. Students are introduced to a range of economic questions and goals, to basic empirical and theoretical tools, and to the basic activities and institutions of a modern economy.

- **Part II, "Microeconomic Analysis: Consumption, Production, and Markets,"** introduces basic supply and demand analysis, along with chapters on consumer behavior, firm behavior, market structures, and the labor market. Most of this material will look very familiar to teachers of economics, although this text gives greater recognition than is typical to real-world market institutions. The chapter on consumer behavior is based on the latest studies in behavioral economics and includes the topic of consumerism. The chapter on market structures describes the idealized model of perfect competition, along with models of market power, and the labor chapter discusses the changing nature of work and contemporary labor market challenges.

- **Part III, "Macroeconomic Theory and Policy,"** introduces basic macroeconomic definitions and accounting methods and explores the issue of macroeconomic fluctuations. This part begins with a chapter on accounting systems, including traditional measures (growth, inflation, and unemployment), as well as new accounting measures that consider economic contributions of the natural environment, unpaid household labor, and other previously uncounted factors. This is followed by chapters presenting Keynesian and classical theories of the determination of aggregate demand and the effects of fiscal and monetary policies. This section also develops a dynamic aggregate supply/aggregate demand model of output and inflation, with inflation rather than price level on the vertical axis, and extensive examples of real-world applications.

- **Part IV, "The Global Economy, Development, and Sustainability,"** addresses the contemporary issues of financial instability, inequality, trade, globalization, economic development, and the environment. While the first chapter of this part is presented from a largely U.S. perspective, the remaining three chapters widen the lens to explore current global issues of globalization and trade, poverty and inequality, economic growth, human development, and global environmental challenges.

In order to focus on "contextual" discussions, we have generally placed more formal instruction in algebraic modeling techniques in optional *online appendices* to the chapters, which can be accessed at **www.bu.edu/eci/education-materials/**

textbooks/essentials-of-economics-in-context/. Contextual themes include prominent consideration of new thinking in behavioral economics; analysis of financial instability and market bubbles; social and environmental issues; and policy responses to problems of unemployment, inequality, and environmental damage.

WHAT MAKES THIS BOOK DIFFERENT FROM OTHER TEXTS?

This text covers the traditional topics included in most economics texts but treats them from a broader, more holistic perspective. The following chapter-by-chapter synopsis shows how this book manages both to be "similar enough" to fit into a standard curriculum and "different enough" to respond to commonly expressed needs and dissatisfactions.

Chapter 0, "Economics and Well-Being," presents graphically illustrated data on 16 variables, including data for the United States as well as international comparisons, using a selected set of countries. The related website **www.bu.edu/ eci/education-materials/textbooks/essentials-of-economics-in-context/** allows users to see the same variables listed in order for all countries in the world where such data are available. This innovative chapter can be used in a variety of ways, including as an introduction to later topics, as a reference for use with other chapters, or as material to draw on in designing research projects.

Chapter 1, "Economic Activity in Context," defines economics as "the study of how people manage their resources to meet their needs and enhance their well-being," which immediately sets economics within a broader context, with the overarching concept of "well-being" encompassing social, environmental, and other dimensions. Most textbooks discuss three essential activities—production, distribution, and consumption—but we add the activity of "resource management" to draw attention to the importance of maintaining capital stocks, including stocks of natural (environmental) capital. Basic concepts of abundance, scarcity, tradeoffs, and opportunity costs are introduced and illustrated with production possibility curve analysis.

Chapter 2, "Foundations of Economic Analysis," introduces standard concepts of economic modeling. It includes a review of graphing techniques and the use of empirical data. In addition to the usual economic "circular flow" diagram, this chapter presents a model of economic activity as embedded in social and physical contexts and relates this approach to issues of economic concern. Economic activity is described in terms of three "spheres": business, public purpose, and "core" or household/community spheres. The final section presents the definitions and the key institutional requirements of the market. We describe the operation of market systems by introducing the concepts of market power, externalities, transaction costs, information and expectations, and concern for human needs and equity. The early introduction of these topics allows us to demonstrate why markets, while useful, are not on their own sufficient for organizing economic life in the service of well-being.

Chapter 3, "Supply and Demand," presents basic supply and demand analysis, including discussions of the slopes of the curves, factors that shift the curves, equilibrium and market adjustment, and the signaling and rationing functions of prices.

The chapter also includes discussions of price elasticities of demand and supply and income elasticity of demand. Our contextual approach, however, leads to some subtle shifts in presentation. The model is explicitly presented as a thought experiment—a human-created analytical tool that may help us gain insight—rather than as a set of "laws" about "the way the world works." Instead of concentrating solely on the efficiency effects of markets, the contextual approach demands that distributional consequences and power issues also be raised.

Chapter 4, "Consumption and Decision-Making," begins by presenting the traditional utility-theoretic model of consumer behavior and elaborating on the topics of individual choice, rationality, and self-interest. It updates and amplifies standard expositions, drawing on studies of human economic behavior by scholars such as Herbert Simon and Daniel Kahneman, and introduces issues of organizational structure and behavior. We also delve into topics of "consumer society," including influences of social and environmental contexts on consumer behavior. The final section presents policy inferences from our contextual model of consumer behavior.

In **Chapter 5, "Production,"** we focus on the costs of production. We present the traditional model of a firm's cost structure, with a focus on marginal costs. The chapter includes a discussion of fixed and variable inputs; diminishing, constant, and increasing returns; total and marginal costs; and short-run versus long-run issues. We set this model in context in two important ways. First, the chapter encourages students to reflect on the idea that because of externalities, private and social net benefits from production may not be equivalent. Second, the chapter offers examples of cases where other economic actors (besides firms) make production decisions and cases where other methods of decision-making are necessary.

Chapter 6, "Market Structure," discusses the theoretic characteristics and the zero-economic-profit and efficiency outcomes of perfectly competitive markets, along with traditional models of monopoly, monopolistic competition, and oligopoly. These different market structures are presented along a competitiveness continuum, with perfect competition and pure monopoly the "ideal types" representing the opposite extremes. Rather than simply concluding that perfectly competitive markets are always efficient, it balances the perfectly competitive model with a discussion of efficiency and equity, including the topics of path dependence and network externalities.

Chapter 7, "Markets for Labor," includes the traditional derivation of profit-maximizing labor demand by a perfectly informed and perfectly competitive firm and the upward-sloping and backward-bending individual paid labor supply curves. The chapter also offers additional ways of understanding how wages are determined, including theories of compensating wage differentials, market power, worker motivation, and labor market discrimination.

Chapter 8, "Macroeconomic Measurement," presents an introduction to national income accounting, including the definitions and measurements for GDP growth, unemployment, and inflation as key macroeconomic metrics. The chapter then discusses the limitations of GDP as a measure of economic progress and notes how the production and investments undertaken in the "household and institutions" and government sectors have historically been deemphasized in national accounting.

The chapter gives an introduction to alternative measures of economic performance, including the Genuine Progress Indicator, the Better Life Index, the Human Development Index, and other current approaches that consider the contributions of unpaid work, natural environment, and other factors that affect our well-being.

Chapter 9, "Economic Fluctuations and Macroeconomic Theory," introduces the analysis of business cycles, presents the classical theory of savings-investment balance through the market for loanable funds, and develops Keynesian aggregate demand analysis. Our contextual approach emphasizes the possibility of instability and unemployment rather than focusing primarily on adjustment to full-employment equilibrium. These issues are placed in historical context, including discussions on the Great Depression and the crisis of the 1970s, along with more recent developments and challenges for the twenty-first century.

Chapter 10, "Fiscal Policy," balances formal analysis of fiscal policy with real-world data and examples. The chapter discusses taxation specifically in the United States. It presents the basic Keynesian analysis on the impacts of changes in taxes and government spending on equilibrium income. The text also discusses classical and supply-side perspectives and the issue of "crowding out" and "crowding in." The section on debt and deficit should give students a basic understanding of deficits, debt, and how these affect the economy. The difference between automatic stabilizers and discretionary policy is made clear, and recent fiscal policies are discussed.

Chapter 11, "Money and Monetary Policy," presents the basics of money and the banking system. Students are introduced to the process of money creation by banks through the fractional reserve system. We discuss the Federal Reserve's structure, functions, and monetary policy tools that it employs to create money. The chapter also spotlights the monetary economy in the United States since the year 2000, with particular attention to the role of monetary policy in the 2007–2008 financial crisis and the nature of the monetary response to the crisis. The final section discusses classical, Keynesian, and monetarist theories and policy issues.

Chapter 12, "Aggregate Supply, Aggregate Demand, and Inflation: Putting It All Together," addresses the tricky problem of how to teach the relationship between output and inflation to introductory students in a way that is simple yet intellectually defensible. The model presented in this chapter has many features that will be familiar to instructors. But unlike *AS/AD* models that put the price level on the vertical axis, implying a static equilibrium at a certain level of prices, this model has the inflation rate on the vertical axis, which makes it more relevant for discussing historical examples as well as current events.* Rather than focusing on long-run full-employment equilibrium output, we emphasize how the macroeconomy adjusts dynamically to often-unpredictable economic events. (More classically oriented approaches are also discussed in the chapter.)

Chapter 13, "Financial Instability and Economic Inequality," applies many of the insights introduced in earlier chapters to explain some of the causes and consequences of the financial crisis that led to the Great Recession, including excessive reliance on finance and growing inequality. It presents theories of financial instability and discusses financial reforms needed to avoid such crises in the future. The chapter also includes definitions and measurements of inequality and discusses the underlying causes of inequality in the United States and possible policy responses.

Chapter 14, "The Global Economy and Policy," covers the gains–from–trade story that is important in discussing topical issues of global commerce. We also discuss some possible negative impacts of trade as they may affect both developed and developing countries and put these in the context of the globalized world as it differs from the historical example of trade between England and Portugal. The circular-flow picture of our macroeconomic model is completed in this chapter with the inclusion of the foreign sector. This chapter also provides a detailed treatment of the factors that influence currency exchange rates worldwide.

Chapter 15, "How Economies Grow and Develop," presents basic concepts related to economic growth, such as the Rostow and Harrod-Domar models, which emphasize the importance of investment in manufactured capital. The chapter also focuses on broader concepts of development and provides examples of how investment in other types of capital—for example, human or natural capital—can be equally, if not more, important. Discussions of dependency theory and export-oriented development strategies are included in the chapter. Country diversity is a central theme, and data on growth, poverty, and inequality levels across countries are presented to provide a global perspective. The chapter highlights that the "one size fits all" approach to economic development emphasizing structural reforms—such as those embodied in the Washington Consensus—has produced disappointing results and that different approaches are required to meet sustainable development goals.

Chapter 16, "Economics of the Environment," examines global ecological challenges, including population growth, depletion of renewable and nonrenewable resources, and pollution. The chapter shows how an understanding of externalities makes supply-and-demand analysis more relevant and raises the problem of the valuation of externalities. The chapter also discusses the activity of resource management, with specific focus on the management of common property resources and public goods. While it covers standard theories such as the environmental Kuznets curve, it raises serious challenges to the belief that economic growth and markets can solve this century's social and environmental problems on their own. The chapter presents ideas for alternative approaches, including "green Keynesianism" and sustainable employment strategies. The final section presents economic analysis on global climate change and discusses policy responses to address the current climate crisis.

SPECIAL FEATURES

Each chapter in this text contains many features designed to enhance student learning.

- *Key terms* are highlighted in boldface throughout the text, and important ideas and definitions are set off from the main text.
- *Discussion Questions* at the end of each section encourage immediate review of what has been read and relate the material to the students' own experience. The frequent appearance of these questions throughout each chapter helps students review manageable portions of material and thus boosts comprehension. The questions can be used for participatory exercises involving the entire class or for small-group discussion.

- *End-of-Chapter Review Questions* are designed to encourage students to create their own summary of concepts. They also serve as helpful guidelines to the importance of various points.
- *End-of-Chapter Exercises* encourage students to work with and apply the material, thereby gaining increased mastery of concepts, models, and investigative techniques.
- Throughout the chapters, boxes enliven the material with real-world illustrations drawn from a variety of sources regarding applications of economic concepts and recent economic developments.
- In order to make the chapters as lively and accessible as possible, some formal and technical material (suitable for inclusion in some but not all course designs) is carefully and concisely explained in online chapter appendices, available at the book's website: **www.bu.edu/eci/education-materials/textbooks/essentials-of-economics-in-context/**
- A glossary at the end of the book contains all key terms, their definitions, and the number of the chapter(s) in which each was first used and defined.

SUPPLEMENTS

The supplements package for this book includes an *Instructor's Resource Manual* and *Test Bank* to accompany *Essentials of Economics in Context*. To access these electronically, send a request via e-mail to **eci@bu.edu** with information to verify your instructor status.

For each chapter, the *Instructor's Resource Manual* includes a statement of objectives for student learning, a list of key terms, a lecture outline, and answers to all review questions and end-of-chapter exercises. In addition, the "Notes on Discussion Questions" section provides not only suggested answers to these questions but also ideas on how the questions might be used in the classroom. Sections titled "Web Resources" and "Extensions" provide supplementary material and links to other passages in the book or other materials that can be used to enrich lectures and discussion.

The Test Bank includes multiple-choice and true/false questions for each chapter. The correct answer for each question is indicated.

PowerPoint slides of figures and tables from the text and a *Student Study Guide* that provides ample opportunity for students to review and practice the key concepts are available for free download at: **www.bu.edu/eci/education-materials/textbooks/essentials-of-economics-in-context/**.

HOW TO USE THIS TEXT

This textbook has been written with the goal of providing students with an introduction to key concepts in microeconomics and macroeconomics. This text draws from the two-semester *Principles of Economics in Context* textbook. However, unlike most one-semester textbooks that simply exclude specific chapters from the two-semester version, this text has been specifically designed to meet the requirements of a one-semester course.

The feedback that we have received from instructors who have used our *In Context* textbooks has been enthusiastic and gratifying. We have found that this book works in a variety of courses with a variety of approaches, and we would like to share some of these instructors' suggestions on tailoring this book to meet your own course needs.

On pages xxxi–xxxiv, you will find several possible course plans based on different emphases (such as ecological, social, global, and human development). We hope that this will help in planning the course that will best suit the needs of instructors and students.

NOTE

* Regarding the theoretical underpinnings of our model, our downward-sloped *AD* curve is based on the *AD* curve developed by David Romer ["Keynesian Macroeconomics without the LM Curve," *Journal of Economic Perspectives* 14:2 (2000): 149–169] and adopted by other introductory textbooks writers, including John B. Taylor (*Principles of Macroeconomics,* Houghton Mifflin, various editions). Our curved *AS* is based on the notion of an expectations-augmented Phillips curve, translated into inflation and output space. The idea of a dynamically evolving economy, rather than one always headed toward settling at full employment, is an approach based on Keynes's own (rather than new Keynesian) thought.

Acknowledgments

Essentials of Economics in Context was written under the auspices of the Economics in Context Initiative (ECI) at Boston University's Global Development Policy Center and the Global Development and Environment Institute (GDAE) at Tufts University. All contributors of written materials were paid through grants raised by the Global Development and Environment Institute.

This text has been a long time in the making, and many people have been involved along the way. First, we would like to thank Wassily Leontief, who initially urged us to write a book on economic principles for students in transitional economies. He provided inspiration and encouragement during those early years. We also are enormously grateful to Kelvin Lancaster, who allowed us to use *Modern Economics: Principles and Policy* (a textbook that he and Ronald Dulany wrote in the 1970s) as a jumping-off point for our work.

We would also like to express immense gratitude to Dr. Julie Nelson, Professor Emeritus of Economics at University of Massachusetts Boston, and Dr. Mariano Torras, Professor of Economics at Adelphi University, for their contributions to our *Macroeconomics in Context* and *Microeconomics in Context* textbooks. This textbook draws on the material from these other textbooks, where they have been our co-authors.

Dr. James Devine of Loyola Marymount University, Los Angeles, contributed to the macro modeling chapters, and Ben Beachy contributed to Chapter 13 on financial crisis.

We thank a number of instructors who were exceptionally generous in giving us detailed comments, including Alison Butler, Willamette University; Gary Flomenhoft, University of Vermont; Robin King, Georgetown University; Dennis Leyden, University of North Carolina, Greenville; Valerie Luzadis, SUNY-ESF, Syracuse; Eric Nilsson, California State University San Bernardino; Chiara Piovani, University of Utah; Rebecca Smith, Mississippi State University; Saranna Thornton, Hampden-Sydney College; Marjolein van der Veen, Bellevue Community College; and Thomas White, Assumption College.

David Garman, of the Tufts University Economics Department, arranged an opportunity for us to class-test a very early draft of the micro portion of the text. Other faculty who assisted in the developmental stage of this text include Steven Cohn (Knox College), Julie Heath (University of Memphis), and Geoffrey Schneider (Bucknell University).

We would also like to thank Robert Scott Gassler (Vesalius College of the Vrije Universiteit Brussels), Julie Matthaei (Wellesley College), and Adrian Meuller (CEPE Centre for Energy Policy and Economics), who, among others, provided helpful comments on an early draft of the text.

This early draft also formed the basis for editions designed for transitional economies, which were translated and published in Russia (Russian State University for the Humanities, 2002) and Vietnam (Hanoi Commercial University, 2002). Economists who contributed ideas to the transitional economies texts included Oleg Ananyin (Institute of Economics and Higher School of Economics, Moscow), Pham Vu Luan and Hoang Van Kinh (Hanoi Commercial University), Peter Dorman (Evergreen College), Susan Feiner (University of Southern Maine), Drucilla Barker (Hollins College), Robert McIntyre (Smith College), Andrew Zimbalist (Smith College), Cheryl Lehman (Hofstra University), and Raymond Benton (Loyola University).

Among the many faculty who provided valuable comments on earlier editions of the micro and macro sections, we would like to thank Sandy Baum (Skidmore College), Jose Juan Bautista (Xavier University of Louisiana), Gary Ferrier (University of Arkansas), Ronald L. Friesen (Bluffton College), Abu N. M. Wahid (Tennessee State University), Fred Curtis (Drew University), James Devine (Loyola Marymount University), Richard England (University of New Hampshire), Mehrene Larudee (Bates College), Akira Motomura (Stonehill College), Shyamala Raman (Saint Joseph College), Judith K. Robinson (Castleton State College), Marjolein van der Veen (Bellevue Community College), Timothy E. Burson (Queens University of Charlotte), Will Cummings (Grossmont College), Dennis Debrecht (Carroll College), Amy McCormick Diduch (Mary Baldwin College), Miren Ivankovic (Southern Wesleyan University), Eric P. Mitchell (Randolph-Macon Woman's College), Malcolm Robinson (Thomas More College), June Roux (Salem Community College), Edward K. Zajicek (Kalamazoo College), Steve Balkin (Roosevelt University), Ernest Diedrich (College of St. Benedict/St. John's University), Mark Maier (Glendale Community College), Ken Meter (Kennedy School of Government), Sigrid Stagl (University of Leeds), Myra Strober (Stanford University), David Ciscel (University of Memphis), Polly Cleveland (Columbia University), Judex Hyppolite (Indiana University), Bruce Logan (Lesley College), Valerie Luzadis (SUNY-ESF), Maeve Powlick (Skidmore College), Mark Wenzel (Wayne State University), Rachel Bouvier (University of Southern Maine), and Armagan Gezici (Keene State College).

Special thanks go to the many students who provided feedback on previous editions, including Brian Cotroneo and Marc McDunch of Boston College; Castleton State College students Kevin Boucher, April L. Cole, Shawn Corey, Lisa Dydo, Tim Florentine, Roger Gillies, Ashley Kennedy, Nicole LaDuc, Matt Lane, Noah Bartmess, Joesph O'Reilly, Kevin Perry, James Riehl, Jessica Schoof, Josh Teresco, Jennifer Trombey, Monica Tuckerman, Craig Wetzel, and Liza Wimble; Colby College student Eric Seidel; Drew University students Sigourney Giblin, Erin Hoffman, Jennifer Marsico, Leo A. Mihalkovitz, Peter Nagy, and Sofia Novozilova; Catherine Hazzard, a student at Saint Joseph College; Stonehill College student Anthony Budri; Sarah Barthelmes, Kathryn Cash, Aris Dinitraropolous, Jen Hanley, Krista Leopold, Mary Pat Reed, E. Rose, Kaitlyn Skelley, and Ryan Tewksbury from the University of New

Hampshire; Rebecca Clausen of the University of Oregon; and students from Will Cummings's class at Grossmont College.

Essential support work on research and manuscript preparation, including data analysis for Chapter 0, was provided by GDAE Research Coordinator Mitchell Stallman, Max Schmulewitz, and Hannah Mirviss. Administrative and outreach support at the Global Development and Environment Institute was provided by Angela Trowbridge, Monica Barros, and Erin Coutts. We also thank the staff at Routledge for their enthusiasm and meticulous work in getting this book to press.

Finally, we would like to thank the many students we've had the privilege to teach over the years—you continually inspire us and provide hope for a bright future.

Sample Course Outlines

Providing both standard and innovative materials for introductory economics, *Essentials of Economics in Context* can be used as the basis for a variety of approaches, depending on which topics and approaches are of particular interest.

To help identify the chapter assignments that make the most sense for a particular class, we have put together some ideas for course outlines subsequently. Arranged in terms of broad selections and more specific emphases, they are designed to help instructors choose among chapters when there is not enough time to cover everything in this textbook.

We understand that in many departments, one primary objective of the introductory course is to teach in some detail "how (neoclassical) economists think." For instructors who choose to focus primarily on neoclassical content, the most traditional combination of the selections described subsequently—the Base Chapters, combined with some or all of the Basic Microeconomics and Basic Macroeconomics Selection and the Neoclassical Emphasis and Macro-Modeling Emphasis chapters—will provide what you need. This combination of chapters does not come close to exploiting fully the richness of *Essentials of Economics in Context*, but the contextual discussions (a hallmark of this text) that are woven into the standard material will broaden the students' understanding of economic theory and provide tools for critical thinking.

Many instructors seek to combine coverage of traditional neoclassical ideas with other material. Addressing such users of *Essentials of Economics in Context*, we suggest that you make use of the special structure of the book, which enables you to introduce traditional concepts in your introductory course while still reserving class time for other areas of interest. Ecological sustainability, for example, is an issue of increasing importance and is deeply linked to the functioning of the economy. For this focus, the Base Chapters Selection and most of the Basic Microeconomics and Basic Macroeconomics Selection could be combined with the "Ecological Emphasis" Selection.

Some instructors and students may have less interest in the formalities of economic modeling, in which case it might make sense to cover the Base Chapters Selection, some material from the Basic Microeconomics and Basic Macroeconomics Selection, and much more material from the topical emphases such as "Human Development" and "Poverty/Inequality/Social Justice." For coverage of alternative and critical perspectives, the "Critiques of Traditional Approaches" and "Keynesian/Post-Keynesian/Institutionalist" Selection will be useful.

The data presented in Chapter 0 cover a wide variety of topics and applications, and it may be appropriate to refer back to this chapter for almost any of the selections subsequently.

BASE CHAPTERS SELECTION

- Chapter 1, "Economic Activity in Context"
- Chapter 2, "Foundations of Economic Analysis"
- Chapter 3, "Supply and Demand"

BASIC MICROECONOMICS SELECTION

- Chapter 4, "Consumption and Decision-Making," Sections 1 and 2
- Chapter 5, "Production"
- Chapter 6, "Market Structure," Sections 2–5
- Chapter 7, "Markets for Labor," Sections 1 and 2

BASIC MACROECONOMICS SELECTION

- Chapter 8, "Macroeconomic Measurement," Sections 1–3
- Chapter 9, "Economic Fluctuations and Macroeconomic Theory"
- Chapter 10, "Fiscal Policy"
- Chapter 11, "Money and Monetary Policy"
- Chapter 12, "Aggregate Supply, Aggregate Demand, and Inflation: Putting It All Together"
- Chapter 15, "How Economies Grow and Develop"

TRADITIONAL EMPHASIS

- Chapter 4, "Consumption and Decision-Making," Sections 1 and 2 and online Appendix
- Chapter 6, "Market Structure," Section 2 and online Appendix
- Chapter 7, "Markets for Labor," Section 1 and online Appendix

EMPHASIS ON CRITIQUES OF TRADITIONAL APPROACHES

- Chapter 1, "Economic Activity in Context," Section 2
- Chapter 2, "Foundations of Economic Analysis," Section 2
- Chapter 3, "Supply and Demand," Section 6
- Chapter 4, "Consumption and Decision-Making," Sections 3 and 6
- Chapter 6, "Market Structure," Sections 1 and 6
- Chapter 7, "Markets for Labor," Section 3
- Chapter 8, "Macroeconomic Measurement," Section 4
- Chapter 14, "The Global Economy and Policy," Section 3

APPLIED ECONOMICS/POLICY EMPHASIS

- Chapter 4, "Consumption and Decision-Making," Section 6
- Chapter 6, "Market Structure," Section 6
- Chapter 7, "Markets for Labor," Sections 3 and 4
- Chapter 10, "Fiscal Policy," Sections 1, 3, and 4
- Chapter 13, "Financial Instability and Economic Inequality," Section 4
- Chapter 14, "The Global Economy and Policy," Section 4
- Chapter 16, "The Economics of the Environment," Section 5

ECOLOGICAL EMPHASIS

- Chapter 4, "Consumption and Decision-Making," Section 5
- Chapter 8, "Macroeconomic Measurement," Section 4
- Chapter 16, "The Economics of the Environment"

GLOBAL EMPHASIS

- Chapter 14, "The Global Economy and Policy"
- Chapter 15, "How Economies Grow and Develop"
- Chapter 16, "The Economics of the Environment"

HUMAN DEVELOPMENT EMPHASIS

- Chapter 8, "Macroeconomic Measurement," Section 4
- Chapter 15, "How Economies Grow and Develop"

BEHAVIORAL ECONOMICS EMPHASIS

- Chapter 4, "Consumption and Decision-Making," Sections 3, 4, and 6

KEYNESIAN/POST-KEYNESIAN/INSTITUTIONALIST EMPHASIS

- Chapter 9, "Economic Fluctuations and Macroeconomic Theory," Sections 3 and 4
- Chapter 12, "Aggregate Supply, Aggregate Demand, and Inflation: Putting it All Together," Section 4 and online Appendix
- Chapter 13, "Financial Instability and Economic Inequality"

MACRO-MODELING EMPHASIS

- Chapter 9, "Economic Fluctuation and Aggregate Demand," online Appendix, "An Algebraic Approach to the Multiplier"
- Chapter 10, "Fiscal Policy," online Appendix, "More Algebraic Approaches to the Multiplier"
- Chapter 12, "Aggregate Supply, Aggregate Demand, and Inflation: Putting it All Together," online Appendix, "More Schools of Macroeconomics"
- Chapter 15, "How Economies Grow and Develop," Section 1

MONEY AND FINANCE EMPHASIS

- Chapter 11, "Money and Monetary Policy"
- Chapter 13, "Financial Instability and Economic Inequality," Sections 1 and 2

POVERTY/INEQUALITY/SOCIAL JUSTICE EMPHASIS

- Chapter 1, "Economic Activity in Context," Section 2
- Chapter 4, "Consumption and Decision-Making," Section 4
- Chapter 6, "Market Structure," Section 6
- Chapter 7, "Markets for Labor," Sections 2 and 3
- Chapter 8, "Macroeconomic Measurement," Section 4
- Chapter 13, "Financial Instability and Economic Inequality," Section 3
- Chapter 15, "How Economies Grow and Develop"

CONTRASTING SCHOOLS OF THOUGHT EMPHASIS

- Chapter 9, "Economic Fluctuations and Macroeconomic Theory," Sections 2, 3, and 4
- Chapter 12, "Aggregate Supply, Aggregate Demand, and Inflation: Putting it All Together," Section 4, and online Appendix, "More Schools of Macroeconomics"
- Chapter 16, "Economics of the Environment," Sections 4 and 5

Part I

The Context for Economic Analysis

Economics and Well-Being

What comes to your mind when you think of the word "economics"? Perhaps you think about things like money, the stock market, unemployment, gross domestic product (GDP), and supply and demand. These things are definitely important in our study of economics, and we will spend much of our time in this book studying these concepts.

But the goals of economics are about much more than these. As we will see in Chapter 1, economics is *the study of how people manage their resources to meet their needs and enhance their well-being*. The term "well-being" can mean different things to different people. Traditional economic indicators like growth, income, inflation, and unemployment clearly affect our well-being. But so does our health, the quality of our environment, our leisure time, our perceptions of fairness and justice, and many other factors. In this book, we will take an inclusive approach to well-being. Our study of economics will help you better understand many of the policies and outcomes we observe and think about ways that we might be able to improve things. Many of the topics that we will study relate to current economic and political debates, such as economic inequality, the environment, taxes, and globalization.

The purpose of this introductory chapter is to provide an overview of many of the topics we will cover in more detail later in the book. You may find some of this information surprising. Sometimes data-based results differ from common perceptions and media representations. But we have tried to be as objective as possible by presenting a wide range of data from reliable sources. Good data are essential for informed debates about how to enhance well-being in our communities.

The information in this chapter is divided into two sections:

1. Time trends graphs presenting **time-series** data that show how a particular variable changes over time; and
2. Bar graphs presenting **cross-sectional** data that show observations on a particular variable for many subjects (such as individuals, firms, countries, or regions) at one point in time. In this chapter, we look at cross-sectional data for different countries to make international comparisons on specific economic variables, but

you will see similar graphs comparing individuals or firms at several points in the book. While we mainly focus on the United States here, and in much of the rest of the book, it is important to see individual country data within the global context. If you are interested in the performance of specific countries we have not included here, detailed tables are available on the book's companion website: www.bu.edu/eci.

---

time-series data: observations of how a numerical variable changes over time
cross-sectional data: observations on a variable for different subjects at one point in time

---

The graphs that appear in this chapter are:

Time Trend Graphs

1. U.S. GDP per Capita
2. U.S. Unemployment Rate
3. U.S. Inflation Rate
4. U.S. Income Inequality
5. Gender-Based Earnings Inequality
6. Global International Trade
7. Global Carbon Dioxide Emissions

Bar Graphs: International Comparisons

8. GDP per Capita
9. Unemployment Rate
10. Inflation Rate
11. Trade Balance
12. Income Inequality
13. Absolute Poverty
14. Educational Performance
15. Life Expectancy
16. Carbon Dioxide Emissions per Capita

International comparison rankings are based on the available data, including the highest and lowest values for each variable. While there are over 200 countries in the world, data are not available for all countries for each variable, so the number of countries ranked for each variable differs.[1] The countries shown here have been chosen to convey the full range of results, with a focus on the United States (the U.S. results are always highlighted). Major countries, such as China, India, and the United Kingdom, are also included in most figures. Country rankings are provided based on the available data, with the "highest" rank at the top and the "lowest" at the bottom. However, this does not always mean that it is best to be at the top. For example, we present graphs showing unemployment rate, the percentage of people living in absolute poverty, and carbon dioxide emissions per capita. Obviously, it is not a good thing to be ranked first (the highest) for these variables.

BOX 0.1 U.S. GDP PER CAPITA

What it is: GDP, or gross domestic product, is a measure of the total value of goods and services produced in a country. As discussed in Chapter 8, GDP is widely used as a measure of a nation's economic development. However, GDP only measures market activities and ignores aspects such as health, education, inequality, and environmental sustainability that are central to economic well-being. Hence, using GDP as a measure of well-being is highly controversial. GDP per capita, shown here, is GDP divided by the country's population, and the time trend of GDP per capita shows how average income changes over time.

The results: U.S. GDP per capita has increased more than threefold since 1960. The progression has not been entirely smooth, with pauses and declines, especially during periods of economic recession, but the overall trend is upwards. One of the largest breaks in this trend was the recession of 2007–2009, discussed in detail in Chapter 13. As the graph shows, growth of GDP per capita started to recover after 2010. GDP per capita has continued to grow, reaching over $54,000 in 2018.

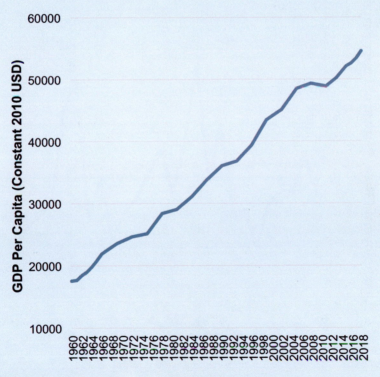

Figure 0.1 *GDP per Capita, 1960–2018 (Constant 2010 USD)*

Source: World Bank, World Development Indicators database.

BOX 0.2 U.S. UNEMPLOYMENT RATE

What it is: The unemployment rate is a measure of the proportion of people in the labor force who are seeking jobs but unable to find them (discussed in Chapters 7 and 8). The measure does not include people who have part-time work but would like full-time work, nor does it include "discouraged workers" who have given up looking for work. The unemployment rate typically falls during economic expansions and rises during and immediately after economic recessions.

The results: U.S. unemployment has varied since 1960 between about 3 and 10 percent. In expansionary periods such as the late 1960s and the late 1990s, it was between 3.5 and 5 percent. In recessions, it has typically risen above 6 percent, with peaks of nearly 10 percent in 1982 and 2009, resulting from severe recessions. Since 2016, the unemployment rate has remained below 5 percent, and in 2018 it reached a nearly five-decade low of 3.9 percent, suggesting strong labor market conditions.

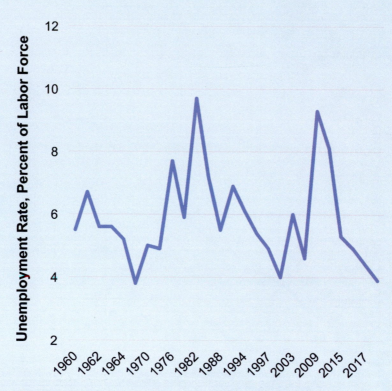

Figure 0.2 *Unemployment Rate (Annual Average), 1960–2018*

Source: U.S. Bureau of Labor Statistics, Current Population Survey, 2019.

BOX 0.3 U.S. INFLATION RATE

What it is: The inflation rate is a measure of the average increase in prices between one year and the next. It is measured by the change in the consumer price index (CPI), discussed in Chapter 8. There are various versions of the CPI; the graph presented here is based on the CPI-U, which measures the cost of living in urban areas.

The results: The U.S. inflation rate has varied considerably since 1960, with noticeable peaks in the late 1970s and early 1980s. At these times, the inflation rate rose above 10 percent (referred to as "double-digit inflation"). This level of inflation is considered significantly harmful to an economy, as discussed in Chapter 9. Since 1992, inflation rates in the United States have generally been fairly low, not rising above 4 percent, and averaging around 2 percent. During the 2007–2009 recession, inflation briefly fell to zero, arousing concern about deflation—negative inflation or generally falling prices. (Although some might think that falling prices would be a good thing, sustained deflation can be very damaging to businesses and reduce employment, as occurred during the Great Depression of the 1930s.)

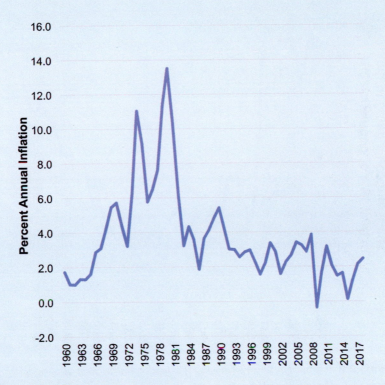

Figure 0.3 *Inflation Rate, 1960–2018*

Source: U.S. Bureau of Labor Statistics, Consumer Price Index (CPI-U), 2019.

BOX 0.4 INCOME INEQUALITY

What it is: The graph presented here shows the trend in income inequality in the United States between 1925 and 2014. Percentage share of income going to the richest 10 percent of the population is used as an indicator of inequality. A decline in the value of this indicator implies lower inequality, with a greater share of income going to the bottom 90 percent of the population.

The results: Income inequality in the United States has varied considerably over time. It declined sharply in the early 1940s, with the economic prosperity during and after World War II, along with the implementation of New Deal policies. While inequality remained relatively stable until the 1960s, it has been increasing since then, reaching almost as high as the peak inequality levels right before the Great Depression. This trend in inequality can be explained by the changes in tax and labor market policies, among other things, as will be discussed in detail in Chapter 13.

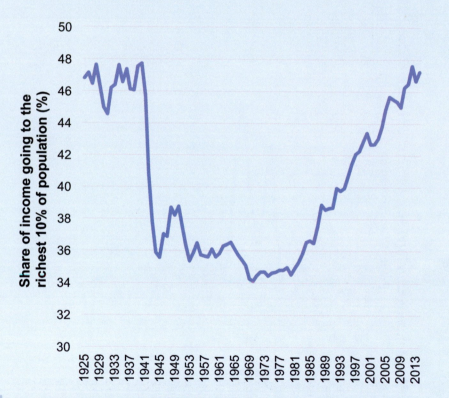

Figure 0.4 *Percentage Share of Income Earned by the Richest 10 Percent of Population, 1925–2014*

Source: Thomas Piketty, Emmanuel Saez, and Gabriel Zucman. "Distributional National Accounts: Methods and Estimates for the United States," Appendix II: Detailed Distributional Series. http://gabriel-zucman.eu/usdina/

BOX 0.5 GENDER-BASED EARNINGS INEQUALITY

What it is: The "gender wage gap" is the difference in median earnings between men and women who work full-time. The graph presented here shows women's median earnings in the United States as a percentage of men's median earnings, over the period 1979 to 2017.

The results: In 1979, women working full-time in the United States only earned 62 percent of what men earned. During the 1970s and 1980s, the gender wage gap closed considerably. By the early 2000s, women working full-time earned about 80 percent of what men earned. Since then, the wage gap has remained relatively constant. In 2017, women earned 81.8 percent of what men earned. Is this clear evidence of gender discrimination? We'll discuss this topic in more detail in Chapter 7.

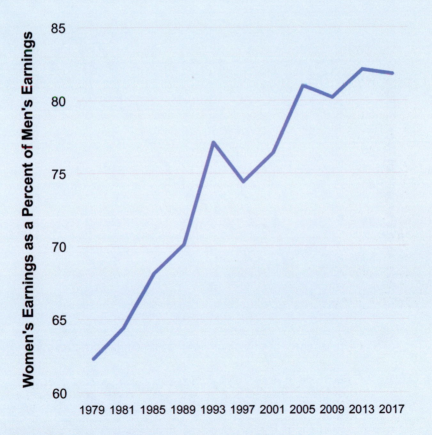

Figure 0.5 *Gender-Based Earnings Inequality, 1979–2017*

Source: U.S. Bureau of Labor Statistics. 2018. "Highlights of Women's Earnings in 2017." Report 1075.

BOX 0.6 GLOBAL INTERNATIONAL TRADE

What it is: The graph presented here shows the volume of international trade (sum of exports and imports) as a percentage of world economic production between 1960 and 2017. This is one way to get a quick, partial snapshot of the degree of "globalization."

The results: At least as measured by international trade, the world has clearly become more globalized in recent decades. About 24 percent of all goods and services produced in the world were traded in 1960. Currently about 58 percent of world production is traded internationally. We can see that the global financial crisis of 2007–2009 temporarily reduced international trade but that it has since recovered to previous levels. We will discuss the topic of international trade further in Chapter 14.

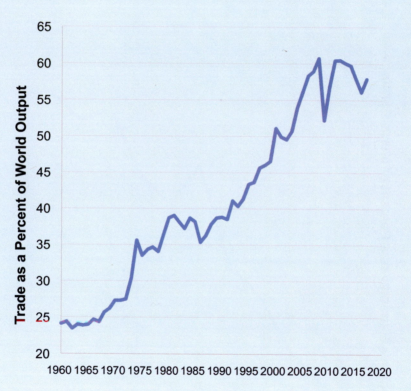

Figure 0.6 *Global International Trade, 1960–2017*

Source: World Bank, World Development Indicators database.

BOX 0.7 GLOBAL CARBON DIOXIDE EMISSIONS

What it is: The vast majority of scientists believe that human activities are impacting the global climate. Carbon dioxide emissions, which result when oil, coal, and natural gas are burned, have been identified as the primary cause of global climate change. The graph presented here shows global carbon dioxide emissions from 1960 to 2017, measured in gigatons (a gigaton is a billion metric tons).

The results: We see that global carbon dioxide emissions increased from about 10 gigatons in 1960 to just over 35 gigatons recently. While most projections indicate that global carbon dioxide emissions will continue to increase in the future, scientists note that emissions will need to decrease substantially in the next few decades to avoid significant negative consequences to the global ecosystem and to human societies. We will discuss global climate change in more detail in Chapter 16.

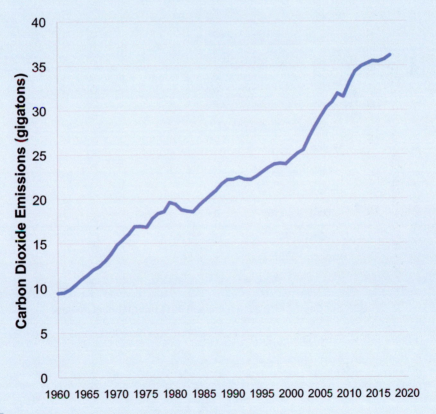

Figure 0.7 *Global Carbon Dioxide Emissions, 1960–2017*

Source: Global Carbon Project. Global Carbon Atlas. www.globalcarbonatlas.org/en/content/welcome-carbon-atlas

BOX 0.8 GDP PER CAPITA

What it is: Media stories of economic performance frequently refer to GDP. A country's GDP per capita measures economic production per person per year, which gives us an idea of the average material living standards in the country. While GDP is perhaps the most commonly used macroeconomic metric, it does not necessarily measure well-being. We discuss how GDP is calculated in Chapter 8, along with a discussion of its limitations and alternative economic measures.

The results: The United States ranks 12th, with a GDP per capita of $55,681. Qatar has the world's highest GDP per capita at around $112,531, with the country's economy driven by its oil and gas sectors. Burundi has the lowest GDP per capita at only $660.

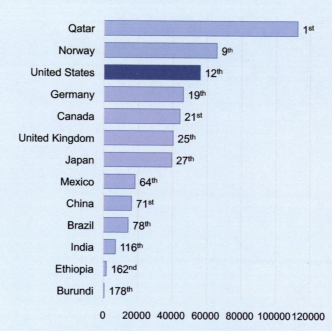

GDP per Capita, PPP 2018 (constant 2011 international dollars)

Figure 0.8 *GDP per Capita, 2018*

Source: World Bank, World Development Indicators database.

Note: Data are adjusted for purchasing power differences across countries (e.g., a dollar in India buys more than a dollar in the United States).

BOX 0.9 UNEMPLOYMENT RATE (PERCENT OF LABOR FORCE)

What it is: The unemployment rate in a country is an important macroeconomic metric. Not only does having a job provide a source of income, but it also provides a sense of identity and contributes to overall well-being. Estimating the unemployment rate is somewhat complex, and the method used to measure unemployment rate may differ across countries. In Chapters 7 and 8, we discuss issues involved in estimating the unemployment rate, including defining what it means to be in the workforce.

The results: Unemployment rates vary tremendously across countries, and they also fluctuate a lot over time. In 2018, Qatar had the lowest official unemployment rate at 0.1 percent, and South Africa had the highest unemployment rate at about 27 percent. While many developing countries, such as Lesotho, Botswana, and Libya, have very high unemployment rates (15 percent or more), other developing countries have rather low unemployment rates, at around 3 percent. The unemployment rate in the United States, usually in the range of 4–6 percent, rose considerably in the 2007–2009 recession but has since declined slowly to about 3.9 percent in 2018.

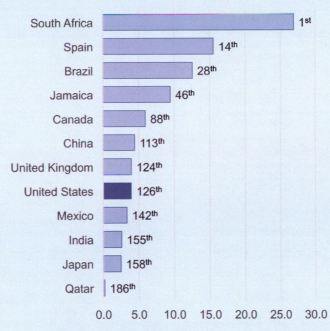

Unemployment Rate, 2018 (Percent of Labor Force)

Figure 0.9 *Unemployment Rate, 2018 (Percent of Labor Force)*

Source: World Bank, World Development Indicators database.

BOX 0.10 INFLATION

What it is: The rate of inflation summarizes how average prices change in a country in one year. For example, an inflation rate of 5 percent means that average prices increased by 5 percent that year. In Chapter 8, we discuss how to adjust data from different years for inflation, and we focus on macroeconomic theories of inflation in Chapters 11 and 12.

The results: Over the period 2009–2018, Switzerland and Japan had the lowest inflation rates in the world, with prices actually declining slightly during some years and hardly increasing overall. However, this is not necessarily a good thing, as we see later in the book. A low and stable—but not negative—inflation rate is generally considered an important macroeconomic policy goal. Most developed countries have generally been successful in controlling inflation in recent years. High and fluctuating inflation rates in a country are a sign of macroeconomic instability. With average inflation rates of over 80 percent between 2009 and 2018, South Sudan had the highest inflation rate over this period. Extremely high inflation rates of over 800 percent in Venezuela and over 24,000 percent in Zimbabwe have been observed in recent years.

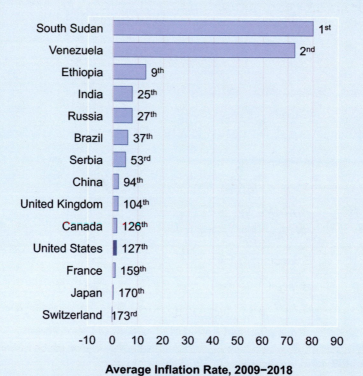

Figure 0.10 *Average Annual Inflation Rate, 2009–2018*

Source: World Bank, World Development Indicators database.

Note: The average inflation rate is calculated as the average of the inflation rate for each year from 2009 to 2018.

BOX 0.11 TRADE BALANCE (PERCENT OF GDP)

What it is: Economists refer to a country's trade balance as the dollar value of its exports minus its imports, normally expressed as a percentage of GDP. Thus, a negative trade balance indicates a trade deficit. A positive trade balance indicates a trade surplus. The trade deficit of the United States is often considered a cause for concern in media stories. We discuss trade balances, and other trade issues, in more detail in Chapter 14.

The results: Of the 178 countries with available data, 71 have a positive trade balance (exports exceed imports) and 107 have a negative trade balance. Those countries with the largest trade surpluses tend to be smaller countries (such as Luxembourg and Singapore) or oil-producing countries (such as Qatar and the United Arab Emirates). The U.S. trade deficit is about 3 percent of GDP, with other countries, such as Canada, in a similar range. The countries with the largest trade deficits tend to be poorer countries, although some poor countries do have trade surpluses.

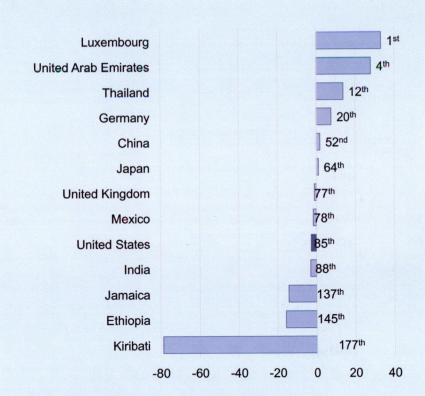

Trade Balance on Goods and Services, 2017 (Percent of GDP)

Figure 0.11 *Trade Balance, 2017 (Percent of GDP)*

Source: World Bank, World Development Indicators database.

BOX 0.12 INCOME INEQUALITY (GINI COEFFICIENT)

What it is: A Gini coefficient is a measure of economic inequality in a country. It is most commonly calculated according to the distribution of income, but it can also be calculated according to wealth distribution or other variables. It can range from 0 (everyone in the country has the same exact income) to 1 (one person receives all the income in a country). We learn more about Gini coefficients and economic inequality in Chapter 13.

The results: Scandinavian countries such as Sweden, Norway, and Finland tend to be the most equal countries in the world, by income (with the lowest Gini coefficients). Several African countries, including Botswana, Lesotho, Namibia, and South Africa, are the most unequal countries in the world. In general, countries with high GDP per capita have lower inequality than those with low GDP per capita. However, this is not always true. The United States, for example, is among the most economically unequal of the developed countries.

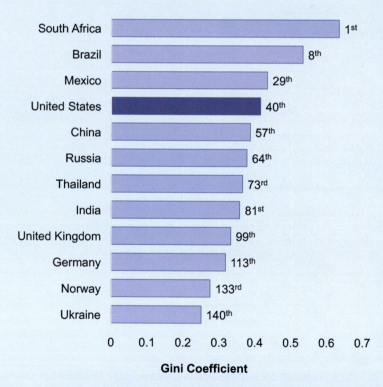

Figure 0.12 *Income Inequality (Gini Coefficient—Least Equal to Most Equal)*

Source: World Bank, World Development Indicators database.

Note: Data for the most recent year available, between 2010 and 2017.

BOX 0.13 ABSOLUTE POVERTY

What it is: The $1.90-per-day poverty line has been defined by the United Nations as a measure of absolute poverty. One of the Sustainable Development Goals set by the United Nations is to eradicate absolute poverty worldwide. Formerly, under the Millennium Development Goals, the UN had aimed at halving the number of people in the world living in absolute poverty between 1990 and 2015. This goal has already been met, mainly due to progress in China and India. We discuss poverty and economic development in Chapter 15.

The results: Note that this is the only graph in this chapter that does not include the United States or any other developed countries (few people in developed countries live below the $1.90-a-day poverty line, though homelessness and food insecurity continue to plague many cities in the United States). A majority of people do live below that poverty line in countries such as Madagascar, Democratic Republic of Congo, Rwanda, Zambia, Mozambique, Malawi, and Burundi. A small portion of the population lives in absolute poverty in some upper middle-income countries such as Argentina, Costa Rica, and Turkey.

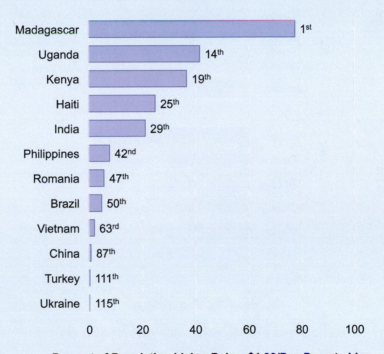

Percent of Population Living Below $1.90/Day Poverty Line

Figure 0.13 *Percent of Population Living Below $1.90/Day Poverty Line*

Source: World Bank, World Development Indicators database. Data are for the most recent year available, between 2011 and 2017.

BOX 0.14 EDUCATIONAL PERFORMANCE

What it is: To compare the educational performance of students in different countries, we present data from the Programme for International Student Assessment (PISA), which administers standardized math, science, and reading tests to 15-year-olds in over 60 countries every three years. The subsequent graph provides results from the science test. The country rankings were relatively similar for the math and reading tests, with some variations (e.g., the United States ranked 21st on the reading test and 35th on the math test).

The results: Students in Asian countries tended to achieve the highest test scores, including China, Singapore, Japan, and South Korea. Among European countries, students received high scores in Finland, the Netherlands, and Germany. The scores from the United States were average for developed countries. For less developed countries, scores tended to be lower.

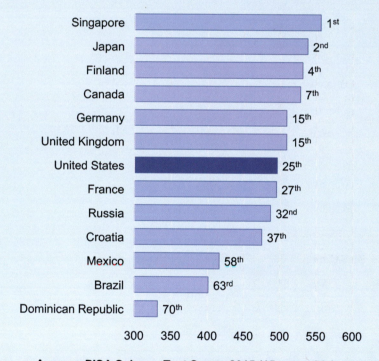

Average PISA Science Test Score, 2015 (15-year-olds)

Figure 0.14 *Average PISA Science Test Score, 2015 (15-Year-Olds)*

Source: Organisation for Economic Co-operation and Development, Programme for International Student Assessment, PISA 2015 Key Findings.

BOX 0.15 LIFE EXPECTANCY

What it is: Average life expectancy at birth is a common measure of health outcomes in a country. We discuss health as one component of well-being indices in Chapter 1.

The results: Life expectancy at birth now exceeds 80 years in over 34 countries, including Japan, France, Spain, and Greece. In 2010, only 20 countries had life expectancy at birth that exceeded 80 years. For a developed country, the United States has a comparatively low life expectancy, even lower than some middle-income countries such as Costa Rica and Cuba. Life expectancy is the lowest, below 55 years, in six African countries, including Sierra Leone, Lesotho, and Central African Republic.

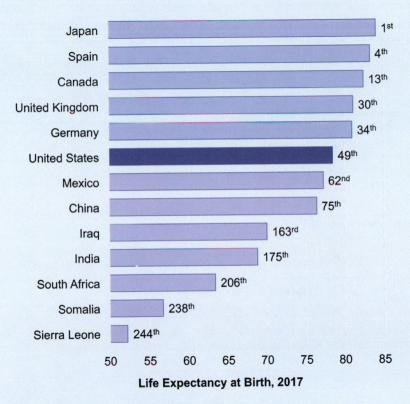

Figure 0.15 *Life Expectancy at Birth, 2017*

Source: World Bank, World Development Indicators database.

BOX 0.16 CARBON DIOXIDE EMISSIONS PER CAPITA

What it is: Carbon dioxide (CO_2) is the most important gas responsible for global climate change. CO_2 is emitted whenever fossil fuels are burned. Scientific analysis indicates that the accumulation of CO_2 in the atmosphere is raising global temperatures, leading to serious negative impacts on human societies and ecosystems. CO_2 per capita gives us an idea of how much the average person in a country is affecting the environment. We learn more about CO_2 and climate change in Chapter 16.

The results: The countries with the highest CO_2 emissions per capita are several oil-producing countries, including Qatar (the highest, at over 40 tons per person), Kuwait, and Bahrain. The United States has the eleventh-highest emissions per capita, around 16.5 tons per person. Emissions per person in European countries such as the United Kingdom and Germany are about half of U.S. levels. While China is the world's largest emitter of CO_2 overall, on a per capita basis, its emissions are less than half of those in the United States. CO_2 emissions per capita are negligible in the world's poorest countries.

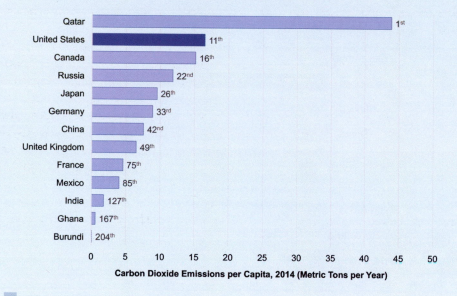

Carbon Dioxide Emissions per Capita, 2014 (Metric Tons per Year)

Figure 0.16 *Carbon Dioxide Emissions per Capita, 2014 (Metric Tons per Year)*

Source: World Bank, World Development Indicators database.

NOTE

1. In our discussion of bar graphs showing international comparisons, we use the classification provided by the World Bank to categorize countries into high-income, middle-income, and low-income groups based on their gross national income (GNI) per capita. Countries with GNI per capita of $1,025 or less in 2015 are categorized as low income. Countries with GNI per capita between $1,026 and $4,035 are categorized as lower middle-income, and those with GNI per capita between $4,036 and $12,475 are categorized as upper middle-income. Countries with GNI per capita above $12,475 are categorized as high-income countries.

Chapter 1

Economic Activity in Context

Welcome to economics! This discipline can help you understand many issues that are likely to be important in your life, such as the job market, the environment, and health care (to take just a few examples). Indeed, because the economic system is a crucial subsystem of our broader social and environmental systems, economic decisions pervade nearly all aspects of our world and strongly affect our experiences as consumers, employees, business owners, and citizens.

It is not an exaggeration to say that our *ideas* about the economy can make a significant difference in how the economy actually functions. In recent history, economic beliefs, advice, and policies have been notably influential in shaping the kind of world we live in. The overall goal of this book is to help you understand how the economy works. It may also help you to explore different ideas about what a "better" economy might be and how it could be best achieved. Another important goal of this book is to explain different economic concepts and types of analysis, showing their limitations as well as their strengths. Many of the ideas that have been put forth by economists can have a direct and material impact on your welfare and on the world in general. Studying economics will allow you to explore and develop your own views and will also enable you to better weigh the ideas of others.

1. OUR STARTING POINT

Why does economics matter? We believe the answer is closely related to why the economy matters. A useful way to understand the importance and nature of the economy is to inquire into its goals and critically look at its workings to see whether these goals are met. As we shall see, there are competing ideas concerning what goals are viable and desirable and how particular goals are best pursued.

We begin our study of economics with its definition. Most twentieth-century definitions of economics emphasize choice and scarcity: economics was defined as the discipline that could help people make optimal choices under conditions of scarcity. These definitions raised implicitly, but did not address explicitly, the issue of the basis on which choices are made: why is one choice considered, by the chooser, to be better than the other? For this reason, we prefer a definition that includes the goal of **economics** and define it as the study of how people manage their resources to meet their needs and enhance their well-being.

> **economics:** the study of how people manage their resources to meet their needs and enhance their well-being

Other definitions of economics have said that the activities of special economic interest are production, distribution, and consumption. To this our definition adds the important activity of resource management. The resources that we have to manage include natural resources such as forests, soils, water, and air, as well as human-made productive resources such as factories, trucks, computers, and roads. Our resources also include our time, knowledge, and skills; financial resources; and even the social relationships that improve the quality of our lives. Economists refer to these as different types of capital; we will look more closely at each type of capital later in this chapter.

In our definition, the term **well-being** refers broadly to a good quality of life. Our well-being is closely connected to meeting our basic needs, such as for food, shelter, and physical security, but it also goes beyond "needs." Virtually everyone desires such things as a decent income, enough leisure time, good family and friends, freedom to express one's opinions, a clean environment, and access to good education and health care. Some people may place a higher emphasis on some of these goals than others, and people clearly have different opinions on the best ways to improve our well-being. People's perception of what constitutes a need and what will promote well-being is also influenced by social forces, individual personality, and value judgments. We discuss some key components of well-being in Section 2.2.

> **well-being:** a term used broadly to describe a good quality of life

At this point, it is useful to discuss briefly how economics, as a discipline, has been organized over the last century for purposes of teaching and analysis. Studies of smaller-scale actors in the economy—that is, individuals as well as subnational organizations such as firms and households—occur under the heading **micro-economics,** while the study of the whole economy, considering national and international trends, is generally conducted under the term **macroeconomics.** Part II of this text focuses mostly on microeconomic issues, and Part III covers topics categorized under macroeconomics. If you go on to take other courses in economics, you may find yourself making choices among classes with one of these names or the other.

> **microeconomics:** the subfield of economics that focuses on activities that take place within and among individuals, households, businesses, and other groups at the subnational level
>
> **macroeconomics:** the subfield of economics that focuses on how economic activities at all levels create a national (and global) economic environment

Discussion Questions

1. What current issues are you most interested in? How do you think economics might help you understand these issues?
2. In what ways do you think economics might help to provide solutions to social problems and improve overall well-being? Are there ways in which the workings of the economic system may *create* social problems or make them worse?

2. THE GOALS OF AN ECONOMY

Virtually all definitions of economics have implied something about goals or criteria for choosing one thing over another. When we ask about the goals of an economy or, indeed, when we use such terms as "need" or "well-being," we come up against a basic issue for all the sciences: Are we only going to ask questions about hard facts (those are called **positive questions**)—or is it also relevant to ask questions about how things should be? The second kind are often referred to as **normative questions**.

---

positive questions: questions about how things are
normative questions: questions about how things should be

Consider a positive question about a particular fact: "How many people live below the poverty line in our country?" Compare this to a normative question such as "How much effort should be given to poverty reduction?" Both of these require that we start with a definition of poverty. To achieve this, we need to combine positive facts about income and wealth with a normative assessment of where to draw the poverty line. Life rarely offers us a neat distinction between "what is" and "what ought to be." More often, we have to deal with a combination of the two. Although much of this textbook is concerned with positive issues, we believe it is not always possible to avoid discussion of normative issues. Good economic analysis recognizes and responds to the intertwining of the normative and positive, helping you to understand how your own values, or someone else's values, are present in particular types of analysis. This is also a more interesting approach to analysis than attempting to talk about the real world in ways that avoid mention of the goals and values that motivate people.

A useful way to look at different goals is to rank them in a kind of hierarchy. Some are **intermediate goals**—that is, they are not primarily ends in themselves but are mainly important because they are expected to serve as the means to further ends. Goals that are sought for their own sake, rather than because they lead to something else, are called **final goals**. For example, you might strive to achieve high grades as a final goal—it just makes you feel good to excel (but maybe feeling good is the final goal in this case?). Or maybe it is an intermediate goal toward the final goal of getting a good job. Of course, we might also think of the goal of "getting a good job" as itself being intermediate to other final goals, such as obtaining income, status, or overall satisfaction with life.

> **intermediate goal:** a goal that is primarily desirable because its achievement will bring you closer to your final goal(s)
> **final goal:** a goal that requires no further justification; it is an end in itself

For a long time, economists have mostly focused on the goal of increasing income and wealth. We take the position that these are intermediate goals, which help achieve broader final goals of attaining a good standard of living and creating a stable and sustainable economic environment. We first discuss the goals that economics has traditionally focused on and then consider broader goals of well-being.

2.1 Traditional Economic Goals

The Goal of Gross Domestic Product Growth

A goal that has been assumed by most economists in the last century was to increase **gross domestic product (GDP)**. This is a measure of the market value of all final goods and services produced within a country's borders over a specific time period, normally one year.

> **gross domestic product (GDP):** the market value of all final goods and services produced within a country's borders over a specific time period, normally one year

GDP can be an important means of promoting well-being. A country with high GDP per person (GDP per capita) is usually able to provide its citizens with quality health care, food security, national defense, and a cleaner environment. Increasing GDP levels may be particularly important in contexts where people lack sufficient financial resources to meet their basic needs. About 10 percent of the world's population lives in absolute poverty, defined by the World Bank as an income below $1.90 per person per day.[1] For the global poor, increased production—more food, better housing, more schools, or more health centers—is clearly necessary as a means toward improved well-being.

However, this is best considered an intermediate goal rather than a final goal. In other words, GDP can be a means to achieve other goals, but there are good arguments for why it should *not* be considered the end goal of the economy. GDP only measures marketed production. As such, it is unable to incorporate other aspects essential to well-being such as access to health or education resources, clean environment, or equal treatment of all persons under the law. GDP tells us nothing about how total income is distributed within the country. GDP has also become an increasingly questionable proxy for well-being in more affluent parts of the world, where production and consumption levels are already relatively high, and more production may not necessarily mean increased well-being.

There are at least three reasons not to equate GDP with well-being. First, where there is abundant income and wealth, pursuit of other goals may have more potential to contribute to well-being. Second, there is now much evidence to suggest that countries with more equal incomes can sometimes have a higher degree of well-being, even if their GDP is relatively low.[2] Third, the capacities of the natural environment to support rapid economic growth are clearly finite. There is growing evidence that economic growth as conventionally understood is damaging the environment in ways that endanger present and future well-being. Given all this, it is unsurprising that in recent years, new quantitative metrics that go beyond GDP have been developed. We will discuss such metrics in Chapter 8.

The Goal of Efficiency

A second traditional goal in economics is **efficiency**. An efficient process is one that uses the *minimum value of resources* to achieve a desired result. Or, to put it another way, efficiency is achieved when the *maximum value of output* is produced from a given set of inputs.

> **efficiency:** the use of resources, or inputs, such that they yield the highest possible value of output, or the production of a given output using the lowest possible value of inputs

Given this definition, efficiency is often thought of as a purely technical and scientific exercise, based only on positive analysis. This is not actually the case, however, because a standard of value must be adopted before the definition of efficiency can be applied.

Money is the standard of value that has traditionally been used in economics. Specifically, the commonest economic definition of value has been that of *market value*—that is, price. Using this standard, an economist would say that resources are being used most efficiently when the market value of production is maximized. It is often very useful to analyze efficiency through the measuring stick of money, and later chapters of this textbook will help you with this skill. However, like most (if not all) tools of analysis in economics and the social sciences, there are some limitations inherent in the tool. For example, a person's *willingness* to pay for something is obviously influenced by their *ability* to pay. As a consequence, those with the most money will disproportionately determine what is economically "efficient" for a society to produce. This could mean that if wealth is unevenly distributed, the "efficient" outcome may be production of luxury cars for the few and a lack of basic health care for the many.

Setting efficiency as a goal also assumes that nothing has value unless humans are willing to pay for it. But perhaps certain things should have intrinsic value, such as the rights of nonhuman species to exist or goals like freedom or fairness. Thus, thinking of efficiency only in terms of market value can lead to neglect of other, perhaps more urgent, needs and goals (see Box 1.1).

BOX 1.1 EFFICIENT AT WHAT?

The point that efficiency defined in terms of market value is rarely the only important goal is vividly illustrated in a story from a now-eminent economist.

Right after he finished graduate school, this young man's first job was to advise the government of a rice-growing country where it should put its research efforts. He was told that two modern techniques for rice milling had been developed elsewhere and was asked to calculate which of these two technologies should be selected. The young economist analyzed the requirements for producing a ton of rice under each of the two competing technologies, including labor, machinery, fuel, and raw materials. He calculated the monetary costs for these inputs, and, finding that Technology A could produce a ton of rice at slightly less cost than Technology B, he recommended that the government invest in the more "efficient" Technology A.

Returning a few years later, the economist was horrified to discover what had happened when the country implemented his suggestion. It turned out that the traditions of that country included strict norms for the division of labor: specifically, what work women were allowed to do and what was defined as men's work. Technology B would have been neutral in this regard, maintaining the same ratio of "male jobs" to "female jobs" as had existed before. Technology A, however, eliminated most of the women's work opportunities. In a society where women's earnings were a major contributor to food and education for children, the result was a perceptible decline in children's nutrition levels and school attendance.

Charged with determining which technology was best, the young economist had not asked, "efficient at doing what?" Instead, he made an implicit assumption that the only final goal was maximizing output and that the only intermediate goal he had to worry about was efficiency in resource use. He has subsequently told several generations of economics students, "Nobody told me to look beyond efficiency, defined in terms of market costs—but I'll never neglect the family and employment effects again, even when my employer doesn't ask about them."

Efficiency remains an important goal for economics, but we do much better analysis when we pay attention to what is being measured—market value—and broaden the scope of our concern with what we are trying to accomplish.

2.2 Moving Beyond the Traditional Goals

Having discussed some of the limitations of the traditional economic goals, we now present some broader goals that may better represent the purpose of an economy. We begin this discussion by offering, in Table 1.1, one possible list of what someone might believe to be the final goals of economic activity. The first five goals on the list are primarily individual concerns, while the last five are more related to societal concerns. Some of the goals involve *making life possible*, some involve *making life worthwhile*, and yet others involve both of these types of goals. Of course, opinions about goals will differ; you may believe that some of the goals on this list could be omitted or that some important goals are missing. In any event, our purpose is not to achieve a precise definition of well-being but to emphasize that well-being is a fundamentally multidimensional concept. In the discussion that follows, we will focus on three important components of well-being—good living standards, stability and security, and sustainability.

Table 1.1 A Potential List of Final Goals

1. **Satisfaction of basic physical needs**, including nutrition and care adequate for survival, as well as a comfortable living environment.
2. **Security:** assurance that one's basic needs will continue to be met throughout all stages of life, as well as security against aggression or unjust persecution.
3. **Happiness:** adequate opportunity to experience feelings of contentment, pleasure, enjoyment, and peace of mind.
4. **Ability to realize one's potential**, including one's physical, intellectual, social, aesthetic, and spiritual potential.
5. **A sense of meaning:** a purpose to one's life.
6. **Fairness:** fair and equal treatment by others and within social institutions.
7. **Freedom:** the ability to make personal decisions while not infringing on the freedom of others.
8. **Participation:** opportunity to participate in the processes in which decisions are made that affect one's society.
9. **Good social relations:** having satisfying and trustful relations with friends, family, fellow citizens, and business associates, as well as peaceful relations among larger groups (such as nations).
10. **Ecological balance:** protecting natural resources and, where necessary, restoring them to a healthy state.

The Goal of Good Living Standards

Achieving good living standards refers to people being able to live long, healthy, and enjoyable lives, with access to opportunities to accomplish things that they believe give meaning to their lives.

> **standard of living:** the quality of people's diet; housing; medical care; education; working conditions; and access to transportation, communication, entertainment, and other amenities

The most basic living standard issues relate to the quality of people's diets and housing, their access to means of transportation and communication, and the quality of medical attention that they receive. Taking a somewhat broader view, we might also include less tangible aspects of life, such as the quality of education that people receive and the variety of entertainment and other non-work-related activities that they can enjoy.

In addition, the way in which people participate in producing and consuming goods and services—as well as the amount of leisure they enjoy—has important implications for their health and happiness. So, for working-age people, the quality of their working lives is part of their standard of living. And for people who cannot do much work because they are too young, old, ill, or handicapped, the quality of the hands-on care that they receive is a major component of their living standard.

For a long time, "raising living standards" was considered nearly synonymous with "achieving economic growth" (increasing GDP). This means increasing the dollar value of what is produced. However, as we discussed above, this may not always be a good measure. In wealthier regions of the world where the population is not growing and where the majority of families already enjoy decent housing, safe water, plenty of food, readily available heating and refrigeration, and a car or two (or more), it may seem more desirable to switch national priorities away from increasing production toward making sure that production is designed to increase well-being. For example, a focus on improving cultural, educational, and environmental conditions; raising the quality of work-life; and promoting an equitable allocation of economic rewards may help achieve *living standards growth* even in the absence of *economic growth*.

The Goal of Stability, or Security

While closely linked to goals for living standards, the goal of stability and security brings in a dimension that we have not yet discussed. Imagine two scenarios in which you can say that *on average*, you enjoyed a good living standard. In the first scenario, you might enjoy a fairly steady, and gently rising, living standard and always be able to plan confidently for the future. In the second scenario, you might be quite successful at some points (getting a good job, buying a house) but also periodically face the possibility of "losing it all" (being unemployed, losing your house, or losing your savings in stock market). Even if, "over the long run," you might have done OK, the uncertainty and anxiety of living with economic fluctuations in the second scenario would take a toll on your overall well-being relative to the more stable case.

Unpredictable fluctuations in employment levels and rates of inflation, interest rates, and foreign exchange rates make it difficult—and, in the worst cases, impossible—for individuals and organizations to make productive and economically sensible plans for the future.

One reason that such fluctuations may occur is changes in the level of production in the economy. Periods of strong economic growth (sometimes called booms, expansions, or recoveries) and their attendant problem of rapidly rising prices alternate with periods of recessions (sometimes called contractions, busts, or slumps), which often bring problems such as high unemployment. This pattern is called the **business cycle**.

> **business cycle:** recurrent fluctuations in the level of national production, with alternating periods of recession and boom

The severity of the fluctuations could range from the minor to the catastrophic. Even if these problems are often "short run," such fluctuations can cause problems that persist for a few months to a few years and can also leave longer-lasting economic and social problems. For example, periods of high unemployment are associated with many indicators of individual and social stress, such as increased rates of suicide, domestic violence, stress-related illnesses, and crime. Clearly, minimizing and better managing such instability in order to create a stable, secure economic environment is an important economic goal. We look more at economic stability in Chapter 13.

In light of new knowledge about our dependence on the natural world, which is undergoing radical alterations due to human economic activity, the goal of security now must also include a much longer time horizon, recognizing a serious responsibility to future generations. This leads us to our third goal: sustainability.

The Goal of Sustainability

We want good living standards and stability, not only for ourselves right now but also for ourselves later in our lives and for our children, grandchildren, and other generations to come. In order to understand how well we are achieving the goal of sustainability, we must address the questions:

- Are economic activities *financially* sustainable into the future? Or is a country incurring such a high amount of debt that it may create a heavy burden on its future inhabitants?
- Are economic activities *socially* sustainable into the future? Are disparities between the "haves" and the "have-nots" accelerating or diminishing? Are they based on justifiable causes or on unequal power relations? Are young people receiving the upbringing and education required to enable them to contribute to a healthy economy and society? Or is the current structure of economic activity setting the stage for future social, political, and economic strife?
- Are economic activities *ecologically* sustainable into the future? Is the natural environment that supports life being treated in a way that will sustain its quality into the future? Or is it becoming depleted or degraded?

For many generations, it seemed that **technological progress** and economic growth were magical keys that unlocked the door to unlimited improvements in the standard of living. For example, real output per person in the United States in 1980 was about ten times what it had been in 1840, and it was 1.9 times greater in 2018 than it was in 1980.

> **technological progress:** the development of new products and new, more efficient methods of production

Can we rely on ever-increasing economic growth and technological progress to deliver financial, social, and ecological sustainability?

Some argue that sustainability problems can be remedied by *more* GDP growth. For example, they believe that the issue of social sustainability can be resolved by increasing the overall income level and reason that the bigger the pie, the bigger everyone's share can be. Regarding ecological issues, some economists see growth as the means to achieve technological improvements that are presumed to lower our environmental impact.

In contrast, some have argued that growth might instead *contribute* to these problems. Continuous expansion in production levels is in reality environmentally unsustainable. The earth is a finite, essentially closed system, which cannot indefinitely sustain the growth of any subsystem, such as human economic systems. The inescapable consequence of overstepping natural limits is *social* and *economic* unsustainability. Researchers have estimated that giving everyone in the world an American lifestyle (which is one of the most resource-consuming lifestyles in the world), including a meat-rich diet and multiple cars per family, would require an extra two to four planets to supply resources and absorb waste. Such research appears to suggest that dwellers in rich countries will be unable to *maintain* current consumption patterns, let alone *increase* them.

These arguments point to the need to adjust our consumption patterns so that we consume enough to allow us to promote our individual and collective well-being while also properly considering the impacts of our consumption behavior on others and on the planet. The notion of **conscious consumption** involves understanding the costs of our consumption on the environment and making consumption decisions responsibly to reduce waste and achieve a more sustainable lifestyle.

> **conscious consumption:** being aware of the costs of consumption on others and on the planet and making consumption decisions responsibly to minimize waste and achieve a more sustainable lifestyle

A further question that we must consider is whether it is sufficient to sustain the financial, economic, and ecological systems *as they are now*. Some of the ecological systems that support economic activity may already be severely degraded. In such cases, it is not enough to sustain what exists now—rather, we need to take on a goal of **restorative development**, to rebuild systems that are no longer supporting well-being in the present and the future.

> **restorative development:** economic progress that restores economic, financial, social, or ecological systems that have been degraded and are no longer adequately supportive of human well-being in the present and the future

Many economists in the twentieth century were content in the belief that economic growth would naturally contribute to the achievement of any other goals that we might choose. We have found it helpful to view the economy as though it exists with a purpose, and that purpose is not simply growth in output but, more broadly, human well-being in the present and the future. This requires learning how to balance ideas about achieving economic growth with questions about what kinds of growth actually contribute to well-being and ideas on how present and future well-being can be enhanced by restorative development. This broader approach may be referred to as **contextual economics**—economics viewed in the context of social and environmental realities—and is the approach taken throughout this text.

> **contextual economics:** economic analysis that takes into account the social and environmental realities within which the economic system operates

Discussion Questions

1. You have evidently decided to dedicate some of your personal resources in time and money to studying economics. Which of the goals listed in Table 1.1 was most important to you in making this decision? If you were to write up a list of your own final goals, how would it differ from Table 1.1?
2. How can economic systems deal with the problems caused when some goals conflict with others? For example, what if a goal of increased GDP growth causes growing environmental damage, with some people enjoying higher income levels but others suffering from the effects of pollution?

3. THE ISSUES THAT DEFINE ECONOMICS

In discussing goals, we have addressed the question of what economics is *for*—what its purpose is. Now we summarize what economics is *about*: what activities it covers and which questions it addresses.

3.1 The Four Essential Economic Activities

We think of an activity as "economic" when it involves one or more of four essential tasks that allow us to meet our needs and enhance our well-being. The four essential economic activities are resource management and the production, distribution, and consumption of goods and services.

Resource Management

Resource management means tending to, preserving, or improving the resources that contribute to the enhancement of well-being for current and future generations. These stocks of resources, which are valued for their potential economic contributions, are referred to as **capital**, or "capital assets."

> **resource management:** preserving or improving the resources that contribute to the enhancement of well-being, including natural, manufactured, human, and social resources
>
> **capital:** any resource that is valued for its potential economic contributions

We can identify five types of capital that contribute to an economy's productivity. **Natural capital** refers to physical assets provided by nature, such as land that is suitable for agriculture or other human uses, fresh water sources, healthy ocean ecologies, a resilient and diverse stock of wild animals and plants, and stocks of minerals and fossil fuels that are still in the ground. **Manufactured capital** means physical assets that are generated by applying human productive activities to natural capital. These include such things as buildings, machinery, stocks of refined oil, transportation infrastructure, and inventories of produced goods that are waiting to be sold or to be used in further production. **Human capital** refers to individual people's capacity for productive work, particularly the knowledge and skills each can personally bring to his or her work. **Social capital** means the existing institutions and the stock of trust, mutual understanding, shared values, and socially held knowledge that facilitates the social coordination of economic activity.

> **natural capital:** physical assets provided by nature
> **manufactured capital:** all physical assets that have been produced by humans using natural capital
> **human capital:** people's capacity for engaging in productive activities and their individual knowledge and skills
> **social capital:** the institutions and the stock of trust, mutual understanding, shared values, and socially held knowledge that facilitates the social coordination of economic activity

Last, there is a fifth sort of resource, **financial capital**, which is a fund of purchasing power available to economic actors. While financial capital is not part of any physical production activity, it indirectly contributes to production by making it possible for people to produce goods and services in advance of getting paid for them. It also facilitates the activities of distribution and consumption. An example of financial capital would be a bank checking account, filled with funds that have been either saved up by the economic agent who owns it or loaned to the agent by a bank.

> **financial capital:** funds of purchasing power available to purchase goods and services or facilitate economic activity

Notice that economists' description of "capital" is different from what you might hear in everyday use, where people sometimes take "capital" to mean *only* financial capital. We hear this in everyday references to "capital markets," "undercapitalized businesses," "venture capital," and so on. Economists take a broader view that includes all five types of capital stocks.

Capital stocks may increase or decrease as a consequence of natural forces, as in the case of a natural forest, or they may be deliberately managed by humans in order to provide needed inputs for the production of goods and services. When people work to increase the quantity or quality of resources in order to make benefits possible in the future, this is what economists mean by **investment**. Advances in technology also expand or improve the stocks of capital, including manufactured, human, and social capital, thereby increasing the productivity of economic activity.

> **investment:** an activity intended to increase the quantity or quality of a resource over time

Production

Production is the conversion of resources into usable products, which may be either goods or services. Goods are tangible objects, such as bread and books; services are intangibles, such as TV broadcasting, teaching, and haircuts. Popular bands performing music, recording companies producing digital music for sale, local governments building roads, and individuals cooking meals at home are all engaged in the economic activity of production.

The economic activity of production converts some resources, which we call **inputs**, into new goods and services, which we refer to as **outputs**. This conversion is a flow that takes place over a period of time (see Box 1.2). Some goods, such as machines and computers, are produced to assist in the production of other goods and services. The way in which production occurs depends on available technologies. Production processes can also lead to undesirable outputs, such as pollution and **waste products**. We consider only *useful* outputs to be economic goods and services.

> **production:** the conversion of resources into usable products, which may be either goods or services
> **inputs:** resources that go into production
> **outputs:** the goods and services that result from production
> **waste products:** outputs that are not used either for consumption or in a further production process

Distribution

Distribution is the sharing of products and resources among people. In contemporary economies, distribution activities take two main forms: **exchange** and **transfer**. When you hand over money in exchange for goods and services, you are engaging in exchange. People are generally much better off if they specialize in the production of a limited range of goods and services and meet most of their needs through exchange than if they try to produce everything that they need themselves. Distribution also takes place through one-way transfers, in which something is given with nothing specific expected in return. Social Security payments are an example of a transfer payment, and transfers can also take place among individuals. Parents are engaged in transfer when they provide their children with goods and services. Gifts and inheritances are also transfers. Local school boards, for example, distribute education services to students in their districts, tuition-free (although public education is, of course, supported by tax revenues). These sorts of nonmonetary transfers are called **in-kind transfers**.

> **distribution:** the sharing of products and resources among people
> **exchange:** the trading of one thing for another
> **transfer:** the giving of something, with nothing specific expected in return
> **in-kind transfers:** transfers of goods or services

BOX 1.2 STOCKS VERSUS FLOWS

When non-economists use the term "stock," they usually mean ownership shares in enterprises that are traded on the "stock market." To an economist, however, the concept of a **stock** refers to something as it is measured at a particular point in time. For example, the amount of water in a bathtub can be measured at one particular instant, and that quantity would be considered a stock. The balance in your checking account at the beginning of the month is a stock value. The number of computers in an office at ten o'clock on Tuesday morning is a stock, as is the number of trees in a forest at two o'clock on Saturday afternoon.

In contrast to stocks, **flows** are measured *over* a period of time. For example, the water that goes into a bathtub from a faucet is a flow that occurs over a period of time; its quantity can be measured per minute or per hour. The deposits and withdrawals you make to your checking account can be understood as flows; your bank statement will tell you what the various flows were during a month. The number of computers purchased by an office over the course of this month or this year is a flow. As trees grow or are cut down or felled by lightning, these flows add to or subtract from forest resources.

Figure 1.1 is a "bathtub"-style **stock-flow diagram**. It represents the relation of stocks and flows, showing a stock at only *one* point in time. Like water flowing through the tap (additions) and the drain (subtractions) of a bathtub, flows raise or lower the level of the water in the tub (stock).

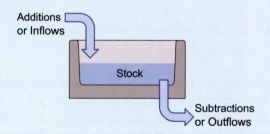

Figure 1.1 *"Bathtub"-Style Stock Flow Diagram*

stock: the quantity of something at a particular point in time
flow: something whose quantity is measured over a period of time
stock-flow diagram: an illustration of how stocks can be changed over time by flows

Consumption

Consumption is the process by which goods and services are put to final use by people. In some cases, such as eating a meal or burning gasoline in a car, goods are literally "consumed" in the sense that they are used up and are no longer available for other uses. In other cases, such as enjoying art in a museum, the experience may be "consumed" without excluding others or using up material resources.

In economics, the activity of consumption is frequently contrasted with the resource-management activity of investment. **Consumption** is spending on final goods and services, whereas investment, as defined previously, can be understood as spending for the purpose of increasing or maintaining the capacity to produce final goods and services. The two activities are linked by the activity of **saving**, or refraining from consumption today in order to gain benefits in the future.

> **consumption:** the final use of a good or service
> **saving:** refraining from consumption in the current period

For example, suppose that a subsistence farmer grows a crop of corn. To the extent that the farmer eats some of the corn, the farmer *consumes*—the corn is used up in the process of eating and is not available for future use. To the extent that the farmer sets aside seeds from this year's corn crop for planting next season, the farmer *saves*. This is an example in which saving is directly turned into *investment:* It puts aside a resource that will aid production in the future.

Many real-world economic undertakings involve more than one of the four economic activities. A steelmaking firm, for example, engages in *production* of steel while also *distributing* the revenues from sales among its employees, managers, and stockholders. A family that grows crops for its own use is engaged first in *production* and then *consumption*.

Resource management in particular often overlaps with production, consumption, and distribution. For example, the production of paper using recycled materials can be classified as both production, because a good is being produced, and resource management, because natural resource use is reduced.

A final point on the relationship between resource management and the other economic activities is that sometimes resource management means *not* engaging in production, consumption, or distribution. For example, people who make voluntary decisions to minimize their unnecessary consumption are managing resources to reduce their ecological impacts. Although this may look like *inactivity*, including resource management as an economic activity implies that minimizing some kinds of production or consumption can contribute to well-being.

3.2 The Three Basic Economic Questions

The four economic activities that we have listed give rise, in turn, to the three basic economic questions:

1. *What* should be produced?
2. *How* should production take place?
3. *For whom* should economic activity be undertaken?

For example, a family faces the problem of how much of its economic resources (money, credit, and so on) to use now and how much to preserve for future use.

Suppose that members of a family decide to spend some of their money on a dinner party. They will have to decide "what" foods to prepare. The "how" question includes who is going to cook and what recipes to use. Answering the "for whom" question means deciding who will be invited for dinner and how to take into account the food preferences and needs of the various individuals. Finally, these decisions may all have implications for resource management, such as whether organic products are purchased and how much energy is used to cook the foods.

The complexity of decision-making and the number of people involved rise steeply as we move to higher levels of economic organization, but the questions remain the same. Businesses, schools, community groups, governments, and international organizations all have to settle the questions of *what, how*, and *for whom*. These questions clearly overlap. For example, "what" and "for whom" may be intertwined— choosing whether to produce luxury goods or necessities like food and medicine may be affected by whether the economic system tilts toward production for the rich or whether production is socially determined. "How" may also have implications for "what"; choosing to produce in an environmentally sound manner may mean that certain goods, such as highly toxic pesticides, should not be produced at all. And "for whom" should include both present and future generations, illustrating the need for resource-saving production.

Discussion Questions

1. Think of a common activity that you enjoy. For example, perhaps you like to get together with friends and listen to music on your smartphone while popping popcorn in the microwave. List the stocks of natural, manufactured, human, and social capital that you draw on while engaging in this activity.
2. Classify each of the following according to which economic activity, or activities, it involves, from this list: production, resource management, distribution, and consumption. If any seem to include aspects of more than one activity, name the activities and explain your reasoning.
    a. Harvesting a crop of corn
    b. Attending college
    c. Building an addition onto a factory
    d. Receiving a Social Security payment
    e. Cutting someone's hair

4. ECONOMIC TRADEOFFS

Tradeoffs are a central concept in economics. When we have limited resources, we have to decide how to allocate them to meet competing goals. If we allocate more resources toward one objective, then fewer are available to meet other goals. This is particularly important when we recognize that progress in one dimension can sometimes come at the expense of other dimensions.

In some cases, resources for economic activity may be available in **abundance**— meaning that there are more than enough to meet our goals. More commonly, we experience **scarcity** due to limits on available resources. Economics can help us make decisions on how to allocate these resources in a way that enhances well-being for both current and future generations.

> **abundance:** resources are abundant to the extent that they exist in plentiful supply for meeting various goals
>
> **scarcity:** the concept that resources are not sufficient to allow all goals to be accomplished at once

4.1 Society's Production-Possibilities Frontier

Economists have developed a simple model to illustrate the concept of tradeoffs. Let us assume that society is considering only two possible choices of what to produce over the coming year from its available resources. The classic example is to take "guns" as one output and "butter" as the other. In more general terms, the guns-versus-butter tradeoff can refer to the general choice of a society between becoming more militarized ("guns") and becoming more civilian- or consumer-oriented ("butter").

With limited resources, our simple imagined society can only produce a given quantity of guns or butter. Also, if we allocate more resources toward one output, we will have fewer resources available to produce the other output. For example, if more labor resources go into gun production, fewer workers will be available to make butter. Economists represent these concepts graphically using a **production-possibilities frontier (PPF)**, which shows all the combinations of two outputs that can be produced by a society in a given time period.

> **production-possibilities frontier (PPF):** a curve showing the maximum amounts of two outputs that society could produce from given resources over a given period

Figure 1.2 shows a PPF for guns and butter. In this graph, the quantity of "butter" produced over a year is measured on the horizontal (or x-) axis. The quantity of

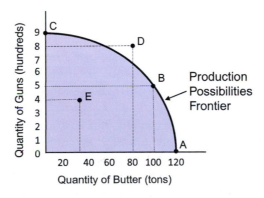

Figure 1.2 *Society's Production Possibilities Frontier*

"guns" is measured on the vertical (or y-) axis. We measure butter in tons and guns in hundreds. The points on the PPF curve illustrate various maximum quantities of guns and butter that the society could produce. For example, point A, where the curve intersects the x-axis, shows that this society can produce 120 tons of butter if it directs all its resources into butter production. If it wants to also produce some guns, it must give up some butter production. Point B illustrates production, over the year, of 100 tons of butter and 500 guns, and point C illustrates that the society can produce 900 guns if it decides to produce no butter. While it is obviously highly unrealistic to think about a society that only produces two goods, this PPF is a thought experiment that is helpful for illustrating three important economic concepts:

1. *Scarcity:* Point D in Figure 1.2 represents a production combination (80 tons of butter and 800 guns) that is not attainable given existing resources and technology. To produce at that point would take more resources, or better technology, than the society currently has. The PPF is specifically defined so that only those points on or inside it (the blue-shaded region) represent outputs that can actually be produced.

2. *Tradeoffs:* All the points that lie on the boundaries of the PPF illustrate the important notion that scarcity creates a need for tradeoffs. Along the frontier, one can get more of one output only by "trading off" some of the other. Figure 1.2 illustrates the important concept of **opportunity costs**. Opportunity cost is the value of the best alternative to the choice that one actually makes. In this case, the cost of increasing gun production is less butter. For example, suppose the economy is at Point A, producing 120 tons of butter and no guns, but then decides that it needs to produce 500 guns. Point B illustrates that after some resources have been moved from butter production into producing the 500 guns, the maximum amount of butter that can be produced is 100 tons. The gain of 500 guns comes at a "cost" to the economy of a loss of 20 tons of butter. Likewise, starting from a point where the economy is producing only guns, the "cost" of producing more butter would be fewer guns.

> **opportunity cost:** the value of the best alternative that is forgone when a choice is made

3. *Efficiency:* Resources are used efficiently when they are used in a way that does not involve any waste. Points that lie *on* the PPF illustrate the maximum combinations that a society can produce from its given resources if these are used efficiently. But for points *inside* the frontier, such as point E, the economy is not producing as much as it could. It is producing 30 tons of butter and 400 guns, even though it *could* produce more of one or the other, or even more of both. Some resources are apparently being wasted at point E. This could occur for at least three reasons, all of which are very often present in real-world economies:
   ■ The resources may be wasted because they are being left idle. For example, workers may be left unemployed, cows could be left unmilked, and existing capital may not be fully utilized.
   ■ Resources may not be used in optimal ways. For example, the gun factory may be poorly designed, so a lot of the workers' time is wasted moving parts from

one area to another. In this case, a better, more efficient organization of the work flow could increase production with no increase in resources.

■ The allocation of resources between the two outputs might not be optimal. For example, locating gun factories on the best pasture land would not be optimal if it means cows are grazing on poor land that would be fine for gun factories.

Thus, our society could move from point E to a point on the PPF, such as point B, by using any idle resources and making better use of its available resources.

The bowed-out shape of the PPF curve comes from the fact that some resources are likely to be more suited for production of one good than for the other. Suppose our society is initially producing only butter, at point A. We can see that it can get the first 500 guns by giving up just 20 tons of butter production. In shifting its resources from butter to guns, we assume the society will start with those resources that are best suited for gun production and least suited for butter production. For example, we would locate our first gun factories on land that is poorly suited for grazing. We would start making guns with workers who have better gun-making skills than butter-making skills. So we don't need to give up much butter production in order to make the first 500 guns.

But the more we shift resources from butter to gun production, the more we will have to remove resources from butter production that are better suited for butter production. We will have to eventually give up good pasture land and shift workers that have better butter-making skills than gun-making skills. So in order to produce 400 more guns (to go from point B to point C along the PPF), we will have to give up all the remaining 100 tons of butter! So the rate of the tradeoff (the opportunity cost) between guns and butter varies at different points along the PPF; this explains why the slope of the PPF is not constant.

Of course, we could use a PPF to show the tradeoffs between many other pairs of outputs besides guns and butter. We could look at the tradeoff between soda and pizza, cars and bicycles, or health care and highways. This classic example, however, is a good one because in the real world, such guns/butter or militarization/peacetime tradeoffs are real and significant (see Box 1.3).

What precise combination of outputs, such as guns versus butter or health versus highways, should society choose to produce? The PPF does *not* answer this question. The curve shows the range of efficient possibilities, such as points A, B, or C, but does not tell us which one of these combinations of outputs would maximize social well-being. To determine this, we would have to know more about the society's requirements and priorities. Is food security a high priority? Then the society would lean toward production of butter. Does the society fear attack by a foreign power? Perhaps then it would choose a point closer to the guns axis. For good social decision-making, production decisions need to take into account a full array of questions about resource management, distribution, and consumption, because all have effects on well-being. In a society with free speech and democratic discussion, there is wide room for disagreement about what the best mix of outputs might be.

BOX 1.3 THE OPPORTUNITY COST OF MILITARY EXPENDITURES

What do military buildups and wars really cost? One way to look at this is to consider what else could have been bought with the money spent on the military.

World military expenditures were $1.82 trillion in 2018, or 2.1 percent of world economic output.[3] The United States is by far the biggest spender; with $649 billion in spending, it accounts for 36 percent of the global total. China was second ($250 billion), followed by Saudi Arabia ($68 billion) and India ($56 billion). Many poor countries spend a significant share of their economic output on the military. For example, Algeria spends 5.3 percent of its GDP on the military and Zimbabwe 3.2 percent (about the same share as the United States).[4] The United States is the world's largest arms exporter, producing 36 percent of global arms, with 52 percent of these exports going to the Middle East.[5]

Military spending comes at the expense of other objectives. In 2015, the United Nations approved a set of 17 Sustainable Development Goals (SDGs) to "end poverty, protect the planet, and ensure prosperity for all," including global goals related to education, gender equality, health, clean energy, and reduced inequality.[6] According to a 2015 analysis,[7] many of these goals could be met for a fraction of world military expenditures. For example, meeting SDG Goal #3—ensuring healthy lives, including reducing maternal and infant mortality and providing universal health coverage—would cost an estimated $70–$90 billion per year, or about 5 percent of annual military expenditures. Providing universal access to safe water and sanitation (SDG Goal #6) would cost about $40 billion annually. Overall, the entire set of SDGs could be achieved with an annual investment of about $1.4 trillion, which is still less than the world's total military spending.

As U.S. president Dwight D. Eisenhower said in 1953, "Every gun that is made, every warship launched, every rocket fired, signifies in the final sense a theft from those who hunger and are not fed, those who are cold and are not clothed."

4.2 Tradeoffs Over Time

A PPF reflects possible production combinations for a given set of resources and technology at a given point in time. Should a society look at *all* the resources it has at a point in time and then strive to employ them to produce the *maximum quantity* of valued outputs over the coming year?

Recall that our economic question of *how* to produce has implications for resource management. If, say, we cut down all our forests or extract all our oil in order to maximize immediate production, that leaves fewer resources available for the future. The economic question of *for whom* asks how we allocate the outputs of production among various possible claimants in the present. It also, importantly, directs us to look at allocations between the present and the future. Sometimes this choice is between "me, now" and "me, in the future." For example, when a student gets some additional years of education, she is giving up current income from working full-time to gain higher skills and possibly earn a higher income in the future.

At other times, the allocation decision between present and future may be a question of using all our resources for the people who are around today vs. directing some resources to benefit others in the future. The flow of output from some production activities adds to the stock of resources available for the future. Investments in plant and equipment can provide productive capacity not just for a few months but often for years. Production of goods and services that preserve or restore natural resources and encourage the development of new forms of knowledge and social organization also lead to an improved resource base. Such production activities are also resource-management activities.

Technological progress, in which new methods are devised to convert resources into products, can lead to long-run improvements in efficiency and productive capacity and *add* to the production possibilities for the future. The PPF may expand over time, out and to the right, making previously unobtainable points obtainable, as shown in Figure 1.3. With the initial PPF, points A, B, and C are attainable, but points D and E are unattainable. With technological progress and an expanded PPF, points D and E could become attainable.

Some productive activities create an ongoing flow of outputs without drawing down the stock of resources, such as organic farming that maintains the nutrient levels in soil. Many other productive activities, however, lead to resource depletion or degradation. The intensive use of fossil fuels depletes petroleum reserves, degrades air quality, and contributes to global climate change. Production processes that destroy important watersheds and wildlife habitats are also resource depleting. Mind–numbing drudgery, work in dangerous circumstances, or excessively long hours of work can degrade human resources by leaving people exhausted or in poor mental or physical health. These kinds of productive activities are at odds with good resource management.

Taking a longer-term view, then, it is clear that getting the absolute most current production is generally not a wise social goal. Decisions such as our guns versus butter example need to be accompanied by another decision about *now* versus *later*.

The choice between current and future production can be presented in terms of a different PPF, as shown in Figure 1.4. In this case, the tradeoff is between current production and resource availability for the future. If society chooses point A,

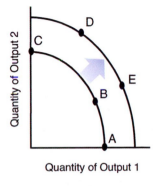

Figure 1.3 *An Expanded Production Possibilities Frontier*

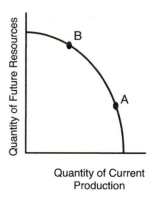

Figure 1.4 *Society's Choice Between Current Production and Future Resource Availability*

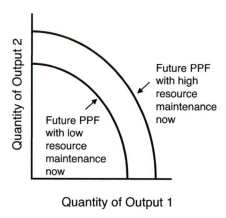

Figure 1.5 *Potential Future Production Possibility Frontiers*

current production is high, but resource availability for the future is low. However, choosing Point B reduces current production but results in significantly greater resource availability in the future.

The consequences of choosing between Points A and B are illustrated in Figure 1.5, where once again we portray a two-output PPF (such as guns versus butter). Now, however, the graph illustrates how future conditions are affected by the current choice between A and B in Figure 1.4. As Figure 1.5 shows, a decision to maintain more resources for the future, by choosing Point B in Figure 1.4, leads to a larger set of production possibilities in future years. A decision to engage in less resource management, shown by point A in Figure 1.4, leads to the smaller future PPF shown in Figure 1.5.

Some people may suggest that PPFs are always expanding outward as a result of technological progress and new investment in productive capacity and that we need not worry much about conserving resources. For example, we might not worry about depleting reserves of an important mineral based on the view that a substitute will be discovered in the future. But this is no more than an assertion of belief about what may or may not occur. In any event, much depends on *what* technology is developed and *what* substitute becomes viable. If technological progress does not materialize in the required form, in the required time, then overly exploiting resources in the present may lead to large-scale and irreversible consequences in the future. Hence, sustaining well-being over time requires technological progress *and* good resource management.

Discussion Questions

1. Suppose that your "resources" for studying can be devoted to either or both of two subjects: this class and another class you are taking. Would the PPF for your "production" have the shape portrayed in Figure 1.2? Discuss.
2. Consider the following possible productive activities. Which ones do you think will tend to expand the PPF in the future? Which ones will tend to contract it? (There may be room for disagreement on some points.)
   a. Increasing educational opportunities
   b. Manufacturing lawn mowers
   c. Building a nuclear power plant
   d. Restoring wetlands
   e. Building a new interstate highway
   f. Expanding internet capacity

REVIEW QUESTIONS

1. What is the definition of economics?
2. How does macroeconomics differ from microeconomics?
3. What is the difference between positive and normative questions? Give a couple of examples of each.
4. What is the difference between final and intermediate goals?
5. What is the goal of efficiency?
6. What are some examples of final goals?
7. What is meant by "living standards growth"? Is this the same as "economic growth"?
8. Why are macroeconomic fluctuations a cause for concern?
9. What global developments have caused financial, social, and ecological sustainability or restoration to become increasingly prominent as macroeconomic concerns?
10. Name the four essential economic activities.
11. What five types of capital contribute to productivity? Describe them.
12. How does economists' use of the term "capital" differ from common use?
13. Describe the difference between a stock and a flow, giving examples.
14. Describe the economic activity of production.
15. What are the two main forms that the activity of distribution takes? Describe.
16. How do abundance and scarcity create the possibility of, and the necessity for, economic decision-making?
17. Draw a societal PPF and use it to explain the concepts of tradeoffs (opportunity cost), attainable and unattainable output combinations, and efficiency.
18. What kinds of decisions would make a PPF expand over time? What kinds of decisions would make it contract over time?
19. What is the relationship between a society's PPF and resource management?

EXERCISES

1. In each of the following, indicate which of the four essential economic activities is taking place.
   a. Ms. Katar, an executive at Acme Manufacturing, directs the cleanup of one of the company's old industrial waste dump sites.
   b. Mr. Ridge plants a garden in his yard.
   c. Ms. Fuller hands an unemployed worker a bag of groceries at a local food pantry.
   d. Mr. Hernandez eats lunch at a cafeteria.

2. Which of the following are flows? Which are stocks? If a flow, which of the five major kind(s) of capital does it increase or decrease? If a stock, what kind of capital is it?
   a. The fish in a lake
   b. The output of a factory during a year
   c. The income that you receive in a month
   d. The reputation of a business among its customers
   e. The assets of a bank
   f. The equipment in a factory
   g. A process of diplomatic negotiations
   h. The discussion in an economics class

3. Which of the following are examples of exchange? Of transfer?
   a. De Beers mining company sells diamonds to wholesalers
   b. De Beers mining company takes diamonds from the mines
   c. You pay interest on credit card balances
   d. Your bank donates posters for a local community fair

4. The notion of scarcity reflects the idea that resources cannot be stretched to achieve all the goals that people desire. But what makes a particular resource "scarce"? If a resource seems to be in greater supply than is needed (like desert sand), is it scarce? If it is freely open to the use of many people at once (like music on the radio), is it scarce? What about resources such as social attitudes of trust and respect? Make a list of a few resources that clearly *are* scarce in the economic sense. Make another list of a few resources that are *not* scarce.

5. How is the concept of efficiency related to the concept of scarcity? Consider, for example, your own use of time. When do you feel that time is more, and when less, scarce? Do you think about how to use your time differently during exam week than you do when you are on vacation?

6. Suppose that society could produce the following combinations of pizzas and books:

Alternative	Quantity of pizzas	Quantity of books
A	50	0
B	40	10
C	30	18
D	20	24
E	10	28
F	0	30

   a. Using graph paper (or a computer program), draw the PPF for pizza and books, being as exact and neat as possible. (Put books on the horizontal axis. Assume that the dots define a complete curve.)
   b. Is it possible or efficient for this society to produce 25 pizzas and 25 books?

c.   Is it possible or efficient for this society to produce 42 pizzas and 1 book?

d.   If society is currently producing alternative B, then the opportunity cost of moving to alternative A (and getting 10 more pizzas) is _____ books.

e.   Is the opportunity cost of producing pizzas higher or lower moving from alternative F to E than moving from alternative B to A? Why is this likely to be so?

Suppose that the technologies used in producing both pizzas and books improve. Draw one possible new PPF in the previous graph that represents the results of this change. Indicate the direction of the change that occurs with an arrow.

7.   Match each concept in Column A with an example in Column B.

Column A	Column B
a. Manufactured capital	1. You should spend more time studying economics
b. An essential economic activity	2. A shared language within a community
c. A final goal	3. A factory building
d. An intermediate goal	4. The current unemployment rate is 7 percent
e. A normative statement	5. You are studying economics in order to get a good job
f. A positive statement	6. If you spend more time studying economics, you will have less time to sleep
g. An opportunity cost	7. Resource management
h. Social capital	8. A fair and just society

NOTES

1. World Bank. 2018. "Decline of Global Extreme Poverty Continues but Has Slowed: World Bank." World Bank Press Release, September 19.

2. Wilkinson, Richard G., and Kate Pickett. 2011. *The Spirit Level: Why Greater Equality Makes Societies Stronger.* Allen Lane, London.

3. Military Spending Data from the Stockholm International Peace Research Institute. www.sipri. org/research/armament-and-disarmament/arms-transfers-and-military-spending/military-expenditure

4. Ibid.

5. Ibid.

6. The United Nations Sustainable Development Goals: https://sustainabledevelopment.un.org/sdgs

7. Schmidt-Traub, Guido. 2015. "Investment Needs to Achieve the Sustainable Development Goals." Sustainable Development Solutions Network, SDSN Working Paper, November 12.

Chapter 2

Foundations of Economic Analysis

This chapter presents a number of important concepts that are useful in understanding how the economy works and in thinking about how we might make it work better as citizens and through government action. We start by describing different ways to investigate economic phenomena. This is followed by an examination of two models that offer different approaches to defining and understanding the economy. The final section provides an introduction to the nature of markets. The concepts discussed in this chapter provide much of the foundational knowledge for later chapters.

1. OUR TOOLS FOR UNDERSTANDING

Explanations of economic phenomena draw on two different approaches to seeking knowledge: empiricism and rationalism.

1.1 Empiricism

An empiricist argues that knowledge primarily comes to us from the five senses (seeing, hearing, touching, tasting, and smelling). In economics, **empirical investigation** is mainly about making observations that are then represented in words or images, as well as collecting numerical data. The time-series and cross-sectional data for various economic indicators, presented in Chapter 0, are a good example of empirical investigation.

> **empirical investigation:** analysis based on observation and recording of specific events, represented in words, images, or numerical data

Historical investigation, which involves using knowledge of historical events to help explain economic phenomena, is also empirical. The Great Depression of the 1930s, major wars, changing roles of women in the workforce, the invention of computers, and the financial crash of 2007–2008—all are examples of historical events that have had a significant economic impact.

> **historical investigation:** study of past events

Induction is a central tool of empiricism. For example, if we observe that swan number 1 is white, swan number 2 is white, and all the rest up to swan number 10,000 are also white, we see a pattern that may prompt us to claim that all swans are white. Of course, if we observe the existence of a black swan, this would disprove our initial claim. Similarly, if we regularly observe that when the price of a good rises, sales of that good will fall, then we might say that this constitutes a general relationship between price and demand for a good. However, if we find cases where price and demand rise together (as sometimes occurs), then this disproves the idea that the relationship between price and demand is fixed. As you can see, empiricism is about real-world evidence.

Empirical investigation is often useful in studying relationships between economic variables. If two economic variables seem empirically related to each other (or "correlated," to use the statistical term) such that they fluctuate together, it might be tempting to think that changes in one variable are *causing* changes in the other. Sometimes this is true. But two variables may also be related empirically *without* there being a well-defined causal relationship between them. For example, countries with higher GDP tend to have higher reported levels of cancer. But before we conclude that higher GDP causes cancer, we should consider other possibilities. For example, higher GDP is broadly associated with longer life expectancy, and people living longer are more likely to develop cancer at some point in their lives. Or there may be other factors (including diet, exercise, and a host of other variables) that connect these two observations—cancer and GDP. Economists take seriously the warning that "correlation does not necessarily imply causation." In other words, the existence of an observable relationship between two economic variables does not imply that changes in one variable *cause* the changes in the other.

BOX 2.1 GRAPHING REVIEW

Graphs provide a useful way to explore the relationship between two variables and test specific economic hypotheses. Based on Table 2.1, we might form the hypothesis that unemployment rates tend to be higher when GDP growth rates are lower. We call this a **negative, or inverse, relationship**—when an increase in one variable is associated with a

Table 2.1 Unemployment Rate and Real GDP Growth Rate, United States, 2008–2018 (in Percent)

	Unemployment rate	Real GDP growth rate
2008	5.8	−0.3
2009	9.3	−2.8
2010	9.6	2.5
2011	8.9	1.6
2012	8.1	2.2
2013	7.4	1.7
2014	6.2	2.4
2015	5.3	2.6
2016	4.9	1.6
2017	4.4	2.2
2018	3.9	2.9

Sources: U.S. Bureau of Economic Analysis and U.S. Bureau of Labor Statistics.

decrease in another variable (or, vice versa, when a decrease in one variable is associated with an increase in another variable).

> **negative (or inverse) relationship:** the relationship between two variables if an increase in one variable is associated with a decrease in the other variable (or vice versa)

Figure 2.1 plots the relationship between unemployment rates and GDP growth rates. Each "data point" on the graph tells us the values of *both* variables for a specific year. In the graph, we have kept the real GDP growth rate on the *x*-axis and the unemployment rate on the *y*-axis. So the data point for 2016, for example, indicates that the GDP growth rate was 1.6 percent (by reading across the *x*-axis) and the unemployment rate was 4.9 percent (by reading down the *y*-axis).

A visual inspection of Figure 2.1 shows relatively high unemployment rates when GDP growth rates were low or negative. In general, the graph seems to support our hypothesis of an inverse relationship between unemployment and GDP growth, but there are some exceptions.

Figure 2.1 can tell us whether our two variables are "correlated," but we cannot determine whether there is a causal relationship between them. While low GDP growth could cause high unemployment, the causality could potentially be in the opposite direction—that high unemployment causes low GDP growth. Even if the variables seem related in a graph, the relationship could be random, or "spurious." For example, you may have read stories about how the outcomes of sporting events are correlated with the performance of the stock market. But it is highly unlikely that such relationships are causal.

The opposite of an inverse relationship is a **positive, or direct, relationship.** In this case, an increase in one variable is associated with an increase in another variable—or a decrease in one variable is associated with a decrease in another variable.

> **positive (or direct) relationship:** the relationship between two variables when an increase in one variable is associated with an increase in the other variable or a decrease in one variable is associated with a decrease in the other variable

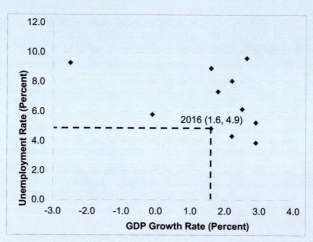

Figure 2.1 *Relationship Between Unemployment and GDP Growth Rate, United States, 2008–2018*

Sources: U.S. Bureau of Economic Analysis and U.S. Bureau of Labor Statistics.

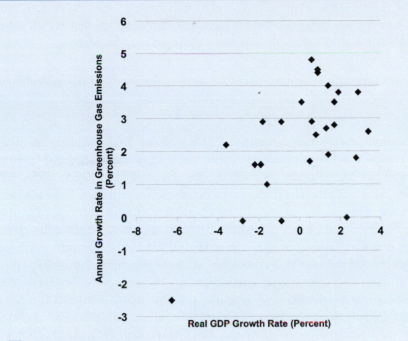

Figure 2.2 *Relationship Between GDP Growth Rate and Greenhouse Gas Emissions Growth Rate, United States, 1991–2015*

Source: Greenhouse gas data from United States Environmental Protection Agency.

A good example of a positive relationship is between the growth rate of GDP and the growth rate of greenhouse gas emissions, such as carbon dioxide and methane. When the economy is growing, greenhouse gas emissions increase as manufacturing industries tend to produce more goods, people tend to fly and drive more, and construction activity tends to increase. The relationship between GDP growth and the growth of greenhouse gas emission is shown in Figure 2.2. In this case, we see a reasonably clear positive relationship—when the economy is growing rapidly, greenhouse gas emissions tend to increase. However, as discussed previously, we cannot demonstrate causality just by looking at a graph.

While empirical evidence creates the foundation of economic analysis, a purely empirical investigation is unlikely to explain causation. Furthermore, we often need guidance in how to sift through the often overwhelming amount of empirical evidence available to us. Thus more tools are clearly needed for economists to try to *explain*, rather than simply describe, economic phenomena.

1.2 Rationalism

In contrast to an empiricist, a **rationalist** directs us to look to reason and logic in order to find knowledge. A dedicated rationalist would argue that observation (and the use of our senses) is not necessary. Consider an example. If we accept as a premise that all people are mortal, and Joe Bloggs is a person, then logical deduction dictates that Joe

Bloggs *must* be mortal. There is no requirement to wait around for many years in order to *empirically* observe Joe Bloggs's death, as logic and reason tell us that if our *premise* is correct and our *reasoning* is logical, then our conclusion *must* be correct.

> **rationalist investigation:** analysis based on abstract thought and the use of logic and reason

Much economic analysis uses rationalism. This tool can be particularly useful for determining causation between variables. Economists tend to use a rationalist approach to create theories based on assumptions about economic agents, from which, with careful reasoning, they draw out potential implications for economic behavior. For example, if we start from the premise that individuals are completely rational and fully informed, then we can use logic and reason to predict that they will make a particular choice. This choice is necessarily *optimal* because the individual has all the relevant information and can weigh this information in a completely accurate and rational manner.

A rationalist approach to pursuing knowledge can be very useful, but rationalism has its limitations. In particular, if your initial premise is not accurate, then your conclusion is unlikely to be correct. For example, if an individual is not fully informed or fully rational (as is often the case), then that individual's choice is unlikely to be optimal, even if our use of reasoning and logic seems correct.

1.3 Theory and Evidence

Most analysis is (or at least should be) a mix of empiricism and rationalism. On one hand, we need reason and logic to make sense of, and to organize, a vast jumble of empirical observations. On the other hand, purely rationalist theorizing without any recourse to empirical evidence is likely to produce misleading and irrelevant lines of analysis. A good economic theory is thus informed by empirical evidence as well as rationalist investigation.

Let us now say a little about the nature of economic theory. It should be stressed at the outset that a theory can never be as complex and rich as the reality it seeks to explain, so theory is about simplification. How to simplify is a difficult and somewhat uncertain task. This is one reason there are sometimes competing theories and disagreements within economics. It is important to understand the strengths and weaknesses of particular theories and to be open to considering alternative theories.

Theories often give rise to models. A **model** is an analytical tool that highlights some aspects of reality while ignoring others (in economics, what is ignored is often a portion of the larger historical, social, and environmental context). A model can take the form of a simplified story, an image, a figure, a graph, or a set of equations, and it always involves simplifying assumptions. We look at examples of two basic economic models in Section 2. Other models appear throughout this text.

> **model:** an analytical tool that highlights some aspects of reality while ignoring others

An important part of many models is the assumption of **ceteris paribus**, a Latin phrase that means "other things equal" or "all else constant." In order to focus on one or two variables, we assume that no other variables change. Of course, in the real world, many things are usually changing at the same time. Often, after a basic model is constructed, we can vary the *ceteris paribus* assumption to see how changes in other variables will affect the model's conclusions.

> **ceteris paribus:** a Latin phrase meaning "other things equal" or "all else constant"

Theories and models essentially simplify reality. Is this justifiable? It is if it gives us greater insight into how things actually work. A model plane, for example, cannot carry passengers or freight, but it can give aerodynamic engineers insights into how a real plane works and help them to design better features for real aircraft. In the same way, simplified models can help economists to understand the working of very complex real-world economies. The question is not whether simplification should occur but whether a particular model's simplifications are reasonable.

Discussion Questions

1. Consider the following examples of investigation. For each one, indicate which mode of investigation it most closely matches, empirical or rational.
   a. A biologist tries to determine the number of different species of plants found on a plot of rainforest
   b. Albert Einstein develops his theory of relativity
   c. An economist measures how GDP varies across countries
   d. A sociologist examines the impact of movements for equal pay for women on women's social and economic status
   e. An economist states that a rise in investment will lead to a fall in unemployment
2. Model building is sometimes compared to map making. If someone asks you how to get to your house, what will you put on the map you draw for them? What if the question asked has to do with the location of the highest point in town, the town's political boundaries, the public transit system, or how your dwelling links up to the local sewer system? Is it possible for a single, readable map to answer every possible question? Does the goal you have in mind for the map affect what you put on it?

2. DIFFERENT ECONOMIC THEORIES: EXAMPLES OF TWO BASIC MODELS

The discipline of economics, like most other areas of academic and public discussion, has a history of varying approaches, beliefs, and conclusions. We will discuss these different approaches in later chapters, but here we present two theoretical models for understanding the economy: the neoclassical model, which has dominated much of standard economics throughout the twentieth century, and the contextual model, which incorporates post-twentieth-century advances in economic research. The contextual model is central to this text. These two approaches have some

overlap, but they have different scope and emphasis and can lead to different under-
standings of economic theory and policy.

2.1 The Basic Neoclassical Model

The **basic neoclassical model** is a model of market exchange that—while abstract-
ing away from many real-world factors—portrays some important aspects of markets
in a simple way. Neoclassical economics is based on the idea that economies can
be thought of as a collection of profit-maximizing firms and utility-maximizing
households interacting in perfectly competitive markets. This idea is expressed in
terms of formalized assumptions, equations, and graphs.

> **basic neoclassical model:** a model that portrays the economy as a collection
> of profit-maximizing firms and utility-maximizing households interacting in
> perfectly competitive markets

This model can be portrayed in the **circular-flow diagram**, as shown in Figure 2.3.
In this model, the world is simplified to two kinds of economic actors: households
and firms, represented by two rectangles. The activity of exchange between the two
actors is illustrated using the blue arrows. Households are assumed to consume

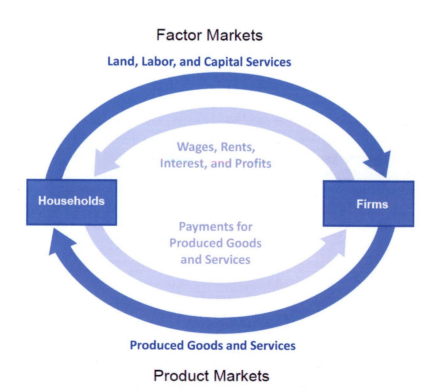

Figure 2.3 *The Circular Flow Diagram for the Basic Neoclassical Model*

goods and services with the single (though rather abstract) goal of maximizing their **utility** (or satisfaction). Firms are assumed to produce with the single goal of maximizing profits. Households are considered the ultimate owners of all resources of land, labor, and capital, called "factors of production" by economists. Households rent the services of these productive factors to firms through **factor markets** (dark blue arrow from households to firms), receiving monetary payments in the form of wages, rents, interests, and profits (light blue arrow from the firms to households). Firms produce goods and services, which they sell to households on **product markets** (dark blue arrow from firms to households) in return for monetary payments (light blue arrow from households to firms). The model further assumes that there are so many firms and households involved in the market for any good or service that a situation of "perfect competition" reigns, in which prices are determined purely by forces of supply and demand.

> **circular flow diagram:** a graphical representation of the traditional view of an economy consisting of households and firms engaging in exchange
> **utility:** the level of usefulness or satisfaction gained from a particular activity such as consumption of a good or service
> **factor markets:** markets for the services of land, labor, and capital
> **product markets:** markets for newly produced goods and services

The circular flow diagram is useful in portraying, in a very simplified way, two of the major actors (households and firms) and three of the major activities (production, exchange, and consumption) involved in economic life. However, it is important to recognize that the model leaves out some key actors and activities.

For example, while "land" is included as a factor of production, the fact that natural resources can be used up or polluted is not shown. Because of this, the circular flow diagram is a little like a "perpetual motion machine"; the economy it portrays can apparently keep on generating products forever without any inputs of materials or energy. The necessity of resource management activities is not included.

Also, the diagram only takes into account flows of goods or resources that are paid for through the market. This ignores unpaid work and free use of natural resources, among other things. The roles of sociocultural norms and historical factors in influencing economic behavior are also neglected in this model. You will also notice that there is no role for government in this diagram. While this oversimplification has some value in allowing us to focus only on the workings of specific markets, it limits our ability to present a broader picture that considers the context in which economic activities occur.

2.2 The Contextual Model

The traditional circular flow model ignores the *environmental* and *social contexts* within which economic activities take place. We therefore need a more inclusive, and more realistic, model than the one presented in Figure 2.3. We present such a model in Figure 2.4.

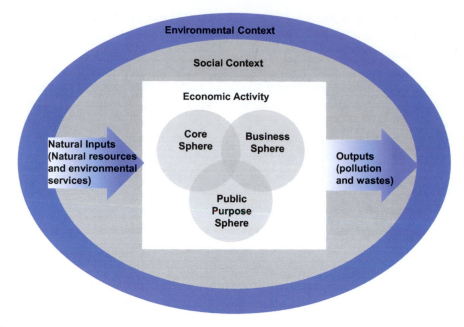

Figure 2.4 *Social and Environmental Contexts of Economic Activity*

Because all economic production requires the input of natural resources and generates some wastes, the economy operates in an *environmental context*. For example, if we overburden a river with toxic chemicals, the water may not be usable in the future for drinking water supplies. Sometimes economic activity can also generate some positive externalities (unintended spill overs), such as restorative care for farms and rangelands that make them more productive over time.

The economy also operates in a *social context* created and maintained by human beings; this includes history, politics, culture, ethics, and other human motivations. The social context determines what constitutes acceptable economic activity. For example, we do not allow legal markets for human organs or certain drugs. It also determines the relative weight that a society attaches to the different goals discussed in Chapter 1, such as how to identify and assess a potential tradeoff between ecological sustainability and increasing material living standards.

As we will see in the discussion of markets in Section 3, much economic activity would become impossible without aspects of the social context such as laws, norms, trust, and honesty. Like the environment, society is also the recipient of both positive and negative outputs from the economy, such as inventions, products, services, and perceptions about what is a "good life." Some of these may be truly well-being enhancing, while others may run counter to actual well-being.

In Figure 2.4, we show the social context as existing inside the environmental context because all human activities—not only those of the economic system—are ultimately dependent on the environmental context. A useful understanding of economics must consider the most critical interactions between the economy and its contexts, showing how the economy is in various ways enabled and constrained by these contexts and how the environmental and social influences are affected *by* the economy.

The contextual approach presents economic activity as occurring within three spheres: core, public purpose, and business. The core sphere includes households, families, and community institutions. The public purpose sphere includes government and other local, national, and international organizations that seek to enhance human well-being. And the business sphere includes firms producing goods and services for profitable sale. Individuals may move among these three spheres; for example, a woman may be a wife and mother in the core sphere, a volunteer for an environmental group in the public purpose sphere, and a business executive in the business sphere. Thus, Figure 2.4 shows the three spheres overlapping. We discuss economic activity in the three spheres in more detail next.

Core Sphere

The **core sphere** includes households, families, and community institutions that undertake economic activities, usually on a small scale and largely without the use of money. Traditionally, economists have focused on the core sphere as consumers and workers in their interactions with businesses. But important economic activity occurs *within* the core sphere. For example, the core sphere is the primary site for raising children; preparing meals; maintaining homes; organizing leisure time; and caring for individuals who are sick, elderly, or needy but not in institutions such as hospitals or nursing homes.

> **core sphere:** households, families, and informal community groups

Conversion of many goods and services (often bought in markets) into forms suitable for final use, such as cooking pasta or planting grass seeds, occurs within the core sphere. Decisions on how to allocate income among consumption, savings, or financial investments are made within the core sphere. So are decisions on allocating time between labor and leisure. As we will see in later chapters, such decisions play an important role in determining economic outcomes.

One distinguishing characteristic of the core sphere is that economic activities are rewarded by what it produces instead of earning money. For example, work in a home garden is rewarded with tomatoes, and the reward from good child care is a happy and healthy child. Activities in the core sphere respond not only to *wants* but also to *needs*—unlike market activities, which respond to what people are able and willing to pay for, regardless of need. The core sphere is critical for subsistence economies, where extended families and villages may produce for themselves most of what they consume, with little outside trading.

Core sphere activities are sometimes described as noneconomic or nonproductive because they generally do not produce goods and services for trade through a market. But this can be misleading. Consider the activity of providing care to family members. According to a 2015 analysis, the estimated economic value of this unpaid labor in 2013 was $470 billion.[1] A different study found that the value of unpaid care work by women in the United States was even higher, at $1.5 trillion per year.[2]

When the core sphere is working effectively to support human well-being, important goods and services are provided to many people, even if the scale of production in each case is quite small. Of course, core spheres can also work inadequately. The requirements of caring for children or elderly and ill people may overwhelm the resources of impoverished families and communities. One extreme example is the situation of families and communities in sub-Saharan Africa trying to care for the large number of children orphaned by HIV/AIDS or by war, without adequate resources to feed and clothe the children, let alone provide for education and safety. There are limits to what can be accomplished within small-scale, largely informal networks of personal relations. The public purpose sphere, with more formal and larger-scale organizations, is uniquely capable of meeting broader well-being needs.

The Public Purpose Sphere

The **public purpose sphere** includes government agencies, as well as nonprofit organizations such as charities, religious organizations, professional associations, and international institutions such as the World Bank and the United Nations. They may be as large as a national government or an international scientific organization or as small as a local chapter of the Cub Scouts. The distinguishing characteristic of these institutions is that they exist for an explicit purpose related to the public good—that is, the common good of some group larger than a household or informal community—and they do not aim at making a profit.

> **public purpose sphere:** governments and other local, national, and international organizations established for a public purpose beyond individual or family self-interest and not operating with the goal of making a profit

We can break down the economic functions of public purpose organizations into two general categories: *regulation* and *direct provision*.

Regulation

One very basic function of public purpose organizations is to **regulate** economic activities—that is, to set the standards and "rules of the game" by which other economic actors "play"—so as to create the legal, informational, and social infrastructure for economic activity. Though many people think of "regulation" entirely in terms of "government regulation," many nonprofit groups also participate in regulating economic activity, particularly in the area of standard setting. For example, standardized exams like the AP, SAT I or II, GRE, GMAT, or TOEFL are all developed and administered by the Educational Testing Service, which is a large private nonprofit organization.

> **regulation:** setting standards or laws to govern behavior

Direct Public Provision

Direct public provision is often used to supply goods or services that cannot be supplied equitably or efficiently by core sphere institutions and businesses alone. Some of the goods and services provided by the public purpose sphere are what economists call public goods. A **public good** (or service) is a good whose benefits are freely available to all (**non-excludable**), and whose use by some does not reduce the quantity available to others (**non-rival**).

> **direct public provision:** the supply of goods or services from government or nonprofit institutions
>
> **public good:** a good whose benefits are freely available to anyone and whose use by one person does not diminish its usefulness to others
>
> **non-excludable good:** a good whose benefits are freely available to all
>
> **non-rival good:** a good whose use by one person does not reduce the quantity or quality available to others

For example, when a local police force helps to make a neighborhood safe, all the residents benefit. Public roads (at least those that are not congested and have no tolls) are also public goods, as is national defense. Some of the larger public purpose organizations, often associated with some level of government, are charged with purposes such as relieving poverty, providing formal health care and education, protecting the natural environment, and stabilizing global financial markets. Religious organizations are other well-known public purpose organizations. Small and large nonprofits exist to promote various causes, ranging from protecting natural resources to providing the homeless with shelter to lobbying for equality based on race and sexual orientation. Some things are provided by the public purpose sphere because, as a society, we believe that everyone should have access to them, regardless of their ability to pay. Public schooling from kindergarten through high school is a primary example.

In some instances, public purpose organizations offer goods and services for sale as businesses do, but this is generally not their primary focus. They usually raise much of their support by soliciting monetary contributions or, in the case of governments, requiring such contributions in the form of taxes or fees. Your college or university, if it is operated by a nonprofit or government entity, would be part of the public purpose sphere. For-profit universities, however, would fall in the business sphere.

The main strength of public purpose institutions is that (like core institutions) they provide goods and services of high intrinsic value, but (unlike core institutions) they are big enough, or sufficiently well-organized, to take on jobs that require broader social coordination. Unlike in the business sphere, the provision of goods and services itself, and not the financial results of these activities, remains the primary intended focus of public purpose organizations.

The public purpose sphere has its weaknesses, of course. Institutions in the public purpose sphere are sometimes accused of being rigid, slow to adapt, and inefficient because of excessive regulation and bloated bureaucracy. Organizations can lose sight

57

of the intrinsic, common-good goal of providing "public service" and become more focused on increasing their organizational budget. Many current debates about reforms in governments and nonprofits concern how incentives for efficiency can be improved without eroding these organizations' orientation toward providing goods and services of high intrinsic value.

The Business Sphere

The **business sphere** is made up of firms that are expected to look for opportunities to buy and manage resources in such a way that, after their product is sold, the owners of the firm will earn profits. Whereas the core sphere responds to direct needs, and the public purpose sphere responds to its constituents, business firms are responsive to demands for goods and services, as expressed through markets by people who have the resources to buy the firms' products.

---

business sphere: firms that produce goods and services for profitable sale

---

It is sometimes thought that maximizing profits is the *only* goal of businesses. But firms may have motivations beyond profit maximization. They may consider social and ethical aspects in making business decisions and may aim to be good "corporate citizens" with regard to their workers, communities, or the environment. Additionally, the activities of "the firm" are made up of the activities of many people, including its stockholders, board of directors, mid- and top-level managers, and employees. The interests of the various individuals and suborganizations may be in conflict. Sometimes, top officers and managers may act, for example, not in the profit-making interest of the owners but according to their *personal* self-interest, such as maximizing their own prestige and income. Profits, and even the long-term survival of the company itself, may be sacrificed in a race for individual high salaries and lucrative bonuses.

One strength of businesses is that because they have at least one clear goal—making a profit—their efficiency in reaching that goal may be greater than the efficiency of actors in the other two spheres. The profit motive of businesses also encourages *innovation:* People are motivated to come up with clever new ideas when they know that they may reap financial rewards. We all benefit from innovations when they bring us improved products at lower prices. We should note, however, that the public purpose sphere has also often played a critical role in innovation (see Box 2.2).

The relative weakness of the business sphere comes from the fact that business interests do not necessarily coincide with overall social well-being. Firms *may* act to enhance social well-being—for example, by making decisions that consider the needs of their customers and their workers, as well as taking into account environmental impacts—but business sphere production has no *built-in* correction for adverse social and environment impacts. A more detailed discussion on some of the key limitations of the business sphere can be found in Section 3.4.

BOX 2.2 THE GOVERNMENT'S ROLE IN INNOVATION

Much economic analysis focuses on entrepreneurship and innovations in the business sector as the key drivers of the economy. Proponents of the free market sometimes argue that the private sector—motivated by the profit-maximizing goal—is more efficient and more innovative than the public sector. They therefore advocate for an expansion of the private sector into sectors like education and health care. Others argue that these activities are normally better undertaken in the public sector, as universal access to education and health care are essential for a healthy society.

Evidence indicates that government plays a key role in supporting the business sector in the United States. Not only does the public sector provide the physical and informational infrastructure on which businesses rely, but also many well-known success stories in the business sector have depended on government inventions.

Take, for example, the case of iPhone. The success of iPhone has been largely attributed to Apple—a private corporation. However, each of its core technologies, including capacitive sensors, solid-state memory, the click-wheel, GPS, internet, cellular communications, Siri, microchips, and touchscreen, are innovations that came from research supported by the U.S. government and military. Economist Mariana Mazzucato argues that long-term and steady government funding in technological research has been a nearly invariable prerequisite for breakthrough innovations. She points out that the public sector is, in fact, often more innovative than the private sector, as the government is more willing to make riskier investments.[3]

In the health care sector, also, the government has taken a lead in research and innovation, with almost 75 percent of all important new drugs coming from funding through the National Institutes of Health. Major pharmaceutical companies do develop innovative drugs, but they also invest heavily in advertising and in developing "me-too" drugs to try to undercut their competitors. Data from GlobalData, a health care research firm, shows that nine out of the top ten pharmaceutical companies spent more on advertising than on research.[4] This is partly the result of the United States being one of only two countries where it is legal to market prescription drugs directly to consumers.[5]

The Size of the Three Spheres

Figure 2.5 presents estimates of the monetary value of the annual production of goods and services in the United States by the three spheres in 2018 in dollar and percentage terms. The business sphere contributed 64.6 percent of production, the core sphere 21.1 percent, and the public purpose sphere 14.3 percent. The dollar figures add up to more than the GDP in that year ($20.6 trillion) because an estimate of the value of unpaid household labor as equal to 18 percent of GDP has been included.[6] This differs from government estimates of GDP in the United States, which do not currently include the value of household production.

While the business sphere comprises the majority of economic activity in the United States, that is not the case in all countries. For example, some rough estimates indicate that the largest sphere in France is the public purpose sphere, at about 40

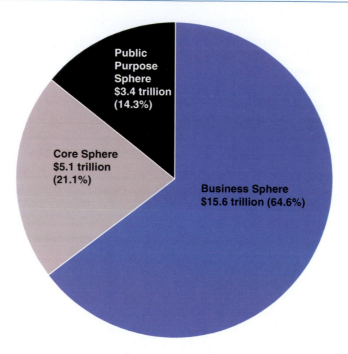

Figure 2.5 *Estimates of the Size of the Three Spheres in the United States, 2018*

Sources: U.S. Bureau of Economic Analysis, GDP and Personal Income database, and authors' calculations.

percent of the overall economy. Also, the value of unpaid labor in the United Kingdom is officially estimated to be equivalent to 63 percent of GDP, suggesting a relatively large core sphere.[7]

In addition to the three spheres discussed so far, all countries have, to some extent, an informal sphere. The **informal sphere** is composed of market enterprises, normally small in scale, operating outside government oversight. Although this sphere could be classified as "business" because it involves private production for sale, it is also similar to the core sphere in that the activities are very small scale and often depend on family and community connections. Economic activities in the informal sphere may be illegal, as in the case of illicit drugs or prostitution. Other informal sphere activities are legal but do not appear in GDP statistics, such as housecleaning services provided "off the books." Barter transactions are also part of the informal sphere.

> **informal sphere:** businesses, usually small in scale, operating outside government oversight and regulation

Though accurate data on the size of the informal sphere are difficult to obtain, the average size of the informal economy in 158 countries between 1991 and 2015 was estimated to be 31.9 percent.[8] A 2018 study estimates that 60 percent of the world's employed population are in the informal economy, with 93 percent of those living in emerging and developing countries.[9]

Discussion Questions

1. Education is sometimes provided within the core sphere (at-home preschool activities and home schooling), often provided by the public purpose sphere (public and nonprofit schools), and sometimes provided by for-profit firms ("charter schools" or firms offering specific training programs). Can you think of some possible advantages and disadvantages of each of these three ways of providing education?

2. Describe three situations in which economic activities could affect their environmental context and three ways in which economic behavior could affect their social context. How might these influences that the economy exerts on its contexts result in changing how the contexts, in turn, affect (either support or constrain) economic activity?

3. THE ROLE OF MARKETS

Having discussed the three major spheres of economic activity, we now take up the more specific issue of how markets work. We begin by defining precisely what we mean by "markets." Then we look at ways to make markets work smoothly and consider the various advantages and limitations of markets as a way to conduct economic activities.

3.1 The Meaning of Markets

When you think of the word "market," you probably think of a store where you buy groceries. But in economics, the word "market" is defined more broadly and has at least three different meanings, ranging from very concrete to very abstract. The appropriate meaning of market must be judged from the context in which it appears.

The most concrete and commonsense definition of a **market** is that it is a *place* where people interact physically or virtually to buy and sell things. Historically, markets have been physical locations such as the Grand Bazaar in Istanbul, Turkey, or African village produce stands where people meet and engage in exchange transactions. In the modern age, the market "location" could be a physical place such as a shopping mall or a stock exchange building. But it could also be virtual, such as Amazon or eBay, where buyers and sellers can come together to make market transactions. Most stock exchanges have also moved to electronic trading, although a role remains for brokers on the floor of the New York Stock Exchange.

> **market (first meaning):** a physical place or Web location where there is a reasonable expectation of finding both buyers and sellers for the same product or service

A more general definition of **market** is that it is a concept that covers broad product categories. For example, we can speak of the "real estate market" in a particular city, the market for used cars, or the market for wind turbines. Economists often study trends in specific markets, such as heating oil or AT&T bonds, to try to forecast what might happen in the future or advise on the specifics of market structures.

> **market (second meaning):** the interaction of buyers and sellers defined within the bounds of broad product categories, such as the market for used cars or the real estate market

In the most abstract terms, people refer to markets as an economic system, for example, describing the United States as having a "**market economy**" or indicating a preference for "free markets." In this macroeconomic sense, a market economy is one that relies heavily on markets (according to both our first and second definitions) to conduct economic activities.

> **market (third meaning):** an economic system (a "market economy") that relies on markets to conduct many economic activities

One alternative to a market economy is a system that relies on central planning to conduct economic activities, as was the case in the Soviet Union. China retains many elements of a central planning system, though the role of markets in China has expanded significantly in recent decades. But even in modern market economies, not all activities are structured by markets. For example, the distribution of resources within the core sphere is mainly based on social or family relationships, and decisions about resource management are often based on scientific evidence or political preferences rather than market forces.

Differing views on the role of markets within an economic system underlie many current debates in economics. Economists who have a "pro-market" view believe that market systems function fairly smoothly and are largely self-regulated and that a **laissez-faire economy** (one with very little government regulation) is most likely to lead to economic growth and prosperity. Other economists recognize the effectiveness of markets but believe that problems such as poverty, inequality, environmental degradation, and declining social ethics may be caused or exacerbated by unregulated markets. They therefore advocate for government policies and other forces of culture and ethics to ensure that markets serve the broader goals of human well-being. As we examine different issues throughout this book, we frequently refer to these perspectives.

> **laissez-faire economy:** an economy with little government regulation

3.2 The Institutional Requirements of Markets

Contemporary markets do an amazing thing: They allow many separate decision-makers, acting on decentralized information, to coordinate their behavior, resulting in highly complex patterns of economic activity. However, markets depend on institutions to operate smoothly. An **institution** refers to a formal or informal rule that structures human interactions. They include laws, customs, norms, routines, and operating procedures. In other words, they encompass everything from a national constitution to table manners.

Organizations (for example, a hospital) are sometimes called institutions, but it makes more sense to consider organizations as *sets* of particular institutions. For example, a hospital's operations are structured by federal and state laws; customary procedures for doctor visits; and rules and procedures concerning patient admissions, care, and discharges. Organizations are usually housed in buildings and contain physical infrastructure, yet an organization's essence is represented by the formal and informal institutions that govern it, not physical infrastructure. This is why even when an organization relocates to a different building, it can essentially be the same organization.

> **institutions:** formal and informal rules that structure the relationship between individuals and groups

Many institutions help markets work more smoothly. For example, credit cards are an institution that facilitates purchases without the use of cash. Consumer protection laws are an institution that defines certain exploitative business practices as illegal. The ability to return purchased items for a refund can also be viewed as a widely accepted institution. We classify institutions that facilitate the functioning of markets into three broad groups:

1. institutions related to property and decision-making
2. social institutions of trust
3. money as a medium of exchange.

Institutions Related to Property and Decision-Making

For markets to work, people need to know what belongs to whom or at least who can or cannot have access and control over something. Ownership is usually defined through systems of property rights set out in law and enforced by courts and police. **Private property** is the ownership of physical or financial assets by nongovernment economic actors. **Common property** is ownership of physical or financial assets by the government or particular subsections of society.

> **private property:** ownership of assets by nongovernment economic actors
> **common property:** ownership of assets by government or particular subsections of society

Within a market economy, actors must be allowed to make their own decisions about how to allocate and exchange resources that belong to them. Prices, in particular, must not be controlled by a central planning agency; generally, they should be set by the interactions of market participants themselves.

63

The institutions of private property and individual decision-making exist both formally, in codes of law, and informally, in social and cultural norms. For example, some Western economists expected markets to grow quickly in the countries of the former Soviet Union as soon as communism was dismantled and opportunities for markets opened up. This failed to occur, partly because many people living in these countries were accustomed to being told by the state where to work and what to do. Norms of individual initiative and entrepreneurship, it turns out, do not just arise naturally but need to be fostered. Nor did other sorts of market infrastructure appear quickly, and the post-Soviet Russian economy went into a severe decline for some time. When market institutions did develop, they were often designed to facilitate the concentration of power and oligarchy (control by a few very wealthy people). The difficult transition to capitalism in the former Soviet Union indicates that institutions matter and that good institutions do not emerge quickly, naturally, or easily.

Social Institutions of Trust

A degree of trust must exist between buyers and sellers. When a buyer puts down her payment, she must trust that the seller will hand over the merchandise and that it will be of the expected quality. A seller must be able to trust that the payment offered is valid, whether it is in the form of currency, a personal check, credit card, online payment, or a promise of future payment such as an installment loan.

The establishment of direct, one-on-one exchanges between customers and businesses help to build trust and make future transactions smoother. Consumers are more likely to choose sellers with whom they have had good experiences in the past. They may also rely on reputation of firms based on online reviews such as Yelp or on perceptions about the quality and prices associated with brand names to make consumption decisions. Cultural norms and ethical or religious codes can also help to establish and maintain an atmosphere of trustworthiness.

In some cases, the terms of trade between different parties may be established informally, based on verbal terms or cultural and social expectations. However, in cases where market transactions take place in large, complex, mobile societies where buyers and sellers may not know each other, a more formal, usually written, contract may be needed to legally enforce the terms of exchange. Hence, legal institutions provide an important basis for many market transactions.

Even with a system of formal contracts, social norms are still essential, as it is costly to write and enforce detailed formal contracts, and it is impossible to cover every conceivable contingency. The legal system can work smoothly only if most people willingly obey most laws and believe that it is dishonorable to cheat. In other words, formal institutions usually depend quite heavily on the presence of good informal institutions, particularly good norms of behavior.

In highly marketized economies, many other institutions have evolved to deal with the issue of trust. For example, credit bureaus keep track of consumer credit trustworthiness, Better Business Bureaus keep track of complaints against businesses, and money-back guarantees give consumers a chance to test the quality of a good before they commit to purchasing. Government agencies such as the U.S. Food and Drug Administration and local boards of health are charged with monitoring the quality and purity of many goods that are sold.

Clearly, relationships, social norms, and government-created laws are all institutions that are essential to make market activity possible.

Money as a Medium of Exchange

The final basic institution required to facilitate the operation of markets is a generally accepted form of money. Many different things, such as carved stones or particular types of seashells, have been used as money in the past. Gold, silver, and other metal coins were the most common choice for many centuries. More recently, paper currency became important. Today, the use of checks, credit cards, debit cards, and electronic payment systems further facilitates making payments for goods and services.

What makes something **money**? Three criteria are necessary for something to be defined as money in a market economy.

1. Money must be widely accepted as *a medium of exchange.*
2. Money must provide *a durable store of value.* Imagine the problems that would occur if heads of lettuce, which rot within a week or two, were proposed as money. The value of money must be relatively stable over time, and money *must have minimal handling and storage costs.* By this criterion, paper currency is better than coins, and electronic transactions are better still.
3. Money must be accepted as a *unit of account.* When people say that something is worth $1,000, that does not necessarily mean that they are proposing to buy or sell the item. Money serves as a way of valuing things, even if no market exchange takes place.

> **money:** a medium of exchange that is widely accepted, durable as a store of value, has minimal handling and storage costs, and serves as a unit of account

In most cases, money is created by the banking system, with oversight by national governments. However, this is not always the case. For example, cigarettes have been used as a form of money by prisoners of war. Also, communities smaller than national governments can create their own money. These local currencies are typically exchangeable for goods and services within the community by participating merchants and individuals. In recent years, local "time-banking" currencies have appeared in some communities in the United States and elsewhere. People earn time dollars by performing valuable services for others or for the community as a whole, such as child care, tutoring, or building repairs. Time dollars can then be used to pay for other services or used instead of "normal" dollars to purchase products from local merchants (see Box 2.3).

BOX 2.3 TIME BANKING

Time banking is a system of exchange where time, not money, is the unit of value. Time banks bring together unused human resources with unmet human needs.[10] When you join a time bank, you indicate what services you might be able to offer others: financial planning, computer debugging, handyman repairs, child care, and so on. For each hour (or fraction of an hour) you spend helping others, you accrue "deposits" in the time bank. Then when you require services, you can "withdraw" accumulated time to request help from others.

Time banks differ from exchange through markets in several important ways. First, everybody's time is normally considered equally valuable. Whether one is performing nursing services, tutoring new immigrants in English, or driving someone on errands, all activities earn time credits at the same rate (1 hour = 1 credit). Second, exchange through time banks helps build social relationships and community spirit. Many time bank members note that performing activities eventually become viewed as spending time with friends rather than work. In fact, according to one time bank director, a majority of members don't claim credit for all hours logged.[11] Another interesting feature is that time banks can particularly flourish during economic downturns when traditional employment is difficult to find. Thus participants can still feel they are contributing to society and accruing credit for needed services without paid employment.

According to the organization TimeBanks, there are about 1,000 time banks in the world, with about half of these being in the United States.[12] In 2017, a time bank was created in the United Kingdom, partially funded by the UK government, to provide care and companionship for elderly people. In this system, people contribute time helping others to eventually be redeemed when they themselves need assistance later in life.[13] Time banking has become popular in New Zealand, where businesses and organizations can also participate, offering goods and services in exchange for time credits rather than money.[14]

3.3 Infrastructure for Flow of Goods and Information

Another requirement of markets is physical infrastructure to enable the smooth flow of goods, services, and information. **Physical infrastructure** includes such things as roads, ports, railroads, and warehouses, but also telecommunications and utilities.

> **physical infrastructure:** roads, ports, railroads, warehouses, and other tangible structures that provide the foundation for economic activity

The function of infrastructure is not just to allow the movement of goods; it is also required for information to flow freely. Producers and sellers need information on what, and how much, their customers want to buy to be able to decide on what, and how much, should be produced and offered for sale. At the same time, consumers need to know what is available and how much they will have to pay to get the products that are on the market. Ideally, consumers should be able to compare *all* potential purchases to decide what will best suit their needs. It seems unlikely that this condition for perfect markets will ever be reached, but Web-based exchange systems such as Amazon and eBay have brought it much closer to realization.

Note that infrastructure can be provided by both private and government entities. While private companies normally own things like warehouses, delivery trucks, and computers, governments normally construct and maintain roads, ensure air traffic safety, and make bandwidth available on the internet. Even in an economic system that primarily relies on private markets, the role of government is critical in supporting market activity.

3.4 Types of Markets

Markets take a wide variety of forms. The two basic market types—product and factor markets—that we defined in the neoclassical model can be further categorized into different groups based on what is sold, as described in Table 2.2.

Table 2.2 Different Types of Markets

Market Type	Description
Retail markets	Markets where goods and services are purchased by consumers from businesses, generally in small quantities. Retail markets deal in tangible goods such as food, books, and clothes, as well as non-tangible objects, including services such as banking or a haircut.
Wholesale markets	Markets where final goods are purchased by retailers from suppliers, normally in large quantities. For example, Wal-Mart and most other retailers don't actually produce the goods they sell but purchase them in bulk from suppliers in wholesale markets.
Intermediate goods markets	Markets where unfinished products are exchanged between businesses, such as the purchase of sheet metal by an automobile company.
Resale markets	Product markets for items that have been previously owned. Examples include used-car markets and markets for antique furniture. Most shares traded in stock markets are also being resold, having been previously owned by other investors.
Commodities markets	Markets where raw materials such as agricultural products, minerals, or petroleum are bought and sold.
Labor markets	A type of factor market, defined as the set of institutions through which people who wish to work offer to sell their services to employers. Unlike a physical object, labor cannot be produced first and then handed to the buyer; rather, the worker promises to do something in return for a promised payment of wages.
Financial markets	Markets for loans, equity finance, and financial assets such as stocks and bonds. Chapter 13 will focus on financial markets.
Underground markets (black markets)	Illegal markets, where either the good or service traded is illegal (such as heroin or smuggled antiquities) or the goods and services are legitimate but the trading occurs through illegal ways. For example, smugglers may sell cigarettes or imported perfume at prices that do not include payment of required taxes.
Auction markets	Markets in which an item is sold to the highest bidder. Auction markets are often used when the price for an item is relatively unknown and there are many possible buyers or sellers. Although auction markets were commonly limited to goods such as antiques and artwork in the past, the advent of online auction sites such as eBay have made auction markets much more prevalent.

Markets can also be categorized based on how prices are determined. At first glance, it might seem as if many prices set in consumer retail markets do not involve interactions of market participants themselves. In an open-air bazaar or flea market, buyers and sellers haggle about prices. But in a typical retail setting in an industrialized society, you do not "interact" directly with the retailer. The price is listed on the shelf, a tag, or directly on the product. Either you pay the **posted price** set by the seller, or you do not buy the item.

> **posted prices:** prices set by a seller

Even though you do not haggle with the cashier at the supermarket, the fact that you *can* decide whether to buy is itself a form of interaction. Over time, retailers will take note of what moves off the shelf most quickly and will then order more of it and may also raise its price. They will also take note of what does not sell so quickly and will then reduce their order from wholesalers or mark the items down. The retailers' purchases from the wholesalers, in turn, give the suppliers information that they can use in deciding how much to order or produce and how to set *their* prices.

So while you may not be able to bargain directly, your actions, in combination with the actions of other customers, ultimately affect the prices and quantities offered in the market. These adjustments should tend, at least in theory, to lead posted prices to reflect what economists call the market-determined price, or **market price**, of the item. Market price, discussed in detail in Chapter 3, is the prevailing price for a specific good or service at a particular time in a given market. The posted price will normally reflect the market price if markets are competitive, the flow of information is good, the adjustment process is given enough time, and no big changes in market conditions occur in the meantime.

> **market price:** the prevailing price for a specific good or service at a particular time in a given market

In some cases, a single buyer and a single seller negotiate the price of an item through **bargaining**. Residential real estate, for example, is generally sold by using such negotiated agreements, as are used cars. (Sometimes there is also a posted price, but both parties understand that it is merely a starting point for negotiation.) Salaries of high-level managers, professionals, and unionized employees—and, notably, of sports and entertainment stars—are commonly set by bargaining. The presence of *potential* other buyers and sellers, however, is obviously important in determining the relative bargaining strength of the two parties. A seller who knows that he or she can easily find other eager buyers, for example, will quickly walk away from an unfavorable deal. A seller with fewer options will have less ability to hold out for good terms.

> **bargaining:** an activity in which a single buyer and a single seller negotiate the terms of their exchange

3.5 The Advantages and Limitations of Markets

Markets clearly have many advantages. Competition among sellers in markets means that goods and services can often be provided to people at affordable prices. Markets often encourage innovation, continually leading to new products such as iPhones, electric cars, and streaming video. Of course, many workers have jobs producing goods and services for sale in markets.

Markets also foster a steady flow of information, in terms of prices and volumes of sales, that encourages producers to respond flexibly to consumer desires. Profits provide feedback to sellers about whether resources are being used in ways that individuals are willing (and able) to pay for. Markets also give people a considerable amount of freedom in deciding which activities to engage in, although this freedom may be severely constrained by the resources to which people have access. Markets can also be thought of as a type of democracy in which all participants can express their views by buying some items and not others.

Against these advantages, markets have a number of limitations. As we have noted, the idealized model of a completely free private market (as in the basic neoclassical model) rarely exists in practice. Actual market-oriented economies always include a mixture of decentralized private decision-making and more public-oriented decision-making. This is because real-world economies include a number of important, complex factors that are not taken into account in the basic neoclassical model. These include social and environmental issues, as well as problems in the way that markets work in certain circumstances. We will briefly discuss some of these issues here and will expand on them more fully in later chapters.

Public Goods

Recall from our discussion earlier in the chapter that a public good (or service) is one whose use by one person does not diminish the ability of another person to benefit from it and whose benefit it would be difficult to keep any individuals from enjoying. Examples of public goods include public roads, parks, libraries, schools, clean air and water, other environmental goods and services, police protection, and the national defense system.

Because it is difficult to exclude anyone from benefiting from public goods, they are generally not offered through markets. Even if individual actors would be willing to pay for them if necessary, they have little incentive to pay because they cannot be excluded from the benefit. Economists call people who seek to enjoy a benefit without paying for it **free riders**. Because of the problem of free riders, it often makes sense to provide public goods through government agencies, supported by taxes, so that the cost of the public benefit is also borne by the public at large.

> **free riders:** people who seek to enjoy the benefit of a good without paying for it

Externalities

Some market activities create **externalities**—spillover effects on parties that are not directly participating in the market exchange. These effects can be either beneficial ("positive externalities") or harmful ("negative externalities"). Sometimes positive externalities are referred to as "external benefits," and negative externalities are referred to as "external costs." Externalities are one of the primary reasons the true *social* value of a good or service can differ from its *market* value.

> **externalities:** side effects in which the market does not make economic actors feel the full consequences of their actions—consequences that, however, are felt by unrelated persons or entities (such as the environment)

Examples of negative externalities include a situation of a manufacturing firm that dumps pollutants in a river, degrading water quality downstream, or a bar that plays loud music that annoys its neighbors. Examples of activities that have positive externalities include child rearing by parents who, out of love for their children, raise them to become law-abiding citizens, thereby creating benefits for society at large; and providing habitats for beneficial insects (such as bees and other pollinators), which then provide services to neighboring landowners. In both of these cases, individual actions have social benefits. Well-educated, productive citizens are an asset to the community as well as to their own families, and without pollinators and other beneficial insects, many crops would fail.

Some of the most important externalities relate to the economic activity of resource management. Relying on markets alone to coordinate economic activities may allow activities that deplete the natural environment to take place, because the cost of pollution may not be felt by the economic actor that created it. Environmental regulations attempt to counteract this, using fines or other disincentives to allocate the true social cost to the economic agents creating those costs. If economic activities affected only the actors directly involved in decision-making, we might be able to think about economic activity primarily in terms of individuals making decisions for their own benefit. But our economic activities are embedded in a social and ecological context, in which actions, interactions, and consequences are generally both widespread and interrelated. If decisions are left purely to individual self-interest, then from a societal point of view, too many negative externalities and too few positive externalities will be created. The streets might be strewn with industrial wastes, while children might be taught to be honest in dealings within their family but not outside it. Market values and human or social values do not always coincide.

Transaction Costs

Transaction costs are the costs of arranging economic activities. In the basic neoclassical model, transaction costs are assumed to be zero. If a firm wants to hire a worker, for example, it is assumed that the only cost involved is the wage paid. In the real world, however, the activity of reaching a hiring agreement may involve its own set of costs. The firm may need to pay costs related to searching, such as placing an ad or paying for the services of a recruiting company. The prospective worker may need to pay for résumé preparation or transportation to an interview. Because of the existence of such costs, some economic interactions that might lead to greater efficiency, and that would occur in an idealized, transaction cost-free, frictionless world, may not happen in the real world.

> **transaction costs:** the costs of arranging economic activities

Market Power

In the basic neoclassical model, all markets are assumed to be "perfectly competitive," such that no one buyer or seller has the power to influence the prices or other market conditions that they face. In the real world, however, we see that many firms have **market power**. For example, when there is only one firm (a monopolist) or a few firms selling a good, they may be able to increase their prices and their profits, creating inefficient allocations of resources. Workers may also be able to gain a degree of market power by joining together to negotiate as a labor union. A government, too, can have market power, for example, when the Department of Defense is the sole purchaser of military equipment from private firms.

> **market power:** the ability to control, or at least affect, the terms and conditions of a market exchange

The potential for social harm grows when firms gain excessive market power—that is, when they come to dominate the market in their area. They may then be able to charge socially inefficient prices or to squelch socially advantageous innovations by competing firms. Large firms also have considerable power to harm the natural environment on which they ultimately depend.

Businesses may also gain power by their sheer size. The decisions of individual large corporations can have substantial effects on the employment levels, economic growth, living standards, and economic stability of regions and countries. Governments may need to factor in the responses of powerful business groups in making their macroeconomic decisions. National or state leaders may fear, for example, that raising business tax rates or the national minimum wage may cause companies to leave their country or state and go elsewhere. Corporations frequently also try to influence government policies directly, through lobbying, campaign contributions, and other methods. We explore the implications of corporate size at more length in Chapter 6.

Information and Expectations

In the basic neoclassical model, in which purely decentralized decisions lead to efficient outcomes, people are assumed to have easy access to all the information that they need to make good choices. This analysis does not consider the time taken to obtain information or make decisions. In the real world, obtaining good

71

information and dealing with future uncertainties may make economic decision-making difficult.

A manufacturing business, for example, might be considering whether to borrow funds to build an additional factory. If the company's managers were able to know exactly what the demand for its products will be like in the future and what interest rates will be—along with additional information about things such as future wages, energy costs, and returns on alternative investments—the decision would be a simple matter of mathematical calculation.

But the managers will have to guess at most of these things. They will form expectations about the future, but these expectations may turn out to be incorrect. If their expectations are optimistic, they will tend to make the new investment and hire new workers. Often optimism is "contagious," and if a lot of *other* business leaders become optimistic, too, then the economy will boom. If, however, people share an attitude of pessimism, they may all tend to cut back on spending and hiring, thus precipitating the very downturn they feared.

Because no one business wants to take the risk of jumping the gun by expanding too soon, it can be very difficult to get a decentralized market economy out of a slump. How people get their information, how they time their actions, and how they form their expectations of the future are all important topics that are not addressed in the basic neoclassical model. Taking these factors into account suggests why markets sometimes do not work as smoothly as that model suggests.

Human Needs and Equity

Another important issue concerns distribution of income and the ability to pay for goods and services. In the basic neoclassical model, the only consumer demands for goods and services that can affect the market are those that are backed up by a consumer's ability to pay. This has several implications.

First, there is nothing in the model that ensures that resources are distributed in such a way that people can meet their basic human needs. If a few rich people have a lot of money to spend on diamonds, for example, while a great number of poor people lack the money to pay for basic health care, "free markets" will motivate producers to respond to the demand for diamonds but not to the need for basic health care.

For this reason, governments often adopt more deliberate policies of economic development, government provision, subsidies, or income redistribution to try to ensure that decent living standards become more widespread. These policies can sometimes incorporate market mechanisms and sometimes replace them.

Second, the model does not take into account nonmarketed production, such as the care given to children, the sick, and the elderly by family and friends. There is nothing in the basic neoclassical model that ensures that these sorts of production will be supplied in adequate quantities and quality. Nor does the market model recognize the ways in which caring activities may be disadvantaged by a market culture in which these activities are considered greatly inferior to the status and money gained through formal employment.

Last, it is also the case that problems such as unemployment and inflation tend to affect some people more than others, so how a country deals with these problems also has distributional consequences.

Clearly, although market systems have strong advantages in some areas, they cannot solve all economic problems. Economists sometimes use the term **market failure** to refer to a situation in which a market form of organization leads to inefficient or harmful results. Because of the various limitations of markets discussed previously, economic systems cannot rely on "free markets" alone if they are to contribute effectively to present and future human well-being.

> **market failure:** situations in which markets yield inefficient or inappropriate outcomes

To some extent, *private* nonmarket institutions may help remedy "market failure." For example, a group of privately owned factories located around a lake may voluntarily decide to restrict their waste emissions, because too much deterioration in water quality hurts them all. Likewise, a widespread custom of private charitable giving may help alleviate poverty. But sometimes the problems are so large or widespread that only government, *public* actions at the national or international levels seem to offer a solution. Exactly how much government action is required, and exactly what governments should do, has been a much-debated question within contemporary economics.

Market economies today face a major conundrum: How can societies continue to benefit from the strengths of the business sphere while ensuring that this sphere supports the kind of world that will sustain the livelihoods and the well-being of future generations? This question suggests that it is necessary to think both about regulatory issues as they apply to the business sphere and about what goods and services should be provided by the business sphere and which ones should instead be provided by either the core or public purpose spheres.

3.6 Assessing Market Outcomes

Unfortunately, too often the debate about markets comes down to one side being "pro-market" while the other side is "anti-market." We seek to avoid such a polarizing and simplistic distinction in this text. Such broad generalizations often reflect a lack of knowledge about when markets do, and do not, work effectively at enhancing well-being.

So rather than trying to decide whether you are "pro-market" or "anti-market," we encourage you to think of the following three broad categories of market outcomes:

1. Situations in which market outcomes are reasonably efficient, fair, and sustainable, with only limited government involvement required. The market for T-shirts in the United States, for example, would fall into this category. Significant competition among many producers means that T-shirt prices are low and virtually

anyone can afford them. Though there are some environmental impacts of producing and transporting T-shirts, and labor standards need to be upheld, there is limited government involvement in the T-shirt market.

2. Situations in which market outcomes are reasonably efficient, fair, and sustainable only with significant government involvement. The market for gasoline in Europe is a good example in this category. While gasoline is provided by private companies in European markets, it is heavily taxed (typically $3–$4 per gallon) to account for its negative externality of environmental pollution.[15] An unregulated gasoline market outcomes is both inefficient and unsustainable.

3. Situations in which market outcomes are not efficient, fair, and/or sustainable, necessitating provision through non-market institutions (such as government). Goods such as national defense and major highways—which are nearly always provided by governments rather than private markets—fall in this category. In many countries, services such as education or health care are provided by the government and funded by taxes. In the United States, health care in particular is often provided by private markets, but whether these markets are efficient and fair is a subject of debate.

In short, we need to assess markets contextually. We need to understand the contexts in which markets work well, the contexts in which government regulation of markets is needed, and the contexts in which markets do not result in acceptable outcomes.

Discussion Questions

1. When you shop online, how do you know that you can trust the seller to deliver the goods as promised? What is necessary for the social institution of trust to work, and how might in break down, in online transactions?
2. On a sheet of paper, draw two columns. In one column, list some historical and contemporary advantages of market exchanges, and in the other, list some disadvantages. Can you give examples beyond those listed in the text?

REVIEW QUESTIONS

1. What are the two main modes of economic investigation? Describe each.
2. What is a positive (direct) relationship? What is a negative (inverse) relationship?
3. What is a model? How does the *ceteris paribus* assumption simplify the creation of a model?
4. What are some of the assumptions of the basic neoclassical model? Why are markets said to be efficient according to this model?
5. What are some of the shortcomings of the neoclassical model? In what ways does the contextual model overcome these shortcomings?
6. What are the three spheres of economic activity?

7. What are some major characteristics and functions of the core sphere?
8. What are some major characteristics and functions of the public purpose sphere?
9. What are some major characteristics, and strengths and weaknesses, of the business sphere?
10. What is the informal sphere? Where is it most significant?
11. What are the three different meanings of the term "markets"?
12. What are the four institutional requirements of markets?
13. What is a public good? Why will private markets generally undersupply public goods?
14. What are negative and positive externalities? Give examples of each.
15. Besides public goods and externalities, describe four real-world factors that can cause market outcomes to be less than ideal.

EXERCISES

1. Consider the following data, taken from the Federal Reserve Bank's website. Perform the graphing exercises subsequently using either pencil and graph paper or a computer spreadsheet or presentation program.

Year	Unemployment rate (%)	Inflation (% per year)
2009	9.3	−0.4
2010	9.6	1.6
2011	8.9	3.2
2012	8.1	2.1
2013	7.4	1.5
2014	6.2	1.6
2015	5.3	0.1
2016	4.9	1.3
2017	4.4	2.1
2018	3.9	2.4

a. Looking at the data listed in the chart, can you detect a trend in the unemployment rate during these years? In the inflation rate? If so, what sort of trends do you see?
b. Create a time-series graph for the unemployment rate during 2009–2018.
c. Create a scatter-plot graph with the unemployment rate on the horizontal axis and inflation on the vertical axis.
d. Using your graph in part (c), do the two variables seem to have an empirical relationship during this period, or do the points seem to be randomly scattered? If there appears to be an empirical relationship, is it inverse or direct?

2. Identify the sphere in which each of the following activities takes place. Could some involve more than one sphere?
a. Recycling is picked up at curbside in a community
b. Tomatoes are grown in a home garden
c. A fire department answers an emergency call
d. People purchase groceries at a supermarket
e. An environmental protection group lobbies for stronger pollution control laws

3. Match each concept in Column A with an example in Column B.

Column A	Column B
a. Theoretical investigation	1. The apple tree that you plant for your own enjoyment also pleases people passing by
b. A core sphere activity	2. Perfectly competitive markets
c. A positive externality	3. The production of apple pie creates water pollution that harms downstream communities
d. A public purpose sphere activity	4. Einstein develops the theory of relativity
e. A public good	5. Police services
f. An assumption of the basic neoclassical model	6. There is only one apple producer, who is able to make very high profits
g. *Ceteris paribus*	7. Home care for the elderly
h. Historical investigation	8. All variables except one are held constant
i. Negative externality	9. An economist studies the Great Depression
j. Market power	10. A city park

NOTES

1. Reinhard, Susan C., Lynn Friss Feinberg, Rita Choula, and Ari Houser. 2015. "Valuing the Invaluable: 2015 Update." AARP Public Policy Institute, July.
2. McKinsey & Company. 2015. "The Power of Parity: How Advancing Women's Equality Can Add $12 Trillion to Global Growth." McKinsey Global Institute, September.
3. Mazzucato, Mariana. 2018. *The Entrepreneurial State: Debunking Private Sector versus Public Sector Myths.* Penguin, London.
4. Swanson, Ana. 2015. "Big Pharmaceutical Companies Are Spending Far More on Marketing Than Research." *The Washington Post,* February 11.
5. Harvard Men's Health Watch. 2017. "Do Not Get Sold on Drug Advertising." February. www.health.harvard.edu/drugs-and-medications/do-not-get-sold-on-drug-advertising
6. Folbre, Nancy. 2015. "Valuing Non-Market Work." UNDP Human Development Report Office Think Piece.
7. Office for National Statistics. 2018. "Household Satellite Account, UK: 2015 and 2016." www.ons.gov.uk/economy/nationalaccounts/satelliteaccounts/articles/householdsatelliteaccounts/2015and2016estimates#main-points
8. Medina, Leandro, and Friedrich Shadow Schneider. 2018. "Shadow Economies around the World: What Did We Learn over the Last 20 Years?" IMF Working Paper WP/18/17.
9. International Labor Organization. 2018. "More Than 60 Percent of the World's Employed Population Are in the Informal Economy." Press Release, April 30. www.ilo.org/global/about-the-ilo/newsroom/news/WCMS_627189/lang--en/index.htm
10. Goodwin, Neva, and Edgar Cahn. 2018. "Unmet Needs and Unused Capacities: Time Banking as a Solution." *Interdisciplinary Journal of Partnership Studies,* 5(1), Article 3.
11. Rosenburg, Tim. 2011. "Where All Work Is Created Equal." *New York Times,* September 15.

12. Thorpe, Devin. 2018. "Time Banking Helps Build Individuals, Organizations and Communities." *Forbes*, March 21.
13. Anonymous. 2016. "Time Is Money." *The Economist*, December 17.
14. Borroughs, David. 2017. "Timebanking Taking Off as Thousands of Kiwis Donate Their Time to Each Other." *Stuff*, June 11.
15. Watson, Garret. 2019. "How High Are Other Nations' Gas Taxes?" Tax Foundation, May 2. https://taxfoundation.org/oecd-gas-tax/

Part II

Microeconomic Analysis

Consumption, Production, and Markets

Chapter 3

Supply and Demand

Understanding how prices are determined in the market and how they change over time is central to our study of economics. Prices matter because they affect who can afford to access particular goods or services. Closely related to *prices*, as something economists study, are the *quantities* of things that are produced and sold in markets. Quantities matter because the undersupply or oversupply of goods and services creates shortages or waste. To understand changes in prices and quantities in the market, it is useful to look at the traditional model of supply and demand. This is the focus of this chapter. You will notice that the model makes some quite strong simplifying assumptions that are at odds with a more complex reality. However, the simple model is still a good place to start, as it provides a foundation for later chapters to build a more complete and contextual understanding of how markets operate and adjust.

Think of the basic supply and demand model as a "thought experiment" that seeks to describe, in abstract terms, how people make decisions about buying and selling. The basic concept, as you will see, is quite simple: Sellers (on the "supply" side) will want to supply more of what they sell if they can get higher prices, while on the "demand" side, buyers will generally be willing to buy more when prices are lower. Sellers and buyers thus want to see prices move in opposite ways. Where, then, does the price end up? In this basic model, prices are determined through some sort of balance, or equilibrium, between supply and demand.

Note that as we continue to discuss this supply/demand relationship, we use the term **demand** to indicate the willingness and ability of purchasers to buy goods and services, while **supply** means the willingness of producers to produce, and merchandisers to sell, goods and services.

> **demand:** the willingness and ability of purchasers to buy goods or services
> **supply:** the willingness of producers and merchandisers to provide goods and services

1. INTRODUCTION TO THE MICROECONOMIC MARKET MODEL

The basic microeconomic market model considers two "**market outcomes**":

- **Market price:** the prevailing price for a specific good or service at a particular time in a given market. To keep things simple, it is assumed that all sellers charge the same price for an identical version of each type of good or service. Each individual item is called a "unit" of that good or service.

■ **Market quantity sold:** the number of "units" of a specific good or service sold in a given market during a particular period.

---

market price: the prevailing price for a specific good or service at a particular time in a given market

market quantity sold: the number of "units" of a specific good or service sold in a given market during a particular period

---

The basic microeconomic model involves the interaction of two economic actors: buyers (consumers) and sellers (producers or merchandisers). We can think of consumers as individuals, households, or even businesses buying supplies or raw inputs to produce goods and services for sale. Sellers are normally thought of as businesses, but this is not always the case. For example, the "sellers" in labor markets are individuals offering their labor services.

An important feature of our microeconomic model is that both buyers and sellers are assumed to be enhancing their own well-being. Money is used as a proxy for well-being. Hence, buyers enhance their well-being by purchasing things that are worth more to them than the price they pay for it, and sellers enhance their well-being by earning profits.

The market imagined in this basic model has two noteworthy characteristics. First, markets are envisioned as being **perfectly competitive**, such that there are many buyers and sellers of a good, all units of the good are identical, anyone can enter or leave the market at will, and everyone has complete information about the products being sold and their prices. Second, markets are assumed to be **self-correcting**, such that imbalances between buyers and sellers are eliminated through natural adjustments in price or quantity.

---

perfectly competitive market: a market in which there are many buyers and sellers, all units of the good are identical, and there is free entry and exit and perfect information

self-correcting market: a market that automatically adjusts to any imbalances between sellers and buyers

---

In the real world, no market is perfectly competitive in the literal sense (although some are far more competitive than others), and although markets do tend to be self-correcting, in many cases, imbalances persist for some time. We will discuss such real-world complications in the final section of this chapter as well as in later chapters. Here we begin by examining the behavior of buyers and sellers in the perfectly competitive and self-correcting markets. Specifically, we look at the relationship between market prices and quantities first from the point of view of sellers and then from the consumer perspective. After that, we see what happens when buyers and sellers interact in markets.

Discussion Questions

1. Discuss some ways in which the assumptions made in the microeconomic market model do not reflect the behavior of consumers and firms in the real world.
2. Think about a case recently in which you exchanged money for a good or service. Was that market "perfectly competitive"?

2. THE THEORY OF SUPPLY

We introduce the microeconomic market model by considering how it applies to coffee markets. Let's assume we are looking at the market for a regular cup of coffee in the vicinity of your campus. We also assume that businesses in this area sell identical cups of coffee and that all coffee sellers are well informed and interested in making profits. Let's define the time period of our analysis as a week. We will consider how the market changes week to week, but within each week, the price does not vary.

At the beginning of each week, each coffee business must make a decision about how much coffee it will offer to sell in the coming week—buying the appropriate quantity of coffee supplies, establishing employee work schedules, and so on. How would we expect changes in the prevailing market price of a cup of coffee to influence the quantity of coffee offered for sale each week?

It is likely that sellers are motivated to offer more coffee if the market price of a cup of coffee is rising. Conversely, if the market price of a cup of coffee is falling, sellers will be less interested in selling coffee and may decide to sell more of other products such as hot chocolate or doughnuts. Hence, common sense suggests that sellers should offer more coffee when prices are relatively high and less coffee when prices are relatively low; that is, there is a positive relationship between prices and quantity supplied. Note that we can talk about the quantity supplied at either the individual level or the market level. The **individual supply** is the quantity supplied by one particular seller. The **market** (or **aggregate**) **supply** is the quantity supplied by all sellers in the market.

> **individual supply:** the amount supplied by one particular seller
> **market (or aggregate) supply:** the amount supplied by all sellers in a particular market

2.1 The Supply Schedule and Supply Curve

We have been talking about the relationship between price and the quantity of coffee supplied only in abstract terms so far. Now let's suppose that we have studied the coffee market around campus by speaking with different coffee sellers and can estimate how the quantity supplied will vary with price. We present our results as shown in Table 3.1. We call a table representing the relationship between price and the quantity supplied a **supply schedule**. In the case of coffee, we have the supply schedule for a physical good. But we can also think of a supply schedule for a marketed service, such as housecleaning, babysitting, or a college education.

83

> **supply schedule:** a table showing the relationship between price and quantity supplied

Just as we might expect, the quantity of coffee supplied increases with higher prices. For example, at a relatively low price of $0.80 per cup, only 400 cups are supplied per week in our market. But if the price rises to $1.00 per cup, then 600 cups are supplied. Note that Table 3.1 is a simplification in that it shows only the cups supplied at $0.10 increments.

From a supply schedule, we can graph a **supply curve**, as shown in Figure 3.1. This is *exactly* the same information in Table 3.1, presented in graphical form. It is standard in economics to place the quantity on the horizontal axis and the price on the vertical axis. We see, for example, that at a price of $1.00 per cup, coffee sellers are willing to supply 600 cups of coffee per week.

> **supply curve:** a curve indicating the quantities that sellers are willing to supply at various prices

Note that the supply curve in Figure 3.1 slopes upward, illustrating the positive relationship between prices and quantity supplied. Sometimes this positive

Table 3.1 Supply Schedule for Cups of Coffee

Price of coffee ($/cup)	0.70	0.80	0.90	1.00	1.10	1.20	1.30	1.40	1.50	1.60
Cups of coffee supplied per week	300	400	500	600	700	800	900	1,000	1,100	1,200

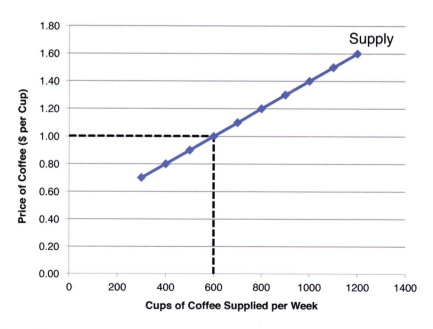

Figure 3.1 *Market Supply Curve for Cups of Coffee*

relationship is referred to as the "law of supply." However, as we will see in later chapters, especially when we discuss the issue of labor supply, this "law" does not hold everywhere. So it is better regarded as a general principle rather than a law.

We now need to introduce an important distinction in market analysis. When quantity supplied changes due to price changes, we move *along* a supply curve. So if the price increased from $0.80 to $1.00 per cup, we would move up from a quantity supplied of 400 cups to 600 cups. Another term for movement along a supply curve is a **change in the quantity supplied**. We *would not* say that this is a "change in supply" because that occurs when the entire supply curve shifts—a topic that we address in the next section.

> **change in the quantity supplied:** movement *along* a supply curve in response to a price change

Test yourself by answering this question with reference to Table 3.1 or Figure 3.1: By how much does the *quantity supplied* change when the price changes from $1.20 to $1.40 per cup?[1]

It is very important when going through this example to imagine that price is the *only* thing changing. Recall from Chapter 2 that this technique of assuming that only one variable changes at a time is termed *ceteris paribus*, meaning "all else constant." This is a basic research technique used in other disciplines as well. For example, when medical researchers try to determine the effect of diet *alone* on a disease, they usually choose as research subjects people whose gender, age, and level of exercise ("all else") are nearly identical ("constant"). If we were to try to estimate a real-world supply curve, we would ideally try to hold everything else in the market constant while varying just the price and observe how the quantity supplied changes. Of course, this cannot be done in the real world, and economists have to rely on statistical techniques to try to isolate the effect of price alone.

2.2 Changes in Supply

In contrast to a "change in quantity supplied," which is a response to a price change, we say that there has been a **change in supply** when something other than price changes and the entire supply curve shifts.

> **change in supply:** a shift of the entire supply curve in response to something changing other than price

Why might the whole curve shift? We can define six **nonprice determinants of supply** that would shift the entire supply curve:

1. a change in the number of sellers
2. a change in the technology of production
3. a change in input prices

4. a change in seller expectations about the future
5. a change in the prices of related goods and services
6. a change in the physical supply of a natural resource

> **nonprice determinants of supply:** any factor that affects the quantity supplied, other than the price of the good or service offered for sale

If a new coffee seller enters the market, then at any given price, more coffee would be supplied, as shown in Figure 3.2. The addition of a new coffee supplier shifts the entire supply curve from S_1 to S_2. So if the prevailing price of coffee were $1.00 per cup, the change in supply would result in 1,000 cups of coffee being offered for sale each week instead of the original quantity of 600 cups, as shown in the graph. Indeed, at every price point, more coffee will be sold, so it can only be the case the entire supply curve has to shift to S_2.

We can describe this increase in supply by saying either that "supply has increased (or risen)" or that "the supply curve has shifted out." It may seem initially confusing that a supply *increase* shifts the supply curve *down*. However, any confusion should dissolve if you read across horizontally along the quantity axis at any chosen price. Then you will notice that as the supply curve shifts out from S_1 to S_2, the number on the quantity axis increases.

We would see a similar result if there were a change in the technology used to make coffee that allowed coffee to be produced at lower cost. With lower production costs, at a prevailing price of $1.00/cup, supplying coffee becomes more appealing (i.e., profitable) to sellers. Thus, they are willing to supply more coffee at the same price. So, the supply curve would shift outward (to the right), as in Figure 3.2.

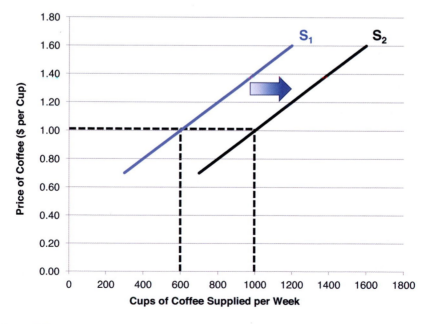

Figure 3.2 *An Increase in Supply*

Another way to think about lower production costs is to note that lower costs imply that sellers can accept a lower price for coffee and still make a profit. In Figure 3.2, we see that with the original supply curve at S_1, sellers would be willing to supply 1,000 cups of coffee at a price of $1.40. Now suppose a decrease in production costs means that sellers would be willing to supply 1,000 cups of coffee at a price of only $1.00 per cup; again, this is reflected in the shift of the supply to curve S_2.

A change in input prices (nonprice determinant #3 in our list) includes the price of coffee beans, labor, milk, sugar, coffee cups, electricity, rent, and any other resource that is an input into the coffee production process. Let's suppose that rental prices for commercial space increase around campus. In this case, selling coffee becomes less profitable, and the local supply of coffee will decrease, as shown in Figure 3.3. If the prevailing coffee price were $1.20/cup, the quantity supplied would decrease from 800 to 400 cups per week. We would refer to this shift as a "decrease in supply" or say that "the supply curve has shifted back."

The effect of seller expectations about the future (nonprice determinant #4) can be tricky. If coffee sellers expect that coffee bean prices will increase soon (perhaps they have been following the news on weather conditions in coffee-growing regions of South America), they might hold back some coffee bean inventory for now, to sell later when coffee prices increase—thus leading to a decrease in supply in the short term. On the other hand, if some coffee sellers hear that other coffee sellers are adopting a new technology that will lower production costs, they might be eager to sell as much coffee as possible now before the price is driven down—thus increasing short-term supply.

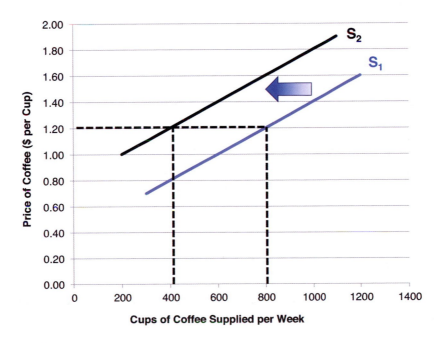

Figure 3.3 *A Decrease in Supply*

Suppose that some coffee sellers notice that many people are switching from coffee to tea and are willing to pay high prices for gourmet teas. These sellers may decide to supply more tea and less coffee. In this case, the price of a related good (nonprice determinant #5) has induced these sellers to reduce their output of coffee, causing a decrease in the market supply of coffee similar to what is shown in Figure 3.3.

Finally, in markets for natural resources such as agricultural crops, oil, or minerals, the supply curve may shift as a result of physical supply factors like weather conditions or absolute availability. Unusually arid weather in Brazil and Vietnam (the two top coffee-producing countries in the world) in 2016 decreased coffee crop yields, causing a direct reduction in the physical supply of coffee beans.[2] The reduction in supply caused the price of coffee beans to increase by about 25 percent. As another example, supplies of recoverable oil are ultimately limited and may someday lead to reductions in supply.

Discussion Questions

1. Verbally explain the difference between a change in "quantity supplied" and a change in supply. Considering the supply side of the market for lawn-mowing services, what kind of change (*increase* or *decrease*, in *quantity supplied* or *supply*) would each of the following events cause?
   a. There is a rise in the price of gasoline used to run power mowers.
   b. There is a rise in the going price for lawn-mowing services.
   c. More people decide to offer to mow lawns.
   d. A new lawn mower is invented that is cheap and makes it possible to mow lawns at a lower cost.
2. Sketch a supply curve graph illustrating a student's willingness to offer tutoring services. The student, call her Lena, is willing to tutor for three hours per week if she receives $10/hour. If Lena receives $15 per hour, she is willing to tutor for five hours per week. If she can charge $20 per hour, she would tutor for seven hours per week. Last, if Lena receives $25 per hour, she is willing to tutor for nine hours per week. Carefully label the vertical and horizontal axes. Then describe one situation that would increase Lena's supply of tutoring services and one situation that would decrease Lena's tutoring supply.

3. THE THEORY OF DEMAND

We now turn to the coffee market from the perspective of coffee buyers. Unlike sellers, consumers find low prices attractive. So it seems reasonable to expect that people will want to purchase more cups of coffee per week when prices are lower. Note that while the consumers in our coffee example are individuals, demand can also arise from, for example, businesses looking to purchase raw materials or to hire employees.

3.1 The Demand Schedule and Demand Curve

Just as with supply, we can present a **demand schedule** showing the quantity that consumers would be willing to buy at different prices, that is, the relationship between price and quantity demanded. In Table 3.2, we see that as the prevailing price of a cup of coffee goes up, the quantity demanded goes down.

> **demand schedule:** a table showing the relationship between price and quantity demanded

From the demand schedule, we can graph a **demand curve**, as shown in Figure 3.4, which shows the quantities that buyers are willing to purchase at various prices. So we see, for example, that at a price of $1.40 per cup, consumers would demand 600 cups of coffee per week.

> **demand curve:** a curve indicating the quantities that buyers are willing to purchase at various prices

It is important to keep in mind that someone's willingness to buy a good or service is not only a function of her preferences but also of her income or wealth. Economists sometimes use the term "effective demand" to stress that they are talking about demand backed up by enough money to pay the prevailing price. But in general, virtually anywhere that the economic term "demand" is used, it refers to this specific meaning: that is, *both* a willingness *and* an ability to pay.

Some people who might want to buy a cup of coffee every day may decide not to because they do not believe that they can afford it and decide instead to make

Table 3.2 Demand Schedule for Cups of Coffee

Price of coffee ($/cup)	0.20	0.50	0.80	1.10	1.40	1.70	2.00	2.30
Cups of coffee demanded per week	1,000	900	800	700	600	500	400	300

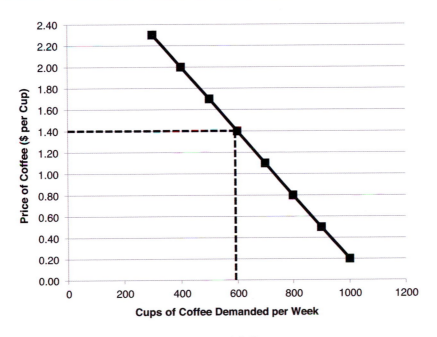

Figure 3.4 *Market Demand Curve for Cups of Coffee*

their own coffee. Although the inability of people to pay for daily cups of coffee at a coffee shop may not be a cause for public concern or a policy response, the inability of people to pay for things such as health care, adequate nutrition, or a college education may create sufficient motivation for government involvement. It is important to remember that markets do not, by their nature, take into account wants or needs that are not backed up by the ability to pay.

Note that the demand curve in Figure 3.4 slopes downward. Again, it is consistent with common sense that, generally, the higher the price of a good, the less willing people will be to buy it. If a book is very expensive, you might look for it in the library rather than buying it. If an accounting firm raises its rates, some of its clients may consider hiring a different accountant. Price and quantity have a negative (or inverse) relationship along a demand curve; that is, when price rises, quantity demanded falls. (This is sometimes called the "law of demand." Like the "law of supply," it does not always hold. Sometimes, for example, a marketer will find that buyers will want more of a good as its price rises if it is sold as a "prestige" or "snob" good.)

The curve that we have drawn is the entire **market** (or **aggregate**) **demand** curve in our local market for coffee. As was the case with supply, the market demand is obtained by aggregating the **individual demand** of each consumer in the market.

> **market (or aggregate) demand:** the amount demanded by all buyers in a particular market
> **individual demand:** the amount demanded by one particular buyer

Again, we need to differentiate between movement *along* a demand curve and a *shifting* demand curve. Movement along a demand curve is always referred to as a **change in the quantity demanded**. So if the prevailing price of coffee in our example rises from $1.40 per cup to $1.70, we would say that the quantity demanded declines from 600 cups to 500 cups per week.

> **change in the quantity demanded:** movement along a demand curve in response to a price change

Check yourself by answering this question with reference to Table 3.2 or Figure 3.4: By how much does the "quantity demanded" change when the price changes from $1.10 to $0.50 per cup?[3]

3.2 Changes in Demand

As with supply, we distinguish between a change in "quantity demanded" resulting from a change in price and a **change in demand**. When there is a change in demand, the whole demand curve shifts. A key way to distinguish between change in "quantity demanded" and a "change in demand" is that the former results from a change in price and the latter from a change in one or more *non-price* variables.

> **change in demand:** a shift of the entire demand curve in response to something changing other than price

Why might the whole demand curve shift? We can identify five **nonprice determinants of demand** that can shift the entire demand curve:

1. a change in the number of buyers in the market
2. changes in buyers' tastes and preferences
3. changes in buyers' income and other assets
4. changes in the prices of related goods and services
5. changes in buyers' expectations about the future

> **nonprice determinants of demand:** any factor that affects the quantity demanded, other than the price of the good or service being demanded

Suppose that our demand curve in Figure 3.4 is based on buying patterns at the beginning of a semester. During final exams, we might expect the overall demand for coffee to increase as more students stay up late to study.[4] Such a change in demand is presented in Figure 3.5. Our initial demand curve is D_1, with a quantity demanded of 600 cups per week when the price is $1.40 per cup. But during the final exam period, the demand curve shifts to D_2, with a quantity demanded of 900 cups per week at the same price of $1.40. In this case, we would say that "demand

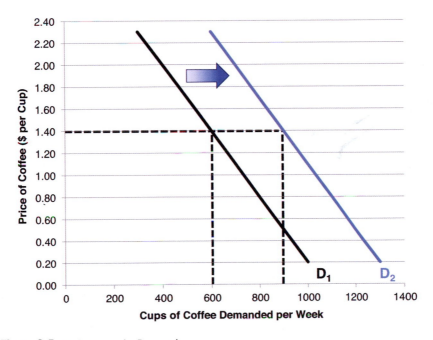

Figure 3.5 *An Increase in Demand*

has risen (or increased)" or that "the demand curve has shifted out." (Because of the curve's negative slope, in this case shifting out also means shifting up, but again the normal approach in economics is to refer to market curves moving horizontally rather than vertically.)

Suppose that a news story comes out that says drinking more than one cup of coffee per day is harmful to your health. This can change buyers' preferences, leading to a decrease in demand as coffee drinkers decide to cut back on their consumption. Such a decrease in demand is illustrated in Figure 3.6. In this case, the demand curve shifts back (to the left) to D_2, and at a price of $1.40 per cup, the demand falls from 600 to 400 cups per week. As another example of changing preferences, marketers seek to increase demand through advertising campaigns, such as the ads for new Apple products that can lead to many consumers waiting in line to buy something the day that it becomes available.

A change in buyers' income can also shift market demand curves. For example, the 2007–2008 recession in the United States reduced income for many households and thus their demand for various products such as restaurant meals and new automobiles.

We can define two types of "related" goods and services (nonprice determinant #4). First, there exist **substitute goods** for most products, meaning goods that can be used in place of another good. For coffee, substitutes include tea and caffeinated energy drinks. If the price of tea were to increase significantly, say as a result of poor weather conditions in tea-exporting countries such as Sri Lanka and India, we would expect the demand for coffee to increase. Meanwhile, if the price of tea were to fall, we would expect the demand for coffee to decrease as some coffee drinkers switch to tea instead.

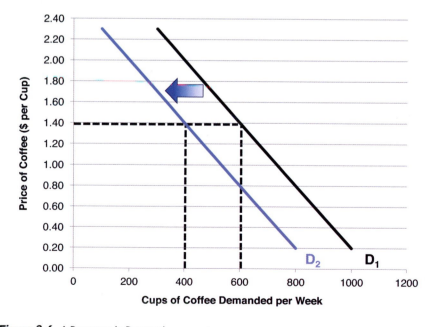

Figure 3.6 *A Decrease in Demand*

substitute good: a good that can be used in place of another good

The other type of related goods are **complementary goods**, or goods that tend to be used along with other goods. Examples of complementary goods for coffee include cream and doughnuts. If someone frequently purchases coffee along with a doughnut, a significant increase in doughnut prices may cause that person to also reduce his demand for coffee.

complementary good: a good that is used along with another good

Like suppliers, buyers can adjust their behavior based on future expectations (nonprice determinant #5). For example, if people expect that prices of houses in a certain neighborhood will rise during the next few years, they may be more inclined to buy now to lock in a lower price.

Discussion Questions

1. Explain verbally why the demand curve slopes downward.
2. Explain the difference between a change in "quantity demanded" and a change in demand. Considering the demand side of the market for lawn-mowing services, what kind of change (*increase* or *decrease*, in *quantity demanded* or *demand*) would each of the following events cause?
    a. A new office park, surrounded by several acres of lawn, is built.
    b. A drought is declared, and lawn watering is banned.
    c. The going price for lawn-mowing services rises.
    d. A more natural, wild yard becomes the "in" thing, as people become concerned about the effects of fertilizers and pesticides on the environment.

4. THE THEORY OF MARKET ADJUSTMENT

Now that we have considered sellers and the buyers separately, it is time to bring them together. Remember that with our relatively simple model, we assume that all cups of coffee in our market are identical and will sell for the same price. We are now ready to ask: How many cups of coffee will be sold in the market and at what price?

4.1 Surplus, Shortage, and Equilibrium

Using the original supply and demand curves, reproduced here in Figure 3.7, we can determine the answer. Let's suppose that the price of coffee is initially at $1.40 per cup. As we see in Figure 3.7, at this relatively high price, coffee sellers are prepared to sell 1,000 cups of coffee per week, but buyers are interested in buying only 600 cups. (You can check these numbers in Tables 3.1. and 3.2.) Economists call a situation in which the quantity supplied is greater than the quantity demanded a

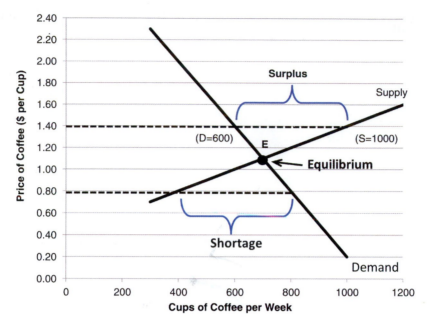

Figure 3.7 *Surplus, Shortage, and Equilibrium in the Market*

surplus. This is illustrated in the upper part of Figure 3.7, where there is a surplus, or excess supply, of 400 cups of coffee per week.

> **surplus:** a situation in which the quantity that sellers are prepared to sell at a particular price exceeds the quantity that buyers are willing to buy at that price

If a market is in a situation of surplus, what would we expect to happen? Imagine that at the start of the week, coffee sellers are equipped to sell 1,000 cups of coffee. At the end of the week, they find that they have sold only 600 cups, and they have a large leftover inventory of coffee supplies. Coffee sellers realize that they need to attract more customers, so they will respond to the surplus by lowering their price. Assuming that all sellers respond equally (which is unlikely in the real world, but it simplifies our model at this point), the prevailing price will be somewhat lower the next week.[5]

Let's say that the next week, the prevailing price is lowered from $1.40 to $1.30. At $1.30, a surplus still occurs—900 cups of coffee are supplied at that price, but the market demands less than 700, so there will be further downward pressure on the price. When the price finally reaches $1.10, each and every cup made available will find a buyer. The number of cups of coffee supplied and demanded is equal to 700. The market price is $1.10. Economists call this a situation in which the "market clears" and an **equilibrium** is reached. "Equilibrium" describes a situation that has reached a resting point, where there are no forces acting to change it. (Economists borrowed the concept of equilibrium from nineteenth-century physics.) In a market situation, equilibrium is reached when the quantity supplied is equal to the quantity demanded and prices stop falling. Figure 3.7 illustrates the **market-clearing equilibrium** point, labeled E.

> **equilibrium:** a situation of rest, in which there are no forces that create change
> **market-clearing equilibrium:** a situation in which quantity supplied equals quantity demanded

What if the price had started out too low, for example, at $0.80 per cup? As shown in the lower part of Figure 3.7, at this price, sellers are prepared to sell only 400 cups per week, while the quantity demanded is 800 cups. A situation in which the quantity demanded exceeds the quantity supplied is referred to as a **shortage**.

> **shortage:** a situation in which the quantity demanded at a particular price exceeds the quantity that sellers are willing to supply

What would we expect to happen in a market with a shortage? Before we even get to the end of the week, the suppliers' inventory will be depleted and they will end up turning away customers who want to buy coffee. Realizing that there is excess demand for coffee, sellers will conclude that they can probably charge a little more for coffee and still have a sufficient number of customers. So whenever there is a situation of shortage, there will be upward pressure on prices.[6] As the price rises, quantity demanded will fall, while quantity supplied will increase. At $1.10, demand is just 700 cups, exactly matched by a supply of 700.

The **theory of market adjustment** says that market forces will tend to make price and quantity move toward the equilibrium point. Surpluses will lead to falling prices, and shortages will lead to rising prices. Surplus and shortage are both instances of **market disequilibrium**. Only at the equilibrium price and quantity is there no tendency for market adjustment. In this example, the equilibrium price is $1.10 per cup and the equilibrium quantity is 700 cups per week.

> **theory of market adjustment:** the theory that market forces will tend to make shortages and surpluses disappear
> **market disequilibrium:** a situation of either shortage or surplus

4.2 Market Forces and Other Considerations

We know that market forces will tend to push the price of coffee toward the equilibrium price, but how long will this adjustment process take? Just a couple of weeks, a month, maybe longer? We do not know, as our simple model doesn't address this issue.[7] In the real world, some markets have adjustment processes that lead rapidly to equilibrium. In highly organized stock markets and other auction-like markets, thousands of trades may take place every minute, as buyers and sellers find each other and quickly negotiate a price. Such a market can probably be thought of as in equilibrium, or moving quickly toward equilibrium, nearly all the time, though the equilibrium point itself may be a "moving target" due to a range of factors. When we look at stock markets, it is evident that the price/quantity combinations that constitute equilibrium now may be quite different from the conditions for equilibrium tomorrow—or even 15 minutes from now.

In other markets, however, adjustment to equilibrium may take years—if it happens at all. The market forces that we have just examined are not the only forces in the world. For example, hospital administrators have complained for decades about a shortage of nurses. The obvious solution, from the point of view of labor supply and demand, would be for hospitals to offer higher wages, thus increasing the incentives for people to enter (and stay in) nursing careers while also reducing the quantity demanded. As in Figure 3.7, market forces would then move us from shortage to equilibrium.

If you study the strategies used by hospitals to combat the shortage, however, you will note that offering higher wages is rarely one of them. Instead, larger training programs, signing bonuses, and forced overtime (which reduces the quality of life for workers and the quality of patient care) have often been used to try to fill the gap. Various explanations have been suggested as to why the nursing wage is not rising to clear the market. On the demand side, hospital management may discount the importance of nurses to patient well-being, preferring to devote financial resources to high-tech medicine. On the supply side, unionizing and fighting for higher wages can be emotionally and ethically difficult for health care personnel, because striking can mean refusing help to people in need. Our simple model of supply and demand cannot account for these types of real-world complexities.

More generally, the forces that can work against quick movement toward equilibrium include such human characteristics as habit or ignorance. Slow production processes and long-term contracts may also slow down or prevent market adjustment. A seller may keep a good at its accustomed price long after it has failed to clear or the back orders have begun to mount, simply because she is slow to change. A common reason for slow adjustment is a lack of information. To be sure, the corner grocer knows which products are or are not moving; increasingly, sophisticated computerized systems are feeding this information back up the supply chain to speed up price adjustment. However, in many parts of the world, and in some industries even in industrialized countries, information is slow to get to those who make some of the essential pricing decisions. Consumers, too, often lack information or behave on the basis of habit rather than constant reappraisal and recalculation.

Equilibrium analysis has it uses, but it is also limited by the reality of constant change in the world where nonmarket forces may effectively combat the equilibrating tendency of market forces. Market adjustment analysis can still make a contribution to our understanding provided it is used carefully and with regard to its limitations.

4.3 Shifts in Supply and Demand

Our model predicts that once we reach equilibrium, the price and quantity sold will stay the same unless something changes. In the real world, of course, things are constantly changing. For example, the median price of a house in the United States increased from about $170,000 in 2000 to about $260,000 in 2007, fell to less than $210,000 at the bottom of the housing crisis in 2009, and then rose to more than $307,700 by the first quarter of 2019.[8] Such price fluctuations are also common in prices for fossil fuels, minerals such as gold and copper, and consumer electronics. Even coffee prices do vary considerably over time.

Nonetheless, many price changes can be largely explained, and in some cases even predicted, by using our basic microeconomic market model. We can determine how a shift in one (or both) of our curves, as a result of a change in one or more non-price determinants, will lead to a change in the equilibrium price and quantity.

Returning to our coffee market, let's suppose that a new seller enters the market. As we discussed earlier, this is a change in a nonprice determinant of supply and will shift the supply curve out (to the right). This is shown in Figure 3.8 with the supply curve shifting from S_1 to S_2. Our initial equilibrium is point E_1 with a price of $1.10 and a quantity of 700 cups per week. But note that with the entry of the new coffee seller shifting the supply curve to S_2, and assuming that initially price stays at $1.10, we go from equilibrium to a situation of surplus (as shown in Figure 3.8). At a price of $1.10 per cup, the quantity supplied exceeds the quantity demanded with the new supply curve of S_2.

Just as before, a situation of surplus creates downward pressure on prices. As sellers lower their prices, the quantity demanded increases as we move along the demand curve. The quantity supplied also falls (along the new supply curve) as lower prices reduce incentives for producers. Thus, the difference between quantity supplied and quantity demanded decreases. As long as a surplus continues to exist, there is downward pressure on prices, leading to further movement along both the

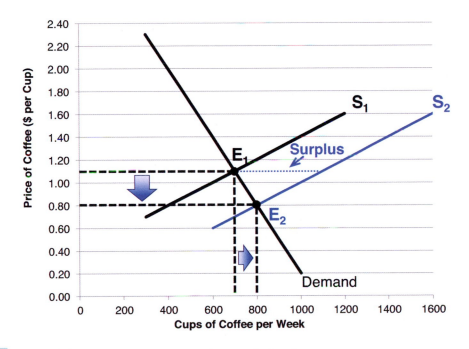

Figure 3.8 *Market Adjustment to an Increase in Supply*

demand curve and the new supply curve. The surplus is eventually eliminated when we reach point E_2, the new equilibrium. The increase in supply has resulted in:

■ a decrease in the equilibrium price
■ an increase in the equilibrium quantity

What if, instead, we have a decrease in supply? Suppose one coffee seller decides to stop selling coffee. In this case, the supply curve would shift to the left. The new equilibrium would result in a higher price and a lower quantity sold. (Try this yourself by drawing a graph similar to Figure 3.8 but with the supply curve shifting in the opposite direction.)

Now let's consider what happens when the demand curve shifts. Suppose we have an increase in demand for coffee as a result of a large incoming freshman class. Figure 3.9 shows an increase in demand (the demand curve shifts to the right) from D_1 to D_2. This creates a temporary situation of a shortage, in which the quantity demanded exceeds the quantity supplied. Sellers perceive the shortage and respond by raising prices. With the higher prices, we move along the supply curve as sellers are willing to supply more coffee. At the same time, the quantity demanded is reduced as students respond to higher coffee prices by buying fewer cups of coffee (a movement along the new demand curve).

As long as the shortage persists, we have continued upward pressure on prices and further movement along the supply curve and the new demand curve. The shortage is eventually eliminated when we reach point E_2, the new market-clearing equilibrium. The increase in demand has resulted in:

■ an increase in the equilibrium quantity
■ an increase in the equilibrium price

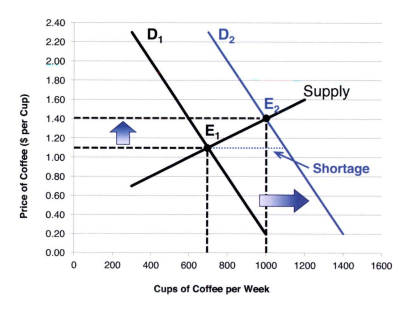

Figure 3.9 *Market Adjustment to an Increase in Demand*

Note that with either an increase in supply or an increase in demand, the equilibrium quantity increases. But the effect on price differs—prices rise with an increase in demand but fall with an increase in supply. This should align with your expectations even before you took this class. If people want more of a product, it makes sense that prices should rise and more will be sold. An increase in the availability (supply) of something should drive prices down while also leading to more being sold. Our microeconomic model tells a commonsense story about market adjustment, although perhaps in a somewhat complex manner.

What would we expect if demand instead decreases, say due to a news story that indicates that drinking coffee is harmful to your health? The demand curve would shift inward (to the left), and we would expect a lower equilibrium price and a lower equilibrium quantity.

Note that when the supply curve shifts, the resulting change in equilibrium price and quantity are always in the *opposite* direction. But when the demand curve shifts, price and quantity always change in the *same* direction. We can summarize what happens when one of the market curves shift in Table 3.3. We recommend that you don't try to memorize this table but work to understand the microeconomic model sufficiently so you can easily arrive at these answers using graphs and commonsense reasoning.

What if *both* curves shift at the same time? What if, for example, there is a concurrent increase in the number of sellers of coffee *and* an increase in the number of buyers? We analyze this situation in Figure 3.10. Supply increases from

Table 3.3 Summary of the Market Effects of Shifts in Supply or Demand

Market Change	Effect on Equilibrium Price	Effect on Equilibrium Quantity
Increase in supply	Decrease	Increase
Decrease in supply	Increase	Decrease
Increase in demand	Increase	Increase
Decrease in demand	Decrease	Decrease

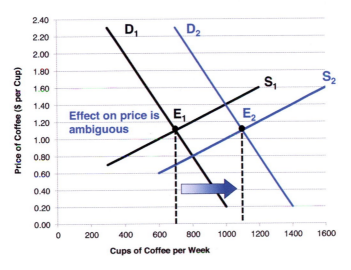

Figure 3.10 *Market Adjustment With an Increase in Both Supply and Demand*

S_1 to S_2, and demand increases from D_1 to D_2. The initial equilibrium is E_1, and the new equilibrium, once the market fully adjusts, is E_2. Both shifts tend to increase equilibrium quantity (see Table 3.3), so we can unambiguously state that the overall result will be an increase in the quantity of coffee sold, as shown in Figure 3.10. (See Box 3.1 for some examples of changes in the real–world market for coffee.)

But in this case, the effect on price is more difficult to discern. An increase in demand tends to increase the equilibrium price, but an increase in supply tends to decrease prices. Looking at Figure 3.10, we cannot tell whether the net effect is an increase or decrease in price. In other cases, it may be the change in the price that is clear but the change in equilibrium quantity that is ambiguous.

Whenever both curves shift at the same time, we can make an unambiguous statement about how one of our market variables (price or quantity) will change but not the other. The net effect on one variable will depend on two factors: how far each of the curve shifts and how steep each of the curves is (the second of these is related to the price elasticity of supply or demand, a concept that is discussed in

BOX 3.1 COFFEE MARKETS IN THE REAL WORLD

The global coffee market went through a particularly tumultuous period from 2011 to 2013. After reaching a 14-year high in May 2011, wholesale coffee bean prices began to tumble. By July 2013, prices for arabica beans, the most-consumed coffee in the world, had fallen over 60 percent. How can our market model provide insights into changing coffee prices in the real world?

Our model suggests that falling prices can occur either due to an increase in supply or a decrease in demand or both. According to data from the United States Department of Agriculture, global coffee supplies increased over this time period. At the same time, consumption in coffee-growing countries and coffee exports both increased.[9] These data suggest that the main reason prices fell so much over 2011–2013 was an increase in the supply of coffee. Even though there was some demand increase, which by itself would tend to raise prices, the supply increase was much larger.

In the 2012/2013 growing season Brazil, the world's largest coffee producer, had a bumper crop, with production up 14 percent over the previous year. Vietnam, the world's second-largest producer, had also scaled up its coffee production. Between 2010 and 2012, production there increased nearly 30 percent. Other major coffee-producing countries, including Colombia and Indonesia, also had production gains.

With coffee bean prices falling by so much, you may wonder why in June 2013 Starbucks announced that it was *increasing* its prices.[10] According to a Starbucks spokesman, the reasons for the price increase included higher costs for labor, raw materials, and rent. The cost of the actual coffee beans represents a minor portion of the total cost of producing a retail cup of coffee. So Starbucks raising its coffee prices can be explained by an increase in input prices, which would be modeled as a shift of their supply curve. The price increase could also reflect a response to an increase in the demand for Starbucks coffee.

Table 3.4 Summary of the Market Effects When Both Supply and Demand Shift

Market Change	Effect on Equilibrium Price	Effect on Equilibrium Quantity
Increase in supply, increase in demand	Ambiguous	Increase
Increase in supply, decrease in demand	Decrease	Ambiguous
Decrease in supply, increase in demand	Increase	Ambiguous
Decrease in supply, decrease in demand	Ambiguous	Decrease

the next section). Table 3.4 summarizes the market results if both curves shift. Again, you shouldn't try to memorize the table but be able to confirm these conclusions based on drawing market graphs of your own.

Discussion Questions

1. Think about the market for high-quality basketballs. In each of the following cases, determine which curve will shift and in which direction. Also draw a graph and describe, in words, the changes in price and quantity. (Treat each case separately.)
   a. A rise in consumers' incomes
   b. An increase in the wages paid to workers who make basketballs
   c. A decrease in the price of basketball shoes and other basketball gear
   d. The country is becoming obsessed with soccer
2. Have you ever found yourself shut out of a class that you wanted to take because it was already full? Or has this happened to a friend of yours? Analyze this situation in terms of surplus or shortage. Do you think classes are supplied through "a market" similar to what has been described in this chapter?

5. ELASTICITY

In this section, we introduce the concept of elasticity. Elasticity measures the *responsiveness* of the quantity demanded, or quantity supplied, to changes in market factors, including price and income. We will discuss different types of elasticities and their importance in making price-setting decisions.

> **elasticity:** a measure of the responsiveness of an economic actor to changes in market factors, including price and income

5.1 The Price Elasticity of Demand

The **price elasticity of demand** (often just called the "elasticity of demand") measures the responsiveness of the quantity demanded to a change in price. The larger the quantity response is, relative to the size of the price change, the "more elastic" demand is said to be. If the response is small, demand is said to be relatively "price inelastic."

> **price elasticity of demand:** the responsiveness of the quantity demanded to a change in price

The extent of responsiveness of the quantity demanded to price changes is dependent on the steepness of the demand curve. Figure 3.11 graphs two different demand curves, along with identical supply curves. In Figure 3.11 (a), with the relatively flat demand curve, we see that there is a large drop in the quantity demanded associated with a small increase in price. In Figure 3.11 (b), by contrast, with a relatively steep demand curve, only a small decrease in quantity demanded is associated with a substantial increase in price. The difference derives from the fact that the demand curve shown in (a) is much more price elastic than the demand curve in (b).

Demand for a good is **price inelastic** if the effect of a price change on the quantity demanded is fairly small. Goods or services for which there are very few good, close substitutes or those that are needed rather than just wanted tend to have relatively price inelastic demand. For example, gasoline has no good, close substitutes for powering nonelectric motor vehicles. When gas prices rise, most drivers still need to use their vehicles to get to work, run errands, and so on. So gasoline is an example of a good that is price inelastic because of the lack of any good substitutes and also because people believe that they need it. Other examples of goods that tend to be price inelastic for these reasons include water for basic needs, essential health care, and electricity.

> **price-inelastic demand:** a relationship between price and quantity demanded characterized by relatively weak responses of buyers to price changes

Some goods are price inelastic because expenditures on them represent such a small portion of people's incomes that most consumers are not affected much by a change in prices. Consider that a 50 percent increase in the price of dental floss is not likely to reduce the quantity demanded significantly.

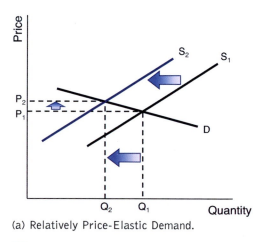

(a) Relatively Price-Elastic Demand.

(b) Relatively Price-Inelastic Demand.

Figure 3.11 *Price Elasticity of Demand*

Conversely, demand for a good is **price elastic** if the effect of a price change on the quantity demanded is fairly large. Goods or services for which there are many good substitutes, which are merely wanted rather than needed or which make up a large part of the budget of the buyer are likely to have relatively price-elastic demand. Different brands of beverage, for example, will tend to be price elastic, because they can readily substitute for one another and are not a necessity for most people. Demand for automobiles is also price elastic—because a car is such a large expense buyers will tend to be sensitive to price.

> **price-elastic demand:** a relationship between price and quantity demanded characterized by relatively strong responses of buyers to price changes

5.2 Measuring Elasticity

The elasticity of demand is mathematically calculated as:

$$\textit{Price elasticity of demand} = \frac{\textit{Percentage change in quantity demanded}}{\textit{Percentage change in price}}$$

Suppose a publishing company is trying to decide on the price for a new book of poetry. After doing some market research, it finds that if it raises the price of the book from \$5 to \$10, the quantity demanded will decline from 1,000 to 800. In order to calculate the price elasticity of demand for the book, we need to calculate the percentage change in quantity demanded and price. The percentage change for any variable is calculated as:

$$\textit{Percentage change} = \left[\frac{\textit{New value} - \textit{Base value}}{\textit{Base value}}\right] \times \textit{100}$$

where "base" value is the starting value and "new" value is the ending value for any variable. So, going from a base of \$5 to a new value of \$10, the percentage change in price is:

$$
\begin{aligned}
\textit{Percentage change in price} &= [(\$10 - \$5)/\$5] \times 100 \\
&= [\$5/\$5 \times 100] \\
&= 1 \times 100 \\
&= 100\%
\end{aligned}
$$

Similarly, the percentage change in quantity with base value of 1,000 and new value of 800 is:

$$
\begin{aligned}
\textit{Percentage change in quantity} &= [(800 - 1,000)/1,000] \times 100 \\
&= [-200/1,000] \times 100 \\
&= -0.2 \times 100 \\
&= -20\%
\end{aligned}
$$

103

We can then calculate the elasticity of demand as the percentage change in quantity demanded divided by the percentage change in price, or:

$$Elasticity = -20\%/100\%$$
$$= -0.2$$

In this example, notice that the percentage change in the quantity demanded is less than the percentage change in price. Whenever this is the case, the elasticity value will be less than 1 in absolute value. This is the **technical definition of price-inelastic demand**. The **technical definition of price-elastic demand** is that the percentage change in the quantity demanded is larger than the percentage change in price, such that the elasticity value will be more than 1 in absolute value. When the percentage change in the quantity demanded is exactly equal to the percentage change in price, we call it **unit-elastic demand**, and the elasticity value is −1.

---

price-inelastic demand (technical definition): the percentage change in the quantity demanded is smaller than the percentage change in price. The elasticity value is less than 1 in absolute value

price-elastic demand (technical definition): the percentage change in the quantity demanded is larger than the percentage change in price. The elasticity value is more than 1 in absolute value

unit-elastic demand: the percentage change in the quantity demanded is exactly equal to the percentage change in price. The elasticity value is −1

Note that price and the quantity demanded normally change in opposite directions (an inverse relationship), so price elasticity of demand will almost always be a negative number. For example, if price increases (a positive sign in the denominator of the fraction), we would expect the quantity demanded to decrease (a negative sign in the numerator of the fraction). So after dividing, we would end up with a negative number. In most cases, economists report price elasticity of demand values after taking the absolute value (i.e., getting rid of the negative sign). We will follow this convention and refer to the absolute value of the price elasticity of demand. But you should always assume that price and quantity are moving in the opposite direction when interpreting a price elasticity of demand value, unless stated otherwise.

5.3 Elasticity and Revenues

A common application of elasticity estimates is predicting how a company's revenues will change in response to a price change. A business can use an elasticity estimate to determine what price it should charge to maximize its revenues. Why is this? The revenues that a business (or government agency) will receive from selling a good or service at a specific price is simply that price multiplied by the quantity sold:

Revenues = Price (P) × Quantity (Q) Sold

Let us consider how revenue will change depending on whether a good or service is elastic or inelastic. As already discussed, if a good is elastic, it means quantity is quite sensitive to changes in price. In other words, the percentage change in quantity is always going to be larger than the percentage change in price. In this case, a small increase in price will have a large impact on quantity sold; hence, the revenue will drop.

Imagine, for example, that a book seller raises the price of a book with price-elastic demand from $10 to $11 (a 10% increase), and the quantity sold drops from 100 books to 85 books (a 15% drop). In this case, the revenue declines from $1,000 ($10 × 100 books) to $935 (11 × 85 books). Hence, there is *less* money in the book seller's cash register as a consequence of raising prices. This does not create much of an incentive to raise prices.

Alternatively, suppose the same book seller had lowered prices from $10 to $9 (a 10% drop), and quantity sold had increased from 100 books to 115 books (a 15% increase). In this case, revenue has increased from $1,000 ($10 × 100 books) to $1,035 ($9 × 115 books). In other words, there is more money in the book seller's cash register as a consequence of lowering prices, thus creating an incentive to lower prices.

If the good is inelastic, the percentage change in quantity sold (Q) is less than the percentage change in price (P). For example, suppose the quantity of books sold drops from 100 to 95 (a 5% decrease) when the book seller raises the price of a book from $10 to $11 (a 10% increase). In this case, the revenues will increase from $1,000 ($10 × 100 books) to $ 1,045 ($11 × 95 books). Hence, raising prices has increased revenues. By contrast, if the book seller reduces prices, they will lose money because the percentage increase in sales will be less than the percentage decrease in price.

If the elasticity value for a good or service is −1 (unit elastic), it means that the percentage change in quantity sold is equal to the percentage change in price (but in opposite directions). So, doubling the prices would reduce the quantity demanded by half. Hence, price changes will have no impact on revenue because any proportional change in price will be exactly offset by the same proportional change in quantity sold.

5.4 Price Elasticity of Supply

The price elasticity of supply measures the same sort of responsiveness but this time on the part of sellers. When suppliers respond to a small increase in price by offering a much larger quantity of goods, we say that supply is relatively elastic. If they hardly react at all, supply is relatively inelastic. Mathematically, it is defined as the percentage change in quantity supplied divided by the percentage change in price.

$$\textit{Price elasticity of supply} = \frac{\textit{Percentage change in quantity supplied}}{\textit{Percentage change in price}}$$

> **price elasticity of supply:** a measure of the responsiveness of quantity supplied to changes in price

Given that supply curves normally slope upward, price and quantity supplied change in the same direction, and thus taking the absolute value is not required. If the price elasticity of supply is greater than 1, we would say the supply curve is price elastic. If the price elasticity of supply is less than 1, we would say the supply curve is price inelastic. A price elasticity of supply equal to 1 is "unit elastic."

5.5 Income Elasticity of Demand

The final kind of elasticity that we consider in this chapter is the **income elasticity of demand**. This measures how much the quantity demanded changes when income changes but price remains constant. Recall from earlier in the chapter that income is a nonprice determinant of demand that shifts the entire demand curve.

> **income elasticity of demand:** a measure of the responsiveness of demand to changes in income, holding price constant

Similar to the equations for price elasticity of demand and supply, income elasticity is calculated as:

Income elasticity of demand = Percentage change in quantity demanded/
Percentage change in income

For most goods, when income increases, demand also increases. Thus, income elasticity is positive. Goods for which demand rises when a household's income rises are called **normal goods**. As people can afford more, they tend to buy more. However, demand for some goods may fall when incomes rise; these goods are called **inferior goods**. Individuals and families tend to buy less of goods like ramen noodles or second hand clothes as incomes rise. For an inferior good, the income elasticity of demand is negative.

> **normal goods:** goods for which demand increases when incomes rise and decreases when incomes fall
> **inferior goods:** goods for which demand decreases when incomes rise and increases when incomes fall

When income elasticity is positive but less than 1, demand is called income inelastic. Spending rises with income but less than proportionately. For example, when income rises by 10 percent, spending on a particular good may rise by only 5 percent. When income elasticity is positive and greater than 1, a good is called income elastic. In this case, expenditures on that good will increase by a greater proportion than the increase in income. For example, income may rise by 10 percent, but spending on the good rises by 20 percent.

The income elasticity of a good or service is a very important variable. For example, some countries have sought to develop industries that produce goods and services that have high income elasticity of demand. Why? Policymakers have reasoned that it makes sense to produce goods where demand will increase more strongly than world income. For example, world income might increase by 10 percent, but purchases of the good or service in question will increase by more than 10 percent. This is likely to be a superior strategy to producing inferior goods with negative income elasticity or to producing goods that have income *in*elastic demand, where the rise in demand will not keep up with the rise in world income. For example, world income might rise by 10 percent, yet demand will increase by less than this amount.

Discussion Questions

1. Can you think of some reasons the demand for cigarettes, eggs, and rice is inelastic?
2. Suppose that your income increases. Which goods and services would you buy more of (i.e., normal goods)? Which goods and services would you buy less of (i.e., inferior goods)?

6. TOPICS IN MARKET ANALYSIS

Now that we understand the basic functioning of microeconomic markets, we can begin to assess market models in terms of their ability to explain real-world economic outcomes and also their ability to produce conditions that truly enhance well-being. As we proceed through this book, further developing and analyzing our market model, we will gain insights into situations where markets currently function well, where markets can be made to function better, and where markets do not offer the best way to allocate society's resources.

6.1 Real-World Prices

The workings of markets in the real world may differ in some ways from the assumptions in the model constructed previously. First, there are costs associated with changing prices that are not considered in our simple model. One type of cost is related to the fact that market exchange occurs within an ethical context. For example, customers may be offended by seeing prices change "opportunistically." If an umbrella shop doubles its prices as soon as it starts raining, this may be seen as being unethical and thus risks giving the shop a bad reputation that damages sales. Other types of costs may also be associated with changing prices. For example, a restaurant with printed menus may keep prices fixed even though demand increases because the cost of printing new menus would offset the additional revenue.

In fact, much evidence indicates that rather than immediately changing prices according to each small change in supply or demand that might affect them, many retailers commonly set prices using **markup (or cost-plus) pricing**. Using this method, they determine how much it costs them to make or supply a product and then add a "markup" (a percentage increase over the costs, for example, 30 percent) and commit to this price for at least the short term regardless of any day-to-day fluctuations in demand.

> **markup (or cost–plus) pricing:** a method of setting prices in which the seller adds a fixed percentage amount to his or her costs of production

In some cases, retailers lower their prices on some products so much that they actually lose money on each sale. These so–called loss leaders exist to attract customers to the store who will hopefully also buy other, nondiscounted products so that overall profits will increase. This is the strategy that many retailers use, for example, during the holiday season when they lower the price on their *electronics* and expect to increase their profits by attracting more customers who may purchase some of their other products that are not on discount.

In the real world, prices may also be set to take advantage of differences among consumers' willingness or ability to pay. For example, the cost of airline travel is usually higher during holidays, when more people are likely to travel, than during other times. This is because the relatively inelastic demand for airline tickets during holidays means that an airline can fill its planes at relatively high prices. It may have an incentive to lower prices and attract more customers during non-busy travel periods.

6.2 Markets and Equity

Markets are one way to ration resources. Specifically, markets allow anyone who is both willing and able to purchase something at the equilibrium prices to do so. As such, one can argue that markets produce about the "right" amount of many goods and services, such as televisions, backpacks, haircuts, and pencils. However, given that people's ability to buy is dependent on their income or wealth levels, this outcome is less straightforward. Poorer people might be very *willing* to purchase a life-saving medication but not actually *able* to do so because of their low income. Fewer seemingly luxury goods like yachts may be produced at the equilibrium price, yet this may be more of a reflection of the ability of the super rich to pay for them than an articulation of the needs and wants of society as a whole.

It is useful at this point to differentiate between market value and social value. **Market value** is defined according to effective demand—the maximum amount that economic actors are both willing and *able* to pay for something. Market value can, in theory, be measured positively, without normative judgments. **Social value** is more difficult to define and measure. We broadly define the social value of an outcome according to the extent to which it moves us toward our final goals. So if "fairness" is one of our final goals, then it should be part of how we assess the social value of an economic outcome. But even if we had an accepted way to measure fairness, we would still need to make a normative judgment about how much fairness is appropriate.

> **market value:** the maximum amount that economic actors are willing and able to pay for a good or service (i.e., effective demand)
> **social value:** the extent to which an outcome moves us toward our final goals

Although yacht production may maximize the market value of production, it may not maximize social value. Devoting yacht-building resources to public transportation, basic health care, or public education may yield greater social value.

6.3 Scarcity and Inadequacy

A fundamental scarcity of resources relative to everything that people might need or want requires individuals and societies to make choices. Scarcity is about an imbalance between what is available and what people would *like* to have, regardless of what they can afford. Perhaps many people would *like* to have a Rolls-Royce, but Rolls-Royces are scarce because not everyone can buy one. But even cups of coffee are scarce in that price acts as a rationing mechanism in which some people decide not to buy all the coffee that they might theoretically want. In other words, at equilibrium, there is technically no shortage of coffee according to economics, but coffee is still a scarce resource.

Not all kinds of scarcity are alike. We tend to feel differently about the scarcity of Rolls-Royces (there are still plenty of other cars that people can purchase to meet their transportation needs) and the scarcity of affordable housing. We use the term **inadequacy** to refer to scarcity when it involves something that is necessary for minimal human well-being but is not obtainable by everyone who needs it. Food, shelter, and basic health care, for example, can be in inadequate supply relative to needs even when the markets for these goods are in equilibrium and no shortage exists in the economic sense. The problem in this case is a lack of what we have called effective demand—people who are very poor cannot afford to purchase even essential goods.

> **inadequacy:** a situation in which there is not enough of a good or service, provided at prices people can afford, to meet minimal requirements for human well-being

While markets can eliminate shortages, and general scarcity is a fact of life, markets normally do not address problems of inadequacy. However, if economics is truly about meeting needs and enhancing well-being, then we need mechanisms to supplement markets in order to reduce problems of inadequacy. As we discussed last chapter, in going through the book, we will identify situations in which markets may not be the best way to provide certain goods and services.

Discussion Questions

1. In Chapter 1, we discussed the three basic economic questions: *What* should be produced? *How* should production be conducted? *For whom* should economic activity be undertaken? Discuss how the workings of markets provide some answers to these questions, also considering the implications for resource management.
2. For each example subsequently, discuss whether it is a situation of scarcity or inadequacy.
   a. Jasmine cannot afford to go to a doctor.
   b. Rafe can think of dozens of songs he would like to download, but he also would like to buy some new clothing.

REVIEW QUESTIONS

1. Define and sketch a supply curve.
2. Illustrate on a graph: (a) a decrease in quantity supplied and (b) a decrease in supply.
3. Name the six nonprice determinants of supply.
4. Define and sketch a demand curve.
5. Illustrate on a graph: (a) a decrease in quantity demanded and (b) a decrease in demand.
6. Name the five nonprice determinants of demand.
7. Draw a graph illustrating surplus, shortage, and equilibrium.
8. Illustrate what happens to equilibrium price and quantity when either the supply curve or demand curve shifts.
9. Illustrate what happens to equilibrium price and quantity when both the supply and demand curve shift. (Explore different combinations of shifting curves.)
10. List three reasons the demand for a good or service may be elastic. List three reasons the demand for a good may be inelastic.
11. What is the formula for the price elasticity of demand?
12. What is the "technical definition" of a price-elastic demand? What is the technical definition of a price-inelastic demand?
13. What are examples of goods that are price elastic? What are some examples of price-inelastic goods?
14. What is the income elasticity of demand?
15. Explain the difference between market value and social value.

EXERCISES

1. Explain in words why the supply curve slopes upward.
2. Explain in words why the demand curve slopes downward.
3. Suppose that the supply and demand schedules for a local electric utility are as follows:

Price	17	16	15	14	13	12	11
Quantity supplied	9	7	5	3	1	—	—
Quantity demanded	3	4	5	6	7	8	9

The price is in cents per kilowatt hour (kWh), and the quantities are in millions of kilowatt hours. The utility does not operate at prices less than 13 cents per kWh.

a. Using graph paper and a ruler or a computer spreadsheet or presentation program, carefully graph and label the supply curve and the demand curve for electricity.

b. What is the equilibrium price of electricity? The equilibrium quantity? Label this point on your graph.

c. At a price of 17 cents per kWh, what is the quantity supplied? What is the quantity demanded? What is the relationship between quantity supplied and quantity demanded? What term do economists use to describe this situation?

d. At a price of 14 cents per kWh, what is the relationship between quantity supplied and quantity demanded? What term do economists use to describe this situation?

e. Sometimes cities experience "blackouts," in which the demands on the utility are so high relative to its capacity to produce electricity that the system shuts down, leaving everyone in the dark. Using the analysis that you have just completed, describe an *economic* factor that could make blackouts more likely to occur.

4. Continuing on from the previous problem (in question 3), suppose that new innovations in energy efficiency reduce people's need for electricity. The supply side of the market does not change, but at each price, buyers now demand 3 million kilowatt hours fewer than before. For example, at a price of 11 cents per kWh, buyers now demand only 6 kWh instead of 9 kWh.

a. On a new graph, draw supply and demand curves corresponding to prices of 16 cents per kWh or less after the innovations in efficiency. Also, for reference, mark the old equilibrium point from the previous exercise, labeling it E_1.

b. If the price were to remain at the old equilibrium level (determined in part (c) of Exercise 3), what sort of situation would result?

c. What is the new equilibrium price, with the new demand curve? The new equilibrium quantity? Give this point on your graph the label E_2.

d. Has there been a change in demand? Has a change in the price (relative to the original situation) led to a change in the quantity demanded?

e. Has there been a change in supply? Has a change in the price (relative to the original situation) led to a change in the quantity supplied?

5. Using your understanding of the nonprice determinants of supply and of demand, analyze each of the following market cases. Draw a graph showing what happens in each situation, indicate what happens to equilibrium price and quantity, and explain why, following this example from the market for gasoline: A hurricane hits the Gulf of Mexico, destroying many refineries that produce gasoline from crude oil.

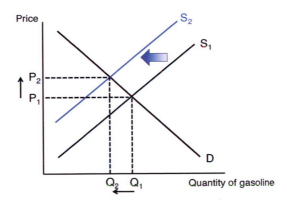

The hurricane reduces the number of producers, which shifts the supply curve back (to the left) from S_1 to S_2; price rises from P_1 to P_2, and quantity falls from Q_1 to Q_2.

a. Market for bananas: New health reports indicate that people can gain important health benefits from eating bananas.

b. Market for shoes: A new technology for shoe making means that shoes can be made at a lower cost per pair.

c. Market for grapes *from California:* A freeze in Chile, usually a major world provider of fresh fruit, raises the price of Chilean grapes.

d. Market for internet design services: Several thousand new graduates of design schools enter the market, ready to supply their services, *at the same time* many firms want to create new Web sites.

111

    e.   Market for bananas: New health reports indicate that people can gain important health benefits from eating bananas, while *at the same time* an infestation of insects reduces the banana harvest in several areas.

6. Suppose that a newspaper report indicates that the price of wheat has fallen. For each of the following events, draw a supply-and-demand graph showing the event's effect on the market for wheat. Then state whether the event could explain the observed fall in the price of wheat.

    a.   A drought has hit wheat-growing areas.

    b.   The price of rice has risen, so consumers look for alternatives.

    c.   As a consequence of increasing health concerns, tobacco farmers have begun to plant other crops.

    d.   The government has a price floor for wheat and increases it.

7. For each of the following items, discuss whether you think the demand that the seller faces will be price inelastic or price elastic, and explain why.

    a.   A new song by an extremely popular recording artist

    b.   One share of stock, when there are millions of shares for that company outstanding

    c.   Bottled drinking water at a town in the desert

    d.   Your used textbooks at the end of the term

8. Calculate the price elasticity of demand for the following cases:

    a.   When price rises by 5 percent, quantity demanded drops by 10 percent.

    b.   When price rises by 10 percent, quantity demanded drops by 2 percent.

    c.   When price falls by 10 percent, quantity demanded rises by 2 percent.

9. Calculate the percentage change in revenue that would result from each of the actions in question 8 previously. Assume that the initial price in all cases is $100 per unit, and the initial quantity demanded is 1,000 units.

10. Use the formulas for elasticity to answer the following questions.

    a.   When Mariba's income rises by 10 percent, her expenditures on carrots rise 12 percent. What is Mariba's income elasticity of demand for carrots? Are carrots, for her, a normal or an inferior good?

    b.   Suppose that the price elasticity of demand for milk is 0.6. If a grocer raises the price of milk by 15 percent, by what percentage will milk sales decrease as a result of the price increase? Will the grocer's revenue from milk sales go up or down?

    c.   Suppose that the price elasticity of supply for paper is 1.5. You notice that the quantity of paper supplied decreases by 6 percent as the result of a change in the price of paper. Determine by what percentage the price of paper must have declined.

11. Match each concept in Column A with the corresponding fact or example in Column B.

Column A	Column B
a. Substitute goods	1. Income elasticity of 1.4
b. A nonprice determinant of demand	2. Tea and coffee
c. A nonprice determinant of supply	3. A change in technology
d. Markup pricing	4. Hunger
e. Income-elastic demand	5. Expenditures on a good increase when your income rises
f. Price-inelastic demand	6. Consumer income
g. Inadequacy	7. Revenues rise as a seller increases her price
h. Normal good	8. Setting price equal to cost plus 20 percent

NOTES

1. The quantity supplied changes from 800 to 1,000 cups per week, an increase of 200 cups.
2. International Coffee Organization. 2019. *Historical Data on the Global Coffee Trade*. www.ico.org/new_historical.asp. Accessed 20 July 2019.
3. The quantity demanded changes from 700 to 900 cups per week, an increase of 200 cups.
4. There is surprisingly little research on the relationship between caffeine consumption and academic performance. The studies we found indicate that higher caffeine consumption is actually associated with *reduced* academic performance. See Pettit, Michele, and Kathy A. DeBarr. 2011. "Perceived Stress, Energy Drink Consumption, and Academic Performance among College Students." *Journal of American College Health*, 59(5): 335–341; Champlin, Sara E., Keryn E. Pasch, and Cheryl L. Perry. 2016. "Is the Consumption of Energy Drinks Associated with Academic Achievement among College Students?" *The Journal of Primary Prevention*, 37(4): 345–359.
5. If one particular coffee seller lowers his price in response to the surplus, pressure will be created on other sellers to lower their prices as well, at the risk of losing customers. Thus the most likely outcome in response to the surplus would be lower prices in general.
6. Because there are many buyers who are willing to pay more than $0.80 for coffee, it is easy for some sellers to raise prices. So even if everyone does not raise prices immediately, the overall tendency will be toward higher prices in general in a situation of shortage.
7. More advanced market models do consider the period required for adjustment.
8. Median Housing Prices Data from the Federal Reserve Bank of St. Louis. https://fred.stlouisfed.org/series/MSPUS
9. U.S. Department of Agriculture. 2013. "Coffee: World Markets and Trade." Foreign Agricultural Service, June.
10. Kavilanz, Parija. 2013. "Next Week You'll Pay More for a Starbucks Latte." CNN Money, June 21.

Chapter 4

Consumption and Decision-Making

In Chapter 1, we defined economic actors, or economic agents, as people or organizations engaged in any of the four essential economic activities: production, distribution, consumption, and resource management. Economics is about how these actors behave and interact as they engage in economic activities. We begin this chapter with a brief overview of the classical and neoclassical perspectives on economic behavior. The rest of the chapter focuses specifically on consumer behavior—how individuals make decisions on what goods and services to consume. We look at both traditional and contemporary approaches to understanding consumer behavior.

1. HISTORICAL PERSPECTIVES ON ECONOMIC BEHAVIOR

Economics is a *social* science—it is about people and how we organize ourselves to meet our needs and enhance our well-being. All economic outcomes are ultimately determined by human behavior. Thus, economists have traditionally used as a starting point some kind of statement about the motivations behind economic actions.

1.1 Classical Economic Views of Human Nature

The classical economic view of human behavior is largely based on the theoretical framework presented in Adam Smith's *An Inquiry Into the Nature and Causes of the Wealth of Nations*, published in 1776. In this book, Smith suggests that an economic system based on markets can effectively promote the general welfare of society. He reasoned that a businessman who is interested in maximizing his own monetary gain would nonetheless serve the social good *if* the best available means for his monetary gain was to produce high-quality goods at a competitive price.

The idea that self-interest can unintentionally promote the social good is an important and valuable one. However, it is often taken out of context to mean that if people *only* behave with self-interest, they will also always do what is best for the entire society. This interpretation would have astonished Smith, who, in his other famous book, *The Theory of Moral Sentiments*, emphasized the desire of people to maintain their own self-respect and earn the respect of others. He assumes that this desire motivates people to act honorably, justly, and with empathy for others in their community. Smith recognized that self-interest is important, but he also believed that narrow self-interest will be held in check by people's "moral sentiments" (the universal desire for self-respect and the respect of others). Thus Smith's vision of human motivation was one in which individual self-interest was mixed with social motives.

Smith was followed by other economists, such as David Ricardo, John Stuart Mill, and Alfred Marshall, who held similarly complex views of human nature and thought quite deeply about ethics. For example, Marshall viewed human motivations as being influenced by a desire to improve the human condition. He specifically focused on the reduction of poverty so as to allow people to develop their higher moral and intellectual faculties rather than being condemned to lives of desperate effort for simple survival.

1.2 The Neoclassical Model

In the twentieth century, the **neoclassical model** came to dominate economic thinking. This approach took a narrower and simpler view of human motivations. Recall from Chapter 2 that the basic neoclassical model only considers two main types of economic actors—firms and households. This model assumes that firms maximize their profits from producing and selling goods and services, and households maximize their utility (or satisfaction) from consuming goods and services. Economic actors are assumed to be self-interested and "rational," meaning that people generally make logical decisions that produce the best outcomes for themselves. Also, firms and households are assumed to interact in perfectly competitive markets. In this model, competition (rather than Smith's "moral sentiments") is regarded as the check on self-interested behavior of individuals and firms. Competition is understood as being able to prevent firms from charging too much for their product or producing poor-quality goods.

> **neoclassical model:** a model that portrays the economy as composed of profit-maximizing firms and utility-maximizing households interacting through perfectly competitive markets

Some benefits can be gained from looking at economic behavior in this way. The assumptions reduce the actual (very complicated) economy to something that is much more limited but also easier to analyze. With some additional assumptions, the model can be elegantly expressed in figures, equations, and graphs. This traditional model is particularly well suited for analyzing the determination of prices, the volume of trade, and economic efficiency in certain cases. We will take a closer look at the neoclassical model of consumer behavior in Section 2.

Moving into the twenty-first century, most economists have accepted that human motivations are much more complex. As we will see in Section 3, in recent years, economists have devised many creative experiments to explore how people make actual economic decisions, typically showing how context can influence decisions. While this model of economic behavior can't necessarily be summed up in tidy mathematical equations and graphs, it is more comprehensive, and often more accurate, than the neoclassical model.

115

Discussion Questions

1. Discuss, with an example, how individuals acting in their own self-interest may sometimes lead to outcomes that serve the social good.
2. Do you agree with the assumption of the neoclassical model that human behavior is rational and self-interested? Can you think of some examples of economic behavior that might contradict these assumptions?

2. THE NEOCLASSICAL THEORY OF CONSUMER BEHAVIOR

We start our analysis of consumption behavior with the neoclassical model. As mentioned previously, this model is based on simplistic assumptions, but it provides some useful insights.

2.1 Consumer Sovereignty

Consumer sovereignty refers to the notion that satisfaction of consumers' needs and wants is the ultimate economic goal and that firms will always seek to organize their production solely in response to better meeting consumer desires. For example, consider the increase in the sales of sport utility vehicles (SUVs) in the United States in recent decades. The theory of consumer sovereignty would suggest that the primary reason for the growth of SUV sales is a change in consumers' preferences for larger vehicles over cars. Consumer sovereignty stands in direct contrast to the idea that some firms can manipulate consumer desires through advertising or that some firms might be largely unresponsive to what consumers actually want.

> **consumer sovereignty:** the idea that consumers' needs and wants determine the shape of all economic activities

2.2 The Budget Line

Consumers are constrained in their spending by the amount of their total budget. We can represent this in a simple model in which consumers have only two goods from which to choose. In Figure 4.1 we present a **budget line**, which shows the combinations of two goods—chocolate bars and bags of nuts—that a consumer can purchase. In this example, our consumer—let's call him Quong—has a budget of $8. The price of chocolate bars is $1 each, and nuts sell for $2 per bag.

> **budget line:** a line showing the possible combinations of two goods that a consumer can purchase

If Quong spends his $8 only on chocolate, he can buy 8 bars, as indicated by the point where the budget line touches the vertical axis. If he buys only nuts, he can buy 4 bags, as indicated by the (4, 0) point on the horizontal axis. He can also buy any combination in between. For example, the point (2, 4), which indicates

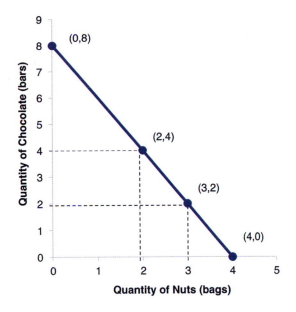

Figure 4.1 *The Budget Line*

2 bags of nuts and 4 chocolate bars, is also achievable. This is because (2 × $2) + (4 × $1) = $8. (Note that to keep things simple we assume that Quong can buy only whole bars and whole bags, not fractions of them—for example, he can't buy 2.5 bars of chocolate. However, we draw the budget line as continuous to reflect the more general case with many more alternatives.)

A budget line is similar to the concept of a production-possibilities frontier, which we discussed in Chapter 1. A budget line defines the choices that are *possible* for Quong. Points above and to the right of the budget line are not affordable. Points below and to the left of the budget line are affordable but do not use up the total budget. This simple model assumes that people always want more of at least one of the goods in question; hence, consuming below the budget line would be inefficient. Therefore, a rational consumer will always choose to consume at a point on the budget line.

The position of the budget line depends on the size of the total budget (income) and on the prices of the two goods. For example, if Quong has $10 to spend instead of $8, the line would shift outward in a parallel manner, as shown in Figure 4.2. He could now consume more nuts, or more chocolate, or a more generous combination of both.

A change in the price of one of the goods will cause the budget line to rotate around a point on one of the axes. So if the price of nuts dropped to $1 per bag (and Quong's income was again $8), the budget line would rotate out, as shown in Figure 4.3. Now, if Quong bought only nuts, he could buy 8 bags instead of 4. With the price of chocolate unchanged, however, he still could not buy more than 8 chocolate bars.

Note that if both prices change, the budget line could shift in any direction, depending on how the two prices changed. If both prices changed by the same

117

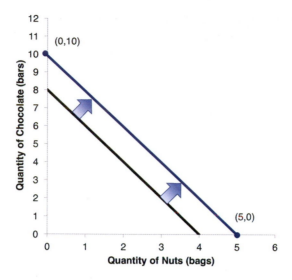

Figure 4.2 *Effect of an Increase in Income*

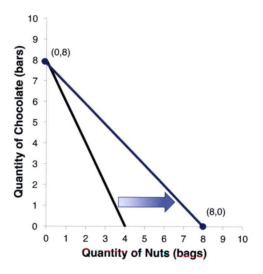

Figure 4.3 *Effect of a Fall in the Price of One Good*

percentage, then the new budget line would be parallel to the original, similar to a change in income. Draw some graphs to prove this to yourself.

A budget line tells us all the combinations of purchases that are possible. However, it does not tell us which combination the consumer will choose. To get to this, we must add the theory of utility.

2.3 Consumer Utility

The neoclassical model assumes that individuals have certain preferences (or tastes) for certain goods and services. Consumers seek to satisfy these preferences and thereby derive **utility**, which is defined as the pleasure or satisfaction received from

consuming goods, services, or experiences. Consumers cannot satisfy all their preferences because they are constrained by their budget, so they have to think carefully
about what goods to purchase in order to maximize the amount of utility from
their given budget.

> **utility:** the level of usefulness or satisfaction gained from a particular activity, such
> as the consumption of a good or service

Utility is a somewhat vague concept, like well-being, and cannot be measured
quantitatively in the real world. However, for the purposes of this model we assume
that we can measure utility in some imaginary unit of "satisfaction." Table 4.1
presents the total utility that Quong obtains from purchasing different quantities of
chocolate bars in a given period, say a day.

We can then plot Quong's total utility from consuming chocolate bars in Figure 4.4. This relationship between utility and the quantity outlined in Figure 4.4 is
an example of a **utility function**, or a **total utility curve**.

Table 4.1 Quong's Utility From Consuming Chocolate Bars

Quantity of chocolate bars	Total utility	Marginal utility
0	0	—
1	10	10
2	18	8
3	24	6
4	28	4
5	30	2
6	29	−1

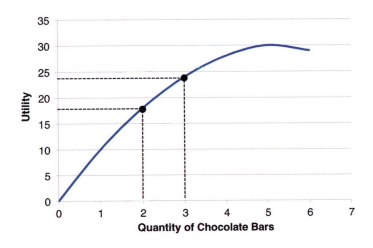

Figure 4.4 Quong's Utility Function for Chocolate Bars

> **utility function (or total utility curve):** a curve showing the relation of utility levels to consumption levels

Rather than just looking at total utility, economists tend to focus on how utility changes from one level of consumption to another. The change in utility for a one-unit change in consumption is known as **marginal utility**. The word "marginal" puts the focus on incremental change rather than total change.

> **marginal utility:** the change in a consumer's utility when consumption of something changes by one unit

We can determine Quong's marginal utility by referring to Table 4.1. We see that Quong obtains 10 units of "satisfaction" from consuming his first chocolate bar. When he eats an additional chocolate bar, his total utility increases from 10 to 18 units (10 + 8 = 18). Here, his total utility is the units of satisfaction obtained from consuming the two bars, while his *marginal* utility from consuming the second chocolate bar is only 8 units. Consuming his third chocolate bar, he obtains a marginal utility of 6 units. Total utility continues to increase, but in smaller installments since the marginal utility is progressively decreasing. If marginal utility becomes negative, total utility decreases.

Figure 4.4 provides a visual picture of how Quong's utility curve levels off as his consumption of chocolate bars increases. This is generally expected—that successive units of something consumed provide less utility than the previous unit. In other words, consumers' utility functions generally display **diminishing marginal utility**. Notice that after six bars of chocolate the marginal utility is negative. In other words, the sixth bar of chocolate has left Quong with negative pleasure (i.e., pain). Perhaps that sixth bar of chocolate gave him an upset stomach.

> **diminishing marginal utility:** the tendency for additional units of consumption to add less to utility than did previous units of consumption

We can now apply the concept of utility to the budget line that Quong faces. Realize that Quong will also have a utility function for bags of nuts, which will display a similar pattern of diminishing marginal utility. Let's assume that his first bag of nuts provides him with 20 units of utility, his second bag with 15 additional units, and his third bag with 10 additional units (more bags result in even fewer units of utility). How can Quong allocate his limited budget to provide him with the highest amount of total utility?

We provide a formal model of utility maximization in an online Appendix to this chapter, but using marginal thinking, we can easily see how Quong can approach his problem in a purely rational manner. Suppose that Quong is thinking about how he will spend his first $2. With $2, he can buy either two chocolate bars or one bag of nuts. If he buys two chocolate bars, he will obtain 18 total units of utility, as shown in Table 4.1. If he buys one bag of nuts instead, he will obtain 20 units of utility. Thus, Quong will receive greater utility by spending his first $2 on a bag of nuts.

What about his next $2? If he spends this on his second bag of nuts, he obtains an additional 15 units of utility. But if he instead purchases his first two chocolate bars, he will obtain 18 units of utility. So, by spending his next $2 on chocolate bars, he increases his utility by a greater amount. After spending $4, Quong has purchased one bag of nuts and two chocolate bars, thus obtaining a total utility of 38 units. Quong can continue to apply marginal thinking to maximize his utility until he has eventually spent his entire budget. (Test yourself: How will Quong spend his third $2, by buying another bag of nuts or two more bars of chocolate?)[1] The basic decision rule to maximize utility is to allocate each additional dollar on the good or service that provides the greatest marginal utility for that dollar.[2]

We suspect that you have never thought about how to spend your money in a manner similar to Quong's marginal analysis of chocolate and nuts. As we will see in the following sections, people may not always act rationally by maximizing their utility, as suggested by the neoclassical model. Additionally, this model does not tell us anything interesting about *why* consumers make particular choices; that is, preferences are taken as given. The contemporary models, which we discuss in the following sections, present a more realistic analysis of consumer behavior by considering how preferences may be influenced by contextual factors.

Discussion Questions

1. Budget lines can be used to analyze various kinds of tradeoffs. Suppose that you have a total "time budget" for recreation of two hours. Think of two activities you might like to do for recreation, and draw a budget line diagram illustrating the recreational opportunities open to you. What if you had a time budget of three hours instead?
2. Explain in words why the total utility curve has the shape that it does in Figure 4.4.

3. MODERN PERSPECTIVES ON CONSUMER BEHAVIOR

Over the past few decades, the neoclassical view of human behavior is being increasingly replaced by an alternative approach that is commonly called **behavioral economics**. Behavioral economics gathers insights from numerous disciplines, including economics, psychology, sociology, anthropology, neuroscience, and biology, to predict how people actually make decisions. Behavioral economics tests theories by conducting experiments and gathering empirical evidence. This work has proven valuable in explaining behavior that may appear to be irrational.

> **behavioral economics:** a subfield of economics that uses insights from various social and biological sciences to explore how people make actual economic decisions

3.1 Behavioral Economics and Rationality

Let us start by examining the neoclassical assumption that people are completely rational, meaning they have *all* the information about the costs and benefits of every single choice available to them and that they can accurately calculate the optimal choice that maximizes their utility. While it may be possible to make a rational choice between a chocolate bar and a bag of nuts, as discussed in the example previously, it becomes much more complicated when we are faced with a wide set of choices. We may not have complete information about each choice. Furthermore, we may not even be able to accurately process and weigh the information that we do possess.

Consider a famous experiment. Researchers at a supermarket in California set up a display table with six different flavors of jam. Shoppers could taste any (or all) of the six flavors and receive a discount coupon to purchase any flavor. About 30 percent of those who tried one or more jams ended up buying some.[3] The researchers then repeated this experiment but instead offered 24 flavors of jam for tasting. In this case, *only 3 percent* of those who tasted a jam went on to buy some. In theory, it would seem that more choice would increase the chances of finding a jam that one really liked and would be willing to buy. But, instead, the additional choices decreased one's motivation to make a decision to buy a jam.

Because we often have trouble processing all the available information, we often employ mental **heuristics**, which are rules of thumb or mental shortcuts that we use to make decisions. While heuristics can often help us make quick and effective decisions, they can often lead to biases based on people's viewpoints or thinking process. Research by Nobel Laureate Daniel Kahneman has found that people tend to give excessive weight to information that is easily available or vivid, something he called the **availability heuristic**. For example, if you regularly watch crime shows on television, you may over rate the risk of being a victim of crime yourself.

> **heuristic:** a rule of thumb or mental shortcut that we use to make decisions
> **availability heuristic:** placing undue importance on particular information because it is readily available or vivid

Kahneman has also shown that the way a decision is presented to people can significantly influence their choices, an effect he refers to as **framing**. For example, consider a gas station that advertises a special 5-cent-per-gallon discount for paying cash. Meanwhile, another station with the same price instead indicates that they charge a 5-cent-per-gallon surcharge to customers who pay by credit card. Although the prices end up exactly the same, experiments suggest that consumers respond more favorably to the station that advertises the apparent discount.

> **framing:** changing the way a particular decision is presented to people in order to influence their behavior

Advertisers and politicians have long been known to use framing techniques to influence the behavior of consumers and voters. For example, beverage or automobile companies show their products in beautiful natural settings or with beautiful female models to make the consumer feel as if purchasing these products will bring the feelings of pleasure or well-being they may associate with natural or human beauty. Similarly, politicians are also often adept at framing issues to trigger emotions of greed or fear rather than offering sound information on which voters can make good decisions.

An effect similar to framing is known as **anchoring**, in which people rely on a piece of information that is not necessarily relevant as a reference point in making a decision. In one powerful example, graduate students at the MIT Sloan School of Management were first asked to write down the last two digits of their Social Security numbers. A short time later, they were asked whether they would pay this amount, in dollars, for various products. The subjects with the highest Social Security numbers indicated a willingness to pay about 300 percent more than those with the lowest numbers! The students had unconsciously used their Social Security numbers as an "anchor" in evaluating the worth of the products.[4] In a real-world example of anchoring, the kitchen equipment company Williams Sonoma was able to increase the sales of its $279 bread maker after it introduced a "deluxe" model for $429. The introduction of the deluxe model created an anchoring effect that made the $279 bread maker seem like a relative bargain.[5]

> **anchoring effect:** overreliance on a piece of information that may or may not be relevant as a reference point when making a decision

In some circumstances, people tend to go with the "default option" when presented with a choice, even if the default option is not necessarily the rational choice. One classic example of the power of defaults looks at whether people are registered to donate their organs at death.[6] In some European countries, such as Austria, Belgium, and France, people are automatically registered as organ donors, but can opt out if they choose to. In these countries, about 98–99 percent of people stay registered. But in other European countries, such as Denmark, Germany, and the United Kingdom, people must sign up to be organ donors. In other words, the default option is that they are not registered. In these countries, less than 20 percent of people register to be organ donors. Such cases, where people prefer things to stay the same by doing nothing or favor the option that is familiar or expected, is referred to as **status quo bias**.

> **status quo bias:** a cognitive bias in favor of that which is familiar, expected, or automatic

3.2 The Role of Time, Emotions, and Other Influential Factors

Much evidence suggests that people seem to place undue emphasis on gains or benefits received today without considering the implications of their decisions for the future. A good example of this is the large number of people who have acquired significant high-interest credit card debt due to excessive spending. According to one study, about 6 percent of Americans are considered "compulsive shoppers," who seek instant gratification with little concern for the troublesome consequences of running up a great deal of debt.

Economists say that someone who does not pay much attention to the future consequences of his or her actions has a high **time discount rate**. This means that in his or her mind, future events are heavily discounted when weighed against the pleasures of today. On the other hand, people who have a low time discount rate would place more relevance on future consequences. For example, people who invest in a college education have a relatively low time discount rate, because they are willing to forgo current income or relaxation, and pay substantial tuition, to study for some expected future gain. Various studies have shown how people who have high discount rates are more likely to make seemingly irrational, or unhealthy choices inconsistent with their long-term goals. A 2016 study reported that those with high time discount rates are consistently found to be more likely to smoke, abuse alcohol, take illicit drugs, and engage in risky sexual behaviors.[7]

> **time discount rate:** an economic concept describing the relative weighting of present benefits or costs compared to future benefits or costs

The choices we make are also influenced by our emotions. The conventional view is that emotions get in the way of good decision-making, as they tend to interfere with logical reasoning. But again, research from behavioral economics suggests a more nuanced reality. It does not seem to be true that decisions based on logical reasoning are always "better" than those based on emotion or intuition. Instead, studies suggest that reasoning is most effective when used for making relatively simple economic decisions, but for more complex decisions, we can become overwhelmed by too much information. In such cases, emotions or intuition can sometimes help us make better decisions.[8]

For example, an experiment with college students involved their tasting five brands of strawberry jam.[9] In one case, students simply ranked the jams from best to worst. The student rankings were highly correlated with the results of independent testing by *Consumer Reports*, suggesting that the students' rankings were reasonable. But in another case, students were asked to fill out a written questionnaire explaining their preferences. As a result of the additional deliberation, students' rankings were no longer significantly correlated with the *Consumer Report* rankings. The researcher concluded that overthinking might cut individuals off from the wisdom of their emotions, which are sometimes much better at assessing actual preferences.[10]

Altruism, meaning a concern of the well-being of others without thought about oneself, can also motivate our behavior. Although it would be idealistic to assume that altruism is the prime mover in human behavior, it is reasonable to assert that some elements of altruism enter into most people's decision-making—contrary to the neoclassical assumption of rational, self-interested individuals. Especially relevant to economics is the fact that much economic behavior may be motivated by a desire to advance the **common good**—the general good of society, of which one's own interests are only a part. People are often willing to participate in the creation of social benefits, even if this involves some personal sacrifice, as long as they feel that others are also contributing.

> **altruism:** actions focused on the well-being of others, without thought about oneself
> **common good:** the general well-being of society, including one's own well-being

A well-functioning economy cannot rely only on self-interest. Without such values as honesty, for example, even the simplest transaction would require costly and elaborate safeguards or policing. Imagine if you were afraid to put down your money before having in your hands the merchandise that you wished to purchase— and the merchant was afraid that as soon as you had what you wanted, you would run out of the store without paying. Such a situation would require police in every store—but what if the police themselves were unethical? Without ethical values that promote trust, inefficiencies would overwhelm any economic system. Fortunately, behavioral economics experiments demonstrate that people really *do* pay attention to social norms, even when this has a cost in terms of their narrow self-interest, as discussed in Box 4.1.

Other recent evidence suggests that pursuing pure self-interest does not lead to happiness. A 2017 journal article by economist Tom Lane reviewed dozens of studies that looked at the relationship between happiness levels and economic behavior and concluded that: "happiness tends to result from pro-social behavior,"

BOX 4.1 THE ULTIMATUM GAME

The "Ultimatum Game" is a behavioral economics experiment in which two people are told that they will be given a sum of money, say $20, to share. The first person gets to propose a way of splitting the sum. This person may offer to give $10 to the second person, or only $8, or $1, and keep the rest. The second person cannot offer any input to this decision but has the power to decide whether to accept the offer or reject it. If the second person rejects the offer, both people will walk away empty-handed. If the offer is accepted, they get the money and split it as the first person indicated.

If the two individuals act only from narrow financial self-interest, then the first person should offer the second person the smallest possible amount—say $1—in order to keep the most for himself or herself. The second person should accept this offer because, from the point of view of pure financial self-interest, $1 is better than nothing.

Contrary to such predictions, researchers find that deals that vary too far from a 50–50 split tend to be rejected. Specifically, offers of around 40 percent or more are almost always accepted, while offers of 20 percent or less are almost always rejected.[11] People would rather walk away with nothing than be treated in a way that they perceive as unfair. Also, whether out of a sense of fairness or a fear of rejection, individuals who propose a split often offer something close to 50–50. Such behavior suggests we have cooperative inclinations along with our more self-interested inclinations.

including trust and generosity.[12] Meanwhile, there "is clear evidence of a negative relationship between happiness and selfishness." These results indicate that if one wants to be happy in life, being trustful and generous might be more "rational" than being selfish.

Finally, our brains, physiology, and genetics also play a role in influencing our decision-making. Referred to as **neuroeconomics**, this relatively new interdisciplinary field is based on approaches, such as using brain imaging, or a functional magnetic resonance imaging (fMRI) machine, to study the brain and predict human behavior. For example, one research study that used an fMRI machine to study the brain confirms the findings discussed previously—that when people engage in cooperative behavior, regions of the brain associated with positive emotions are activated.[13] On the other hand, when observing others being treated unfairly, our brains react as if we ourselves had been treated unfairly.[14]

> **neuroeconomics:** the interdisciplinary field that studies the role our brains, physiology, and genetics play in how we make economic decisions

Now that we have considered several factors influencing economic behavior, we can present a model based on behavioral economics using concepts that have been suggested as alternatives to self-interested and rational behavior.

3.3 Consumer Behavior in Contextual Economics

Recent research has generally refuted the neoclassical view of self-interested people making economic decisions that maximize their utility (or profits, in the case of businesses). We now use the lessons from the previous discussion to develop a more modern and accurate model of consumer behavior.

One important factor in an economic model of behavior is *information*. Consider the decision to purchase a new automobile. Numerous factors go into such a decision, such as the cost of the car, the importance of fuel economy, safety features, the resale value, and maintenance costs. Making a rational decision requires that you first obtain all this information. The neoclassical approach tends to assume that rational economic actors have "complete information" concerning each choice in front of them. A variation on this assumption is that people will optimize by collecting information until the perceived costs of acquiring additional information exceed the perceived benefits. However, there is a logical problem with this assumption, as Nobel Laureate Herbert Simon points out: one cannot know if that extra information was worth the cost of gathering it until it has been gathered! Maybe some additional searching will yield valuable information, or maybe it won't.

Simon showed that one first needs to have complete knowledge of all choices in order to identify the optimal point at which one should cease gathering additional information. Accordingly, Simon maintained, people rarely optimize. Instead they do what he called **satisficing**; they choose an outcome that would be satisfactory (rather than optimal) and then seek an option that reaches that standard. In other words, they identify an option that is "good enough" rather than continuing to search for the ideal.

> **satisfice:** to choose an outcome that would be satisfactory and then seek an option that at least reaches that standard

Economic decisions are always made subject to constraints, including limits on income and other resources and on physical or intellectual capacities. A universal constraint, for example, is time—you only have 24 hours in a day to allocate among competing activities such as sleeping, studying, eating, or entertainment. Given such constraints, satisficing seems to be a reasonable behavior. If an individual finds that the "satisfactory" level was set too low, a search for options that meet that level will result in a "solution" rather quickly. In this case, the level may then be adjusted to a higher standard. Conversely, if the level is set too high, a long search will not yield an acceptable outcome, and the "satisficer" may lower his or her expectations for the outcome.

Another deviation from maximizing behavior as traditionally defined has been called **meliorating**—defined as starting from the present level of well-being and finding opportunities to do better. A simple example is a line fisherwoman who has found a whole school of haddock but wants to keep only one for her supper. She first catches a fish. She doesn't stop there but goes on to catch a second fish, which she compares to the first one—keeping the larger and releasing the other. Each subsequent catch is compared to the one she has retained as the largest so far. At the end of the day, the fish that she takes home will be the largest of all those caught.

> **meliorating:** starting from the present level of well-being and continuously attempting to do better

One result of using melioration as the real-world substitute for optimization is its implication that *history matters*: people view each successive choice in relation to their previous experience. It is commonly observed that people are reluctant to accept a situation that they perceive as inferior to previous situations. For example, workers are likely to resist pay cuts or switch to jobs with lower wages.

Satisficing and meliorating may both be included under the term **bounded rationality**. The general idea is that, instead of considering all possible options, people limit their attention to some more-or-less arbitrarily defined subset of the universe of possibilities. With satisficing or meliorating behavior, people may not choose the "best" choices available to them, but they at least make decisions that move them toward their goals.

> **bounded rationality:** the hypothesis that people make choices among a somewhat arbitrary subset of all possible options due to limits on information, time, or cognitive abilities

Let us now summarize the current thinking about consumer behavior, in five core principles, based on two recent journal articles and contrast it to the neoclassical model presented in Section 2.[15]

1. People may try to engage in maximizing behavior, but they often aren't successful due to insufficient or inaccurate information, poor judgment, limited resources, and other issues. We might think of economic decisions as being a somewhat "muddled" process rather than the maximizing process envisioned by the neoclassical model.
2. People make economic decisions using various reference points to help them. We saw previously how framing and anchoring can influence economic decisions.
3. Most people have a "present bias" when making decisions with long-term impacts. Running up large credit card debts and under-investing in education are examples of "present-bias."
4. While people often engage in self-interested behavior, they also care about the welfare of others, even people they do not know. People may care about others in order to increase their own well-being or out of true altruism and concern for the common good. Any model that assumes only self-interested behavior is inadequate.
5. The fact that people's preferences are often not fixed or even fully known to them means that their decisions can be influenced through framing, anchoring, or present bias. We have discussed how these techniques may be used by advertisers or politicians to influence people's behavior. But such approaches may also be used to design policies that might encourage people to make healthier and wiser choices, as we will discuss in the final section of this chapter.

The model just described is supported by many scientific studies, and it is also consistent with experience and common sense. We are all human beings, often far from perfect, normally with good intentions but subject to many influential factors.

Discussion Questions

1. Can you think of any economic situations where people seem to make irrational decisions? For the most part, do you think people are rational or irrational?
2. Discuss how one or more conclusions reached by behavioral economists help you to understand an experience that you have had making an economic decision.

4. CONSUMPTION IN SOCIAL CONTEXT

In modern societies, consumption is as much a social activity as an economic activity. Consumption is closely tied to personal identity, and it has become a means of communicating social messages. We are immersed in the culture of **consumerism**, where people's sense of identity and meaning are often defined through their purchase of consumer goods and services. An increasing range of social interactions are influenced by consumerist values.

> **consumerism:** having one's sense of identity and meaning significantly defined through the purchase and use of consumer goods and services

The rise of consumerism is also deeply connected to capitalism, where the profit-driven nature of market competition imposes strong pressure on firms to increase their production and sales. As we will see, firms often devote an enormous amount of resources to advertising and other marketing strategies to encourage consumption.

Consumption behavior has evolved over time, with influences from various cultural, religious, political, and social forces, as well as from the availability of environmental resources. Consumerism is often traced back to the Industrial Revolution, when technological advances in mass production made it possible to increase consumption levels. The rise of consumerism is also related to other historical developments such as the invention of department stores, the expansion of consumer credit (with the invention of credit cards), and changes in work ethics as workers came to see themselves as consumers and became more inclined to work full-time or even overtime (instead of advocating for a shorter work week) in order to increase their consumption.

Despite these developments, consumerism has not become a global phenomenon even in the twenty-first century. Many people around the world are still simply too poor to be considered modern consumers. Over 700 million people, about 10 percent of humanity, lives in "extreme" poverty, defined by the World Bank as living on less than $1.90 per day.[16] Poverty is about more than just low income. The United Nations defines **absolute deprivation** as "a condition characterized by severe deprivation of basic human needs, including food, safe drinking water, sanitation facilities, health, shelter, education and information."[17] The poorest of developing countries, particularly in sub-Saharan Africa and Southern Asia, often lack the resources needed to lift their populations out of absolute deprivation.

> **absolute deprivation:** severe deprivation of basic human needs

Additionally, in numerous places around the world, cultural and religious values exist that seek to restrain the consumer society. For example, Buddhism teaches a "middle path" that emphasizes material simplicity, nonviolence, and inner peace. Even in the United States, some Americans are motivated to lower their consumption levels with the goal of reducing environmental impacts and focusing more on social connections. In this section, we discuss some social aspects that influence consumer behavior.

4.1 Social Comparisons

As social beings, we compare ourselves to other people. In a consumer society, such comparison is commonly in terms of income and consumption levels. We are often motivated to maintain a material lifestyle that is comparable to a **reference group**, which includes people around us who influence our behavior because we compare ourselves to them. Most people have various reference groups, traditionally including our neighbors, our coworkers, and other members of our family. We are also influenced as consumers by **aspirational groups**, groups to which a consumer *wishes* he or she could belong. People often buy, dress, and behave like the group—corporate executives, rock stars, athletes, or whoever—with whom they would like to identify.

> **reference group:** the group to which an individual compares himself or herself
> **aspirational group:** the group to which an individual aspires to belong

This tendency to compare ourselves with a reference group has evolved over time. Economist Juliet Schor suggests that in the 1950s and 1960s, people usually compared themselves to individuals with similar incomes and backgrounds, but in recent decades, people have become "more likely to compare themselves with, or aspire to the lifestyle of, those far above them in the economic hierarchy."[18] One reason for this might be the transformation in media representation, which has over time become increasingly depicted by upper-class lifestyles. Schor's research indicates that the more television one watches, the more he or she is likely to spend, holding other variables, such as income, constant.

Schor concludes that identifying with unrealistic aspirational groups leads many people to consume well above their means, acquiring large debts and suffering frustration, as they attempt to join those groups through their consumption patterns but fail to achieve the income to sustain them. Because people tend to evaluate themselves relative to reference and aspirational groups, increasing inequality may result in people feeling as if they are falling behind even when their incomes are actually increasing. Schor goes on to note that:

> The problem is not just that more consumption doesn't yield more satisfaction, but that it always has a cost. The extra hours we have to work to earn the money cut into personal and family time. Whatever we consume has an ecological impact. . . . We find ourselves skimping on invisibles such as insurance, college funds, and retirement savings as the visible commodities somehow become indispensable. . . . We are impoverishing ourselves in pursuit of a consumption goal that is inherently unattainable.[19]

Modern technology means that nearly everyone has some exposure to the "lifestyles of the rich and famous" engaging in conspicuous consumption. The result is the creation of widespread feelings of **relative deprivation**, that is, the sense that one's own condition is inadequate because it is inferior to someone else's circumstances. Such feelings can diminish individual well-being and one's sense of self-respect and self-confidence. Relative deprivation is a condition that exists in all countries to some extent, but it is more extreme in countries where the gap between rich and poor is greatest.

> **relative deprivation:** the feeling of insufficiency that comes from comparing oneself with someone who has more

4.2 Advertising

Advertising is central to the rise of consumerism. As Christopher Lasch writes,

> The importance of advertising is not that it invariably succeeds in its immediate purpose, . . . but simply that it surrounds people with images of the good life in which happiness depends on consumption. The ubiquity of such images leaves little space for competing conceptions of the good life.[20]

Though advertising is often justified as a source of information about the goods and services available in the market, a vast amount of advertising sells consumer culture and influences consumers' values and their spending behavior. Recent research shows that advertising is associated with problems such as obesity, attention deficit disorder, heart disease, and other negative consequences. Furthermore, advertising commonly portrays unrealistic body images, traditionally for women but more recently for men as well. (See Box 4.2.)

Global advertising expenditures were about $520 billion in 2016, equivalent to the national economy of Argentina or Sweden. About one-third of global advertising spending takes place in the United States. According to one estimate, Americans are exposed to around 5,000 commercial messages per day, up from around 2,000 per day in 1980s.[21] China recently became the world's second-largest advertising market.

BOX 4.2 WOMEN AND ADVERTISING

A 2007 report by the American Psychological Association concluded that advertising and other media images encourage girls to focus on physical appearance and sexuality, with harmful results for their emotional and physical well-being.[22] The research project reviewed data from numerous media sources and found that 85 percent of the sexualized images of children were of girls. The lead author of the report, Dr. Eileen L. Zurbriggen, points out that the sexualization of girls in media is likely to have negative effects on girls in a variety of domains, including cognitive functioning, physical and mental health, and healthy sexual development. She concludes, "As a society, we need to replace all of these sexualized images with ones showing girls in positive settings—ones that show the uniqueness and competence of girls."

Three of the most common mental health problems associated with exposure to sexualized images and unrealistic body ideals are eating disorders, low self-esteem, and depression. It is estimated that 8 million Americans suffer from an eating disorder—7 million of them women.[23] According to a 2012 article, most female models would be considered anorexic according to their body mass index. Twenty years ago, the average model weighed 8 percent less than the average woman; now it is 23 percent less.[24]

Jean Kilbourne, an author and filmmaker, has been lobbying for advertising reforms since the 1960s. She has produced four documentaries on the negative effects of advertising on women, most recently in 2010, under the title *Killing Us Softly*. Kilbourne notes that virtually all photos of models in advertisements have been touched up, eliminating wrinkles, blemishes, extra weight, and even skin pores. She believes that we need to change the environment of advertising through public policy.[25]

4.3 Private Versus Public Consumption

The growth of consumerism has altered the balance between private and public consumption. Public infrastructure has been shaped by the drive to sell and consume new products, and the availability of public and private options, in turn, shapes individual consumer choices.

In the early 1930s, for example, many major U.S. cities—including Los Angeles— had extensive and nonpolluting electric streetcar systems. However, due to a range of factors, including unsupportive policies, poor city planning, and the actions of companies such as General Motors in buying up streetcar systems and then converting many of them to bus lines, the presence of streetcars declined in many U.S. cities.[26] The ongoing viability of streetcar systems elsewhere in the United States, and across the world, suggests that many of the streetcar systems could have continued had the playing field been more level. U.S. government support for highway construction in the 1950s further hastened the decline of rail transportation, made possible the spread of suburbs far removed from workplaces, and encouraged the purchase of automobiles.

These examples illustrate that many of the choices that you have, as an individual, depend on decisions made for you by businesses and governments. Living in Los Angeles today would be significantly different if it had better maintained and supported its streetcar system rather than cars and buses. As more people carry cell phones and bottled water, pay telephones and drinking fountains either cease to exist or become less well maintained, leading more people to carry cell phones and bottled water. The tradeoffs between public infrastructure and private consumption are significant. As economist Robert Frank notes, "at a time when our spending on luxury goods is growing four times as fast as overall spending, our highways, bridges, water supply systems, and other parts of our public infrastructure are deteriorating, placing lives in danger."[27]

4.4 Affluenza and Voluntary Simplicity

One of the main lessons of economics is that we should always weigh the marginal benefits of something against its marginal costs. In the case of consumerism, these costs include less time for leisure, friends, and family; greater environmental impacts; and negative psychological and physical effects. In short, there can be such a thing as too much consumption—when the marginal benefits of additional consumption are exceeded by the associated marginal costs.

Two public television specials, as well as a book,[28] refer to the problem of "affluenza"—a "disease" with symptoms of "overload, debt, anxiety and waste resulting from the dogged pursuit of more." Some people see the solution to affluenza as rejecting consumerism as a primary goal in life. The term **voluntary simplicity** refers to a conscious decision to live with a limited or reduced level of consumption in order to increase one's quality of life.

> **voluntary simplicity:** a conscious decision to live with a limited or reduced level of consumption in order to increase one's quality of life

BOX 4.3 VOLUNTARY SIMPLICITY

Greg Foyster had a good job in advertising in Australia. But in 2012, he and his partner Sophie Chishkovsky decided to give up their consumer lifestyles and bicycle along the coast of Australia, interviewing people who have decided to embrace voluntary simplicity and eventually writing a book about their experience.

Voluntary simplicity is a growing movement in Australia, with several popular websites and a regular column on the topic in the *Australian Women's Weekly*. Foyster explains:

> The overall idea is that you should step out of the consumer economy that we're all plugged into and start doing things for yourself because that is how you'll find happiness. The best way to think of it is as an exchange. In our society people trade their time for money, and then they spend that money on consumer items. . . . It's really about stepping back and deciding what's important to you in your life.

Foyster found that his career in advertising conflicted with his personal sense of ethics. His "eureka" moment came during an advertising awards event when he saw colleagues being praised for their efforts to sell people products they didn't need or even want. He realized that most of the world's environmental problems stem from overconsumption, not overpopulation. He says:

> When I worked in advertising, I had a decent income, I had a prestigious job, and I was miserable. I chose to leave the industry because it wasn't making me happy; it wasn't my purpose in life. And now I have a much lower income; I work as a freelance writer, which isn't the most prestigious job. But I am so much more happy because I know what is important to me and I'm doing what I love and I have everything I need.[29]

The motivations for voluntary simplicity vary, including environmental concerns, a desire to have more free time to travel or raise a family, and to focus on non-consumer goals. Voluntary simplicity does not necessarily mean rejecting progress or living a life of poverty. Some people ascribing to voluntary simplicity have left high-paying jobs after many years, while others are young people content to live on less.

Perhaps the unifying theme for those practicing voluntary simplicity is that they seek to determine what is "enough"—a point beyond which further accumulation of consumer goods is either not worth the personal, ecological, and social costs or simply not desirable. Unlike traditional economics, which has assumed that people always want more goods and services, voluntary simplicity sees these as only intermediate goals toward more meaningful final goals. (See Box 4.3.)

Discussion Questions

1. What are your reference groups? Describe why you consider these your reference groups. What are your aspirational groups? Why do you aspire to be a member of these groups?

2. Think about at least one fashion item you own, such as an item of clothing, jewelry, or accessory, that you think says a lot about who you are. What do you think it says about you? Do you think others interpret the item in the same way that you do? How much do you think that you were influenced by advertising or other media in your views about the item?

5. CONSUMPTION IN AN ENVIRONMENTAL CONTEXT

The production process that creates every consumer product requires natural resources and generates some waste and pollution. However, we are normally only vaguely aware of the ecological impact of the processes that supply us with consumer goods. Most of us are unaware that, for example, it requires about 600 gallons of water to make a quarter-pound hamburger or that making a computer chip generates 4,500 times its weight in waste.[30] (See Box 4.4.)

BOX 4.4 THE ENVIRONMENTAL STORY OF A T-SHIRT

T-shirts are perhaps the most ubiquitous article of clothing. What are the environmental impacts of one T-shirt?[31]

Consider a cotton/polyester blend T-shirt, weighing about 4 ounces. Polyester is made from petroleum—a few tablespoons are required to make a T-shirt. During the extraction and refining of the petroleum, one-fourth of the polyester's weight is released in air pollution, including nitrogen oxides, particulates, carbon monoxide, and heavy metals. About *ten times* the polyester's weight is released in carbon dioxide, contributing to global climate change.

Cotton grown with nonorganic methods relies heavily on chemical inputs. Cotton accounts for 10 percent of the world's use of pesticides. A typical cotton crop requires six applications of pesticides, commonly organophosphates that can damage the central nervous system. Cotton is also one of the most intensely irrigated crops in the world, contributing to water shortages for other uses.

T-shirt fabric is bleached and dyed with chemicals including chlorine, chromium, and formaldehyde. Cotton resists coloring, so about one-third of the dye may be carried off in the waste stream. Most T-shirts are manufactured in Asia and then shipped by boat to their destination, with further transportation by train and truck. Each transportation step involves the release of additional air pollution and carbon dioxide.

Despite the impacts of T-shirt production and distribution, most of the environmental impact associated with T-shirts occurs *after purchase*. Washing and drying a T-shirt just ten times requires about as much energy as was needed to manufacture the shirt. Laundering will also generate more solid waste than the production of the shirt, mainly from sewage sludge and detergent packaging.

How can one reduce the environmental impacts of T-shirts? One obvious step is to avoid buying too many shirts in the first place. Buy shirts made of organic cotton or recycled polyester, or consider buying used clothing. Wash clothes only when they need washing, not necessarily every time you wear something. Make sure that you wash only full loads of laundry, and wash using cold water whenever possible. Finally, avoid using a clothes dryer—clothes dry naturally for free by hanging on a clothesline or a drying rack.

5.1 The Link Between Consumption and the Environment

One measure used to quantify the ecological impacts of consumerism is the amount of "trash" generated by an economy. In 2014, the U.S. economy generated over 250 million tons of municipal solid waste, which consisted mostly of paper, food waste, and yard waste.[32] But most of the waste generation in a consumer society occurs during the extraction, processing, or manufacturing stages—impacts normally hidden from consumers. According to a 2012 analysis, the U.S. economy requires about 8 billion tons of material inputs annually, which is equivalent to more than *25 tons per person.*[33] The vast majority of this material is discarded as mining waste, crop residue, logging waste, chemical runoff, and other waste prior to the consumption stage.

Perhaps the most comprehensive attempt to quantify the overall ecological impact of consumption is the **ecological footprint** measure. This approach estimates how much land area a human society requires, both to provide all that it takes from nature and to absorb the society's waste and pollution. Although the details of ecological footprint calculations are subject to debate, it does provide a useful way to compare the overall ecological impact of consumption in different countries.

> **ecological footprint:** a measure of the human impact on the environment, measured as the land area required to supply a society's resources and assimilate its waste and pollution

We see in Figure 4.5 that the ecological footprint per capita varies significantly across countries. The United States has one of the highest per capita ecological footprints (the per capita footprints of only six countries are higher, the highest

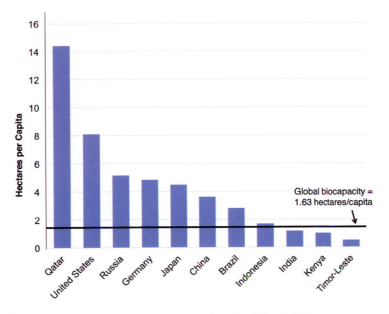

Figure 4.5 *Ecological Footprint per Capita, Select Countries, 2016*

Source: Global Footprint Network, 2019.

being Qatar).[34] The average European has a footprint about 40 percent lower than the average American, while the average Chinese has a footprint that is only one-quarter of that of a U.S. citizen.

Perhaps the most significant implication of the ecological footprint research is that the world is now in a situation of "overshoot"—our global use of resources and generation of waste exceeds the global capacity to supply resources and assimilate waste, by about 60 percent. As seen in Figure 4.5, the total amount of productive area available on earth (the average "biocapacity") is only 1.63 hectares per person. In other words, for humans to live in an ecologically sustainable manner, the average person's ecological impacts could only be about that of the average Indonesian. However, an increasing number of people in the world seek to consume at a level equivalent to a typical American. We would require five earths to provide the resources needed and assimilate the waste to meet such a demand.

5.2 Green Consumerism

Green consumerism means making consumption decisions at least partly on the basis of environmental criteria. Clearly, green consumerism is increasing: more people are recycling, using reusable shopping bags and water containers, buying hybrid or electric cars, and so on. Yet some people see green consumerism as an oxymoron—that the culture of consumerism is simply incompatible with environmental sustainability.

> **green consumerism:** making consumption decisions at least partly on the basis of environmental criteria

Green consumerism comes in two basic types:

1. "Shallow" green consumerism: consumers seek to purchase "ecofriendly" alternatives but do not necessarily change their overall level of consumption
2. "Deep" green consumerism: consumers seek to purchase ecofriendly alternatives but also, more importantly, seek to reduce their overall level of consumption

Someone who adheres to shallow green consumerism might buy a hybrid or electric car instead of a car with a gasoline engine or a shirt made with organic cotton instead of cotton grown with the use of chemical pesticides. But those practicing deep green consumerism would, when feasible, take public transportation instead of buying a car and question whether they really need another shirt. In other words, in shallow green consumerism, the emphasis is on substitution, while in deep green consumerism, the emphasis is on a reduction in consumption.

Ecolabeling helps consumers make environmentally conscious decisions. An ecolabel can provide summary information about environmental impacts. For example, stickers on new cars in the United States rate the vehicle's smog emissions on a scale from one to ten. Ecolabels are placed on products that meet certain certification standards. One example is the U.S. Environmental Protection Agency's Energy Star program, which certifies products that are highly energy efficient.

> **ecolabeling:** product labels that provide information about environmental impacts or indicate certification

In addition to environmental awareness by consumers, many businesses are seeking to reduce the environmental impacts of their production processes. Of course, some of the motivation may be to increase profits or improve public relations, but companies are also becoming more transparent about their environmental impacts. The Global Reporting Initiative (GRI) is a nonprofit organization that promotes a standardized approach to environmental impact reporting. In 2017, 82 percent of the world's 250 largest corporations used the GRI methodology, including Coca-Cola, Wal-Mart, Apple, and Verizon.

Discussion Questions

1. Think about one product you have purchased recently and list the environmental impacts of this product, considering the production, consumption, and eventual disposal of it. What steps do you think could be taken to reduce the environmental impacts associated with this product?
2. Do you think that green consumerism is an oxymoron? Do you think that your own consumer behaviors are environmentally sustainable? Why or why not?

6. POLICY INFERENCES FROM OUR MODEL OF CONSUMER BEHAVIOR

If one assumes that individuals always have perfect information and that they use that information to make the best choice, then one tends to see little role for government. For example, why would we require consumer protection law if consumers know the full consequences of buying something and always choose well? The model of economic behavior presented in this chapter, however, indicates that economic actors often do not behave rationally or have complete information and stable preferences. Their behavior is often significantly influenced by various contextual factors. Adopting a contextual model of behavior justifies the need for a more active role of government policy in affecting market outcomes.

6.1 Predictable Irrationality and Nudges

It is important to realize that while economic behavior is often irrational, it is not random. Deviations from "optimal" behavior are typically in a specific direction. For example, most people irrationally under-save for retirement rather than over-save. People tend to place too little value on the future and tend to eat foods that aren't healthy enough. Leading behavioral economist Dan Ariely notes that rationality is the exception rather than rule:

> We are all far less rational in our decision making than standard economic theory assumes. Our irrational behaviors are neither random nor senseless—they are

systematic and predictable. We all make the same types of mistakes over and over, because of the basic wiring of our brains.[35]

So if people continually make mistakes in the same direction, how can policies be devised to help them make "better" decisions? One answer comes from the 2008 book *Nudge*, by Richard Thaler and Cass Sunstein.[36] They advocate for policy "nudges" that encourage, but don't force, people to make certain decisions—an approach they refer to as **libertarian paternalism**. While they recognize that these two terms may seem unappealing and contradictory, they argue that the libertarian aspect of their strategies lies in the insistence that policies should be designed to maintain or increase freedom of choice. The paternalism aspect lies in the claim that it is desirable to design policies and present choices to motivate people to make better choices.

> **libertarian paternalism:** the policy approach advocated in the 2008 book *Nudge*, where people remain free to make their own choices but are nudged toward specific choices by the way policies are designed and choices are presented

Thaler and Sunstein provide numerous examples in their book related to decisions about health, financial management, education, and the environment. Take the problem of insufficient saving for retirement. They note that many people intend to increase the amount they save for retirement but never get around to it. Recognizing this, the book describes the "Save More Tomorrow" idea, where workers enroll in a program that automatically increases the percent of their income that is set aside for their retirement each time they get a raise. As increased saving is timed to correspond with pay raises, workers don't see their take-home pay go down. Workers enrolled in the program can opt out of it any time, but most don't. Evidence shows that the program is very effective. In one case, implementation of this program increased workers' retirement savings from an average of 3.5 percent of their income to 13.6 percent in four years.

Take another example—how to get people to reduce their home energy use. An experiment in California gave some residents a small electronic ball that would glow red when energy usage exceeded a given level but glowed green with moderate usage. The results showed that the ball led to energy use reductions of 40 percent during peak-use periods, while text and e-mail notifications were ineffective. The key seems to be that the ball makes one's energy use more visible and provides an "anchor" for decision-making about energy use.

Governments around the world are increasingly devising policies based on the findings of behavioral economics, nudging people to make better decisions. For example, in 2007, New Zealand implemented the KiwiSaver program, which automatically enrolls workers in a national savings plan for retirement, with a default contribution of 3 percent. Workers have the freedom to opt out or choose a higher contribution rate. In 2010, the government of the United Kingdom set up the Behavioral Insights Team, commonly known as the "Nudge Unit," with the objectives of "improving outcomes by introducing a more realistic model of human behaviour to policy" and "enabling people to make 'better choices for themselves'."[37]

One of the issues studied by the Nudge Unit has been ways to reduce rates of tax evasion.[38] To encourage people to pay their taxes on time, they experimented with various versions of a reminder letter sent to people who hadn't yet paid their taxes. Making the letter as simple as possible did not significantly affect response rates. However, response rates nearly doubled when people were reminded of social norms such as "9 out of 10 people pay their taxes on time." This illustrates that people's behavior can be influenced when they are nudged to think of themselves in comparison to others.

As another example, government officials in Bogotá, Colombia, initially responded to a water shortage by sending residents information about the crisis and asking them to reduce their usage. Not only was the appeal ineffective, water consumption actually *increased* as many people began stockpiling water. The government then changed its strategy, trying to make water conservation a new social norm. They distributed free stickers with water conservation messages, to be placed on faucets at offices and schools. Households with exceptional water savings were presented with small awards and praised in the local media. This latter strategy proved to be much more effective.

6.2 Consumption and Public Policy

While government regulations could help address the problem of overconsumption to an extent, some people may argue that government intrusion into personal consumption decisions is unwarranted. But current government regulations already influence consumer decisions—for instance, high taxes on products such as tobacco and alcohol discourage their consumption to some extent. On the other hand, subsidies are often used to increase the demand for certain products. Buyers of new electric vehicles in the United States may be eligible to receive a $7,500 federal tax credit, a subsidy that reduces the environmental externalities of transportation and encourages a shift away from fossil fuels. Taxes and subsidies can be justified for several reasons, including as a response to externalities or to achieve some social goal. Thoughtful regulations can encourage people to make choices that better align with social and personal well-being. We now consider a range of different policy ideas for responding to concerns about overconsumption.

Flexible Work Hours

One specific policy to reduce the pressure toward consumerism is to allow for more flexibility in working hours. Current employment norms, particularly in the United States, create a strong incentive for full-time employment. Employees typically have the option of seeking either a full-time job, with decent pay and fringe benefits, or a part-time job with lower hourly pay and perhaps no benefits at all. Thus, even those who would prefer to work less than full-time and make a somewhat lower salary, say, in order to spend more time with their family, in school, or in other activities, may feel the imperative to seek full-time employment. With a full-time job, working longer hours with higher stress, one may be more likely to engage in "retail therapy" as compensation.

Europe is leading the way in instituting policies that allow flexible working arrangements. Legislation in Germany and the Netherlands gives workers the right to reduce their work hours, with a comparable reduction in pay. Sweden and Norway give parents the right to work part-time when their children are young. Such policies encourage "time affluence" instead of material affluence. Juliet Schor argues that policies to allow for shorter work hours are also one of the most effective ways to address environmental problems such as climate change.[39] Those who voluntarily decide to work shorter hours will be likely to consume less and thus have a smaller ecological footprint.

Advertising Regulations

Another policy approach to discourage overconsumption is to focus on advertising regulations. Government regulations in most countries already restrict the content and types of ads that are allowed, such as the prohibition of cigarette advertising on television in the United States. Additional regulations could expand truth-in-advertising laws, ensuring that all claims made in ads are valid. For example, laws in the United States already restrict what foods can be labeled "low-fat" or "organic." Again, European regulations are leading the way with stricter advertising regulations, especially for children. For example, Norway has banned all advertising targeted at children under 12 years old. Regulations in Germany and Belgium prohibit commercials during children's TV shows. At least eight countries, including India, Mexico, France, and Japan, have instituted policies to limit children's exposure to junk food ads.

Another option is to change the tax regulations regarding advertising expenditures. In the United States, companies are generally able to treat all advertising costs as tax-exempt business expenses. Restricting the amount of this tax deduction (or eliminating the deduction entirely) would create an incentive for companies to reduce their advertising.

Consumption Taxation

One of the ways to reduce the extent of any activity is to tax it. Taxes on foods considered unhealthy are increasingly common. For example, taxes on sugary drinks have been implemented in several countries, including France, Mexico, and Hungary. Other taxes can target specific luxury items that are seen as representing conspicuous consumption—consumption primarily for the display of high economic status. For example, from 1992 to 2002, the United States imposed luxury taxes on new automobiles that cost more than $30,000.

Rather than classifying particular goods and services as luxuries, some economists prefer broader tax reforms. In his 2001 book *Luxury Fever*, Robert Frank proposes replacing the current emphasis in the United States on taxing income with taxes on consumption. Under his proposal, the tax on a household would be determined by the amount it spends each year. A certain amount of spending would be exempt from taxation so that low-income households would be exempt from the tax—Frank suggests $30,000 per family. Beyond that, consumption would be taxed at successively higher rates. For example, while the first $30,000 of spending would be nontaxable, he suggests that the next $40,000 of spending be taxed at a 20 percent rate. Then the next $10,000 of spending might be taxed at a 22 percent rate. In his example, consumption tax rates on spending above $500,000 rise to 70 percent. He argues that such high tax rates on conspicuous consumption are necessary "to curb the waste that springs from excessive spending on conspicuous consumption."[40]

Frank notes that both conservatives and liberals have expressed support for a shift from taxation of income to taxation of consumption, although they disagree on the details. Frank argues that exempting all savings from taxation would increase savings rates, which he suggests is reason enough for the shift. But the main objective would be to reduce the pressures toward consumerism and promote well-being.

Discussion Questions

1. Do you believe that the government has a right to influence or otherwise interfere in consumer decisions? What additional policies, if any, do you think are needed regarding consumer behaviors?
2. What do you think about libertarian paternalism as a way to guide policies? Do you think there are any problems with this approach?

REVIEW QUESTIONS

1. Is it accurate to describe Adam Smith as an uncritical champion of selfish behavior?
2. What are some of the key assumptions of the neoclassical model?
3. What is consumer sovereignty?
4. What is a budget line? How can we show one on a graph?
5. How does a budget line change when one's income changes?
6. How does a budget line change when the price of one of the items changes?
7. What is a utility function? How can we represent one on a graph?
8. What is marginal utility?
9. What is diminishing marginal utility? What does it imply about the shape of a utility function?
10. What are some of the limitations of the neoclassical consumer model?
11. What is behavioral economics?
12. What is the availability heuristic?
13. How can "framing" affect decision-making?
14. What is the anchoring effect?
15. What is the difference between a high and low time discount rate?
16. Does the evidence suggest that people should always make economic decisions without relying upon their emotions?
17. Does empirical evidence indicate that people act only out of self-interest?
18. What are some of the insights from neuroeconomics?
19. Explain the concept of bounded rationality.
20. Summarize the model of economic behavior in contextual economics.

21. What is the difference between absolute and relative deprivation?
22. What are reference and aspirational groups?
23. What is voluntary simplicity?
24. What is the ecological footprint approach to quantifying environmental impacts? What are some of the findings of ecological footprint research?
25. What is green consumerism? What is the difference between "deep" and "shallow" green consumerism?
26. What are the policy implications of behavioral economics?
27. What are some policy examples of "nudges"?
28. How can flexible work-hour policies reduce excessive consumerism?
29. How would consumption taxation work?

EXERCISES

1. Monica plans to spend her income on concert tickets and movie tickets. Suppose that she has an income of $100. The price of a concert ticket is $20, and the price of a movie ticket is $10.
   a. Draw, and carefully label, a budget line diagram illustrating the consumption combinations that she can afford.
   b. Can she afford 6 movie tickets and 1 concert ticket? Label this point on your graph.
   c. Can she afford 2 movie tickets and 6 concert tickets? Label this point on your graph.
   d. Can she afford 4 movie tickets and 3 concert tickets? Label this point on your graph.
   e. Which of the combinations mentioned uses up all her income?
2. Continuing from the previous exercise, suppose that Monica's income rises to $120. Add her new budget line to the previous graph.
3. Next, suppose that Monica's income stays at $100, but the price of concert tickets drops from $20 to $12.50 each.
   a. Draw and carefully label both her original and her new budget lines.
   b. Can she afford 2 movie tickets and 6 concert tickets after the price drop?
4. Suppose that Antonio's total utility from different quantities of snacks per day is given by the table subsequently.

Quantity of snacks per day	Total utility	Marginal utility
0	0	
1	20	
2	40	
3	60	
4	75	
5	85	
6	90	
7	85	
8	75	

   a. Draw and label Antonio's utility function for snacks.
   b. Fill in the last column of the table above, calculating Antonio's marginal utility from snacks.
   c. Does Antonio always display diminishing marginal utility in his satisfaction from snacks?

d. Assuming Antonio is rational, what is the maximum number of snacks that he could choose to consume per day?

5. Various U.S. government agencies, among them the Food and Drug Administration (FDA) and the Environmental Protection Agency (EPA), include "consumer protection" as one of their goals. The FDA, for example, decides whether drugs that pharmaceutical companies want to sell are safe and effective, and the EPA decides whether particular pesticides are safe for consumer use. Some people believe that such government oversight unnecessarily interferes with companies' freedom to sell their goods and with consumers' freedom to buy what they want. Indicate how you think each of the following individuals would evaluate consumer protection policies, in general.

a. Someone who believes strongly in consumer sovereignty

b. Someone who believes strongly that consumers make rational choices

c. Someone who believes that consumers sometimes have less than perfect information about what they are buying

d. Someone who believes that consumers can be overly influenced by marketing campaigns

6. Which of the following is consistent with the view of human behavior as purely self-interested? Which may indicate the presence of broader motivations?

a. Michael sells his car on eBay.

b. Jane joins a community clean-up group.

c. Ramon studies to become a doctor.

d. Joe buys a birthday present for his daughter.

e. Susan buys a new pair of shoes for herself.

7. Consider the process of applying to college and choosing a college to attend if admitted. Would you say that this process involves:

a. Maximizing behavior

b. Satisficing behavior

c. Meliorating behavior

d. Bounded rationality

Could it involve a combination of them? Could this differ from person to person?

8. How does time discounting affect your own decision-making? Do you do things today with a view toward future benefits, or do you look mainly for short-term satisfaction? Does your time discount rate differ in different areas of your life?

9. Consider a rational, profit-maximizing business firm. What motivations might the firm have that are not directly related to making a profit? For example, what if the firm made a donation to a community organization or voluntarily cleaned up pollution resulting from its production process? Why might it do this? How about if it offered employees a good health care plan or subsidized day care? Are these actions all ultimately directed at making more profit, or could there be something else involved?

10. Match each concept in Column A with an example in Column B.

Column A	Column B
a. Self-interest	1. Finding a restaurant that is close by and has food that is "good enough"
b. Altruism	2. You start getting bored after watching your third TV show in a row
c. Satisficing	3. You decide that you have enough clothing and do not need any more

continued

Column A	Column B
d. Availability heuristic	4. Looking for a job that's better than your current job
e. Deep green consumerism	5. You buy clothing made with organic cotton instead of cotton produced with pesticides
f. Utility maximizing	6. Choosing a college because your older brother or sister went there and really recommends it
g. Optimizing	7. How households act in the neoclassical model
h. Diminishing marginal utility	8. Seeking the highest-paying job possible
i. Shallow green consumerism	9. Volunteering at a homeless shelter
j. Meliorating	10. Carefully examining all available automobile models to select the one that is best for you

NOTES

1. If he buys his second bag of nuts, he will obtain 15 units of utility. If he buys two more chocolate bars, he will obtain 10 units of utility (6 units for his third bar, and 4 for his fourth bar). Thus, he is better off buying another bag of nuts.
2. As most goods and services are not available in $1 increments, such as bags of nuts, consumers in this model will not always be able to allocate every single dollar in a way that maximizes utility.
3. Iyengar, S. S., and M. R. Lepper. 2000. "When Choice Is Demotivating: Can One Desire Too Much of a Good Thing?" *Journal of Personality and Social Psychology*, 79(6): 995–1006.
4. Ariely, Dan. 2010. *Predictably Irrational: The Hidden Forces That Shape Our Decisions.* Harper Perennial, New York.
5. Lee, Paul. 2013. "The Williams-Sonoma Bread Maker: A Case Study." *The Wall Street Journal*, April 10.
6. Johnson, Eric J., and Daniel Goldstein. 2003. "Do Defaults Save Lives?" *Science*, 302: 1338–1339.
7. Story, Giles W., Ivo Vlaev, Ben Seymour, Ara Darzi, and Raymond J. Dolan. 2016. "Does Temporal Discounting Explain Unhealthy Behavior? A Systematic Review and Reinforcement Learning Perspective." *Frontiers in Behavioral Neuroscience*, 8(76): 1–20.
8. Dijksterhuis, Ap, Maarten W. Bos, Loran F. Nordgren, and Rick B. van Baaren. 2006. "On Making the Right Choice: The Deliberation-without-Attention Effect." *Science*, 311(5763): 1005–1007.
9. Lehrer, Jonah. 2009. *How We Decide.* Mariner/Houghton-Mifflin, Boston.
10. Ibid., pp. 142–143.
11. Güth, Werner, and Martin G. Kocher. 2014. "More Than Thirty Years of Ultimatum Bargaining Experiments: Motives, Variations, and a Survey of the Recent Literature." *Journal of Economic Behavior and Organization*, 108: 396–409.
12. Lane, Tom. 2017. "How Does Happiness Relate to Economic Behavior? A Review of the Literature." *Journal of Behavioral and Experimental Economics*, 68: 62–78.
13. Stanca, Luca. 2011. "Social Science and Neuroscience: How Can They Inform Each Other?" *International Review of Economics*, 58: 243–256.

14. Kable, Joseph W. 2012. "Neuroeconomics: How Neuroscience Can Inform the Social Sciences." In *Grounding Social Sciences in Cognitive Sciences* (Ron Sun, editor). The MIT Press, Cambridge, MA.

15. Brzezicka, Justyna, and Radoslaw Wisniewski. 2013. "Homo Oeconomicus and Behavioral Economics." *Contemporary Economics*, 8(4): 353–364; Laibson, David, and John A. List. 2015. "Principles of (Behavioral) Economics." *American Economic Review: Papers and Proceedings*, 105(5): 385–390.

16. World Bank Poverty and Equity Data Portal. 2018. http://povertydata.worldbank.org/poverty/home/. Accessed 15 July 2019.

17. United Nations, World Summit for Social Development Programme of Action. www.un.org/esa/socdev/wssd/text-version/agreements/poach2.htm

18. Schor, Juliet. 1999. "What's Wrong with Consumer Society?" In *Consuming Desires: Consumption, Culture, and the Pursuit of Happiness* (Roger Rosenblatt, editor). Island Press, Washington, DC. p. 43.

19. Schor, Juliet B. 1998. *The Overspent American*. Harper Perennial, New York. pp. 107–109.

20. Goodman, Douglas J., and Mirelle Cohen. 2004. *Consumer Culture*. ABC-CLIO, Santa Barbara, CA. pp. 39–40.

21. Story, Louis. 2007. "Anywhere the Eye Can See, It's Likely to See an Ad." *New York Times*, January 15.

22. American Psychological Association. 2007. "Sexualization of Girls Is Linked to Common Mental Health Problems in Girls and Women—Eating Disorders, Low Self-Esteem, and Depression." APA Press Release, February 19.

23. South Carolina Department of Mental Health, Eating Disorder Statistics. www.state.sc.us/dmh/anorexia/statistics.htm

24. Lovett, Edward. 2012. "Most Models Meet Criteria for Anorexia, Size 6 Is Plus Size: Magazine." ABC News, January 12.

25. Jean Kilbourne Web site. www.jeankilbourne.com

26. Stromberg, Joseph. 2015. "The Real Story Behind the Demise of America's Once-Mighty Streetcars." Vox, May 7.

27. Frank, Robert H. 2010. *Luxury Fever: Why Money Fails to Satisfy in an Era of Excess*. Free Press, New York. p. 5.

28. de Graaf, John, David Wann, and Thomas H. Naylor. 2005. *Affluenza: The All-Consuming Epidemic*. Berrett-Koehler, San Francisco.

29. Material for Box 4.3 from Short, Michael. 2012. "Seeking a Simple Life." *The Age* (Australia), July 9.

30. Ryan, John C., and Alan Thein Durning. 1997. *Stuff: The Secret Lives of Everyday Things*. Northwest Environment Watch, Seattle.

31. Material drawn from Ryan and Durning, 1997.

32. U.S. Environmental Protection Authority, 2016.

33. Gierlinger, Sylvia, and Fridolin Krausmann. 2012. "The Physical Economy of the United States of America: Extraction, Trade, and Consumption of Materials from 1870 to 2005." *Journal of Industrial Ecology*, 16(3): 365–377.

34. Global Footprint Network. 2016. "Ecological Footprint and Biocapacity in 2016." www.footprintnetwork.org

35. Ariely, Dan. 2010. *Predictably Irrational: The Hidden Forces That Shape Our Decisions*. Harper Perennial, New York.

36. Thaler, Richard H., and Cass R. Sunstein. 2008. *Nudge: Improving Decisions about Health, Wealth, and Happiness*. Penguin Books, London.

37. The Behavioural Insights Team. 2019. *About Us*. www.behaviouralinsights.co.uk/about-us/

38. Neatu, Alina Maria. 2015. "The Use of Behavioral Economics in Promoting Public Policy." *Theoretical and Applied Economics*, 22(2): 255–264.

39. Schor, Juliet. 1999. "What's Wrong with Consumer Society?" In *Consuming Desires: Consumption, Culture, and the Pursuit of Happiness* (Roger Rosenblatt, editor). Island Press, Washington, DC.

40. Frank, Robert H. 2010. *Luxury Fever: Why Money Fails to Satisfy in an Era of Excess*. Free Press, New York.

Chapter 5

Production

The United States is home to about 30 million businesses,[1] ranging in size from the largest corporation in the world (in 2018, this was Wal-Mart, which had revenues of half a *trillion* dollars)[2] to numerous businesses that consist of a single individual, and everything in between. Every day many of these businesses are faced with decisions about what to produce, how to produce it, how to market it, and how much to sell it for. In this chapter, we focus on the economic activity of production: the conversion of resources into goods and services.

Although we focus on the production process of for-profit businesses, economic production takes place in all three spheres: business, core, and public purpose. According to published statistics on GDP, just over 11 percent of economic production in the United States in 2018 was attributed to government, including federal, state, and local governments.[3] Another 12.5 percent of economic production took place in households and institutions. However, these statistics understate the amount of production that occurs in the public purpose and core spheres, because they fail to include production that is not distributed through markets. We develop a model of production costs based on a for-profit firm. Some, but not all, of the lessons of this model are applicable to public purpose and core production as well.

1. AN OVERVIEW OF PRODUCTION

Before we begin our analysis of production costs, we first consider the goals of production and define some important concepts.

1.1 The Goals of Production

In the business sphere, one of the goals of production is to make a profit. But the generation of profit is not the only goal pursued by businesses. Many companies balance social and environmental objectives with profit-making. As one remarkable example, in 2011, the outdoor clothing and gear company Patagonia took out an ad in the *New York Times* advising readers: "Don't buy what you don't need. Think twice before buying anything," based on concern about the environmental impacts of all production. The company has since gone on to make significant donations to "grassroots organizations working in local communities to protect our air, water and soil for future generations."[4]

At the same time, every period of history provides examples of businesses that have behaved unethically in the pursuit of profits, including violence against workers. However, norms of what is generally acceptable change over time, sometimes swinging toward more social disapproval of harsh business practices, and at other times accepting—even celebrating—a "culture of greed," as is sometimes the case today.

Economic analysis of production has tended to emphasize the objective of profit-making. Starting in the 1960s, some economists began to argue that business managers should *only* seek to maximize profits, without concern for any broader social or environmental objectives. The Nobel Prize–winning economist Milton Friedman once wrote:

> [T]here is one and only one social responsibility of business—to use its resources and engage in activities designed to increase its profits so long as it stays within the rules of the game.[5]

Such statements beg multiple questions, including who gets to influence and decide what the rules of the game are. In any event, businesses are increasingly operating with a broader set of objectives, often referred to as the **triple bottom line**. This perspective reflects a commitment to social and environmental goals, as well as making profits.

> **triple bottom line:** an assessment of the performance of a business according to social and environmental as well as financial performance

Looking further back in history, before the Civil War in the United States, corporations were fully accountable to the public to ensure that they acted in a manner that served the public good. Corporate charters could be revoked for failing to serve the public interest and were valid for only a certain period of time. For example, in 1831, a Delaware constitutional amendment specified that all corporations were limited to a 20-year life span.[6]

More recently, an emphasis on externalities is giving renewed attention to the question of whether particular productive activities are consistent with social and environmental well-being. This question requires considering *all* costs and benefits of the production process. For example, a business that increases its profits by making its employees work overtime without pay is creating a negative social externality not reflected in the prices of the products that it sells. Lawsuits have been brought against Wal-Mart in several U.S. states that found the corporation guilty of forcing some employees to work without pay.[7] The negative social externality resulting from Wal-Mart's minimizing what it pays workers extends to policies of hiring employees to work just below the number of hours that would qualify them for full-time benefits, including health insurance coverage. Lacking employer-provided health care benefits, such workers rely on government-subsidized coverage or go without any insurance at all. Further, the cost of emergency room visits by uninsured patients represents another example of an external cost imposed on society.

In principle, we can use the technique of **cost–benefit analysis**, which involves estimating all the costs and benefits of business production or a policy proposal in monetary values to determine the net social impact. One problem with implementing such an analysis, however, arises from the fact that some costs and benefits are easier to measure than others. It is relatively easy, for example, to determine how many jobs will be created if a large retailer builds a new store in an area. It may even be relatively easy to convert the number of jobs gained into a benefit that can be expressed in dollars. It is harder to quantify the costs to social well-being from any environmental damages associated with the store or the loss of community as people become less likely to shop at "mom-and-pop" competitors.

> **cost–benefit analysis:** a technique to analyze a policy or project proposal in which all costs and benefits are converted to monetary estimates, if possible, to determine the net social value

So, although much of our discussion about production costs and decisions is in the context of making profits, we also keep in mind the broader environmental and social context in which all production occurs.

1.2 An Economic Perspective on Production

As we have stated before, production involves the conversion of resources into goods and services. We define **inputs** as the resources that go into production and **outputs** as the goods and services that result from production. In addition to desired goods and services, all production processes also generate waste, including pollution, waste materials, and waste heat.

> **inputs:** the resources that go into production
> **outputs:** the goods and services that result from production

We tend to think of production in terms of physical goods. For example, cotton goes into a textile mill as fiber and comes out as fabric. This fabric is then shipped to another location, printed with small red hearts, cut into pieces, sewn into boxer shorts, distributed through wholesalers, and eventually marketed by retailers. Or households may purchase cotton fabric and use it to produce homemade curtains or Halloween costumes. To most people, the various stages of manufacturing would be regarded as production, but the transport, distribution, and sale that are involved would not.

Economists think of production more broadly, including any activity involved in the conversion of resources into final goods and services. For example, Texas oil "producers" do not actually make oil; they merely transport it from its natural state under the ground to the nearest refinery. Yet this activity is still considered production in a broad economic sense. Similarly, such activities as storage, packaging, and retailing all can be interpreted as forms of production.

Nor is production confined to processes that involve tangible goods. Production also includes providing services. From an economist's point of view, physicians, child-care providers, mechanics, musicians, park rangers, lawyers, professors, house cleaners, tax auditors, and massage therapists are all engaged in production, even though they don't produce a physical product. In the United States, and in many other countries, the production of services constitutes a larger percentage of GDP than the production of goods.

Another important concept in thinking about production from an economic perspective is **marginal analysis**, which involves thinking about incremental changes. We have already seen the importance of marginal thinking in Chapter 4. When we apply marginal analysis to production decisions, we ask whether it makes economic sense to produce one more unit of a good or service. In other words, we compare the marginal benefits of a decision to its marginal costs.

> **marginal analysis:** analysis based on incremental changes, comparing marginal benefits to marginal costs

As long as marginal benefits exceed marginal costs, it makes sense for a business to expand production. But after the marginal costs rise to the level of marginal benefits, the firm should stop increasing production. We spend much of the remainder of the chapter introducing an economic model of marginal production costs. We will then use this model in the next chapter to illustrate how a hypothetical firm can maximize its profits. But as we have discussed previously, a model is a simplification of the real world that focuses on some issues while ignoring others.

Discussion Questions

1. What distinguishes the economic activity of production from the activity of resource management? Of consumption? Of distribution?
2. Think about the processes involved in producing this textbook. Describe these processes, considering all the steps of production from an economic perspective. What inputs were required? What waste was generated?

2. TYPES OF PRODUCTION COSTS

We begin our analysis by differentiating between different types of costs. As with several other topics explored here, economists view production costs from a perspective that differs somewhat from that of noneconomists.

2.1 Fixed Versus Variable Costs

Consider the production costs of farming. A farmer who grows corn, let's call her Gail, needs to purchase various inputs, such as seed, fertilizer, and fuel for machinery. To some extent, Gail can vary the amount of these inputs that she purchases. For example, she can use a little fertilizer or a lot. The amount that she spends on fertilizer will also depend on the type of fertilizer that she applies. Her options may include purchasing a chemical fertilizer, purchasing compost, or putting in time and effort to obtain compost from her own farm residues.

The production costs that Gail can easily adjust are called **variable costs**. Variable costs can be adjusted relatively quickly in response to changes in market conditions, production targets, or other circumstances. Another way to define variable costs is that these costs do not need to be incurred if, for some reason, Gail decides not to produce corn.

> **variable costs:** production costs that can be adjusted relatively quickly and that do not need to be incurred if no production occurs

Gail has other costs to pay regardless of whether she decides to produce corn. These are called **fixed costs**, which include such expenses as a mortgage and monthly payments on machinery. Another term economists use for fixed costs is "sunk costs." Regardless of how much corn Gail produces, she cannot avoid paying these costs, at least not in the short term. If corn prices go down, she has the option of spending nothing on corn seed (because that is a variable cost), but in the absence of any corn production at all, she still must pay the mortgage on her farm and other fixed costs.

> **fixed costs (sunk costs):** production costs that cannot be adjusted quickly and that must be paid even if no production occurs

The distinction between fixed and variable costs is not always clear. Gail could decide to sell all her farm machinery, so in this sense machinery becomes a variable cost, but it may take some time for her to find buyers. Given enough time, *all* production costs become variable, as a business could decide to shut down entirely and sell off all its resources.

2.2 Accounting Versus Economic Costs

The costs just discussed are all actual monetary costs paid by a producer. When Gail completes her tax return and calculates her farming profits, she (or her accountant) can list all these costs—both fixed and variable—as valid businesses expenses. **Accounting costs** can also include some items that are not actual out-of-pocket expenditures but that are understood to reduce the value of the stock of capital owned by the business; the most common example is depreciation of buildings or equipment. Table 5.1 presents an example of Gail's accounting costs.

> **accounting costs:** actual monetary costs paid by a producer as well as estimated reduction in the value of the producer's capital stock

We can take a broader perspective on Gail's costs of farming by considering other costs that, like depreciation, do not appear as monetary outflows. Perhaps the most

Table 5.1 Gail's Cost of Farming

Accounting Costs		
Seeds	$20,000	
Fertilizer	$3,000	
Fuel	$5,000	
Interest on bank loan	$15,000	
Depreciation of equipment	$5,000	
Total accounting costs		$48,000
Opportunity Costs		
Forgone salary	$30,000	
Forgone return on equity capital	$12,000	
Total opportunity costs		$42,000
Total economic costs		$90,000
Externality Costs		
Pollution damage	$5,000	
Total social costs		$95,000

obvious example is the value of Gail's time. If Gail is a full-time farmer, she is giving up the opportunity to work at a different job, say, as an engineer or a teacher. The salary that she could obtain at her next-best option is the opportunity cost of Gail's decision to be a farmer. So if Gail's best alternative to farming is to be a teacher and earn $30,000 per year, this forgone salary also represents a production cost, as shown in Table 5.1.

Economic costs include accounting costs but also add in the value of forgone opportunities. In addition to a forgone salary, another economic cost would be the value of forgone investments. Suppose that, in addition to taking out a bank loan, Gail also uses her own savings to finance some of the costs of farming. Her next-best alternative may have been to invest that money in the stock market and make a return on her investment. Her forgone investment returns are another economic cost, as shown in Table 5.1.

> **economic cost:** the total cost of production, including both accounting and opportunity costs

If Gail looks at the full economic costs of farming—rather than just at the accounting costs—she will find that farming is more costly than she may have initially thought. Whereas her account books show costs of $48,000, when we consider her opportunity costs, we see that it is really costing her $90,000 to farm.

The same concept applies to the costs of production in other spheres of the economy. For example, think about the government of an economically depressed region, which is considering whether to invest in building a new highway. The project will hire people and pay them a salary. The *accounting* costs for this labor, included in the project's budget, will be the actual salary paid. To calculate the *economic* costs of this labor, however, from the perspective of society's production possibilities, you have to think about how much this highway project pulls out of other productive activities that would otherwise have been undertaken. If the workers would otherwise have been unemployed and not productively engaged at home or in their communities, the answer might be that not very much is lost elsewhere. But if the workers could have otherwise been building needed new schools or hospitals, it may be that the economic costs are much higher than the accounting costs.

The advantage of considering economic costs, rather than just accounting costs, is that we have a more complete framework for making production decisions. Producers should always weigh the benefits of a decision against its costs, both its financial costs and the costs of what must be given up.

2.3 Private Versus External Costs

Suppose that Gail's farming practices result in fertilizer runoff that pollutes a river, reducing downstream fishing and swimming opportunities and harming the ecosystem—this represents a negative externality. Gail is unlikely to take such costs into account when making production decisions. She will probably consider only her private costs—her accounting costs and perhaps her economic costs as well.

The pollution Gail produces represents a real cost imposed on society. Suppose that we estimate the negative externality costs of Gail's farming at $5,000 per year. From the perspective of society as whole, this is an additional cost of farming, as shown in Table 5.1. The true social cost of farming would be the sum of the economic and externality costs. In an ideal world, there would be ways of ensuring that externality costs are internalized. For example, if Gail had to pay a "farming tax" of $5,000 per year to compensate society for the pollution damage, then the tax would be an accounting cost and thus enter directly into Gail's production decisions. Such a tax is likely to motivate her to reduce the level of pollution by cutting down farm production, implementing better farm management techniques, or using new technologies.

The distinction between private and external costs is important because a production process chosen by a producer that may appear to be the least expensive based on accounting, and perhaps economic, costs may not be the least-cost option when externalities are considered. In the absence of any motivation to consider the social or environmental externalities, Gail may conclude that her optimal production decision is to rely on chemical fertilizers to grow corn. But the optimal production decision from the perspective of society may be that she should replace some chemical fertilizer with organic farming techniques. This case exemplifies the fact that private production decisions may not always align with the best choice in terms of social well-being and environmental sustainability.

Discussion Questions

1. In order to take this course, you have paid tuition and bought this book. What other costs should be added in to calculate the *economic* costs of this course to

you personally? (*Hint:* What is your best alternative to spending time taking this course? How are you financing your education?) Also, does your taking this course entail any externality costs in addition to your private economic costs?

2. What fairness issues arise when producers are required to take social or environmental costs into account in their decision-making? For example, suppose that Gail is just barely making ends meet, using proceeds from the sale of her farm's output to feed and house her family—while the neighbors who are suffering the consequences of runoff from her fertilizer applications are mostly better off than she is. Should government policies take this into consideration? Who should make such a decision?

3. THE PRODUCTION FUNCTION

Actual production decisions are often a matter of trial and error. Firms might experiment with different levels of various inputs to determine which production processes are the least costly. Often the results will be difficult to predict in advance, and firms can make costly mistakes. But with our model of production, we assume for now that firms have accurate information about the relationship between the levels of various inputs and output. This enables us to define a **production function**, an equation or graph that represents the relationship between a set of inputs and the amount of output that a firm (or other economic actor) can produce over a given period. Think of a production function as a type of cooking recipe that specifies what certain quantities of inputs will combine to produce a particular quantity of output. Production functions typically do not exist in the real-world economy, but this concept can help us think about certain aspects of production in a very simple, and sometimes useful, way.

> **production function:** an equation or graph that represents a relationship between types and quantities of inputs and the quantity of output

3.1 Thinking About Inputs and Outputs

Many inputs go into real-world production processes. We continue to use the example of farming because it is relatively easy to produce fairly realistic, easy-to-comprehend production functions for farms, at least for some inputs—and because there have been many studies of farming production functions. The normal inputs include land (a type of natural capital), machinery (manufactured capital), and labor (human capital). Human capital, as we have seen in earlier chapters, is more than just hours of labor; it also includes a component of formal education that has become increasingly important for modern farmers. Social capital can also be considered a farming input in terms of the strength and quality of relations among farm workers and managers and with their buyers. Financial capital is also needed by most farmers in terms of loans to finance the purchase of land, equipment, and other inputs.

In a very general sense, we can define a production function using the following mathematical equation:

$Y = f(natural\ capital,\ manufactured\ capital,\ human\ capital,\ social\ capital,\ financial\ capital)$

where Y represents a quantity of output, $f()$ is read "is a function of," and the inputs include the levels of different types of capital discussed previously. This equation generally holds true for all kinds of production. We can define a more specific production function, in the case of corn production, as:

$Y = f(seeds,\ fertilizer,\ pesticides,\ labor,\ land,\ equipment\ .\ .\ .)$

This equation means that the quantity of output (say, bushels of corn) is a function of the number of seeds planted, the amount of fertilizer applied, the amount of pesticides applied, the amount of labor allocated to corn production, the amount of land used for corn production, the type of equipment used, and so on.

Extending our discussion about fixed and variable costs, we can correspondingly define various inputs as fixed or variable. **Fixed inputs** by definition are those for which the quantities do not change, regardless of the level of production. An example of a fixed input is a field that has been leased by a farmer for the growing season. If the farmer already signed a lease for the use of the field, she is not able *right now* to avoid paying for this input. By contrast, **variable inputs** are those for which the quantities can be changed quickly, resulting in changes in the level of production. In our farming example, fertilizers and pesticides are variable inputs because a farmer can change her use of these inputs relatively quickly.

> **fixed input:** a production input that is fixed in quantity, regardless of the level of production
>
> **variable input:** a production input whose quantity can be changed relatively quickly, resulting in changes in the level of production

As mentioned earlier, over a very long period, all inputs might be considered variable. So economists try to make the distinction more specific by defining the **short run** as a period in which at least one production input is fixed in quantity. A farmer, for example, may be temporarily constrained by the size of her land holdings and by the amount of equipment she owns but can vary many other inputs, such as seeds, fertilizers, and labor. In other production processes, an organization may be constrained by a lack of space, a shortage of materials, a dearth of suitably talented workers, or any other production input. The key aspect is that a **limiting factor** creates a constraint to increasing production. Even with access to unlimited amounts of all the *variable* inputs, production can go only so far, because of this one limiting factor.

> **short run:** (in terms of production processes) a period in which at least one production input has a fixed quantity

> **limiting factor:** a fixed input that creates a constraint to increasing production

In the **long run**, the quantities of all production inputs may be varied. In the case of farming, this means the amount of time (perhaps several months) in which more land can be purchased, more machinery purchased, and more labor hired. In other situations, it might take years for a business to increase or decrease (or eliminate) the quantities of all inputs.

> **long run:** (in terms of production processes) a period in which all production inputs can be varied in quantity

3.2 Graphing Production Functions

As with supply and demand in Chapter 3, we can represent a production function using either a table or a graph. We keep our model simple by focusing on just one input at a time. One production relationship that has been studied by numerous researchers is the impact of different fertilizer levels on crop yields. Table 5.2 presents the results of one such study, showing the effect of applying various amounts of nitrogen fertilizer on corn yields over a season. The study was performed in Missouri in the late 1990s.[8] The researchers varied the amount of fertilizer used on different fields in increments of 20 pounds per acre. At harvest time, the corn yield was recorded in bushels per acre. For mathematical simplicity, we call each 20-pound increment a "bag" of fertilizer and express all values in per-acre terms.

In this case, nitrogen fertilizer is a variable input, and corn is the output. Corn yields increase as more fertilizer is added. We can take the data in Table 5.2 and convert it to a graph, as shown in Figure 5.1. So, we can see, for example, that when 3 bags of fertilizer are applied per acre, corn yields are 137 bushels per acre. Note that we have started the vertical axes at 80 bushels per acre for graphical convenience to focus on the range where corn yields occur in the study.

Table 5.2 Corn Production Function

Quantity of nitrogen fertilizer (bags per acre)	Corn yield (bushels per acre)
0	100
1	115
2	127
3	137
4	145
5	150
6	154
7	157
8	159

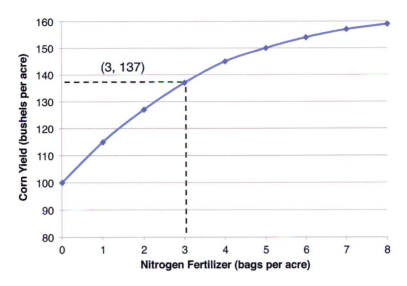

Figure 5.1 *Corn Production Function*

For this production function, we are only measuring the impact of one variable input—nitrogen fertilizer. The researchers in this case tried to keep all other variable inputs, such as the amount of seed applied, the amount of water, soil quality, and so on, unchanged across the various corn fields to isolate the impact of one variable input. Recall from Chapter 2 that in economics, when we want to isolate the effect of one particular variable, we hope to study the particular relationship *ceteris paribus*, or "with all else constant." You can see in Figure 5.1 that nitrogen and crop yields have a positive relationship, though the curve goes upward less steeply as one moves to the right.

3.3 Production in the Short Run

Another term that economists use to describe the production function in Figure 5.1 is a **total product curve**. A total product curve shows the total amount of product (i.e., output) as a function of one variable input, holding all other inputs constant. But, as we mentioned earlier in the chapter, we are assuming that production decisions are based on marginal analysis. So, we focus on how much corn output changes with each additional bag of fertilizer. We call the additional corn output with each additional bag of fertilizer (holding all other inputs constant) the **marginal product**. We can take the data in Table 5.2 and calculate the marginal product for each additional bag of fertilizer, as shown in Table 5.3.

> **total product curve:** a curve showing the total amount of output produced with different levels of one variable input, holding all other inputs constant
> **marginal product:** the additional quantity of output produced by increasing the level of a variable input by one, holding all other inputs constant

Table 5.3 Calculating Marginal Product

Quantity of nitrogen fertilizer (bags per acre)	Corn yield (bushels per acre)	Marginal product
0	100	—
1	115	= 115 − 100 = 15
2	127	= 127 − 115 = 12
3	137	10
4	145	??
5	150	5
6	154	4
7	157	3
8	159	2

Table 5.3 shows that adding the first bag of fertilizer increases corn yields from 100 bushels per acre to 115 bushels per acre, for a marginal product of 15 bushels. The marginal product going from 1 to 2 bags of fertilizer is 12 bushels, shown in the table as the difference between 127 and 115 bushels. You can calculate the marginal product for the fourth bag of fertilizer yourself for practice.

Table 5.3 indicates that the marginal product of additional fertilizer is constantly declining, referred to by economists as **diminishing marginal returns**. For each additional unit of an input, the marginal product (or return) increases by a smaller amount. Note that we can also see this in Figure 5.1—corn output increases with additional fertilizer but at a decreasing rate.

> **diminishing marginal returns:** a situation in which each successive unit of a variable input produces a smaller marginal product

We should not be surprised that the production function for corn displays diminishing marginal returns. If there were *not* diminishing marginal returns, you could feed the whole world from one farmer's field just by adding more and more nitrogen fertilizer forever! But, in reality, as more and more nitrogen is added to the same amount of land, eventually the corn plants become unable to make use of the extra nutrient. Eventually, if excessive fertilizer were added, the graph in Figure 5.1 would turn *downward*, with a negative slope, as the crop yield would diminish due to high level of fertilizer damaging plant growth.

In a case of diminishing marginal returns, as we have seen for corn production, the total product curve gets flatter as you move out to the right. Not all production functions display diminishing marginal returns, at least not throughout the entire production range. Suppose that we consider a production function for handmade shoes. Let's assume that one worker can make two shoes a day. So, if we have only one worker (our variable input), two shoes per day can be produced. If we have two workers, then four shoes can be produced per day. Three workers can produce six shoes per day. In this case, each additional unit of our variable input (workers) results in the same marginal product—two additional shoes per day. Economists refer to this as a case of **constant marginal returns**.

> **constant marginal returns:** a situation in which each successive unit of a variable input produces an increasing marginal product

Finally, a production function can display **increasing marginal returns**. This can occur in our shoemaking example if adding workers allows for specialization and an overall increase in efficiency. For example, one worker might specialize in cutting leather, another might make only soles, and a third could focus on stitching. In this case, the total product curve would increase at an increasing rate, at least up to a certain number of workers.

> **increasing marginal returns:** a situation in which each successive unit of a variable input produces a larger marginal product

Figure 5.2 illustrates production functions with constant and increasing marginal returns. For constant marginal returns, the total product curve is a straight line sloping upward. For increasing marginal returns, the total product curve becomes steeper as we move to the right.

It is possible for a production process to exhibit *all* three patterns of marginal returns when we consider the entire range of production levels available to a firm. Figure 5.3 shows increasing marginal returns at very low levels of the input, constant marginal returns for moderate levels of the input, and then decreasing marginal returns for high levels of the input. Such a production function may be common in the real world. Consider a restaurant. If there is only one worker to take orders, cook the food, and wash dishes, production is

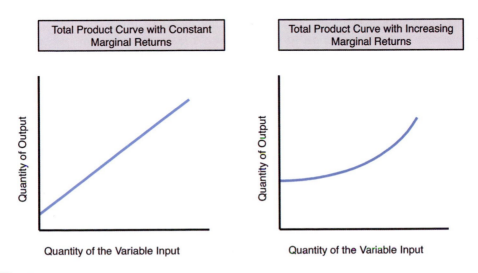

Figure 5.2 *Total Product Curves With Constant and Increasing Marginal Returns*

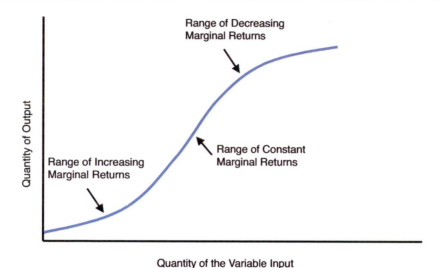

Figure 5.3 *A Total Product Curve With Increasing, Constant, and Decreasing Marginal Returns*

likely to be very inefficient. Adding more workers allows for specialization and increasing marginal returns. Once a restaurant has enough workers for each separate task, then perhaps doubling the number of workers (e.g., increasing from one cook to two cooks) might exactly double total production. However, eventually hiring more workers leads to decreasing marginal returns as the kitchen becomes too crowded to allow for effective production. As the old saying goes, "too many cooks spoil the broth."

4. PRODUCTION COSTS

In this section, we will combine information about production costs with a production function to determine the costs of different levels of production. We will differentiate between production in the short run and in the long run.

4.1 Production Costs in the Short Run

Now that we understand the physical side of production, we can turn back to the topic of production costs. Variable costs change when we increase or decrease the quantity of a variable input. In our farming example, Gail's variable costs will increase when she decides to apply more fertilizer. Meanwhile, fixed costs depend on the quantity of fixed inputs, which do not change in the short run. Gail's mortgage payments on her farm are fixed, as she cannot vary the amount of land that she owns in the short run.

Total cost is simply the sum of fixed and variable costs. We can apply this concept to our example of nitrogen fertilizer. Let's suppose that the cost of nitrogen fertilizer is $15 per bag. For simplicity, we assume that this is our only variable cost. All other costs of producing corn are considered fixed in the short run and

Table 5.4 Cost of Corn Production

Quantity of nitrogen fertilizer (bags per acre)	Corn yield (bushels per acre)	Fixed costs ($)	Variable costs ($15 per bag of fertilizer)	Total costs ($)
0	100	500	0	500
1	115	500	15	515
2	127	500	30	530
3	137	500	45	545
4	145	500	60	560
5	150	500	75	575
6	154	500	90	590
7	157	500	105	605
8	159	500	120	620

total $500 per acre. Table 5.4 calculates the fixed and variable cost of applying different amounts of nitrogen fertilizer. For each additional bag of fertilizer, total costs increase by $15. In other words, the marginal cost of each additional bag of fertilizer is $15.

total cost: the sum of fixed and variable costs

We can take the data in Table 5.4 and graph a **total cost curve**, which relates the total cost of production to the level of output, as shown in Figure 5.4. We see that the slope becomes steeper as we move to the right. This makes sense, as it becomes increasingly expensive to produce an additional bushel of corn per acre. In other words, the higher the level of corn production, the more fertilizer needs to be added to produce one more bushel per acre. This is consistent with a total product curve with diminishing marginal returns.

total cost curve: a graph showing the relationship between the total cost of production and the level of output

We can examine the total cost curve in more detail to determine the marginal cost of producing corn. Specifically, we can use the total cost curve, and the data in Table 5.4, to determine the marginal cost of producing one more bushel of corn. This will vary depending on the level of corn production. Note that this is fundamentally different from the marginal cost of a bag of nitrogen fertilizer, which is always $15 per bag.

Let's determine what the marginal cost of corn production is as we go from producing 145 bushels per acre to 150 bushels. We see in Table 5.4 that total costs increase from $560 to $575 as we go from adding 4 bags of fertilizer per acre to 5 bags. As it costs an additional $15 to produce 5 more bushels of corn, the marginal cost *per bushel* is $3, obtained by dividing the additional cost of $15 by five bushels, as shown in Figure 5.4.

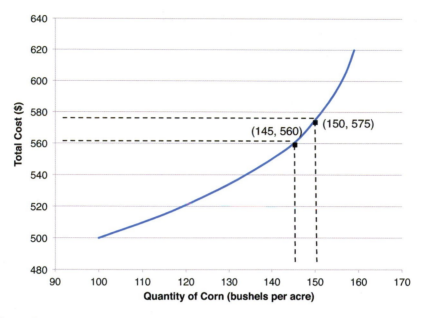

Figure 5.4 *Total Cost Curve for Corn Production*

Table 5.5 Marginal Cost of Corn Production

Quantity of nitrogen fertilizer (bags per acre)	Corn yield (bushels per acre)	Marginal product of additional nitrogen (bushels of corn)	Cost of additional nitrogen ($ per bag)	Marginal cost ($ per bushel of corn)
0	100	—	—	—
1	115	15	15	15 ÷ 15 = 1.00
2	127	12	15	15 ÷ 12 = 1.25
3	137	10	15	15 ÷ 10 = 1.50
4	145	8	15	15 ÷ 8 = 1.88
5	150	5	15	15 ÷ 5 = 3.00
6	154	4	15	15 ÷ 4 = 3.75
7	157	3	15	??
8	159	2	15	15 ÷ 2 = 7.50

We can calculate the marginal cost for other levels of corn production, as shown in the last column of Table 5.5. You can test yourself by calculating the marginal cost of corn production going from 154 to 157 bushels per acre.

We can see that the marginal cost of producing corn increases as production levels increase. Diminishing marginal returns to fertilizer application have resulted in **increasing marginal costs** for corn production. In other words, the cost of producing one more bushel of corn rises as more output is produced.

> **increasing marginal costs:** the situation in which the cost of producing one additional unit of output rises as more output is produced

In computing the marginal costs, we ignored the fixed costs. This is correct, because we assumed that fixed costs would be paid regardless of whether any nitrogen fertilizer was used, and we were interested only in the cost of the "additional" or "marginal" bushel of corn production.

The significant implication for producer behavior is that in situations characterized by diminishing marginal returns and increasing marginal costs, the quantity of production will tend to be naturally limited. Diminishing returns mean that it is not possible for the farmer to try to feed the whole world from one plot. Increasing costs mean that at some point, production will become too expensive relative to the additional revenues that can be obtained. In Chapter 6, we will see that diminishing returns are assumed in the case of the profit-maximizing competitive firm. Because marginal costs are increasing, whereas the price that the firm receives for its output is constant, the traditional microeconomic model gives a neat diagrammatic explanation of how a firm will choose a unique, profit-maximizing level of output.

What if marginal returns are constant, as illustrated in the left-hand graph in Figure 5.2? Then we will have **constant marginal costs**. In this case, each unit of the variable input (which has a constant price) adds exactly the same amount to output, so the cost for each additional unit of output is the same. The total cost curve will be a straight line.

> **constant marginal costs:** the situation in which the cost of producing one additional unit of output stays the same as more output is produced

What if marginal returns are increasing, as illustrated in the right-hand graph in Figure 5.2? Then we will have **decreasing marginal costs**. To portray a total cost curve with increasing marginal returns, you would draw a line that rises but also *flattens out* or curves toward the horizontal axis as you move to the right. Increasing marginal returns means decreasing marginal costs, because additional production is getting *cheaper* as output increases. Many manufactured goods have increasing marginal returns to production. This explains why manufacturing firms are often large in size.

> **decreasing marginal costs:** the situation in which the cost of producing one additional unit of output falls as more output is produced

Sometimes all these cost patterns are combined in one graph, as shown in Figure 5.5. Figure 5.5 shows the pattern of total and marginal costs that corresponds to the pattern of marginal returns that we saw in Figure 5.3. First, consider how total costs are related to quantity of output, as shown in the top graph. When production levels are low, marginal returns are increasing (refer back to Figure 5.3), which means that total cost is rising but at a decreasing rate. Then, as we move into the range of constant marginal returns, total costs rise at a constant rate. Finally, in the range of decreasing marginal returns, total costs rise rather steeply, as it becomes increasingly expensive to produce additional output with more variable inputs.

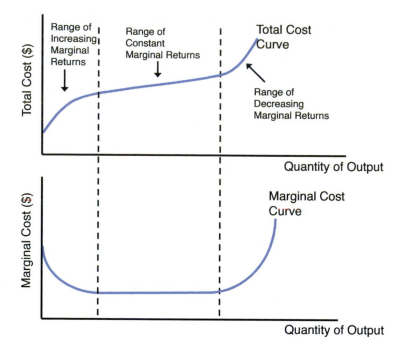

Figure 5.5 *Relationship Between Total and Marginal Costs*

In the lower figure, we see how changes in the slope of the total cost curve translate to changes in marginal costs. In the first production stage, moving left to right, with increasing marginal returns, total costs are rising at a decreasing rate, meaning that marginal costs are declining. Next, as total costs increase at a constant rate, marginal costs are constant. Finally, when total costs rise at an increasing rate, marginal costs are increasing.

For certain production processes, such as the application of fertilizer to corn, curves like these can actually be quite accurately graphed on the basis of real-world studies done by researchers. In most cases, however, these curves are only hypothetical. Rarely would lone producers, concerned with providing for a family or staying in business, have the luxury of being able to conduct such a study. While they were holding some inputs constant and varying others from zero up to high amounts in order to find out what exactly their total product curve and total cost curve were, they could easily go out of business!

These graphs do, however, give us a visual image that can help us think about the many ways in which production and cost may be related, for many producers. We will see that the concepts of diminishing returns and increasing returns, in particular, are important throughout the study of economics.

4.2 Production Costs in the Long Run

In the long run, as we noted earlier, all inputs are variable. A farmer can buy or rent more land or equipment. A factory owner can build a new factory. More engineers can be trained in software development, if skilled engineers are a short-run fixed input. A child-care enterprise can expand from a private home to a larger center, if facing space constraints.

Given sufficient time to acquire equipment, workers, or other resources, a producer should be able to remove all obstacles to getting the highest net benefits (profits) from production. Then a question arises: How big should an enterprise get?

Why do we observe, for example, small neighborhood child-care centers and single-worker locksmith businesses, but not small neighborhood steel foundries or hospitals? Many factors can contribute to the explanation of enterprise size, including factors related to history, culture, and the level of demand for a producer's output. Here we focus on technological and cost-related reasons why one size, or scale, may be more advantageous than another.

Because we are now looking at these issues with a long-term perspective, marginal cost—discussed previously for the case of the short run, in which one input is fixed—is no longer the relevant concept, because now *all* inputs can be varied. It is, however, relevant to calculate the **average cost** (or **average total cost**) per unit of production. This can be done simply by dividing total cost by the quantity of output produced, at any production level. For example, if it costs $500 to produce 100 bushels of corn, the average cost per bushel at this level of production is simply $500/100 bushels = $5 per bushel.

> **average cost (or average total cost):** cost per unit of output, computed as total cost divided by the quantity of output produced

The relevant type of cost when the entire scale of production can be varied is the **long-run average cost**, which is the cost per unit of output when all inputs are variable. It is logical to think that, to whatever extent possible, enterprises will tend to grow to the size where the long-run average costs are lowest. Enterprises that are bigger or smaller than this optimal size would be unnecessarily expensive to run.

> **long-run average cost:** the cost of production per unit of output when all inputs can be varied in quantity

For example, to go into business, a locksmith needs primarily a set of tools and a van. To double the output of a single-locksmith enterprise would require a second locksmith, another set of tools, and another van. Except for perhaps some small savings in costs, such as advertising or billing, there is no reason to believe that the larger firm would be any cheaper to run, per unit of output, than the original, smaller one. In fact, if the new locksmith has to service customers who are farther away from the head office, it may be more expensive per unit of output. It may therefore make more sense for each neighborhood to have its own local locksmith. Bigger is not necessarily better in this case.

By contrast, a steel foundry requires a sizable investment in plant and equipment, and a hospital that has only a few beds would be either exceedingly expensive to run (as a consequence of underutilization of skilled labor and laboratory facilities) or exceedingly limited in its services. Enterprises in such industries tend to be big because of what economists call **economies of scale**. A process exhibits economies of scale when, in the long run, average production costs decline as the size of the enterprise increases. You could build a single foundry furnace to turn out a few pounds of steel a year—but it might cost its weight in gold to produce each pound of steel. A foundry reaches a stage of low costs per unit only when it is producing steel in much larger quantities.

> **economies of scale:** situations in which the long-run average cost of production falls as the size of the enterprise increases

A production process exhibits **constant returns to scale** over the range where the long-run average cost is constant as the size of the enterprise changes. Finally, a process exhibits **diseconomies of scale** if the long-run average cost rises with the size of an enterprise. Similar to our previous discussion, a production process can display all three types of returns to scale. This is illustrated as a U-shaped long-run average cost curve in Figure 5.6.

> **constant returns to scale:** situations in which the long-run average cost of production stays the same as the size of the enterprise increases
> **diseconomies of scale:** situations in which the long-run average cost of production rises as the size of the enterprise increases

What might cause diseconomies of scale? It is generally thought that, despite numerous reasons for economies of scale, for most enterprises, there is a point at

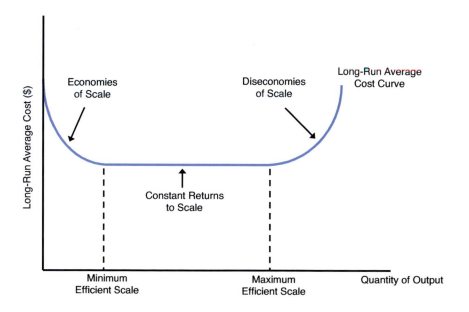

Figure 5.6 *Long-Run Average Costs*

which they are just too big and too complex for all the human beings and all the functions involved to be managed effectively. Anyone who has the experience of working inside any large organization (private or public) is likely to be able to tell at least a few stories about confronting instances of inefficiency, dysfunction, and irrationality they encountered. Some of the big business mergers in recent decades were inspired by hopes of reaping economies of scale (as well as market power or simply in the belief that bigger would be better). Such hopes were sometimes dashed, with the failure of such megamergers as AOL and Time Warner in 2001 and Bank of America and Merrill Lynch in 2009.

Many production processes appear to have a **minimum efficient scale**. This is the point at which the long-run average cost curve begins to bottom out, as shown in Figure 5.6. For locksmiths, the minimum efficient scale might be the output level corresponding to a one-person shop; for an automobile company, it may be several hundred thousand vehicles per year. Levels of output *less* than these will leave per unit production costs higher than they would otherwise be. This means the firm is less competitive against its rivals. This level of output is less efficient, as some resources are underemployed, thus creating the downward-sloping portion of the long-run average cost curve. Given the problems of managing very large organizations, one can also posit the existence of a **maximum efficient scale**—which is the largest an enterprise can be and still benefit from low long-run average costs.

> **minimum efficient scale:** the smallest size an enterprise can be and still benefit from low long-run average costs
> **maximum efficient scale:** the largest size an enterprise can be and still benefit from low long-run average costs

4.3 Production Process Choice

Another important issue in the economics of production is the choice of production process. If two or more processes exist that can make the same output, which should be chosen? Producers, to be economically efficient, should choose the process that entails the lowest cost.

Because various technologies are available, producers can engage in **input substitution**, using less of one input and more of another while producing the same good or service, as costs and availability change. As we mentioned earlier, in the case of corn farming, nitrogen can be obtained from renewable, organic sources such as manure and alfalfa or from chemical fertilizer produced using nonrenewable natural gas. Generally, whenever prices change, producers will want to substitute cheaper inputs for inputs that have become more expensive. From a public welfare perspective, input substitution will enhance well-being when the choices that are made take into account external as well as internal costs.

> **input substitution:** increasing the use of some inputs, and decreasing that of others, while producing the same good or service

Of particular importance, historically, has been the process of substituting the use of machinery for human labor. This is dramatically exemplified in the American folk hero John Henry, the railway worker who pitted himself against the new steam drill that threatened to take jobs away from him and his fellows. In his heroic effort, John Henry fulfilled his promise to "die with a hammer in my hand."

Yet even with modern production methods that rely heavily on machines, labor remains an important input cost. Because of globalization and the possibility of moving production to any part of the world, an increasingly important question has been *where* to produce. Low wages in countries such as China, Vietnam, and Bangladesh have motivated many companies to locate production facilities in those countries. Often the cost savings associated with production in a low-wage country outweigh the increased costs of transporting goods long distances to market. However, wage trends are beginning to reverse in some cases, and manufacturing in the United States may be making a comeback, as discussed in Box 5.1.

BOX 5.1 MADE IN THE USA AGAIN?

Low production costs, particularly labor costs, motivated numerous American companies to move production facilities overseas in recent years. This wave of "offshoring" is estimated to have caused the loss of 3.4 million U.S. manufacturing jobs to China alone between 2001 and 2016.[9] The rapid economic growth in China has caused manufacturing wages in China to triple between 2005 and 2016.[10] Meanwhile, wage growth in the United States has stagnated. Thus, the relative wage advantage of producing in China has declined or been eliminated.

As a result, many American companies are finding that it makes economic sense to bring manufacturing facilities and jobs back to the United States from overseas—a trend referred to as "reshoring." For example, General Electric decided to shift production of water heaters from China to a plant in Louisville, Kentucky, reshoring hundreds of manufacturing and engineering jobs. In 2013, Wal-Mart announced a "Made in the USA" program, which has supported the return of thousands of jobs.[11] For the first time in decades, in 2016, more manufacturing jobs came back to the United States than left, with most of those returning jobs coming from China.[12] In 2018, the number of U.S. companies reporting new reshoring and foreign companies reporting foreign direct investment (FDI) was at its highest ever level.[13]

Still, the number of jobs that have returned is relatively small, and it is unclear whether the reshoring trend will gain significant momentum. Optimistic projections suggest that up to half of the manufacturing jobs that moved overseas could return.[14] Others are more cautious, such as University of Pennsylvania professor Morris Cohen, who notes that reshoring is generally limited to select industries and that, while it makes sense for some companies to reshore jobs, "there are other situations where companies continue to offshore, either to Asia or to other parts of the world."[15] He concludes:

> The extent to which [recent reshoring is] truly a sign of an American manufacturing renaissance or merely a pause from the ongoing departure of [jobs] from U.S. shores is still unclear. One certainty is that it will take more than a few thousand jobs to reverse the trend of decades of offshoring and heavy reliance on foreign imports.[16]

Discussion Questions

1. Explain in your own words why a firm's marginal cost curve may initially decline, but then increase, as the quantity of output increases.
2. Diminishing marginal returns is a valuable concept, not only in economics, but in many other areas of life: an obvious example (which we saw in Chapter 4, on consumption) was the diminishing pleasure received by eating successive units of the same food. Suggest two other areas in life that exhibit diminishing marginal returns. Can you also think of some examples in your own life where there are constant or increasing returns to scale (i.e., you get the same, or more, psychic or other "returns" from each additional increment of something)?

REVIEW QUESTIONS

1. What is the "triple bottom line," and how does it differ from the traditional economic assumption about the goal of production?
2. What is the difference between fixed costs and variable costs?
3. What is the difference between accounting costs and economic costs?
4. Name all the categories that make up economic costs.
5. What is the difference between private costs and external costs?
6. What is a production function?
7. What is a limiting factor in production?
8. What distinguishes the short run from the long run?
9. How can we express a production function graphically?
10. What is marginal product?
11. Describe the meaning of diminishing returns, constant returns, and increasing marginal returns, and explain how each might come about.
12. Sketch a total product curve illustrating increasing returns, constant returns, and diminishing returns.
13. Distinguish among fixed cost, variable cost, total cost, and marginal cost.
14. Sketch a total cost curve illustrating fixed cost and decreasing, constant, and increasing marginal costs.
15. What are average costs?
16. What are economies of scale?
17. Sketch a long-run average cost curve illustrating economies of scale, constant returns to scale, and diseconomies of scale.
18. How do we define the efficient scale of production?

EXERCISES

1. Kai's records show that last month, he spent $5,000 on rent for his shop, $3,000 on materials, $3,000 on wages and benefits for an employee, and $500 in interest on the loan that he used to start his business. He quit a job that had paid him $3,000 a month to devote himself full-time

to this business. Suppose that he has to pay the lease on his shop and the interest on the loan regardless of whether he produces. However, suppose that at any time, he can change the amount of materials that he buys and the hours that his employee works and that he can also go back to his old job (perhaps part-time).

a. What are the accounting costs of operating his shop for the month?

b. What are the economic costs?

c. Which types of costs of running his business for a month are fixed? Which are variable?

2. A nonprofit organization dedicated to health care wants to open a new hospital near a residential neighborhood. A group of residents of that neighborhood protests this decision, claiming that traffic caused by the hospital will increase noise and auto emissions. The hospital rejects the idea of building a wall to contain the noise and fumes, claiming that this would be too expensive. Describe in a few sentences, using at least two terms introduced in this chapter, how an economist might describe this situation.

3. The production relationship between the number of chapters that Tiffany studies in her history book (the variable input) and the number of points that she will earn on a history exam (the output) is as follows:

Input: number of chapters studied	0	1	2	3
Output: test score	15	35	60	95

a. Using graph paper or a computer spreadsheet or presentation program, graph the total product curve for exam points. Label clearly.

b. What is the marginal return of the first chapter that Tiffany reads? And what is the marginal return of the third chapter that she reads?

c. How would you describe this pattern of returns?

4. Suppose that you have started a small business offering computer consulting. Match each concept in Column A with an example in Column B.

Column A		Column B	
a.	Fixed input	1.	The more months that you work at consulting, the better you become at it
b.	Variable input	2.	The way that you irritate your roommate by working late at night
c.	Opportunity cost	3.	The lost salary that you could have had as an employee elsewhere
d.	External cost	4.	The more hours you work without a break, the less effectively you work
e.	Increasing returns	5.	The time that you spend consulting
f.	Diminishing returns	6.	The computer that you initially purchased when you started the business

5. Ramona designs Web pages and needs the jolt that she gets from the caffeine in cola drinks to keep herself awake and alert. The total product curve for the relationship between her cola consumption per day and the number of pages that she can design in one day is given in the following figure.

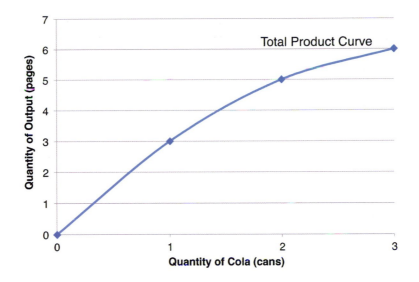

a. Fill out Columns (2) and (3) of the table subsequently, referring to the previous graph.

Quantity of variable input (cans of cola)	(2) Quantity of output (pages)	(3) Marginal product (pages)	Fixed cost ($)	Variable cost ($)	Total cost ($)
0					
1					
2					
3					

b. Ramona's employer pays her $50 per day regardless of whether she is productive and provides her with all the cola that she wants to drink. Cola costs her employer $2 per can. Add to your table information on the fixed, variable, and total costs of Ramona's producing from 0 to 3 Web pages.

c. Using graph paper or a spreadsheet or presentation program, graph the total cost curve. (What is measured on the horizontal axis? The vertical axis?)

d. Using information on the marginal product from your previous table, calculate the marginal cost per page of output at each level of soda consumption.

6. Suppose that in her first hour of work, Lynn can hand-knit four pairs of mittens. During her second consecutive hour, Lynn can hand-knit three additional pairs of mittens, and during her third hour of work, as a consequence of fatigue, she can hand-knit only one additional pair. Suppose that she works for up to three hours and makes a wage of $15 per hour.

a. Create a table relating the number of hours worked to the *total* number of pairs of mittens produced, and graph the *total* product curve for the production of pairs of mittens. Label clearly.

b. Looking at labor costs only (ignoring, for the purposes of this exercise, the cost of the yarn that she uses and any fixed costs), make a table relating costs to the number of pairs of mittens produced. Graph the total (labor) cost curve for the production of mittens. Label clearly.

c. How would you describe in words the pattern of marginal returns? The pattern of marginal costs?

d. What is the marginal product, in pairs of mittens per hour, of her second hour of work? Of her third hour of work?

e. What is the marginal cost, in dollars per pairs of mittens, as she goes from an output of four pairs of mittens to an output of seven pairs of mittens? What is the marginal cost of the eighth pair of mittens?

NOTES

1. Small Business Administration. 2018. *Small Business Profile*. Office of Advocacy, Small Business Association, Washington, DC.
2. Wal-Mart Incorporated. 2018. *Income Statement*. NASDAQ.com. Accessed July 2019.
3. U.S. Bureau of Economic Analysis, Table 1.3.5. *Gross Value Added by Sector*. https://apps.bea.gov/national/pdf/SNTables.pdf. Accessed 27 June 2019.
4. Cave, Andrew. 2016. "'Don't Buy This Jacket': Patagonia to Give Away All Retail Revenues on Black Friday." *Forbes*, November 21.
5. Friedman, Milton. 1970. "The Social Responsibility of Business Is to Increase Its Profits." *New York Times Magazine*, September 13.
6. Danaher, Kevin, and Jason Mark. 2003. *Insurrection: Citizen Challenges to Corporate Power*. Routledge, Abingdon, UK.
7. See, for example, Morran, Chris. 2014. "Court Affirms $151M Ruling against Wal-Mart for Making Employees Work Off the Clock." *Consumerist*, December 16.
8. Scharf, Peter, and Bill Wiebold. 2001. "Nitrogen Prices: How Do They Affect Optimum Nitrogen Management?" *Integrated Pest & Crop Management Newsletter*, 11(2).
9. Economic Policy Institute. 2018. "The Growing Trade Deficit with China Has Led to a Loss of 3.4 Million U.S. Jobs between 2001 and 2017." Press Release, October 13.
10. Worstall, Tim. 2017. "Chinese Wages Are Showing Paul Krugman Is Right Once Again." *Forbes*, March 1.
11. Sauter, Michael B., and Samuel Stebbins. 2015. "Manufacturers Bringing the Most Jobs Back to America." *USA Today*, April 23.
12. Glaser, April. 2017. "Why Manufacturing Jobs Are Coming Back to the U.S.: Even as Companies Buy More Robots." Recode, May 26.
13. Moser, Harry. 2019. "Reshoring Was at Record Levels in 2018: Is It Enough?" Industry Week, July 8.
14. Moser, Harry, and Sandy Montalbano. 2017. "How the U.S. Could Bring Back Up to Half the Manufacturing Jobs That Moved Overseas." MarketWatch, May 29.
15. Anonymous. 2015. "Is the Reshoring of U.S. Manufacturing a Myth?" Knowledge@Wharton, University of Pennsylvania, May 5. http://knowledge.wharton.upenn.edu/article/offshoring-gets-a-rethink/
16. Sauter, Michael B., and Samuel Stebbins. 2015. "Manufacturers Bringing the Most Jobs Back to America." *USA Today*, April 23.

Chapter 6

Market Structure

Economists have traditionally described four basic market structures based on the number of sellers participating in that market and the types of products that they sell. These four types of market structure are:

- perfect competition: the situation in which there are many sellers, selling identical goods
- pure monopoly: the situation in which there is only one seller
- monopolistic competition: the situation in which there are many sellers, but they sell slightly different things
- oligopoly: the situation in which there are so few sellers that each needs to watch, and respond to, what the other sellers are doing

These four market structures exist along a "competitiveness spectrum" where perfectly competitive markets with no market power are at one end of the spectrum, while pure monopoly with *all* the market power for a particular good or service is at the other end. In between we have the other two market types—monopolistic competition and oligopoly.

In this chapter, we present economic models of each of the four market structures, giving particular emphasis to implications of these market structures for social welfare, fairness, and public policy.

1. UNDERSTANDING MARKET POWER AND COMPETITION

Having power means having the ability to influence something. **Market power** is the ability to control, or at least affect, the terms and conditions of a market exchange.

> **market power:** the ability to control, or at least affect, the terms and conditions of a market exchange

Market power is related to the degree of competition in a market. A general rule of thumb is that the more competitive a market is (i.e., the more sellers present in that market), the less market power is held by any individual seller. But what exactly do we mean by "competition"? Let us look at potential definitions of competition and how they relate to market power from the perspectives of four different groups—businesses, consumers, citizens, and economists.

1.1 The Business Perspective on Competition and Market Power

From the point of view of an individual business, competition is generally a *bad* thing—something to be reduced or eliminated. Competition means that other businesses are working to reduce your sales and profits. It also means that you have to be aware of what your competitors are charging for their goods and services, and you may have to adjust your prices to reflect what your competitors are doing.

From the perspective of businesses, market power is a good thing because businesses want to be able to influence people's consumption decisions, command lower prices for the resources they buy, set a high price for their own products, and capture a larger share of the market.

1.2 The Consumer Perspective on Competition and Market Power

To consumers, competition is generally a good thing. Competition among businesses tends to drive prices down, making goods and services more affordable to consumers. Having several competing stores to choose from means that consumers are more likely to find bargains. Consumers generally do not benefit when sellers possess market power, as sellers with market power are likely to charge higher prices for their products. (For more on competition from the perspective of both businesses and consumers, see Box 6.1.)

BOX 6.1 AMAZON AND MARKET COMPETITION

Amazon is the world's top online retailer, with 2018 global revenues of more than $232.8 billion.[1] In the United States, Amazon dominates e-commerce, accounting for 44 percent of all online spending in 2017.[2] Amazon's founder, Jeff Bezos, started the company out of his garage in 1994, initially only selling books. With Amazon's success, Bezos became the world's first person to achieve a net worth of $100 billion, in November 2017.[3]

Amazon's success is based largely on its ability to offer a lower price than its competitors, especially "brick-and-mortar" competitors that must pay the cost of operating physical stores. Consumers benefit from Amazon's low prices and free shipping on many orders. As other retailers have sought to increase their online presence, Amazon has maintained a competitive advantage through innovation. Its Amazon Prime service, launched in 2005, provides its members with free two-day shipping on most items and access to streaming video content.

According to a 2016 article, Amazon's most overlooked competitive advantage may be its ability to link online consumers to numerous third-party sellers.[4] Many non-Amazon merchants seek to have their products listed on Amazon because of Amazon's unparalleled online traffic. Thus more and more consumers are able to find exactly what they want on Amazon, leading to a virtuous cycle where Amazon attracts customers, which attracts third-party merchants, which attracts even more customers, which attracts even more merchants, and so on.

1.3 The Citizen Perspective on Competition and Market Power

People are both consumers and citizens. Sometimes their goals as consumers may not align with their views as concerned citizens. Competition and market power is one such issue. While consumers generally approve of competition because it tends to lead to lower prices, as concerned citizens, they may perceive competitive pressures as the cause of undesirable social and environmental impacts. For example, concerned citizens may worry about businesses that cite the "need to stay competitive" as their reason for eliminating jobs, taking over smaller companies, refusing to implement voluntary pollution controls, or moving their production overseas, all of which are perceived as harmful. Citizens may also be concerned that businesses with large market power are more likely to disproportionately influence public policy to obtain tax breaks, subsidies, or exemptions from environmental regulations or to act unethically by raising prices or by forcing workers to accept low wages.

From the point of view of a concerned citizen, neither intense competition nor market power serves the interests of a peaceful and humane society. Many concerned citizens would prefer to see markets based on decentralized power and effective regulation that maintains ethical boundaries and better serves the common good.

1.4 The Economists' Perspective on Competition and Market Power

To an economist, competition implies the case in which so many buyers and sellers interact in a market that none are able to exercise significant market power. In such markets, firms are always trying to attract customers away from their competitors, which keeps them on their toes. Hence, competition between firms incentivizes them to run their organizations efficiently. The traditional neoclassical view, focused almost entirely on efficiency goals, argues that market power can create economic inefficiencies. Hence, economists often emphasize the benefits of competition and perceive market power as being largely harmful.

However, if competition drives businesses to treat their workers poorly or ignore environmental regulations, these costs must be included in evaluating economic outcomes. Well-crafted regulations that consider social and environmental externalities can encourage "healthy" competition to enhance social efficiency. As economists, we may also be concerned about whether competitive markets lead to just outcomes, based on normative views of fairness.

Discussion Questions

1. To which of the four views of market power and competition do you most relate? Do you think all four views are valid, or is one view more worthwhile or "correct" than the others?
2. Can you think of an example of an economic actor that is *not* a business firm but that has "market power" in the sense defined in the text?

2. PERFECT COMPETITION

The economic model of perfect competition relies on particular assumptions and leads to certain conclusions about how firms behave. Though this model is somewhat abstract, it is influential in policymaking and can function as the first step toward understanding market structures that have more real-world relevance.

2.1 The Conditions of Perfect Competition

The model of **perfect competition** is based on the following key assumptions:

1. There are *numerous small sellers* and *buyers*. Each buyer and seller is so small relative to the size of the relevant market that none can affect the market price.
2. Within any particular market, only one kind of good or service is traded and all units of the good or service offered for sale *are identical*. Therefore, buyers will make their purchasing decisions based solely on price.
3. Firms can freely enter or exit the industry. There are no barriers preventing a new firm from joining the market or preventing an existing one from leaving the market.
4. Buyers and sellers all have *perfect information* about where goods are available, at what prices they are offered, and what profits are being made.

> **perfect competition:** a market for the exchange of identical units of a good or service in which there are numerous small sellers and buyers, all of whom have perfect information

Another assumption is that the long-run minimum efficient scale (discussed in Chapter 5) of a producer in this industry is small, relative to total market demand. In other words, production is generally characterized by diminishing or constant returns to scale, not by economies of scale. This is important because, if it were *not* the case, the market might not be large enough for the many efficient firms assumed by the theory.

In a perfectly competitive market, there is no market power, meaning that every individual seller is a **price taker**. If a firm raises its price even just a little above the market-determined price, *no one* will buy from them because consumers can purchase identical items for a lower price from their competitors.

> **price taker:** a seller that has no market power to set price. Price is determined solely by the interaction of market supply and market demand.

Being a price taker means that you face a perfectly elastic demand curve, where any increase in price, no matter how small, eliminates all the demand for the good. This is shown in Figure 6.1. A seller can sell all it wants at the market price of $P*$. At any price above $P*$, however, it will sell nothing. There is also no reason to sell at any price below $P*$ because it can sell as much as it wants at $P*$.

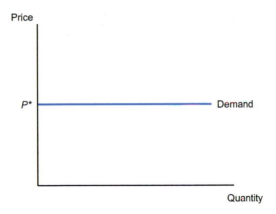

Figure 6.1 *The Demand Curve for a Perfectly Competitive Seller*

While each individual seller in a perfectly competitive market faces a perfectly elastic demand curve, the *market* demand curve is less elastic, or perhaps inelastic. Hence, the market demand curve has the normal downward slope.

Examples of perfectly competitive markets in the real world are hard to come by. One example of a market that closely approaches perfect competition is a financial resale market, such as the stock market. The shares of stock of a particular company are all identical. Because this is a financial resale market, the cost of "production" is irrelevant, so there are no barriers to entry. The going price of stocks is generally common knowledge, and the trading of few shares does not perceptibly affect the share price if many shares of stock are outstanding. Also, because individual sellers can only sell shares of the stock at the going market price, the demand curve faced by individual sellers is horizontal.

In some labor markets as well, conditions may approximate perfect competition. Workers with general skills, such as flipping burgers or sweeping floors, may provide nearly identical services from an employer's point of view. When there are many such "sellers," they may find that they have a choice of a job at "the going wage" or no job at all.

2.2 Profit Maximization Under Perfect Competition

We now consider the production decisions of perfectly competitive sellers. Although a perfectly competitive seller can *theoretically* sell all they want at a given price, selling beyond a certain volume will not be profitable. We illustrate profit maximization with an example of an individual corn farmer selling into a perfectly competitive market. We present a more formal model of production decisions in an online Appendix to this chapter.

Revenues and Profits

In Chapter 5, we discussed production costs. We now consider revenues—the money that sellers receive from their sales. If all units sell for the same price, **total revenues** are simply equal to price multiplied by the quantity sold. So, if the price of corn were $4 per bushel and a farmer sold 1,000 bushels of corn, her total revenues would be $4,000 ($4 ×1,000).

> **total revenues:** the total amount of money received by a seller, equal to price times quantity sold

We can now define **profits** as the difference between total revenues and total costs. But recall from Chapter 5 that we have two different definitions of costs—accounting costs and economic costs. The difference is that economic costs include all opportunity costs, such as the wages that one could potentially earn doing something else. Comparably, we also have two definitions of profits. **Accounting profits** are calculated as the difference between total revenues and accounting costs, while **economic profits** are the difference between total revenues and economic costs. Accounting profits are higher than economic profits, because economic costs are higher than accounting costs.

> **profits:** the difference between total revenues and total costs
> **accounting profits:** the difference between total revenues and accounting costs
> **economic profits:** the difference between total revenues and economic costs

The standard neoclassical model of perfect competition assumes that each seller seeks to maximize his or her profits. In the numerical model that we present here, we assume that costs means economic costs, and thus any profits are economic profits.

We also need to define **marginal revenue**, which is the *additional* revenue obtained by selling one more unit. In a perfectly competitive market, marginal revenue is simply the market price. So if the price of corn is $4 per bushel, the marginal revenue from selling one more bushel is simply $4, which is constant regardless of how much corn a farmer sells.

> **marginal revenue:** the additional revenue obtained by selling one more unit. In a perfectly competitive market, marginal revenue equals the market price

We can represent total revenues graphically, as shown in Figure 6.2. The total revenue curve is a straight line because marginal revenue is constant at $4 per bushel. So if a farmer sells 100 bushels of corn, for example, total revenues will be $400; if she sells 140 bushels of corn, total revenues will be $560, as shown in the figure.

Profit Maximization Example

In order to determine the level of corn production that will result in the maximum profit, we combine our information from Chapter 5 about production costs with the fact that corn sells for $4 per bushel to produce Table 6.1. We have calculated

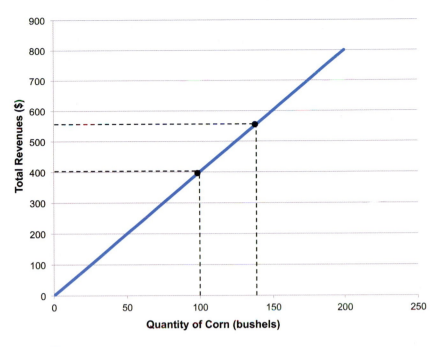

Figure 6.2 *Total Revenues*

Table 6.1 Profit Maximization, Based on Analysis of Total Costs and Total Revenues

Quantity of nitrogen fertilizer (bags/acre)	Corn yield (bushels per acre)	Fixed costs ($)	Variable costs ($15 per bag of fertilizer)	Total costs ($)	Total revenues ($)	Economic profit/loss ($)
0	100	500	0	500	400	−100
1	115	500	15	515	460	−55
2	127	500	30	530	508	−22
3	137	500	45	545	548	3
4	145	500	60	560	580	20
5	150	500	75	575	600	25
6	154	500	90	590	616	26
7	157	500	105	605	628	23
8	159	500	120	620	636	16

the profit (or loss) of each level of corn production based on different levels of fertilizer application. Note that Table 6.1 repeats the information from Table 5.4 but adds columns for total revenue and profit. We assume that there is a fixed cost of $500 per acre.

We see that the farmer's profits are maximized at a production level of 154 bushels per acre, applying 6 bags of fertilizer per acre. At this point, economic profits are $26 per acre. Any other level of production results in lower (or negative) profits.

Profit maximization can be shown graphically as the difference between total revenues and total costs, as shown in Figure 6.3. In this figure, we have combined

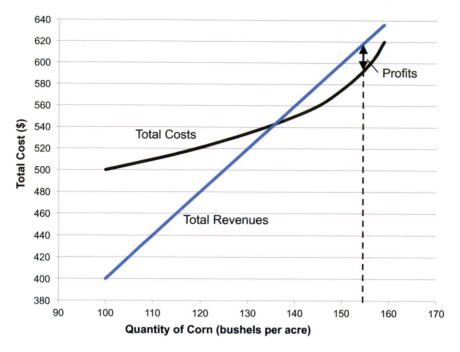

Figure 6.3 *Profit Maximization, Based on Analysis of Total Costs and Total Revenues*

Table 6.2 Profit Maximization, Based on Analysis of Marginal Costs and Marginal Revenues

Quantity of nitrogen fertilizer (bags per acre)	Corn yield (bushels per acre)	Marginal product of additional nitrogen (bushels of corn)	Cost of additional nitrogen ($ per bag)	Marginal cost ($ per bushel of corn)	Marginal revenue ($ per bushel of corn)
0	100	—	—	—	4
1	115	15	15	15 ÷ 15 = 1.00	4
2	127	12	15	15 ÷ 12 = 1.25	4
3	137	10	15	15 ÷ 10 = 1.50	4
4	145	8	15	15 ÷ 8 = 1.88	4
5	150	5	15	15 ÷ 5 = 3.00	4
6	154	4	15	15 ÷ 4 = 3.75	4
7	157	3	15	15 ÷ 3 = 5.00	4
8	159	2	15	15 ÷ 2 = 7.50	4

Figure 6.2, showing total revenues, with our total cost curve from Figure 5.4. The vertical distance between the total revenue curve and the total cost curve represents profits. This vertical distance is greatest, and profits are maximized, at 154 bushels per acre.

In addition to determining the profit-maximizing level of production using a table or a graph of total revenues and total costs, we can also use marginal analysis. Recall that in Chapter 5, we calculated the marginal cost of producing one more bushel of corn at each level of fertilizer application (Table 5.5). We repeat this table here as Table 6.2, with the addition of a column indicating the marginal revenue from selling corn, which is constant at $4 per bushel.

Marginal analysis tells us that it makes economic sense to do something as long as the marginal benefits are greater than the marginal costs. In this case, it makes economic sense for the farmer to add a bag of fertilizer as long as the marginal revenues (from selling more corn) exceed the marginal cost of adding fertilizer, because profits are increasing. So, for example, we can see that adding the third bag of fertilizer increases profits because marginal revenues per bushel of $4.00 exceed the marginal cost of $1.50 per bushel.

Marginal revenues exceed marginal cost for every production level up to six bags of fertilizer. For the seventh bag of fertilizer, the marginal cost of $5 exceeds the marginal revenue of $4. By adding the seventh bag of fertilizer, the farmer loses money. So the profit-maximizing level of fertilizer application is 6 bags, at which the farmer is producing 154 bushels of corn per acre. This is the same answer that we obtained previously based on tabular and graphical analysis of total costs and revenues.

We can also illustrate profit maximization using a graph of marginal costs and marginal revenues, shown in Figure 6.4. We see that marginal revenue is constant at $4 per bushel. The marginal cost of corn production is increasing, as we discussed in Chapter 5. The profit-maximizing level of corn production is 154 bushels, again up to the point where the marginal revenue equals marginal cost.

We can now state the general rule for **profit maximization under perfect competition**: a seller should increase production up to the point where marginal

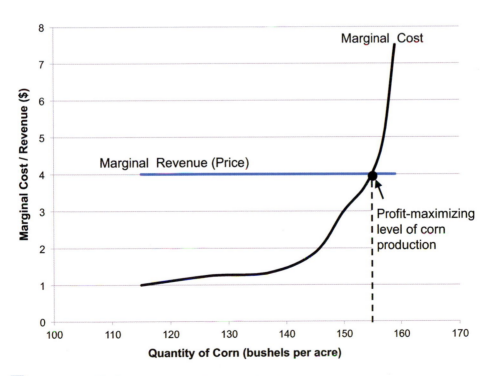

Figure 6.4 *Profit Maximization Based on Marginal Analysis*

revenues equal marginal costs, expressed as $MR = MC$. Given that marginal revenue is always equal to price under perfect competition, we can also state that profit maximizing means setting $P = MC$.

> **profit maximization (under perfect competition):** a seller should increase production up to the point where $MR = MC$. As $MR = P$ under perfect competition, we can also define the profit-maximizing solution by setting $P = MC$

Profits Under Perfect Competition

In Table 6.1, we found that at the profit-maximizing level of production (154 bushels of corn per acre), the farmer is making $26 per acre in economic profits. The existence of such profits would create an incentive for new suppliers to enter the market, resulting in an increase in the *market supply* of corn. This increase in supply lowers price, reducing the economic profits made by each farmer. The entry of new farmers into the market will continue as long as economic profits exist. Eventually, we reach a point where prices decline to a level where economic profits fall to zero. Hence, economic profits would not persist under perfect competition. The end result, where all firms are making zero economic profit, is called the **perfectly competitive market equilibrium**. Note that even though economic profits are zero at this equilibrium, each farmer is still making an accounting profit.

> **perfectly competitive market equilibrium:** the market equilibrium in a perfectly competitive market in which the economic profits of each individual seller are zero, and there is no incentive for entry or exit

2.3 Losses and Exit

In our corn example, each farmer will continue to farm (or be indifferent between farming and the next-best alternative) as long as he or she is making a positive or zero economic profit. But what happens if a farmer is making negative economic profits?

Let's suppose that the price of corn decreased to $3.60 per bushel, perhaps due to a decrease in the demand for corn. The impact of this on an individual farmer is shown in Table 6.3. This is the same as Table 6.1, except that total revenues are now calculated based on a corn price of $3.60 per bushel instead of $4.00 per bushel. The fixed and variable costs of corn production have stayed the same.

We see that at the lower corn price, the "profit-maximizing" level of corn production, now at 150 bushels per acre with five bags of fertilizer, is actually an economic loss. The best that the farmer can do is to lose $35 per acre!

Would it ever make sense for a farmer to stay in business in such circumstances? The decision depends on whether the farmer is willing and able to accept temporary losses, with the hope of making profits in the future, or quit farming. To understand how a rational business person will behave, we have to recall, from Chapter 5, the

Table 6.3 Impact of a Decrease in Corn Prices

Quantity of nitrogen fertilizer (bags/acre)	Corn yield (bushels per acre)	Fixed costs ($)	Variable costs ($15 per bag of fertilizer)	Total costs ($)	Total revenues ($)	Economic profit/loss ($)
0	100	500	0	500	360	−140
1	115	500	15	515	414	−101
2	127	500	30	530	457	−73
3	137	500	45	545	493	−52
4	145	500	60	560	522	−38
5	150	500	75	575	540	−35
6	154	500	90	590	554	−36
7	157	500	105	605	565	−40
8	159	500	120	620	572	−48

distinction between the short run and the long run. In the short run, at least one input is fixed in quantity, and thus the cost of paying for any fixed inputs must be paid regardless of production levels. In the long run, all inputs are variable, and thus a seller can avoid paying all costs simply by leaving the market.

In our corn example, the fixed cost of $500 must be paid in the short term, regardless of the level of corn production. Even if the farmer decides to produce no corn, she must still pay this fixed cost. So the farmer's short-term production decision comes down to two options:

1. continue to produce some corn, even at a loss
2. produce no corn at all and just pay the fixed costs

Table 6.3 shows that at 150 bushels of corn (the best the farmer can do), the farmer loses $35 per acre—total costs are $575, and total revenues are $540. But if she decides not to produce any corn at all, she will still have to pay her fixed cost of $500 per acre. She avoids having to pay any variable costs, but she also receives no revenues, so her losses will be $500 per acre. Obviously, it is better to lose only $35 per acre than to lose $500 per acre. By producing some corn, rather than none, she can more than cover her variable costs, recovering a large portion of her fixed costs as well. Thus, in the short term, it makes economic sense for her to continue production if she can cover her variable costs and recoup some of her fixed costs, even if, overall, losses are occurring.

This is a specific example of a more general economic principle concerning production decisions. *Sunk costs should not affect short-run production decisions.* A **sunk cost** is a cost that, in the short run, has already been incurred (or committed to) and cannot be reversed. This principle often seems to contradict common sense. Humans seem to have an economically illogical but psychologically strong tendency to want to make past investments "pay off." And the larger the past investment, the more likely people are to be influenced by sunk costs. This is true not only of production decisions but of economic behavior in general. This is yet another example of seemingly irrational economic behavior that was discussed in Chapter 4.

> **sunk cost:** an expenditure that was incurred or committed to in the past and is irreversible in the short run

In the long run, all costs are variable, so the farmer can avoid having to pay the fixed cost of $500 per acre simply by exiting the corn market—she can sell her land and machinery and take up a different profession. In a perfectly competitive market, or any market, short-term losses may be rational, but in the long run, exit becomes preferable to losing money.

Markets are rarely as competitive as described under the conditions of perfect competition. Indeed, many industries—from transportation and utilities to agriculture and health care—are characterized by a considerable degree of market power. In the following three sections, we present economic models of markets with varying degrees of market power.

Discussion Questions

1. Suppose you are thinking of starting your own business. Would you want to start a business in a perfectly competitive market? What do you think are the advantages and disadvantages of selling in a perfectly competitive market?
2. How useful do you think the model of a perfectly competitive market is in explaining economic behavior in the real world? What do you think is the most relevant insight from the model?

3. PURE MONOPOLY: ONE SELLER

The case that is diametrically opposed to perfect competition is pure monopoly, in which there is only one seller. As in the case of perfect competition, the traditional model of profit maximization for monopoly leads to clear predictions, but the predicted outcomes are very different from those of the perfectly competitive model.

3.1 The Conditions of Monopoly

Monopoly is characterized by the following conditions:

1. There is only *one seller.*
2. The good or service being sold has *no close substitutes.* This means that buyers must buy from the monopolist or not at all.
3. *Barriers to entry* prevent other firms from starting to produce the good or service.

Because the monopolist is the only seller in the market, it faces no competition from other firms. The condition of "no close substitutes" means that the product that the monopolist sells must be substantially different from anything else, so the monopolist does not have to worry about losing buyers to markets for similar products. Of course, if a monopolist can make an economic profit, in principle, other firms would want to enter the market. However, **barriers to entry** keep those other firms out of the market. There are three major kinds of barriers to entry: economic barriers, legal barriers, and deliberate barriers.

> **barriers to entry:** economic, legal, or deliberately created or maintained obstacles that keep new sellers from entering a market

Economic Barriers

Economic barriers derive primarily from the nature of the production technology, which may be characterized by high fixed costs, economies of scale, or network externalities.

High fixed costs prevent potential competitors from entering the industry on a small scale and expanding, because while they are small, they cannot generate enough revenue to recover the sizable fixed costs. Competitors must therefore enter as very large-scale operations, which may be a difficult and risky thing to do. For example, the large initial investment required to build facilities that can produce specialized military aircraft make it difficult for any potential entrant to challenge existing firms.

The size of the market relative to the minimum efficient scale of a firm is also important. A monopoly will likely arise if the minimum efficient scale is large enough to constitute a majority of a particular market. In such situations, any firm with less than the majority of the market will be producing at higher per-unit costs than a firm that is producing above the minimum efficient scale. Ultimately, these smaller competitors will be uncompetitive compared to a firm with monopoly power. A monopoly that emerges because of economies of scale is called a **natural monopoly**.

> **natural monopoly:** a monopoly that arises because the minimum efficient scale of the producing unit is large relative to the total market demand

Monopolization may also result from production technology characterized by a **network externality**, where as more people adopt a given technology, the more likely it is that *other* people will adopt it. A common example of network externality is the widespread use of Microsoft's Windows operating systems on personal computers. Although other operating systems, such as Linux and Chrome, exist and offer some advantages, the vast majority of computers have a Windows operating system mainly because that is what other users have adopted. As Microsoft Windows became more common, more software was designed for Windows, making it more difficult for new operating systems to gain market share.

> **network externality:** (in production) a situation in which a particular technology or production process is more likely to be adopted because other economic actors have already adopted it

Legal Barriers

Legal barriers include copyrights (which protect creative works), franchises and concessions (which directly prohibit entry into a particular market), patents (which prevent other firms from using innovations), and trademarks (which protect brand names). Legal barriers provide the oldest and most secure foundations for monopoly. In the United States, patent protection allows a firm exclusive use of an invention for an extended period, usually 17 to 20 years. If the invention produces a new and unique good or facilitates production at much lower costs than competitors incur, a monopoly can result.

While patent protections may encourage innovations, critics often argue that the government is excessively generous in providing patents or trademarks, which can stifle market competition. Also, a well-endowed firm with market power has resources available to lobby the government to grant such concessions.

Deliberate Barriers

A deliberate barrier is created when a producer finds a way to exclude competitors through physical, financial, or political means. Not surprisingly, many such "barriers" are illegal. For example, a monopolist might induce the supplier of an essential raw material not to supply potential competitors, or it might get a distributor to agree not to distribute products produced by a rival. A powerful monopolist might also discourage potential competitors by engaging in **predatory pricing**. Whenever competitors enter the market, the monopolist may *temporarily* lower the price of its product to a level so low that it does not cover costs in order to drive its new rivals out of business.

> **predatory pricing:** a powerful seller's temporary pricing of its goods or services below cost in order to drive weaker competitors out of business

A powerful monopolist might also threaten smaller potential competitors with unfounded (but very expensive) lawsuits in attempts to intimidate or bankrupt them. Acts of violence have been used as barriers to entry, most obviously in monopolies run by organized crime.

3.2 Examples of Monopoly

Traditional examples of monopoly include railroads, utility companies (e.g., water utilities, electricity providers, natural gas utilities), and telecommunication companies. Some examples of monopoly are **local monopolies**, meaning that a firm possesses monopoly power in a specific geographic area. For example, a small, isolated town may have only one hardware store, which has a local monopoly for the sale of certain products. Local monopolies frequently exist for cable television, electricity, and flights out of particular airports.

> **local monopoly:** a monopoly limited to a specific geographic area

Governments can also be considered monopolists in the provision of certain goods and services, such as national defense or highways. The U.S. government once held a monopoly in the delivery of mail, but the creation of UPS, FedEx, and other delivery companies has added competition to this market. In other markets, technological innovations reducing barriers to entry have eliminated monopoly conditions. For example, the spread of cell phones has eliminated the monopoly that landline phone providers once held.

Where private companies maintain monopoly power, they often operate as **regulated monopolies**—that is, private companies run under government supervision. The government controls what prices regulated monopolies can charge their customers and stipulates minimum service requirements, as in the case of private utility companies that provide water or electricity. Prices can be set to limit the profits that a private monopolist can earn or on the basis of fairness so that all people can afford basic services.

> **regulated monopoly:** a monopoly run under government supervision

3.3 Profit Maximization for a Monopolist

In choosing what level of output to produce, a monopolistic firm follows the general pattern of behavior of a profit-maximizing firm as described previously, seeking the level at which its marginal cost is equal to its marginal revenue ($MC = MR$). But although its costs are determined in the same way as those of a perfectly competitive firm, its revenues are significantly different.

In contrast to the price-taking firm in perfectly competitive markets that has no impact on the overall market price, a monopolist is the sole supplier of a given product, and it possesses the power, in principle, to set price at whatever level it chooses. However, that doesn't mean it can charge an infinitely high price, as a monopolist is still dependent upon consumer demand for its product. Whereas the demand curve for the price-taking firm is horizontal, the demand curve for the monopolist's output is identical to the overall market demand curve for that product. In other words, it slopes downward.

The monopolist can sell more only by inducing consumers as a group to buy more. To sell more, it must either mount an effective advertising campaign or offer its product at a lower price. Another way to look at the difference is to note that the monopolist can raise its price, losing some sales but obtaining more revenue per unit for those remaining. In contrast, the price-taking firm in a competitive market will sell absolutely nothing if it raises its price above the existing market level. In short, a monopolist is a **price maker**, not a price taker. It can set both price and quantity, although the price–quantity combinations that it can choose are constrained by market demand.

> **price maker:** a seller that can set the selling price, constrained only by demand conditions

Table 6.4 Total and Marginal Revenue for a Monopolist

Quantity of output	Selling price ($)	Total revenue ($)	Marginal revenue ($)
1	44	44	44
2	40	80	36
3	36	108	28
4	32	128	20
5	28	140	12
6	24	144	4
7	20	140	−4
8	16	128	−12
9	12	108	−20

Consider how a producer would behave if, instead of receiving a flat amount for each unit of output sold, it were a monopolist and its demand schedule was the market demand schedule. Table 6.4 presents a simple example of a monopolistic firm. In order to sell a higher quantity of its product, the firm must lower its price. For example, it can sell 1 unit if it sets the price at $44, but if it wants to sell 2 units, it must drop the price to $40 per unit. The first two columns of Table 6.4 thus describe the demand curve for this good.

The third column of Table 6.4 calculates the total revenue of the firm for each level of output, multiplying quantity by price. The fourth column in Table 6.4 indicates how much *extra* revenue the monopolist gains by producing and selling an additional unit. Although total revenue for selling 1 unit is $44, if the monopolist wants instead to sell 2 units, it must sell *both* units at the lower price of $40, receiving total revenue of $80. It thus gains $40 from selling the second unit but also loses the $4 (from the original $44) that it would have gotten from selling the first unit alone. Marginal revenue from the second unit, then, is only $36 (40 minus 4 or, what amounts to the same thing, 80 minus 44).

Marginal revenue for other levels of output is similarly calculated. Note that after the monopolist sells 6 units, total revenue starts to go *down* (from its peak at $144), and marginal revenue becomes negative. We can use the data from Table 6.4 to construct a demand curve for the good, as well as a marginal revenue curve. These are shown in Figure 6.5. The marginal revenue curve lies below the demand curve (after the first unit) and falls off more steeply, entering the negative part of the graph after 6 units.

Figure 6.5 also shows the marginal cost curve for the good, which is the same as the cost curves we derived in Chapter 5. (The cost curves are the same whether a producer is competitive or a monopolist; only the demand side of the market is different.) The monopolist will maximize profits by producing the quantity at which $MR = MC$; this occurs at point A in Figure 6.5. This is an output level of 5 units. Reading horizontally from the MC curve, you see that the marginal cost of producing the fifth unit is $12. The graph and table show that the marginal revenue from the fifth unit is also $12.

The monopolist, however, will not charge its customers $12 per unit. Reading up from a quantity of 5 to the demand curve in Figure 6.5, we see that customers

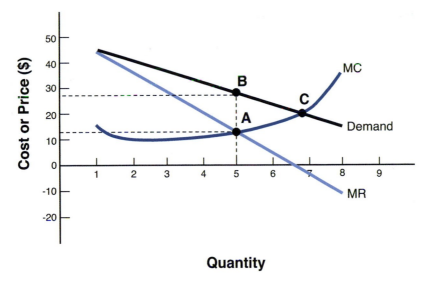

Figure 6.5 *Profit Maximization for a Monopoly Firm*

are willing to pay up to $28 each for the 5 units produced, as shown by point B on the demand curve (see also the "Selling price" column in Table 6.4). The monopolist will produce at a marginal cost to itself of $12 per unit but can clearly take the opportunity to charge customers $28 per unit to maximize profits.

What level of profits will the monopolist make in the long run? Unlike in the perfectly competitive case, where economic profits are driven to zero by the entrance of new producers, monopolists *can* make sustained positive economic profits, as long as barriers to entry keep potential competitors out. To determine the actual level of profits, you need to know more about the cost structure of the firm. This is investigated in the online Appendix to this chapter. If the monopolist's cost structure is such that it makes economic *losses*, presumably in the long run, it will choose to exit the industry.

We should also consider what monopolists do with their positive economic profits. A monopolist may, in fact, need to spend most or all of the profits merely keeping entry barriers up. For instance, when monopolies are generated by exclusive concessions or licenses given out by governments, producers might spend much or all of their economic profits on lobbying and bribing government officials in order to maintain their exclusive right to produce a good.

3.4 Monopoly and Inefficiency

Monopoly power generally leads to inefficiencies. Because the monopolist produces at an output level at which price exceeds marginal cost, society could gain from increased output of the product. In other words, from the point of view of society, the cost to the monopolist of producing additional units is less than the additional benefits consumers would receive from buying those units. Monopolies may also have less incentive to please customers, manage costs efficiently, and adopt new ideas

189

than a firm that has its survival on the line. Hence, monopolies often lead to inefficiencies when compared to a competitive outcome.

While monopolies aren't economically efficient, sometimes people justify monopolies on the grounds that they create situations that foster innovation. Other justifications note that, in the 1950s and 1960s, the large U.S. firms in the steel and automotive industries shared some of their monopoly profits with their workers, providing levels of wages and benefits that helped cast large firms with such market power in positive lights. Such benefits could not, however, be maintained where foreign competition forced them to cut costs to remain profitable.

In some situations, the economic efficiency loss from a monopoly may not be significant, and sometimes monopoly can even be more beneficial than a competitive market. We now consider some specific types of monopolies.

Natural Monopoly

We have already mentioned one case in which a single big firm may be preferable to many small ones: natural monopoly. Small firms in a competitive market structure would face per-unit costs that are unnecessarily high, but a monopolist can exploit its economies of scale to produce output at lower cost. Of course, with no competitors, the monopolist faces few (if any) incentives to pass such production savings on to consumers. Given the potential for a natural monopoly to exploit its customers, natural monopolies are often government owned or tightly regulated.

If the natural monopoly is government owned, the government is in a position to control the company's pricing and operation. If the government regulates a privately owned natural monopoly, it will likely mandate that it produce at higher levels, and sell at lower prices, than the firm would choose on its own. One prominent example of a natural monopoly is the Metropolitan Transportation Authority in the New York City area. As a private company that provides a variety of public transportation services, it is fundamentally a monopoly, but the local government regulates its pricing policy.

Regulated monopolies can, nonetheless, present the government with a dilemma, especially when substantial economies of scale are present. Often the marginal cost of production is very low and below average total cost. For example, on a passenger railroad line, the marginal cost of adding another car is very low after the rails, engines, and schedules are all in place. However, efficiently setting the price of a ticket equal to the marginal cost of providing a ride, and in particular, at less than average cost, would mean that the monopolist's revenues would not cover its costs at this level of production, making its business untenable.

Sometimes, in such cases, the government subsidizes the monopolist to encourage socially beneficial price setting and levels of production. But such subsidies are politically unpopular: many taxpayers resent having their tax dollars go to private companies. Rather than regulating price, government might also regulate the company's profit rate or its output level, though each comes with its own problems. Compelling companies not to exceed a specified profit rate creates an incentive to engage in wasteful spending (e.g., excess administration or perks for company executives). And requiring companies to provide a minimum level of output to meet the

BOX 6.2 PRIVATIZATION OF MUNICIPAL WATER SUPPLIES

Municipal water supply is a common example of a natural monopoly. The significant fixed cost of water treatment facilities and supply pipes means that the minimum efficient scale is normally so large that it forms an effective barrier to entry for potential competitors. Municipal water has been traditionally supplied either by nonprofit public utilities or by highly regulated private companies that are limited in the prices that they can charge their customers.

In recent decades, some economists have proposed increased privatization of municipal water supplies, with fewer regulations on the prices that companies can charge. Proponents of privatization contend that for-profit companies will be motivated to operate water supply systems more efficiently than public utilities.

Privatization of water supplies has been highly controversial in developing countries. In the late 1990s, the World Bank pushed scores of poor countries to privatize their water supplies as a condition for receiving much-needed economic assistance. In several cases, most infamously Bolivia, private companies raised the price of water so much that poor families could not afford enough to meet basic needs.[5] Given such consequences, privatization may work best when combined with policies ensuring that the poorest can afford enough water to meet their basic needs. For example, in the South African system, a minimum supply of water is provided for free to all households to ensure that basic needs can be met.

needs of society creates an incentive to skimp on quality of service and materials used. So although it is certainly true that natural monopolies make sense in certain industries and that such monopolies must be regulated, there is no single optimal method of regulation.

Despite the economic case in favor of natural monopolies in some instances, some economists argue that *all* monopolies should be discouraged, if not abolished, because of their belief that competition always leads to more efficient outcomes and, invariably, lower prices. In recent decades, significant deregulation and privatization of natural monopolies has taken place in the United States and other countries. (See Box 6.2 for an example.)

Intellectual Property

The development of new technologies and drugs can be very expensive; hence, firms argue that they need a period of exclusive high profits to recover the cost of research. Patents, copyrights, and other protections of intellectual property are granted by the government to *encourage* research and innovation.

Of course, patents also have a social cost in that they restrict the production of some important and valuable goods while raising their price. The cost can be extremely high: in many cases, exorbitant prices for certain indispensable medications result in unnecessary human suffering—see Box 6.3. Also, as societies become more concerned about climate change, there is concern that allowing new low-emission energy technologies to be patented could slow their rates of adoption, as

BOX 6.3 MONOPOLY POWER AND DRUG PRICE INCREASES

The prices of prescription drugs in the United States have been increasing much faster than inflation.[6] In September 2015, the price of Daraprim—a critical drug for AIDS and transplant patients—increased by almost 5,500 percent overnight from $13.50 to $750 per tablet. The price of EpiPen—an injection for treating severe allergic reactions—increased from $94 to over $700 between 2006 and 2016.[7] Such large price hikes in the drug market are partly explained by the relatively inelastic demand for drugs and the immense market power that pharmaceutical companies have over controlling market prices. For example, Mylan—the drug company supplying EpiPen—controls about 90 percent of the market for drugs to treat severe allergic reactions. As prices of drugs increase, they become less accessible—especially to the poor. Should prices of such commodities that are essential for survival be dependent on one's ability to pay?

Some economists argue that it is essential for the government to control prices in certain circumstances to protect consumers and producers from rapidly increasing or declining prices. In the case of the market for prescription drugs, the government could set price ceilings for drugs or give Medicare the power to negotiate drug prices. Such controls on drug prices have been shown to increase accessibility in other developed countries.[8] While the critics of price controls point out that such controls could reduce the ability of the pharmaceutical industry to invest in research and come up with new drugs, it is worth noting that in the United States, the federal government funds most of the risky investments for medical research.

the owner of the patent would produce such technologies based on maximum profit, not social need.

Other forms of government action have been suggested as ways of encouraging invention that would not carry the patent system's harmful effects. These include direct funding of research, offering research prizes, and buying patents from companies for a one-time fee.

Pressure to Appear Competitive

Without regulation, a monopolist is free to maximize profits with no concern for the social consequences. But even if a monopolist faces neither a serious rival nor any meaningful government restriction, it may fear *potential* competitors or government action and set production levels and prices in a way that resembles a competitive firm. Most countries have created government agencies charged with investigating cases of monopoly power. Governments may take over monopolies, regulate them, or break them up into smaller companies if their existence is found to be socially harmful. For example, in 1911, the U.S. Supreme Court ordered the breakup of the Standard Oil Company, founded by John D. Rockefeller, into 34 smaller companies for violation of antitrust laws.[9] More recently, in 2013, Apple was found to have violated antitrust laws by conspiring with book publishers to gain exclusive rights to provide certain e-books and thus the monopoly power to charge high prices.[10]

Often, the barriers protecting a monopoly can be bypassed by producing a similar, though not identical, product. Monopolies held by American railroads in the early twentieth century, for example, were weakened not by competing railroads but by truck and airline competition that increased the elasticity of demand for railroad transportation. Microsoft has argued that even though it currently enjoys a near-monopoly, it is "competitive" in a dynamic sense because new technologies could arise at any time to upset its dominance in the market for PC operating systems.

Price Discrimination

We usually think of firms as charging the same price to all buyers. But this need not be the case. A **"price-discriminating"** monopolist charges different prices to different buyers, depending on their ability and willingness to pay. How can a seller do this? One way is to keep the prices a secret. In the real world, car salespeople often carry out a version of price discrimination, offering a price that is closer to the list price and pressing more options on a buyer who comes into the showroom dressed in expensive clothing, while more rapidly offering discounts to a less-affluent-looking client. Airline companies characteristically do something similar, charging business travelers—who are generally quite inflexible about when they must fly—a higher price, on average, than vacationers. A clever way of doing this is by offering discounts for flights that require a weekend stay away (because doing so generally excludes business travelers).

> **price discrimination:** the practice of charging different customers different prices for the same good or service

Another way is to offer discounts structured so that some people but—importantly—not others will pass them up. For example, when stores offer bulk discounts, "two for the price of one" sales, or discounts on particular "sale days," they are trying to separate the price-unresponsive customers (who will buy anyway at full price) from the price-responsive ones, who will take the time and trouble to find discounted sales, mail in coupons for rebates, and so on.

The equity consequences of price discrimination are interesting. Price discrimination seems unfair to consumers when monopolists reap large profits at consumers' expense. However, price discrimination may sometimes just allow a producer to break even. The only nonprofit mental health clinic in town, for example, may offer its services on a "sliding scale," in which the price charged to a client rises with his or her income. The care given to lower-income clients is thus subsidized by the higher prices paid by those with a higher ability to pay. If it were forced to charge only a single price, the clinic might have to close or turn away its poorest clients.

Discussion Questions

1. On many campuses, the official college or university bookstores used to have monopoly power in selling textbooks to students. What would you call this kind of monopoly? Is it still the case at your institution? Why or why not?

2. What are some of the issues that policymakers need to consider if they are to make wise decisions in regard to the regulation of monopolies?

4. MONOPOLISTIC COMPETITION

Monopolistic competition shares characteristics with both perfect competition and monopoly. Many students understandably confuse monopolistic *competition* with monopoly, but monopolistic competition is actually closer to the competitive end of the spectrum.

4.1 The Conditions of Monopolistic Competition

Monopolistic competition is generally characterized by the following conditions:

1. There are numerous small buyers and sellers.
2. The sellers produce goods that are close substitutes but are not identical. Products are often *differentiated*, which means that each seller's product is somewhat different from that offered by the other sellers.
3. Producers of the good or service can freely enter or exit the industry.
4. Buyers and sellers have perfect information.

These conditions are identical to those of perfect competition, except that products are differentiated instead of identical. In the case of monopolistic competition, buyers care which producer they buy from.

Situations of monopolistic competition are ubiquitous in contemporary industrialized societies. There are many firms competing to sell us slightly different varieties of the same goods and services. For example, different brands of gasoline, with slightly different products, different levels of service, or different complementary products or services (e.g., a convenience store or a car wash), may be offered at the same busy intersection. You might find the same book at different prices at a newsstand, a bookstore, and online, offering a different mix of location, convenience, and delivery costs. Such differences in product offerings, however slight, often are sufficient to elicit a degree of brand loyalty on the part of the consumer.

4.2 Profit Maximization With Monopolistic Competition

Product differentiation means that each seller is, in a limited sense, a miniature monopoly, producing a good with no *exact* substitutes. Whereas perfectly competitive sellers will lose *all* their customers if they raise their prices above the prevailing market price, a firm that sells a differentiated product may have a little more leeway to raise prices as they face a downward-sloping demand curve for their particular product. For example, some people might claim that McDonald's hamburgers are superior to Wendy's and might be willing to continue to buy from McDonald's even if it raises its prices.

The fact that such firms face a downward-sloping demand curve means that their profit-maximization problem somewhat resembles that of a monopolist (refer back to Figure 6.5). They also face marginal revenue curves that lie below the demand curve. A monopolistic competitor with good information about their sales and production costs will maximize profits by setting $MR = MC$ at point A and will charge customers a markup on top of that by charging at the price set by the demand curve, at point B in Figure 6.5.

Unlike what occurs in the case of monopoly, however, the demand for such a firm's product is affected by the availability of close substitutes. If a Wendy's restaurant shuts down, demand at McDonald's, Burger King, and other restaurants and franchises nearby is likely to rise. If a new Burger King opens up, demand at many existing nearby restaurants may fall. Even though no other firm produces an *identical* good, substitutes often are close enough to induce meaningful changes in the market.

The fact that entry and exit are easy means that if any monopolistically competitive firm is making positive economic profits, new producers will be attracted to the market and will begin to sell similar goods (e.g., other hamburgers). As new firms, making similar products, enter the market, the demand for a company's specific product (e.g., a McDonald's hamburger) will fall, as illustrated in Figure 6.6. This will cut into the existing firms' revenues and profits. How many new firms will enter, and how much will demand fall for any one firm? In theory, demand will fall just up to the point where every firm is making zero economic profits. (See the online Appendix to this chapter for a graphical explanation.)

Like the monopolist, the monopolistically competitive firm faces a downward-sloping demand curve and so produces less, and charges a higher price, than a perfectly competitive firm. As in the case of a perfectly competitive firm, however, free entry and exit in monopolistically competitive markets mean that any positive economic profits to be gained should only be temporary, as new competitors move in to exploit new opportunities to earn profits.

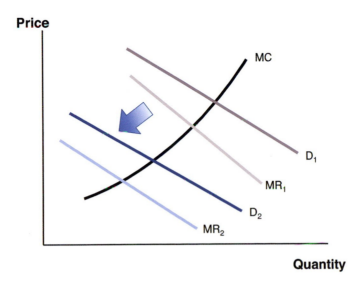

Figure 6.6 *The Effect of Firm Entry on the Demand Curve for a Monopolistically Competitive Firm*

4.3 Monopolistic Competition and Long-Run Efficiency

Compared to perfectly competitive firms, monopolistically competitive firms produce lower levels of output and charge higher prices. It can also be shown (and *is* shown in the online Appendix to this chapter) that such firms have higher unit costs than would occur in a perfectly competitive market. In short, they operate inefficiently.

Monopolistically competitive firms may, like monopolists, expend considerable resources to protect their miniature monopoly. While perhaps unable to keep competitors from entering their general industry, they can try, increasingly, to differentiate their product. Firms in this kind of market structure are observed to engage in a great deal of **nonprice competition**. That is, they use strategies such as advertising heavily, using attractive signs and packaging, selecting better locations, and varying hours of operation to compete with other producers.

> **nonprice competition:** competition through activities other than setting prices, such as advertising and location

In terms of social benefit, it seems evident that resources would be better spent producing fewer varieties of goods and services, at lower costs, and with less advertising. Yet some argue that inefficiencies in production are merely the price that must be paid to satisfy consumers' desire for variety. Although probably not the whole story, it may very well be that the highest social benefit lies somewhere between dull, completely standardized products and the extreme proliferation of (almost identical) consumer goods that we currently observe.

Discussion Questions

1. Think of a somewhat differentiated good or service that you can buy locally in any number of different places—for example, a gallon of gasoline or a cup of coffee. Do you observe differences in prices? What differences might lead to these variations in prices? (Or is the assumption of perfect information violated? Does everyone know where the cheapest version can be found?) What examples of nonprice competition can you identify among the various sellers?
2. Do you think that the amount of variety in the goods and services that you are offered as a consumer is excessive? Just about right? Too limited? Do some forms of nonprice competition have consequences for the retail price of the product as well as for long-term well-being and sustainability?

5. OLIGOPOLY

Oligopoly markets include a relatively small number of sellers who each possess a sizable share of the market. Oligopoly markets have a high degree of market power and are likely to have significant economic and political clout on local and national levels.

196

5.1 Market Structure of an Oligopolistic Industry

The oligopolistic market structure is characterized by the following conditions:

1. The market is dominated by *only a few* sellers, at least some of which control enough of the market to be able to influence the market price.
2. Entry is difficult.

The products produced by oligopolists may be either standardized or differentiated. Oligopoly is a very common (perhaps the most common) market structure. Car manufacturing, airlines, and newspapers are good examples of oligopolies. The most important characteristic of an oligopoly is that the actions of each firm have effects on the market that rival firms cannot ignore. If a firm acts, rivals may respond in ways that, in turn, require a response from the original firm(s). Oligopolistic firms have to constantly consider their actions in relation to possible reactions of rival firms.

Remember that in perfect competition, the seller need not be concerned at all with the actions of other firms—all that such a seller needs to know is the market price. In the case of monopoly, of course, there are no other sellers to worry about. And, in the case of monopolistic competition, the effect of the action of any one seller is spread out over many other sellers.

5.2 Oligopoly and the Behavior of Firms

The behavior of an oligopolistic firm is truly *social* in the sense of being interdependent with the behavior of other actors. Oligopolistic firms can be expected to act strategically against one another. They often engage in "competition" in an active sense by choosing prices, marketing strategies, and the like with an eye to "beating out" specific rivals and gaining greater market share at their expense. Hence, a model of social behavior may be more relevant (than a supply and demand model) to understanding the behavior of oligopolies.

Let us consider a market with two sellers, also known as a **duopoly**. If the first firm (Firm 1) lowers its prices in order to gain greater market share, this may well induce the second firm (Firm 2) to lower its prices to maintain its market share. The end result may be that both firms have lowered their prices (and thus their profits), yet their respective market shares have not changed. In such circumstances, Firm 1 may well regret its initial move to lower prices. Firm 2 may also be frustrated that it is now also worse off.

Alternatively, the firms could engage in **collusion** and make a binding agreement to raise their prices. This would likely result in higher profits for both firms and also allow each firm to retain its market share. In this case, the firms get together and essentially form a monopoly (at least a local one) for pricing purposes, even though they keep their production activities separate. Cartels such as the Organization of Petroleum Exporting Countries (OPEC) are examples of explicit collusion. OPEC did not try to keep its collusion a secret but instead announced its formation and its high prices.

> **duopoly:** a market with only two sellers
> **collusion:** cooperation among potential rivals to gain market power as a group

Tacit collusion takes place when sellers collude more subtly, without creation of a cartel. Because cartels are by and large illegal in many industrialized countries, sellers must often pass information around on the sly. An industry association may collect information and post it on the Web so that all members will know what price the others are charging. Such flows of information make it easier to cooperate and to monitor compliance with tacit **price fixing**, in which all sellers implicitly agree to maintain a common price. One form of implicit collusion is **price leadership**, in which everyone in the industry looks to one firm, raising their prices when it does and lowering them likewise. Such price leadership, many believe, characterized the U.S. steel and airline industries for years. Price leadership tends to be more common when the firms all sell identical, standardized products.

> **tacit collusion:** collusion that takes place without creation of a cartel
> **price fixing:** a form of collusion in which a group of sellers implicitly agrees to maintain a common price
> **price leadership:** a form of collusion in which many sellers follow the price changes instituted by one particular seller

As participants in OPEC discovered, collusion can be hard to sustain. Each seller has an incentive to undercut the agreed set price in order to sell a little more. Nevertheless, collusion has sometimes been persistent. Members may realize that it is in their greater long-term interest to stick with the collusive price rather than to risk losing everything by starting a price war.

5.3 Examples of Oligopoly

Economists frequently refer to data on market shares to determine whether an industry is an oligopoly. The **concentration ratio** is the share of the market, based on revenues, output, or value added, attributed to the largest producers in an industry. Concentration ratios are typically calculated for the largest four or eight firms in an industry. For example, a four-firm concentration ratio of 0.60 indicates that the largest four firms in that industry possess 60 percent of the market. Despite the absence of a precise definition, economists generally conclude that an oligopoly exists wherever four or eight firms account for more than approximately half the entire market.

> **concentration ratio:** the share of the market, based on revenues, output, or value added, attributed to the largest producers in an industry

Figure 6.7 presents the four- and eight-firm concentration ratios for select industries in the United States. We see that several industries, such as cellular

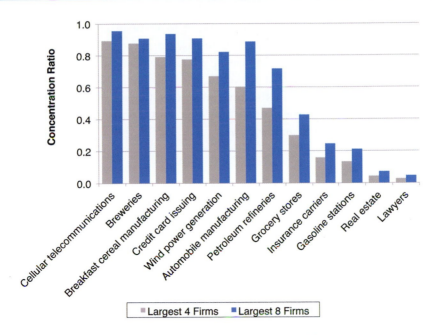

Figure 6.7 *Concentration Ratios for Select Industries, United States, 2012*

Source: U.S. Census Bureau, 2012 Economic Census.

Note: Manufacturing concentration ratios based on value added. All other concentration ratios based on revenues.

telecommunications and credit card issuing, are dominated by just a few companies, which collectively account for 80 or 90 percent of the market; the concentration ratio in these cases is 0.80 or 0.90. Other industries, such as automobile manufacturing and petroleum refining, are not quite as concentrated but still may be considered oligopolies. Finally, industries such as gasoline stations and law are clearly not oligopolies, with concentration ratios of 0.20 or lower.

Discussion Questions

1. What would it mean for two sellers to act noncooperatively? What, instead, would it mean for these two sellers to collude? What real-world examples can you think of?
2. If the government decided to ban advertising in an oligopolistic market (as it has, in the past, banned advertising of cigarettes and alcohol in various media), would that help or hurt the companies' profits?

6. MARKET POWER, EFFICIENCY, AND EQUITY

The traditional models presented in this chapter do not consider the externalities associated with the production and consumption of goods or services. Also, these models ignore the influences of lack of information on production and consumption decisions. However, in the real world, externalities are common, and information is often lacking (and even intentionally distorted to serve other economic interests). Additionally, competitive pressures on firms can lead to job cuts and other cost-minimizing decisions (instead of increasing efficiency) that create social disruptions. Such limitations of the traditional economic models must be considered when making policy decisions that are in the best interest of the society. In this section, we discuss some limitations of the models presented above, with specific focus on issues related to power, efficiency, and equity.

6.1 Market Inefficiencies

One of the implications of the model for perfectly competitive markets is that any firm that does not act in an economically efficient manner will be forced out of the market. But in the real world, inefficiencies may be quite common, even in markets that approach the conditions of perfect competition. We now consider examples of inefficiencies that may exist in any kind of market structure.

Path Dependence

Path dependence, a term borrowed from mathematics, basically means that "history matters" in determining how production technologies—and even entire economies—develop. The development of a path-dependent process is crucially dependent on "initial conditions" and past events. The present state of manufactured capital or human capital, for example, can be thought of as making up part of the initial conditions for current production decisions.

> **path dependence:** the idea that the state of a system such as the economy is strongly shaped by its history

Agriculture offers a good example of path dependence. For example, in the western part of Germany, farms tend to be relatively small, but in the eastern part of Germany, farms tend to be much larger. The explanation has nothing to do with a difference in the minimum efficient scale in the two regions. Instead, it is a result of history—until 1990, Germany was split into two countries, and in East Germany, farms were organized by the government as large collectives.[11]

Health care in the United States is heavily shaped by the forces of path dependency.[12] As part of the New Deal legislation in the 1930s, President Franklin Roosevelt supported universal public health-insurance coverage, but it was defeated in Congress. Then, during World War II, wage controls were implemented that prevented businesses from increasing wages. To attract workers while they were unable to offer higher wages, some firms began to offer health-insurance coverage as a fringe benefit. Labor unions then began to demand health-insurance coverage from employers. As employer-provided health insurance became more common, interest in universal health care faded. The United States now spends more than any other country on health care, as a percentage of GDP, yet many of its health outcomes are rather mediocre when compared to other developed countries that spend less on health care.

Network Externalities

As discussed previously, a production technology is characterized by a network externality if people are more likely to adopt it the more *other* people have adopted it. Take, for example, a city that is trying to increase the use of public transportation in order to decrease road congestion and pollution. If most of the people in the city use the public transportation system, as in New York City and many European cities, it will seem like a normal thing to do; residential and workplace location patterns will reflect the availability of public transportation, the buses and subways will run frequently, and service may be so good that people freely choose it over using a private car. By contrast, if few people use public transportation, it may be stigmatized, routes and services will (in the absence of massive subsidies) tend to be very limited and inconvenient, residences and workplaces will tend to sprawl, and thus ridership will be further discouraged.

Network externalities create another way in which rational decision-making by individuals can lead to inefficient production processes and a failure to maximize long-run social welfare. In other words, the exercise of individual rationality can sometimes produce a collectively irrational outcome. (See Box 6.4 for another example of path dependence and network externalities.)

6.2 Market Power and Politics

The standard economic model of oligopoly suggests two possible conclusions. First, strategic behavior by individual firms in an oligopoly market may limit the negative consequences of market power on consumers. For example, oligopolistic firms may have an incentive to keep their prices low, since raising prices could result in a loss

---

BOX 6.4 THE QWERTY KEYBOARD

A classic example of path dependency is the layout of typewriters and computer keyboards. The conventional QWERTY layout, developed in the nineteenth century, was actually designed to *slow down* typing in order to prevent the keys from jamming on old-fashioned typewriters![13] Studies with modern typewriters and computer keyboards have shown that the QWERTY layout is far from the most efficient.

Alternative keyboard designs have been developed that, with sufficient practice, increase typing speeds and reduce errors. For example, the "Dvorak Simplified Keyboard," patented in the 1930s, groups common letter combinations together and places most of the key strokes on the row where people commonly rest their fingers, making it more ergonomic. However, efforts to market an alternative keyboard layout have consistently failed. The major reason for this failure is that the QWERTY layout has historically been built into an interlinked, economy-wide structure of equipment and training. A shift to a more efficient layout would entail substantial costs in time and money, even though long-run efficiency gains could be achieved.

In sum, you type on a QWERTY keyboard not because it is the most efficient layout but because of a historical quirk and the fact that everyone else is using it.

in market share. Hence, there may be little need for regulations to limit market power.

On the other hand, if the firms cooperate, then market power can be exercised to keep prices, and profits, higher. In this case, the market outcome is likely to result in a reduced level of social well-being, and a stronger argument can be made for regulations that increase economic efficiency or fairness.

The standard economic model of oligopoly focuses on firm cooperation only in terms of setting prices. But instances of firms cooperating with each other to set prices high are relatively rare, and such collusion is generally illegal. Instead, oligopoly firms may actively compete with each other while still effectively exerting market power in other ways to keep profits high. In particular, large firms may acquire the political power to pressure government to enact policies that protect their profits and limit competition. Also, the standard oligopoly model does not address other relevant issues, such as externalities, labor issues, and economic inequality. Thus we need to look beyond this simple model in order to understand oligopoly in the real world.

While we saw previously that many sectors of the U.S. economy can be characterized as oligopolistic, we should also consider whether the U.S. economy as a whole is becoming more concentrated. According to a 2017 analysis, over 75 percent of U.S. industries have become more concentrated over the last couple of decades.[14] The authors conclude that the two main factors driving increased market concentration are lax enforcement of antitrust laws and increased technological barriers to entry. The analysis found that industrial concentration is correlated with higher profit margins for the remaining firms. These findings contradict an optimistic view of markets as self-regulating and competitive, keeping profits at a modest level.

Further evidence indicates that the outcome of most oligopoly markets is not the modest profit levels predicted by the standard model. A 2016 article in *The Economist* expressed concern over the persistence of "exceptional" profits in the U.S. economy.[15] As we've discussed, the existence of economic profits should attract competition that tends to reduce profits over time. But U.S. companies with abnormally high profits seem increasingly able to maintain those high profits while stifling competition. For example, in the 1990s, companies with very high profits (defined as a rate of return in excess of 25 percent) were about 50 percent likely to maintain such profit levels ten years later. More recently, however, highly profitable companies are more than 80 percent likely to sustain those profits over a ten-year period.

The *Economist* article estimates that about one-third of the profits in the U.S. economy are exceptional—well above the return rates on capital that investors generally seek. While profits are necessary in a capitalistic economy, and can provide social benefits through investment and employment, exceptional profits represent a transfer from the rest of society to business owners and executives. Further, these exceptional profits are concentrated in two major sectors: health care and technology. It is likely no coincidence that these are two of the sectors with the highest lobbying expenditures.[16] Exceptional profits can be used to fund intensive lobbying efforts, leading to even higher future profits and barriers to entry for existing or potential competitors.

Nobel Prize–winning economist Joseph Stiglitz has pointed out the relationship between market power, corporate profits, and rising inequality. In 2017, he wrote:

> [M]uch of the increase in inequality [is a result of] redistribution from workers and ordinary savers to the owners of oligopolies and monopolies. . . . We used to think that high profits were a sign of the successful working of the American economy, a better product, a better service. But now we know that higher profits can arise from a better way of exploiting consumers, a better way of price discrimination, extracting consumer surplus, the main effect of which is to redistribute income from consumers to our new super-wealthy. . . . What is required is a panoply of reforms—rewriting the rules of the American economy to make it more competitive and dynamic, fairer and more equal.[17]

What reforms might be able to reverse the trend of the U.S. economy, away from competition, so as to achieve greater equality, and weakening of economic and political power? One obvious area would be stronger enforcement of existing antitrust regulation, along with resistance to efforts to weaken such regulations. Antitrust laws are designed to restrict mergers and acquisitions that significantly reduce market competition and harm consumers.

A second area for reform addresses the relationship between lobbying by companies and other special-interest groups and excessive concentration of economic and political power. In the United States, lobbying is generally highly effective at influencing government policies. According to one study, those companies that spend the most on government lobbying tend to earn significantly higher-than-average profit margins.[18] While all stakeholders in the political process should be entitled to voice their opinions in a functioning democracy, lobbying is currently dominated by corporate interests. Spending on lobbying by corporations exceeds spending by labor unions and other public-interest groups 34 to 1.[19] This imbalance contributes to an economic and political system that serves one segment of society—the largest corporations—at the expense of most small businesses and the general public.

In summary, oligopolistic markets are pervasive in the modern economy. They are not necessarily or inherently problematic. However, they require careful supervision and regulation so that instances of collusion are identified and remedied. Furthermore, because the economic size and power of large oligopolistic firms easily translates to undue influence over policymakers, particular attention needs to be given to insulating the political process from such pressures.

Discussion Questions

1. Try to think of other examples, not mentioned in the text, of path dependence or network externalities. Do you think that these situations are inefficient? Do you think that government policy should play a role in eliminating path dependence and network externalities?

2. An interesting book published in the 1990s, titled *No Contest*, argues for the restructuring of society to promote cooperation rather than competition. The book contends that the pervasive existence of competition in society actually destroys social capital, creates anxiety, and lowers productivity. Do you think that there could be a viable alternative to an economy based on competitive pressures? Should government policies promote competition, cooperation, neither, or both?

REVIEW QUESTIONS

1. List and briefly define the four types of market structures.
2. Describe how consumers, businesses, citizens, and economists view competition and market power.
3. What are the four conditions of perfect competition?
4. What is the difference between accounting and economic profits?
5. How do we determine the profit-maximizing level of production using analysis of total costs and total revenues?
6. What is the rule for profit maximization using marginal analysis in a perfectly competitive market?
7. What happens to economic profits in a perfectly competitive market in the long run?
8. What is the perfectly competitive market equilibrium?
9. What is a sunk cost? How does it influence production decisions, according to economic theory?
10. How should a producer decide whether to operate at a loss or shut down production in the short run?
11. What market conditions characterize pure monopoly?
12. Describe three types of barriers to entry, giving examples of each.
13. How does a pure monopolist maximize profits?
14. In what ways are monopolies inefficient? In what cases might monopolies be efficient?
15. Explain, with a graph, how a price-discriminating seller behaves.
16. What market conditions characterize monopolistic competition?
17. How is a monopolistically competitive firm supposed to maximize profits?
18. Are monopolistically competitive markets efficient? Explain.
19. What market conditions characterize oligopoly?
20. How can firms in oligopoly markets cooperate to increase profits?
21. What are concentration ratios, and how can they determine whether an industry is oligopolistic?
22. What is path dependence?
23. What are network externalities?
24. What is some of the evidence suggesting further regulation of market concentration is warranted?
25. How can government lobbying be reformed to reduce the negative social impacts of market power?

EXERCISES

1. The Top Notch Grill's marginal costs of producing take-out meals are described subsequently.

Quantity of meals	Marginal cost ($)
0	—
1	6
2	5
3	7
4	10
5	12
6	17

   a. Assuming that the Grill has fixed costs of $7, what is its total cost at each level of production? (Add a column to the table.)

   b. Assume that meals sell for $10 each and the Grill is a perfectly competitive firm. What is the Grill's total revenue (price × quantity), marginal revenue, and total profit (total revenue − total cost) at each level of production? (Add three more columns to the table.)

   c. How many meals should the Grill produce to maximize profits? Explain in a sentence or two how you arrived at your answer.

2. Suppose a firm that manufactures bicycles has the following cost structure:

Quantity of bicycles	Total cost ($)
0	50
1	100
2	200
3	400
4	800

   a. How much does this firm have in fixed costs?

   b. Using graph paper or a computer program, graph the total cost curve for this firm. Suppose that bicycles sell for $200 each, and the firm is a price taker. Create a table showing the marginal cost, total cost, marginal revenue, total revenue (price × quantity), and total profit (total revenue − total cost) at each level of production.

   c. Add a total revenue curve to the graph that you created in (b). Indicate with arrows the approximate quantity at which the vertical distance between the two curves is the greatest.

   d. Would the firm make a profit by producing and selling only one bicycle? Would one bicycle be the best output level for the firm? What is the output level that maximizes profits?

3. Continuing with the bicycle firm described in the previous problem, consider how the firm's decision-making will change as the price of bicycles changes. For each of the following, make a new table.

   a. If the price per bicycle were $100, what would the profit-maximizing level of output be? How much profit would the firm make?

   b. If the price per bicycle were $20, what would the profit-maximizing level of output be? How much profit would the firm make?

4. Suppose that a perfectly competitive firm manufactures gizmos with the following cost structure (including all opportunity costs):

Quantity of gizmos	Total cost ($)
0	75
1	150
2	250
3	425
4	675

a. Calculate the marginal cost schedule for this firm in a table, and then graph the marginal cost curve.

b. If the price of gizmos on the market is $175 each, how many gizmos should the firm produce to maximize profits? What is the level of the firm's revenues at its chosen output level? How much does it make in profit?

c. Suppose that more firms start producing gizmos, and the market price drops to $125. How many gizmos should this firm now produce to maximize profits? (*Note:* In the case of discrete quantities such as these, interpret the $P = MC$ rule as "produce as long as price *is at least as great as* marginal cost.") What is this firm's new revenue level? How much does it make in profits?

d. When the price is $125, will more firms want to enter the market? Will existing firms want to exit?

5. When Braeburn Publishing priced its poetry book at $5, it sold 5 books, and when it priced the volume at $8, it sold 4 books. You can calculate that its revenues were higher with the higher price. Suppose that, from further test marketing, this firm determines that it faces the demand curve described by the following schedule.

Quantity of output (demanded)	Selling price ($)	Total revenue ($)	Marginal revenue ($)
1	17		—
2	14		
3	11		
4	8		
5	5		

a. Graph the demand curve for the poetry book, labeling carefully. (Compare your graph to Figure 6.1.)

b. Calculate total revenue and marginal revenue at each output level, and add a marginal revenue curve to your graph.

c. Can the $8 price be Braeburn's profit-maximizing choice? Why or why not?

d. Suppose that, thanks to computerized, on-demand publishing technology, Braeburn can produce any number of books at a constant cost of $5 each. (That is, average cost and marginal cost are both $5 for any quantity of books, and total costs are simply the number of books times $5.) Add a marginal cost curve to your graph. (It will *not* look like the "usual" *MC* curve—it will be horizontal.)

e. What are Braeburn's profit-maximizing price and output levels for the poetry book? State these, and label them on the graph.

f. What level of profit would Braeburn earn with the $8 price? (Recall that profits equal total revenue minus total cost.) What is the level of profit with the price you just found that maximizes profit?

6. Match each concept in Column A with an example in Column B.

Column A	Column B
a. A legal barrier to entry	1. History matters
b. Predatory pricing	2. Patent rights
c. Path dependence	3. Each firm is a price taker
d. Nonprice competition	4. Cornflakes in different-colored boxes
e. Product differentiation	5. I buy an iPhone because everyone else has iPhones
f. Price fixing	6. Cooperating with a rival to charge the same price
g. Condition for perfect competition	7. Advertising
h. Network externality	8. Cutting prices to below cost to drive out a rival

NOTES

1. https://en.wikipedia.org/wiki/Amazon_(company)
2. Molla, Rani. 2017. "Amazon Could Be Responsible for Nearly Half of U.S. E-Commerce Sales in 2017." Recode, October 24. www.recode.net/2017/10/24/16534100/amazon-market-share-ebay-walmart-apple-ecommerce-sales-2017
3. https://en.wikipedia.org/wiki/Jeff_Bezos
4. Levy, Adam. 2016. "Amazon's Most Overlooked Competitive Advantage." Fox Business, November 27.
5. Interlandi, Jeneen. 2010. "The New Oil: Should Private Companies Control Our Most Precious Natural Resource?" Newsweek, October 18.
6. McKiski, Kayla. March 3, 2020. "U.S. Drug Prices Have Risen Three Times Faster than Inflation." U.S. News and World Report.
7. O'Donnell, Jayne. 2016. "Family Matters: EpiPens Had High-Level Help Getting into Schools." USA Today, September 20. www.usatoday.com/story/news/politics/2016/09/20/family-matters-epipens-had-help-getting-schools-manchin-bresch/90435218/
8. Bernstein, Jared. 2016. "Drug Price Controls Are Vital in a Market That's Not Free." New York Times, June 29.
9. https://en.wikipedia.org/wiki/Standard_Oil
10. Fung, Brian. 2013. "Apple's Violation of Antitrust Law, Explained in 6 Bullet Points." The Atlantic, July 10.
11. Ostermeyer, Arlette, and Alfons Balmann. 2011. "Perception of Dairy Farming from Different Views: Results of a Stakeholder Discussion in the Region Altmark, Germany." Paper presented at the EAAE 2011 Congress, Change and Uncertainty, Zurich, Switzerland, August 30–September 2.
12. Page, Scott E. 2006. "Path Dependence." Quarterly Journal of Political Science, 1: 87–115.
13. David, Paul A. 1985. "Clio and the Economics of QWERTY." American Economic Review, 75(2): 332–337.
14. Grullon, Gustavo, Yelena Larkin, and Roni Michaely. 2017. "Are U.S. Industries Becoming More Concentrated?" SSRN, August. https://ssrn.com/abstract=2612047

15. Anonymous. 2016. "Too Much of a Good Thing." *The Economist*, March 26.

16. Sectoral Data on Lobbying Expenses from the Center on Responsive Politics. www.opensecrets.org/

17. Stiglitz, Joseph. 2017. "America Has a Monopoly Problem—And It's Huge." *The Nation*, October 23.

18. Anonymous. 2011. "Money and Politics: Ask What Your Country Can Do for You." *The Economist*, October 1.

19. Drutman, Lee. 2015. "How Corporate Lobbyists Conquered American Democracy." *The Atlantic*, April 20.

Chapter 7

Markets for Labor

For most people, few things are more important than the ability to secure a good job with an adequate wage or salary. The work that we do is central to our well-being. Research shows that those who are more satisfied with their jobs tend to have higher life satisfaction.[1] Meanwhile, being unemployed has significant negative impacts on one's mental and physical health.[2] For these reasons, issues of employment, unemployment, and wages are central to the study of economics. In this chapter, we will present the basic economic theory of labor markets and take a detailed look at how labor markets function. We will also offer some perspectives on current challenges in the labor market and discuss future prospects on how employment might look for workers and societies at large.

1. ECONOMIC THEORY OF LABOR MARKETS

The markets for labor are different from other markets in many ways. For a start, what is sold in labor markets is not people (that would be slavery) but the willingness of people to undertake paid work. This is sometimes called "labor power"—that is, what a given person is able and willing to do in a given amount of time. An employer who hires a certain amount of labor power (X number of people working for Y hours) expects that it will produce a certain level of output. But it is not the actual output that is being purchased in this market—it is the contribution that employees make toward the production of output. This makes labor markets different from markets for the things that labor produces, such as sweaters, jet planes, or haircuts.

The neoclassical model of labor starts with a familiar idea—that the market is based on the interaction of supply and demand. It assumes that in some ways labor markets *are* similar to markets for other things. The demand side of labor markets is composed of firms seeking to maximize their profits. The supply side is composed of people seeking to maximize their utility, in this case by exchanging their labor power for payment.

Like the neoclassical consumer model in Chapter 4, the neoclassical labor model ignores the significance of historical and social contexts in influencing market outcomes. For example, it assumes that people seek employment purely in order to earn money, disregarding any intrinsic motivations or benefits associated with work. Just like any other market model, the labor market model is used to study prices and quantities. Thus it is concerned with estimating how much labor will be supplied and purchased, and at what price (wage). To determine this using the neoclassical model, we need a theory both of the demand and the supply of labor.

1.1 The Firm's Decision to Hire Labor

On the demand side of the labor market, a profit-maximizing firm would have an incentive to hire labor only if an additional person–hour of labor will increase its profits, but not otherwise. When a firm hires an additional person–hour, its cost increases by the amount of additional wage paid. At the same time, the additional labor increases the firm's potential revenue by raising its output. As long as the firm gets *more* additional revenue than it has to pay out in additional wages, its profit increases, and hence it should keep hiring workers. But if it is getting *less* in additional revenue than it is paying out in additional wages, its profit declines, and it should reduce the number of workers that it hires. The profit-maximizing decision rule for the firm can thus be expressed as hiring labor up to the point where:

$$MRP_L = MFC_L$$

where MRP_L is the **marginal revenue product of labor**, or the amount that an additional unit of labor contributes to revenues, and MFC_L is the **marginal factor cost of labor**, or the amount that the additional unit of labor adds to the firm's costs. Note that hiring an additional unit of labor clearly adds to the wages the firm must pay, but it may also increase other costs, such as energy and supplies. However, for simplicity, let us assume that the MFC_L is just the additional wages and that for the individual firm, hiring another unit of labor doesn't change the wages paid to any other workers. A formal derivation of this rule is described in an online Appendix to this chapter.

> **marginal revenue product of labor (MRP_L):** the amount that a unit of additional labor contributes to the revenues of the firm
> **marginal factor cost of labor (MFC_L):** the amount that a unit of additional labor adds to the firm's costs

If the firm buys labor services in a competitive market, MFC_L will simply be the competitively determined market wage, and the rule will simplify to:

$$MRP_L = \text{Wage}$$

In most situations, the marginal revenue product of labor will decline as more workers are hired. A factory, for example, may be able to increase output by hiring more workers, but beyond a certain point, additional workers will usually bring less benefit in terms of increased production. This may be due to several reasons, including the possibility that the workplace is becoming crowded and there is no longer sufficient equipment to give to each worker. A firm will typically expand hiring

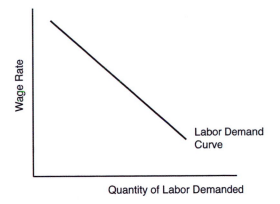

Figure 7.1 *An Individual Firm's Labor Demand Curve*

so long as the MRP_L is above the wage the firm has to pay. This creates a downward-sloping demand curve for labor, as shown in Figure 7.1.

1.2 The Individual's Decision to Supply Labor

We now consider how much time an individual is willing to work, given different wage levels, assuming that people seek to maximize their utility. This simple model also assumes that the potential labor market participant has perfect information regarding available jobs and wages, and is free to vary his or her hours of paid work. The hours of paid work that an individual can supply is, however, limited by the amount of available time (i.e., 24 hours per day, 7 days per week, etc.). An individual can spend his or her time either on paid work or on unpaid work and leisure.

Hours "spent" on paid labor result in wages, which in turn give opportunities for consumption. Hours spent on other activities yield utility either directly (as in the case of leisure) or indirectly through unpaid production such as cooking and cleaning. In the neoclassical model, paid work is generally assumed to yield no direct utility. The potential labor market participant will choose the level of paid labor market participation that maximizes his or her utility.

We look at the decision of an individual to supply various amounts of work hours over a given time period—say, a week—assuming, for the moment, that the worker can find a paid job. For now, we only focus on the decision about how much time to put into paid work given a certain wage rate. A reasonable first thought is that a labor supply curve will slope upward since as the wage rate increases, paid work becomes more attractive relative to other activities. The opportunity cost of *not* working also increases as the wage rate goes up. We can think of a substitution effect, where workers substitute away from leisure and other activities, and toward more work, as the wage rate increases. We show this in Figure 7.2, where the wage rate is on the vertical axis and the quantity of labor, measured in time units, is on the horizontal axis.

But as the wage gets higher and higher, will the person *always* want to work more and more? Probably not. As people earn higher incomes, they may also want

211

Figure 7.2 *Upward-Sloping Labor Supply Curve*

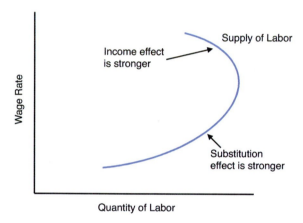

Figure 7.3 *Backward-Bending Individual Labor Supply Curve*

more time to enjoy the fruits of their labor. So we also need to consider an income effect: the higher the market wage, the more leisure (and other unpaid activities) people will want to "buy." Imagine you are already making a good wage rate, and you get a raise. You may well decide to work less rather than more, assuming you have the choice. In this case, a higher wage rate leads to a lower quantity of labor supplied and a backwards-sloping labor supply curve!

Economists usually believe that, at relatively low wage rates, the substitution effect will dominate. But eventually, when wages rise enough, the income effect will dominate. The overall result is a **backward-bending individual paid labor supply curve**, as shown in Figure 7.3. So the existence of the income effect means that the individual labor supply curve looks rather different from our normal supply curve in previous chapters.

> **backward-bending individual paid labor supply curve:** a labor supply curve that arises because, beyond some level of wages, income effects outweigh substitution effects in determining individuals' decisions about how much to work

1.3 The Market Supply for Labor

We now broaden our thinking, moving from labor demand by an individual firm and labor supply by an individual worker to the market level. We first extend our analysis of labor supply and then consider market-level labor demand.

The supply of labor to a particular market, such as the national market for aerospace engineers or the market for restaurant wait staff in Chicago, can be thought of as the horizontal sum of the supply curves of those individuals who could participate in the market. Although the supply curves of some individuals might bend backward, the supply curve for a particular market can generally be assumed to have the usual upward slope, similar to Figure 7.2. This is because employers can obtain a larger quantity of labor either by persuading workers already in the market to supply more hours or by attracting more workers to enter the particular market by drawing them away from other jobs or drawing them into the paid labor force from other activities. For most of these workers, we can assume that the substitution effect dominates, and so the supply curve will slope upward.

Market labor supply is relatively wage elastic if a variation in the wage brings a large change in the quantity of labor supplied. Markets for types of labor that use general or more easily acquired skills generally tend to have relatively elastic supply curves. If the local wage for restaurant wait staff rises, for example, people may leave jobs as salesclerks in order to offer their services to restaurants. If the wages paid by restaurants fall, wait staff may look for jobs as salesclerks and drivers.

Market labor supply is relatively wage inelastic, however, if a variation in the wage brings little change in the quantity of labor supplied. At the extreme, the supply of labor might be "fixed" for some occupations, at least in the short run. For example, there are only so many aerospace engineers in the United States at any point in time. Raising the wage might draw a few engineers out of retirement or self-employment, but it cannot instantly produce a large quantity of new engineers, because obtaining the skills necessary for this job requires many years of education. In such cases, changes in labor supply will occur only over the long run, as high wages attract more students to train for the job or low wages cause more engineers to retrain for something else. For a real-world example of a labor shortage, see Box 7.1.

We can also think of the supply of labor not just in terms of the market for a specific type of job, such as aerospace engineers, but with regard to the labor market for an entire region or country. In this case, we are considering the total number of people willing to supply their labor as a function of the average wage rate. Economists define the percentage of adults willing to work at current wages as the **labor force participation rate**. In the United States, the labor force participation rate in 2019 was about 63 percent. That is lower than it was in the early 2000s but higher than it was in the 1950s and 1960s.[3] We will discuss trends in labor force participation in more detail in Section 3.

> **labor force participation rate:** the percentage of the adult, noninstitutionalized population that is either working at a paid job or actively seeking paid work

> ### BOX 7.1 A SHORTAGE OF DOCTORS
>
> Even before the Covid-19 pandemic, the shortage of doctors in the United States was expected to worsen, due to changes on both the demand and supply side. According to a 2019 study, before the pandemic, the shortfall of doctors was predicted to be between 46,900 and 121,900 by 2032.[4] A long-run change on the demand side is the aging of the American population, given that health care needs generally increase with age. By 2032, the number of Americans over age 65 is predicted to increase by 48 percent.
>
> On the supply side, one problem is that the supply of doctors is relatively inelastic in the short term. It commonly takes about 10 to 15 years from the time an undergraduate decides to become a doctor to the time when he or she can actually start practicing.[5] Another problem is that about one in four doctors in the United States are foreign born. Tighter immigration policies being pursued by the Trump administration could restrict the supply of foreign-born doctors, exacerbating the shortage. Finally, the predicted doctor shortage will be even larger if steps are taken to reduce health care inequalities in the country. Expanding health insurance coverage and reducing economic inequalities, particularly related to race, would further increase the demand for doctors.

Labor supply curves can also *shift* in response to nonprice factors, just like the shifts in other supply curves that we studied in Chapter 3. For the economy as a whole, for example, labor supply curves tend to shift outward over time because of population growth. Changes in gender norms and household technology have resulted in outward shifts in labor supply curves for professions such as law and medicine as increasing numbers of women have entered those fields.

1.4 Market Demand Curves

The demand curve for paid labor—whether for a specific job type (e.g., the demand for aerospace engineers) or for the entire labor market—can generally be thought of as downward sloping, like the demand curves we examined in Chapter 3. This is true for the individual firm's demand for labor, as well as for the market demand curve for labor, made up of the horizontal sum of the demand curves of individual firms. The reason for the downward slope is that when wages are high employers have incentives to economize on the use of labor. They may cut back on production or try to substitute other inputs (e.g., machinery or computerization) for the type of labor whose wage is high. But when wages are low employers may be able to expand production or substitute relatively cheap labor for other inputs. In terms of the marginal revenue product logic discussed previously, we can say that firms are willing to accept a lower marginal revenue product of labor when wages are low but will insist on a high marginal revenue product when wages are high.

Labor demand will tend to be relatively wage elastic if there are good substitute inputs available and if the wage bill is a large proportion of total production costs (so that the employers are motivated to seek out substitutes). Labor demand will tend to be relatively inelastic if no good substitute inputs are available and the wage bill is a small proportion of total costs. A 2015 meta-analysis based on over 100 studies from all regions of the world finds that labor demand tends to be inelastic, averaging around 0.20 in the short run and 0.40 in the long run.[6] We would expect labor demand to be more elastic in the long run as employers have more time to find substitutes for relatively expensive labor. The article also found that demand is more elastic for low-skilled workers, as it is easier to find substitutes for workers without specialized skills.

The labor demand curve may shift if there is a change in the demand for the good or service that it is used to produce, if technological developments alter the production process, if the number of employers changes, or if the price or availability of other inputs changes. For example, when an organization experiences a fall in demand for its products, its labor demand curve will shift back as well.

1.5 Market Adjustment

We can now examine how market forces might influence wage rates and the quantity of labor employed. For example, Figure 7.4 depicts a stylized labor market for real estate agents in the United States. In the early 2000s, housing sales were booming, and demand for the services of real estate agents was high, as depicted by demand curve D_1. Stories in the newspapers at the time touted the fat salaries real estate agents could make, as many people were buying homes in order to "flip" them in a short time period at a profit.

When the housing bubble burst in 2006 and 2007, home sales declined by about half, and the demand for real estate agents similarly declined. The labor market for real estate agents went from boom to bust. We can think of this as the demand curve shifting to D_2.

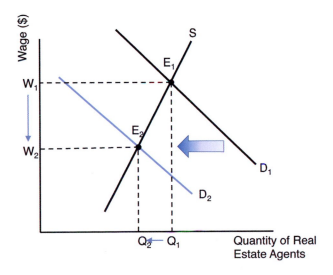

Figure 7.4 *The Labor Market for Real Estate Agents*

Comparing equilibrium E_1 to equilibrium E_2, we can see that the model predicts that the number of real estate agents will fall and that the wage will fall as well. In fact, employment for real estate agents declined by more than 25 percent during the Great Recession and real wages did decline.[7] More recently, employment and wages for real estate agents have started to rise again as the housing market has recovered. (How would this appear in Figure 7.4?)

Labor market adjustment takes time—the movement from E_1 to E_2 is not instantaneous. It takes time for workers to change their career plans and for employers to adjust wages and salaries, which may be set by labor contracts. Given that labor market conditions are constantly changing, it may be unclear whether a particular labor market is in equilibrium. Much of the recent labor economics research has focused on the persistence of "friction" in labor markets, which slows the transition of workers from one job to another. In particular, unemployed workers may spend considerable time searching for a job that meets their specific requirements.

The existence of labor market friction means that a significant number of job openings typically exist, even during periods of unemployment. For example, in February 2019, unemployment was 3.8 percent in the United States and 6.2 million people were unemployed, but there were also 7.1 million job openings.[8]

Discussion Questions

1. Suppose that your college or university substantially raises the wages that it offers to pay students who tend computer laboratories. What do you think would happen to the quantity of labor supplied? Why? Where would the extra labor hours come from? Do you think the supply of this kind of labor is elastic or inelastic? Why?

2. Opticians fit people who have poor eyesight with glasses or contact lenses. Beginning in the 1990s, technological developments in laser eye surgery made surgery an increasingly popular way of correcting bad eyesight. What effect do you think this development had on the market for opticians? Draw a graph, carefully showing whether the shift is in demand or supply and showing the resulting predicted changes in the quantity of labor demanded and in the wage.

2. EXPLAINING VARIATIONS IN WAGES

Among the things that economists are especially eager to understand about labor markets are differences in wages. Why do professional basketball players (average annual salary over $6 million in 2016)[9] make so much more than aerospace engineers (average salary of $112,000), who in turn earn so much more than preschool teachers (average salary of $40,000)?[10] In addition, within the same job definition, it is possible to find workers who receive very different compensation, even though they seem to have equivalent qualifications and are hired from the same job market. Women in the United States are paid, on average, only 85 percent of male wages.[11] Are such patterns of wage differentials irresistibly determined by the logic of markets? If not, what other forces affect them?

2.1 Wage Variations in the Neoclassical Labor Model

In the neoclassical labor model, the demand for labor—the employers' willingness to pay for different types of labor services—is solely a function of how productive workers are. This emphasis requires a number of restrictive assumptions: that people behave in a rational, purely self-interested way; that market forces are strong; and that markets are fully competitive. Employers pay their workers based on their contribution to production—what we have called the marginal revenue product of labor.

According to this model, the main reason for variations in labor productivity, and hence in wages, is human capital. This consists of people's knowledge and skills, which is affected by their education, training, and experiences, as well as their physical and mental health. The wages for skilled occupations, such as aerospace engineers (e.g., compared to farm manual laborers), reflect in part the fact that aerospace engineers have normally engaged in formal training to acquire skills and credentials, whereas farm laborers largely use more common skills that, it is assumed, most people possess. A worker's productivity may also depend on several other factors, such as the level of effort with which workers work and the resources available to each worker.

Early economic thinkers put forth the idea that extra pay is required to attract workers to take jobs that are especially unappealing compared to other work that is available for people at the same skill level. For example, jobs with an elevated risk of injury or death, such as commercial fisher, logger, or roofer, tend to pay more than other jobs that require similar human capital levels. On the other hand, people may sometimes accept a lower wage to perform an especially appealing job. The example that professors usually give is the job of being a professor; for those who like the intellectual life, it may be a very rewarding job, even though the pay is often below what professors believe that they could earn elsewhere.

All these are examples that illustrate the theory of **compensating wage differentials**. This theory states that extra compensation is needed to attract people to particularly unattractive jobs, while workers may be willing to accept relatively low pay for jobs with desirable characteristics. But it is certainly not true in general that unpleasant or dangerous jobs have higher pay. You have probably noticed that many of the least attractive jobs in a society—such as garbage collection, agricultural work, and boring and repetitive work in clothing manufacture or meat processing— are found at the lowest end of the pay scale. This is partly because they require relatively little in the way of formal qualifications. To the extent that this is true, the low wages do not violate the theory of compensating wage differentials; this theory compares only jobs of equal skill. But even within the class of jobs that require few qualifications, some jobs pay particularly badly, especially when workers belong to particular groups—usually minority or female, nonunionized, and often immigrants. This suggests that we may need to consider other factors than the simple neoclassical theory of productivity to understand wage differentials.

> **compensating wage differentials:** the theory that, all else being equal, workers will be willing to accept lower wages for jobs with better characteristics and will demand higher wages for jobs with unappealing characteristics

2.2 Social Norms, Wage Regulations, and Bargaining Power

As suggested by some of the examples that we have already mentioned, the neoclassical labor model does not explain all variations in wages across occupations and across workers. We now turn to various other factors that influence wages.

One factor that may prevent wages from reaching equilibrium is minimum wage laws. As illustrated in Figure 7.5, if employers are required to pay a minimum wage of $W*$, which is above the equilibrium wage, employers' demand for workers (L_D) will be lower than the number of people seeking jobs (L_S). Hence, there is a situation of labor surplus (that is, people are unemployed) because legal restrictions on employers prevent the market from adjusting to equilibrium. The standard microeconomic reasoning thus suggests that minimum wages cause substantial unemployment.

However, in a well-known study, economists David Card and Alan Krueger found that a moderate increase in the minimum wage in New Jersey did not cause low-wage employment to decline and may have even increased it.[12] The economic logic behind this result is that the rise in minimum wages could increase people's income and consumption levels, which increases the demand for goods and services in the economy and leads to job creation. This reasoning is based on the Keynesian theory, which will be introduced in Chapter 9. The Card and Krueger study, however, came under fire from some neoclassical economists who believed that such a result simply could not be true based on the theory of supply and demand.

Another factor that may prevent wages from adjusting downward due to market forces is social norms. According to the neoclassical labor model, wages should adjust downward when demand decreases or supply increases. In reality, employers are usually slow to impose significant wage reductions either because they don't want to cause hardship among employees or because they may fear that workers will resist such a move—perhaps with strikes and other labor actions such as putting in less effort at work. Because the social norm is for wages to adjust upward, not downward, there could be psychological resistance to wage cuts. Often when businesses find that their revenue does not readily support the existing payroll, instead of lowering wages, some workers are laid off.

In addition to social norms, an essential aspect of most labor markets is the bargaining power on each side. Firms may be able to keep wages low if they have a

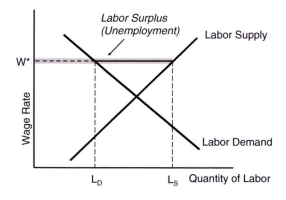

Figure 7.5 Unemployment due to Minimum Wage Regulations

greater bargaining power. This could occur, for instance, under the condition of **monopsony**, where a firm is the only employer to whom a certain group of workers can look for work. In the 1900s, for example, some manufacturing companies (including Hershey's for chocolate) set up "company towns" in which they were the sole major employer. In such cases, workers may have to accept the company's low wages as the price of keeping their jobs—unless they have the ability and the determination to leave the area.

More common in labor markets are cases of **oligopsony**, in which there are just a few employers. For example, someone looking for work as a supermarket stocker may have little power to bargain over their wages since there are just a few major supermarket chains, and these large employers have considerable power in setting wages. In theory, even a few large employers could compete against each other for employees, thereby bidding wages up, but in situations where the employees do not have specialized skills, this is unlikely.

> **monopsony:** a situation in which there is only one buyer but many sellers. This situation occurs in a labor market in which there are many potential workers but only one employer
>
> **oligopsony:** a situation in which there are only a few major buyers but many sellers. This situation occurs in a labor market when there are many potential workers but just a few large employers

Labor unions are legally recognized organizations that collectively bargain for their members regarding wages, benefits, and working conditions. As seen in Figure 7.6, membership in labor unions in the United States peaked in the mid-1950s,

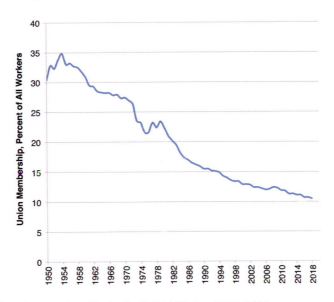

Figure 7.6 *Union Membership in the United States, 1950–2018*

Sources: Mayer, Gerald. 2004. "Union Membership Trends in the United States." Congressional Research Service, Washington, DC. U.S. Bureau of Labor Statistics, 2019.

when over one-third of all wage and salary workers were unionized. Since then, membership in unions has gradually but steadily declined. In 2018, less than 11 percent of workers in the United States belonged to a union.

One of the reasons for the decline in union membership in the United States in recent decades has been an anti-union regulatory environment. For example, states such as Wisconsin and Indiana have passed new laws limiting the power of labor unions since 2011. Another reason for the decline of labor unions has been a shift in employment from traditional unionized occupations such as manufacturing to service occupations, such as retail and restaurant workers, in which it is more difficult to unionize.

> **labor unions:** legally recognized organizations that collectively bargain for their members (workers) regarding wages, benefits, and working conditions

Union membership rates are higher in most other industrialized countries. For example, union membership is 17 percent in Japan, 29 percent in Canada, 36 percent in Italy, 52 percent in Norway, and 67 percent in Sweden.[13] However, in most countries, union membership rates have been declining in recent years.

Labor unions have been effective at providing good-paying jobs and improving working conditions for their members. According to the U.S. Bureau of Labor Statistics, the average weekly earnings of unionized private-sector workers in 2018 were $1,051 per week, compared to earnings of $860 for non-union workers.[14] Union workers are also more likely to have employer-provided benefits such as health insurance and paid vacations. Based on such evidence, some economists see labor unions as a way for workers to bargain on an equal footing with management. The decline of unions is widely considered a contributing factor in the rise of economic inequality in the United States, which we discuss in more detail in Chapter 13.

Some economists see the decline in labor union membership as a positive development, arguing that unions had pushed wages to above-market levels.[15] According to this view, while unions were probably necessary to counter the excessive power of corporations in the first half of the twentieth century, they had become a source of market inefficiency by the end of the century.

2.3 Efficiency Wages and Dual Labor Markets

Economists have theorized that employers may sometimes pay wages somewhat above the market-determined level as a way of motivating and retaining workers. **Efficiency wage theory** proposes that workers will work harder and "smarter" when they know that their present employer is paying them more than they could receive elsewhere. The higher wages might prompt workers to feel more valued and to see their employer as generous, thus incentivizing them to work harder. Furthermore, because these wages are above the market-clearing level, there is likely to be a queue of potential workers who would like to get the relatively high wages. This fact may also add to employee motivation, because they understand that if they were

BOX 7.2 GOOD JOBS ARE GOOD FOR BUSINESS

According to a 2012 study,[16] providing employees with "good" jobs and paying efficiency wages can frequently be good for business, too. This idea runs counter to prevailing notion that companies have no choice but to offer "bad" jobs—especially retailers, whose business models entail competition for customers by offering low prices. If retailers invest more in employees, customers will have to pay more, so the assumption goes.

Several businesses in the study provide their employees with "good" jobs, including Trader Joe's and Costco. Trader Joe's starting salary of around $40,000 per year is about twice what many of its competitors offer. Costco's wages are about 40 percent higher than those of its main competitor, Wal-Mart's Sam's Clubs. Turnover at both Trader Joe's and Costco is low, and employee morale is relatively high. These companies are also known for high-quality customer service. The study found that, rather than hurting these firms' profits, they actually financially outperform their competitors. For example, annual revenues per square foot are $986 at Costco but only $588 at Sam's Club. Sales at Trader Joe's are about three times that of a typical U.S. supermarket. Hence, companies may be able to increase profits by offering higher wages to their workers and promoting worker efficiency and dedication.

to shirk, they could be easily replaced, and they might have to take another job with lower wages. Thus, it is theorized that efficiency wages can be profit maximizing: The cost to the firm of the extra wages may be more than made up for by the superior work effort and loyalty that they elicit. (See Box 7.2 for more on the potential benefits of efficiency wages.)

efficiency wage theory: the theory that an employer can motivate workers to put forth more effort by paying them somewhat more than they could get elsewhere

The theory of **dual labor markets** is based on the idea that labor markets are segmented between a "primary" sector with relatively high wages, opportunities for advancement, job security, and perhaps other favorable working conditions, and a "secondary" sector with none of these characteristics. Various issues of class background, education, and employment experience could get some workers stuck in the secondary sector or else make it relatively easy for more fortunate workers to enter, and stay in, a primary sector.

dual labor markets: a situation in which *primary* sector workers enjoy high wages, opportunities for advancement, and job security, while *secondary* sector workers are generally hired with low wages, no opportunities for advancement, and little job security

Such labor market segmentation may take place across firms or within a single organization. Contemporary versions of this theory emphasize the difference between

---

BOX 7.3 THE LOSS OF GOOD JOBS

A 2012 report from the Center for Economic and Policy Research defines "a good job" as "one that pays at least $37,000 per year, has employer-provided health insurance, and an employer-sponsored retirement plan." By this definition, the share of workers with a "good job" fell from 27.4 percent in 1979 to 24.6 percent in 2010. The writers go on to say that:

> if technological change were behind the decline in good jobs, then we would expect that a higher—probably substantially higher—share of workers with a four-year college degree or more would have good jobs today. Instead, at every age level, workers with four years or more of college are actually less likely to have a good job now than three decades ago.

The writers conclude that the decline in good jobs is "related to a deterioration in the bargaining power of workers, especially those at the middle and the bottom of the income scale."[17] Along similar lines, economic writer Neil Irwin commented in September 2017 that:

> as more companies have outsourced more functions over more time, a strong body of evidence is emerging that it's not just about efficiency. It seems to be a way for big companies to reduce compensation costs.
>
> . . . Pay for janitors fell by 4 to 7 percent and for security guards by 8 to 24 percent in American companies that outsourced, Arindrajit Dube of the University of Massachusetts-Amherst and Ethan Kaplan of Stockholm University found in a 2010 paper.[18]

---

workers who have a (fairly) secure relationship with the employer and those who are taken on "as needed." Examples of the latter include alternative employment arrangements such as contract work, on-call work, temporary help agencies, and others in the "gig" economy, where employment isn't defined by a steady, full-time job but by shorter-term freelance or contract projects. According to estimates from a Gallup poll, about 29 percent of all U.S. workers have an alternative work arrangement as their primary job.[19]

2.4 Discrimination

Labor market discrimination exists when, among similarly qualified people, some are treated disadvantageously in employment on the basis of race, sex, age, sexual preference, physical appearance, or disability. Workers who belong to disfavored groups may be paid less for the same work, may be denied promotions, or may simply be excluded from higher-paying and higher-status occupations.

> **labor market discrimination:** a condition that exists when, among similarly qualified people, some are treated disadvantageously in employment on the basis of race, sex, age, sexual preference, physical appearance, or disability

Historically, much labor market discrimination, particularly against African Americans and other minorities, was based on racist beliefs that certain groups were innately inferior. Some discrimination against women was similarly based on sexist notions of inferiority. Gender discrimination is also historically rooted in social norms that reserved better-paying jobs for men (who were assumed to be supporting families), while making women (who were assumed to have husbands to rely on) solely responsible for providing unpaid household labor and family care.

In Figure 7.7, we compare median weekly earnings in the United States of full-time, year-round workers in various groups, using government data from 2018. *Median* earnings are at a level where half the people in the group make more and half less. We see that median earnings vary significantly by both race and sex. The median earnings of black male workers were only about 73 percent of the earnings of their white male counterparts, and the median earnings of Hispanic male workers were only 70 percent of white male earnings. Disparities among female workers of different races also exist, although the differences are somewhat less pronounced. White female workers only earn about 80 percent of the earnings of their white male counterparts. Gender disparities are also evident among male and female workers of other races.

The data in Figure 7.7 are not necessarily evidence of wage discrimination. Some variations in wages may be due to factors outside the labor market itself, such as differences in experience, education, and occupational choice (although some of these differences may also be a result of discrimination). For example, educational

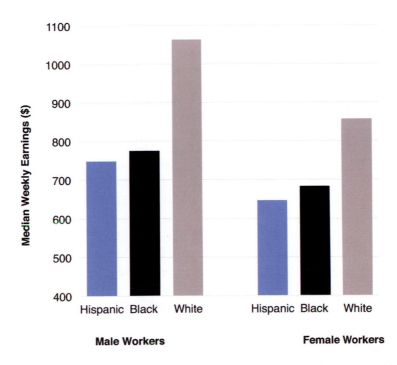

Figure 7.7 *Median Weekly Earnings, Select Groups of U.S. Workers, Age 25 and Over, 2018*

Source: U.S. Bureau of Labor Statistics, 2019.

levels vary by race—about 33 percent of white individuals have a bachelor's degree or higher, compared to 23 percent of black and 16 percent of Hispanic individuals.[20] Such differences in educational attainment can have a significant impact on earnings.

Educational attainment does not vary significantly by gender in the United States (actually, a slightly higher percentage of women have a college degree).[21] So the differences in earnings by gender in Figure 7.7 cannot be attributed to differences in education. Part of the explanation for women's lower earnings is that women have traditionally had less work experience than men, on average. While men tend to work more continuously at their jobs, women often work less than full time or not at all to attend to family responsibilities, especially when their children are young.

Another important factor in explaining earnings differences by gender is **occupational segregation**—the tendency of men and women to be found in different kinds of jobs. For example, in the United States, jobs like bookkeeper, dental hygienist, child-care worker, registered nurse, and preschool teacher are held overwhelmingly by women. Meanwhile, men dominate in occupations such as construction trades, metal working, truck driving, and engineering. Occupational segregation could be a result of differences in preferences, or it could also reflect discrimination. For example, existing stereotypes may lead more women to become nurses, while doctors are more likely to be men.

> **occupational segregation:** the tendency of men and women to be employed in different occupations
>
> **gender wage gap:** the difference in average wages between men and women; women are paid, on average, less than men

The **gender wage gap**—the difference in average wages between men and women—has declined in the United States in recent decades.[22] In 1980, women's average wages were 64 percent of men's wages. By 2018, women's wages were about 85 percent of men's wages. Despite this progress, the gender wage gap in the United States is still larger than some other industrialized nations such as Norway, Belgium, and New Zealand, where women earn about 93 percent of what men earn.[23]

According to a 2016 analysis, about half of the difference between men's and women's pay in the United States is associated with differences in industry and occupation choice.[24] Another factor explaining the gender wage gap is workforce interruptions, such as taking time off to care for family members. However, even after accounting for gender differences in education, experience, occupational choice, and other variables, about 40 percent of the gender pay gap remains unexplained. At least part of this unexplained difference can be attributed to discrimination.

As shown in Figure 7.7, the gap in wages based on race is larger than the gap based on gender. While the gap in wages between black and white workers in the United States narrowed in the 1990s due to low unemployment and minimum wage increases, it has increased since 2000 as black workers were more negatively impacted by the Great Recession.[25] Economists have used statistical studies to test if discrimination is a factor in explaining the difference in wages between workers of different races. A 2017 paper that reviewed the results of 28 studies found that applicants with white-sounding names receive, on average, 36 percent more callbacks than black applicants and 24 percent more callbacks than Latinos.[26] The authors conclude that the results "document a striking persistence of racial discrimination in U.S. labor markets."

Discussion Questions

1. According to the U.S. Bureau of Labor Statistics, the hourly median wage in 2017 is $10.87 for home health aides, $24.29 for firefighters, $38.39 for computer programmers, $56.81 for lawyers, and $76.81 for dentists.[27] Based on the information in this section, try to explain why the wages for these various occupations differ. Do you think these wage differences are justified based on market forces? Also, do you think these wage differences are fair, based on the social contribution of each job?
2. What do you think society should be doing, if anything, to reduce labor market discrimination? Do you have any experience with discrimination in the workplace?

3. SPECIAL ISSUES FOR THE TWENTY-FIRST CENTURY

For the remainder of this chapter, we consider several issues that reflect recent changes in labor markets. The six topics covered in this section are:

1. Changes in labor force participation rates
2. Labor market flexibility
3. Labor markets and immigration
4. Cooperatives
5. Work–life balance
6. Technology, productivity, work, and leisure

3.1 Labor Force Participation Rates

As discussed previously, the labor force participation (LFP) rate is the percentage of noninstitutionalized adults that are either working or seeking a job. Of course, many people don't want, or may not need, a job, such as students, retirees, or those taking time off from working for personal reasons such as child care or health concerns. The U.S. labor force participation rate in 2018 was 63 percent, but looking at Figure 7.8, we see that this rate differs significantly between men and women. Labor force participation for men has been steadily declining since 1960. Female labor participation steadily increased up to 2000, leveled off, and then began to decline more recently.

What factors explain these trends? The increase in female labor participation up to 2000 largely reflects increased work opportunities for women. The women's rights

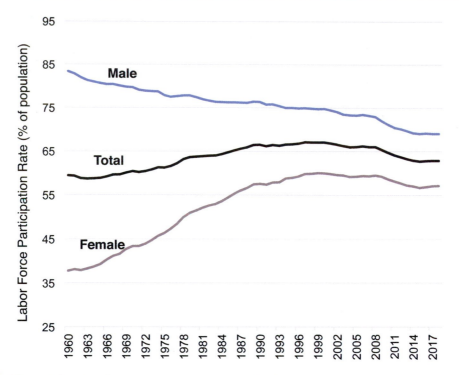

Figure 7.8 *Labor Force Participation Rates, 1960–2018*

Source: U.S. Bureau of Labor Statistics, 2019.

movement during the 1960s and 1970s, along with the expansion of the service sector and reductions in the average number of children per family, all contributed to an increase in women's labor market activities. In addition, the reduction in the gender pay gap meant that the opportunity cost to women of not working increased, thus increasing female labor supply.

To some extent, the decline in male labor force participation in the 1960s and 1970s can also be attributed to a greater gender balance in paid work within families. But more recently, labor force participation has been declining for both men and women, particularly after the Great Recession. Over the last several decades, the United States has gone from having one of the highest labor force participation rates among industrialized countries to one of the lowest.[28] Economists attribute this recent decline to two main factors: that many people have dropped out of the labor force from being unable to find acceptable jobs and other difficulties, and that various demographic changes are putting downward pressure on labor force participation.[29]

The demographic changes include an aging population and higher educational attainment. An increasing share of Americans are retired and thus voluntarily out of the labor force (although this group could include some who involuntarily retired early due to lack of job opportunities). Also, a higher proportion of young (and some older) people are attending college and graduate school, voluntarily removing themselves from the labor force.

BOX 7.4 LABOR FORCE PARTICIPATION OF PRIME-AGE MEN

In the past 60 years, the share of men between the ages of 25 and 54 either working or actively seeking work, also known as the prime-age male labor force participation rate, has been falling. While over 96 percent of prime-age men were in the labor force until the 1960s, this number has gradually declined to about 89 percent today.[30] The decline has been steepest, and the rate remains lowest, for prime-age black men, who suffer the highest rates of unemployment.

These data raise some obvious questions; for one, how are these individuals getting by? If we assume that the workforce drop-outs are dependent on a working spouse, data from the Council of Economic Advisors (CEA) show that less than a quarter of these men have a working spouse, and that figure has actually *decreased* during the last 50 years. In case we suppose that these workforce drop-outs have other sources of income, CEA data show that more than 35 percent of prime-age men not in the labor force lived in poverty in 2014.[31] If we assume that these men may be receiving generous public assistance, it must be noted that government benefits for those out of work have become increasingly hard to access, especially for those without children.

Some labor market researchers are also looking at the opioid crisis as an explanation for the decline in labor force participation, particularly among males of prime working age with lower education levels. According to a 2017 paper, about half of the prime-age men not in the labor force take pain medication on a daily basis.[32] Labor force participation rates have declined the most in areas of the country where opioid use is highest. It is also possible that the causation runs the other way—loss of good jobs could be leading to higher rates of opioid use.

Amid strengthening labor market conditions in recent years, the LFP of prime-age men has increased slightly since 2015. With low unemployment rates, an increasing proportion of the population has been pulled into the labor force. The question of whether this is just a rebound from a cyclical low or an actual reversal of the long-term decline in LFP rates is now greatly complicated by the difficulty of predicting how the loss of jobs during the Covid-19 crisis will affect future trends in labor relations, laws, and so forth.[33]

3.2 Labor Market Flexibility

For most of the twentieth century, Americans generally thought of "a job" (or at least a good job) as something that you typically did Monday through Friday, 40 hours a week, for a wage or salary and benefits (such as health insurance and pension plans). People often expected to stay in the same job for years or even decades. In recent years, however, the structure of the labor market has transformed, with employment becoming more "flexible" from the point of view of both the worker and the employer.

For workers, increased flexibility could mean having greater control over their work arrangements, such as being able to adjust their work hours, job sharing, working from home at times, or participating in the "gig" economy by taking up short-term contract jobs. Gig work has become the fastest-growing category of new jobs across America, with estimates of around a quarter of the American workforce being in the gig economy.[34] Such employment arrangements might be attractive to workers who may not want a regular full-time job, such as students, stay-at-home parents, or retirees. In the gig economy, workers with specialized skills and experience can often garner high compensation while retaining a high level of autonomy and flexibility. Research shows that not only are flexible workers more satisfied with their jobs, but they also tend to be more productive and take sick leave less often.[35]

But many workers are forced into gig jobs because they cannot find "regular" jobs and end up making low wages with no benefits. A recent report from the Federal Reserve found that in 2018, workers who supported themselves through the gig economy struggled financially far more than the average person.[36] Many gig economy workers are part-timers doing freelance work to supplement their primary income. But about 15.3 million workers are estimated to be employed full-time in the gig economy, where they are not entitled to minimum wage regulations or health care benefits.[37]

Employment "flexibility" from the perspective of the employer generally refers to having more control over setting workers' hours and pay, offering few or no benefits, and being able to terminate employees quickly and without fuss. Laws that regulate how easy it is to terminate employees can affect a firm's hiring decisions. Firms might be more willing to hire workers when it is easier to terminate them. For example, in 2016, France instituted labor law changes that gave firms greater discretion when terminating employees, to encourage hiring.[38] While such policies are beneficial to employers and may create jobs, they also increase job insecurity for workers and put them in a more vulnerable position.

It is likely that a desire for flexibility from the employer perspective is driving the gig economy at least as much as the demand side by workers. Gig workers are estimated to be about 30 percent cheaper, and hence more profitable for corporations, than regular workers.[39] Employers avoid providing benefits such as health care and retirement plans and can adjust the hours of gig workers, or terminate them, as economic conditions change, much more easily than with traditional employees. Workers in the gig economy bear the full burden of social insurance taxes, while firms must contribute half of these taxes for regular workers. Increased flexibility for employers at the expense of lower employment protection for the workers could also be a factor in the rise in inequality in the United States in recent years.

3.3 Labor Markets and Immigration

One of the most controversial topics in discussions of labor markets is the impact of immigration, particularly the immigration of workers seeking low-wage jobs. According to the neoclassical labor model, an influx of unskilled workers willing to work for relatively low wages (an increase in labor supply) will drive down equilibrium wages in markets for unskilled labor and displace some domestic workers. But greater labor supply may also increase economic output and productivity.

Most economists find that immigration into the United States does not have a negative impact on the wages of most U.S.-born workers.[40] In many cases, immigrants and native-born workers do not compete for the same jobs and may actually complement each other. For example, low-skilled immigrants tend to be concentrated in sectors such as agriculture and hospitality, with native-born workers concentrated in other sectors of the economy. Also, immigrants' demand for goods and services supports many jobs, driving up wages in some labor markets.

A 2017 report by the National Academies of Science, Engineering, and Medicine[41] reviews hundreds of studies on the impacts of immigration and concludes that immigration has little impact on the wages or employment levels of native-born Americans. Low-skilled immigrants reduce prices for consumers in certain sectors, including child care, construction, and house cleaning. As immigrants tend to be younger than average Americans, they also help balance the overall aging of the American population. A recent consensus has also emerged that educated immigrants actually increase the wages of native-born workers, based on the productivity gains resulting from innovation and worker interactions.[42]

Note that the previous analyses consider immigration as a whole, both legal and illegal. Much of the political debate on immigration focuses on illegal, or undocumented, immigration. Economic research has found that undocumented immigrants depress the wages of native-born workers without a high school degree by between 1 and 7 percent.[43] But the net impact on the country is generally positive, for several reasons. With undocumented workers concentrated in low-skilled positions, other workers focus on higher-productivity tasks.

3.4 Cooperatives

The dominant model of the firm today is one in which much of the economy consists of large enterprises that are owned by a small percentage of the population who make decisions on whom to hire and how to distribute the income generated from production. In reality, this structure is just one of the many possible ways to organize work.

One alternative way to organize work is through a cooperative model. This model includes worker cooperatives, employee-owned firms, credit unions, community land trusts, foundation-owned companies, and any form of organization that is owned and controlled by its workers or community. Worker cooperatives are for-profit businesses that are owned and run by workers. Unlike traditional corporations, where profits are distributed among stockholders who often have little connection with or knowledge of the business, profits from cooperatives go to their workers. Workers also control the decision-making process in cooperatives, either through individual votes or by electing a board of members. This allows workers to participate in the decisions related to their working conditions, wages, and job security.

Having a more democratic work space where workers control production and distribution processes can encourage workers to work harder and be more innovative and also help reduce disparities in income levels. According to one estimate, the pay ratio between highest- and lowest-paid workers in cooperatives is between 3:1 and 5:1, compared to the CEO-to-average-worker pay in corporations being as high as 287:1.[44] In terms of worker productivity, cooperatives can perform at least as well as traditional capitalist companies.[45] Also, worker cooperatives are more likely to offer regular work hours, health insurance, and other benefits than conventional companies.[46] And during economic downturns workers are more likely to decide on working fewer hours rather than laying off people, hence distributing work and income as well as the costs of the economic downturn more evenly.[47]

The cooperative model, like any other form of economic and social organization, is not perfect. Though the democratic process may mitigate inequalities, the structure can be less efficient, and conflicts between workers' interests can present significant challenges. Also, not all employees may want to share the risks of ownership, and it might be difficult for some workers to go against the system of corporate hierarchy.[48] Additionally, having to compete with capitalist firms that focus on cost-cutting and profit maximization may put pressure on worker cooperatives.

Worker cooperatives are still quite marginal in the United States. According to the U.S. Federation of Worker Cooperatives, of the approximately 5.7 million U.S. firms with employees, roughly 350 are worker-owned cooperatives employing about 5,000 workers. Employee ownership in the form of employee stock ownership plans (ESOPs) is much more common in the United States, with roughly 7,000 ESOPs benefiting more than 13 million workers.[49] The ESOPs, however, only provide employees with shares of stock over time; they may not have control over company operations, as there is no requirement for democratic governance. The cooperative model is better developed in some other countries, mainly in Europe. For example, the world's largest cooperative, the Mondragon Corporation, with more than 75,000 employees, is in Spain. Italy has about 8,000 worker cooperatives, and France has nearly 2,000.

3.5 Work–Life Balance

Paid work can both enhance and reduce well-being. But even for those who truly enjoy their work, a balance is needed between working and other activities that enhance well-being. One aspect of work–life balance concerns the amount of time the average worker spends working. In the United States, workers spend an average of about 34 hours per week on the job.[50] While workers in low- and middle-income countries tend to work the most hours per year, Americans work more hours per year, on average, than most other industrialized countries, as shown in Figure 7.9. Americans work, on average, about 106 hours more than Japanese workers, 266 hours more than French workers, and 423 hours more than German workers. Note that the difference between American and German workers equates to about ten full 40-hour workweeks per year!

National policies regarding paid vacation and holidays explain much of the differences shown in Figure 7.9. The United States is the only OECD nation that does not federally mandate any paid vacation days or holidays. About one in four workers in the United States don't get any paid vacation at all. This particularly affects low-income workers, part-time employees, and small business workers. Meanwhile, every country in the European Union has at least 20 vacation days per year, with some countries mandating as many as 25 to 30 days per year. National laws entitle all employees to at least 25 paid days off per year in Japan, 19 days in Canada, and 28 days in Australia.[51] Movements in Europe toward shorter standard working hours

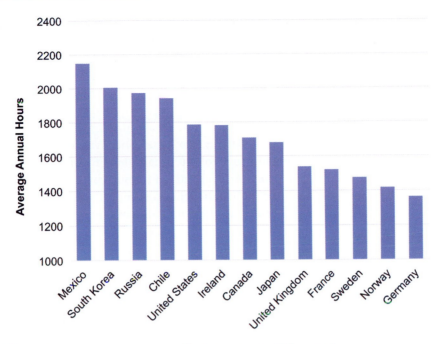

Figure 7.9 *Average Annual Hours Worked, Select Countries, 2018*

Source: OECD, OECD.Stat, "Average Annual Hours Actually Worked per Worker."

have often been motivated by macroeconomic considerations, with the goal of reducing unemployment. Also, unions tend to be more prominent in European countries, effectively advocating for workers' rights.

Even when American workers are able to take paid vacations, many do not fully utilize them over concerns about falling behind or appearing unproductive. According to one survey, more than half of U.S. workers who receive vacation days use half or less of their available time off. And even when Americans do take time off, most indicate that they end up doing some work during their vacations.[52] Research has shown that the well-being benefits of vacations include reduced stress, lower risk of heart disease, improved mental health, and even better relationships.[53]

The United States is also the only industrialized nation that does not mandate employers to provide paid leave to new parents. According to the Family and Medical Leave Act of 1993, U.S. workers are entitled to up to 12 weeks of *unpaid* time off to care for a new child or for a personal or family medical reason. But workers in other nations receive paid time off for these reasons and for much longer periods. For example, in France, new mothers are entitled to 42 weeks of leave at an average of 45 percent of their normal salary. In Germany, new mothers receive 58 weeks off at 73 percent of their normal salary.[54] Many nations also allocate some paid parental leave specifically to fathers. Japan entitles new fathers to up to 30 weeks of paid parental leave, while Norway, Portugal, and Iceland provide them with around two months of paid leave.[55]

The OECD ranks countries according to work–life balance, considering the percentage of employees who work long hours (50 or more per week) and the amount of time that is available for leisure.[56] Of 38 countries evaluated, the top countries were, in order: the Netherlands, Italy, Denmark, Spain, and France. The United States ranked 29th, behind Brazil but ahead of Australia, Japan, and South Korea.

3.6 Technological Change, Productivity, Work, and Leisure

Technological change undoubtedly affects the types and availability of jobs in the labor market. Advancements in technology usually lead to higher productivity, which could reduce the demand for labor and result in unemployment as workers are replaced by machines. This raises the question: If future technological advancements continue to reduce the need for human workers, will people be able to get jobs to support themselves and their families and improve their standards of living?

Change is happening so rapidly at this time, it is not possible to predict how technology may affect overall employment. While technological innovation may destroy some jobs, it also creates new ones. Additionally, technological change increases efficiency, which results in an increase in the overall wealth of society, because the same resources can produce a greater output. More efficient production is likely to reduce the cost of production, lower prices, and increase the overall demand for goods and services. Hence, even if technological innovation reduces the need for labor in one sector, there could be an increase in the need for aggregate labor inputs.

This reasoning may be generalized to the whole economy, suggesting that, as productivity increases generally, a given income will be able to purchase more goods and services. This indeed is what occurred during much of the second half of the twentieth century, when productivity increases resulted in higher income, so that, on average, workers and their families saw their standard of living more than double.

Since about 1980, however, this trend has changed, as shown in Figure 7.10. While productivity has continued to increase, the rate of growth in wages has lagged significantly behind that of productivity growth. This change is a major reason for growing inequality, as will be discussed in Chapter 13. In addition, there is the possibility that the demand for workers is actually shrinking. Some observers, looking at past and projected technology-induced productivity gains, fear that the economy's potential to produce goods and services could outstrip demand for these products.

A very different take on productivity gains is that they could be the basis for reducing work hours in ways that do not increase inequality or reduce quality of life. Figure 7.10 shows that labor productivity doubled between 1980 and 2016. One interpretation of this result is that the United States can now produce twice the quantity of goods and services with the same amount of labor used in 1980. But an alternative possibility is that we can now produce the *same quantity* of goods and services produced in 1980 but with *half the amount of labor.*

Consider this statement in light of the notion of labor flexibility. Suppose that workers had the choice between taking productivity gains as either wage increases

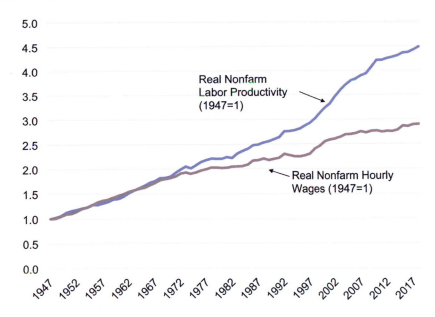

Figure 7.10 *Real Nonfarm Median Wages and Labor Productivity, 1947–2018*

Source: U.S. Bureau of Labor Statistics, Labor Productivity and Costs online database.

or labor time decreases. Theoretically, American workers could be living at the same material living standards of the 1970s but working only six months of every year! Of course, some workers may always choose more pay over shorter hours, but allowing for more work choice accords with standard economic theory, stated as follows:

> According to economic theory, we should let each worker choose how many hours to work. If workers choose shorter hours, it is because they get greater satisfaction from more free time than they would get from more income. According to the basic principle of market economics, interfering with individuals' choices between more free time and more income reduces total well-being, just as interfering with individuals' choices between two products would reduce total well-being by forcing some people to buy the product that gives them less.[57]

If it turns out that many workers are willing to work shorter hours for an equivalent reduction in pay, a choice for more leisure rather than more consumption could have important environmental benefits in rates of natural resource degradation and extraction.

Unfortunately, in the United States, part-time jobs are generally much less attractive than full-time jobs, because hourly wages are often low and few benefits are provided. Some countries have enacted policies to promote higher-quality part-time jobs. One example is the Netherlands, where discrimination against part-time workers is illegal and employers must offer the same pay to all workers who are doing the same kind of work, whether they work part time or full time, unless the business can prove that hiring part-time workers would impose an economic hardship. Another approach is taken in Denmark, where, in the 1990s, "flexicurity" policies were designed to help workers cope with rapid changes in what employers are looking for in their worker force. These policies combine lifelong learning with income support to workers as they transition between skills and jobs.

Discussion Questions

1. What evidence have you seen—in your own experience, others' experiences, or through the media—of increasing "flexibility" in labor markets? Do you think that these changes have been beneficial, harmful, or both?
2. Do you think having more worker cooperatives might help mitigate economic inequality in the United States? What might be some of the challenges in encouraging firms to adopt this model?

4. LABOR MARKETS, INEQUALITY, AND POWER

In this final section, we consider labor markets in a broader context of the business sphere and political power. Figure 7.11 shows the time trend for real (inflation-adjusted) median weekly wages and corporate profits in the United States from 1980 to 2018. After adjusting for inflation, median weekly wages in 2018, around $890,

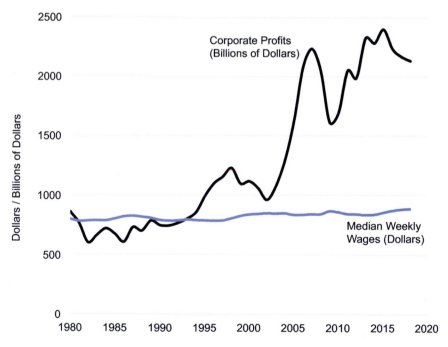

Figure 7.11 *Real Median Weekly Wages Versus Real Corporate Profits, United States, 1980–2018*

Sources: U.S. Bureau of Economic Analysis, National Income and Products Accounts, Corporate Profits before Tax, Table 6.17; U.S. Bureau of Labor Statistics, weekly and hourly earnings data from the current population survey.

were only slightly higher than they were in 1980. Meanwhile, corporate profits (also adjusted for inflation) nearly tripled, reaching more than $2 trillion.

One interpretation of Figure 7.11 is that the economic gains in the business sphere over the last several decades were almost entirely "captured" as profits to corporations rather than wage increases for workers. Some rough calculations suggest that if half of the increase in corporate profits from 1980 to 2018 had instead been allocated to increasing employees' wages, workers' incomes would be at least 10 percent higher than they are today. As we will see in Chapter 13, the stagnation of workers' wages is a leading reason for the increase in economic inequality in the United States since the 1970s. Stagnation of wages could also inhibit consumption and hurt economic growth. On this basis, it is argued that the United States should pursue wage-led, rather than profit-led, growth.[58]

Historical data indicate that American workers fared much better earlier in the twentieth century. According to the U.S. Census Bureau, real average annual earnings increased by a factor of about four between 1900 and 1970.[59] During the 1970s, real earnings essentially stopped increasing. *Household* income continued to increase slightly beyond the 1970s, only because more people per household entered the labor force.

Figure 7.11 suggests that corporations have effectively been able to increase their profits dramatically in the past few decades without having to pay their workers higher wages and salaries. Meanwhile, the incomes of management executives, particularly those at the very top, have soared. The average compensation of chief executive officers (CEOs) of large U.S. corporations in 1965 was 20 times the pay of an average worker. But, as noted earlier, in 2018, CEO average compensation stood at 287 times the pay of an average worker.[60]

Are CEOs really worth so much more today than they were 50 years ago, as a result of an increase in their marginal revenue product? Nobel Prize–winning economist Joseph Stiglitz notes the evidence that the extremely high incomes of CEOs accurately reflect the marginal revenue increases they earn for their companies "remains thin."[61] It is more likely that these trends indicate a shift in economic power, away from workers and toward corporate profits and executive compensation. American workers have lost economic power as a result of various factors, including globalization, technological change, and weakening of labor unions, as we will discuss in Chapter 13.

Economic power is closely related to political power. Prior to the 1970s, corporate influence on American politics was more limited, with lobbying by corporations that was partly balanced by the efforts of labor unions and organizations advocating for broader public interests. But the balance of political power began to shift dramatically in the 1970s and 1980s as corporations ramped up their lobbying efforts:

[B]usiness lobbying has built itself up over time, and the self-reinforcing quality of corporate lobbying has increasingly come to overwhelm every other potentially countervailing force. It has also fundamentally changed how corporations interact with government—rather than trying to keep government out of its business (as they did for a long time), companies are now increasingly bringing government in as a partner, looking to see what the country can do for them.[62]

Thus, the explanation for the stagnation of median wages in Figure 7.11 is found in a mix of both market forces and political power. Some policies for promoting a more equal distribution of economic gains include raising minimum wages, increasing investment in public infrastructure to create well-paying jobs, strengthening workers' rights to collective bargaining, and reducing gender- and race-based inequalities.[63] We will discuss these policies in more detail in Chapter 13, where we take a closer look at the issue of economic inequality.

Discussion Questions

1. Do you think that the relative wages of average workers and top executives reflect their respective marginal revenue product? What kinds of policies would you favor regarding worker pay and executive compensation?
2. Discuss the relationship between economic power and political power. How might these power structures influence economic inequality?

REVIEW QUESTIONS

1. In the neoclassical labor model, how does a firm decide on the quantity of labor to hire?
2. Why might the individual labor supply curve bend backward?
3. Why can we generally assume that market labor supply curves will slope upward?
4. In what types of labor markets might labor supply be relatively wage elastic? In what types of markets might labor supply be relatively wage inelastic?
5. How can we use a supply-and-demand graph to illustrate the operation of a labor market?
6. How does the neoclassical labor model explain variations in wages?
7. What are compensating wage differentials?
8. What is monopsony?
9. What is oligopsony?
10. What is efficiency wage theory?
11. What are dual labor markets?
12. How can we identify labor discrimination?
13. What is occupational segregation?
14. How has labor market participation changed in the United States in recent decades?
15. What is employment flexibility from the perspective of workers? From the perspective of employers?
16. What is the economic evidence about how immigration affects wages?
17. What are worker cooperatives? What are some of the advantages and limitations of the cooperative firm structure?
18. How do average work hours per year in the United States compare to most other countries?

19. What has been the trend in median wages in the United States in the past few decades? How does this compare with the trend in corporate profits?

20. What is the role of political power in explaining the stagnation of median wages in the United States in recent decades?

EXERCISES

1. Illustrate on a labor market graph the following examples that were described in the text.
   a. A virtually "fixed" supply of aerospace engineers, in the short run.
   b. The effect on the supply of lawyers of the reduction of barriers to women's participation in the practice of the law.
   c. The effect on the market for wait staff of a rise in the wage of salesclerks.
   d. The effect of a drop in demand for the organization's product.
   e. The effect of a rise in the price of other inputs that have been used as substitutes for labor.

2. Suppose that you observe that the wages for accountants in your town have gone up and that the number of accountants employed has also gone up. Which one of the following conditions could explain this? Illustrate your answer with a graph and explain in a brief paragraph.
   a. Businesses are failing, reducing the need for accountants.
   b. Many accountants are leaving the field in order to train to become financial analysts instead.
   c. A rash of business scandals has increased the demand for auditing services performed by accountants.
   d. The local university has just graduated an unusually large group of accountants.

3. The U.S. Bureau of Labor Statistics keeps track of the average wages and number of workers involved in various occupations over time and also makes projections about what jobs may show the most growth in the future. Using data available at the bureau's Web site, www.bls.gov, try to look up information on an occupation that interests you. How does it pay compared to other jobs? Is demand projected to rise in the future?

4. Match each concept in Column A with an example in Column B.

Column A	Column B
a. An alternative to wage employment	1. "Insurance adjustor" jobs are traditionally given to men, while "insurance representative" jobs go to women
b. The income effect on individual labor supply	2. Isabella cuts back her hours at her job after she gets a raise
c. A cause of a shift in the demand for professors	3. Many professors reach retirement age
d. A cause of a shift in the supply of professors	4. A rising college-student-age population
e. Occupational segregation	5. Acme Corp. pays above prevailing market wages to motivate and retain its employees
f. Efficiency wages	6. Westinghouse is the major employer in the county
g. Labor market monopsony	7. Resident assistants get a rent-free apartment but little pay
h. Compensating wage differential	8. Household production

NOTES

1. Bowling, Nathan A., Kevin J. Eschleman, and Qiang Wang. 2010. "A Meta-Analytic Examination of the Relationship between Job Satisfaction and Subjective Well-Being." *Journal of Occupational and Organizational Psychology*, 83: 915–934.

2. Goldsmith, Arthur, and Timothy Diette. 2012. "Exploring the Link between Unemployment and Mental Health Outcomes." *The Socioeconomic Status Indicator* (American Psychological Association), April.
   Martikainen, Pekka, and Tapani Valkonen. 1996. "Excess Mortality of Unemployed Men and Women during a Period of Rapidly Increasing Unemployment." *The Lancet*, 348(9032): 909–912.

3. U.S. Bureau of Labor Statistics, Labor Force Participation Rate Series from the Current Population Survey.

4. Association of American Medical Colleges. 2019. "New Findings Confirm Predictions on Physician Shortage." AAMC News, Press Releases, April 23. https://news.aamc.org/press-releases/article/2019-workforce-projections-update/

5. Editorial Board. 2013. "Nevada Must Get Creative Solutions for Doctor Shortages." *Reno Gazette-Journal*, August 3.

6. Lichter, Andreas, Andreas Peichl, and Sebastian Siegloch. 2015. "The Own-Wage Elasticity of Labor Demand: A Meta-Regression Analysis." *European Economic Review*, 80: 94–119.

7. U.S. Bureau of Labor Statistics, employment and wage data.

8. Bureau of Labor Statistics, 2019.

9. Gaines, Cork. 2016. "NBA Players Have the Highest Salaries in the World but No League Spends More on Players Than the NFL." *Business Insider*, November 14. www.businessinsider.com/nfl-mlb-nba-nhl-average-sports-salaries-2016-11

10. Average annual salaries for aerospace engineers and preschool teachers from the U.S. Bureau of Labor Statistics, May 2016 National Occupational Employment and Wage Estimates.

11. Graf, Nikki, Anna Brown, and Eileen Patten. 2019. "The Narrowing, but Persistent, Gender Gap in Pay." Pew Research Center, March 22.

12. Card, David, and Alan B. Krueger. 1994. "Minimum Wages and Employment: A Case Study of the Fast-Food Industry in New Jersey and Pennsylvania." *American Economic Review*, 84(4): 774–775.

13. OECD, Trade Union Density, OECD.Stat.

14. U.S. Bureau of Labor Statistics. 2017. Economic News Release, Union Membership, Table 4. January 26.

15. See, for example, Watchner, Michael. 2007. "The Rise and Decline of Unions." *The Washington Post*, July 18.

16. Ton, Zeynep. 2012. "Why Good Jobs Are Good for Retailers." *Harvard Business Review*, 90(1–2): 124.

17. Schmitt, John, and Janelle Jones. 2012. "Where Have All the Good Jobs Gone?" Center for Economic and Policy Research, Washington, DC, July.

18. Irwin, Neil. 2017. "To Understand Rising Inequality, Consider the Janitors at Two Top Companies, Then and Now." *New York Times*, September 3, 2017.

19. Gallup. 2018. "The Gig Economy and Alternative Work Arrangements." https://www.gallup. com/file/workplace/240878/Gig_Economy_Paper_2018.pdf

20. Ryan, Camille L., and Kurt Bauman. 2016. "Educational Attainment in the United States: 2015." U.S. Census Bureau, Current Population Reports, P20–578, March.

21. Ibid.

22. Graf, Nikki, Anna Brown, and Eileen Patten. 2019. "The Narrowing, but Persistent, Gender Gap in Pay." *Pew Research Center*, March 22.

23. Oyedele, Akin. 2016. "There's No Country Where Women Make More Than Men." *Business Insider*, March 23.

24. Blau, Francine D., and Lawrence M. Kahn. 2016. "The Gender Wage Gap: Extent, Trends, and Explanations." National Bureau of Economic Research, Working Paper 21913, Washington, DC, January.

25. Wilson, Valerie, and William M. Rodgers III. 2016. "Black-White Wage Gaps Expand with Rising Wage Inequality." Economic Policy Institute, Washington, DC, September 19.

26. Quillian, Lincoln, Devah Pager, Ole Hexel, and Arnfinn H. Midtbøen. 2017. "Meta-Analysis of Field Experiments Shows No Change in Racial Discrimination in Hiring over Time." *Proceedings of the National Academy of Sciences*, 114(41): 10870–10875.

27. Bureau of Labor Statistics. 2019. "National Occupational Employment and Wage Estimates United States." www.bls.gov/oes/current/oes_nat.htm

28. Krause, Eleanor, and Isabel Sawhill. 2017. "What We Know and Don't Know about Declining Labor Force Participation: A Review." Brookings Institution, May 2017.

29. Arias, Maria A., and Paulina Restrepo-Echavarria. 2016. "Demographics Help Explain the Fall in the Labor Force Participation Rate." *The Regional Economist*, 24(4): 16–18.

30. U.S. Bureau of Labor Statistics database.

31. Council of Economic Advisors (CEA). 2016. "The Long-Term Decline in Prime-Age Male Labor Force Participation." Washington: Office of the President, July. https://obamawhitehouse. archives.gov/sites/default/files/docs/labor_force_participation_report.pdf

32. Krueger, Alan B. 2017. "Where Have All the Workers Gone? An Inquiry into the Decline of the U.S. Labor Force Participation Rate." Brookings Institution, September 7.

33. Breitwieser, Audrey, Ryan Nunn, and Jay Shambaugh. 2018. "The Recent Rebound in Prime-Age Labor Force Participation." Brookings Institution, August 2. www.brookings.edu/blog/up-front/2018/08/02/the-recent-rebound-in-prime-age-labor-force-participation/

34. Reich, Robert. 2019. "The Gig Is Up: America's Booming Economy Is Built on Hollow Promises." *The Guardian*, June 2.

35. Gaskell, Adi. 2016. "Why a Flexible Worker Is a Happy and Productive Worker." *Forbes*, January 15.

36. Federal Reserve Bank. 2019. "Report on the Economic Well-Being of U.S. Households in 2018." Board of Governors of the Federal Reserve System, Washington, DC, May.

37. The State of Independence in America. 2019: The Changing Nature of the American Workforce, MBO Partners.

38. Kelly, Joshua. 2016. "France Wants to Make It Easier to Fire Workers so Employers Will Stop Harassing Them into Quitting." PRI (Public Radio International), May 13.

39. Reich, Robert. 2019. "The Gig Is Up: America's Booming Economy Is Built on Hollow Promises." *The Guardian*, June 2.

40. Greenstone, Michael, and Adam Looney. 2012. "What Immigration Means for U.S. Employment and Wages." The Hamilton Project, May 4.

41. Blau, Francine D., and Christopher Mackie (editors). 2017. "The Economic and Fiscal Consequences of Immigration." Panel on the Economic and Fiscal Consequences of Immigration, The National Academies of Science, Engineering, and Medicine, Washington, DC.

42. Ibid., pp. 6–7.

43. Davidson, Adam. 2013. "Do Illegal Immigrants Actually Hurt the U.S. Economy?" *New York Times,* February 12.

44. Estimate on highest-to-lowest-paid worker in cooperative is from Austin, Jennifer Jones. 2014. "Worker Cooperatives for New York City: A Vision for Addressing Income Inequality." Federation of Protestant Welfare Agencies, January. Estimate on CEO to average employee in corporations is from AFL-CIO. 2018. "Executive Paywatch." https://aflcio.org/paywatch

45. Doucouliagos, Chris. 1995. "Worker Participation and Productivity in Labor-Managed and Participatory Capitalist Firms: A Meta-Analysis." *Industrial and Labor Relations Review,* 49(1): 58–77.

46. Gillies, Benjamin. 2016. "Worker Cooperatives: A Bipartisan Solution to America's Growing Income Inequality." *Kennedy School Review,* June 15.

47. Rieger, Shannon. 2016. "Reducing Economic Inequality through Democratic Worker-Ownership." The Century Foundation, August 10. https://tcf.org/content/report/reducing-economic-inequality-democratic-worker-ownership/

48. Gillies, Benjamin. 2016. "Worker Cooperatives: A Bipartisan Solution to America's Growing Income Inequality." *Kennedy School Review,* June 15.

49. Cortese, Amy. 2017. "The Many Faces of Employee Ownership." *B Magazine,* March 31. https://bthechange.com/the-many-faces-of-employee-ownership-aa048ba262af

50. U.S. Bureau of Labor Statistics. 2017. Economic News Release, Average Weekly Hours and Overtime of All Employees on Private Nonfarm Payrolls, Table B-2, October 6.

51. Maye, Adewale. 2019. "No-Vacation Nation, Revised." Center for Economic and Policy Research, May.

52. Calfas, Jennifer. 2017. "Why Most Americans Aren't Using All of Their Vacation Days." *Time,* May 29.

53. Ferguson, Jill L. 2017. "Health Benefits of Taking a Vacation." *Huffpost,* March 5.

54. Organisation for Economic Co-Operation and Development (OECD). 2017. "Key Characteristics of Parental Leave Systems." OECD Family Database. www.oecd.org/els/family/database.htm

55. Livingston, Gretchen. 2016. "Among 41 Nations, U.S. Is the Outlier When It Comes to Paid Parental Leave." Pew Research Center, September 26.

56. OECD. Better Life Index. www.oecdbetterlifeindex.org/topics/work-life-balance/

57. Siegel, Charles. 2006. *The End of Economic Growth.* Preservation Institute, Berkeley, CA. p. 29.

58. Palley, Thomas I. "Wage- vs. Profit-Led Growth: The Role of the Distribution of Wages in Determining Regime Character." *Cambridge Journal of Economics,* 41(1), January 1: 49–61.

59. U.S. Census Bureau. 1976. *Bicentennial Edition: Historical Statistics of the United States, Colonial Times to 1970.* U.S. Department of Commerce, Washington, DC. Series D.
U.S. Census Bureau. 1982. *Statistical Abstract of the United States 1982–1983.* U.S. Department of Commerce, Washington, DC. Table 667.

60. AFL-CIO. 2018. "Executive Paywatch." https://aflcio.org/paywatch

61. Stiglitz, Joseph E. 2011. "Of the 1%, by the 1%, for the 1%." *Vanity Fair*, March 31.

62. Drutman, Lee. 2015. "How Corporate Lobbyists Conquered American Democracy." *The Atlantic*, April 20.

63. Mishel, Lawrence, and Ross Eisenbrey. 2015. "How to Raise Wages: Policies That Work and Policies That Don't." Economic Policy Institute, Briefing Paper #391, March 19. p. 2.

Part III

Macroeconomic Theory and Policy

Chapter 8

Macroeconomic Measurement

In order to make good economic policy choices, we need to have reliable information on how the economy is performing. The metrics that are most often cited to assess overall economic performance are gross domestic product (GDP), the unemployment level, and the inflation rate. GDP measures all marketable goods and services produced in a country over a certain time period. Rising GDP is often associated with declining unemployment, since expansion in production is expected to create jobs. Rapid increases in GDP could, however, cause labor and input shortages and result in increased inflation. These are the sorts of relationships we examine in macroeconomics. However, before studying such interactions, we need to understand what these variables mean and how they are measured. We will present the definitions and measures of these variables in this chapter. We also discuss the limitations of GDP as a measure of economic well-being and describe some alternative measures in order to place our discussion of GDP "in context" with our broader discussion of well-being.

1. AN OVERVIEW OF NATIONAL ACCOUNTING

The first set of U.S. national accounts was created in 1937, during the Great Depression, when the economy experienced a severe decline. Without a set of national accounts, policymakers had little way of knowing whether the policies that they were trying to implement were actually helping the economy to rebound. Today every functioning country maintains a system of **National Income and Product Accounts** (NIPA) that collects data on production, income, spending, prices, and employment. In the United States, the national accounts are maintained by a federal agency, the **Bureau of Economic Analysis** (BEA).

> **National Income and Product Accounts (NIPA):** a set of statistics compiled by the BEA concerning production, income, spending, prices, and employment
> **Bureau of Economic Analysis (BEA):** the agency in the United States in charge of compiling and publishing the national accounts

In order to try to make the accounts as standardized and comparable across different countries and time periods as possible, agencies maintaining the national accounts adopt a set of common practices or conventions. One such convention concerns how the entire economy is divided into four national accounting sectors. These sectors, as defined by the BEA, are:

1. *Households and institutions sector:* This includes households and nonprofit institutions that serve households, such as nonprofit hospitals, universities, museums, trade unions, and charities.
2. *Business sector:* The BEA business sector includes all for-profit businesses, along with certain business-serving nonprofit organizations, such as trade associations and chambers of commerce and government agencies that produce goods and services for sale, such as the U.S. Postal Service, municipal gas and electric companies, and airports.
3. *Government sector:* The government sector includes all federal, state, and local government entities, except for the "business-like" government enterprises mentioned previously.
4. *Foreign sector:* The entities in the first three sectors include, for the national accounts, only those located in the United States. The foreign sector (or "rest of the world") includes all entities—household, nonprofit, business, or government—located outside the borders of the United States. An individual in another country who buys imported U.S. products, for example, or a company located abroad that sells goods or services to the United States figures into U.S. accounts as part of the foreign sector.

Other conventions adopted in standardizing the national accounts concern what is measured and how data are categorized. For example, although natural, manufactured, human, and social capital are all crucial resources for economic activity, it is primarily *manufactured* capital that is currently included in the accounting of national nonfinancial assets.

There are also accounting conventions related to how investment is measured. Economists generally use the term "investment" to mean additions to stocks of *non*financial assets. This contrasts with the common use of the term "investment" to refer to financial investment, such as the purchase of stocks and bonds. Also, investment represents a *flow*; hence its value is counted only in the year it is installed. A machine that was added to a factory in 2018, for example, is counted as an investment only in 2018.

Because the value of capital stocks may **depreciate** over time due to wear and tear or obsolescence, we need to distinguish between **gross investment**, which measures the total value of flows into the capital stock over a period, and **net investment**, which adjusts the gross investment measure to account for the depreciation of capital stock. For example, suppose that an office complex built in 1980 is torn down this year and replaced by a new, larger office complex. Measured gross investment for this year would include the full value of the new office complex. Net investment for this year would be calculated as the value of the new office complex *minus* the value of the depreciated building that was torn down.

> **depreciation:** a decrease in the quantity or quality of a stock of capital due to wear and tear or obsolescence
>
> **gross investment:** all flows into the capital stock over a period of time
>
> **net investment:** gross investment minus an adjustment for depreciation of the capital stock

Discussion Questions

1. To which national accounting sector might the BEA assign each of the following entities? Why?
    a. A local city government–owned golf course that charges fees similar to those at local private courses
    b. A large nonprofit hospital
    c. A U.S.-owned movie company whose offices and studio are in Japan
    d. A nonprofit trade association, such as the Chocolate Manufacturers Association
2. Under the BEA definitions, would spending on education be counted as investment? Would buying shares in a company be considered investment? Why?

2. GROSS DOMESTIC PRODUCT

GDP is the most-referenced single number that comes out of the national accounts. Businesses, policymakers, and media outlets often await the announcement of newly published figures on GDP with great anticipation. The growth rate of GDP is often taken to signal the success or failure of macroeconomic policymaking.

2.1 Defining Gross Domestic Product

According to the BEA, **GDP** is supposed to measure the total market value of final goods and services newly produced within a country's borders over a period of time (usually one year).

> **gross domestic product (GDP) (BEA definition):** a measure of the total market value of final goods and services newly produced within a country's borders over a period of time (usually one year)

This definition contains several key phrases. Let us consider each of them.

"Market value": We measure GDP in terms of the market value of goods and services produced in order to have a common unit of measurement—U.S. dollars—for comparing and adding the contribution of various goods and services to the economy. Converting everything into their dollar values makes it possible to aggregate pizzas, cars, and health care into one measure. In some cases, when we do not have market prices for certain goods and services, we use the method of **imputations**, which involves making an educated guess, usually based on the

market value of similar products or the cost of production. For example, in order to make the value of owner-occupied housing in the GDP comparable to tenant housing, an imputation based on rental values is made for the value of owner-occupied housing. The value of goods and services produced by the government and not sold in the market, such as highways, parks, national defense, and public education, is imputed by adding up the cost of inputs, which includes wages paid to the workers, spending on intermediate goods and services, and allowance for depreciation of fixed assets.

> **imputation:** a procedure of assigning values for a category of products, usually based on the market values of related products or the cost of inputs

"Final goods and services": A **final good** is one that is ready for use. That is, no further productive activity needs to occur before the good can be consumed (if it is a good that is used up as it is put to use) or put to work producing other goods and services (e.g., if it is a piece of equipment). The reason for limiting measurement to *final* goods and services is to avoid double counting. Double counting would create a misleadingly large estimate of GDP. For example, suppose that over the course of a year, paper is produced by one company and sold to another company that uses it to make books. The books are then sold to their final buyers. Books in this case are the final goods, while the paper used in them is an **intermediate good**. By limiting the accounting to final goods, production is only counted once—the paper is only counted as part of the books.

> **final good:** a good that is ready for use, needing no further processing
> **intermediate good:** a good that will undergo further processing

"Over a period of time": Since GDP measures a flow, it must be measured over a time period. Macroeconomists usually work with GDP measured on a yearly basis. Estimates of GDP are released more often than once a year—generally on a quarterly basis. However, even quarterly data on GDP growth rates are usually expressed in annual terms, to provide an estimate of how much the economy would grow if it were to continue to expand for the entire year at the speed reported for the three-month period.

"Newly produced": Only new goods and services are counted. For example, if you buy a book published in 2010 at a used bookshop, the value of the book itself is not included in this year's GDP. Only the retail services provided by the used bookshop are "newly produced" and are part of this year's GDP.

"Within a country's borders": This means that the goods and services are produced within the physical borders of the country. Production of goods and services by U.S. citizens working abroad is *not* part of U.S. GDP. But the work of a Japanese citizen at a Japanese-owned factory located in the United States *is* part of U.S. GDP.[1]

2.2 Measuring Gross Domestic Product

Imagine a simple economy that has the following characteristics: all the profits that companies earn end up in the bank accounts of households, all the goods produced by businesses are bought by households (i.e., there are no leftover inventories), the capital stock does not depreciate, and there is no foreign sector. In this case, three quite different measures of counting GDP would in theory all add up to the same number:

Value of Production = Value of Income = Value of Spending

Using a *production approach*, which might seem to be the most direct method, we could sum up the dollar value of all final goods and services produced in each national accounting sector—by household and institutions, businesses, and the government. For example, if the business sector produces 1 million automobiles that are then sold to final users for $20,000 each, this production contributes $20 billion (1 million automobiles × $20,000 = $20 billion) to GDP. Note, however, that production of goods and services within households for their own use, such as unpaid child care, cooking, and cleaning, is not included in the national accounts. (See Box 8.1.)

We could just as easily calculate GDP by using an *income approach*. In this simple economy, everyone who is involved in production also receives monetary payment for their contribution to production. Using this approach, the aggregate level of production is measured by adding the value of wages and benefits earned by workers, along with profits, rents, interests, and subsidies earned by investors, creditors, and owners of land or capital, as well as taxes received by the government.

Last, using the *spending approach*, we could look at who *buys* the final goods and services that have been produced. Since we assumed that no goods are carried as inventory in this very simple economy, everything produced must be bought. Totaling the dollar value of spending on goods and services provides a third and final way of arriving at the figure for GDP. In our simple imaginary economy, the total value of production, income, and spending are equal; hence economists sometimes use the three terms interchangeably. Measuring GDP using the spending approach provides a useful way of examining how changes in spending by different economic actors (households, firms, or government) affect the overall level of demand in the economy. Hence, we describe this approach in some detail.

In the spending approach, GDP is categorized into four components based on *who* is doing the spending: consumption, investment, government spending, and net exports. **Consumption** spending includes purchases of goods and services by households and nonprofit institutions serving households. Spending by businesses undertaken to increase or maintain their productive capacity in order to produce final goods and services for sale is called **investment**. For example, the spending on a new coffee machine by a café to expand its production of coffee is counted as investment. **Government spending** includes expenditures (consumption and investments) made by the government sector at the federal, state, and local levels.

> **consumption:** purchases of goods and services by the households and institutions sector
> **investment:** spending by businesses undertaken to increase or maintain their productive capacity in order to produce final goods and services for sale
> **government spending:** expenditures made by the government at the federal, state, and local levels

Remember that our simple imaginary economy was a **closed economy**, with no foreign sector. However, real-world economies are connected through trade, international finance, and migration of labor and capital. For example, the United States has an **open economy**, where some of the goods and services produced inside its borders are bought by entities in the foreign sector (exports), and some domestic spending is for goods and services produced abroad (imports). In an open economy, our calculation of GDP must include the value of spending on goods that we export to other countries (because exports are produced in *our* country) and *subtract* spending on imports from GDP (because imports are pro-duced *outside* our country). The difference between exports and imports is called **net exports**.

Net exports = Exports − Imports

> **closed economy:** an economy with no foreign sector
> **open economy:** an economy with a foreign sector
> **net exports:** the value of exports less the value of imports

Based on the spending by different sectors, we can summarize the spending approach with the identity:

GDP = Personal consumption
  + Private investment
  + Government spending
  + Net exports

We see from Table 8.1 that the total GDP for 2018 was $20.58 trillion. Con-sumption spending was the largest component (68 percent) of GDP. Note that net exports may be either positive (if exports > imports) or negative (if imports > exports). In 2018, for example, the United States imported goods and services worth $0.64 trillion (or $640 billion) more than the value of the goods and services exported. Hence, that year, U.S. net exports were negative. Between 1960 and 2018, U.S. net exports have been positive only for 13 years. The last time the United States had positive net exports was in 1975.

Table 8.1 Gross Domestic Product, Spending Approach, 2018

Sector and type of spending	Spending by sector (trillions of dollars)	Spending by type (trillions of dollars)
Household and institutions spending (*personal consumption expenditures*)	13.99	
Durable goods		1.48
Nondurable goods		2.89
Services		9.63
Business spending (*gross private domestic investment*)	3.63	
Fixed investment		3.57
Change in private inventories		0.05
Government spending (*government consumption expenditures and gross investment*)	3.59	
Federal		1.35
State and local		2.24
Net foreign sector spending (*net exports of goods and services*)	0.64	
Exports		2.51
Less: Imports		3.15
Total: Gross domestic product	20.58	

Source: U.S. Bureau of Economic Analysis, National Income and Products Account, Table 1.1.5, October 4, 2019.

Note: Totals may not add up exactly due to rounding.

BOX 8.1 WHAT ARE STAY-AT-HOME MOMS REALLY WORTH?

What is the fair market value of all the work a typical stay-at-home mom does in a year? To answer this question, we can multiply the hours spent at different tasks by the typical wage paid to workers who perform those tasks. For example, if the typical mom spends 14 hours per week cooking and the average wage for cooks is $9 per hour, the annual value of a mom's cooking labor is over $6,000. Applying the same approach to other household tasks, including child care, cleaning, and yard work, the annual value of a full-time stay-at-home mom is estimated to be over $64,000, based on a 2012 research by insure.com. Similar research by salary.com comes up with an even larger market value—about $113,000 annually![2]

An analysis of 27 mostly high-income countries shows that the value of unpaid labor equates to an average of more than 25 percent of GDP.[3] The UK Office of National Statistics estimated that the value of unpaid labor in 2014 was equivalent to 56 percent of GDP, with the largest components of the value of unpaid work being child care and transportation.[4] Notably, the majority of this work is done by women. Estimates from the United Nations indicate that globally women do nearly 2.5 times the amount of unpaid care and domestic work than men.[5] Recognizing the value of unpaid work is important if we are to make a comprehensive assessment of well-being.

2.3 Nominal and Real Gross Domestic Product

The measure of GDP discussed in the previous section is **nominal or current-dollar GDP**, or GDP expressed in terms of the prices of goods and services that were current at the time of measurement.

> **nominal (current-dollar) GDP:** the dollar value of all final goods and services produced in a year in that year's prices

In 2018, the nominal GDP in the United States was 20,580 billion dollars, more than three times its 1990 value of 5,979 billion dollars. Does this mean that the production level in the United States increased by more than three times in 28 years? No, some of the increase in the value of nominal GDP comes from the increase in the *prices at which output is valued*. To measure the change in the level of production, we need to separate price changes from changes in the amount of production.

Suppose a very simple economy produces only two goods, apples and oranges, as shown in Table 8.2. Column (2) shows the price of each good in each year, while Column (3) gives the physical quantity of production, measured in pounds. Nominal GDP, calculated in Column (4), is just the sum of the dollar values of the goods produced in a year, evaluated at the prices in that same year:

Nominal GDP = Total production valued at current prices

As we can see in Table 8.2, the value of nominal GDP increases from $200 in Year 1 to $300 in Year 2. This $100 increase, taken by itself, can be misleading since only part of the change in nominal GDP is due to an increase in production (quantity of oranges produced has increased). The rest of the increase in nominal GDP is due to the rise in *price* of apples, from $1.00 to $1.50. In order to measure the change in production level from year to year, we construct the **real GDP**—a

Table 8.2 Calculation of Nominal GDP in an "Apples-and-Oranges" Economy

(1)	(2)	(3)	(4)
Description	Price per pound ($)	Quantity (pounds)	Contribution to nominal GDP [column (2) × column (3)] ($)
Year 1			
Apples	$1.00	100	$100
Oranges	$2.00	50	$100
			$200
Year 2			
Apples	$1.50	100	$150
Oranges	$2.00	75	$150
			$300

measure of actual value of goods and services produced—by removing the effect of changes in prices.

> **real GDP:** a measure of gross domestic product that seeks to reflect the actual value of goods and services produced by removing the effect of changes in prices over time

A relatively simple way of calculating real GDP is called the "constant-dollar method." This method uses prices from one particular year, called the **base year**, to evaluate the value of production in all years.

> **base year (in the constant-dollar method of estimating GDP):** the year whose prices are chosen for evaluating production in all years

Constant-dollar real GDP is calculated by doing the same sort of multiplying and summing exercise as shown in Table 8.2 but using the *same* prices (the prices from the base year) for all years:

Constant-Dollar Real GDP = Total production valued at base year prices

Applying the constant-dollar method to our simple "apples-and-oranges" example, for instance, we might take Year 1 as the base year and express GDP in both Year 1 and Year 2 in terms of Year 1's prices, as shown in Table 8.3. While the quantities in Column (3) are the same as in Table 8.2, the prices in Column (2) are *all from Year 1*. GDP in Year 2 expressed in "constant (Year 1) dollars" is the sum of quantities in Year 2 multiplied by prices in Year 1. This comes out to be $250. So the change in real GDP between Year 1 and Year 2 is $50, significantly less than the change in nominal GDP of $100 shown in Table 8.2.

Table 8.3 Calculation of Constant-Dollar Real GDP

(1)	(2)	(3)	(4)
Description	*Price per pound in base year ($)*	*Quantity (pounds)*	*Contribution to real GDP [Column (2) × Column (3)] ($)*
Year 1 **(Base)**			
Apples	$1.00	100	$100
Oranges	$2.00	50	$100
			$200
Year 2			
Apples	**$1.00**	100	$100
Oranges	**$2.00**	75	$150
			$250

*Bold type indicates base year *prices*.

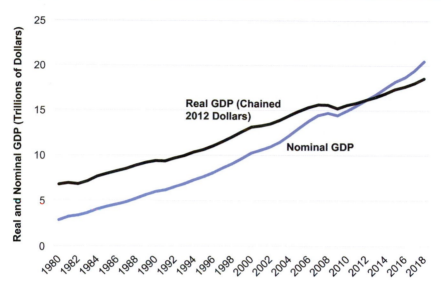

Figure 8.1 *Real Versus Nominal GDP, Chained 2009 Dollars, 1980–2018*

Source: U.S. Bureau of Economic Analysis National Income and Product Accounts, Tables 1.1.5 and 1.1.6.

The convention of using "constant dollars," however, has a number of problems. Its main weakness is that the value of the rate of change in real GDP is dependent on the year chosen as base year. This method also suffers from various other biases, which arise from differences in relative prices and spending patterns between the base year and a current year.

As a way to address these problems, the BEA now uses a more sophisticated "chained dollar" method to measure real economic growth. Because the "chained dollar" approach requires a steep jump in computational complexity, we will not cover it here. It is, however, important to note that the concept behind the two approaches is still the same—real GDP should measure output changes free of the influence of price changes. The real GDP is currently expressed in BEA publications in terms of "chained (2012) dollars."

In Figure 8.1, you can see how measures of real and nominal GDP diverge. Because prices were generally rising over the period 1980–2018, nominal GDP grew faster than real GDP, as shown by the more steeply rising line. But if we are interested in knowing how fast the economy was actually expanding in terms of production, the real GDP line gives a more accurate picture. Note that the reference year in Figure 8.1 is 2012; thus, real and nominal GDP are the same in that year.

Discussion Questions

1. The previous section explained why a country's "production" and "income" can be thought of as roughly equal in a conceptual sense. Why, in practice, does the value of domestic production actually differ from the total of domestic incomes?

2. The "constant-dollar" method of estimating real GDP uses prices for one year to calculate measures of GDP for all years. Why is it sometimes important to evaluate GDP in the current year using prices from some other year? Explain.

3. KEY MACROECONOMIC INDICATORS: GROSS DOMESTIC PRODUCT GROWTH, INFLATION, AND UNEMPLOYMENT

3.1 Gross Domestic Product Growth

Policymakers are interested in not just the level of GDP but the rate at which it is changing. The rate of change in GDP, referred to as GDP growth, shows how fast the economy is expanding or contracting. We use the real GDP to calculate the GDP growth rate in order to estimate the actual change in production level so as to eliminate the impact of price changes.

The rate of change in percentage terms can be calculated using the standard percentage change formula. For something that takes $Value_1$ in Year 1 and $Value_2$ in Year 2, this is:

$$Percentage\ change = \frac{Value_2 - Value_1}{Value_1} \times 100$$

Using this formula, the percentage change in real GDP (i.e., the growth rate of GDP) from, say, 2017 to 2018 can be calculated as:

$$growth\ rate\ of\ GDP = \frac{real\ GDP_{2018} - real\ GDP_{2017}}{real\ GDP_{2017}} \times 100$$

The real GDP values in the United States in 2017 and 2018 were estimated at $18.05 trillion and $18.57 trillion, respectively. Hence, the rate of growth of GDP in 2018 is given by:

$$\begin{aligned} growth\ rate\ of\ GDP &= \frac{18.57 - 18.05}{18.05} \times 100\% \\ &= .029 \times 100\% \\ &= 2.9\% \end{aligned}$$

3.2 Price Indexes and Inflation Rates

Price indexes assist us in better determining and understanding real GDP and inflation. An **index number** measures the change in a given magnitude, in this case the price level, compared to another period. Generally, the value of the index number in the reference or base year is set at 100, though sometimes other values (such as 1 or 10) are used.

> **index number:** a figure that measures the change in magnitude of a variable, such as a quantity or price, compared to another period

Economists mainly look at two *price indexes*: the GDP deflator and the consumer price index (CPI). The GDP deflator is derived from the measurement of GDP, and it estimates the average price of goods and services produced in an economy. The CPI, on the other hand, is a measure of the average price of goods and services purchased by the average consumer. An increase in the general level of prices, measured by either of these indices, is called **inflation**. Let us now look at each of these two measures in turn.

> **inflation:** a rise in the general level of prices

GDP Deflator

We have discussed how changes in nominal GDP can come both from changes in production levels and from changes in prices. If prices are rising, nominal GDP increases faster than real GDP, and if prices are falling, real GDP rises faster than nominal GDP. Hence, in order to get from nominal GDP to real GDP, we need to adjust nominal GDP by a measure based on the change in prices. A **GDP deflator** is a price index that is used to make this adjustment. For a specific year, GDP deflator is the ratio of nominal GDP to the real GDP in that year.

$$GDP\ deflator = \frac{Nominal\ GDP}{Real\ GDP}$$

> **GDP deflator:** price index for measuring the general level of prices and defined as the ratio of nominal GDP to real GDP

Note that the GDP deflator provides a simple way of calculating the real GDP from the nominal GDP. The GDP deflator is an index, and its level is based on price changes relative to the reference (base) year. The GDP deflator for the reference year, when the nominal and real GDPs are equal, is 1.

The rate at which the GDP deflator changes shows the movement of price levels in the economy in general. To measure the rate of change in prices, we look at the percentage change in GDP deflator from year to year, using the percentage change formula. So the rate of change in price between two years, referred to as the inflation rate when prices rise and deflation rate when prices fall, is given by:

$$\frac{GDP\ deflator_{Year2} - GDP\ deflator_{Year1}}{GDP\ deflator_{Year1}} \times 100$$

For example, between 2017 and 2018, the value of the GDP deflator increased from 107.9 to 110.3. The inflation rate can thus be calculated as:

$$\frac{110.3 - 107.9}{107.9} \times 100\%$$
$$= 2.22\%$$

Consumer Price Index

The price index most often reported in the news is the **consumer price index** (CPI), calculated by the U.S. Bureau of Labor Statistics (BLS). The CPI measures changes in a particular basket of prices of goods and services bought by average household. There are eight major categories of goods and services in the basket: food and beverages, housing, apparel, transportation, medical care, recreation, education and communication, and other goods and services.

> **consumer price index (CPI):** an index measuring changes in the prices of goods and services bought by households

One simple approach to calculating price changes would be to take the *average of price changes for all* the goods and services consumed in an economy. This may, however, be problematic, since some price changes are more significant to consumers than others, either because they purchase more of certain products (such as loaves of bread) or because they spend a large portion of their incomes on something (such as rent). Also, some price changes may not be directly relevant for consumers (for example, price of forklifts and other items mainly purchased by businesses).

Because some goods and services are more significant to consumers, the prices in the basket are brought together as a "weighted average" that gives greater weight to the prices of goods and services that affect consumers the most and less weight to the prices of relatively minor goods and services. The way to do this is to weight each price by the corresponding quantity that is sold at that price. Until recently, the BLS used a *constant-weight method*, choosing quantities bought during one period as the "base," to calculate the CPI. These quantities are said to represent a typical "market basket" of goods bought by households. A constant-weight price index is calculated according to the following formula:

$$Constant\ Weight\ Price\ Index = \frac{sum\ of\ current\ prices\ weighted\ by\ base\ quantities}{sum\ of\ base\ prices\ weighted\ by\ base\ quantities} \times 100$$

The price-index problem is analogous to the calculation of "constant-dollar" GDP, since we face choices about which standards to use to determine the base quantities. In order to get around this problem, the BLS now publishes "chained"-price indexes, involving more complex calculations (which we do not discuss here). The BLS also updates the "market basket" periodically using data from its household expenditures survey. (See Box 8.2.)

The growth rate of consumer prices—that is, the inflation rate affecting consumers—is measured by the growth rate of this price index:

$$Inflation\ rate = \frac{CPI_2 - CPI_1}{CPI_1} \times 100$$

257

BOX 8.2 HOW QUANTITY WEIGHTS CAN LOSE VALIDITY OVER TIME

The CPI is a useful measure, but it is subject to measurement problems. In particular, changes in household expenditure patterns mean that we periodically have to make changes to the basket of goods that are used to benchmark price changes.

In 1901, nearly half the budget of a typical urban, working family went toward food, while 15 percent went toward shelter and an equal proportion toward clothing. Only about 3 percent of the spending was on health care, and the family probably spent nothing at all on cars or gasoline—because automobiles were not yet in wide use.

By 1950, the picture had changed considerably. Now only a third of the family's spending was on food, while spending on shelter and clothing declined to about 11 to 12 percent. Spending on health care had risen to about 5 percent, and about 12 percent of a family's spending was related to private vehicles. Only about 1 percent of the family's spending was on education.[6]

In recent data on consumer expenditures, the share devoted to food has dropped even further—to 12 percent (possibly the lowest ever seen). Expenditures on clothing have dropped to about 3 percent of a household's budget, on average. Meanwhile, families are spending more on shelter (30 to 40 percent of their budget) and private vehicle expenses (16 percent of their budget) than they were in the mid-twentieth century. The proportion of family spending on health care has risen further, to about 8 percent, and spending on education is about 2.5 percent.[7] All of these changes reflect either changes in people's consumption behavior and/or changes in relative prices (for example, food becoming cheaper to produce relative to other goods and services).

Using expenditure patterns from one of these periods to "weight" the CPI in another would clearly result in biased figures. Using the 1901 expenditure pattern nowadays, for example, would mean that auto and gasoline prices would not figure into the CPI at all.

The invention of new goods and services (e.g., electric cars and touchscreen phones) and quality improvements in existing goods (e.g., in products for home entertainment and computing) continue to create special challenges for the economists working to measure price changes.

Between 2017 and 2018, the CPI index increased from 245.1 to 251.1, so the inflation rate is given by:

$$Inflation\,rate = \frac{251.1 - 245.1}{245.1} \times 100\%$$
$$= 2.44\%$$

Note that while the CPI is based on the average price of goods and services purchased by consumers, the GDP deflator gives the average price of output produced in a country. These two indices are different since the set of goods produced in an economy is not the same as the set of goods consumed. For example, some of the consumption goods included in the CPI may be imported, and some goods

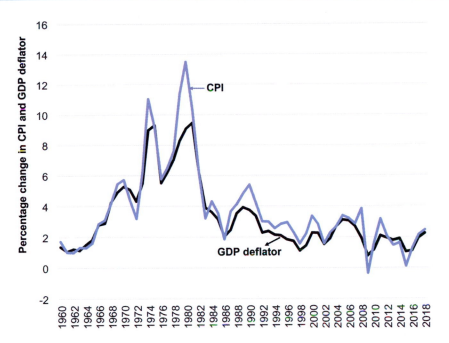

Figure 8.2 *Rate of Change in GDP Deflator vs. CPI, 1960–2018*

Source: U.S. Bureau of Economic Analysis, National Income and Product Accounts, Table 1.1.4, and U.S. Bureau of Labor Statistics, Table on CPI—All urban consumers.

produced may be exported. Also, some of the goods produced may be bought by firms or the government and may not be counted as consumption. In most cases, however, the two price indices move together, as illustrated by Figure 8.2. The sharp deviation of CPI from GDP deflator in the 1970s is explained by the rise in price of oil, most of which was imported and hence not captured by the GDP deflator.

3.3 Measuring Employment and Unemployment

Every month, the U.S. **Bureau of Labor Statistics** (BLS) interviews about 60,000 households and collects data from 40,000 employers to publish monthly data on unemployment. The BLS statistics only include the **civilian noninstitutional population** that consists of persons 16 years or older living in private households. Hence, children are excluded, as are people who are in compulsory military services and those who live in prisons, nursing homes, mental institutions, and long-term care hospitals.

> **Bureau of Labor Statistics (BLS):** in the United States, the government agency that compiles and publishes employment and unemployment statistics
>
> **civilian noninstitutional population (BLS definition):** persons 16 years or older who do not live in institutions (for example, correctional facilities, nursing homes, or long-term care hospitals) and who are not on active military duty

Of the civilian noninstitutional population, those who did any work or had jobs as paid employees or business owners or worked for 15 hours or more at a family business during the reference week are defined as being **employed**. Note that *any* paid work done during the reference week—even if it was for only an hour or two at a casual job—counts as being "employed." Anyone with a paid job, but on a leave during the reference week, is also counted as being employed. The only case where unpaid work counts as being employed is when more than 15 hours of work is done at a family-run business.

> **employed person (BLS definition):** a person who did any work for pay or profit during the week before he or she is surveyed by the BLS or who worked for 15 hours or more in a family business

Unemployed persons, on the other hand, are those in the civilian noninstitutional population who were not employed during the reference week but were available to work and had made specific efforts to find employment sometime in the four-week period ending with the reference week. Activities such as contacting employers and sending out résumés count as an "active" job search. Merely participating in a job-training program or reading employment ads do not. The question about whether you could start a job concerns whether, in fact, you are *available* for work. If, for example, you are a college student searching for a summer job during spring break, but you are not available to start the job until June, you would not be classified as unemployed.

> **unemployed person (BLS definition):** a person who is not employed but who is actively seeking a job and is immediately available for work

If you are either employed or unemployed, the BLS classifies you as part of the **labor force**. The percentage of population in the labor force is what we defined in the last chapter as the labor force participation rate. We can calculate the labor force participation rate by dividing the number of people officially in the labor force by the number of people age 16 or over who are not institutionalized or in the military:

$$LFP\ Rate = \frac{number\ of\ people\ in\ the\ labor\ force}{number\ of\ people\ age\ 16+,not\ institutionalized\ or\ in\ the\ military} \times 100$$

But what if you are neither "employed" nor "unemployed"—if you do not have a job but are not actively seeking one? Then you are classified as "**not in the labor force**." People in this category are often taking care of a home and family, in school, disabled, or retired.

> **labor force (BLS definition):** people who are employed or unemployed
> **"not in the labor force" (BLS definition):** the classification given to people who are neither "employed" nor "unemployed"

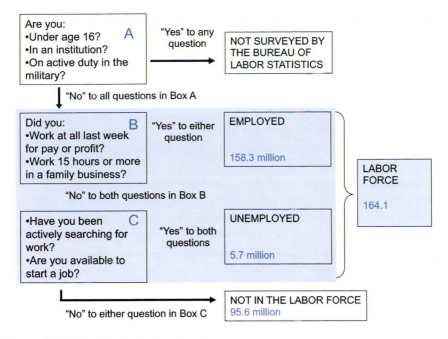

Figure 8.3 *Who Is in the Labor Force?*

Source: U.S. Bureau of Labor Statistics, The Employment Situation—September 2019, News Release.

Notice, in Figure 8.3, that the vast majority of U.S. residents who are not "employed" either are "not in the labor force" (about 95.6 million) or are not part of the surveyed population (about 69.4 million). The latter group includes children under 16 and persons who are institutionalized. In comparison, about 5.7 million people in September 2019 were formally counted as "unemployed."

The Unemployment Rate

Every month, having made estimates of the total number of employed and unemployed people in the country, the BLS calculates the official **unemployment rate**. This is defined according to the formula:

$$unemployment\ rate = \frac{number\ of\ people\ unemployed}{number\ of\ people\ in\ the\ labor\ force} \times 100$$

unemployment rate: the percentage of the labor force made up of people who do not have paid jobs but are immediately available and actively looking for paid jobs

For example, looking at Figure 8.3, you can see that in September 2019 the BLS estimated that 158.3 million people were employed and 5.7 million people were unemployed, so a total of 164.1 million people were in the labor force. The unemployment rate was thus calculated as 3.5 percent:

$$unemployment\ rate = \frac{5.7\ million}{164.1\ million} \times 100 = 3.5\%$$

The unemployment rate represents the fraction of the officially defined labor force that is made up of people who are not currently working at paid jobs but are currently looking for and available for paid work.

The unemployment rate is often "seasonally adjusted." Over the course of a year, some swings in unemployment are fairly predictable. For example, agriculture and construction tend to employ fewer people in the cold winter months, and each year, many students enter the labor force in May and June after graduation. The BLS releases "seasonally adjusted" figures that attempt to reflect only shifts in unemployment that are due to factors *other than* such seasonal patterns.

The BLS also estimates unemployment rates for various demographic groups, occupations, industries, and geographical areas. Historically, unemployment rates have generally been substantially higher for minority populations than for whites, for teenagers than for older people, and for less-educated people than for the more educated. Unemployment rates often have differed somewhat by gender, though not with any consistent pattern. Some representative unemployment rates are given in Table 8.4.

Table 8.4 Unemployment Rates for Different Groups

Group	Unemployment rate
All Workers	3.5
Race and ethnicity＊	
White	3.2
Black/African American	5.5
Hispanic or Latino	3.9
Age	
Teenage (age 16–19)	12.5
Age 55 and older	2.8
Education＊＊	
Less than a high school diploma	4.8
Bachelor's degree and higher	2.0
Gender	
Adult male (20 years and over)	3.2
Adult female (20 years and over)	3.1

Source: BLS News Release, "The Employment Situation—September 2019," October 8, 2019.

＊ People are allowed to indicate more than one racial group. However, data from people who indicated more than one race are not included in these statistics.

＊＊Data on unemployment by education is for the age group 25 years and over.

Discouraged Workers and Underemployment

The fact that some people "not in the labor force" might want jobs but have given up looking for them means that the official unemployment rate *underestimates* people's need for paid jobs. In recent years, the BLS has added survey questions to try to determine how many people who are "not in the labor force" may want employment, even if they are not actively searching for work. Anyone who is available for work, wants to work, and has looked for work in the past 12 months but not in the past 4 weeks is categorized by the BLS as "**marginally attached workers**." In September 2019, marginally attached workers numbered 1.3 million.

> **marginally attached workers:** people who want employment and have looked for work in the past 12 months but not in the past 4 weeks

If these marginally attached workers also say that the reason they are no longer looking for work is that they believe there are no jobs out there for them, they are called **discouraged workers**. They may have become discouraged because their skills do not match available openings, because they have experienced discrimination, or because they have been turned away time after time. In September 2019, the number of discouraged workers in the United States was estimated at about 321,000. Marginally attached workers who are not discouraged workers typically have not looked for work recently because of school attendance or family responsibilities.

> **discouraged workers:** people who want employment but have given up looking because they believe that there are no jobs available for them

Let's also take a closer look at the people classified as "employed." The BLS statistics count anyone who worked even for an hour or two during the reference week as being "employed." Some people prefer part-time work, of course, because it leaves them time for other activities or because of health reasons. But others want and need full-time work and are only settling for part-time work until they can find something better. The household survey asks people the reason for working part-time. In September 2019, 21.5 million people reported working part-time for "noneconomic" reasons such as health or family responsibilities, and an additional 4.4 million people reported working part-time for "economic reasons"—that is, slack business conditions or because part-time work was all they could find.

What indicator, then, should we look at to see whether the national employment situation is "good" or "bad"? The BLS now publishes various measures of labor underutilization that allow you to see the situation from a variety of different perspectives. For example, if the marginally attached workers and people who work part-time involuntarily are added to the number of unemployed, the rate of labor underutilization in September 2019 comes to 6.9 percent, compared to the official unemployment rate of 3.5 percent.

The BLS also counts people as employed even if the kind of work that they did does not match their skills. Suppose that you paint your aunt's living room for cash while you are waiting to hear back on job applications for management positions; the BLS counts you as already employed. People who are working at jobs that underutilize their abilities, as well as those who work fewer hours than they wish to, are said to be **underemployed**.

> **underemployment:** working fewer hours than desired or at a job that does not match one's skills

If we are concerned about human well-being, underemployment as well as unemployment should be of concern. While underemployment due to an underutilization of skills is certainly of considerable concern for both efficiency and quality-of-life reasons, BLS official surveys do not currently attempt to measure this sort of underemployment.

Discussion Questions

1. How would the BLS classify you, personally, on the basis of your activities last week? Can you think of an example where someone you think of as *working* would not be considered officially "employed" by the BLS? Is it true that people who are *not working* are generally counted as "unemployed"?
2. Would you say that the official unemployment rate provides an accurate estimate of the actual labor market conditions in the economy? What are some of the issues with the way in which this number is calculated? How has the BLS addressed some of these issues?

4. ALTERNATIVE MEASURES OF ECONOMIC WELL-BEING

As discussed previously, GDP numbers are widely used as a proxy for national success. However, GDP was never intended to play such a role. Economists dating back to Simon Kuznets, the originator of U.S. national accounting systems, have warned that GDP is a specialized tool for measuring market activity, which should not be confused with national well-being. National well-being is affected by social and environmental factors, such as inequality, political participation, security, quality of health care and education, and access to clean air and water, which are no less important than marketed economic activity. We need to account for these factors in order to develop a more comprehensive measure of well-being.

In this section, we examine the problems that arise from focusing only on the money value of output, with little attention to what is being produced and how it affects human well-being. In order to understand this more complete picture of the economy, national governments need to start gathering new kinds of data and creating new indicators. The use of such indicators may have important implications for policymaking, as discussed subsequently.

Before we begin to discuss alternatives to GDP, we first need to ask ourselves three important questions:

1. *What should we measure?* GDP measures only market production. Are there some things that GDP excludes that should be included as a component of well-being? Should some parts of GDP be excluded because they harm well-being?
2. *What should be used as the unit of measurement?* Although GDP is measured in dollars, what units should be used to measure other variables affecting well-being, such as education, health, or environmental quality?
3. *Should we combine disparate well-being indicators into a single number, or should we keep the variables disaggregated (i.e., split up into component categories)?* While it is tempting to convert all variables to dollars to allow for comparability, how can variables such as environmental quality or social capital be translated into dollar values?

4.1 Why Gross Domestic Product Is Not a Measure of Well-Being

As already mentioned, GDP was never designed or intended to measure well-being. Indeed, it can sometimes be quite perverse in this respect. As outlined in Box 8.3, GDP often rises with increases in things that most people would want to have less of, while it fails to rise with positive contributions to individual and social

---

BOX 8.3 THERE'S NO G-D-P IN "A BETTER ECONOMY"

The United States is the largest economy in the world, ranked by total GDP. In terms of GDP per capita (GDP divided by population), it still ranks highly but falls below some other countries such as Luxembourg, Norway, and Switzerland.[8] (See Figure 0.8.) What should we make of such measurements?

> Gross domestic product has become the most watched and most misinterpreted of all economic indicators. It's a measure of economic activity—of money changing hands. Despite the mundane nature of this economic indicator, politicians fiercely compete with each other to see who can promise the fastest GDP growth. Government programs and investments in technology get the green light only when they are predicted to spur GDP growth. . . . And while the United States leads in GDP, it also leads in military spending, the number of people in prison, and the percentage of people who are obese. These other first-place finishes seem at odds with America's position atop the GDP standings—that is, until you realize that spending on war, incarceration, and disease, as well as other "defensive expenditures," all count toward GDP. The arithmetic of GDP doesn't consider what the money is actually being spent on, and over time, we've been spending more and more money on remedial activities and calling this "progress."[9]

Alternative measures to GDP have been constructed that correct for these negative aspects of production, as well as taking into account positive factors such as a clean environment, household production, or volunteer work that contribute to well-being. Such indicators have drawn increasing interest from economists and policymakers in recent years.

---

well-being that are not bought and sold in markets. Even if a particular increase in GDP contributes to increasing well-being, *ceteris paribus*, many other factors may be equally or more important in determining well-being levels. In fact, overall social well-being may be declining if GDP growth is accompanied by increasing inequality and environmental degradation. As discussed in Chapter 1, well-being is clearly multidimensional. Accordingly, it is desirable to consider factors other than GDP if we wish to formulate and evaluate policies that enhance well-being.

Some limitations of GDP as a measure of well-being include:

■ It does not account for *household production*. While standard accounting measures include the paid labor from such household activities as child care and gardening, these very significant services are not counted when they are unpaid. (See Box 8.1.)

■ Standard measures do not count the benefits of *volunteer work* and the free services provided by nonprofit organizations, even though such work contributes to social well-being.

■ Some significant *services provided for free*, such as internet services, including Wikipedia, Gmail, or YouTube, are not counted, even though they might increase well-being.

■ *Leisure* is another important neglected factor. A rise in output might come about because people spend more time on paid work. The resulting increase in output does not consider the fact that more work can make people tired and stressed and can lower their well-being. People's well-being might increase from spending more time as leisure, but this is not reflected in GDP.

■ Also inadequately reflected are issues around loss (or gain) of *human and social capital formation*. Factors such as health and education levels, political participation, and issues of trust and corruption may significantly affect well-being, but these are not counted in GDP.

■ Interactions between the economy and the natural world, such as environmental degradation and resource depletion, are also often ignored by the GDP measure. (See Box 8.4.)

■ Some outputs merely compensate for, or defend against, harmful events that result, directly or indirectly, from the economic activity represented in GDP. Referred to as **defensive expenditures**, these show up as positive contributions to GDP, but we do not account for the associated negative impacts. Consider, for example, the billions of dollars spent cleaning up after the 2010 Deepwater Horizon oil spill in the Gulf of Mexico. This spending turned up as positive additions to GDP, while the environmental and human losses were not reflected. When environmental issues are mostly invisible, there can be an appearance of economic growth even as the ecological basis for future economic health is being seriously undermined.

> **defensive expenditures:** money spent to counteract economic activities that have caused harm to human or environmental health

- *Products or production methods that reduce, rather than increase, well-being* may show up as additions to GDP. Unhealthy foods and drugs and dangerous equipment may lower overall well-being. If people are miserable at their jobs, suffering boring, degrading, unpleasant, or harmful working conditions, their well-being is compromised. In spite of these factors, however, all paid work contributes to increasing GDP.
- Rises in consumption levels show up as additions to GDP, even if this consumption is financed by unsustainably large debt levels that may require painful changes in future consumption and affect future well-being.
- Finally, increased economic activity counts as an addition to GDP even if it *increases inequality*. An increase in GDP by $10 million counts as the same societal gain, whether this income goes to the richest 5 percent or to the poorest 50 percent of the population. Obviously, the gains from production being distributed among a larger proportion of the poorer population is likely to have a much greater impact on improving overall well-being.

BOX 8.4 ACCOUNTING FOR THE ENVIRONMENT

The natural environment underpins all economic activities—it provides resources and environmental services as inputs to economic activities and absorbs waste products. If a country's forests are cut down, its soil fertility depleted, and its water supplies polluted, surely the country becomes poorer. But national income accounting will merely record the market value of the timber, agricultural produce, and industrial output as positive contributions to GDP. Omitting such important environmental considerations from our measures of success could seriously undermine our goals for sustainability. But how should we go about estimating the value of environmental services received from the trees on the hillside or from clean air and water?

The most basic approach to "green" accounting is to start with traditional measures and make adjustments that reflect environmental concerns. The current national accounting methods produce estimates of net domestic product (NDP), which deducts the annual depreciation value of existing manufactured, fixed capital such as buildings and machinery from GDP value. Extending this logic, we can estimate the value of net annual change in natural capital and add or subtract it from NDP to obtain an environmentally adjusted measure of national product, or **Green GDP**. Thus:

$$Green\ GDP = GDP - D_m - D_n$$

where D_m is the depreciation of manufactured capital and D_n is the depreciation of natural capital.

Green GDP: GDP less depreciation of both manufactured and natural capital

This measure requires estimating natural capital depreciation in monetary terms rather than physical units such as biomass volume or habitat area. Methods of imputation can theoretically be used to estimate such values. Often the costs of damage from withdrawing an environmental service (for example, measuring the value of unpolluted air in terms of the cost of pollution on human health) or the cost of maintaining environmental resources (for example, cost of devices for controlling pollution) are used as monetary estimates of environmental services. But to estimate all types of natural capital depreciation in monetary terms is a daunting task; hence, estimates of Green GDP generally focus on only a few categories of natural capital depreciation.

Attempts to estimate Green GDP date back to the 1980s. A 2001 analysis in Sweden looked at a broader set of natural resource categories, including soil erosion, recreation values, metal ores, and water quality, and found that accounting for these factors would reduce GDP by about 1–2 percent for 1993 and 1997.[10]

The foregoing examples all indicate the dangers of pursuing policies geared only to raising GDP. A narrow national focus solely on increasing output may result in decreased leisure and less time for parenting, friendships, and community relations; it can increase levels of stress and mental illness or raise economic inequality to a socially destructive level. For all these reasons, improvements are needed in the design of measures of national success and in defining and gathering the data needed for such measures.

4.2 A Broader View of National Income Accounting

Approaches to creating alternative indicators include refining national measures by supplementing the National Income and Product Accounts framework with information on resources and environmental impacts, developing separate indicators for the different aspects of well-being, or creating wholly new indicators based on a set of variables measuring different aspects of well-being. Examples of some of these approaches and indicators are presented here.

Satellite Accounts

Satellite accounts are intended to supplement standard national income accounts by tracking data on well-being indicators, such as health, education, and other aspects of social and environmental well-being.[11] For example, the United Kingdom maintains environmental accounts that track data on forested area, oil and gas reserves, waste generation, greenhouse gas emissions, and expenditures on environmental protection. Proponents of this approach agree that GDP is a useful measure of national output but believe that GDP tells us only one of the things that we want to know about the economy. Some of the things that it does not include are important, and they deserve to have their own indicators.

> **satellite accounts:** additional accounting systems that provide measures of social and environmental factors in physical terms, without necessarily including monetary valuation

The BEA uses dollar–denominated satellite accounts to highlight certain existing components of GDP.[12] Currently, BEA satellite accounts include separate indicators for transportation, travel and tourism, health care, arts and cultural production, and outdoor recreation. These satellite accounts eliminate some of the obscurity in the aggregate GDP measure by estimating the contributions of particular sectors to the national income. Future uses of satellite accounts in the BEA may start experimenting with valuing household labor or counting environmental damages as losses.

Measuring Well-Being

Recognizing the need to develop indicators that incorporate social and environmental factors, in 2008, French president Nicolas Sarkozy created the Commission on the Measurement of Economic Performance and Social Progress (CMEPSP).[13] In September 2009, the commission presented its report advocating for the need to shift from an emphasis on measuring economic production to measuring well-being. The report defined eight dimensions of well-being: material living standards, health, education, work and personal activities, political voice, social connections, economic and physical security or insecurity, and the environment.[14]

For some of these dimensions, objective data from indicators such as average life expectancy, literacy rates, and air pollution levels can be collected. However, such data still do not tell us exactly how these factors relate to well-being. This is partly explained by the subjective nature of well-being. We can, however, take a much more intuitive approach and simply ask people about their well-being.

The **subjective well-being** (SWB) approach involves surveying individuals and asking them a question such as: "All things considered, how satisfied are you with your life as a whole these days?" Respondents then answer based on a scale from 1 (dissatisfied) to 10 (satisfied). Although this approach may seem unscientific, a large body of recent scientific research has suggested that data on SWB provide meaningful information regarding factors that influence well-being. The CMEPSP recommended using SWB data in combination with quantitative data on various well-being dimensions such as income levels and health outcomes to obtain a more comprehensive picture of well-being.

> **subjective well-being (SWB):** a measure of welfare based on survey questions asking people about their own degree of life satisfaction

A wide variety of efforts, such as the World Happiness Report from Columbia University's Earth Institute,[15] the Gallup World Poll, and the European Quality of Life Survey, have come up with remarkably consistent measures of "happiness" or "life satisfaction." Figure 8.4 plots average SWB against per capita GDP, adjusted for differences in purchasing power, for 60 countries. In general, SWB is positively

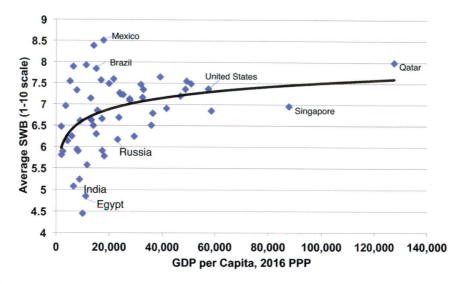

Figure 8.4 *Average Subjective Well-Being and GDP per Capita*

Sources: SWB from World Values Survey online data analysis, 2005–2008 survey wave; GDP from World Development Indicators database.

Note: The trendline is a statistically fitted line showing a "best fit" estimate of the relationship between the two variables on the graph, GDP per capita and SWB.

correlated with higher levels of GDP per capita, but the benefits of income gains decline at higher income levels, as shown by the curved trendline.[16] However, SWB can be high in both rich and poor countries. In fact, the countries with the highest SWB levels are Mexico and Colombia, both middle-income countries. Figure 8.4 also shows that all developed countries have relatively high SWB. There are no countries above a per capita GDP of US$20,000 per year that have an average SWB below 6.0, and many poorer countries have an average SWB below 6.0. Thus, it appears from this graph that for at least some developing countries, increasing GDP could lead to higher SWB levels, though much would depend on that GDP growth also being accompanied by other characteristics pertaining to issues such as income distribution, environmental protections, and so on.

The Genuine Progress Indicator

The genuine progress indicator (GPI) is one of the most ambitious attempts to date to design a replacement to GDP. It is a monetary measure of economic well-being for a given population in a given year that includes many benefits and costs that are not included in GDP.[17] GPI has three main components: market-based welfare, services from essential capital, and environmental and social costs.[18]

Market-based welfare is based on the household's consumption levels represented by personal consumption expenditures (PCE). Components of PCE that have zero or negative contribution to the household's well-being, including defensive expenditures on medical care, insurance, or food and energy wastes, are subtracted from PCE. Expenditures on household investments that may contribute to long-term sustainability, such as spending on consumer durables or household maintenance, are also subtracted from PCE to keep a focus on current well-being. Next, an adjustment is made for income inequality to reflect the negative impact of inequality on well-being. And, finally, benefits from provision of public goods and services are added to PCE to obtain a value of total market-based welfare.

Unlike GDP, which mostly focuses on manufactured capital, GPI accounts for welfare benefits from services of human, social, and natural capital. Hence, benefits from knowledge and skills, the value of household and volunteer work, leisure time, free internet services, gains from consumer durables, and home improvement and infrastructure, as well as benefits from environmental services such as provision of food and medicine and benefits from lakes, forests, wetlands, and other ecosystems are added to the market-based welfare component of GPI.

Finally, social and environmental activities that have a negative effect on well-being are subtracted from PCE. Social costs include homelessness, underemployment, increasing crime rates, and vehicle accidents. Environmental costs include depletion of natural capital such as the loss of wetlands, soil erosion, groundwater depletion, increases in air pollutants, greenhouse gas emissions, noise pollution, and water pollution. The adjustments made to PCE in order to arrive at the GPI for the United States in 2014 are shown in Table 8.5.

Table 8.5 Genuine Progress Indicator ($2012 per Capita), United States 2014

Indicator	Value
Market-based welfare	
Household budget expenditures (HBE)	$25,529.42
Defensive and regrettable expenditures	−$3,966.90
Household investments	−$7,278.06
Costs of income inequality	−$3,121.57
Public provision of goods and services	+$7,025.23
Total market-based welfare	*$18,188.12*
Services from essential capital	
Services from human capital	+$5,223.68
Services from social capital	+$12,856.93
Services from built capital	+$6,041.57
Services from protected natural capital	+$1,554.65
Total services from essential capital	*$25,676.65*
Environmental and social costs	
Depletion of natural capital	−$6,495.60
Costs of pollution	−$3,714.65
Social costs of economic activity	−$5,195.44
Total environmental and social costs	*$15,405.69*
GPI per capita total	$28,459.09

Source: Talberth, John, and Michael Weisdorf. 2017. "Genuine Progress Indicator 2.0: Pilot Accounts for the US, Maryland, and City of Baltimore 2012–2014." *Ecological Economics,* 142, December: 1–11.

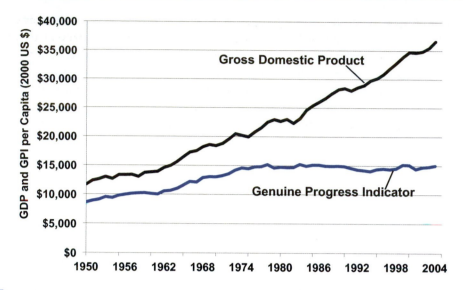

Figure 8.5 *GPI vs. GDP per Capita, 1950–2004*

Source: Talberth, John, Clifford Cobb, and Noah Slattery. 2007. "The Genuine Progress Indicator 2006: A Tool For Sustainable Development." Redefining Progress. February 2007.

As we might expect, the GPI differs significantly from GDP. The largest positive adjustments to GPI come from the increases in social capital, and the largest deductions come from the depletion of natural capital. Figure 8.5 compares the trends in GPI per capita and GDP per capita between 1950 and 2004.[19] We see that the value of GPI per capita is much lower than GDP per capita. Also, while GDP per capita and GPI per capita both increased from 1950 to about 1978, in recent decades, GPI has flatlined, while GDP continued to grow, indicating that environmental and social costs omitted from GDP have been increasing faster than the value of the omitted benefits. Relying on the GPI instead of GDP might often suggest significantly different policy recommendations, focusing more on reducing environmental damage, preserving natural renewable energy resources, and redressing rising inequality.

The states of Maryland and Vermont and the city of Baltimore also measure their GPI. In Maryland, while economic contributions to the GPI rose steadily over the period 1960–2010, the net social contributions increased only slightly, and the environmental costs more than doubled (based on an earlier variation of GPI). In Vermont, GPI per capita was 40 percent less than state GDP in 2011 due to rising income inequality and a strong dependence on fossil fuels.[20] GPI estimates have also been developed for countries other than the United States, including Australia, China, Germany, India, Japan, Italy, and Brazil.

The Better Life Index

One of the challenges of using multiple indicators to evaluate well-being is that it is sometimes difficult to communicate the results. How do we assess overall well-being if the poverty rate falls by two percentage points but the emission of greenhouse gases increases by 3 percent? Summing up production, inequality, and environmental and social costs in one single index, as is done with the GPI measure, requires assigning monetary values to each dimension, which is also difficult to do. The Organization for Economic Cooperation and Development (OECD) has thus tried a mixed approach.[21] With its **Better Life Index** (BLI), it combines a large number of dimensions, many of which cannot easily be valued in monetary terms, into one single indicator using different possible weights for each dimension.

> **Better Life Index (BLI):** an index developed by the OECD to measure national welfare using 11 well-being dimensions

BLI considers well-being a function of the following 11 dimensions: income, wealth, and inequality; jobs and earnings; housing conditions; health status; work and life balance; education and skills; social connections; civic engagement and governance; environmental quality; personal security; and subjective well-being. The results for each dimension are standardized across countries, resulting in a score from 0 to 10. The BLI Web site allows users to select their own weights for each of the dimensions (see www.oecdbetterlifeindex.org), and the OECD collects user input to gain a better understanding of the factors that are most important for measuring well-being.

Based on input collected from over 100,000 users about their preferred weight for each dimension, the OCED 2015 report shows a considerable variation in the importance of the 11 well-being dimensions across regions. The highest-ranked dimensions are education in Latin America; life satisfaction in North America; health, education, and environment in Europe; safety in Asia-Pacific; and work-life balance in Australia.[22] Such findings suggest that when a dimension is particularly poorly met in one region, it is likely to be rated as a more important issue.

The BLI has been measured for 38 countries, including the OECD member countries, along with Brazil, South Africa, and Russia. Figure 8.6 shows the total BLI for eight countries. Among these countries, Norway and Australia show the greatest life satisfaction, scoring highly on employment levels, quality of jobs, and health of the population. Countries with low employment levels and low life expectancy have the lowest life satisfaction. The United States performs well in terms of household income, status of housing and sanitation, and long-term unemployment. It falls somewhere around the OECD average in terms of work-life balance, social connections, civic engagement, quality of working environment, literacy and cognitive skills, and exposure to pollution. But it ranks among the lowest in terms of inequality in income and health outcomes.[23]

The BLI provides a comprehensive view of the many factors that influence well-being. Income is not presented as a dominant feature but as one component of many. One of the criteria used to choose the BLI variables is their capacity to be influenced by government policy. Several of the dimensions, such as education, housing, and environmental quality, can be directly improved with effective policies, although the linkage between other dimensions (such as subjective well-being) and policies needs further study.

273

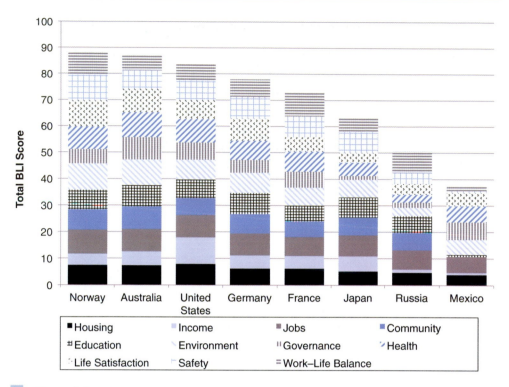

Figure 8.6 *BLI for Selected Countries, 2015*

Source: OECD, 2015.

The Human Development Index

In contrast to the BLI, the United Nations **Human Development Index (HDI)** is calculated based on only three components of well-being: life expectancy at birth, years of formal education, and real gross national income per capita. Since these are denominated in different units, relative performance is presented in a scaled index (Figure 8.7).

> **Human Development Index (HDI):** a national accounting measure developed by the United Nations based on three factors: GNI per capita level, education, and life expectancy

Like the BLI, the HDI then faces the issue of how to assign relative weights. The standard HDI approach is to give equal weight to each of the three indicators, although the GNI measure is modified to account for the principle that additional income is worth more to a person with lower income than to a person with higher income. Notwithstanding these modifications to GNI, the inclusion of this standard measure of income as one-third of the indicator makes it highly, although not perfectly, correlated with GDP; of the 30 countries with the highest HDI scores in 2015, all but one were also ranked in the top 40 by national income per capita. At

Human Development Index (Scale 1 – 100)	
90 – 95	Norway, Australia, Germany, Denmark, Netherlands, Canada, **United States**, New Zealand, Sweden, United Kingdom, Japan
85 – 89.9	Israel, France, Finland, Austria, Italy, Spain, Greece, Qatar, Poland
80 – 84.9	Chile, Saudi Arabia, Portugal, Hungary, Argentina, Russia
75 – 79.9	Bulgaria, Malaysia, Cuba, Turkey, Mexico, Brazil
70 – 74.9	Ukraine, Peru, Thailand, China, Colombia
65 – 69.9	Egypt, Vietnam, Philippines, El Salvador, South Africa
60 – 64.9	Iraq, Guatemala, India, Bhutan
55 – 59.9	Ghana, Kenya, Pakistan
50 – 54.9	Nigeria, Zimbabwe
45 – 49.9	Rwanda, Haiti, Afghanistan
40 – 44.9	Ethiopia, South Sudan
35 – 39.9	Niger, Central African Republic

Figure 8.7 *Selected Countries as Ranked in the Human Development Index*

Source: UNDP, Human Development Report, 2016 data.

the same time, the results often show that countries with similar income levels measured by GNI per capita vary dramatically in overall human welfare, as measured by the HDI. For example, Jamaica, the Philippines, and Swaziland have similar levels of GNI per capita, but their HDI scores vary significantly.

The relative simplicity of the HDI has made it much easier to apply in countries with less money to spend on data collection; hence, it has been especially valuable for developing countries. It has been an annual feature of every UN *Human Development Report* since 1990. The HDI is one of the most referenced quality-of-life indices, and it continues to be modified, with new versions that adjust for inequality and gender equity.

One lesson from these alternative measures is that there is not necessarily a positive correlation between the GDP value and other measures of well-being. In many instances, GDP is rising while other measures stay flat or fall. Another observation we can make is that no single approach has yet emerged as the "best" way to adjust, replace, or supplement GDP. No one—and especially not their creators—would argue that alternative macroeconomic indicators have been perfected. As we have seen, any macroeconomic indicator, including GDP, involves numerous assumptions and contains numerous limitations. However, the new measures allow users to see how the results change under different assumptions. The alternative approaches discussed in this section also clearly show that reliance on a single traditional GDP measure omits or distorts many crucial variables. Thus, all the alternative approaches discussed here have some value in providing broader perspectives on the measurement of well-being.

Discussion Questions

1. Of the various alternative indicators presented in this section, which one would you advocate as the best approach for measuring economic well-being? What do you think are the strengths and weaknesses of this indicator? How do you think using this would change specific policy debates in your country?
2. Give examples of each of the following:

   - Efforts to supplement GDP
   - Efforts to adjust GDP
   - Efforts to replace GDP

   Are there some alternatives discussed previously that would fit into more than one of these categories? Are there some that are difficult to fit into any of them? Would you suggest any other ways of categorizing efforts that are being made to improve how we measure the success of an economy in achieving well-being for present and future people?

REVIEW QUESTIONS

1. What are the four accounting sectors of the economy, according to the BEA? What sorts of entities are included in each sector?
2. What forms of capital assets are tracked by the BEA?
3. Explain four key phrases that appear in the definition of GDP.
4. What are the three approaches to GDP measurement?
5. Explain why, in a simple economy, the three approaches would yield the same figure for the value of total production.
6. Describe the components of GDP according to the spending approach.
7. Describe the reasoning behind the "constant-dollar" approach to calculating real GDP.
8. Define GDP deflator and consumer price index. What are some of the key differences between the two price indices?
9. What population is included in the official household survey that measures employment and unemployment?
10. What is the BLS definition of "employment" and "unemployment"?
11. How is the unemployment rate calculated?
12. What are marginally attached workers? Discouraged workers?
13. What is the labor force participation rate and how is it calculated?
14. What are some of the main critiques of GDP as a measure of well-being?
15. What are satellite accounts?
16. What is subjective well-being (SWB), and how is it commonly measured?
17. What is the genuine progress indicator (GPI), and how is it measured?
18. What is the relationship between GDP per capita and GPI per capita in the United States over the past several decades?
19. What is the Better Life Index, and what components are used to construct it?
20. What is the Human Development Index?

EXERCISES

1. In which line (or lines) of Table 8.1 would the value of each of the following be counted? "Not counted in any category" is also an option.
   a. A new refrigerator bought by a family
   b. A book newly produced in Indiana and bought by a store in Mexico
   c. New computers, manufactured in Asia, bought by a U.S. accounting company
   d. New computers, produced in the United States, bought by a U.S. computer retail chain and not yet sold by the end of the year
   e. A three-year-old couch bought by a used furniture store in Arizona
   f. Cleaning services bought by a nonprofit hospital in New York
   g. The services of volunteers in an environmental action campaign

2. Answer the following questions, using information in the following table, for an extremely simple economy that produces only two goods, pillows and rugs.

		Quantity Produced	Price ($)
Year 1	Pillows	50	$5
	Rugs	11	$50
Year 2	Pillows	56	$5
	Rugs	12	$60

   a. What is nominal GDP in each of the two years?
   b. What is real GDP in each year, expressed in terms of constant Year 1 dollars?
   c. What is the growth rate of real GDP (in constant Year 1 dollars)?
   d. What is the growth rate of real GDP (in constant Year 2 dollars)?
   e. Are the growth rates calculated in parts (c) and (d) the same or different?

3. Complete the following table.

Year	Nominal GDP (in billions of dollars)	Real GDP (in billions of chained 2009 dollars)	GDP deflator	GDP growth rate	Inflation rate
2012	16,155.3	15,354.6		2.2%	—
2013		15,612.2	1.07		
2014	17,427.6			2.6%	

4. List the key simplifying assumptions of the traditional macro model concerning:
   a. The forms of capital included in the model
   b. The sectors of the economy
   c. Who in the economy produces and invests

5. Go to the Bureau of Economic Analysis Web site (www.bea.gov). What are the latest figures for real GDP, current dollar GDP, and the growth rate of GDP? What time period do these represent? In what sort of dollars is real GDP expressed?

6. Go to the Bureau of Labor Statistics Web site (www.bls.gov) and locate its information on the Consumer Price Index for All Urban Consumers (called the "CPI-U"). What is its current value? What month is this for? How does its value in this month compare to its value for the same month a year ago? (That is, by what percentage has the index risen? Use the "seasonally adjusted" number.)

7. Locate the most recent news release on employment and unemployment statistics at the Bureau of Labor Statistics Web site (www.bls.gov). In a paragraph, describe how the labor force, the overall unemployment rate, and unemployment rates by race and ethnicity, gender, age, and education differ from the numbers (for September 2019) given in the text.

8. The small country of Nederland has a population of 350 people. Of the 350 people, 70 are under age 16, 190 are employed in paid work, and 80 are adults who are not doing paid work or looking for work because they are doing full-time family care, are retired or disabled, or are in school. The rest are unemployed. (No one is institutionalized, and the country has no military.) Calculate the following:
   a. The number of unemployed
   b. The size of the labor force
   c. The unemployment rate
   d. The labor force participation rate (overall, for both sexes)

9. The population of Tatoonia is very small. Luis works full-time for pay. Robin works one shift a week as counter help at a fast-food restaurant. Sheila is retired. Shawna does not work for pay, but is thinking about getting a job and has been looking through employment postings to see what is available. Bob has given up looking for work, after months of not finding anything. Ana, the only child in the country, is 12 years old.
   a. How would a household survey, following U.S. methods, classify each person?
   b. What is the labor force participation rate in Tatoonia?
   c. What is the unemployment rate in Tatoonia?

10. Describe in a short paragraph why measures of *output* do not always measure *well-being*. Include some specific examples beyond those given in the text.

11. Indicate whether each of the following actions or impacts would increase GDP.
   a. An individual purchases bottled water to avoid a contaminated municipal water supply.
   b. An individual obtains her drinking water from a water fountain at her workplace to avoid a contaminated municipal water supply.
   c. A homeowner pays a lawn-care company for landscaping services.
   d. A neighbor agrees to help a homeowner with landscaping work in exchange for assistance with plumbing work.
   e. An environmental organization provides volunteers to plant trees.

12. Go to the OECD's Web site for the Better Life Index (www.oecdbetterlifeindex.org). Note that you can adjust the weights applied to each of the 11 well-being dimensions using a sliding scale. Adjust the weights based on your personal opinions. To which factors do you assign the most weight? To which factors do you assign the least weight? Briefly summarize the rationale for your weights. Also, which countries rank the highest according to your weighted BLI?

13. Match each concept in Column A with a definition or example in Column B:

Column A	Column B
a. A negative (subtracted) item in GDP	1. The year in which real and nominal values are equal
b. "Not in the labor force"	2. Comparison with GDP supports the diminishing marginal utility of income
c. Marginally attached workers	3. A retired person
d. An entity in the government sector	4. Unpaid household production
e. Reflects the prices of all goods and services counted in GDP	5. GDP deflator
f. Base year	6. Better Life Index
g. Unemployed	7. Spending on imported cheese
h. Something not counted by the BEA in calculating GDP	8. A measure that seeks to remove the effects of price changes
i. Real GDP	9. Uses a fixed "market basket"
j. An indicator of well-being including 11 dimensions	10. Want to work and have looked in the past year but not the past month
k. A constant-weight price index	11. Immediately available for and currently looking for paid work
l. Subjective well-being	12. A state university

NOTES

1. A closely related measure is gross national product (GNP). The difference between GNP and GDP concerns whether foreign earnings are included. GNP includes the earnings of a country's citizens and corporations regardless of where they are located in the world. GDP includes all earnings within a country's borders, even the earnings of foreign citizens and corporations. GDP is used more commonly in international comparisons.

2. Briody, Blaire. 2012. "What Are Stay-at-Home Moms Really Worth?" *Fiscal Times*, May 4.

3. Folbre, Nancy. 2015. "Valuing Nonmarket Work." 2015 UNDP Human Development Report Office Think Piece.

4. Peachy, Kevin. 2016. "The Value of Unpaid Chores at Home." BBC News, April 7.

5. UN Women. 2015. "Progress of the World's Women 2015–2016: Transforming Economies, Realizing Rights." https://www.unwomen.org/en/digital-library/publications/2015/4/progress-of-the-worlds-women-2015

6. Jacobs, Eva, and Stephanie Shipp. 1990. "How Family Spending Has Changed in the U.S." *Monthly Labor Review*, March: 20–27.

7. U.S. Bureau of Labor Statistics. *Consumer Expenditure Survey 2016*, data tables; and authors' calculations.

8. International Monetary Fund (IMF). 2017. *World Economic Outlook Database*. Database updated on April 12. Accessed 21 April 2017.

9. Dietz, Rob, and Dan O'Neill. 2013. "There's No G-D-P in 'A Better Economy'." Stanford Social Innovation Review, January 7.

10. Skånberg, Kristian. 2001. *Constructing a Partially Environmentally Adjusted Net Domestic Product for Sweden 1993 and 1997*. National Institute of Economic Research, Stockholm, Sweden.

11. The United Nations differentiates between "internal" satellite accounts (those that are linked to standard accounts and typically measured in monetary units) and "external" satellite accounts (not necessarily linked and measured in either physical or monetary units). See: http://unstats.un.org/unsd/nationalaccount/AEG/papers/m4SatelliteAccounts.pdf

12. Information on BEA satellite accounts is available at: www.bea.gov/industry/#satellite

13. The commission included several distinguished social scientists and was headed by prominent economists Joseph Stiglitz, Amartya Sen, and Jean-Paul Fitoussi.

14. Stiglitz, Joseph E., Amartya Sen, and Jean-Paul Fitoussi. 2009. *Report by the Commission on the Measurement of Economic Performance and Social Progress*. Commission on the Measurement of Economic Performance and Social Progress, Paris. https://ec.europa.eu/eurostat/documents/118025/118123/Fitoussi+Commission+report

15. Helliwell, John, Richard Layard, and Jeffrey Sachs. 2017. "World Happiness Report 2017." Sustainable Development Solutions Network, New York.

16. A trendline represents the statistical "best fit" showing the relationship between the two variables on the graph.

17. Talberth, John, and Michael Weisdorf. 2017. "Genuine Progress Indicator 2.0: Pilot Accounts for the US, Maryland, and City of Baltimore 2012–2014." *Ecological Economics*, 142, December: 1–11, 142.

18. Note that the GPI measure has been modified over time to respond to theoretical critiques and valuation methods. The version discussed here is the most recent variation, termed GPI 2.0.

19. Note that this study is based on an earlier variation of GPI, but the underlying methodology of estimation—taking the PCE, adding positive contributions, and subtracting negative ones—is the same.

20. Ceroni, Marta. 2014. "Beyond GDP: US States Have Adopted Genuine Progress Indicators." *Guardian*, September 23.

21. The OECD is a group of the world's advanced industrialized countries, now including some developing countries, such as Mexico.

22. Organization for Economic Co-Operation and Development (OECD). 2016. "The Path to Happiness Lies in Good Health and a Good Job, the 'Better Life Index' Shows." May 31. https://www.oecd.org/social/the-path-to-happiness-lies-in-good-health-and-a-good-job-the-better-life-index-shows.htm

23. Organization for Economic Co-Operation and Development (OECD). 2015. *How's Life? 2015: Measuring Well-Being*. OECD Publishing, Paris.

Chapter 9

Economic Fluctuations and Macroeconomic Theory

What makes an economy experience GDP expansion or contraction, high or low employment, and good or bad business conditions? One factor that affects economic conditions is the level of **aggregate demand** in the economy—the amount that individuals and businesses want to spend. A decline in demand for goods and services by consumers and businesses generally leads to recessionary conditions and higher unemployment. Recovering demand promotes economic growth but can also sometimes lead to inflation. The level of aggregate demand in the economy, in turn, is affected by conditions in the labor market and price changes. In this chapter, we consider the interactions between these macroeconomic variables.

> **aggregate demand:** the total demand for all goods and services in a national economy

1. THE BUSINESS CYCLE

In Chapter 1, we introduced the concept of business cycles as recurrent fluctuations in the level of production in an economy. We see such fluctuations in the pattern of real GDP growth in the United States over the period 1985–2019 in Figure 9.1. During three periods—1990–1991, 2001, and 2007–2009, GDP declined sharply. The decline was most severe between 2007 and 2009 when the level of real GDP went *down* from one calendar quarter to the next. The economy is said to be in a **recession** when economic activity declines for at least two consecutive quarters.

> **recession:** a downturn in economic activity, usually defined as lasting for two consecutive calendar quarters or more

In other periods, GDP grew quite steadily. The positive GDP growth beginning in 2002 shown in Figure 9.1 continued well into 2007, when the economy plunged into a severe recession. Since the recession ended, there has been a steady increase in GDP, though it took several years for GDP to recover to its previous level, and high unemployment lingered much longer. The goal of macroeconomic stabilization policy is to smooth out such variations.

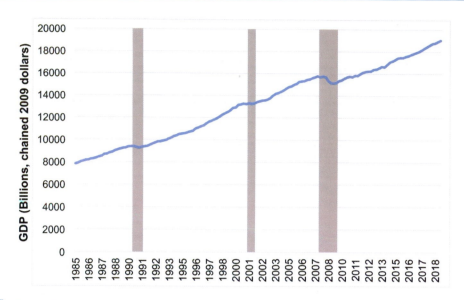

Figure 9.1 *U.S. Real GDP and Recessions*

Source: Bureau of Economic Analysis quarterly data 1985–2019, and National Bureau of Economic Research.

1.1 Stylized Facts

As we discuss the ins and outs of stabilization policy, you need to keep in mind two "stylized facts." A "stylized fact" refers to something that is a general tendency or relationship but one that may not always hold exactly in all circumstances.

Stylized Fact #1: During an economic downturn or contraction, unemployment rises, while in a recovery or expansion, unemployment falls. This is fairly easy to understand, since, when production in an economy is falling, it would seem natural to assume that producers need fewer workers. Similarly, in an expansion, unemployment falls. This relationship is sometimes expressed by an equation called **Okun's law**, which states that a one-percentage-point drop in the unemployment rate is associated with an approximately three-percentage-point boost to real GDP. The equation for Okun's "law" has been estimated many times since then, and in many different variations, and is best regarded as a stylized fact rather than a "law."

> **Okun's "law":** an empirical inverse relationship between the unemployment rate and real GDP growth

We can see some strong evidence of this inverse relationship between output growth and employment by comparing Figure 9.1 with Figure 9.2, which shows the unemployment rate from 1985 to 2019, including the three recessions that occurred during this period. As output turns downward in Figure 9.1, unemployment shoots dramatically upward in Figure 9.2. The inverse relation, however, is not

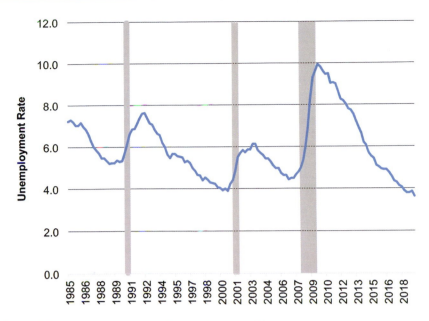

Figure 9.2 *U.S. Unemployment Rate and Recessions*

Source: Bureau of Labor Statistics monthly data 1985–2019, and National Bureau of Economic Research.

perfect and is often characterized by a time lag. In all three recessions, the unemployment rate continued to *increase* even after GDP started to rise again. But with the exception of the periods immediately following a recession, rising GDP is generally associated with increased employment.

Stylized Fact #2: An economic recovery or expansion, if it is very strong, tends to lead to an increase in the inflation rate. During a downturn or contraction, pressure on inflation eases off (and inflation may fall or even become negative). The reasoning behind this result is that, as an economy "heats up," producers increasingly compete with one another over a limited supply of raw materials, labor, and so on. Prices and wages tend to be bid up, and inflation results or intensifies. In a slump, this upward pressure on prices slackens, or even reverses, so inflation may be lower or flat, in some cases, negative (i.e., there is deflation). Figure 9.3 shows the inflation rate over the period 1985–2019, including the same three recessions highlighted in Figures 9.1 and 9.2.

As you can see, the "stylized fact" that inflation tends to fall during a recession seems to be borne out by the actual data for this period. The three recessions shown in Figure 9.3 were accompanied by distinct downturns in the inflation rate. But wide fluctuations in the inflation rate also occurred during other periods, with both increases and downturns occurring during economic upswings. Business cycle–led variations in the degree of competition for workers and resources are only *one* cause—and, in recent decades, not always the most important cause—of variations in inflation.

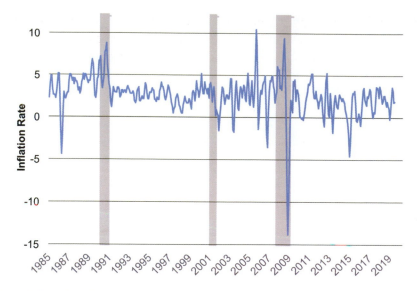

Figure 9.3 *U.S. Inflation Rate and Recessions*

Source: "Economic Report of the President" 1985–2019; rate is calculated as a three-month moving average of the consumer price index; National Bureau of Economic Research.

1.2 A Closer Look at Unemployment

Unemployment due to macroeconomic fluctuations—specifically a decline in GDP—is termed **cyclical unemployment**. This kind of unemployment is expected to decline as the economy recovers. Because cyclical unemployment is caused by economic recessions, it is likely to hurt broad parts of the population. A great deal of macroeconomic theorizing has to do with the causes of cyclical unemployment and the appropriate policy responses, since the incidence of cyclical unemployment can be minimized with macroeconomic stabilization policies.

> **cyclical unemployment:** unemployment caused by a decline in economic output

Some degree of unemployment is, however, expected and even considered healthy in an economy. The fact that some people are unemployed does not necessarily mean that there are no jobs available. In June 2019, for example, even though there were 7.3 million job vacancies, 5.9 million people were unemployed. It takes time for people to find jobs that match their interests and expertise. Unemployment arising from people's transitions between jobs is termed **frictional unemployment**. An unemployment rate of 0 percent could only occur if everyone who wants a job always takes one immediately. For the most part, economists don't worry too much about frictional unemployment, because much of it tends to be short term, and some frictional unemployment—about 2 to 3 percent—is inevitable.

> **frictional unemployment:** unemployment that arises as people are in transition between jobs

A third kind of unemployment, called **structural unemployment**, arises when there is a widespread mismatch between, on the one hand, the kinds of jobs being offered by employers and, on the other, the skills, experience, education, or geographic location of potential employees. One important cause of structural unemployment is sectoral shifts—the decline in agricultural and manufacturing jobs in the United States in recent decades means that those with skills specific to these industries may be unemployed. The U.S. economy may have a lot of new openings for financial analysts in the Southwest, for example. But these will not do you much good if you live in the Northeast and your skills are in engine assembly or Web design.

> **structural unemployment:** unemployment that arises because people's skills, experience, education, or location do not match what employers need

Technological unemployment may be considered a special case of structural unemployment. Ever since the beginning of the Industrial Revolution, technology

---

BOX 9.1 TECHNOLOGICAL CHANGE AND THE FUTURE OF WORK

Is the current situation of rapid technological change substantially different from previous eras? We are in what some call the second wave of the IT revolution, in which cloud-based platforms that deploy increasingly sophisticated forms of artificial intelligence are used to connect buyers and sellers; coordinate robots, drones, and sensors; and provide other services. While the demand for software engineers is expanding, taxi and truck drivers are nervously watching the development of ride-sharing programs and self-driving vehicles, and many professions that had seemed immune from technological unemployment—banking, retail sales, education, health care, and public services—may now also be in danger. Is there a tipping point ahead, where the total number of jobs will fall behind the number of those seeking work?

According to Andres McAfee, an MIT business school researcher, the need for human labor is expected to be greatly reduced by a highly automated and productive economy—"So the optimistic version is that we finally have more hours in our week freed up from toil and drudgery." But he pointed out that "the people at the top of the skill, wage, and income distribution are working more hours," while added leisure is going to those who don't want it—the unemployed.[1]

A 2013 study examining the risks of automation found that some jobs—telemarketers, loan officers, cashiers, taxi-drivers, and fast-food cooks—are more at risk than others such as therapists, mechanics, and health care and social workers.[2] Martin Ford, futurist and author of *Rise of Robots*, explains that the jobs that are most at risk are those which "are on some level routine, repetitive and predictable." Jobs involving "genuine creativity" (artists, scientists) and building complex social relationships (nurses, counselors) and those that are highly unpredictable (first responders) face the lowest risk of automation.[3]

It is important to note that automation does not necessarily lead to a disappearance of jobs overall. Rather, new jobs that require a different skill set could be emerging from automation of some jobs. Also, changes in other areas, such as transition to renewable energy and the rise of the middle class in many emerging markets, could result in creation of new jobs.

has been recognized as a double-edged sword for workers. On the one hand, it has created circumstances wherein each worker has more natural and manufactured capital to work with, raising workers' productivity and hence (potentially, at least) their earnings. On the other hand, technology can replace workers, leading to a situation in which ever fewer workers are needed to produce a given quantity of output.

> **technological unemployment:** unemployment caused by reduced demand for workers because technology has increased the productivity of those who have jobs

Fears of technological unemployment have been raised repeatedly during the last two and a half centuries. While these fears have been valid in specific areas—for example, tractors introduced in the 1920s were clearly a factor in reducing the need for farm labor, and computers have made many secretarial jobs obsolete—the total quantity of jobs has generally not declined as a proportion of the population. Indeed, in the twentieth century, the number of jobs in the United States increased significantly, as women successfully entered the labor force.

Employment is an essential aspect of livelihood, comfort, and well-being, since wages and salaries are the most important source of income for a majority of the population in most countries. In 2018, wages and salaries accounted for 43 percent of the national income in the United States. (The other sources of income—rents, profits, and interests—mostly derive from various kinds and degrees of ownership of productive assets such as buildings, land, or other resources, or stocks, which are ownership "shares" in companies.) Jobs are easiest to find, and often better paid, under conditions of **full employment**, when those who wish to work at prevailing wages are able to find a job readily. But often, the economy does not achieve full employment, and rising unemployment can create hardship for many. We will discuss economic theories on achieving full employment later in this chapter.

> **full employment:** a situation in which those who wish to work at the prevailing wages are able to find work readily

1.3 A Closer Look at Inflation

Business cycles also affect and are affected by the changes in price level in the economy. Rapidly rising prices are considered bad for the economy because high inflation can wipe out the value of people's savings, and it hurts people who are on fixed incomes. People may experience a decline in their standards of living if prices rise faster than wages. Inflation also redistributes wealth from creditors to debtors, since people now repay debts in money that is worth less than the money that they originally borrowed.

On the other hand, decline in prices—also known as **deflation**—is also considered bad. While deflation does indeed make people's savings *more* valuable and *helps* people who are on fixed incomes, it is highly disruptive to the broader economy. With deflation, wealth is redistributed from debtors to creditors. You borrow "cheap" money, but later have to pay back with money that is "expensive," as the real value of the money you owe has increased. This can force consumers and businesses into bankruptcy. This also makes companies less inclined to borrow and invest, which could result in a decline in output and employment levels.

deflation: when the aggregate price level falls

When people come to expect deflation, they may cut back on spending. Why buy a car or a computer now if you believe you will be able to buy them for less next year? Deflation is often touched off by a financial crisis in which many people lose access to loans and possibly even access to their own deposits at banks. This discourages consumer spending and could slow down the economy considerably. With lower consumer spending, business failures follow, which in turn lead to loan defaults and more banking failures, not to mention substantial layoffs.

Many experts feared a deflation in the United States after the 2007–2008 financial crisis. People all over the country were losing their homes and jobs. Fortunately,

---

BOX 9.2 DEFLATION IN JAPAN

Following a banking crisis in 1989, the Japanese economy slid into a situation of recession and deflation, which it has not been able to shake for over two decades. A very slow growth rate has been accompanied by generally falling prices, and consumers have held back on spending with the expectation that the longer they wait, the cheaper goods would become.

In 2013, Japanese prime minister Shinzo Abe tried to revive Japan's deflated economy with economic stimulus and monetary expansion. Since then, deflationary forces have been stabilized, but inflation has remained low (around 0.5 percent as of July 2019). Even though interest rates have been near zero percent (and even negative) for over two decades and unemployment rates have remained below 3 percent since 2017, there has been no sign of reaching the targeted 2 percent inflation. In order for prices to rise, companies need to feel confident to raise prices and consumers need to start spending more. Data confirming these trends are mixed.[4]

In June 2019, Prime Minister Abe defended his economic policies, stating: "It's true that the 2 percent price target hasn't been reached, but while we have a kind of 2 percent stability target, our real objectives, including those for monetary policy, such as spurring job growth to reach full employment, have been achieved."[5]

measures aimed at bailing out failing financial institutions and providing cheaper credit pumped more money into the system, with the result that a severe collapse in economic activity was averted. While inflation remained low, the feared deflation did not materialize. Europe also came close to deflation in the aftermath of the Great Recession but managed to avoid it through changing central banking policies to inject more money into the system.

Deflation can be very damaging when looked at from the perspective of the real potential productivity of an economy. Businesses might have great ideas for expansion, and people might want to work, earn money, and make purchases, but all are held back by a falling price level. With the prospect of debt becoming harder to service over time, companies are far less inclined to borrow. Hence, investment is postponed or even canceled, resulting in rising unemployment. For these reasons, avoiding deflation is a major concern for most governments.

Instability in prices also creates a great deal of uncertainty, which can make it very difficult for households and businesses to make sensible plans regarding savings, retirement, investment, and so on. Price instability also creates menu costs—literally, the cost of time and effort made to update printed menus and other sorts of price lists. For these reasons, stabilization of a country's price level is among the important goals of macroeconomic policy.

1.4 A Stylized Business Cycle

When analyzing business cycles, it is often convenient to separate the issue of economic fluctuations from the issue of economic growth. To do this, we can remove the upward trend in GDP in Figure 9.1 and think of business cycles in terms of the stylized picture shown in Figure 9.4. This stylized business cycle has no scale on the "year" axis, since the timing of the cycle is not regular or predictable.

During a contraction, GDP falls, and unemployment is expected to rise until the economy hits the trough, or lowest point. The biggest downturn in U.S. history was, of course, the Great Depression that started with the stock market crash of 1929 and continued until 1939. During this period, production dropped dramatically, national unemployment topped 25 percent, and prices declined. The increase in aggregate demand precipitated by World War II played a major role in ending the Great Depression. In 2007, another severe economic downturn hit the United States. While not as serious as the Great Depression, this "Great Recession" resembled it in that, unlike most recessions of the past, it persisted for more than a few quarters, and employment growth was very slow, even after the economy formally entered recovery in June 2009.

During an expansion, GDP rises from a trough until it reaches a peak where unemployment is assumed to be at the full employment level. Given the different kinds of unemployment discussed previously, there is some controversy about exactly what "full employment" means over the business cycle, so we have used a range of output levels, represented by the gray area in Figure 9.4, rather than a specific level of GDP here to indicate **full-employment output**.

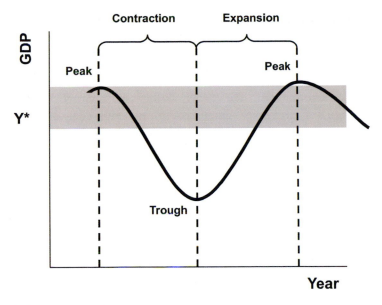

Figure 9.4 *A Stylized Business Cycle*

> **full-employment output:** a level of output that is assumed to correspond to a case of no excessive or burdensome unemployment but the likely existence of at least some transitory unemployment

At full-employment output, the economy is, presumably, not suffering from an unemployment problem. But neither is the unemployment rate actually zero, due to the existence of at least some short-term, frictional, or structural unemployment.

What economists generally do agree on is that there have been—historically, at least—episodes when economies have "overheated" and output has gone above the full employment range, giving rise (by Stylized Fact #2) to inflationary pressures. Thus, Figure 9.4 shows employment at the peak levels at the top of, or possibly slightly exceeding, the "full employment" band. And there have also been times when economies have fallen into troughs, with (in accordance with Stylized Fact #1) unacceptable levels of unemployment. In terms of the business cycle model shown in Figure 9.4, the goal of stabilization policy is to keep an economy in the gray area, avoiding the threats of inflation and unemployment.

Discussion Questions

1. What impressions do you have of the Great Recession that began in 2007? What were its impacts on people whom you know or have heard about?
2. Do you know in what phase of the business cycle we are at present? Is the U.S. economy currently in a recession or an expansion? What does this mean for employment, inflation, and GDP growth?

2. MACROECONOMIC THEORIES

One of the key debates in macroeconomics is between Keynesians, who believe that aggregate demand needs active management by the government if the economy is to be stable, and more classically oriented economists, who believe that aggregate demand can take care of itself. These theories have dominated economic thinking and policymaking for over two centuries. For the remainder of this chapter, we discuss how these two theories describe the behavior of economies that face a threat of *recession* and rising unemployment. While modern macroeconomic models are often not purely "Keynesian" or "classical" anymore,[6] this formulation helps to understand the underlying arguments.

2.1 Simplifying Assumptions

In Chapter 8, we saw that the economy could be described in terms of four sectors: household, business, government, and foreign. Household expenditures on final goods and services were called "consumption," business expenditures were categorized as "investment," spending by the government was called "government spending," and the balance between imports and exports was expressed as "net exports." We added these four components to obtain total GDP.

Note that this approach to measuring GDP simplifies the economy—for example, by assuming that only businesses carry out investment and that all the income generated in the economy goes to households in return for the labor and capital services they provide. (In the real world, businesses often hold onto some of their profits rather than paying them all out to households.) We also assume that prices are stable and that the full-employment output level *does not grow*.

Recall from Chapter 8 that whether GDP is measured by the product approach, the spending approach, or the income approach, the number will be the same (in theory). For the macroeconomic models that we now develop, we will assume that a single variable, which we will denote as "Y," represents GDP expressed as "output," "product," or "income" interchangeably. A macroeconomy is said to be in an *equilibrium* when output, income, and spending are all in balance—when they are linked in an unbroken chain, each supported by the other at the equilibrium level, as illustrated in Figure 9.5. The top arrow in Figure 9.5 illustrates that, in our

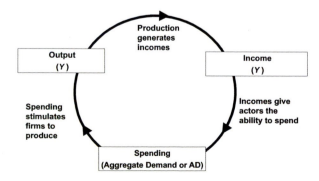

Figure 9.5 *The Output-Income-Spending Flow of an Economy in Equilibrium*

simplified macroeconomy, production by firms generates labor and capital incomes to households. We examine how this income flows into spending to support a given level of output in the economy next.

2.2 The Classical Model

Centuries ago, most people in the world were involved in agriculture or in home production, merchants were a minority, and industrial production and large-scale trade were unknown. All this changed with the coming of the Industrial Revolution in the mid-eighteenth century, when technological progress led to new methods of production, more productive economies, and an improvement in the living standards. Academic thinkers tried to understand and explain how these changes came about— and **classical economics** was born.

> **classical economics:** the school of economics, originating in the eighteenth century, that stressed issues of growth and distribution, based on an image of smoothly functioning markets

The most famous classical economist was the Scottish philosopher Adam Smith (1723–1790), whose 1776 book *An Inquiry Into the Nature and Causes of the Wealth of Nations* set the terms of discussion for centuries to come. Smith attributed the growing "wealth of nations" to various factors. One was changes in the organization of work, particularly the **division of labor** that assigned workers to **specialized**, narrowly defined tasks. By specializing in specific tasks, workers would presumably become more proficient and thereby produce more output per hour, thus increasing **labor productivity**. Another factor was technological progress, such as the invention of new machines powered by burning coal. The third was the accumulation of funds to invest in plants and machinery ("capital accumulation").

> **division of labor:** an approach to production in which a process is broken down into smaller tasks, with each worker assigned only one or a few tasks
> **specialization:** in production, a system of organization in which each worker performs only one type of task
> **labor productivity:** the level of output that can be produced per worker per hour

Classical economists, including Smith, David Ricardo, Thomas Malthus, John Stuart Mill, and Karl Marx, were interested in several questions on economic growth and distribution of society's wealth and income that are still among the most important issues for macroeconomics. Recall from our discussion in Chapter 4 that Smith is particularly known for promulgating the idea that market systems could coordinate the self-interested actions of individuals so that they would ultimately serve the social good. While Smith himself supported a number of government interventions and discussed the moral basis of social and economic behavior at length in other works, the school of classical economics has been popularly identi-fied with the idea that individual self-interest is a positive force and that govern-ments should let markets function without interference—that economies should be **laissez-faire**.[7]

> **laissez-faire economy:** an economy with little government regulation

The classical economists, with the exception of Malthus and Marx, did not much address the problem of economic fluctuations. Most of them thought that a smoothly functioning market system should be entirely self regulating, and full employment should generally prevail. This view was summarized in **Say's law**, named after the French classical economist Jean-Baptiste Say (1767–1832), which states that "supply creates its own demand." The example Say gave was of a tradesman, for example, a shoemaker who sold $100 worth of shoes. Say argued that the shoemaker would naturally want to spend the $100 on other goods, thereby creating a level of demand that was exactly equal in monetary value to the supply of shoes that he had provided.

Say was essentially assuming a barter economy whereby it is actually impossible to supply a good without demanding a good of equal value in return. Unfortunately, this logic breaks down in a modern monetary economy, where one could supply a good *not* in exchange for another good but in exchange for money. If this money is then neither spent on another good nor invested, then there is a mismatch between total supply and total demand.

> **Say's law:** the classical belief that "supply creates its own demand"

In general, when businesses produce goods or services, they pay wages to workers and rents to the owners of capital, creating income for households. Households then use this income to purchase the goods and services produced by businesses. The process of production generates income that creates the demand to consume the goods and services produced. (Recall our two-sector circular flow model from Chapter 2.) According to the logic of Say's law, the quantities demanded and quantities supplied of goods and services will exactly balance at the aggregate level; that is, there will never be insufficient demand for the goods and services produced in the market. From this, Say also deduced that the system would always generate the right number of jobs for those need-ing work.

According to classical economists, the limits to growth could only come from the supply side, where the economy's ability to expand might be limited by the availability of resources such as fertile land, productive labor, or savings. The idea that growth could be limited by inadequate demand or a lack of spending was generally rejected.

Equilibrium in the Goods and Labor Market

In the classical theory, the equilibrium level of full-employment output is determined by the supply and demand for labor. We presented the classical theory of the labor market in Chapter 7. Recall that, according to this model, wages in the labor market move freely to reach an equilibrium where the demand and supply for labor are equal; that is, everyone who wants a job at the going wage gets one. Hence, the classical labor market is always at full employment. The level of output produced by this fully employed labor force determines the equilibrium in the goods market.

In this model, the only way that involuntary unemployment can exist is if something gets in the way of market forces. For example, the presence of a legal minimum wage that keeps wages above the equilibrium wage (as illustrated in Figure 7.5 in Chapter 7) could discourage employers from hiring workers and result in unemployment. A key implication of the classical theory of labor market is that any glut of workers (i.e., unemployment) can be solved by lowering the price of labor (i.e., wages). The problem of unemployment is created and solved within the labor market alone.

In the real world, wages do not adjust freely, as they are often tied into long-term contracts. Also, employers may be less willing to cut workers' wages based on macroeconomic fluctuations, since it is likely that workers might revolt against such pay cuts, which may result in interruptions in production. Additionally, issues of motivations, labor relations, and power are also important in determining both the labor demand and supply.

The Market for Loanable Funds

Say's law assumes that all the income generated in the economy is immediately spent. But what if the households decide to save some of their income? Saving is considered a "leakage" from the output-income-spending cycle, because it represents income that is *not* spent on currently produced goods and services. This is illustrated in Figure 9.6, which shows that some funds are *diverted* from the income-spending part of the cycle into savings.

The classical theory accounts for savings in the market for credit or what economists call *loanable funds*. Because households can earn interest on any savings they deposit in a bank rather than stuff under a mattress, they will prefer the bank. Savings by households create the supply of loanable funds in the market.

Firms are the *demanders* of loanable funds. They borrow loanable funds in order to buy investment goods.[8] In our simple model, we assume that firms must borrow the savings put away by households in order to be able to finance investment projects. You can think of households depositing their savings in banks, with firms taking out loans from the banks to buy structures or equipment. In this way, firms can reinject funds to the spending stream in the form of investment. This "injection" of spending through investment is also illustrated in Figure 9.6.

The classical theory about the market for loanable funds is illustrated in Figure 9.7. The x-axis is the quantity of loanable funds supplied or demanded, and the y-axis

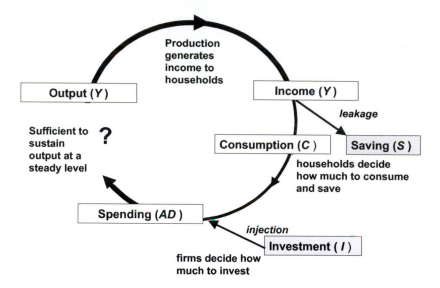

Figure 9.6 *The Output-Income-Spending Flow With Leakages and Injections*

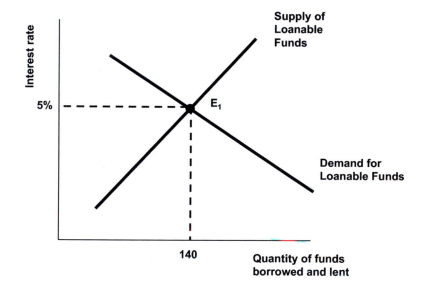

Figure 9.7 *The Classical Model of the Market for Loanable Funds*

is the interest rate paid from firms to households, which acts as the "price" of loanable funds.

Classical economists assume that households make their decisions about how much to save by looking at the going rate of interest in this market. The higher the interest rate, the more worthwhile it is to save, because their savings earn more. The lower the interest rate, the less appealing it is to save. So the supply of loanable funds (savings) curve slopes upward. To firms, however, interest payment is a cost.

So when interest rates are low, firms will want to borrow more because borrowing is inexpensive. High interest rates, in contrast, will discourage firms from borrowing. The demand curve in Figure 9.7 thus slopes downward. Where the curves cross determines the equilibrium "price" of funds and the equilibrium quantity of funds borrowed and lent.

What happens if the demand and supply for loanable funds are not equal? Suppose that the loanable funds market is initially at an equilibrium E_0, as illustrated in Figure 9.8. If businesses suddenly lose confidence about the future and cut back on their investment, there will be an excess supply of loans as the demand curve for loanable funds shifts leftward. If the interest rate remained at 5 percent, we would see a big drop in investment. But because the interest rate falls to 3 percent, part of the drop in investment will be reversed as firms take advantage of the cheaper loans. And because the interest rate is now lower, some households will choose to save less and consume more (indicated by the movement downward along the supply curve). In the end, saving and (both intended and actual) investment will still be equal, though at a lower level—in Figure 9.8, the level drops to 60. The aggregate demand will still be equal to the full-employment level—though now it is made up of somewhat less investment and somewhat more consumption. In short, the fall in intended investment was balanced exactly by an increase in consumer spending (a decrease in saving).

If, on the other hand, investment is unchanged, but households suddenly decide to consume more and save less, so that there is a shortage of loanable funds, interest rates will increase to make savings more attractive. Hence, in this model, any surplus or shortage in the market for loanable funds is eliminated through adjustments in interest rate, and the amount that households want to save is equal to the amount that firms want to invest. With saving and intended investment always in balance, there is no reason to think that the economy would ever diverge from full employment.

In the classical model, the economy is therefore depicted as a self-balancing system that stabilizes at the full-employment equilibrium. Whatever income households

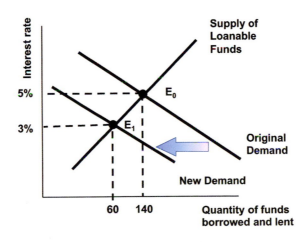

Figure 9.8 *Adjustment to a Reduction in Intended Investment in the Classical Model*

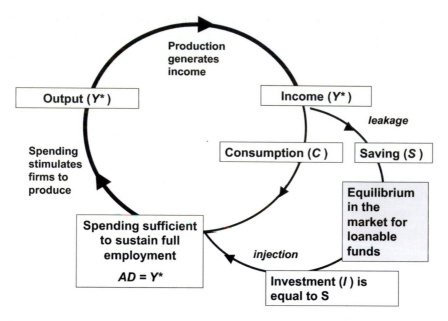

Figure 9.9 *Macroeconomic Equilibrium at Full Employment in the Classical Model*

don't spend in consumption is spent by businesses in investments; hence, the total level of income, expenditures, and production has to be equal. (See Figure 9.9.)

Classical economists acknowledged that the economy often deflects from this equilibrium, creating economic slumps, but they attributed this deflection to exogenous factors such as political upheavals, conflicts, natural disasters, or speculative crises. They assumed that economic downturns and unemployment are short-lived phenomena that should be automatically eliminated through adjustment in market prices if markets are free.

Classical economists also discussed issues related to a country's monetary system but tended to assume that monetary issues affected only the price levels, and not the level of production, in a country. We will discuss the classical monetary theory in Chapter 11.

Discussion Questions

1. Who are the actors in this simple macroeconomic model? What is the role of each in determining the flow of currently produced goods and services? What is the role of each in the classical market for loanable funds?
2. Explain verbally why, in the classical model, the demand curve for loanable funds slopes downward. Explain verbally why the supply curve of loanable funds slopes upward.

3. THE GREAT DEPRESSION AND KEYNES

The classical theory was called into question during the Great Depression, when the economy entered a severe recession and continued declining for almost a decade with no signs for automatic recovery. A great many people in the United States (and much of the rest of the industrialized world) suffered considerable hardship during the Great Depression. Production dropped by about 30 percent between 1929 and 1933, and the unemployment rate topped 25 percent. Most economists in the 1930s, trained in the classical school, reassured public leaders that this sort of cycle was to be expected. They believed that the economy was in the "trough" stage but that it would soon start to expand again. In the long run, they assured officials, the economy would recover by itself, as it had recovered from other downturns in the past.

However, high unemployment persisted throughout the 1930s. Even though wages and prices were *declining*, there were no signs of increasing production or employment. This exposed the flaws in the classical theory of self-adjusting markets with full employment, a perspective that was unable to explain or correct for this long and persistent unemployment.

In response, British economist John Maynard Keynes quipped that "in the long run, we are all dead." He meant that simply waiting for the economy to recover would lead to an unacceptably long period of severe economic damage—which, indeed, is what happened during the Great Depression. In 1936, Keynes presented a theory on how economies can fall into recessions and stay there for a long time, along with some ideas about how public policy might help the economy get out of the trough more quickly, in his book *The General Theory of Employment, Interest, and Money*.

3.1 The Keynesian Theory

Keynes's major contribution was to develop a theory to explain why aggregate demand could stay persistently low. He called it *The General Theory*, because he believed that the case of full employment (Y^*) represents only a special case, one that may not often be achieved. In his book, Keynes argued that Say's law was wrong. It *is* possible, he said, for an economy to have a level of demand for goods that is insufficient to meet the supply from production; that is, the aggregate spending could fall out of balance with income and production flows. In such a case, producers, unable to sell their goods, will cut back on production, laying off workers and thus creating economic slumps. The key to getting out of such a slump, Keynes argued, is to increase aggregate demand—the total demand for goods and services in the national economy as a whole.

As discussed previously, the aggregate demand in the economy is the sum of household expenditures on consumption, business expenditures on investment, government spending, and net foreign spending. Hence, in order to increase aggregate demand, people could be encouraged to consume more, the government could buy more goods and services, or businesses could be encouraged to spend more. In this section, we present his theory using (for the moment) the very simple closed economy with no growth model introduced previously. The topic of aggregate demand in an open economy is taken up in Chapter 14.

Consumption

Consumption expenditure makes up about 60 percent of aggregate demand. Households are able to consume more when the economy is generating higher income. In the Keynesian theory, every dollar increase in income is assumed to result in a proportional change in consumption. The number of *additional* dollars of consumption spending that occurs for every *additional* dollar of aggregate income is termed the "**marginal propensity to consume**" (*mpc*). Using the notation Δ (the Greek letter delta) to mean "change in," *mpc* can be expressed as:

$mpc = \Delta C/\Delta Y =$ *(the change in C resulting from a change in Y) ÷ (the change in Y).*

> **marginal propensity to consume (mpc):** the number of additional dollars of consumption for every additional dollar of income

For example, if the *mpc* is 0.8, it means that for every $1 increase in aggregate income, households will spend an additional 80 cents in consumption. Recall that any income that is not spent in consumption is saved. Hence, the remaining 20 cents of the $1 increase goes into savings. The number of *additional* dollars of saving that occur for every *additional* dollar of aggregate income is termed the "**marginal propensity to save**" (*mps*).

> **marginal propensity to save (mps):** the number of additional dollars saved for each additional dollar of income

Logically, the *mpc* should be no greater than 1. An *mpc* greater than 1 would mean that people increase their consumption by *more* than the addition to their income. The Keynesian consumption function also includes an "autonomous" part not related to income. This can be thought of as a minimum amount that people need to spend for basic needs. In algebraic form, the Keynesian consumption function is expressed as:

$$C = \bar{C} + mpc * Y$$

where $\bar{C}$ is "autonomous" consumption and Y is aggregate income.

A number of factors can cause a change in consumption. For example, an increase in wealth may encourage households to spend more, even if their incomes have not changed. Consumer confidence is another factor—when people feel less confident about the future, perhaps due to political turmoil or the fear of a coming recession, they tend to spend less. Attitudes toward spending and saving, influenced by cultural shifts or health or environmental concerns, could also influence consumer behavior. Government policies to either encourage or discourage savings are another factor that may affect consumption. Consumption level may also be affected by the distribution of income. Since poorer people tend to spend more of their income than wealthier people, a redistribution of income from the rich to the poor could raise consumption and depress saving. While Keynes discusses the influence of these other factors on consumption, the simple Keynesian model focuses only on income.

Note that the classical model assumes that people make their decisions about how much income to consume and how much to save based largely on the interest rate, but the Keynesian model does not mention the interest rate because the effects of interest rates on saving are, in fact, ambiguous. If the interest rate in the loanable funds market is very high, you might want to take advantage of it and increase your savings, at least for a while. But what if you are saving primarily to finance your college education or your retirement, so you have a certain target level of accumulated wealth in mind? Common sense suggests that the amount that people save depends mainly on their ability to save, based on their income as well as their needs and plans, rather than primarily on the current interest rate.

A more significant impact of changes in interest rates on household behavior comes from their effect on what households pay in interest on their *loans* rather than on what households earn on any savings. While the simple classical model assumes that households supply all savings and do not borrow, in reality, households frequently borrow to meet their consumption needs. When interest rates are high, households will face higher repayment costs on loans they have taken out for houses, cars, major appliances, and other consumer durables, so an increase in interest rates may make it more difficult to save. It is for these reasons that the simple Keynesian model leaves out the issue of interest rates entirely.

Investment

The most important factor in explaining aggregate investment spending, Keynes thought, is the general level of optimism or pessimism that investors feel about the future, or what he called "animal spirits." While only making up about a quarter of aggregate demand, investment is by far the most volatile component. This volatility is due to the fact that investment is dependent on expectations about the future economic environment, which is fundamentally uncertain.

If firms' managers believe that they will be able to sell more of the goods or services that they produce in the future, and at a good price, they will want to invest in equipment and structures to maintain and expand their capacity. If they do not see such a rosy future ahead, then why would even a very low interest rate persuade them to invest? Since the borrowed funds will have to be repaid, the major question for the borrower is: "Are my prospects for success good enough to allow me to repay this loan?" The interest rate will marginally change the amount to be repaid but is not the major determinant of the answer to this question.

Because Keynes saw investment as directed not by interest rates but instead by expectations about a fundamentally uncertain future, the simple Keynesian model simply assumes that investors intend to invest whatever investors intend to invest! Investment is thus considered "autonomous" in this model and can be denoted as:

$$I = \overline{I}$$

Of course, in the real world, firms may take into account a number of things when thinking about how much to invest. The cost of borrowing (the interest rate) is certainly one factor, but so are other things, such as the prices of investment goods, their own accumulated assets and debt, and the willingness of investors and banks to lend to them. (Not everyone can qualify for a loan.) Keynes himself conceded that, in the real world, interest rates did have some role in explaining the level of investment. But he argued that, in the case of a severe slowdown of economic activity such as the Great Depression, a low interest rate would not be enough to motivate business firms to invest in building up new capacity.

Government Spending

According to Keynes, the solution to business cycles lay in having the government take more direct control of the level of national investment. Spending by the government directly increases the demand for goods and services and helps with economic recovery. In Keynes's view, capitalist economies are inherently unstable due to the fundamental uncertainty that besets investment decisions, and only a more socially oriented direction of investment can cure this instability. This is one of the main tenets of **Keynesian economics**. However, Keynes's policy prescription outlined in 1936 was not immediately adopted, and the Great Depression continued for the remainder of the 1930s. It was the high government spending associated with national mobilization for World War II that finally brought the Great Depression to an end. While this might be seen as compelling evidence in support of Keynesian theory, war should never be waged as a macroeconomic stabilizer, nor should military spending be justified on macroeconomic grounds alone, given that there are many good options for government spending (such as expansion of public education or health care programs).

> **Keynesian economics:** the school of thought, named after John Maynard Keynes, that argues for an active government involvement in the economy to keep aggregate demand high and employment rates up through changes in government spending and taxation

The Keynesian approach strongly influenced macroeconomic policymaking in the United States and many other countries after World War II. Between 1946 and the 1960s, the U.S. government took an active role in the economy through huge investments in infrastructure development and implementation of various social welfare and anti-poverty programs. This era in the U.S. economy was characterized by strong growth, low unemployment, low inflation, and increases in productivity and wages. The idea became popular that the government might even be able to "fine-tune" the economy, counteracting any tendencies to slump or excessive expansion with policy changes, thereby largely eliminating business cycles. We will study the impacts of changes in government spending and taxation on the level of aggregate demand in the economy in more detail in the next chapter.

3.2 Persistent Unemployment and the Keynesian Labor Market Theory

Now that the pieces of the model have been explained, the model can be put together to illustrate how Keynes explained the Great Depression. At the start of the Great Depression, the 1929 stock market crash and other events caused business and investor confidence to plummet. (Consumer confidence and financial wealth also plummeted, but we are simplifying the story by concentrating on investment by firms.) Firms became very uncertain about whether they would be able to sell what they produced, so they cut back radically on their investment spending.

A similar mechanism can be argued to have worked at the onset of the Great Recession in 2008–2009: the banking crisis in the United States and its global repercussions caused such a high degree of uncertainty and disruption that businesses all over the world cut back their investment plans radically. Such a cut back in investment plans caused a drop in aggregate demand, and the economy moved away from the full-employment equilibrium. With the drop in aggregate demand, income and spending contracted to reach a new equilibrium where output and employment were much below the initial full-employment equilibrium; that is, the new level of production was not sufficient to provide full employment for workers, resulting in unemployment.

In the Keynesian model, there is no automatic mechanism that rescues the economy from this situation. The economy experiences a contraction, settling at a new, persistent, self-reinforcing low-income and high-unemployment equilibrium. The downward economic spiral results from inadequate aggregate demand, shown in Figure 9.10. A crucial thing to understand is that saying that a macroeconomy is "in equilibrium" just means that output, income, and spending are in balance. But achievement of an equilibrium is not the same thing as full employment—the equilibrium level at which output, income, and spending balance may or may not be at full employment. Because Keynes did not equate equilibrium with full employment, he believed that there is often a need for action to stimulate aggregate demand. Such policies are discussed in Chapter 10.

Unlike the classical model that assumes that unemployment is eliminated through adjustment in wages to bring the economy to the full-employment level, there was

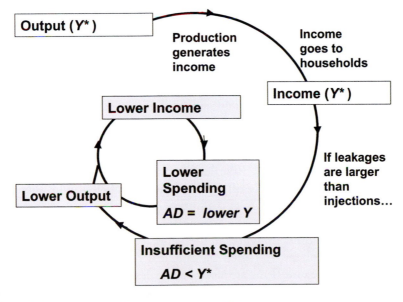

Figure 9.10 *A Keynesian Unemployment Equilibrium*

nothing that would "naturally" or "automatically" happen to pull an economy out of a low-employment situation in Keynes's view. Keynes was one among a number of economists who pointed out that aspects of real-world human psychology, history, and institutions make it unlikely (as well as often undesirable) for wages to fall quickly in response to a labor surplus. Wages may eventually adjust as shown in the classical model, but this adjustment would be too slow to keep the labor market in equilibrium. And even if wages fall, this will not necessarily result in full employment.

The Keynesian perspective challenges the entire classical assertion that unemployment results mainly from wage levels that are too high. Rather than blaming unemployment on high wages, Keynes and his followers focus on the issue of insufficient demand for labor—which they perceive as the direct result of *insufficient aggregate demand for goods and services*. Hence, to Keynesian economists, fixing the problem of unemployment is not just a matter of making labor markets work more smoothly. Rather, aggregate demand for goods and services in the economy has to increase in order to stimulate hiring. Notice how different this explanation of unemployment is from the classical theory, where the problem of unemployment arose due to wages being above the equilibrium.

In a Keynesian analysis, falling wages do not improve labor market conditions but would actually make things worse, because workers have less money to buy goods and services. This lowers consumption expenditure and aggregate demand, resulting in a decline in business sales and further layoffs. Unlike the classical economists, Keynes believed that government policies in stimulating aggregate demand could be effective in response to an economic downturn.

3.3 The Multiplier

Whenever there is an injection or leakage of funds in the economy, the total change in income will be greater than the initial change in spending. So, for example, if investors become pessimistic about future economic outlook and decide to cut investment by $100, the overall decrease in demand will be greater than $100. The intuition behind this argument is that, while the drop in investment spending leads to a drop in aggregate demand, which leads directly to a contraction in output, there are also additional feedback effects through consumption. Because consumption depends on income and income depends on aggregate demand, which depends on consumption, additional effects "echo" back and forth. For example, reducing production in a factory does not merely involve laying off assembly-line workers. The laid-off factory workers now have less income to spend at stores. This means that the stores will also need to lay off some of their employees, who then also have less income. And so on. This process is illustrated in more detail in Figure 9.11.

In the first step in Figure 9.11, we assume that investment drops by $100. This leads to an immediate drop in aggregate demand. Firms see inventories piling up and cut back production by 100 (step 2). But this decreases the income going to households (step 3), because firms are now paying less in wages, interest, dividends, and rents. Consumers react (in step 4) to a change in income. Recall that the change in consumption due to a change in income is dependent on the value of the *mpc*.

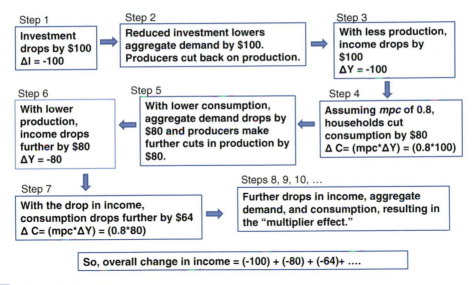

Figure 9.11 *The Multiplier at Work*

Assuming that *mpc* is 0.8, consumption drops by $80 (0.8*100) when income drops by $100. This drop in consumption results in further lowering of aggregate demand, output, and income by $80 (step 5). In the next step (step 6), the drop in income by $80 causes a further drop in consumption by $64 (0.8*80).

The process of decreases in consumption followed by decrease in aggregate demand, output, and income continues further in the following steps (8, 9, 10, and onwards). Note that in each round, the decrease in income (*Y*) gets a little smaller. Fortunately, a convenient result from mathematics means that we do not need to calculate the sum of all these changes in *Y* by continuing to extend this figure (in theory, forever—although the numbers get very tiny after a while). A result from the mathematics of infinite series implies that, in the end, the total change in *Y* is related in the following way to the original change in investment (*I*):

$$\Delta Y = \frac{1}{1 - mpc} \Delta I$$

which means, in this case,

$$\Delta Y = \frac{1}{1 - 0.8}(-100) = \frac{1}{0.2}(-100) = -500$$

The expression $1/(1 - mpc)$ is called "the income/spending multiplier"—or, for short, the multiplier—and is abbreviated *mult*:

$$mult = \frac{1}{1 - mpc}$$

In this case, with $mpc = 0.8$, the multiplier is 5. The initial decrease in intended investment causes, in the end, a decrease in income that is five times its size. We can express this mathematically as $\Delta Y = mult\ \Delta \overline{I}$.

The value of the multiplier would be the same if it had been a decrease in consumer confidence, acting through a change in $\overline{C}$, that started this cascade in incomes, instead of a decrease in investor confidence. Mathematically, this means $\Delta Y = mult\ \Delta \overline{C}$ as well. In Chapter 10, we will consider factors other than investor and consumer confidence that can change aggregate demand, including government policies.

3.4 Comparing Classical and Keynesian Views

In classical economic theory, an economy should never go into a slump—or, at least, it should not stay in one very long. Any deficiency in aggregate demand would be quickly counteracted by adjustments in interest rates and wages. Keynes, by contrast, theorized that deficiencies in aggregate demand, due to drops in investor (or consumer) confidence, could explain the deep, long-term slumps that many countries experienced during the Great Depression. Modern Keynesians argue that this theory also explains the Great Recession that began in 2007.

According to Keynes, any excess of "leakages" over "injections" would lead to progressive rounds of declines in consumption and income, until savings are so low that a new, lower-output-level equilibrium is established. Keynes and his followers believed that in this situation, some kind of government action was required to get the economy out of its slump and to achieve a higher equilibrium level. In Chapter 10, we explore how the U.S. economy did, in fact, get out of the Great Depression, as well as some of the policies that were instituted in response to the Great Recession.

This Keynesian approach turns some classical economics principles upside down. Classical economists, of course, thought that government should interfere in the economy as little as possible, while Keynes suggested that in many circumstances, a government role was essential. Another classical belief, that greater savings would automatically lead to greater investment, which in general would be good for the economy, is also reversed in the Keynesian model. Suppose that consumers become thriftier—that is to say, they decide to save more at every level of income. This pushes the consumption expenditure downward and, other things equal, leads to a *decline* in equilibrium income and, at this lower equilibrium income, *lower* total savings. This has been called the **paradox of thrift**, meaning that a seemingly commendable attempt to put more money away for the future actually leads to lower economic output and lower savings. This could help to explain why recession or depression might persist: feeling pessimistic about the future, people try to save more for a "rainy day," and the resulting decline in spending keeps the economy below its full-employment level.

> **paradox of thrift:** the phenomenon that an increase in intended savings can lead, through a decline in equilibrium income, to lower total savings

Another implication of Keynesian thinking is that the level of investment determines savings, rather than savings determining the level of investment. This is because increase in investments expands the size of the economy and raises real income. As people's income increases, they will save more (remember our earlier discussion of the marginal propensity to consume). This is very different from the classical theory, where the level of savings by households determines the amount available for business to invest.

Discussion Questions

1. If you received a raise of $100 per month, how would you increase your spending per month? How much would you change your saving? What is your *mpc*? What is your *mps*?
2. Describe verbally how, in the Keynesian model, an economy can end up in an equilibrium of persistent unemployment.

4. MACROECONOMIC HISTORY AND RECENT DEVELOPMENTS

4.1 The Crisis of the 1970s and Retreat From Keynesian Economics

In the early 1970s, many industrialized countries began to experience rising unemployment *combined with* increased inflation. Several factors contributed to the economic problems of this era. First, the U.S. economy faced increasing competition from industrialized nations in Europe and Japan, which resulted in declining profits for U.S. businesses. The strengthening of labor unions and the consolidation of corporations in the United States in the decades after the war had created an environment where the demands for wage increases by workers were accommodated through increases in the price of goods, resulting in an inflationary spiral. Also, sharp rises in energy prices due to the oil embargo in 1973 and the high expenditures by the government since the 1940s contributed to the rising inflation. Overall, growth during the 70s and 80s remained sluggish (under 3 percent).

The government was largely blamed for many of the problems of the 1970s. Too much regulation of businesses, high government spending on social programs, high taxes on corporations and individuals, and creation of too much money by the government were seen as the key causes of the crisis. This led to a reorientation of the role of the government in the economy and a revival of the classical idea that individual freedom of choice in market is central to human welfare. It was believed that a free-market economy would drive out market inefficiencies and that a smaller government would unleash private initiative and accelerate growth.

Most notable among those who took this view was University of Chicago economist Milton Friedman. Friedman had strongly challenged Keynesian ideas even before the problems of the 1970s surfaced. His most prominent theory, **monetarism**, argued that a government limited to allowing central banks to keep the nation's money supply growing on a steady path was all that was required to prevent economic downturns. Monetarists also claimed that deliberate efforts by the government to push unemployment levels too low would lead to inflation—a prediction that was seemingly borne out in the problems of the 1970s. Like the classical economists, they believed that the economy would be best left to adjust on its own. As economic conditions worsened in the late 1970s, this set of beliefs gained momentum. We will discuss this theory in more detail in Chapter 11.

> **monetarism:** the school of economic thought that argued that governments should aim for steadiness in the money supply rather than playing an active role

This change in economic ideology led to a decline in regulation of businesses and finance, cuts in social welfare programs, privatization of public services, and a shift in tax burden from corporations to the middle class. The economic effects of this transition have been mixed. Starting in the 1980s, there have been periods with long economic expansions: 1983–1990, 1992–2000, and 2000–2007, though the growth rates were lower than those during the 1940s to 1960s. At the same time, the occurrence of large asset bubbles, driven by speculation, became more common, followed by sharp declines in 1989–1992, 2001, and a huge recession in 2007—the recovery from which required active government involvement. Other notable changes since the 1970s include stagnant real wages, an increase in inequality, and an increase in the size and power of big businesses. We will discuss these issues, and possible policy responses, in later chapters.

Debates on the value of active government policies have continued, with macroeconomists at the classical end of the spectrum starting from the assumptions that people are rational and markets work efficiently. Large governments, they believe, discourage private-sector activities and economic growth. Economists on the Keynesian end of the spectrum, meanwhile, tend to emphasize the way in which unemployment can cause severe human suffering and may persist for a long time. They argue for a more active role for government. Waiting for markets to adjust on their own, they believe, may mean waiting too long. And, as Keynes himself put it, "In the long run, we are all dead."

4.2 Macroeconomics for the Twenty-First Century

The previous discussions illustrate that macroeconomics, as a field of study, is not a set of principles that is set in stone. Rather, the field has evolved over time as new empirical and theoretical techniques have been invented and as historical events have raised new questions for which people have urgently sought answers.

The issues of economic growth and the business cycle that preoccupied macroeconomic thinking for generations are still relevant today, but in the twenty-first century, new developments are demanding new ways of looking at the economic world, most recently great suffering including loss of homes and income resulted from the 2007–8 financial crisis. Deep concerns have arisen over levels of national debt, rising inequalities of wealth and income, increasing size of the financial sector, and the changing nature of the labor market, where more people are taking up temporary and part-time jobs and workers are being replaced by machines.

The environmental impact of fossil fuel–based economic growth has become a major focus of economic, social, and political concern. Most previous economic theories assumed that resources and the capacity of the environment to absorb the by-products of economic growth were essentially unlimited—or at least that continued developments in technology would keep problems of depletion and pollution at bay. This has been increasingly questioned as the scale of human economic activity grows larger. (See Figure 0.7 illustrating the rise in greenhouse emissions.) Such impacts on the environment are expected to result in severe disturbances to agriculture; disruptions in water supply; increase in tropical diseases; and threats from severe weather, including hurricanes, floods, and droughts. Reconciling ecological sustainability and restoration with full employment and growth in living standards is rising in prominence as a macroeconomic issue.

It is also worth taking a moment to consider the implications of the Keynesian model as it relates to contemporary controversies over consumerism and the environment. In the Keynesian model, it does, indeed, appear that keeping consumption and spending at high levels is necessary to keep the economy humming. The idea that cutting back on consumption spending would be "bad for the economy" is based on the Keynesian notion that reductions in aggregate spending lead to recessions or depressions and that these could potentially be deep and persistent. Would our cutting back on the kinds of consumption that are environmentally damaging lead to recession and job losses? Or could we perhaps substitute other kinds of economic activity and job creation? We revisit this assumption in later chapters to see whether it really is the case that what is good for the environment (and for future generations) has to be "bad for the economy."

Discussion Questions

1. Which major historical events influenced the development of macroeconomics as a field of study? In addition to the problems listed in the text, do you think there are other current problems that macroeconomics should be addressing?
2. Have you ever read articles or editorials that claim that high consumption is essential for a healthy economy? Does the Keynesian model seem to confirm or challenge this idea? What are some arguments for the opposite point of view?

REVIEW QUESTIONS

1. During a business-cycle recession, which of the following typically rises: the level of output, the unemployment rate, the level of investment, or the inflation rate?
2. List and describe the three types of unemployment.
3. What is technological unemployment? How might productivity-increasing advances in technology affect employment levels?
4. Explain why both inflation and deflation may be bad for the economy.
5. During the 1930s, how did economists' opinions about the Great Depression differ?
6. In the models laid out in this chapter, who receives income? Who spends? Who saves?

307

7. What is the definition of aggregate demand?

8. What conditions constitute equilibrium in a macroeconomy?

9. How can an increase in saving (if not balanced by an increase in intended investment) cause a shrinkage of the output-income-spending flow?

10. Describe the classical market for loanable funds. Who are the actors, and what do they each do?

11. Describe how the problem of leakages is solved in the classical model.

12. How did Keynes model consumption behavior? List five factors, aside from the level of income, that can affect the level of consumption in a macroeconomy.

13. Why isn't the interest rate included in the Keynesian consumption function?

14. What did Keynes think was the most important factor in determining investment behavior?

15. How can high levels of unemployment be explained in the Keynesian model?

16. Does a macroeconomy's being "in equilibrium" always mean it is in a good state? Why or why not?

17. What is "the income/spending multiplier"? Explain why a drop in autonomous investment, or in autonomous consumption, leads to a much larger drop in equilibrium income.

18. What is monetarism, and how does it differ from Keynesian theory?

19. What major changes in economic policy have taken place since the 1970s, and what new problems have emerged?

20. Why are environmental issues, including climate change, important for twenty-first-century macroeconomics?

EXERCISES

1. Search for the "World Economic Outlook Database" on the internet and locate the most recent version. Use this database to select inflation data (units of percentage change) for Germany, Japan, and the United States for the period 1990 to 2019. Construct a table of annual inflation rates for these countries. Now construct a graph using annual inflation rates on the vertical axis and the year on the horizontal axis. Plot the annual inflation rates from your table in three separate lines on the same graph. How would you compare the experiences of these three countries based on your graph?

2. Carefully draw and label a supply-and-demand diagram for the classical loanable funds market. Assuming that the market starts and ends in equilibrium, indicate what happens if there is a sudden drop in households' desire to consume.
   a. Which curve shifts, and in what direction?
   b. What happens to the equilibrium amount of loanable funds borrowed and lent? (You do not need to put numbers on the graph—just indicate the direction of the change.)
   c. What happens to the equilibrium interest rate?
   d. What happens to the equilibrium amount of investment?

3. Suppose that the marginal propensity to consume in an economy is 0.75.
   a. For each additional dollar that households receive, how much do they save? How much do they spend?
   b. If autonomous consumption increases by $100, by how much does the aggregate income rise?

4. Match each concept in Column A with a definition or example in Column B.

Column A		Column B	
a.	Structural unemployment	1.	Peak
b.	An injection	2.	An inverse relationship between unemployment and rapid GDP growth
c.	Cyclical unemployment	3.	Households save more when income rises
d.	Okun's "law"	4.	The theory that unemployment is caused by insufficient aggregate demand
e.	Classical assumption about saving	5.	The proportion of an additional dollar that households spend on consumption
f.	Keynesian theory	6.	Occurs as people move between jobs
g.	The turning point from a business cycle expansion to contraction	7.	Occurs when the skills, experience, and education of workers do not match job openings
h.	*mpc*	8.	Households save more when the interest rate rises
i.	Frictional unemployment	9.	Occurs during a recession
j.	A Keynesian assumption about saving	10.	Investment

NOTES

1. Regalado, Antonio. 2012. "When Machines Do Your Job: Interview with Andres McAfee." *MIT Technology Review*, July 11.
2. Frey, Carl Benedikt, and Michael A. Osborne. 2013. "The Future of Employment: How Susceptible Are Jobs to Computerisation?" Oxford Martin School, September 17.
3. Mahdawi, Arwa. 2017. "What Jobs Will Still Be around in 20 Years? Read This to Prepare Your Future." *The Guardian*, June 26.
4. Tabuchi, Hiroko. 2013. "Getting Japan to Spend." *New York Times*, June 29.
5. Hirokawa, Takashi. 2019. "Japan's Abe Says His 'Real' Economic Goals Were Met without Hitting 2% Inflation." Bloomberg, June 10.
6. Current schools of thought include "New Keynesian," "Post-Keynesian," "Neoclassical," and "New Classical." See online Appendix to this chapter for a description of these various schools of thought.
7. "Laissez-faire," a French term, means "leave alone" and is pronounced "lez-say fair."
8. Note that we are assuming that businesses do not hold onto any of the income they receive but pass it all along to households as wages, profits, interest, or rents.

Chapter 10

Fiscal Policy

Economic theory has real-world implications, as we can see by looking at some recent economic history. When the economies of the United States and other industrialized countries plummeted in the financial crisis of 2008, many governments responded by passing similar policies, including tax cuts, increased government spending, and increased transfers for the unemployed. The basic economic theory behind such policies is that creating demand for goods and services by encouraging spending expands the level of employment and output.

Some European countries took a different approach to the crisis, instituting "austerity" policies of spending cuts and tax increases with a goal of improving each government's budgetary position. Advocates of austerity policies argued that such policies would improve investors' confidence in the soundness of the economy and produce positive effects for economic growth, while critics argued that large reductions in public expenditure combined with tax increases would push the countries concerned deeper into recession.

In terms of the macroeconomic theory outlined in Chapter 9, these different policy responses reflect the difference between classical and Keynesian views of how the macroeconomy works and what the appropriate role of the government in the economy should be. In this chapter, we examine how the government can influence economic outcomes with a focus on **fiscal policy**—what government spends, how it gets the money that it spends, and the impacts of these activities on the level of employment, output, and aggregate demand in the economy. We begin with a discussion on the components of the government budget. The basic theory of government spending and taxes is presented next. This is followed by a discussion on the policy implications of these theories. The final section examines the issue of government debt.

> **fiscal policy:** government spending and tax policy

1. THE GOVERNMENT'S BUDGET

The government's budget is composed of government spending, transfer payments, and taxes. **Government spending** (G) includes spending on goods and services by federal, state, and local governments. **Transfer payments** (TR) are government grants, subsidies, or gifts to individuals or firms. Examples of transfer payments include unemployment insurance and Social Security payments and subsidies to, for example, energy or agricultural corporations. These two categories—government spending and transfer payments—constitute total government expenditures, or **government outlays**.

Government Outlays = G + TR

government spending (G): the component of GDP that represents spending on goods and services by federal, state, and local governments

transfer payments (TR): payments by government to individuals or firms, including Social Security payments, unemployment compensation, interest payments, and subsidies

government outlays: total government expenditures, including spending on goods and services and transfer payments

On the revenue side, government income comes from taxes (*T*). When revenues are not sufficient to cover outlays, the government borrows to cover the difference. This borrowing is accomplished through the sale of **government bonds**. In the United States, these sales are conducted by the U.S. Treasury. Government bonds are interest-bearing securities that can be bought by firms, individuals, or foreign governments. In effect, a government bond is a promise to pay back, with interest, the amount borrowed at a specific time in the future.

government bond: an interest-bearing security constituting a promise to pay at a specified future time

1.1 Understanding Taxes

Tax policies have important economic consequences, both for the national economy and for particular groups within the economy, as we will discuss in this and later chapters. Taxes can, however, be very complicated to understand. The United States federal tax code is more than 70,000 pages long.[1] Fortunately, one need not comprehend the complexity of tax law to understand the crucial role of taxes on economic outcomes. We now present a brief overview of the structure of taxation in the United States.

Before we discuss the different types of taxes, we need to first define the concept of tax progressivity. A **progressive tax** system is one where the percentage of income an individual (or household) pays in taxes tends to increase with increasing income levels. This system embodies the principle that those with higher incomes should pay more in taxes because of their greater ability to pay without making critical sacrifices. While a very poor household, for example, might have to give up eating some meals in order to pay even a small percentage of their income in taxes, a very rich household could pay a substantially larger percentage without much loss in well-being.

> **progressive tax:** a tax in which the percentage of one's income paid in taxes tends to increase with increasing income levels

A tax can also be either regressive or proportional. A **regressive tax** is one in which the proportion of income paid in taxes tends to decrease as one's income increases. A **proportional tax** means that everyone pays the same tax rate regardless of income. To give some examples, a 10 percent proportional tax would collect $1,000 from someone with an income of $10,000 per year and $100,000 from someone with an income of $1 million per year. If, instead, the system collected 10 percent from the poorer person and more than 10 percent from the richer person, it would be progressive. If the richer person pays a *smaller* percentage, the tax is regressive. Most countries' overall tax system, including that of the United States, includes a mix of progressive, proportional, and regressive taxes, as different taxes are designed with different purposes.

> **regressive tax:** a tax in which the percentage of one's income paid in taxes tends to decrease with increasing income levels
> **proportional tax:** a tax in which all taxpayers pay the same tax rate, regardless of income

Federal Income Tax

The federal income tax is levied on wages and salaries as well as income from many other sources, including interest, dividends, capital gains, self-employment income, alimony, and prizes. Of the total income received by individuals (and couples) from these various sources, a small portion is identified as being nontaxable. Additionally, some expenses can be deducted, including individual retirement account (IRA) contributions, student loan interest, and certain tuition expenses. Federal income taxes are then paid on **taxable income**, which is the income remaining after all deductions.

The federal income tax system in the United States is progressive, since it uses increasing **marginal tax rates** (the tax rate applicable to an additional dollar of income). This means that different tax rates apply to different portions of a person's income. For example, in 2018, a single filer was taxed at 10 percent on the first $9,525 of taxable income, 12 percent on taxable income above $9,525 but less than $19,050, and so on up to a maximum marginal tax rate of 37 percent for income above $500,000.

> **taxable income:** the portion of one's income that is subject to taxation after deductions and exemptions
> **marginal tax rate:** the tax rate applicable to an additional dollar of income

The marginal tax rate is different from the **effective tax rate**, which is the proportion of an individual's total income that is paid in taxes. Mathematically, it is the ratio of the total taxes to total income, expressed as a percentage. For example, assume that you earned $20,000 in 2018, out of which your taxable income was $15,000. Using the marginal tax rates for 2018, you would pay $1,609.5 (10% on the first $9,525 + 12% on the remaining $5,475) in taxes. In this case, your effective tax rate is given by:

$$\frac{\$1,609.5}{\$20,000} \times 100\% = 8.05\%$$

The distinction between marginal and effective tax rates is very useful for understanding tax policies. (See Box 10.1.)

> **effective tax rate:** one's taxes expressed as a percentage of total income

Federal Social Insurance Taxes

Taxes for federal social insurance programs, including Social Security, Medicaid, and Medicare, are collected in addition to federal income taxes. **Social insurance taxes** are levied on salaries and wages, as well as income from self-employment. Federal social insurance taxes include two separate taxes. The first is a tax of 12.4 percent of income, which is used primarily to fund Social Security. Half of this tax (6.2 percent) is deducted from an employee's pay, and the other half is paid by the employer. The other is a tax of 2.9 percent for Medicare and Medicaid, for which the employee and employer again each pay half. Self-employed individuals are responsible for paying the entire share, 15.3 percent, themselves.

> **social insurance taxes:** taxes used to fund social insurance programs such as Social Security, Medicare, and Medicaid

One main difference between these two types of taxes is that the Medicare tax is a proportional tax, since it is paid as a percentage of *all* wages and salaries. Social Security taxes, on the other hand, are capped at $128,700 as of 2018. So, the maximum Social Security tax that could be deducted from an employee's total pay in 2018 was $7,979.40 (6.2 percent of $128,700). The Social Security tax is a proportional tax on the first $128,700 of income but then becomes a regressive tax when we consider income above this limit.

Take, for example, two individuals: Susan, who earns $100,000 annually, and Leah, who makes $200,000 per year. Susan would pay a Social Security tax of 6.2 percent on all her income, or $6,200. Leah would pay the maximum Social Security contribution of $7,979.40, which works out to an effective tax rate of 3.98 percent ($7,979.40/$200,000)—much lower than the tax rate for Susan.

313

Federal Corporate Taxes

Corporations must file federal tax forms that are in many ways similar to the forms that individuals complete. Corporate taxable income is defined as total revenue minus the cost of goods sold, wages and salaries, depreciation, interest paid, and other deductions. Thus, corporations, like individuals, can take advantage of many deductions to reduce their taxable income. In fact, a corporation may have so many deductions that it actually ends up paying no tax at all or even receives a tax rebate check from the federal government despite having paid no taxes in the first place.

Prior to 2018, corporate tax rates were progressive, similar to personal income tax rates, with tax rates ranging from 15 percent to 39 percent. But with the passage of the 2017 Tax Cuts and Jobs Act, the federal corporate tax is now a "flat" 21 percent on all taxable profits. (See Box 10.1.)

Other Federal Taxes

The U.S. federal government collects **excise taxes**, which are a per-unit tax levied on numerous commodities and services, including tires, air travel, transportation fuels,

---

BOX 10.1 CORPORATE TAXES IN THE UNITED STATES: THE USE AND MISUSE OF INFORMATION

In December 2017, the Tax Cuts and Jobs Act was passed into law by the U.S. Congress. Perhaps the biggest policy change in the Act was a reduction in the federal corporate tax rate, down from around 35 percent on significant profits to 21 percent. President Trump argued that a reduction in the corporate tax rate was necessary "so that America can compete on a level playing field."[2] In supporting the plan, Trump administration officials stated that corporate taxes in the United States are the highest among industrialized nations.[3]

Looking only at top marginal rates, it is true that the United States did have the highest corporate tax rate among OECD member countries.[4] But U.S. companies use an array of tax breaks and loopholes and *actually* pay significantly lower taxes than the U.S. statutory tax rate.[5] If we instead look at effective corporate tax rates, we find that corporate taxes in the United States prior to the Tax Cuts and Jobs Act were about average for OECD countries.[6] According to a 2017 analysis by the Congressional Budget Office, the effective corporate tax rate of 18.6 percent in the United States is lower than in Japan and the United Kingdom but higher than in Germany, France, Australia, and Canada.[7]

The difference in opinions about whether the United States had the highest corporate taxes is, in part, driven by whether those making the analysis are looking at marginal tax rates or effective tax rates. Recall our earlier discussion that marginal tax rates determine taxes paid on *additional* income, while effective tax rates indicate total taxes as a percentage of total income and are better indicators of the proportion of income actually paid by corporations in taxes. As with many economic policy issues, claims made by politicians and the media need careful evaluation to determine whether they are presenting misleading or incomplete information.

alcohol, tobacco, and firearms. Consumers may be unaware that they are paying federal excise taxes, as the tax amounts are normally incorporated into the prices of products. For example, the federal excise tax on gasoline is about 18 cents per gallon.

> **excise tax:** a per-unit tax on a good or service

The final federal taxes that we consider are federal estate and gift taxes. The **estate tax** is applied to transfers of large estates to beneficiaries, and the **gift tax** is applied to the transfer of large gifts to beneficiaries. The estate tax and gift tax are complementary because the gift tax essentially prevents people from giving away their estate to beneficiaries tax-free while they are still alive. Like the federal income tax, the estate and gift taxes have exemptions. In 2018, the exemption on estate tax was $11.2 million for a married couple, and gifts under $15,000 per year per recipient were excluded from taxation. The maximum marginal tax rate on estate and gift taxes was 40 percent.

> **estate taxes:** taxes on the transfers of large estates to beneficiaries
> **gift taxes:** taxes on the transfer of large gifts to beneficiaries

The estate and gift taxes (capped at 40 percent) are the most progressive element of federal taxation. However, this high level of progressivity only applies to those with considerable assets. Indeed, fewer than 2 out of every 1,000 estates are subject to any estate tax at all.[8] Moreover, the majority of estate taxes are paid by a very small number of wealthy taxpayers. According to the Tax Policy Center, in 2017, the richest 1 percent of those estates subject to the estate tax paid 61 percent of the total estate tax revenue.[9]

State and Local Taxes

Like the federal government, state and local governments rely on several different tax mechanisms, including income taxes, excise taxes, and corporate taxes. Thus much of the previous discussion applies to the tax structures in place in most states. However, some important differences deserve mention.

First, nearly all states (45 as of 2018) have instituted some type of general sales tax. State sales tax rates range from 2.9 percent (Colorado) to 7.25 percent (California).[10] A few states reduce the tax rate on certain goods considered necessities, such as food and prescription drugs. In most states, municipal localities can charge an additional sales tax, which is generally lower than state sales taxes.

Unlike income taxes, sales taxes tend to be quite regressive, as low-income households tend to spend a larger share of their income on taxable items than do high-income households. Consider gasoline—a product that constitutes a smaller share of total expenditures as income rises. An increase in state taxes on gasoline, measured as a percentage of income, affects low-income households more than high-income households.

Taxes levied at state and local levels include property taxes, which are taxes on real estate, including land, private residences, and commercial properties. Property taxes tend to be regressive, although less regressive than excise and sales taxes, since high-income households tend to have a lower proportion of their assets subjected to property taxes.

Finally, 41 states levy an income tax. While most of these states have several progressive tax brackets, state income taxes tend to be less progressive than the federal income tax.

1.2 Federal Revenue and Outlays

For the purpose of introducing fiscal policy analysis, we will focus on the federal budget for the rest of this chapter (though we will make references to state budget, when relevant). Figures 10.1a and 10.1b show the federal sources of revenue and outlays for fiscal year (FY) 2018, respectively.[11] The major sources of federal revenue are personal income and Social Security taxes. In FY 2018, the federal government borrowed an amount equal to 10.7 percent of the total budget.

The major categories of government spending are Social Security, defense spending, and social programs. Note that because Social Security and Medicare taxes are collected for the provision of Social Security and Medicare benefits, these funds cannot be used to finance any other government programs, such as national defense or social programs.

Figure 10.2 shows the changes in government outlays and revenues for the United States from 1980 to 2018. For most of these years, the government had a

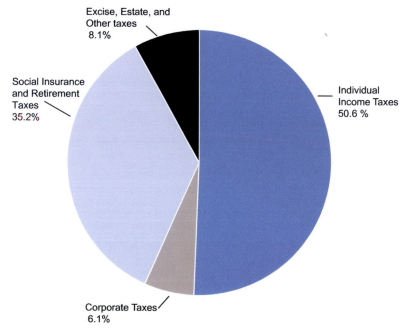

Figure 10.1a *United States Government Source of Funds, Fiscal Year 2018*

Source: Economic Report of the President, 2019. Table 2.2.

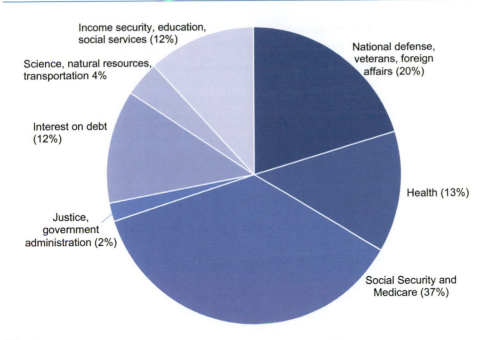

Figure 10.1b *United States Government Source of Outlays, Fiscal Year 2018*

Source: Economic Report of the President, 2019. Table 3.2.

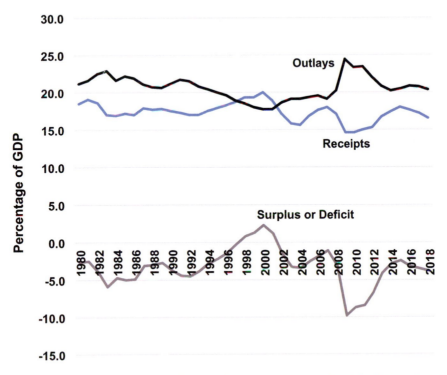

Figure 10.2 *Federal Outlays, Receipts, and Surplus/Deficit, as a Percent of GDP, 1980–2018*

Source: Economic Report of the President, 2019, Table 1.2.

budget deficit, where government outlays were greater than its receipts. The government had a **budget surplus** between 1998 and 2001, when it collected more in revenues than it spent. The government is said to have a **balanced budget** when the total government revenues and total outlays are equal. Mathematically, government budget surplus or deficit is calculated by subtracting total government outlays from total government tax revenues. A positive result indicates a surplus; a negative one a deficit.

$$Budget\ Surplus\ (+)\ or\ Deficit\ (-) = T - Government\ Outlays$$
$$= T - (G + TR)$$

> **budget deficit:** an excess of total government outlays over total government tax revenues
>
> **budget surplus:** an excess of total government tax revenues over total government outlays
>
> **balanced budget:** situation in which the total government outlays are equal to the total government tax revenues

The government's budget deficit is often expressed as a percentage of nominal (rather than real) GDP. This is a simple way to correct for the effects of inflation (since both the debt and nominal GDP are measured in current dollars) and to assess the ability of the economy to handle the deficit. The larger the economy—as measured by GDP—the easier it is to manage a given deficit, since the deficit is likely to be relatively small compared to the size of the economy. A bigger economy means that a larger flow of savings might be available to purchase more government bonds, making it easier for the government to borrow.

Over the years, the U.S. federal budget position has varied from deficit to surplus and back again. As we can see from Figure 10.3, after record deficits during World War II, the budget was briefly in surplus, then ran mostly small deficits until about 1980. Deficits increased in the 1980s. Ronald Reagan's 1980 presidential campaign leaned heavily on the principle that offering more incentives (through tax cuts) to the individuals and groups that held the most productive capital would stimulate rapid investment growth and job creation. (Such policies, referred to as "supply-side" policies, will be covered in more detail in Chapter 12.) According to this principle, tax cuts would pay for themselves through greater revenues from an expanded economy. This idea informed a major policy experiment called the Economic Recovery Act (ERA, 1981), which cut income and corporate tax rates, substantially *reducing* government revenues. At the same time, military spending increased in the 1980s. Consequently, the annual budget deficit increased from 2.7 percent of GDP in 1980 to an annual average of about 4 percent during the Reagan presidency. A portion of the deficits resulted from an unusually deep recession in 1981–1982, but most of it was from the failure of the Reagan-era policies to produce the revenue growth that would supposedly flow from the tax cuts.

In an attempt to address persistent deficits, President George H. W. Bush raised tax rates slightly and signed a bill in 1990 requiring that all spending increases be

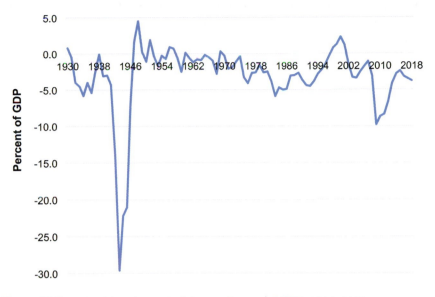

Figure 10.3 *Federal Surplus or Deficit as a Percent of GDP, 1930–2018*

Source: Economic Report of the President, 2019.

matched by either decreases in spending in other areas or tax increases, in a system known as PAYGO ("pay as you go"). Despite the introduction of that system, another recession (1990–91) and the first Iraq war kept deficits in the range of 4 percent of GDP annually. It also did not help matters that sizable sums had to be used to bail out many savings and loan banks that collapsed due to losses from risky and ill-conceived real estate investments.

Bush's PAYGO policy was continued under the administration of Bill Clinton. Congress again raised income tax rates, and the end of the Cold War allowed the federal government to lower military expenditures (relative to GDP, although not in absolute terms). At the same time, the economy emerged from a recession and began a period of sustained growth, generating surpluses in the overall federal budget from 1998 to 2001, a feat that had not been achieved since 1969. This period of budget surpluses, however, was short lived.

During the presidency of George W. Bush (2001–2009), a combination of recession, tax cuts, and increased military expenditures pushed the budget back into deficit. The first Obama administration (2009–2013) was spent responding to the worst recession since the 1930s. During this period, annual deficits averaged around 8 percent of GDP, as the government deployed an $800 billion fiscal policy package to keep the 2007–2009 recession from turning into a full-fledged depression. Tax revenue fell sharply, from $2.5 trillion in 2008 to $2.1 trillion in 2009. In addition to continued military expenses in Iraq and Afghanistan, these changes in revenue and spending led to record deficits of more than $1 trillion.

After 2012, the annual deficit fell to a historically more normal level of around 2.5 to 4 percent of GDP. But with the passage of the 2017 Trump tax cuts, deficits have started to rise again and are projected to exceed \$1 trillion in 2019.[12] (See Box 10.3.)

While the federal government is uniquely empowered to run deficits and borrow funds to meet its expenses, state and local governments are generally required to pay for current spending out of current taxes. Money can be borrowed for investment ("capital") projects such as new schools, bridges, and transit systems, but state and local governments have considerably less flexibility in the conduct of budget operations.

Discussion Questions

1. Do you think it is necessary for the United States to have so many different types of taxes? What would you change about the structure of taxation in the United States?
2. What causes budget deficits? Are budget deficits necessarily a bad thing?

2. THE ROLE OF GOVERNMENT SPENDING AND TAXES

Recall from Chapter 9 that government spending is one of the components of aggregate demand. Hence, changes in government spending directly affect the level of output and employment in the economy. Taxes and transfer payments do not directly affect aggregate demand, but, as we will see, they have an impact indirectly, particularly through their effect on consumption spending. We now examine the role of government spending, taxes, and transfer payments in influencing macroeconomic outcomes.

2.1 A Change in Government Spending

Government spending has a direct impact on the level of GDP. Government purchases of goods and services increase aggregate demand and boost the level of output and employment. In Chapter 9, we showed how a decline in investment (I) lowered the aggregate demand, leading to lower output and income levels. This suggests that government spending might be used as an antidote to low investment spending; that is, a fall in investment could be compensated by an increase in government spending.

Suppose that the economy is initially at an unemployment equilibrium, due to low investment spending (as illustrated in Figure 9.10 in Chapter 9). In this case, additional aggregate demand will be needed to return to full employment. The government could create this demand by increasing its spending. For example, the government could initiate a new building construction program where it spends money on goods such as concrete and steel as well as on wages for workers. This directly increases the income levels in the economy. In addition, there are multiplier effects—construction workers will use their incomes to buy all kinds of consumer goods and services. The multiplier effects add to the original economic stimulus resulting from the government spending.

The effect is similar to the multiplier for investment that we discussed in Chapter 9. An initial increase in government spending (ΔG) leads to an increase in income to individuals (ΔY), which leads to an increase in consumer spending (ΔC) equal to ($mpc * \Delta Y$), which in turn becomes income to other individuals, leading to another round of consumer spending, and so forth. The whole process can be summarized using the same formula as in Chapter 9 but now applied to government spending rather than investment:

$$\Delta Y = \frac{1}{1 - mpc} \Delta G$$

or:

$$\Delta Y = mult\ \Delta G$$

Using the same *mpc* and multiplier as before (*mpc* = 0.8, *mult* = 5) allows us to predict the impact of government spending on economic equilibrium. An increase in government spending of 100 leads to an equilibrium shift of 100 × 5 = 500. Looking at it the other way, if we start with the goal of an increase of 500 in Y, we can divide 500 by 5 to find the needed quantity of ΔG: 500/5 = 100.

Using the multiplier, we can easily calculate the effect of further changes in government spending. For example, suppose that government spending were reduced from 80 to 60. This negative change of 20 in G would lead to a change of (5 × −20 = −100) in equilibrium Y.

So we can see that an increase in government spending will raise the level of economic equilibrium, while a decrease in government spending will lower it. The multiplier effect, which is the same size in both directions, gives the policy extra "bang for the buck"—in this case, a change in government spending leads to five times as great a change in national income.

While we have used a multiplier of 5 to illustrate our hypothetical example, in real life, the multiplier is rarely this large, but there will usually be some multiplier effects from a change in government spending. The exact size of this multiplier is subject to much debate among economists but is generally estimated to be 2.0 or less for the U.S. economy. Note that increased government and consumer spending may make businesses more confident and encourage them to raise their investment levels, which would further increase aggregate demand. However, for the moment, we concentrate on the impact of government spending on income and consumption levels.

2.2 Taxes and Transfer Payments

To complete the picture of fiscal policy, we need to include the role of taxes and transfer payments. Changes in taxes or transfer payments affect people's **disposable income** (Y_d), which is the income available to consumers after paying taxes and receiving transfers:

$$Y_d = Y - T + TR$$

where T is the total of taxes paid in the economy and TR is the total of transfer payments from governments to individuals.

> **disposable income:** income remaining for consumption or saving after subtracting taxes and adding transfer payments

A fiscal tool frequently chosen by policymakers to provide economic stimulus is tax reductions. Lower taxes increase people's disposable income and stimulate consumption. This rise in consumption motivates further increases in income and consumption levels through multiplier effects, resulting in a higher aggregate demand. Increases in transfer payments also raise people's disposable income and have the same positive effect on aggregate demand. The opposite policies—increasing taxes or decreasing transfer payments—would have a negative effect on economic equilibrium, similar to a reduction in government spending.

Note that the mechanism by which changes in tax and transfer payments affect output differs from the process discussed previously for government spending. While government purchases *directly* affect aggregate demand and GDP, the effect of taxes and transfer payments is *indirect*, based on their effect on consumption or investment. There are many kinds of taxes and transfers; however, to keep things simple, let us just focus on the effects of changes in personal income taxes and transfers to individuals.

For example, let's say consumers receive a tax cut of 50 million dollars. If they spent it all, that would add 50 million dollars to aggregate demand. But according to the "marginal propensity to consume" (*mpc*) principle, consumers are likely to use a portion of the tax cut to increase savings or reduce debt. With the *mpc* of 0.8 that we used in Chapter 9, the portion saved will be 0.2 ×50 million dollars = 10 million dollars, leaving 40 million dollars for increased consumption. Thus, the effect on aggregate demand would be only 40 million dollars, not 50 million dollars (since saving is not part of aggregate demand).

The same logic would hold if consumers received extra transfer income of 50 million dollars. They would spend only 40 million dollars and save 10 million dollars. The reverse would be true for a tax increase or a cut in transfer payments. With a tax increase or benefit cut of 50 million dollars, individuals and families would have less to spend and would reduce their consumption by 40 million dollars.

Since only a fraction of the changes in taxes or transfer payments goes into consumption and affects the level of aggregate demand, their impact on economic equilibrium is less than that of government spending, where every single dollar affects aggregate demand directly. For this reason, the multiplier effects of changes in taxes and transfer payments are smaller than the multiplier impacts of government spending. If taxes are "lump sum"—that is, set at a fixed level that does not change with income, then we can write $T = \bar{T}$. The **tax multiplier** for a lump sum tax works in two stages. In the first stage, consumption is reduced by $mpc\,(\Delta \bar{T})$, which can be expressed as:

$$\Delta C = -(mpc)\Delta \bar{T}$$

In the second stage, this reduction in consumption has the regular multiplier effect on equilibrium income. The combined effect can be expressed as:

$$\Delta Y = (mult)\Delta C = -(mult)(mpc)\Delta \overline{T}$$

The tax multiplier is equal to $\Delta Y / \Delta \overline{T} = -(mult)(mpc)$. Mathematically, $(mult)(mpc)$ always works out to exactly 1.0 less than the regular multiplier. (You can use the multiplier formula from Chapter 9 to work out why this is true.) The tax multiplier is negative because an *increase* in taxes leads to a *reduction* in consumption, and a *reduction* in taxes leads to an *increase* in consumption. Using the figures from our previous example, where $mpc = 0.8$ and $mult = 5$, the tax multiplier would be $-(0.8)(5) = -4$.

> **tax multiplier:** the impact of a change in a lump sum tax on economic equilibrium, expressed mathematically as $\Delta Y / \Delta \overline{T}$

Transfer payments also affect the level of output through a similar logic. An increase in transfer payments, like a tax cut, will increase people's disposable income. According to the *mpc* logic, this will result in an increase in consumption, but this increase in consumption is less than the increase in disposable income. The multiplier impact of a change in transfer payments is therefore the same as that of a change in taxes, except in the opposite direction. Hence, an increase in transfer payments, like a reduction in taxes, stimulates the economy. By the same logic, a decline in transfer payments, or an increase in taxes, lowers economic equilibrium.

You might wonder: What would be the effect of an increase in government spending that is exactly balanced by an increase in taxes? Since we have shown that the multiplier effect of taxes goes in the opposite direction from that of government spending, it might appear that the effects would cancel each other out. But this is not the case. Because the tax multiplier is smaller than the government spending multiplier, there is a net positive effect on aggregate demand. The difference between the two multipliers equals 1, so the net multiplier effect will also equal 1. In the example we have used, the government policy multiplier is 5, and the tax multiplier is 4, so the **balanced budget multiplier** $= +5 - 4 = 1$. Thus, the impact on economic equilibrium is exactly equal to the original change in government spending (and taxes). So we can say that $\Delta Y = \Delta G$.[13] For example, an increase of $50 billion in government spending, balanced by an equal increase of $50 billion in taxes, would be expected to lead to a net increase in equilibrium output of $50 billion.

> **balanced budget multiplier:** the impact on equilibrium output of simultaneous increases of equal size in government spending and taxes

2.3 The Circular Flow With Government Spending and Taxes

We can modify the simple circular flow model introduced in Chapter 9 to add government spending and taxes, as shown in Figure 10.4. As noted previously, transfer payments are considered negative taxes, so we do not include a separate arrow for

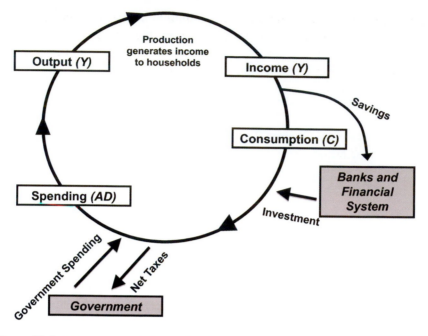

Figure 10.4 *A Macroeconomic Model With Government Spending and Taxes*

transfers. Instead, we show **net taxes**—taxes minus transfer payments—as a leakage from the circular flow and government spending as an injection to the circular flow.

> **net taxes:** taxes minus transfer payments

This model thus has two leakages, savings and net taxes, and two injections, investment and government spending. As discussed in the previous chapter, savings and investment flow through the financial system and may or may not balance. Similarly, taxes and government spending may or may not balance. If the overall leakages and injections balance, the system should be at a full employment equilibrium. From a Keynesian perspective, the object of government policy is to achieve such a balance by varying government spending and net taxes to offset any imbalances in savings and investment. Classically oriented economists are more skeptical about the ability of government to achieve this and more concerned that government action will unbalance, rather than balance, the circular flow.

In Chapter 14, we will introduce one more modification of the circular flow diagram to take into account the foreign sector, showing the effect of imports and exports.

2.4 Expansionary and Contractionary Fiscal Policy

The three fiscal policy tools discussed previously—changes in government spending, changes in tax levels, and changes in transfer payments—affect income and employment levels, as well as inflation rates (discussed further subsequently and in Chapter 12). Increasing government spending and transfer payments or lowering taxes are examples of what economists refer to as **expansionary fiscal policy**. Whether through a direct impact on aggregate demand or through giving consumers more money to spend, these policies should increase aggregate demand and equilibrium output.

> **expansionary fiscal policy:** the use of government spending, transfer payments, or tax cuts to stimulate a higher level of economic activity

If that were the whole story, macroeconomic policy would be simple—just use sufficient government spending or tax cuts to maintain the economy at full employment. But there are complications. One problem is that in order to spend more, the government has to raise taxes or expand borrowing.[14] Raising taxes tends to counteract the expansionary effects of increased spending, and borrowing money creates deficits.

Another problem is that too much government spending may lead to inflation. The goal of expansionary fiscal policy is to achieve the full-employment equilibrium. But what if fiscal policy overshoots this level? It is easy to see how this might occur. For politicians, government spending on popular programs is easy, but raising taxes to pay for them is hard. This can lead to budget deficits, but it can also cause excessive aggregate demand in the economy. Excessive demand could also arise from high consumer or business spending, but government spending, alone or in combination with high consumer and business expenditures, is capable of causing the economy to "overheat" and result in inflation.

According to our basic analysis, the cure for inflation should be fairly straightforward. If the problem is too much aggregate demand, the solution is to reduce aggregate demand. We could do this by lowering government spending on goods and services, by reducing transfer payments, or by increasing taxes. With lower transfer payments or higher taxes, businesses and consumers will have less spending power. Lower spending by government, businesses, and consumers will result in a lower equilibrium output level, and there will no longer be excess demand pressures to create inflation.

Thus, we have identified another important economic policy tool—**contractionary fiscal policy**. This is a weapon that can potentially be used against inflation. However, some caution needs to be exercised at this point. For example, it would generally be unwise to use contractionary fiscal policy at times of high unemployment. (The problem of what to do if unemployment and inflation occur at the same time—something that is not shown in our simple model—is discussed in Chapter 12.) Of course, too large a spending reduction could overshoot in a downward direction, leading to excessive unemployment and, possibly, a recession.

> **contractionary fiscal policy:** reductions in government spending or transfer payments or increases in taxes, leading to a lower level of economic activity

Economists sometimes use the term "**countercyclical**" to describe a federal government policy of increasing spending and cutting taxes in lean times and doing the reverse when the economy strengthens. State and local governments, in contrast, tend to follow a more **procyclical policy**, in which both recessions and booms are reinforced rather than counterbalanced. This is not a deliberate macroeconomic policy but simply the result of the fact that tax revenues usually fall when times are bad. Since the borrowing ability of state and local governments is much more limited than that of the federal government, they tend to cut their expenditures in bad times and use increased tax revenues to increase spending in good times. So in certain respects countercyclical federal fiscal policy works against not only business-cycle fluctuations but also the unintentional reinforcement of such fluctuations by state and local governments.

> **countercyclical policy:** fiscal policy in which taxes are lowered and expenditure is raised when the economy is weak, and the opposite occurs when the economy is strong
>
> **procyclical policy:** fiscal policy in which taxes are lowered and expenditure is raised when the economy is strong, and the opposite is done when the economy is weak

2.5 Automatic Stabilizers and Discretionary Policy

A significant portion of the variations in government spending and tax revenues occurs "automatically," due to mechanisms built into the economic system to help stabilize it. Suppose that the economy is entering a recession. As aggregate demand falls, government revenues from taxes decline since people have less income on which to pay taxes. In addition, government spending on "safety-net" items such as unemployment benefits or food stamp programs increases. This increase in government spending cushions the fall in personal disposable income—and thus the fall in consumer spending. Hence, the recession creates an automatic response of expansionary fiscal impacts that tend to moderate the recession.

Similarly, if aggregate demand is rising during an economic expansion, tax revenues rise. At the same time, fewer people receive unemployment or other transfer payments. This means that personal disposable income does not rise as quickly as national income. This, in turn, puts a damper on increases in consumer spending and limits the inflationary overheating that can arise from increased aggregate demand.

Economists refer to these changes in tax receipts and transfer payments as the **automatic stabilization** effect of government spending and taxes. It refers to the way in which the government budget moderates fluctuations of aggregate demand even without any active decision-making or legislating by the government.

> **automatic stabilizers:** tax and spending institutions that tend to increase government revenues and lower government spending during economic expansions but lower revenues and raise government spending during economic recessions

Automatic stabilizers help to explain why, for example, the U.S. government was able to enjoy budgetary surpluses in the late 1990s. It is true that the policies of the Clinton administration, which included raising some tax rates to try to balance the budget, contributed. But as business revenues and personal incomes soared, the resulting increase in tax revenues allowed the government's coffers to fill.

Sometimes, the automatic stabilization effect of government spending and taxes cannot smooth economic ups and downs as much as is needed. Relatively severe problems of recession or inflation often give rise to proposals to use an active or **discretionary fiscal policy** to remedy the situation. This issue is controversial among economists. Some economists believe that activist fiscal policy is likely to do more harm than good, while others argue that such policies are essential, especially to respond to severe economic problems.

> **discretionary fiscal policy:** changes in government spending and taxation resulting from deliberate policy decisions

The first major experience with expansionary fiscal policy was during the Great Depression (1929–1939) and World War II (1939–1945). During the Great Depression, President Franklin D. Roosevelt's New Deal had initiated some government spending programs intended to put the unemployed to work. As a result of this increased spending, unemployment declined from 25 percent in 1933 to 19 percent in 1938. This spending was dwarfed by the large increase in government spending during World War II, which lowered unemployment much further, to about 2 percent in 1943.

After the war, the beneficial effects of the expanded government role—steady economic growth and low unemployment—seemed to justify high government spending. Economists became so optimistic about the power of fiscal policy that it was suggested that it would be possible for the government to "fine-tune" the economic system using fiscal policy, to ratchet aggregate demand up or down in response to changes in the business climate.

"Fine-tuning" was largely discredited in the 1970s and 1980s, as the economy struggled with inflationary problems that were partly a result of sharp increases in oil prices but were also seen as having been worsened by excessive government spending (we look at this in more detail in Chapter 12). In addition, many economists argued that problems of **time lags** made fiscal policy unwieldy and often counterproductive. It takes time to collect data on economic indicators, identify potential problems, formulate appropriate policy measures, and get them approved by the Congress and the president. Additionally, these legal changes take time to show up in actual tax forms and government budgets. Such delays that occur within the government are called *inside lags*.

> **time lags:** the time that elapses between the formulation of an economic policy and its actual effects on the economy

Once all of these lags have been overcome, there are *outside lags* arising from the time taken for the new policies to affect the economy. Suppose, for example, that the government responds to a rise in unemployment with increased government spending or a tax cut. By the time these policies are in place and create an economic stimulus, the economy may have recovered on its own. In that case, the additional aggregate demand will not be needed and is likely to create inflationary pressures.

Despite these issues with discretionary fiscal policy, governments have continued to use it, with mixed results. Worldwide, using fiscal policy to stabilize the economy made a global revival during the Great Recession of 2007–2009 when many major economies passed large stimulus packages to prevent a further deterioration of the world economy. In the United States, the Obama administration passed a $787 billion stimulus package, including both increased government spending and tax cuts. (See Box 10.2.)

BOX 10.2 THE OBAMA STIMULUS PROGRAM

In February 2009, in response to a severe recession that had pushed the unemployment rate over 8 percent, the Obama administration proposed a $787 billion stimulus package, including $288 billion in tax cuts; $224 billion in extended unemployment benefits, education, and health care; and $275 billion for job creation through federal contracts, grants, and loans. The stimulus, formally known as the American Recovery and Reinvestment Act (ARRA), was enacted by Congress, providing for increased spending and tax reductions over a period of ten years. (In practice, the cost of the stimulus package ended up being slightly larger, about $831 billion.)

The stimulus is an example of expansionary fiscal policy, including all three fiscal policy tools: changes in government spending, including spending on infrastructure investment; changes in tax levels; and changes in transfer payments. According to the economic theories discussed in this chapter, the effects of such a program should be to expand economic activity, boost GDP, and lower unemployment.

Was the stimulus successful? The answer was not immediately obvious, because the recession was severe (unemployment rates peaked in late 2009 at 10 percent) and the subsequent recovery slow, giving many people the impression that the stimulus failed. But there is now sufficient evidence to indicate that in fact it was very effective.

According to the Congressional Budget Office (CBO), the ARRA "added as many as 3.3 million jobs to the economy in the second quarter of 2010, and may have prevented the nation from lapsing back into recession."[15] An analysis by economists Alan Blinder and Mark Zandi in 2010 found that the stimulus "probably averted what could have been called Great Depression 2.0. . . . [W]ithout the government's response, GDP in 2010 would be about 11.5 percent lower [and] payroll employment would be less by some 8½ million jobs." Blinder and Zandi's analysis takes into account negative multiplier effects.[16] Note also the spending did not, and has not subsequently, generated problems of inflation.

What about longer-term effects of the stimulus? The CBO estimated that ARRA would increase budget deficits by about $840 billion over the 2009–2019 period; 95 percent of this impact was realized by December 2014.[17] Without the stimulus, the economy would have been likely to go into a much more severe decline, which would have lowered tax revenues and raised transfer payments, so it is possible that without the stimulus, the deficit would have increased even more.

Discussion Questions

1. What recent changes in government spending or tax policy have been in the news? How would you expect these to affect GDP and employment levels?
2. In general, tax increases are politically unpopular. Would you ever be likely to favor a tax increase? Under what circumstances, if any, might a tax increase be beneficial to the economy?

3. POLICY ISSUES

3.1 Crowding Out and Crowding In

A common concern of fiscal policy critics is that federal government spending gets in the way of private investment. Recall from our discussion in Section 1 that when the government cannot raise enough taxes to finance its expenditures, it must borrow money from the capital markets. Using the theory of loanable funds introduced in Chapter 9, government borrowing in theory could absorb some of the available supply of funds, leaving less money available for private investment. The reduced availability of loanable funds can have the effect of raising interest rates, which, by making borrowing more expensive, makes investment less likely, *ceteris paribus*. Economists therefore say that borrowing to help cover budget deficits may have the effect of "**crowding out**" private investment. Using this argument, economists who favor the classical approach often claim that replacing dynamic private investment with supposedly less efficient government spending is undesirable, as well as ineffective in stimulating the economy.

> **crowding out:** a reduction in the availability of private capital resulting from federal government borrowing to finance budget deficits

Figure 10.5 uses the classical model of the loanable funds market, introduced in Chapter 9, to illustrate how government demand for loanable funds could crowd out private borrowing. The supply curve (S) represents savings or, more concretely, the supply of loanable funds. For a given supply, the interest rate will be pushed up from i_1 to i_2 when the government borrows money to pay for a budget deficit, represented by a shift in the demand curve from D_1 to D_2. The result is that private investment is now more expensive, and saving becomes more attractive.

The difference between Q_2 and Q_3 represents the amount of funds borrowed by the government. Because this additional demand raises the interest rate, private investment becomes less attractive, and some is "crowded out." Q_3 now represents the quantity of loanable funds available for private investment. The amount of "crowding out" is shown on the graph as the difference between Q_1 and Q_3. The implication of this analysis is that government deficit spending is counterproductive to the aim of promoting private investment.

Keynesian economists generally disagree with this conclusion. Keynes himself acknowledged the potential for crowding out. He did not, however, believe that government borrowing would crowd out private investment to a significant degree

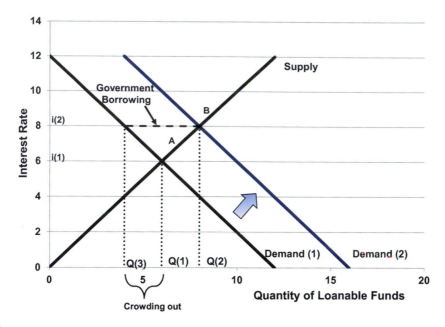

Figure 10.5 *Crowding Out in the Loanable Funds Market*

if, as during the Great Depression, there was considerable slack in the economy. In other words, if businesses are reluctant to invest anyway, there is no reason for government borrowing to drive up interest rates. Remember that in the Keynesian view, recessionary conditions are characterized by an excess of savings over investment, so there is no reason to worry that government borrowing will absorb too much of the available loanable funds.

Keynes also minimized the importance of crowding out for other reasons. First, recall from Chapter 9 that, according to Keynes, investment decisions are dependent not just on the rate of interest but more importantly on expectations of future profit. In good economic times, investors purchase more capital goods because their growing profits reinforce an optimistic outlook about the future. And they are likely to do so despite the historical tendency for interest rates to *rise* in good economic times. The opposite might well be true in recession. Despite low interest rates, business spending will be lower due to growing pessimism. Hence, government borrowing to finance deficits may not raise interest rates during a recession, and even if it does, this might not have any significant effect on investment, since investors will not want to invest until the economy starts to recover. Once the recovery is under way, the prospect of growing demand will encourage "animal spirits" and increased investment.

Modern Keynesian economists also point out that the theory of loanable funds does not really apply to the actual workings of modern financial systems. As will be discussed in Chapter 11, the banking sector can *create* the money demanded by other sectors without first having to accumulate a stock of savings. Therefore, there is no fixed amount of loanable funds. As long as government spending does not lead to overheating the economy by pushing aggregate demand beyond the economy's capacity limits, there will be no crowding out.

In fact, from a more Keynesian point of view, expansionary fiscal policy can potentially lead to the *opposite* of crowding out. This is because there is significant scope for complementarity between public and private investment. According to this argument, certain government expenditures on, say, transportation, energy, or communications networks enhance the potential profits of private investment by providing critical infrastructure. Rather than being a substitute for private investment, government spending supports the productivity of private investment and is therefore likely to encourage more of it. When such government spending generates more private investment, it is called **crowding in**.

> **crowding in:** the process in which government spending leads to more favorable expectations for the economy, thereby inducing greater private investment

During the Great Depression, Keynes argued that the economy could be stuck in a potentially permanent low-level equilibrium (i.e., the unemployment equilibrium we saw in Chapter 9) and that the government needed to run deficits to finance the spending necessary to stimulate aggregate demand and thus attract renewed investment spending on capital goods. This argument was also used to justify the Obama administration's stimulus program of 2009–2012 (Box 10.2).

3.2 Different Multiplier Effects

The multiplier effect outlined in Chapter 9 implies that every additional dollar of government spending increases aggregate demand by more than one dollar. But we have seen that much of the effect can be offset by taxes. In addition, it is unrealistic to assume that different types of government expenditures have the same multiplier effect.

As seen earlier, the larger the *mpc*, the greater the multiplier. Until now, we have assumed that the *mpc* is uniform—that is, that it represents the marginal propensity to consume of all individuals and groups in society. But there may be significant variations in the *mpc* depending on which income groups are involved.

The typical wealthy individual is capable of saving a much greater percentage of income than most lower-income people. Hence, a low-income person's *mpc* tends to be higher than the *mpc* of a high-income person. Because a higher *mpc* translates to a larger multiplier, Keynes argued that, in general, the multiplier is largest when government spending is directed toward those who have the highest *mpc*. Spending or tax cuts that benefit middle- and lower-income people are thus likely to have larger multiplier effects than spending or tax policies that primarily benefit the rich.

Considering both crowding out/crowding in effects and different *mpc* effects, we can conclude that multipliers:

- Are not stable over time but might be larger in a recession, when crowding out is less of a problem.
- Are larger if the spending benefits lower-income households.
- Are larger if the government spends money on investment for infrastructure; in this case, crowding in of private investment might result.

Table 10.1 Different Multiplier Effects

Tax Cuts	Multiplier
Nonrefundable lump-sum tax rebate	1.02
Refundable lump-sum tax rebate	1.26
Temporary Tax Cuts	
Payroll tax holiday	1.29
Across-the-board tax cut	1.03
Accelerated depreciation	0.27
Permanent Tax Cuts	
Extend alternative minimum tax patch	0.48
Make income tax cuts permanent	0.29
Make dividend and capital gains tax cuts permanent	0.37
Cut corporate tax rate	0.30
Spending Increases	
Extend unemployment insurance benefits	1.64
Temporarily increase food stamps	1.73
Issue general aid to state governments	1.36
Increase infrastructure spending	1.59

Source: M. Zandi, "The Economic Impact of the American Recovery and Reinvestment Act," Moody's Economy. com, 2009.

Table 10.1 presents estimates for the multiplier effects of different fiscal policy initiatives that were considered in response to the 2007–2009 recession. Note that unemployment benefits, food stamps, aid to state governments (which help prevent layoffs), and infrastructure spending all have relatively large multiplier effects. The smallest multiplier effects tend to be associated with tax cuts, especially those for wealthy individuals or corporations. As anticipated by Keynes, tax cuts in this case get less "bang for the buck" due to the generally smaller *mpc* exhibited by the beneficiaries of such policies.

Discussion Questions

1. Under what conditions would government spending tend to displace private investment spending? Under what conditions might it contribute to increasing private investment spending?
2. Looking at Table 10.1 on different multiplier effects, which kinds of government fiscal policy do you think are most effective? Which are least effective? What might be some implications for evaluation of the Obama stimulus program (Box 10.2) or the Trump tax cuts (Box 10.3 below)?

4. DEBT AND DEFICITS

You may have seen the national debt clock in New York City that continuously shows how much our debt is increasing by the second. The total amount of the debt, which exceeds $20 trillion, seems very large. But what does it mean? Why does our country borrow so much money? To whom do we owe it all? Is it a serious problem? In this final section, we answer these questions and examine the relationship between the national debt and the economy.

4.1 Deficits and the National Debt

Perhaps because the two terms sound so much alike, many people confuse the government's deficit with the government *debt*. But the two "D words" are very different. The deficit totaled nearly $800 billion in fiscal year 2018, while total federal debt exceeded $21 *trillion* by the end of fiscal year 2018. The reason the second number is much larger than the first is that the debt represents deficits accumulated over many years. The government's debt rises when the government runs a deficit and falls when it runs a surplus.

The total debt outstanding for the federal government is referred to as the national debt or the **gross federal debt**. The gross federal debt includes money that the federal government "borrows" from other government accounts (such as Social Security and Medicare) and the money it borrows from the public by issuing Treasury bonds. The difference between the gross federal debt and the debt owed to other government accounts is **the debt held by the public**.

> **gross federal debt:** total amount owed by the federal government to all claimants, including foreigners, the public in the United States, and other government accounts
> **debt held by the public:** the gross federal debt minus the debt owed to other government accounts

Figure 10.6 shows some recent data on the government's debt, measured as a percentage of GDP. The two lines on the graph indicate the total government debt

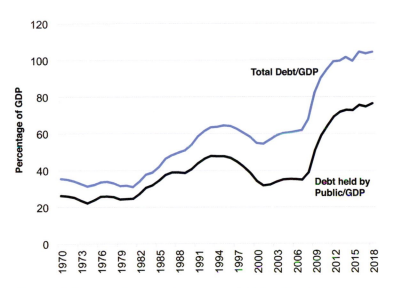

Figure 10.6 *U.S. National Debt as a Percentage of GDP, 1970–2018*

Source: St. Louis Federal Reserve Bank.

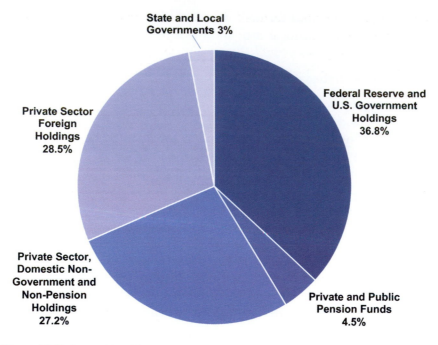

Figure 10.7 *Ownership of Gross Federal Debt, 2016*

Source: Treasury Department, 2016, Table OFS-1; Distribution of Federal Securities by Class of Investors and Type of Issues, Table OFS-2; Estimated Ownership of U.S. Treasury Securities.

and the part of government debt held by the public. After hitting a high of more than 100 percent of GDP during World War II, the debt generally declined as a percentage of GDP until 1980. It rose between 1980 and 1996, then declined again relative to GDP until 2000. Since 2000, the debt has risen, with a particularly sharp increase in the years following the 2007–2009 recession.

Figure 10.7 shows how ownership of the gross federal debt is divided up. Federal Reserve (the U.S. central bank) and U.S. government holdings account for about 37 percent of the debt. State and local governments, perhaps surprisingly, account for another 3 percent of federal debt. States and municipalities with budget surpluses will often buy federal debt, because it is considered mostly risk-free. The domestic private sector owns about 27 percent of the federal debt in the form of bonds, which are found in a variety of locations: banks, pension plans, insurance companies, mutual funds, and others, including households. Finally, foreigners own about 29 percent of all federal debt.

4.2 Government Debt: Potential Problems

One commonly expressed view of the government's debt is that it represents a burden on future generations of citizens. There is some truth to this assertion, but it is also somewhat misleading. It implicitly compares the government's debt to the debt of a private citizen. Certainly, if you personally accumulated a huge debt, it would not be good for your financial future. But government debt is different in some important ways.

First, about half of government debt held by the public is, directly or indirectly, owed to U.S. citizens. When people own Treasury bills (T-bills), Treasury notes, or Treasury bonds, they own government IOUs. From their point of view, the government debt is an asset, a form of wealth.

Second, government debt does not have to be paid off. Old debt can be "rolled over," that is, replaced by new debt. Provided that the size of the debt does not grow too quickly, the government's credit is good—there will always be people interested in buying and holding government bonds. Most economists use the rule of thumb that as long as the rate of increase in government debt is not significantly greater than that of GDP for several years in a row, it does not represent a severe problem for the economy.

Third, the U.S. government pays interest in U.S. dollars. A country such as Argentina that owes money to other countries and must pay interest in a foreign currency (the U.S. dollar) can get into big trouble and eventually be forced to default on its debt. But it is much easier to manage a debt that is denominated in your own currency. Even if some of the debt is owed to foreigners, the United States does not have to obtain foreign currency to pay it. And so long as foreigners are willing to continue holding U.S. government bonds, it will not be necessary to pay it at all—instead, the debt can be rolled over as new bonds replace old ones.

But this should not encourage us to believe that government debt is never a concern. Rising debt creates several significant problems. First, interest must be paid on the debt. This means that a larger share of future budgets must be devoted to paying interest, leaving less for other needs. As of September 2019, the interest rate on a 10-year Treasury bond was 1.6 percent. This is extremely low from a historical perspective, but interest rates are likely to rise in the future, increasing the burden of servicing the debt. In this sense, increasing debt is a burden on future generations in that debt finance detracts from other important functions that the government could be performing. The portion of tax receipts that goes to debt service (paying the interest, if not the principal, of the government's debt) is not available for other uses such as education, health, and so on.

It is also true that the largest holders of government bonds tend to be wealthier people, so most of the interest paid by the government goes to better-off individuals. If this payment is not counteracted by changes in the tax system, it encourages increased income inequality.

Another problem is that in recent years, an increasing proportion of the debt has been borrowed from governments, corporations, and individuals in foreign countries (Figure 10.8). The interest payments on this portion of the debt must be made to those outside the country. That means that the United States must earn enough income from exports and other sources to pay not only for imports but also for interest payments to the rest of the world. Alternatively, the country could borrow more, but it is best to avoid this solution, since it would just make the overall foreign debt problem larger in the long run.

Large foreign holdings of debt also pose another problem—what if those foreign debt holders decided to sell the U.S. bonds that they own? In that case, the

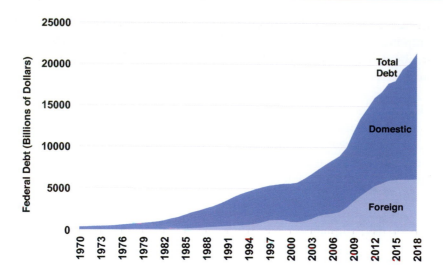

Figure 10.8 *Domestic and Foreign Ownership of U.S. Debt (Billions of Dollars), 1970–2018*

Source: St. Louis Federal Reserve Bank.

government might have trouble finding enough people who are willing to hold government bonds (that is, lend money to the government), which could cause interest rates to rise sharply. The greater the unease over the borrower's ability to pay, the higher the interest rate that the borrower must offer in order to attract lenders. This would push the government budget further into deficit and could tip the economy into a recession.

The question "Is government debt worth it?" can be answered only if we consider what that debt is used to finance. In this respect, an analogy to personal or business debt is appropriate. Our judgment about accumulating consumer and corporate debt depends on the benefits received. For example, if debt is accumulated for gambling, it is a bad idea. If the bet does not pay off, then it is very difficult to pay the interest on the debt (not to mention the principal). But if the government borrows to pay for intelligently planned investment, it can be very beneficial. If the investment leads to economic growth, the government's ability to collect tax revenue is enhanced. This kind of borrowing can pay for itself, as long as the investment is not for wasteful "pork barrel" spending, poorly planned or unnecessary projects, and so on.

Even if the debt finances current spending, it can be justifiable if it is seen as necessary to maintain or protect valuable aspects of life. Most people would not be opposed to borrowing to pay for cleanup after a natural disaster or to contain a deadly pandemic. For example, Congress appropriated $60 billion in relief funds for Hurricane Sandy relief in 2013 and over $100 billion for Hurricanes Harvey, Irma, and Maria, as well as wildfire relief, in 2017.

The argument for adding to federal debt seems stronger if the government spends on programs that produce a high multiplier effect. With low interest rates, the gain from the multiplier effect (in terms of the increase in aggregate demand) is potentially larger than the loss (in terms of adding to the debt burden), which would make the net gain positive. It may be counterproductive, however, to allow the debt to grow if it is financing "low-multiplier" activities. An example is tax cuts for the wealthy, which do not produce as much "bang for the buck" as tax cuts for the poor or new spending on constructive activities.

The management of debt involves standard principles of wise stewardship of finances. When we apply them to government deficits and debt, we need to understand how government debt is different from private debt and weigh the economic benefits of different spending and tax policies.

4.3 The Balanced Budget Debate

If balancing the budget were legally required, the United States could not have accumulated a national debt. Hoping to avoid uncontrolled debt dependence, many in the past have advocated legislation requiring that the budget be balanced. Proponents argue that such a law would prevent the federal government from imprudently running deficits, potentially causing inflation, in good economic times. But there is a very serious downside, in that such an amendment would make the federal government powerless to use countercyclical policy to fight recessions.

Most states have a balanced budget requirement that forces them to cut services and government employees during a recession. The federal government often provides aid to allow states to minimize cost cutting in an attempt to prevent both the state and national economy from weakening further. States often have less recourse to cut spending during a recession because, unlike the federal government, they are unable to create additional funds and may be much more constrained in being able to borrow funds. A balanced budget amendment would effectively make the federal government little different from the states.

In 1985, Congress passed the Balanced Budget and Emergency Deficit Control Act, requiring that a limit be set on the annual deficit and that the limit be reduced until a balanced budget was achieved in 1991. Not meeting the **deficit ceiling** would require spending to be reduced automatically to the point where the deficit was no higher than the prescribed limit for that year. This proved too much for Congress, and even for the Supreme Court, which found the automatic reduction provision unconstitutional.

> **deficit ceiling:** a congressionally mandated limit on the size of the federal budget deficit

In 2011 and again in 2013, the Obama administration faced a potential crisis over the near breaching of what is known as the U.S. **debt ceiling**—a congressionally mandated limit on the size of the gross federal debt. As the debt approached the mandated ceiling, the United States faced the prospect of not being able to borrow fresh funds to pay bonds that were coming due for payment. Amid doubts about the perceived creditworthiness of the United States, Standard and Poor's, one of the major rating agencies, downgraded U.S. government debt from AAA to AA+

in the summer of 2011, the first time in history that this happened. Fortunately for the United States, even with this downgrade, its debt remained very much in demand.

> **debt ceiling:** a congressionally mandated limit on the size of the gross federal debt

Following heated and partisan negotiations, Congress and the president struck a deal in 2011, allowing the debt ceiling to be raised (by about a trillion dollars). Since then, debt ceiling deadlines have become an issue every few years but have generally been resolved without crisis, given the memory of 2011 and broad recognition of the dangers of pushing the country close to the cliff of debt default.

The periodic focus on the debt ceiling is in many ways misleading. If Congress and the president want to avoid increasing the debt, they would have to agree on a balanced budget, in which case the debt ceiling would not become an issue. But that is a lot easier said than done. A balanced budget would either require drastic cutbacks in popular programs such as Social Security or significant tax increases. In the long run, of course, it is important to keep debt levels under control, but it is a mistake to presume that the federal government should maintain zero debt. The ability to use deficits at appropriate times to generate a fiscal stimulus is what sets the federal government apart from the states and cities and possibly protects a weak economy from sinking deeper.

An alternative approach to balanced budgets is the principle of **functional finance**, expounded by economist Abba Lerner, which requires that national governments do their utmost to ensure that aggregate demand remain at a reasonable level, ideally achieving full employment. The assumption behind this principle is that the healthy economic growth that resulted would ensure that the government could sustainably finance its debt with greater tax revenue. The view is in direct conflict with that of deficit "hawks," who would maintain absolute limits on deficit and debt levels.

> **functional finance:** the idea that a sovereign government should finance current needs and provide for adequate aggregate demand to maintain employment levels

4.4 Deficit Projections and Policy Responses

The U.S. annual federal deficit declined from a peak of about 10 percent of GDP in 2009 to a low of 2.4 percent of GDP in 2015 but has since been rising gradually to 3.8 percent of GDP in fiscal year 2018 (Figure 10.3). The Congressional Budget Office, which provides nonpartisan economic analysis for Congress, projects that the deficit will continue to increase to about 5 percent of GDP by 2022 and then remain close to 5 percent for the next six years.[18] This is significantly greater than the annual average over the past 50 years, 3.1 percent, implying a more rapid increase in overall federal debt. One of the key reasons for the expected increase in deficit and debt levels is the tax cuts passed by Congress in December 2017. (See Box 10.3.)

BOX 10.3 THE TRUMP TAX CUTS

In December 2017, a major package of tax cuts known as the Tax Cuts and Jobs Act (TCJA) was passed by Congress and signed into law by President Trump. Major elements of the TCJA included:

- Reductions in personal income tax rates and changes in exemptions and deductions. These changes would deliver major gains to wealthy households with smaller reductions for middle-class and lower-income earners.
- A reduction in the corporate tax rate from 35 percent to 21 percent.
- Repealing the Affordable Care Act's mandate for individuals to purchase health insurance.

While most economists agreed that the tax cuts would exert a stimulative effect on the economy, opinions differed on the mechanisms involved, as well as the overall impact of the Act. Tax cuts tend to increase aggregate demand, but many economists questioned whether excessive stimulus at a time when the economy was close to full employment would increase inflationary pressures. Advocates of the tax cuts envisioned a positive impact on economic growth, with the corporate tax cuts especially anticipated to increase investment.

The tax cuts also came under fire from economists who argued that the TCJA "weakens revenues at a time when the nation needs to raise more revenue."[19] These critics predicted that larger deficits resulting from the tax cuts would make it much more difficult to invest in such priorities as infrastructure, education, and health, while increasing pressure for cutbacks in social programs such as Social Security, Medicare, and Medicaid.

Analysis by the conservative-leaning Tax Foundation concludes that the Act will create more than 300,000 jobs, increase the after-tax incomes by an average of 1.1 percent, and increase the GDP by 1.7 percent over the long term.[20] The liberal-leaning Tax Policy Center, however, finds that the Act will have little effect on GDP in the long term but significantly increase the national deficit as tax revenues decline.[21] The nonpartisan Joint Committee on Taxation estimates that the $1.5 trillion cost of the Act will be partially offset by additional revenues associated with economic growth of about $500 billion. Thus, the net cost to the U.S. government would be about $1 trillion.[22]

Since the individual tax cuts mainly benefit upper-income earners, the multiplier effect is likely to be limited. In addition, the individual tax cuts were slated to expire in 2027, resulting in net tax increases for many taxpayers after that date, while the corporate tax cuts were permanent. The repeal of the ACA individual mandate was also expected to add millions to the number of uninsured Americans and increase health premiums in the individual market. For these reasons, the tax cuts would tend to increase overall inequality. Analysis by the Congressional Budget Office finds that those with incomes of less than $20,000 are made, on net, worse off by the Act, while the largest benefits accrue to those with incomes greater than $100,000.[23]

In addition to the 2017 tax cuts, the CBO has identified factors such as demographic pressures of an aging population, increase in health care costs, increase in federal subsidies for health care, and increase in interest payments on the federal debt as reasons that deficits are projected to remain at relatively high levels even as the economy stabilizes.[24] Note that the first three factors are closely related and suggest that a focus on health care should be an important component of any significant long-term budgetary reforms in the United States. What can be done to address the issue of rising deficits? A range of possible policies for reducing future deficits can be summarized as follows.

Policies for Increasing Revenues

- Expansionary fiscal policies that promote growth may increase tax revenues by raising overall income levels. However, the historical record shows that the overall effect of broad tax cuts yields lower, not higher revenues. This suggests that any lowering of tax rates would need to be accompanied by closing tax loopholes in order to be revenue neutral or revenue positive.
- Increase revenues through repealing tax cuts for upper-income individuals and large corporations. It would also be possible to increase revenues by raising tax rates more broadly, but this would tend to accentuate inequality by penalizing middle- and low-income earners.
- Increase revenue through new, possibly environmentally oriented, taxes such as taxes on carbon emissions or consumption taxes. These taxes could also have a regressive effect unless accompanied by rebates for lower-income taxpayers.

Spending-Side Policies

- Reduce "mandatory" spending on programs such as Social Security, Medicare, Medicaid, and the Affordable Care Act. Cuts to these programs are likely to increase inequity, but spending reductions could be achieved through holding down health care costs, which has already been achieved to some extent in Medicare and through Affordable Care Act provisions.
- Reduce discretionary spending in areas such as military, education, highways, scientific research, and the environment. Non-defense military spending is already declining, and with increased infrastructure spending needs, possibilities for reductions in this area are limited.
- Increase efficiency of spending in health care and other areas, seeking more "bang for the buck," including state/federal and public/private collaboration initiatives.

To the extent that any of the previous policies can be successful in reducing deficits and long-term growth of the debt, interest costs will also be reduced. There is broad agreement that some combination of these policies will be needed to avoid a long-term increase in debt, but which policies to implement remains controversial.

Our review of debt and deficits indicates that neither is inherently bad for the economy and that deficits in times of recession may be essential to helping the economy recover. But some degree of balance is required. Deficits must be limited as a percent of GDP, and long-term increases in the debt burden should be avoided. This represents a major challenge, but policies are available to promote both a healthy economy and a manageable debt, provided such policies can gain sufficient political support.

Discussion Questions

1. What is the difference between the deficit and the national debt? How are they related?
2. "The national debt is a huge burden on our economy." How would you evaluate this statement?

REVIEW QUESTIONS

1. How is the federal budget surplus or deficit defined? How has the federal budget position varied in recent years?
2. What is a progressive tax? A regressive tax? A proportional tax?
3. How do marginal tax rates work in calculating one's income taxes?
4. How is an effective tax rate calculated?
5. What is the impact of a change in government spending on aggregate demand?
6. What is the impact of a lump-sum change in taxes on aggregate demand? How does it differ from a change in government spending?
7. Give some examples of expansionary and contractionary fiscal policy.
8. What is meant by an automatic stabilizer? Give some examples of economic institutions that function as automatic stabilizers.
9. What are some of the advantages and disadvantages of discretionary fiscal policy? Give some examples of the use of discretionary fiscal policy.
10. What is crowding out? How specifically does crowding out happen? What is crowding in?
11. What is the difference between the national debt and a deficit?
12. What factors contributed to the federal surplus during the Clinton administration, and why did it turn into a deficit in the following Bush administration?
13. Summarize some of the potential problems with government debt.
14. What are the pros and cons of a balanced budget amendment?

EXERCISES

1. Consider the following table, which shows the total amount of taxes paid at different total income levels in a society. For each income level, calculate the effective tax rate. Is this tax system progressive or regressive? Explain.

Total income	Total taxes paid
$200,000	$50,000
$100,000	$22,000
$80,000	$16,000
$50,000	$8,000
$40,000	$4,000
$20,000	$1,000

2. If the *marginal propensity to consume* in an economy is 0.75, calculate:
    a. The effect on equilibrium GDP of a government spending level of 100
    b. The effect on equilibrium GDP of a tax increase of 100
    c. The effect on equilibrium GDP if both government spending and tax increase by 100
    d. What does this imply about the impact of a balanced government budget on GDP, compared to government spending alone?

3. Which of the following are examples of automatic stabilizers, and which are examples of discretionary policy? Could some be both? Explain.
    a. Tax revenues rise during an economic expansion
    b. Personal tax rates are reduced
    c. Government spending on highways is increased
    d. Unemployment payments rise during a recession

4. Go to the Federal Reserve Economic Database (http://research.stlouisfed.org/fred2/) and look in categories/national accounts for recent data on the U.S. national debt as a percent of GDP and recent figures on budget deficits. What does this tell you about recent trends? Compare the period 1990–2007 to more recent years. Do the figures indicate that we may be returning to a more "normal" situation regarding debt and deficits?

5. The chapter identifies and explains several reasons it is inappropriate to compare the government debt to the debt of a private citizen. Which of these explanations are consistent with the presentation in the chapter?
    a. Governments have the ability to "roll over" their debt more or less endlessly.
    b. A significant portion of the government debt is owed to U.S. citizens.
    c. The U.S. government pays interest on its debt in dollars that it prints.
    d. Government debt is always used to finance investment.

6. The chapter is very clear that it's dangerous to assume that "government debt is never a concern." Which of the following are reasons articulated in the chapter for why debt can be a concern?
    a. A larger share of future budgets must be devoted to interest payments.
    b. It is always unwise for governments to get into debt.
    c. Interest payments to high-income individuals could exacerbate income inequality.
    d. Deficit spending during a recession will only make the economic downturn worse.

7. Match each concept in Column A with a definition or example in Column B.

Column A	Column B
a. Tax multiplier	1. A congressionally mandated limit on the size of the federal debt
b. Disposable income	2. Unemployment compensation
c. Debt	3. The excess of spending over revenue collections
d. An example of a progressive tax	4. Sales tax
e. Expansionary fiscal policy	5. $Y - T + TR$
f. Contractionary fiscal policy	6. $G + TR$
g. Debt ceiling	7. Reduction in income tax rates
h. Government outlays	8. The accumulation of deficits over many years
i. Automatic stabilizer	9. Intended investment
j. Deficit	10. $-(mult)(mpc)$
k. An example of a regressive tax	11. Estate taxes
l. Injection into the circular flow	12. Reduction in government spending

NOTES

1. Russell, Jason. 2016. "Look at How Many Pages Are in the Federal Tax Code." *Washington Examiner*, April 15.
2. U.S. Treasury Department Press Release. www.treasury.gov/press-center/press-releases/Documents/Tax-Framework_1pager.pdf
3. Kamisar, Ben. 2017. "WH Clarifies Trump's 'Highest Taxed Nation' Claim." *The Hill*, October 10.
4. OECD, OECD.Stat, Table II.1. Statutory Corporate Income Tax Rate.
5. Center on Budget and Policy Priorities (CBPP). 2017. "Actual U.S. Corporate Tax Rates Are in Line with Comparable Countries." Tax Reform Brief, October 10.
6. Gravelle, Jane G. 2014. "International Corporate Tax Rate Comparisons and Policy Implications." Congressional Research Service, January 6.
7. Congressional Budget Office (CBO). 2017. "International Comparisons of Corporate Income Tax Rates." Congress of the United States, March 8. https://www.cbo.gov/publication/52419
8. Adamczyk, Alicia. 2016. "How Many People Pay the Estate Tax?" *Time*, August 9.
9. Tax Policy Center. 2016. The Tax Policy Center's Briefing Book. https://www.taxpolicycenter.org/briefing-book
10. Walczak, Jared, and Scott Drenkard. 2017. "State and Local Sales Tax Rates in 2017." Tax Foundation, January 31.
11. The federal fiscal year runs from October 1 of the prior year through September 30 of the year being described. For example, FY 2018 ran from October 1, 2017 through September 30, 2018.
12. Wasson, Erik, and Sarah McGregor. 2018. "U.S. Deficit to Surpass $1 Trillion." Bloomberg News, April 9.
13. Technically, simultaneous changes in government spending and taxes of equal size do not imply that the overall budget is balanced. What is required for this is that *total* spending and *total* taxes be equal.
14. "Printing money," or increasing the money supply, requires the cooperation of the central bank; this will be discussed in detail in Chapter 11.
15. Montgomery, Lori. 2012. "Congressional Budget Office Defends Stimulus." *Washington Post*, June 6.
16. Blinder, Alan S., and Mark Zandi. 2010. "How the Great Recession Was Brought to an End." www.economy.com/mark-zandi/documents/End-of-Great-Recession.pdf
17. Congressional Budget Office. 2015. "Estimated Impact of the American Recovery and Reinvestment Act on Employment and Economic Output in 2014." February 20. https://www.cbo.gov/publication/49958
18. Congressional Budget Office. 2018. "CBO's Projections of Deficits and Debt for the 2018–2028 Period." April. www.cbo.gov/publication/53781
19. Marr, Chuck, Brendan Duke, and Chye-Ching Huang. 2018. "New Tax Law Is Fundamentally Flawed and Will Require Basic Restructuring." Center on Budget and Policy Priorities, April 9.
20. Tax Foundation. 2017. "Preliminary Details and Analysis of the Tax Cuts and Jobs Act." Special Report No. 241, December.
21. Tax Policy Center. 2017. "Analysis of the Tax Cuts and Jobs Act." www.taxpolicycenter.org/feature/analysis-tax-cuts-and-jobs-act

22. Joint Committee on Taxation. 2017. "Macroeconomic Analysis of the Conference Agreement for H.R. 1, the 'Tax Cuts and Jobs Act'." JCX-69-17, December 22.

23. Congressional Budget Office (CBO). 2017. "Distributional Effects of Changes in Taxes and Spending under the Conference Agreement for H.R. 1." December 21. https://www.cbo.gov/publication/53429

24. Congressional Budget Office. 2012. "Choices for Deficit Reduction." November. www.cbo.gov/publication/43692

Chapter 11

Money and Monetary Policy

So far, this book has said very little about money. This is in line with early views on money, according to which money was seen as a mere facilitator in the process of employing scarce resources to produce goods and services. But in modern economies, money, and the banking system by which money is made available to the public, are crucial to the effective functioning of the economy. In the Great Recession of 2007–2009, people relearned the lesson of the Great Depression of the 1930s: if there are problems in the banking system, deep and long-lasting recession can result. Hence, money and the health of the banking system are important macroeconomic issues.

1. UNDERSTANDING MONEY

1.1 Why Money?

Before we discuss the functions of money in a sophisticated contemporary economy, let's picture a few simpler scenarios, drawn from real-world events, that inform how economists have come to think about money and the macroeconomy.

Let's start with the case of an economy in which inflation is low to moderate and the banking system is in reasonably good shape. You are a businessperson who has a great idea about how to expand your business. Or you are interested in buying a home for your family. But you do not have the cash. You go to a bank and ask for a loan. The bank will evaluate whether lending you the requested amount is sensible within its business strategy and regulatory requirements and then either deny you the loan or offer it to you on particular terms. If you and the bank come to an agreement, you obtain the loan and go out and spend. If you are denied the loan, or if you think the terms offered to you are too unfavorable, you will probably forgo expansion of your business or the purchase of the house. In both cases, less spending in the economy will occur.

If government policy, implemented by the country's central bank, can influence the volume and terms of loans made by banks, then it will influence the level of spending in the economy. We have already seen in Chapters 9 and 10 how the level of spending (or aggregate demand) in an economy can determine the level of output and employment. Hence, policy that affects the behavior of banks (referred to as

monetary policy) can be a significant factor in achieving the goals of macroeconomic stabilization and low unemployment.

> **monetary policy:** the use of policy tools controlled by a nation's central bank to influence interest rates, available credit, and the money supply

Not all economies enjoy low inflation rates and stable banking systems. Consider a country with a very simple government and banking system. The country's government finds it very difficult to collect enough taxes to pay its operating expenses, so it runs a printing press to print paper money and uses this money to pay its employees and its bills. How would such behavior affect the economy? If the national economy were very large and growing in relation to the volume of government expenditures, the fresh bills might just be absorbed into circulation without much impact (there is more money, but also there are more goods to spend that money on). But if the economy were stagnant and government expenditures were significant relative to national output, the result would be inflation caused by too much money "chasing too few goods." If more and more money were put into circulation, prices would rise further.

If this situation continued for long, hyperinflation—often defined as any annual inflation rate higher than 100 percent—would likely result (see Box 11.1). Germany after World War I, Hungary after World War II, Bolivia in the mid-1980s, Argentina during various periods, Ukraine in the early 1990s, Zimbabwe in 2008–2009, and Venezuela in 2016–2019 all experienced notable hyperinflations.

During hyperinflation, it becomes very difficult to keep a modern economy going. People tend to resort to **barter**—exchanging goods, services, or assets directly for other goods, services, or assets—to try to avoid having to deal with a rapidly inflating currency. Normal patterns of saving and lending are disrupted as it becomes difficult to make bank deposits or to get loans. If they can, people may try to

---

BOX 11.1 EXPERIENCES OF HYPERINFLATION

During the German hyperinflation in the 1920s, a story was told of someone taking stacks of deutsche marks (the German currency at the time) to town in a wheelbarrow in order to make a modest purchase, and—after leaving it for a moment—returning to find the wheelbarrow stolen but the bills left stacked on the ground. Other stories told of people in a bar ordering their beers two at a time, because the time it took for the price of beer to rise was less than it would take for the beer to get warm.

After the fall of the Soviet Union, in the 1990s, Russia suffered from severe inflation. Many people who had saved money in cash found that it had become nearly valueless. A Russian colleague told one of the authors of this text how his mother had thought, at the beginning of the 1990s, that she had enough money saved to take care of her in old age. She watched the value of her stash of bills go down and down until finally, in desperation, rather than watch it disappear, she took it to the store and bought a bag of sugar.

acquire—or at least keep their accounts in—a "hard," stable currency issued by a foreign country. Hyperinflation is obviously not a desirable situation; production tends to decline, and unemployment is increased by the chaos that it causes.

> **barter:** exchange of goods, services, or assets directly for other goods, services, or assets, without the use of money

Hyperinflation usually ends when the nearly valueless currency is abandoned and people exchange very large denominations of the old currency for small denominations of a new currency. If the new currency is accompanied by a credible government promise to stop "running the printing press," the episode of hyperinflation draws to a close. This is what happened after the hyperinflation of the early 2000s in Turkey. In 2004, a million Turkish lira was worth about US$0.75. The old lira was abandoned in favor of a new currency that removed six zeros. In 2019, the new Turkish lira had a value of about US$0.18. Recall from our discussion in Chapter 9 that even if price increases do not reach hyperinflation levels, high inflation tends to be disruptive to an economy.

Now consider an economy in the opposite situation, in which insufficient money is entering the system and people are not spending—either because they simply want to hold onto their money or because they are unable to get loans from banks. Such a situation, if sustained, can result in falling prices (deflation). As discussed in Chapter 9, deflation also disrupts consumption and investment activities by creating uncertainties about future prices, redistributing wealth from debtors to creditors, and discouraging borrowing.

The Great Depression in the United States was accompanied by a collapse in the banking system and a drop in price level by 25 percent in just a few years. Falling prices bankrupted business and farmers, thus making conditions even worse. But deflation is not merely "ancient history." We saw in Chapter 9 (Box 9.2) that Japan also experienced deflation touched off by a financial crisis in late 1989. Stability of the monetary system is thus a fundamentally important policy goal—to prevent both rapid inflation *and* deflation.

1.2 What Is Money?

The bills and coins you have in your wallet are obviously "money." And so is the "money" in your bank account that you can spend using a debit card or other electronic payment system. But the cash in your pocket or the balance in your bank account only represent specific *forms* of money. Economists use the term "money" in a much broader sense to refer to a special kind of financial asset that has the following three important functions:

1. *Medium of exchange*: When you buy or sell something, you need money to make the exchange. Without money, an economy would have to operate as a barter system. This could be quite inconvenient—there would have to be what is called a "double coincidence of wants." For example, if you want pizza and can offer Web design services, you would need to spend considerable time finding pizza-makers

347

in need of Web design. Such merchants may or may not exist. With money, you can sell your services to anyone who wants them and use the money you receive to buy pizza from anyone who supplies it.

2. *Store of value*: The pizza-makers, in the previous example, are unlikely to accept your money unless they know that, a month from now, their landlord will also accept the same money when they pay their rent. Hence, money serves as a way of holding wealth. While wealth can also be held in other forms of financial or real capital that is worth something, the thing that makes money distinct from these other assets is its liquidity, that is, the ease with which it can be used in exchange. Money is highly liquid—you can take it to the store and use it immediately. If you own a car or shares in a business, these are also ways of storing your wealth, but they have quite low liquidity: you must convert the value stored in them to money before you can buy something else.

> **liquidity:** the ease of use of an asset as a medium of exchange

3. *Unit of account:* The price of a pizza can be expressed in monetary units that, presumably, reflect the pizza's "value." In this example, money is a unit of account for the pizzeria calculating its revenue and profit and for the household calculating its expenditures. Yet even things that are not actually being bought and sold are often assigned money values. When a firm estimates the value of unsold inventories in its warehouses, for example, or a town assesses the dollar value of a house even though there are no plans for it to be sold, they are using money as a unit of account.

Some ways in which we commonly use the term "money" differ from how economists use it. For example, we might say that someone "makes a lot of money" because she has a high annual *income*. Income, however, is a *flow* variable, measured over a period of time. Money is a *stock* variable—a particular kind of asset (stocks and flows are described in Chapter 1). A person who makes a lot of income over a year may acquire a large stock of money—or she may not if most of that income is quickly spent on goods and services.

We may also say that someone "has a lot of money" if she has accumulated a lot of *wealth*. But this is also not technically correct. A wealthy person may hold a lot of her assets in the form of corporate shares, real estate, or Renaissance paintings, rather than as spendable, highly liquid money. Liquidity issues aside, holding money (a particular financial asset) is not the same as holding a tangible asset with useful physical properties. Money is thus not the same thing as wealth or income (although the concepts can overlap). These distinctions will be useful to better understand the material that follows.

1.3 Types of Money

Historical accounts about the origins of money differ. While economists generally tell a story in which money was introduced simply to eliminate the inconvenience of barter, the truth appears to be more complicated. As noted earlier, barter still exists, not only in situations of hyperinflation but also in vibrant, local communities where, for example, friends or neighbors exchange dog-walking services for tutoring or guitar lessons. Furthermore, it is far from clear that barter was *ever* the principal means of exchanging goods. Indeed, the use of money in the form of debits and credits (also called **credit money**) may even predate the use of gold or other metals as money.

> **credit money:** money that is transferable to another through credit and debit bookkeeping entries

Over significant periods in history, gold and other forms of metal served as important forms of money. Gold is an example of **commodity money**, which is money made up of something that is used in the exchange of goods and services, giving it what economists call **exchange value**, but also contains **intrinsic** value (value based on its own properties). While coins made of gold or silver are probably the most familiar example, decorative beads, shells, fishhooks, and cattle have also served the purpose in some cultures.

> **commodity money:** a good used as money that is also valuable in itself
> **exchange value:** value that corresponds to the value of goods or services for which the item can be exchanged
> **intrinsic value:** value related to the tangible or physical properties of the object

To be used as money, a commodity must be *generally acceptable, standardized, durable, portable, scarce,* and, preferably, easily *divisible.* Standardization is important so that disputes do not arise about the quality and value of the money. Coins stamped by the government indicate that they are of equal weight and purity of mineral content. Gold and silver have historically been popular because of their durability and scarcity. Coins made of, say, wood, in an area with many forests would rapidly lose value, as everyone could just make their own. Divisibility is also important. Heavy gold ingots might work for making a large purchase, or as a "safe haven" investment, but are not very useful for buying pasta for dinner. Smaller coins, and coins made of less valuable minerals, were historically minted to provide a medium of exchange for smaller purchases.

Gold and silver coins, while fairly portable, can still be inconvenient to carry around in large quantities. Individual banks, state governments, and national governments have at various times issued paper monies that represent claims on actual commodities, usually gold or silver. For many years, starting in the late 1880s, government-issued silver certificates were the main form of domestic paper money in the United States. International transactions were, for many years, based on gold reserves, in what came to be known as the **gold standard**. When people carried such a piece of paper, they could think of it as a certificate showing that they owned a bit of a gold ingot in Fort Knox.

> **gold standard:** a monetary system in which the monetary unit is based on some fixed quantity of gold

Such systems in which the value of paper notes is tied to commodities with intrinsic value such as gold and silver were, during their time, considered necessary for people to have faith in the exchange value of the notes and, by extension, for the economy to function smoothly. One problem with this system, however, was that fixing an amount of money to a particular amount of scarce gold or silver (say $1 = 1/32$ ounce of gold) seriously limited the ability of the banking system to create money. Some researchers have blamed the gold standard for major economic downturns of the past, such as the Great Depression.

In the 1960s, due to an increase in the price of silver, the government eliminated silver certificates and replaced them with what is called a "dollar bill" or a Federal Reserve note. At about the same time, the U.S. government also removed silver coins from circulation, replacing them with look-alike coins made from cheaper nickel-clad copper. Finally, in 1971, President Richard Nixon took the U.S. economy off the international gold standard, ushering in a new monetary era that dates to the present.

Did you ever stop and think of what the basis is for the value of the coins and dollar bills we use today? The basis for the value is—precisely and no more than—the expectation that the dollar bill will be acceptable in exchange! The currency and coins we use now are what are called **fiat money**. "Fiat" in Latin means "let it be done," and a legal authority does something "by fiat" when it just declares something to be so. *A dollar bill is money because the government declares it to be money.* In other words, its intrinsic value is no more than the value of the piece of paper of which it is made, but fiat money possesses exchange value, which is the value of the goods or services that such money can pay for in the market. Fiat money is what some people call a "social construction"—something that works in society because of how people think and act toward it, not because of something it intrinsically "is." Fiat money works well as long as people are generally in agreement that it has value.

> **fiat money:** a medium of exchange that is used as money because a government says it has value, and that is accepted by the people using it

As economies have become more and more sophisticated, even carrying around paper money is inconvenient, and transactions are increasingly made electronically. For example, you can pay for your purchases through transfer of electronic funds from your bank account, and commercial banks can create electronic "money" when granting you a loan. So paper money and bank credit can both be considered "money."

1.4 Measures of Money

Because different assets have different degrees of liquidity, it is difficult to draw distinct lines between which assets are actually money (sometimes called "pure money"), which are "near-money," and which are "not money." Economists have devised various ways of defining and measuring the volume of money that is circulating in a given economy.

Coins and bills are obviously money. In the United States today, coins are manufactured by the U.S. Mint in Philadelphia; Denver; San Francisco; and West Point, NY, while bills are created by the Bureau of Engraving and Printing in Washington, DC, and Fort Worth, Texas. When economists measure a country's "money supply," only currency that is *in circulation* is included—that is, not currency sitting in a vault at the Mint or at a bank. In December 2018, currency in circulation in the United States totaled about 1.7 trillion.

But checking accounts are also extremely liquid. People can pay for almost everything using paper checks and, increasingly, debit cards and electronic transfers of funds from their checking accounts. The most commonly used measure of the amount of money in an economy, called M1 or pure money, includes currency in circulation as well as the value of checkable deposits and travelers checks. In December 2018, checkable deposits totaled about $2.12 trillion, and travelers checks amounted to about $1.7 billion, so M1 (cash plus checks and checkable accounts) totaled about $3.8 trillion.

> **M1:** a measure of the money supply that includes currency, checkable deposits, and travelers checks

A measure called **M2** includes everything in M1, plus savings deposits and other funds such as small certificates of deposit and retail money market funds (those owned by individuals and businesses). Many people can now move funds from their savings accounts to their checking accounts with the click of a mouse or make electronic payments directly from their savings accounts. One can, moreover, often write checks against money market accounts, so from a liquidity perspective, they also seem almost indistinguishable from M1. However, the traditional system of classification used by monetary economists has been slow to adapt. Until the system is changed, therefore, savings and money markets, as well as small certificates of deposit, are classified as "near money" and fall into M2. Presently M2 is nearly four times the size of M1 and totaled $14.4 trillion as of December 2018. When economists talk about "the money supply," they usually mean either M1 or M2.

> **M2:** a measure of the money supply that includes all of M1 plus savings deposits, small certificates of deposit, and retail money market funds

If we include large certificates of deposit and money market funds owned or managed by large financial institutions, we arrive at M3. Specialists even use other broader categories of money. The principal reason for the different classifications is to allow for different points on the liquidity continuum that distinguish money from other kinds of assets (see Figure 11.1). While it is clear that currency is money and that real estate is not, the line separating money from non-money assets is not clearly defined.

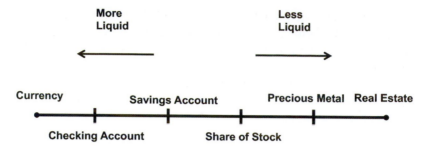

Figure 11.1 *The Liquidity Continuum*

What about using a credit card to make a purchase? From the user's point of view, using a credit card often seems to be like using a debit card or cash from one's pocket. In economists' terms, however, one does *not* use "money" when paying with a credit card. When paying on credit, you are, technically speaking, taking out a temporary loan from the credit card company. Only when you pay your credit card bill from your checking account do you make a "money" transaction.[1]

Discussion Questions

1. Why do dollar bills have value? Are they backed by any commodity such as gold or silver? Are there conditions under which they might lose their value?
2. What do you commonly use to make payments? Cash? Credit cards? Online payments? In which of these cases are you using "money"?

2. THE BANKING SYSTEM

The banking system in the United States includes commercial banks, savings and loans institutions, credit unions, private banks, investment banks, and a central bank—most commonly known as the Federal Reserve (or "Fed," for short). The banks with which most people are familiar are known as commercial banks (also called retail banks). Commercial banks keep money in secure deposits, provide check writing and clearing services, and extend loans. Savings and loan banks are similar to commercial banks but specialize in the provision of home loans to their customers. Credit unions are also similar to commercial banks, except that instead of being privately owned, they are collectively owned by their customers.

Private banks are exclusive, catering to high-net-worth individuals and companies. Their functions range widely from traditional banking to many forms of investment. Investment banks mostly deal with companies instead of individuals. Their principal function is to make asset values grow by managing a diverse portfolio of investments—for example, in growth stocks, corporate bonds, commodities, and so on—that balances moderate to high investment risk with the goal of a considerably higher annual return, on average, than most retail customers obtain.

The central bank exists to regulate the banking system and ensure monetary and interest rate stability in the economy. It determines how much currency should be produced and put into circulation. In the United States, the actions of the Fed, together with actions of commercial banks, create the economy's volume of checkable deposits. For much of Europe, now that many countries have joined together in using the euro as a common currency, the equivalent institution to the Fed is the European Central Bank (ECB). Most countries have combined systems of commercial and central banking, which work at least roughly like the system described in this chapter.

2.1 Commercial Banks[2]

A commercial bank is a type of institution called a **financial intermediary** that connects lenders and borrowers. Individuals and organizations deposit funds with financial intermediaries for safekeeping, to provide the convenience of making bank transfers, paying with debit cards, and writing checks, or to earn interest. These deposits are considered the bank's **liabilities**, because the bank has an obligation to repay these funds to the depositors.

> **financial intermediary:** an institution such as a bank, savings and loan association, or life insurance company that accepts funds from savers and makes loans to borrowers
>
> **liability:** anything that one economic actor owes to another

Financial intermediaries use the funds deposited with them to make loans to individuals and organizations that seek to borrow funds (though, as we shall soon see, banks can create loans *prior* to receiving a matching level of deposits). In any event, banks must keep some funds on hand to meet likely short-term calls, such as depositors' withdrawals. These funds, called **bank reserves**, form the bank's assets and include vault cash as well as deposits made by commercial banks at the Federal Reserve.

> **bank reserves:** funds not lent out or invested by a commercial bank but kept as vault cash or on deposit at the Federal Reserve

A commercial bank is a for-profit business, meaning that it seeks to make earnings on its activities. It does this by charging interest on the loans it makes and perhaps other fees on loans or deposits. One of its functions is to determine the creditworthiness of the parties seeking loans and to set loan conditions (such as demanding physical assets as collateral) to minimize the risks associated with failures to repay loans. For example, mortgages and home-equity loans are collateralized by the value of a house; if the owner defaults on the loan, the bank may take possession of the house. Consumer loans are made on the basis of available income and job security of the applicant. Other loans are made on the basis of an evaluation of, say, the strength of a business plan and a business's record in paying back past loans. Banks may charge different interest rates depending on the riskiness of a loan or deny a loan request outright.

One relatively safe way for the bank to earn some interest on funds not held as reserves is to hold government bonds. Recall from Chapter 10 that the U.S. Treasury borrows from the public when it needs to finance a government deficit or refinance part of the debt. It does this by issuing government bonds, which give the buyer the right to specific payments in the future.[3] Banks tend to keep some of their assets—about one-quarter, on average—in government bonds, because they are among the safest of investments, and they earn interest on these bonds.

The major asset of a commercial bank—and the main way that it makes its earnings—is its portfolio of loans to businesses, households, nonprofits, or nonfederal levels of government. These assets are generally far less liquid than vault cash or government bonds. In difficult times, it could be problematic if banks have made too many loans. The health of a commercial banking system depends on having depositors who are confident about the safety of the funds that they have entrusted to the banking system. If confidence in the banks diminished, and many customers wanted to withdraw their money, some banks might find themselves with insufficient liquidity (i.e., with too many of their assets in long-term loans) to service all requests, further undermining confidence in the system.

2.2 The Federal Reserve System

In 1907, the U.S. economy experienced a bank panic, in which depositors lost trust in banks, tried to withdraw their deposits all at once, and as a result caused many banks to fail. In response, Congress enacted legislation creating the Federal Reserve System in 1913. The Fed is a rather odd organization in that it is not exactly part of the government, nor entirely separate from it. Policy decisions made by the Fed are ostensibly independent from other branches of government, although it is impossible to guarantee that there never is any political influence exerted on it. The Fed is technically "private," in that it has commercial banks as private shareholders that earn dividends on their Fed shares. It is, however, quite different from other private companies or commercial banks in that its primary objectives are to ensure adequate national employment and to maintain stable prices—not to make profits.

The Federal Reserve System consists of a board of governors based in Washington, DC, and 12 regional Federal Reserve Banks based in Atlanta, Boston, Chicago, Cleveland, Dallas, Kansas City (MO), Minneapolis, New York, Philadelphia, Richmond (VA), St. Louis, and San Francisco. The regional Fed banks also have their own branches in many other cities, such as Baltimore, Los Angeles, Miami, and Pittsburgh.

The Fed is overseen by the board of governors, whose seven members are nominated by the president and approved by the Senate. These members serve nonrenewable 14-year terms. One member of the board is chosen by the president to serve as chair for a four-year term (though he or she may serve consecutive terms if renominated). The long terms of service are intended to help insulate the Fed from short-term political pressures.

The Fed performs a number of important functions. It requires banks to hold a certain percentage of their reserves in its account as required reserves. By holding deposits made by commercial banks, the Fed serves as a "banker's bank." The Fed uses these deposits to clear checks that draw funds from one bank and deposit them in another. If a bank is in need of cash to hold in its vault, it can buy currency from the Fed, using the funds in its Fed account. Another of the Fed's important tasks is to attempt to stabilize the rate of exchange between domestic and foreign currencies; this process is detailed in Chapter 14. In addition, the Fed, along with other organizations such as the Federal Deposit Insurance Corporation (FDIC), regulates banks, attempting to ensure that they operate as much as possible without error or fraud.

The Fed keeps close track of the economy and tries to sense whether some adjustment in the money supply or in interest rates might be necessary to increase output and employment or to counteract undesirable changes in the inflation rate. We examine the mechanics of *how* the Fed influences the money supply and interest rates in the next section.

Discussion Questions

1. Does it bother you that banks hold only a small fraction of the value of their deposits on reserve? Why or why not?
2. Is the Federal Reserve truly an independent bank, or is it part of the government? What are its principal functions?

3. HOW BANKS CREATE MONEY

3.1 Commercial Banks and Money Creation

As we saw earlier, the U.S. Mint and the Bureau of Engraving and Printing are responsible for producing the country's supply of *currency*. But there is another way in which money is created, and commercial banks play a critical role in the process.

When you take out a loan from a bank, the money that you borrow is seldom, if ever, delivered to you as a bundle of cash. Rather, the bank credits your bank account for the amount of the loan. Consequently, when banks make loans, they *increase the money supply*, because such transaction accounts make up part of M1 and the broader money supply.

Some of the relationships around money and banking are reasonably straightforward. For example, depositing a check drawn on another bank will simply shift deposits from one bank to another and not affect the level of money supply. Also, depositing currency in the bank simply takes the same amount of currency *out* of circulation, so there is no change in money supply. In this instance, only the composition of money supply is altered—less currency, more transaction deposits. Yet a cash deposit does enable a bank to increase the money supply because the bank can now make new loans—hence, create new money—based on the deposit.

The banking system is a **fractional reserve system** in which only a small percentage of the total value of deposits must be kept on reserve. The portion of bank reserves that are kept to satisfy the minimum requirement is known as **required reserves**. Currently, U.S. banks are required to keep an amount equal to about 10 percent of their checkable deposits as reserves.[4] This means that banks can lend out the other 90 percent. So when you make a deposit at your local bank, 90 percent of its value is classified as **excess reserves**, which a bank is free to lend to other customers.

> **fractional reserve system:** a banking system in which banks are required to keep only a fraction of the total value of their deposits on reserve
> **required reserves:** the portion of bank reserves that banks must keep on reserve
> **excess reserves:** the portion of bank reserves that banks are permitted to lend to their customers

So even though your deposit does not *directly* increase the money supply, it does help increase it to the extent that banks are willing to lend out their excess reserves. Banks are usually eager to lend out excess reserves, because they can earn interest on the loans. But sometimes, in periods of uncertainty or financial crisis, banks prefer to hold onto excess reserves.

When money is created by the banking system, the economy as a whole is essentially taking on more debt. What are the implications of this? Some may argue that the effect is positive, enabling more economic activity. Others may feel that the process may lead to excessive debt, creating risks to the economy including inflation or debt default. We will pursue these issues next, where we consider the Federal Reserve's role in influencing the banking system's process of money creation.

3.2 How the Fed Creates Money

The Federal Reserve has several tools at its disposal to affect the quantity of bank reserves. Historically, the most commonly used tool is open market operations. **Open market operations** involve the buying and selling of U.S. Treasury bonds in order to change the level of bank reserves. Such operations are directed by the **Federal Open Market Committee** (FOMC), which is composed of the board of governors of the Fed and 5 of the 12 regional Fed bank presidents.

> **open market operations:** sales or purchases of U.S. Treasury bonds by the Fed
> **Federal Open Market Committee (FOMC):** the committee that oversees open market operations

When the Fed makes an open market purchase of bonds, its holdings of bonds increase. It generally makes such purchases by buying bonds from a commercial bank, so it pays for the purchase by crediting the bank's account with the Fed by the amount of the purchase. What does it pay *with?* Unlike any other actor in the economy, the Fed can create funds with the proverbial "stroke of a pen" or, these days, adjusting an entry in a computer database. It simply declares that the bank's reserves are now higher by the amount of the bond purchase. This increase in bank reserves expands the bank's ability to make new loans. These new loans will end up as deposits elsewhere in the banking system—that is, new money. When the Fed makes an open market purchase, it increases something called the **monetary base**. This is defined as the sum of total currency in circulation plus bank reserves.

> **monetary base:** the sum of total currency plus bank reserves

Let us illustrate this process with an example. Suppose that the Fed buys $10 million worth of government bonds from ABC Bank. This increases the Fed's holdings of the bonds by $10 million and increases the reserves of ABC bank by $10 million. So far in our story, reserves have risen by $10 million, but the supply of money in circulation (as measured by M1 or other measures) *has not changed*. But if ABC Bank uses this $10 million to make $10 million in new loans to Jane's Construction, and then Jane's Construction deposits the entire amount of the funds at XYZ Bank, then XYZ Bank's checkable deposits and its reserves at the Fed both increase by $10 million.

Note, first, that the money supply *has* now increased. Checkable deposits are part of M1, and there are now $10 million more in total deposits in the economy than there were before. Through an open market purchase of bonds paid for by a "stroke of the pen," the Fed has brought $10 million of new money into being.

Second, note that XYZ Bank now has excess reserves. If required reserves are 10 percent of deposits, it can lend out as much as $9 million of the $10 million in new funds that it has received, while keeping only 10 percent ($1 million) as reserves. (Note that ABC Bank was able to lend out the entire $10 million that it received from the Fed, because there was no corresponding increase in deposits at ABC—they obtained the $10 million by selling bonds.)

These new loans will, in turn, become new deposits in the banking system. Then M1 will have increased by the initial 10 million, plus the second-round $9 million—already an increase totaling $19 million, which is quite a bit larger than the initial $10 million increase.

Now, of course, the banks that receive the $9 million in deposits resulting from XYZ Bank's loans will find that they have excess reserves and will also be able to make new loans, and the process will continue. Where will it all end? If each bank that receives new funds lends out as much as it can (given the 10 percent reserve requirement), the total amount of new money will eventually be $100 million.[5] Table 11.1 summarizes the money multiplier process just described, with the assumption that the initial increase in deposits is $10 million and the required reserve ratio is 10 percent.

The logic is similar to the government spending multiplier in fiscal policy. Just as re-spending by consumers multiplies the original amount of government

Table 11.1 Money Multiplier Effect

	Deposits	Required Reserves	Bank Loans = (Deposit − Required reserves)	Cumulative Increase in Money Supply
Step 1	$10 million	10% of $10 million = $1 million	$10 million − $1 million = $9 million	$10 million
Step 2	$9 million	10% of $9 million = $0.9 million	$9 million − $0.9 million = $8.1 million	$10 million + $9 million = $19 million
Step 3	$8.1 million	10% of $8.1 million = $0.81 million	$8.1 million − $0.81 million = $7.29 million	$19 million + $8.1 million = $27.1 million
Steps 4, 5, 6, . . .	The loan created in the last step becomes the new deposit	10% of the new deposit goes into required reserve	Excess reserve is lent out, and the loans keep decreasing until they reach 0	Total increase in money supply = $100 million

spending, so the creation of new loans by banks multiplies the original creation of new reserves. The story of the money multiplier is, however, more complicated than the spending multiplier because banks often hold excess reserves, and people who take out loans similarly often want to hold some of the funds in cash or in types of deposits that are not part of M1. So not all the money created will translate directly into new deposits and loans, and monetary expansion will not be as dramatic as the example above suggests. Economists define the **money multiplier** as the ratio of the money supply to the monetary base:

$$money\ multiplier = \frac{money\ supply}{monetary\ base}$$

> **money multiplier:** the ratio of the money supply to the monetary base, indicating by how much the money supply will change for a given change in high-powered money

Using M1 as the measure of money, empirical studies have shown the money multiplier in the United States is currently very close to 2. That is, if the Fed acts to increase reserves and currency by $10 million, the total increase in the money supply would be expected to be around double that:

Δmoney = money multiplier × Δmonetary base
$20 million = 2 × $10 million

With the "stroke of a pen," the Fed open market purchase of government bonds increases the money supply by about twice the value of the initial bond purchase.

Note that, looking at the same story in a slightly different way, the action of the Fed can also be seen as increasing the amount of *credit* extended to private actors in the economy. The Fed, in making an open market purchase of government bonds, in essence takes over a portion of the public debt that was previously held by private institutions. The new bank reserves created by the purchase of government bonds allow banks to extend more credit—new loans—to private actors in the economy.

Traditionally, macroeconomists have tended to perceive the story outlined previously as a matter of increasing deposits and hence increasing the money supply. By this account, the Fed takes an active role in money creation by increasing or reducing bank reserves (and currency), thereby facilitating or inhibiting the lending activity that determines the money supply. More recently, however, many macroeconomists stress that money creation is a story of expansion of credit rather than the accumulation of savings. They emphasize that it is the commercial banks' lending proclivities that determine their demand for reserves from the Fed or other banks. This interpretation views the Fed's role in determining the money supply as being more limited. If the economy is booming, financial institutions will lend and invest to the maximum of their capacity. If the economy is slack, banks may hold excess reserves, and there will be less expansion of money and credit.

While the two views are just "two sides of the same coin," looking at the money face of monetary policy tends to draw more attention to people's need for liquidity, while looking at the credit face draws more attention to issues of how financial capital is created and distributed within the economy.

3.3 Other Monetary Policy Tools

While the Fed mostly uses open market operations to expand the money supply, it also has other tools at its disposal. One monetary policy tool available to the Fed is the **discount rate**. This is the interest rate at which commercial banks can borrow funds from the Fed at what is called the Fed's "discount window." In theory, a reduction in the discount rate should increase the money supply, because it would lower the cost to a bank of being found to be below its required level of reserves. A bank could then be somewhat more aggressive about making loans. However, since the Fed has historically frowned on (and penalized) banks found to be low on reserves too often, banks have generally preferred to borrow from one another if they need money in the short term. But in extraordinary circumstances such as the financial crisis, the Fed has taken the opposite approach of encouraging use of the discount window to promote greater liquidity.

> **discount rate:** the interest rate at which banks can borrow reserves at the Fed discount window

Another tool that the Fed has is the required reserve ratio. If it wanted to increase the money supply, the Fed could lower the reserve requirement ratio, which would have the effect of expanding the money supply by allowing banks to make more loans on a smaller base of reserves. If, on the other hand, the Fed wanted to limit continued increases in the money supply, it could increase the ratio of reserves required, thereby restraining bank lending. In practice, the required reserve ratio is rarely altered. The last time the Fed changed the ratio was in 1982.

Since the financial crisis of 2007–2008, the Fed's "toolkit" has increased. The Fed has expanded its operations by purchasing large amounts of assets other than Treasury bonds. For example, the Fed has resorted to an unusual approach known as **quantitative easing** (QE), where it buys diverse financial assets, including what are known as mortgage-backed securities, which are basically "pools" of a variety of private mortgages, from banks and nonbank institutions alike. The main objective of such purchases is to flood the economy with more money, in hopes of provoking the necessary spending to create an economic stimulus. This change in course caused the assets and liabilities on the Fed's balance sheet to balloon from about $800 billion before the crisis to over $4 *trillion* as of 2017, declining slightly since then to $3.7 trillion as of mid-2019.

> **quantitative easing (QE):** the purchase of financial assets, including long-term bonds, by the Fed, creating more monetary reserves and expanding the money supply

Thus far, we have almost exclusively discussed monetary expansion, but the Fed can, of course, cause the money supply (and credit) to contract as well. If instead of making an open market purchase of government bonds, it makes an open market *sale*, everything we have thus far described just happens in reverse. When the Fed sells bonds, the buyer (usually a commercial bank) must pay the Fed. That means the bank has that much less in its reserve account. Overall, commercial banks will now hold *more* in government bonds and *less* in reserves. If banks hold less in reserves, they have to tighten up on loans, which means there will be fewer deposits. The money multiplier also works in reverse, so that the original bond sale has a magnified effect in reducing the total money supply.

The Fed can thus increase the money supply (or expand credit) by making an open market purchase of bonds (or more recently, as noted, other assets), lowering the required reserve ratio, or lowering the discount rate. It can decrease the money supply (or contract credit) by making an open market sale of bonds, raising the required reserve ratio, or raising the discount rate.[6]

In a growing economy, a central bank would rarely want to shrink the money supply in absolute terms. A growing economy, as measured by GDP, means ever more transactions need to be facilitated by readily available liquid assets and generally growing demand by private economic actors for loans. "Loose" monetary policy, in the case of a real-world growing economy, then, usually means making the money supply grow *faster* than the economy has been growing. "Tight" policy does not mean actually making M1 fall; rather, it just means making the money supply grow *more slowly* than the growth rate of the economy.

Discussion Questions

1. Describe in words how a Fed open market operation can increase the volume of money in the economy.
2. How do banks lend their customers money that they do not physically possess? Are they *really* creating money in the process?

4. THE THEORY OF MONEY, INTEREST RATES, AND AGGREGATE DEMAND

In an economy that is experiencing fairly low inflation and that has a healthy banking system, most of the concern with the money supply is really a concern about interest rates, the availability of credit, and their consequences for aggregate demand.

4.1 The Federal Funds Rate and Other Interest Rates

In contemporary discussions of the Fed's monetary policy, attention usually focuses on what is called the **federal funds rate**. This is the going rate of interest determined on a private market of interbank loans. If a bank finds that it has more reserves than it needs to meet its reserve requirements, it offers funds on the "federal funds" market, usually just overnight. If another bank is short on reserves, it borrows on that market and pays back the next day.

> **federal funds rate:** the interest rate determined in the private market for overnight loans of reserves among banks

Although a quick reading of reports in the media often make it sound as though the Fed directly controls the federal funds rate (for example, headlines may read "Fed Announces Increase in Federal Funds Rate of 0.25 Percent"), this is not, in fact, the case. The Fed announces desired *target* or *benchmark* levels for the federal funds rate and then acts on bank reserves to try to achieve that target. Because the Fed is usually quite effective at this, the difference between the (official) target federal funds rate and the (market-determined) actual federal funds rate is generally quite small.

A simplified model of the federal funds market is portrayed in Figure 11.2 (a). The quantity of funds is on the horizontal axis, and the federal funds rate—the price of borrowing on this market—is on the vertical axis. (Note that this is just a specific variant of the sort of "market for loanable funds" discussed in Chapter 9.) The actors on both sides of this market are banks.

The supply curve for federal funds slopes upward, because higher returns in this market mean that banks with excess reserves will be more likely to lend them here rather than finding other ways to lend them out. The demand curve for federal funds slopes downward, because the lower the interest rate, the more willing banks are to borrow. Figure 11.2 (a) portrays a situation in which the federal funds rate at which the market clears is 6 percent.

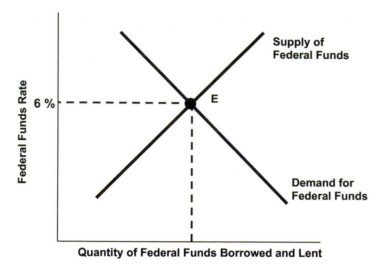

Figure 11.2a *The Market for Federal Funds*

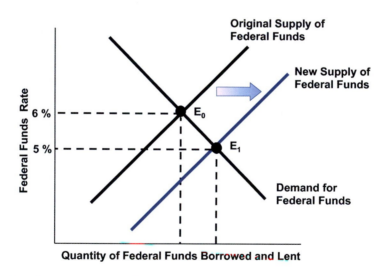

Figure 11.2b *An Open Market Purchase Lowers the Federal Funds Rate*

The Fed undertakes open market operations with the goal of pushing the going rate for loans in that market to the level of its choosing. If, for example, the Fed wanted to lower the federal funds rate, it could make an open market purchase and increase the quantity of reserves that banks hold. All else being equal, this increases the amount of reserves available for private lending in the federal funds market. In Figure 11.2(b), this is shown as the supply curve for federal funds shifting to the right. Thus, the federal funds rate falls to 5 percent.

In today's modern, sophisticated economy, financial markets tend to be closely interlinked, so a drop in an important rate like the federal funds rate tends to carry over into other markets. Interest rates on consumer loans or mortgages are usually much higher than the federal funds rate. There are several reasons for this. First, most consumer loans are relatively long-term loans that run over several months, if not years. Banks usually borrow from the Fed for a few days. Banks therefore must charge a higher rate than they themselves pay as compensation for giving up liquidity for long periods.

Second, the higher interest rate partly compensates commercial banks for the occasional instance when the borrower does not pay back the loan. Indeed, in this sense, the cost of the "bad debts" of customers is ultimately borne by other customers. Finally, the commercial bank needs to make a profit in order to cover costs for credit administration, staff, and services. This also explains why the interest rate on bank loans exceeds the rate it pays depositors on their savings accounts.

As a general rule, an expansionary monetary policy lowers interest rates throughout the economy. Since lower interest rates make loans cheaper, such a policy usually leads to faster credit growth. Conversely, contractionary monetary policy tends to shrink the volume of credit and raise interest rates. Higher interest rates make loans more expensive and lead to slower credit growth or even credit contraction. Therefore, the central bank's monetary policy profoundly affects businesses and individuals throughout the economy.

4.2 Interest Rates and Investment

Economists are particularly interested in interest rates because of their effect on investment. To the extent that individuals or businesses make investments using borrowed funds, higher interest rates make investing more expensive, and hence less attractive. Even if investment were to be financed directly out of savings, in theory, it would still be diminished by a higher rate. With higher interest rates, saving profits in the bank might be more attractive than buying a new piece of machinery or building a house.

Residential investment is especially sensitive to variations in interest rates. Given that residential investments are usually financed by 15- or 30-year mortgages, a small change in the interest rate can add up to a very big difference in the total cost of buying a house.

The impact of interest rate changes on business investment in structures, equipment, and inventories is a bit more mixed. We saw in Chapter 9 that Keynes did not think that changes in the interest rate would be sufficient to encourage investment at times of economic decline when investor pessimism is too deep to respond to lower borrowing costs. (Keynes described such situations as attempting to "push on a string.")

Business fixed investment primarily responds to changes in sales much more than to changes in interest rates. This idea has been called the **accelerator principle**. If businesses see their sales rising, they may need to expand their capacity—that is, invest in new equipment and structures—in order to keep up with demand for their product. Since the best macroeconomic indicator of expanded sales is a rising GDP, this principle says that the best predictor of investment growth is not interest rate but growth in GDP. Conversely, a small decline—or even just slowing down—of demand may lead to a disproportionate drying up of intended investment, as firms come to fear being caught with excess capacity. To the extent the accelerator principle is in force, changes in the interest rate may have only a relatively minor effect on levels of business investment.

> **accelerator principle:** the idea that high GDP growth leads to increasing investment, and low or negative GDP growth leads to declining investment

Given a particular level of optimism or pessimism, however, firms can be expected to pay at least *some* attention to interest rates in deciding how much to invest. Higher interest rates tend to limit the amount of investment by firms that may need to borrow money to invest. Using Keynes's string analogy, it is easier to pull on a string than to push it—tighter monetary policy is likely to restrain overall investment. Combining this logical assumption with the empirically observed sensitivity of residential investment to interest rates, our simple model of macroeconomic stabilization says that, *all else being equal,* lower interest rates will lead to higher intended investment spending (and lower investment for higher interest rates). The quantity of intended investment is inversely related to the interest rate, r, as shown in Figure 11.3.

Keynes emphasized how volatile and unstable investor confidence could be. Changes in investor confidence, related to actual spending (via the accelerator

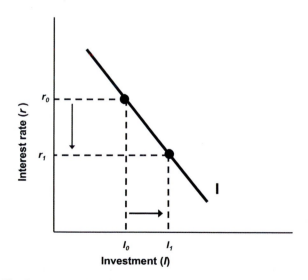

Figure 11.3 *The Investment Schedule*

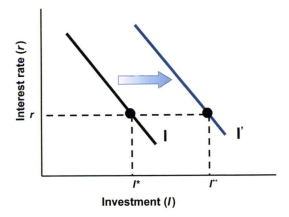

Figure 11.4 *An Increase in Investor Confidence*

principle) or to expected levels of spending, can be portrayed as shifting this investment curve. An increase in investor confidence, for example, shifts the curve to the right (from **I** to **I'**), as shown in Figure 11.4. At any given interest rate, firms now want to invest more (**I**** rather than **I***). A decrease in investor confidence shifts the curve to the left.

4.3 Monetary Policy and Aggregate Demand

In an economy with relatively low inflation and a stable banking system, expansionary monetary policy tends to lower interest rates and consequently raise investment. Because investment spending is part of aggregate demand, the increase in investment results in higher levels of output and employment in the economy.

  If the economy were headed toward a recession, then monetary policy that is relatively loose, increasing the money supply in order to help maintain output, could have a desirable stabilizing effect. Sometimes such an **expansionary monetary policy** is called an **accommodative monetary policy**, especially when the Fed is reacting to a specific economic event that might otherwise tend to send the economy into recession.

---

expansionary monetary policy: the use of monetary policy tools to increase the money supply, lower interest rates, and stimulate a higher level of economic activity
accommodative monetary policy: loose or expansionary monetary policy intended to counteract recessionary tendencies in the economy
contractionary monetary policy: the use of monetary policy tools to limit the money supply, raise interest rates, and encourage a leveling off or reduction in economic activity and inflationary tendencies

---

  Contractionary monetary policy, however, is often prescribed if the economy seems to be heading toward inflation. In response to inflationary pressures, the Fed seeks to slow growth and "cool down" the economy. Thus, it would decrease the rate of growth of the money supply to raise interest rates, lower intended investment, and lower the equilibrium levels of output and employment.

BOX 11.2 MONETARY POLICY IN PRACTICE

History appears to support the idea that, while monetary policy may be effective as a restraint to the economy, it is limited in its ability to stimulate it.

The United States experienced an estimated one-third decrease in its money supply from 1929 to 1933. This coincided with the greatest decline that the U.S. economy has experienced in over a century. Whether the decline in money was actually the main *cause* of the Great Depression remains a topic of controversy. But there is significant evidence that restrictive monetary policy contributed to the severity and duration of the Depression.

The 1970s and early 1980s offer another instance in which recession appears to have been caused by tight money. In this period, the Fed's goal was to counteract inflation, which had reached double digits by the late 1970s. But the resulting application of highly contractionary monetary policy, while effective against inflation, also caused severe recession.

In contrast, the Fed has implemented aggressively expansionary monetary policy in recent decades. The low-interest-rate policy pursued by the Fed in the aftermath of the dot-com bust of 1999–2000 achieved short-term stimulus but sacrificed long-run stability. Several years of low interest rates provoked unsustainable levels of mortgage refinancing and other forms of consumption that were the seeds of the 2007–2008 collapse.

Following the financial crisis of 2007–2008, the Fed used even more expansionary measures, with mixed results. On the one hand, very low interest rates helped to support economic recovery. On the other, the Fed's ability to "push on a string" was clearly limited in that the recovery was painfully slow. Concerns were also raised that the low-interest-rate policy introduced other distortions to the economy, hurting savers, who got almost no return on their investment, while possibly increasing inequality through benefiting primarily affluent investors in stocks, which rose partly as a result of the availability of "cheap money" for investment.

4.4 The Liquidity Trap and Credit Rationing

Following the 2008 financial crisis, the federal funds rate has remained at historically low levels. Despite the low interest rates, recovery from the crisis was very slow. Though the Fed added to the monetary base, this money did not find its way into useful investment and job creation. This experience reinforces the notion that the Fed's influence over money creation is limited: if the banks are not motivated to lend and if consumers and businesses simply hold onto the money instead of spending it, a low interest rate may not translate into new credit and new investment. This problem repeatedly frustrated the Fed's attempts to spark a recovery from the 2007 crisis.

In the 1930s, Keynes introduced the term **liquidity trap** for a situation in which it is impossible for a central bank to drive interest rates down any lower. During the period 2008–2017, the United States appeared to have hit this monetary policy wall.

> **liquidity trap:** a situation in which interest rates are so low that the central bank finds it impossible to reduce them further

Banks may accumulate more funds via the actions of the Fed. However, instead of using these extra funds to make more loans, banks may tend to engage in **credit rationing** in order to ensure their own profitability. This means that they will lend to the customers whom they deem most creditworthy, using restrictive standards to decide who merits getting a loan. If this happens, some firms and individuals will get the funds that they need, while others—and particularly smaller firms and lower-income individuals—may be frozen out. In this case, monetary policy may have significant distributional effects: in the simplest terms, making the rich richer and the poor poorer.

> **credit rationing:** when banks deny loans to some potential borrowers in the interest of maintaining their own profitability

The possibility of a liquidity trap or of reluctance among bankers and investors to lend and borrow means that the Fed faces limits to its ability to stimulate a sluggish economy. This does not necessarily mean that the Fed's efforts are ineffective. The Fed's purchases of existing mortgages from banks through quantitative easing, for example, had the effect of freeing up banks to create new mortgages, improving the situation in the housing market. But at the same time, the creation of so much new money might create inflation in asset and goods prices.

While expansionary monetary policy did not lead to significant increase in goods prices (i.e., price inflation), prices of assets, particularly publicly traded equities, did rise substantially. Concern grew over whether prices reflected in the key stock indexes such as the Dow Jones and the S&P 500 were sustainable. Partly as a result of such concerns, together with a desire to return to more "normal" interest rates and a perception that the economy had improved and was approaching full employment, the Fed, under Chair Janet Yellen, started moving cautiously in 2016–2017 to raise interest rates, as reflected in Figure 11.5. These policies continued in 2018 under new Fed Chair Jerome Powell, together with initial efforts to "unwind" (sell off) the Fed's massive holdings of corporate bonds acquired during the period of quantitative easing. In July 2019, the Fed cut interest rates for the first time in a

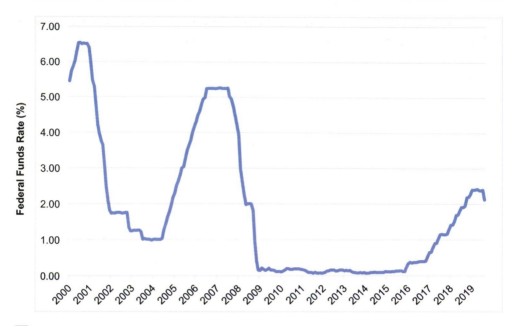

Figure 11.5 *Monetary Policy, 2000–2019*

Source: Federal Reserve and Bureau of Economic Analysis, 2019.

decade, citing slowing global growth, low inflation, and uncertainties from President Trump's trade war.[7]

Discussion Questions

1. Explain the liquidity trap. Do you think that the theory accurately describes the events after the Great Recession?
2. What economic conditions would cause the Fed to shift from an expansionary policy to a policy of raising interest rates? What risks might be involved with a policy that is too expansionary or not expansionary enough?

5. THEORIES OF MONEY AND POLICY COMPLEXITIES

The relationship between money and the "real" economy has long been a source of controversy. In this section, we will review some of the main ways in which economists have conceptualized this relationship and the corresponding implications for government policy.

5.1 The Quantity Equation

One way of thinking about the relationship between the real economy, money, and prices is based on what economists call the **quantity equation**:

$$M \times V = P \times Y$$

In this equation, Y is, as usual, real output or GDP. P indicates the price level as measured by a price index (such as the GDP deflator). The multiplication of these two variables means that the right-hand side of the equation represents nominal output (the difference between nominal and real output was discussed in Chapter 8).

> **quantity equation:** $M \times V = P \times Y$
> where M is the money supply, V is the velocity of money, P is the price level, and Y is real output.

On the left-hand side, M measures the level of money balances, such as the M1 measure discussed previously. V, the only really new variable here, represents the velocity of money. The **velocity of money** is the number of times that a dollar changes hands in a year in order to support the level of output and exchange represented by nominal GDP. In other words, since the money in circulation is insufficient to "purchase" everything entailed by GDP, velocity represents how often, on average, each dollar changes hands in order for there to be sufficient funds to purchase all the goods and services produced in the economy. (Remember that we are talking both about cash and bank deposits—so "changing hands" could be literal, as when you pay for a pizza with cash, or virtual, as when a bank clears a check on one account, making the funds available to another account holder.)

> **velocity of money:** the number of times that a dollar would have to change hands during a year to support nominal GDP, calculated as $V = (P \times Y)/M$

Since nominal GDP and M1 are observable, velocity can be calculated as the ratio of the two,

$$V = \frac{P \times Y}{M}$$

For the quantity equation to become the basis for a *theory*, rather than merely represent definitions of variables, an assumption needs to be made about velocity. Supporters of different macroeconomic theories all have subscribed to the irrefutable arithmetic of the quantity equation. Where they have differed is over assumptions regarding the behavior of one or more of the variables.

Two closely related theories that we discuss subsequently—classical and monetarist—assume that velocity is constant: changing very little, if at all, with changing conditions in the economy. If this is true, then the level of the money supply and the level of nominal GDP will be tightly related. We denote this assumption that velocity is constant by putting a bar over V. The **quantity theory of money**, then, is characterized by the relation

$$M \times \bar{V} = P \times Y$$

369

where $\bar{V}$ is read "V-bar." More Keynesian-oriented theories, however, while they may make use of the quantity equation, do not assume that velocity is constant.

> **quantity theory of money:** the theory that money supply is directly related to nominal GDP, according to the equation $M \times \bar{V} = P \times Y$

5.2 Competing Theories

Classical monetary theory is based on the quantity theory of money, plus the assumption that output is always at or close to its full-employment level.[8] That is,

$$M \times V = P \times Y*$$

where $Y*$, as usual, denotes full-employment output. In this case, changes in the money supply have *no* effect on the level of output. The inability of changes in the money supply to affect real output is called **monetary neutrality**. The only variable on the left-hand side that is not constant is the money supply, while the only variable on the right-hand side that is not constant is the price level. Thus, all that a change in the money supply can do is change prices. Rather than an increase in the money supply increasing output, in this model, an increase in the money supply has no effect other than to cause inflation.

> **monetary neutrality:** the idea that changes in the money supply may affect only prices, while leaving output unchanged

Classical economists, then, tend to see no need for discretionary monetary policy. On the contrary, they consider it counterproductive. In the case of an economy that is not growing, classical theory would prescribe a stable money supply level to avoid unnecessary changes in prices. In a growing economy, classical theory says that the money supply should grow at the same rate as real GDP in order to keep prices stable. If we assume that the rate of real GDP growth is fairly constant, then the money supply should just grow at a fixed rate, say, 3 percent per year. A central bank that enforces this is said to be following a **money supply rule**.

> **money supply rule:** committing to letting the money supply grow at a fixed rate per year

Another famous theory based on the quantity equation is **monetarism**, propounded by Milton Friedman and Anna Jacobson Schwartz in their book *A Monetary History of the United States, 1867–1960*, published in 1963. While Keynes had argued that insufficient investment and aggregate demand caused the Great Depression, Friedman and Schwartz argued that it was caused by a severe contraction in the money supply.

> **monetarism:** a school of economic thought that argues that governments should aim for steadiness in the money supply rather than playing an active role

Friedman had earlier propounded the quantity theory of money and has become known for his saying that "inflation is always and everywhere a monetary phenomenon." Like classical economists, he thought that bad monetary policy could, at least temporarily, have detrimental effects on the real economy. But unlike the pure classical theorists, he thought that it could work both ways; that is, monetary policy could be deflationary as well as inflationary. During the early years of the Great Depression, he and Schwartz pointed out, both the money supply and the level of nominal GDP fell sharply. This empirical observation can be seen as consistent with the quantity theory of money:

$$M \times \underset{\substack{no \\ change}}{\bar{V}} = P \times Y$$
$$\scriptstyle\downarrow \qquad\qquad \downarrow \quad \downarrow$$

Friedman and Schwartz argued that the contraction in the money supply caused reductions in both the price level and real GDP. It is an assertion that remains controversial, and there remains widespread disagreement over whether prices or output are more sensitive to a money supply reduction. Because of his belief in the potential for bad monetary policy to cause harm, Friedman was one of the most vocal proponents of the idea that central banks should simply follow a fixed rule of having the money supply grow at a steady rate. In this regard, he and most classical theorists would have been in agreement.

While the quantity equation can be helpful in thinking about monetary phenomena such as inflation, we get different results if we assume that velocity is variable. For example, an increase in M could be offset by a decrease in V, which is the situation described previously as a liquidity trap. Even though the central bank pursues a policy of monetary expansion, people and banks are pessimistic enough that they hold onto excess reserves of money, in effect neutralizing the desired expansionary policy. This is why Keynesian-leaning economists often prefer expansionary fiscal policy measures to stimulate the economy in situations of high unemployment. Similarly, contractionary fiscal policies would be favored by Keynesian economists to control inflation.

Some economists in the modern Keynesian tradition go further. According to the school known as **modern monetary theory**, it makes little sense even to use the concept of the money supply as being an important determinant of prices. Rather, the direction of causation runs the other way: the real economy, based on private consumption, investment, government spending, and taxes, determines the growth of the money supply. The role of the Fed, in this view, is merely to maintain a target rate of interest by buying or selling bonds. While it is possible to measure the money supply, it is not an independent variable that affects P and Q, as in the monetarist approach. Exponents of modern monetary theory argue that this is, in fact, how central banks operate: they set a target rate of interest and are not much concerned with the level of M.

Even taking this view of a more passive role for the Fed, it seems that monetary policy would have some impact, depending on the choice of the target rate of interest. We therefore need to consider how the Fed can balance the different goals and theories associated with making monetary policy.

> **modern monetary theory:** the belief that fiscal expenditure and taxes determine output and price levels, while money is supplied or withheld merely in response to fiscal policy

Some modern Keynesians also argue that causation in the quantity theory of money actually runs from prices to money. In other words, an increase in prices will cause an increase in the money supply. Of course, this is the reverse of Friedman and Schwartz's view that it is a change in the money supply that is responsible for any change in prices.

5.3 Policy Complications

In the real world, central banks generally have to be concerned about output and inflation, as well as banking regulation and stability, all at the same time. When the goals include *both* stabilization of prices and maintaining output at or near full employment, it complicates the analysis considerably.

When the economy is in a recession, the Fed implements expansionary monetary policy—policies that increase the money supply, lower interest rates, and stimulate investment and output. But if the Fed implements expansionary monetary policy too vigorously or at the wrong time, then it can cause inflation to accelerate. If inflation is "heating up," then the Fed should use contractionary monetary policy—that is, reining in the money supply, raising interest rates, and discouraging investment to "cool off" the economy.

One of the complications with this process is that the exact "full-employment" level of employment at any given time is controversial. If the Fed starts to get nervous about inflation too early in an economic upswing, it may halt the recovery too early and keep unemployment high. If, on the other hand, the Fed lets the recovery continue for too long, the economy might experience inflationary pressures.

There is also considerable controversy over what rates of inflation can be considered acceptable. Some economists find only inflation rates from 0 percent to 2 percent acceptable; others do not see an urgent need for monetary control unless inflation is around 4 percent or higher. There is a continuing debate among economists and policymakers over the proper weight to give to employment goals versus price stabilization goals (see Box 11.3).

Another practical problem is that monetary authorities have to pay attention to issues of timing. A monetary policy decision can generally be made relative quickly as it only requires discussion and agreement among the FOMC's 12 members, unlike the much more extensive discussions required for fiscal policies. But monetary policy only has an effect on aggregate demand as people change their plans (often long-term plans) about investment and spending. So it might take a long time to feel the effects of monetary policy. There is a danger that the effects of a policy intended to counteract a recession may not be felt until the next boom, or the effects of policies intended to counteract a boom might not be felt until the next recession, exacerbating the business cycle instead of flattening it out.

Last, it is not always the case that an economy suffers from *either* recession *or* high inflation. While the phenomenon has not been witnessed in the U.S. economy since about 1980, it is possible for an economy to suffer both recession and inflation

BOX 11.3 BRING ON INFLATION?

A decade after the recovery from the 2008 financial crisis began, unemployment levels have declined to below 4 percent since 2018. Citing concerns about possible inflation from strengthening economic conditions, the Fed gradually started to increase interest rates starting in 2017. While some economists applauded this shift in monetary policy, others felt that the Fed was moving too quickly to tighten monetary policy.

According to Isabel Sawhill, senior fellow at the Brookings Institution, waiting to raise interest rates until inflation begins to rise substantially might bring in benefits, especially for those who haven't gained from economic growth in recent years, that are higher than the costs of inflation. Sawhill notes that "recent experience has shown us that the economy can operate at low levels of unemployment—even lower than 'full employment'—without inflation becoming a serious problem. . . . Even if inflation does creep up above 2 percent, we shouldn't be too worried. The Fed's inflation target is not a ceiling; it's a desirable average. Having operated below it for many years, the economy may not be harmed if it runs for a few years above the target."[9]

Other economists and policymakers worry more about the dangers of allowing inflation to become entrenched. At a meeting of world finance ministers in Davos in January 2018, Axel Weber, chair of Union Bank of Switzerland (UBS), warned that the world financial system is approaching a dangerous "inflection point" on inflation, risking a surge in interest rates and a shock to asset prices.[10] This echoed warnings that some economists have issued for some time about excessively "easy" monetary policy leading to inflation. These predictions were generally wrong during the long period of recovery from the financial crisis, during which inflation remained low despite very expansionary monetary policies by many countries. But in a tighter labor market, close to or at full employment, they are likely to gain greater traction.

at the same time. Because one problem seems to require expansionary policies, while the other calls for contractionary ones, in this case, the dilemma facing the Fed is especially acute.

Given all these caveats about monetary policy, you might think that the Fed would do better just to follow a money supply growth rule, as suggested by the quantity theory of money. Indeed, a number of classically oriented macroeconomists make just this argument.

But the quantity theory has its problems. For one thing, the velocity of money is not as constant as the theory assumes. Because financial markets have many linkages, people's desire to hold some of their assets as money, as opposed to another asset, can cause wide swings in velocity. Financial market innovations, shocks to asset markets, and many other developments in the economy can also affect velocity. The more unpredictable velocity is, the harder it is to make policy based on the assumption of a stable relationship between money supply and nominal GDP.

Nor is it true that output is always at or close to its full-employment level, as we saw when looking at business cycles in Chapter 9. In addition, prices can change due to factors other than monetary policy, such as shortages of productive factors (e.g., oil) or rise in consumer demand. As a result, many macroeconomists argue for a relatively flexible and activist monetary policy stance. Rather than having the Fed locked onto a particular rule—as the monetarists would have it—they suggest that the Fed keep an eye on inflation but also remain flexible, so that it can respond to new developments, including financial market changes, price shocks, and threats of recession.

In Chapter 12, we bring together monetary policy, fiscal policy, and the twin goals of output and price stabilization. We also take into account some of the effects that world events, and policy responses to them, have had on the U.S. economy over the past several decades.

Discussion Questions

1. What are some arguments in favor of having the Fed follow a money supply rule? What are some arguments against it?
2. Has inflation been reported to be a problem in any recent news reports? Check recent inflation data at www.usinflationcalculator.com. How do you think this is related to recent Fed monetary policy?

REVIEW QUESTIONS

1. Describe the three roles played by money.
2. Describe at least three different types of money.
3. Describe at least two measures of money.
4. Explain the process through which the Fed uses open market operations to increase the level of money supply in the economy.

5. Describe how a Fed open market purchase leads to a sequence of loans and deposits and thus a multiplier effect.
6. Describe two tools the Fed can use to affect the money supply, other than open market operations.
7. Describe how a Fed open market purchase changes the federal funds rate.
8. How is investment related to the interest rate? What other factors affect investment? Use a graphical analysis to show these relationships.
9. What is the quantity equation? What is the quantity theory of money?
10. What is monetarism?
11. Discuss how monetary expansion can lead to high inflation, using the quantity equation.
12. What are some of the problems with using a monetary rule?

EXERCISES

1. Suppose that the Fed makes an open market purchase of $200,000 in bonds from QRS Bank.
   a. Show how this affects the assets and liabilities of the Fed and of QRS Bank.
   b. Assume that QRS Bank lends out as much as it can, and the proceeds from those loans are deposited in TUV Bank. If the required reserve ratio is 10 percent, what new opportunity does TUV Bank now face? What is it likely to do?
2. Suppose that the Fed makes an open market *sale* of $15 million in bonds to HIJ Bank.
   a. Show how this affects the assets and liabilities of the Fed and of HIJ bank.
   b. Show in a graph the effect on the market for federal funds. (No numbers are necessary, for this or later sections of this exercise.)
   c. Assuming that the level of business confidence remains unchanged, show on a graph how this open market sale will change the level of investment.
3. Suppose that investor confidence falls, and the Fed is aware of this fact. Using the model presented in this chapter, show (a)–(b) subsequently graphically:
   a. How a fall in investor confidence affects the schedule for intended investment.
   b. What the Fed could do, influencing the federal funds market, to try to counteract this fall in investor confidence.
4. Suppose that the level of nominal GDP ($P \times Y$ in the quantity equation) for Estilvania is $30 billion and the level of the money supply is $10 billion.
   a. What is the velocity of money in Estilvania?
   b. Suppose that the money supply increases to $15 billion and nominal GDP rises to $45 billion. What has happened to velocity?
   c. Suppose that the money supply increases to $15 billion and nominal GDP rises to $40 billion. What has happened to velocity?
   d. Suppose that the money supply decreases to $8 billion and, as a result, both the price level and real GDP fall, leading to a decrease in nominal GDP to $26 billion. What has happened to velocity?
5. The chair of the Federal Reserve semiannually gives testimony before Congress about the state of monetary policy. Search for the most recent such testimony by the Fed chair at www.federalreserve.gov/newsevents.htm. What does the Fed chair identify as the most significant issues facing the economy? How is the Fed proposing to deal with them?

6. Match each concept in Column A with the best definition or example in Column B.

Column A	Column B
a. Expansionary monetary policy	1. The idea that changes in the money supply affect only prices, not output
b. Fiat money	2. The Federal Reserve lowers the discount rate
c. Accelerator principle	3. The portion of bank reserves that banks are permitted to lend to their customers
d. Monetary neutrality	4. A dollar coin made of minerals worth $.10
e. Velocity	5. The ease with which an asset can be used in trade
f. Liquidity	6. Federal Reserve open market sale of bonds
g. Commodity money	7. A silver coin
h. Excess reserves	8. The portion of bank reserves that banks *must* keep on reserve
i. Required reserves	9. Relates investment to GDP growth
j. Contractionary monetary policy	10. The number of times that a unit of money changes hands in a year

NOTES

1. Note that the credit card transaction *could* count as money from a credit money perspective, since the new debt to your credit card company could be considered a transfer of "money." But most economists would not count the debt as money, since it occurs outside the banking system (whereas the use of a check or electronic transfer to pay the bill is within the banking system).

2. What we call a commercial bank is sometimes called a "private bank." To avoid confusion, in this text, we limit the use of the term "private bank" to a specific kind of bank that caters to wealthy customers.

3. We use the term "government bond" to represent any type of federal government security. These securities may be called "bills," "bonds," or "notes," depending on the duration of loan.

4. In truth, there is no "single" reserve requirement ratio, as it varies considerably depending on type of deposit and size of bank (based on total deposits). For example, the U.S. reserve requirement is 0 percent for banks with total transactions accounts of less than $12.4 million, 3 percent for those between $12.4 million and $79.5 million, and 10 percent for those holding deposits exceeding $79.5 million.

5. This can be calculated by using the formula for an infinite series where x is less than one: $(1 + x + x^2 + x^3 + \ldots + x^n) = 1/(1 - x)$. In this case, $x = 0.9$. This "x" corresponds to the portion of new deposits that are loaned out—90% if the reserve ratio is 10%.

6. Selling riskier assets, as described earlier, would be more problematic, as there would be a much smaller pool of buyers. Indeed, many have criticized the Fed's actions in purchasing these assets in the first place, believing that it represented a "handout" to some of the biggest investment banks and insurance companies, since the price paid may have been far in excess of then-market value.

7. Smialek, Jeanna. 2019. "Fed Was Divided about Interest Rate Cut." *New York Times*, August 21.

8. We simplify here, but to be precise, the classical view is that the economy will always *tend* toward full-employment equilibrium in the long run, as discussed in Chapter 9.

9. Sawhill, Isabel. 2018. "Inflation? Bring It On: Workers Could Actually Benefit." *New York Times*, March 8.

10. Evans-Pritchard, Ambrose. 2018. "Inflation Shock Is a Mounting Danger, Warn Finance Chiefs in Davos." *Financial Times*, January 26.

Aggregate Supply, Aggregate Demand, and Inflation

Putting It All Together

If you read the financial pages in any newspaper, you will see discussion about government budgets and deficits, interest rate changes, and how these affect unemployment and inflation. You may also see news about changes in the availability of certain crucial resources—particularly energy resources—and about the impact of changes in resource supplies on the country's economy. How does economic theory help to make sense of it all?

In Chapter 9, we started to build a model of business cycles. In Chapters 10 and 11, we explained economic theories concerning fiscal and monetary policy. So far, most of our macroeconomic analysis has focused on the "demand side," examining how changes in consumption, investment, and government spending might affect the levels of aggregate demand in the economy. In this chapter, we complete this story, with explicit attention to the problem of inflation. Then we move on to "supply-side" issues that determine the productive capacity of the economy and influence the level of output. Finally, we will arrive at a model that puts demand and supply issues together.

1. AGGREGATE DEMAND AND INFLATION

Recall from Chapter 9 that aggregate demand is the total quantity of goods and services demanded by households, businesses, government, and the international sector in the economy. It is represented by the total spending, which is the sum of consumption, investment, government spending, and net exports. Since the level of spending is influenced by the changes in price levels, we use the **aggregate demand (AD) curve** to represent the relationship between the equilibrium level of output and inflation.

> **aggregate demand (AD) curve:** graph showing the relationship between the rate of inflation and the total quantity of goods and services demanded by households, businesses, government, and the international sector

1.1 The Aggregate Demand Curve

The aggregate demand curve is graphically represented with output (denoted by Y) on the horizontal axis and the rate of inflation on the vertical axis (denoted by the symbol π).[1] The AD curve is shown in Figure 12.1. It is downward sloping,

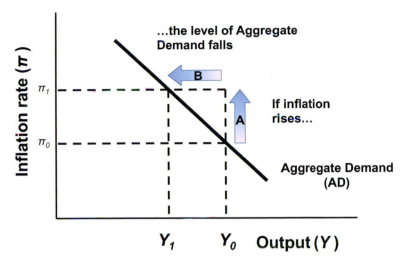

Figure 12.1 *The Aggregate Demand Curve*

indicating that higher inflation rates will tend to reduce total demand. This reasoning is based on the following effects of inflation on total demand:

- When inflation rises, it reduces the value of money assets. Even if this does not reach the level of hyperinflation, it hurts savers and people who have money balances. This **real wealth effect** tends to reduce their consumption, lowering total demand.
- Inflation also lowers the **real money supply**, defined as M/P, where M is the nominal money supply and P is the general price level. This has an effect similar to contractionary monetary policy, raising interest rates, discouraging investment, and lowering aggregate demand.
- Inflation hurts net exports by making domestically produced goods more expensive for foreigners and imports more attractive for domestic consumers. This decreases aggregate demand by decreasing net exports.[2]
- The Federal Reserve generally responds to higher inflation by raising interest rates, as discussed in Chapter 11. This also tends to lower investment and total demand.

> **real wealth effect:** the tendency of consumers to increase or decrease their consumption based on their perceived level of wealth
> **real money supply:** the nominal money supply divided by the general price level (as measured by a price index), expressed as M/P

There is some disagreement among economists about which of these effects are most significant, but there is little doubt about the overall result: higher inflation results in lower aggregate demand levels. Note that every point on the aggregate demand curve is an economic equilibrium, where output, income, and spending are equal. (Recall our discussion on economic equilibrium from Chapter 9.)

1.2 Shifts of the Aggregate Demand Curve: Spending and Taxation

The downward slope of the *AD* curve shown in Figure 12.1 is based on the indirect impacts of inflation on aggregate demand, as discussed previously. What determines the position of the curve? The position of the *AD* curve depends on specific levels of government spending, taxation, autonomous consumption, autonomous investment, and autonomous net exports.[3] Changes in these variables will therefore cause the *AD* curve to shift.

For example, if the government were to undertake expansionary fiscal policy, this would shift the *AD* curve to the right, as illustrated in Figure 12.2. At any level of inflation, there would now be aggregate demand sufficient to support a higher level of output.

An increase in autonomous consumption or investment would have a similar effect, as would an autonomous increase in net exports. Recall that autonomous consumption is the part of household spending that does not depend on income, and autonomous investment is the part of business spending that does not depend on the interest rate. These are often used to represent consumer and business "confidence." Thus, an increase in consumer or investor confidence could also cause the rightward shift in Figure 12.2. Conversely, of course, contractionary fiscal policy, reductions in consumer or investment confidence, or reduction in autonomous net exports would shift the *AD* curve to the left.

1.3 Shifts of the Aggregate Demand Curve: Monetary Policy

As we have noted, the Federal Reserve usually responds to higher inflation by increasing interest rates; this is reflected in the downward slope of the *AD* curve. This policy response by the Federal Reserve, which aims to keep inflation near a target level, is a rather passive sort of monetary policy. A more active form of monetary policy occurs when the Fed changes its inflation target or shifts its focus to fighting unemployment.

For example, in a severe recession, the Fed might decide that the economy requires additional stimulus. If the Fed instituted significant expansionary monetary policies, driving interest rates down (as it did, for example, starting in 2007), this would, in

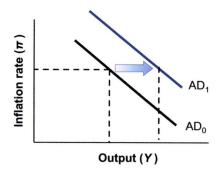

Figure 12.2 *The Effect of Expansionary Fiscal Policy or Increased Confidence on the* AD *Curve*

theory, have the effect of boosting investment and shifting the *AD* curve to the right. Alternatively, if the Fed decided that its policies on inflation have been too lax, it could tighten monetary policy sharply (this happened, for example, in 1982 in response to severe continuing inflation). This would have the effect of shifting the *AD* curve to the left.

To summarize:

■ The *AD* curve indicates levels of equilibrium GDP at different possible rates of inflation.
■ The *AD* curve can be shifted by changes in levels of autonomous consumer spending, autonomous investment, fiscal policy, net exports, or by major changes in monetary policy.

Discussion Questions

1. "The negative slope of the *AD* curve means that higher levels of output will lead to lower levels of inflation." Is this statement correct or not? Discuss.
2. Does the Fed always want the inflation rate to be as low as possible? Why or why not?

2. CAPACITY AND THE AGGREGATE SUPPLY CURVE

As we have noted in earlier chapters, increases in aggregate demand can push output up toward the full-employment level. In our current analysis, an increase in aggregate demand is shown by a rightward shift in the *AD* curve. But what happens when output reaches—or maybe even exceeds—the full-employment level? In a graph such as Figure 12.2, for example, there is nothing in the model that seems to prevent expansionary policies from just shifting the *AD* curve up and up so that any level of output can be achieved.

Obviously, this cannot be true in the real world. At any given time, there are only certain quantities of labor, capital, energy, and other material resources available for use. The U.S. labor force, for example, comprises just over 160 million people. The United States simply cannot, then, produce an output level that would require the work of 200 million people. This is a *hard capacity constraint*. What happens as an economy approaches maximum capacity can be modeled using the **aggregate supply (*AS*) curve**. The *AS* curve shows combinations of output and inflation that can, in fact, occur within an economy, given the reality of capacity constraints.

aggregate supply (*AS*) curve: graph representing the relationship between the rate of inflation and the total goods and services producers are willing to supply, given the reality of capacity constraints

2.1 The Aggregate Supply Curve

Figure 12.3 shows how aggregate supply is related to the rate of inflation. It will be easiest to explain the shape of the curve starting from the right, at high output levels. Moving from right to left, we can identify five important, distinct regions of the diagram.

First (starting on the right in Figure 12.3), the vertical **maximum capacity output** line indicates the hard limit on a macroeconomy's output. Even if every last resource in the economy were put into use, with everybody working flat out to produce the most they could, the economy could not produce to the right of the maximum capacity line.

> **maximum capacity output:** the level of output an economy would produce if every resource in the economy were fully utilized

Just below the maximum capacity level of output, the *AS* curve has a very steep, positive slope. This indicates that, as an economy closely approaches its maximum capacity, it is likely to experience a substantial increase in inflation. If many employers are all trying to hire many workers and buy a lot of machinery, energy, and materials all at once, workers' wages and resource prices will tend to be bid upward. But then, to cover their labor and other costs, producers will need to raise the prices that they charge for their own goods. Then, in turn, if workers find that the purchasing power of their wages is being eroded by rising inflation, they will demand higher wages, which leads to higher prices, and so on. The result is a phenomenon called a **wage–price spiral**, in which higher wages and higher prices lead to a steep rise in self-reinforcing inflation.

> **wage–price spiral:** when upward pressure on wages creates upward pressure on prices and, as a result, further upward pressure on wages

In the real world, such steep increases in inflation are usually the result of dramatic pressures on producers, such as often occur during a national mobilization for war. During World War II, for example, the U.S. government pushed the economy very close to its maximum capacity—placing big orders for munitions and other supplies for the front, mobilizing the necessary resources by encouraging women to enter the paid labor force, encouraging the recycling of materials on an unprecedented scale, encouraging the planting of backyard gardens to increase food production, and in general pushing people's productive efforts far beyond their usual peacetime levels. As a result, unemployment plummeted. The government, knowing that such pressures could lead to sharply rising inflation (as shown in the wage-price spiral region of Figure 12.3), kept inflation from getting out of hand by instituting **wage and price controls**—direct regulations telling firms what they could and could not do in the way of price or wage increases.

> **wage and price controls:** government regulations setting limits on wages and prices or on the rates at which they are permitted to increase

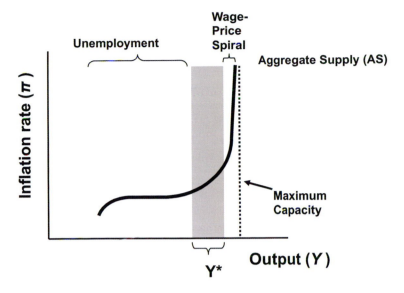

Figure 12.3 *The Aggregate Supply Curve*

The shaded area to the left of the wage-price spiral region in Figure 12.3 indicates a range of full-employment levels of output. While it is controversial to say exactly where that level may be, it can be thought of as an output level high enough that unemployment is not considered a national problem. And because it must be low enough to allow for at least a small measurable level of transitory unemployment, the *full-employment* level of output is slightly lower than the *maximum capacity* level of output.

Within the full-employment range, Figure 12.3 shows a gently rising *AS* curve. This is because, even well before an economy approaches the absolute maximum capacity given *all* its resources, producers may tend to run into "bottlenecks" in the supply of *some* resources. Agricultural workers may be plentiful, for example, but professional and technical workers may be in short supply. Or fuel oil may be plentiful, but there may be a shortage of natural gas. Shortages in the markets for particular kinds of labor and other inputs may lead to an acceleration of inflation in some sectors of the economy. Because the measured inflation rate represents an average for the economy as a whole, some aggregate increase in inflation may be observed.

This sort of increase in inflation that comes with high (but not extremely high) production is what economists expect to happen when the economy nears a business cycle "peak." Note, however, that the *AS* curve has been drawn as flatter toward the left of the Y* range, indicating that combinations of full employment and stable inflation may also be possible.

Moving further to the left, the AS curve shows a region in which the economy is in recession or recovering from a recession. Here output is below its full-employment level. The flat *AS* line shown in Figure 12.3 for this region indicates that, under these conditions, there is assumed to be no tendency for inflation to rise. Because a considerable amount of labor and other resources are unemployed, there is no pressure for higher wages or prices. It is also likely that because wages and prices tend to be slow in adjusting downward, inflation will not fall either—at least not right away.

When the economy is hit not by a regular recession but by a really deep recession, such as one experienced in most industrialized countries in the 2008–2009 global economic crisis, output is so far below the full-employment level that inflation starts to drop and may even become negative (deflation). In this situation, demand is so weak that a large number of companies may fail. Struggling to stay in business, firms are forced to cut prices in order to maintain at least some sales. Also, in such a situation, workers and their unions might agree to wage cuts, which lowers firms' costs and allows them to further reduce their prices. As output falls, the *AS* curve in Figure 12.3 slopes downward as a further fall in aggregate demand accelerates the process of **disinflation** (a decline in the rate of inflation) or even deflation (an absolute decrease in price levels).

---

disinflation: a decline in the rate of inflation

2.2 Shifts of the Aggregate Supply Curve: Inflationary Expectations

When people have experienced inflation, they come to expect it. They then tend to build the level of inflation that they expect into the various contracts into which they enter. If a business expects 4 percent inflation over the coming year, for example, it will add 4 percent to the selling price that it quotes for a product to be delivered a year into the future just to stay even. If workers also expect 4 percent inflation, they will try to get at least a 4 percent cost of living allowance just to stay even. A depositor who expects 4 percent inflation and wants a 4 percent real rate of return will be satisfied only with an 8 percent nominal rate of return.[4]

In this way, an expected rate of inflation can start to become institutionally "built in" to an economy. As a first approximation, it is reasonable to assume that people expect something like the level of inflation that they have recently experienced (an assumption that economists call "adaptive expectations"). Thus, inflation can be, to some degree, self-fulfilling.

Because different contracts come up for renegotiation at different times of the year, the process of building in particular inflationary expectations will take place only over time. Because of the time that it takes for prices and wages to adjust, we need to make a distinction between short-run and medium-run aggregate supply responses.

The *AS* curve in Figure 12.3 was drawn for a particular level of expected inflation in the *short run*. Before people have caught on to the fact that the inflation rate might be changing, their expectations of inflation will continue to reflect their recent experience. The rate of inflation at which the *AS* curve becomes horizontal is the expected inflation rate. In this model, an economy in recession, or on the horizontal part of the *AS* curve, will tend in the short run to roll along at pretty much the same inflation rate as it has experienced in the past. Only tight labor and

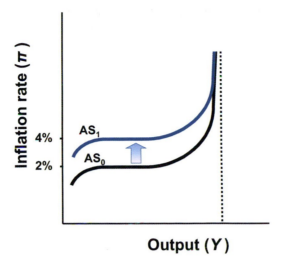

Figure 12.4 *The Effect of an Increase in Inflationary Expectations on the Aggregate Supply Curve*

resource markets caused by a boom will tend to increase inflation, which will come as a surprise to people and will not immediately translate into a change in expectations. For the purposes of this model, you might think of the short run as a period of some weeks or months.

Over an unspecified longer period of time—the *medium run*—however, a rise in inflation due to tight markets tends to increase people's expectation of inflation. If they expected 2 percent inflation, but over a period of time they experience 4 percent inflation, the next time that they renegotiate contracts they may build in a 4 percent rate. Figure 12.4 shows how the *AS* curve shifts upward as people's expectation of inflation rises. Note that in our model, the maximum capacity of the economy has not changed—nothing has happened that would affect the physical capacity of the economy to produce. All that has happened is that now, at any output level, people's expectation of inflation is higher.

Similarly, if people experience low demand in markets for their labor or products or lower inflation due to lack of aggregate demand and recessionary conditions, over the medium run, the expected inflation rate may start to come down. Employers may find that they can still get workers if they offer lower wages. Unions might agree to lower wage increases, as their members might be afraid of unemployment, but only need a small wage increase to guarantee stable purchasing power. Producers may raise their prices less this year than last year or cut prices, because they are having trouble selling in a slow market. When people start to observe wage and price inflation tapering off in some sectors of the economy, they may change their expectations about inflation. As people react to the sluggish aggregate demand that occurs during a recession, they will tend, over time, to lessen their expectations about wage and price increases. The graph for this would be similar to Figure 12.4 but would show the *AS* curve shifting downward instead of upward.

2.3 Shifts of the Aggregate Supply Curve: Supply Shocks

The AS curve also shifts when the capacity of the economy changes. A **supply shock** is something that changes the ability of an economy to produce goods and services. Supply shocks can be beneficial, as when there is a bumper crop in agriculture or a new invention allows more goods or services to be made using a smaller quantity of resources. Increases in labor productivity also allow an economy to produce more goods and services.

> **supply shock:** a change in the productive capacity of an economy

In such cases, the real capacity of the economy expands, as shown in Figure 12.5. The line indicating maximum capacity also shifts to the right, showing that the economy can produce more than before. We model the beneficial supply shock as moving the AS curve both to the right and downward. It moves to the right because capacity has increased. It moves downward because beneficial supply shocks are often accompanied by decreases in prices. As computer technology has improved, for example, the price of any given amount of computing power has dropped rapidly. To the extent that computers play a significant role in the economy, this tends to undermine inflation.

Supply shocks can also be adverse. Natural occurrences, such as hurricanes or droughts, and human–caused situations, such as wars, that destroy capital goods and lives are examples of adverse supply shocks. With regard to energy resources, adverse supply shocks can arise from physical changes such as the exhaustion of an oil reserve. They can also arise for economic reasons such as a successful limitation of oil supply by a cartel (a major factor in promoting inflation during the 1970s). Adverse supply shocks reduce the economy's capacity to produce and, by concentrating demand on the limited supplies of resources that remain, tend to lead to higher inflation. Adverse supply shocks would be illustrated in a graph such as Figure 12.5 but with the direction of all the movements reversed.

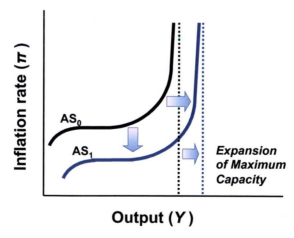

Figure 12.5 *A Beneficial Supply Shock: Expansion of Output Capacity*

Discussion Questions

1. Describe in words how the *AS* curve differs from the *AD* curve. What does each represent? What explains their slopes?
2. Do you get "cost-of-living" raises at your job or know people who do? Why does this practice have important macroeconomic consequences?

3. PUTTING THE AGGREGATE SUPPLY/AGGREGATE DEMAND MODEL TO WORK

Economists invented the *AS/AD* model to illustrate three points about the macroeconomy:

1. Fiscal and monetary policies affect output and inflation:
   - *Expansionary fiscal and monetary policies* tend to push the economy toward higher output. If the economy is approaching its maximum capacity, they are likely to cause inflation to rise.
   - *Contractionary fiscal and monetary policies* tend to push the economy toward lower output. Inflation may not fall quickly, but a persistently lower level of economic activity will tend to lower inflation over the long term.
2. *Supply shocks* may also have significant effects:
   - Adverse supply shocks lower output and raise inflation.
   - Beneficial supply shocks raise output and lower inflation.
3. *Investor and consumer confidence and expectations* also have important effects on output and inflation.

Bearing these principles in mind, we will see how this model helps to explain some major macroeconomic events.

3.1 An Economy in Recession

In Figure 12.6, we bring together the *AS* and *AD* curves for the first time. The (short-run) equilibrium of the economy is shown as point E_0, at the intersection of the two curves. Depending on how we place the curves in the figure, we could illustrate an economy that is in a recession, at full employment, or in a wage-price spiral. (We temporarily omit the maximum capacity line, but we reintroduce it when we discuss inflation.)

In this specific case, the fact that E_0 is well to the left of the full-employment range of output indicates that the economy is in a recession. Private spending, as determined in part by investor and consumer confidence, along with government and foreign sector spending, are not enough to keep the economy at full employment. The fact that the curves intersect on the flat part of the *AS* curve indicates that inflation (in the short run) is stable. So in this situation, unemployment is the major problem. What can be done?

Figure 12.6 models the real-world situation of the U.S. economy in the 2007–2009 recession. Unemployment rose to 10 percent in 2009, but inflation was very low.

387

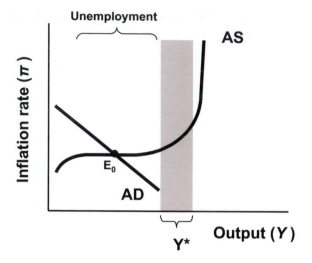

Figure 12.6 *Aggregate Demand and Supply Equilibrium in Recession*

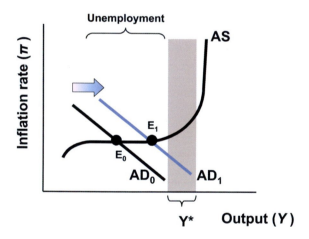

Figure 12.7 *Expansionary Fiscal Policy in Response to a Recession*

In this situation, the administration of President Barack Obama called for a major fiscal stimulus program, which was approved by Congress in early 2009. The goal of the stimulus program, which included $800 billion in increased government spending and tax cuts, was to promote employment both through its direct impact and multiplier effects expanding private spending and employment. This effect is shown in Figure 12.7 as a rightward shift of the *AD* curve.

As noted in Chapter 10, the stimulus plan was responsible for adding millions of jobs to the economy. While economists are not in agreement about how large the multiplier effects of the program were, many argue that without the program, the economy would have continued to plunge deeper into recession.[5] The effects, however, were not large enough to bring the economy back to full employment. The unemployment rate remained above 7 percent until 2013 and only gradually declined to 5 percent in late 2015. This is reflected in Figure 12.7 as an *AD* shift that moves output toward, but not into, the full-employment zone.

What is the effect of this expansionary program on inflation? As the *AS/AD* model would lead us to expect, inflation did not rise because the economy did not move beyond the flat portion of the *AS* curve. Some economists and political commentators warned at the time that such a high level of government spending and deficits would certainly cause serious inflation—but inflation remained low through 2019, ten years after the start of the stimulus program.

Would more macroeconomic stimulus have made sense, given that unemployment was still high and inflation relatively low? Some economists argued that it would, but proposals for further fiscal stimulus were not acted on by Congress, largely out of fear that deficits were already too high. So the Federal Reserve stepped in with the expanded monetary stimulus known as "quantitative easing" (discussed in Chapter 11). The hope was that a combination of this monetary expansion plus recovering confidence on the part of consumers and businesses could lead to a more complete recovery.

When the official unemployment rate reached below 4 percent in early 2018, many economists believed that the U.S. economy had reached or was close to reaching the goal of full employment. This is illustrated in Figure 12.8, where we see that a larger *AD* shift brings the economy back into the full-employment zone. At this point, the model predicts that there could be at least a slight increase in inflation. Detection of such rising inflation would signal the Fed to cut back on its monetary expansion (see Box 12.1 for recent Fed policies).

The achievement of full employment with relatively low inflation could be judged a success (indicated by point E_1 in Figure 12.8). However, the process of recovery

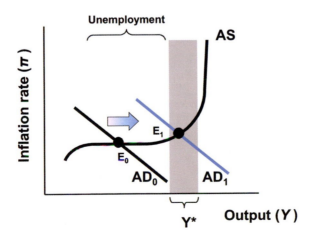

Figure 12.8 *A Greater Expansion of Aggregate Demand*

BOX 12.1 ARE INTEREST RATES TOO LOW OR NOT LOW ENOUGH?

By 2019, the U.S. economy had entered its tenth year of expansion since the crisis of 2008–2009. As of August 2019, the unemployment rate was at 3.7 percent—the lowest since 2000—and hourly wages had increased by about 1.5 percent since the previous year. Despite fears of inflation amid such strong labor market conditions, inflation has continued to remain below 2 percent.

In 2018, when unemployment rates reached below 4 percent for the first time since the 2008 crisis, the Fed raised interest rates four times to address concerns about the possibility of inflation. In fact, the Fed had been raising interest rates gradually since mid-2015, from its low of 0.25 percent in 2008 to 2.5 percent by the end of 2018, due to strengthening economic conditions. However, interest rates are still at historic lows, and some economists have expressed concerns that such prolonged periods of low interest rates create dangerous bubbles. One of the factors leading to the 2008 crisis was the low interest rates that forced investors in desperate search of higher-yield securities to take too much risk for low return. Also, low interest rates often motivate people to take far too much debt. Some economists have warned that there is already a bubble forming in the bond market due to high levels of borrowing.[6]

Despite these concerns about interest rates being too low, the Fed reversed course in 2019 and lowered interest rates twice (as of September), citing possibilities of a looming recession with slowdowns in major economies like China and Germany, declines in manufacturing, and the uncertainties created by Trump's trade and foreign policies. Though the unemployment rate continues to remain low and wages are gradually rising, Fed Chair Jerome Powell argued that the lower rates would "help keep the U.S. economy strong in the face of some notable developments and to provide insurance against ongoing risks."[7]

Some economists have criticized these recent rate cuts, arguing that lowering rates when the economy is still doing well could reduce the Fed's ability to lower rates further if an actual recession hits. However, President Trump has attacked the Fed for not lowering rates enough and pressed the central bank to cut short-term rates to "ZERO, or less" arguing that lower rates would help boost the economy.[8]

was slow, with about 1.39 million workers being long-term unemployed (over 27 weeks) and the unemployment rate including marginally attached workers and those working part-time for economic reasons remaining above 8 percent in February 2018. The uncertainty about whether full employment had really been reached is reflected by our "gray zone" or shaded area denoting a range for what can be considered full employment.

As we see later in this chapter, not all economists agree with this analysis of the impacts of expansionary fiscal and monetary policy in the wake of the Great Recession. Some classically oriented economists argue that inflation has merely been delayed but will eventually cause major problems and perhaps force a return to recession. We will look into the theoretical issues involved later (without providing any definite judgment on the debate).

Although inflation has recently been low in the United States, we do know that there have been other times in economic history when inflation has been a major problem. What does the *AS/AD* model suggest about policy response in such periods? We explore this topic next.

3.2 An Overheated Economy

Problems with inflation were a major issue in the United States starting in the late 1960s. High government spending, in particular spending on the Vietnam war, meant that fiscal policy was excessively expansionary. Monetary policy during this period tended to accommodate the fiscal expansion. Although unemployment was very low as a result, the economy started to "overheat," causing inflation to rise.

This period of history is modeled in Figure 12.9. The *AD* curve moves further to the right due to the increases in government spending. It shifts from AD_0, which at E_0 corresponds to a full-employment equilibrium, to AD_1, which crosses the *AS* curve in the wage-price spiral range. The economy became overheated, moving beyond full employment to E_1.

Our analysis thus far suggests that there is a tradeoff between unemployment and inflation. There is some real-world evidence to support this idea. For example, economist A. W. Phillips, analyzing data from 1861 to 1957, found that for the United Kingdom, periods of high inflation coincided with periods of low unemployment and vice versa. This inverse relationship between unemployment and

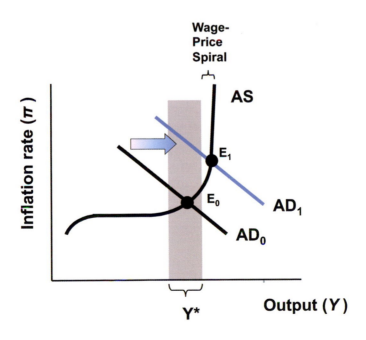

Figure 12.9 *Excessively High Aggregate Demand Causes Inflation*

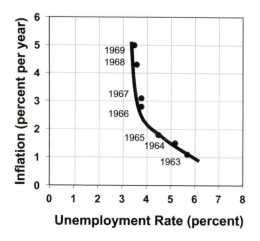

Figure 12.10 *The Phillips Curve in the 1960s*

inflation came to be known as the Phillips curve. The Phillips curve for the United States in the 1960s is shown in Figure 12.10.

As you can see, the shape of the upward-sloping portion of the *AS* curve is essentially a mirror image of the Phillips curve. This is no coincidence. The models that economists developed during the 1960s grew out of observing such a pattern of unemployment and inflation rates and trying to explain why it occurred. Although, as we will see, subsequent events challenged the simple view of the Phillips curve, the concept of an unemployment/inflation tradeoff is still relevant, as evident in recent concerns about rising inflation during periods of economic strength (see Box 12.1).

3.3 Stagflation

Economic history shows that the Phillips curve is not always a reliable guide to policy. The developments of the early 1970s came as a shock to Phillips curve–minded economists and policymakers. From 1969 to 1970, unemployment and inflation *both* rose, and both stayed fairly high through the 1970–1973 period. This combination of economic stagnation (recession) and high inflation came to be known as **stagflation**.

stagflation: a combination of rising inflation and economic stagnation

What happened? As noted, by the late 1960s, rising government spending on the Vietnam war as well as domestic programs had started to push the economy into inflation (the upper portion of the Phillips curve in Figure 12.10). In 1968, worried about rising inflation, President Lyndon Johnson persuaded Congress to enact an income tax surcharge. In our model, we show this contractionary fiscal policy as a leftward shift of the *AD* curve in Figure 12.11.

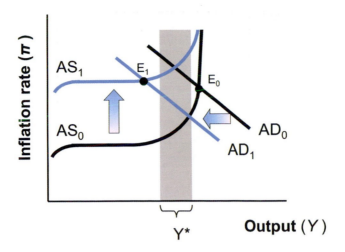

Figure 12.11 *Rising Inflationary Expectations and Contractionary Fiscal Policy*

This policy move is widely considered to have been "too little, too late" to curb consumer and investor spending. By the time the economy started to cool off, inflationary expectations had become firmly implanted. Having recently experienced a wage-price spiral, people had built expectations of higher inflation into their wage and price contracts. As Karl Otto Pohl, former president of the Bundesbank, the German central bank, once commented, inflation is like toothpaste—once you squeeze it out of the tube, you cannot get it back in. Although the fiscal cutbacks contributed to falling GDP and rising unemployment, they did not bring down inflation due to this institutional "ratcheting up" of inflationary expectations.

The increase in inflationary expectations is represented by an upward shift of the AS curve. In Figure 12.11, the combination of the contractionary fiscal policy and the rise in inflationary expectations is shown as moving the economy from an overheated boom point of E_0 to a recessionary, high-inflation point of E_1. This is exactly what happened to the U.S. economy in the early 1970s.

The situation became worse later in the decade. In 1973–1974, the member countries of the Organization of Petroleum Exporting Countries cut production, greatly increased the price at which they sold their oil, and even temporarily stopped shipping oil to certain countries. The price of oil, a key input into many production processes, suddenly quadrupled. What effect did this have on the macroeconomy?

The impact of the oil price shock is shown in Figure 12.12. The economy starts off in a recession at point E_0, which is substantially to the left of the initial maximum capacity line. The cut in foreign oil production meant that the United States (and many other oil-importing countries) now suffered from a reduced capacity to produce goods, which is shown in Figure 12.12 by the maximum capacity line and AS curves shifting to the left. Even if labor resources were fully employed, an economy with reduced access to other inputs would not be able to produce as much. At the same time, the rise in oil prices had an immediate and direct effect

393

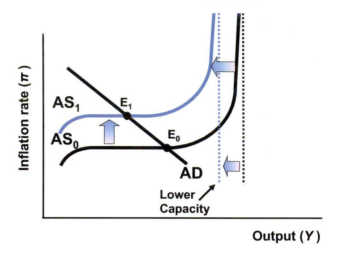

Figure 12.12 *The Effect of the Oil Price Shock of the 1970s*

on inflation, shifting the *AS* curve up as well, as also shown in Figure 12.12. Both inflation and unemployment got worse.

3.4 A Hard Line Against Inflation

This was still not the end of the inflationary story of the 1970s. Although oil prices held steady and inflation moderated during the period 1975–1978, oil prices jumped again in 1979 and 1980. In 1979, the price of oil was *ten* times higher than it had been in 1973. The overall inflation rate in the United States was more than 9 percent in 1979—and exceeded 10 percent (measured at an annual rate) during some months.

The high rates of inflation experienced in the late 1970s were very damaging to the economy. As we noted in Chapter 9, high rates of inflation can wipe out the value of people's savings and make it very difficult for households and business to plan, save, and invest. Because unemployment was also high, as shown in Figure 12.12, it was difficult to see how consumers and businesses could ever recover confidence while inflation seemed out of control.

Even though the economy was already in a recession, and the unemployment rate was above 7 percent, the Federal Reserve, under the chairmanship of Paul Volcker, took drastic action to bring the long-term inflation rate down by increasing interest rates substantially. During Volcker's tenure, the Fed raised the federal funds rate target well into the double digits, where it peaked at over 19 percent in early 1981 and did not fall back to single digits until late 1984. The effects of these "tight money" policies during the early 1980s can be seen in Figure 12.13.

As discussed earlier, contractionary monetary policy shifts the *AD* curve to the left. The *AS/AD* model predicts that the immediate effect of this policy will be to send the economy even deeper into a recession, with output falling even farther below its full-employment level, as shown by equilibrium point E_1. But there is a further effect, on inflationary expectations.

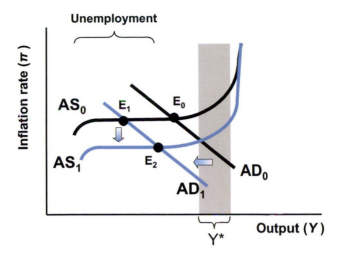

Figure 12.13 *The Effects of the Fed's "Tight Money" Policies in the 1980s*

This contractionary policy was accompanied by many stories in the media about how Volcker was really committed to bringing down inflation, no matter the cost. Because people found this commitment credible, their expectations of inflation also came down. The effect of this decrease in inflationary expectations is shown as a downward shift in the AS curve to AS_1, showing a reduction in inflation. Such a recession with falling inflation is, in fact, what happened during the Volker contraction. By 1983, the inflation rate had fallen to 4 percent, but at a significant human and economic cost. Unemployment during 1982 and 1983 rose to nearly 10 percent. But in the years that followed, the economy recovered and employment increased, as shown by equilibrium point E_2.

The experience of the 1980s suggests that if inflationary expectations become established, they can be difficult to reduce. Furthermore, lowering inflationary expectations via tight monetary policy is likely to cause major economic pain.[9] This has led future policymakers to be very wary of encouraging any new inflationary wage-price spiral. Changes in the global economy in the 1990s, however, made achieving low-inflation goals significantly easier, as discussed in the next section.

3.5 Technology and Globalization

Following the substantial recession and disinflation of the early 1980s, output began to recover again. Fluctuations in unemployment and inflation continued, though within narrower bands than during the earlier years. From 1984 to 2004, unemployment varied from 4 percent to about 8 percent and inflation from 1 percent to about 6 percent; since 1992, inflation has never risen above 4 percent and briefly fell to zero following the Great Recession (raising concerns about the opposite problem of deflation). Unemployment was low throughout the 1990s but peaked again at 10 percent in 2010 following the Great Recession and then declined only slowly (see Figures 12.14 and 12.15).

395

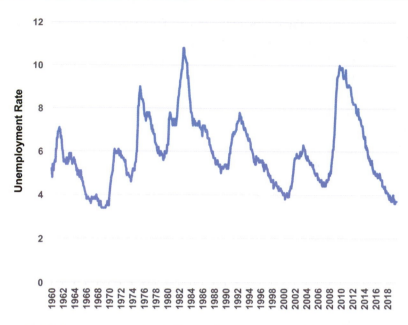

Figure 12.14 *Unemployment Trends 1960–2019 (Percentage of Labor Force)*

Source: Bureau of Labor Statistics, *Current Population Survey*, 2019.

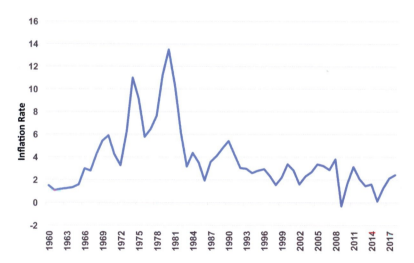

Figure 12.15 *Inflation Trends 1960–2018 (Annual Percent Inflation)*

Source: Bureau of Labor Statistics, Consumer Price Index (CPI-U), 2019.

We can use our *AS/AD* analysis to focus on one more period: the expansion of the 1990s. From 1992 to 1998, unemployment rates and inflation rates steadily fell, as shown in Figures 12.14 and 12.15. In 1998, unemployment was 4.4 percent, the lowest it had been since 1971. Inflation was 1.6 percent, lower than it had been in more than ten years. This was clearly the best macroeconomic performance in decades. Unemployment continued to fall for another two years, reaching 3.9 percent in 2000.

What caused this sustained recovery? Significant advances in innovation—in particular, enormous leaps in information technology, including the advent of widespread use of the internet and information systems for business supplies, deliveries, and product design—provided a major impetus for this period of superior macroeconomic performance. This can be modeled as a period of beneficial supply shocks, as shown in Figure 12.16.

Many economists also point to increasing global competitiveness as a factor in the rising productivity of this period. Competition from foreign firms, they argue, made U.S. firms work harder to become efficient. Meanwhile, competition from foreign workers and anti-union government policies weakened the power of domestic unions. This helped keep wage and price inflation low (though it also had consequences for the U.S. distribution of income, as we will see in Chapter 13).

The strong performance of the macroeconomy in the 1990s inspired economic optimism. A number of commentators wondered whether we were entering a "new economy" in which business cycles would become a thing of the past. Events after 2000 proved otherwise. In 2001–2002, the stock market crashed as the "dot-com" speculative bubble burst. About a year later, the economy slid into recession. Policymakers were worried that the pattern of enthusiastic investment and consumer spending that had fueled GDP growth in the 1990s might be coming to an end. Orders for goods had slowed down. Inventories had built up. Moreover, the global security situation, with the terrorist attack in September of 2001 being followed by the wars in Afghanistan and Iraq, caused uncertainty among the business community and tended to reduce investment.

Expansionary fiscal and monetary policies, including tax rate cuts and low interest rates, helped to promote a recovery from that recession. In late 2000, the federal

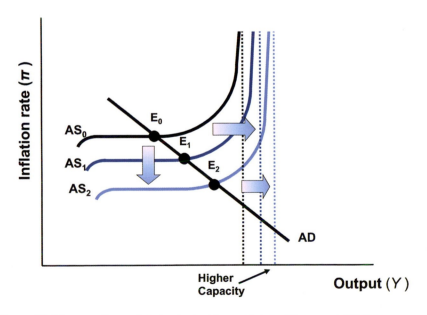

Figure 12.16 *The Effects of Technological Innovation and Increased Efficiency*

funds rate had been at 6.5 percent, reflecting a generally strong economy. In January 2001, the Fed, publicly expressing concern about the growing weakness of the economy, took action to lower the federal funds rate. Throughout the period 2001–2003, the Fed steadily pushed interest rates down (as shown in Figure 11.4 in Chapter 11). The federal funds rate reached a low of 1 percent in early 2004.

By May 2004, the Fed believed that the recovery was well under way and would continue. It returned to focusing on its other main macroeconomic goal: controlling inflation. For the next three years, the Fed steadily increased the federal funds rate in an attempt to keep the economy from "overheating." But in 2007, another even more significant speculative bubble in housing collapsed, leading rapidly to the most severe recession since the 1930s—often referred to as the Great Recession because of its length and severity. The housing bubble and the Great Recession are discussed in much greater detail in Chapter 13.

This brings us back to the first application that we discussed for *AS/AD* analysis—policies to recover from recession. It seems that we have not entered a new, business cycle–free, "recession-proof" economic optimum. Instead, we have relived some of the recessionary problems of previous decades. Although the real productivity gains made during the 1990s did not go away, and the effects of that part of the expansion persist to this day, the kinds of economic fluctuation and policy response that we have modeled with *AS/AD* analysis clearly remain of prime importance to macroeconomics. As the economy moves out of recession and approaches full employment, concerns shift to possible excessive aggregate demand and the need for policies to moderate inflation—but if possible without tipping the economy back into recession.

Discussion Questions

1. Under what circumstances can aggregate demand be increased without leading to problems with inflation? Under what circumstances is an increase in aggregate demand likely to cause inflation?
2. Stagflation—a combination of unemployment and inflation—seems to be the worst of both worlds. What policies were used to respond to the stagflation of the late 1970s and early 1980s? What factors led to improving economic conditions in the later 1980s and the 1990s?

4. COMPETING THEORIES

The *AS/AD* model has given us insight into some of the major macroeconomic fluctuations of the past several decades. But there remains much room for controversy. Was it necessary to enact expansionary fiscal policy in order to get the economy out of the 2007–2008 recession? Was it a good idea for the Federal Reserve to lower interest rates to near zero in 2007–2015 to try to promote recovery? Economists differ greatly in their views on these issues, and their theoretical backgrounds tend to inform their answers to these and other more contemporary questions.

Here we review the ways in which classical and Keynesian economics address these questions. Additional theories—some of which take positions between these two poles—are reviewed in an online Appendix to this chapter.

4.1 Classical Macroeconomics

As discussed in previous chapters, economists with ties to the classical school tend to believe in the self-adjusting properties of a free-market system. In the classical view, labor markets clear at an equilibrium wage, and markets for loanable funds clear at an equilibrium interest rate where savings and investment are equal (Chapter 9). In theory, then, a smoothly functioning economy should never be at anything other than full employment.

In terms of the *AS/AD* model, the classical theory implies an *AS* curve that is vertical, as shown in Figure 12.17. In this model, output is always at or close to its full-employment level (now shown as a distinct value, rather than a range). The *AD* level would merely determine the inflation rate but nothing else.

The rationale for this vertical *AS* curve is as follows. At the full-employment level, people are making their optimizing choices about how much to work, consume, and so on. If, for some reason, the economy were to produce at less than the full-employment level, the unemployed workers would bid down wages, and full employment would be restored. If the economy were to produce at more than its full-employment level, wages would be bid up, and employment would drop back to its full-employment level. Such processes are assumed to work quickly and smoothly, so that the economy will return to full employment fairly quickly.

What, according to the classical model, is the effect of aggregate demand management policies? As we can see in Figure 12.17, expansionary fiscal or monetary policy cannot have an effect on the output level. An increase in aggregate demand can only increase the rate of inflation. Furthermore, classical economists believe that increased government spending just "crowds out" private spending (as discussed in Chapter 10), in particular spending on investment. Because the economy is already at its full-employment level of *Y**, more spending by government just means less spending by consumers and businesses.

The classical model we have just described, and expressed in Figure 12.17, is probably not held by many economists. Even most classically oriented economists acknowledge that there can be short-term variations in employment and temporary effects of fiscal and monetary policies. But they argue that, in the longer run, the economy will achieve its natural equilibrium (*Y** in Figure 12.17), and government stimulatory policies will only lead to inflation.

As we saw in our discussion of classical monetary theory in Chapter 11, the classical prescription is that the central bank should just choose a certain growth

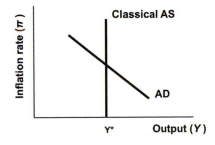

Figure 12.17 *The Classical View of AS/AD*

rate of the money supply or level of the interest rate to support and stick to it, without concerning itself about unemployment and output. Classical theory tends to support politically conservative policies that emphasize small government and strict rules on monetary policy. Classical economists would tend to say that the fiscal expansionary policies put into place in 2009 were unnecessary for the purposes of macroeconomic stabilization but that the Volcker-led monetary contractions of the early 1980s were a good idea.

4.2 Keynesian Macroeconomics

The basic Keynesian position is that that market economies are inherently unstable. The Keynesian notion of the influence of "animal spirits" on investment refers to the fact that since the future is fundamentally uncertain, investors' decisions are volatile and subject to rapidly shifting sentiments and emotions. Hence, private decision-makers may become overly optimistic when the economy is doing well and create unsustainable booms in investment and production. And they may contribute to prolonging or deepening an economic crisis if they become overly pessimistic. Firms that have overextended and overproduced during an upswing need time to regroup, sell off inventory, and so on before they will be ready to go on the upswing again. Households that have overextended and overspent during a boom also need to regroup and perhaps pay down debt before they will be willing to restart an optimistic spending bandwagon.

This view of perpetual business cycles is a fundamentally different worldview from those that presume an automatic "settling down" of the economy at a full-employment equilibrium. Keynes did *not* believe that macroeconomic phenomena could be explained by assuming rational, optimizing behavior by individuals and then extrapolating from models of individual markets to the macroeconomy, because he felt that most of the relevant information that is required for rational decision-making resided in a fundamentally uncertain future. Modern Keynesians argue that this inherent tendency toward market instability requires active government intervention and that the alternative—simply waiting for the market to correct itself—risks major economic damage and long-term depression.

It is important to note that Keynesians do not only favor using fiscal and monetary policies to manage recessions, they also argue that *contractionary* policies can sometimes be used to manage inflation. Keynesians thus find the kind of analysis that we have presented in this chapter very useful for determining what type of policy is needed in different circumstances. The traditional model of Keynesian business cycles must be modified to deal with new events such as supply shocks (discussed previously) and sustainability issues (discussed in Chapter 16). These require models that are flexible enough to address new issues as they arise. Such models are best built on the understanding that economies are subject to a variety of forces, many of which can swamp the simple market equilibrium arguments that would be expected to lead to a classical situation of full-employment equilibrium.

In the modern era, the debate between economists who favor classical approaches and those who argue for Keynesian analysis has continued. The Great Recession and its aftermath have provided new fodder for these arguments about economic analysis and policy (see Box 12.2).

BOX 12.2 CLASSICAL AND KEYNESIAN VIEWS OF RECESSION AND RECOVERY

The Great Recession of 2007–2009, followed by a very slow recovery in the United States, and the euro crisis and its aftermath in Europe, have provided a new arena for the long-running debate between classical and Keynesian views in economics and their impacts on macroeconomic policies.

Two major responses to the recession in the United States—the fiscal stimulus program of 2009–11 and the Federal Reserve policies of ultralow interest rates and "quantitative easing"—are right out of the Keynesian playbook of expansionary fiscal and monetary policy. Many European countries implemented similar expansionary policies when the crisis initially hit in 2008. However, a second crisis (the euro crisis) emerged in Europe as many countries saw their debt levels rise, partly from the increase in fiscal burden and the use of public money to rescue ailing banks. With the revelation that Greece had understated its public debt, investors became aware of the potential for sovereign default and raised interest rates. Risks of sovereign default also escalated in other countries, including Portugal, Ireland, Italy, and Spain, and these countries adopted measures to cut public spending and raise taxes to address the debt crisis.[10]

In response to this sovereign debt crisis, contractionary fiscal policies of "austerity" (drastic spending cutbacks) implemented in many European countries reflect the classical perspective that excessive government spending is a problem, not a solution, and that budget deficits need to be eliminated. Thus, the discussion has focused on the relative success or failure of these policies.

Keynesians argued that the stimulative fiscal and monetary policies implemented in the United States prevented a much worse recession, saving or creating millions of jobs and putting the country on a (slow) road to recovery.[11] They believed that the results, in terms of employment creation, were limited mainly because the stimulus was not large enough and that the stimulus was essentially reversed after the 2010 Republican congressional victories.[12] Although Keynesians generally supported the Fed's expansionary policies, they suggested that they are subject to the "liquidity trap" identified by Keynes—the tendency of banks and individuals to hold onto money in bad times, limiting the effectiveness of expansionary monetary policy. Meanwhile, they pointed to the deepening recession in Europe as proof that the "classical medicine" of budget austerity was counterproductive.[13]

Classical economists, by contrast, saw the government efforts at economic stimulation as a failure, one that would saddle the country with an increased burden of debt. According to Allan Meltzer (2011),[14]

U.S. fiscal and monetary policies are mainly directed at getting a near-term result. The estimated cost of new jobs in President Obama's jobs bill is at least $200,000 per job . . . once the subsidies end, the jobs disappear—but the bonds that financed them remain and must be serviced. Perhaps that's why estimates of the additional spending generated by Keynesian stimulus—the "multiplier effect"—have failed to live up to expectations.

Until 2016, the U.S. economy was performing much better than most European economies, which were still well below their production levels of 2007, with unemployment rates in some countries remaining at Great Depression levels of over 25 percent. Predictions by classical economists of the beneficial effects of budget austerity in Europe, and of accelerating inflation in the United States, had not come true. U.S. budget deficits were falling until 2015—something that Keynesians attributed to the success of their policies, while classical economists pointed to budget cuts imposed as part of the "debt ceiling" deal of 2011.

More recently, the European economy has experienced robust growth and declining unemployment. In 2017, GDP in the EU region rose by 2.6 percent—the fastest since 2007—and the unemployment rate dropped below 8 percent for the first time since 2008.[15] This recent progress in the European economy has been mainly attributed to expansionary policies put in place by the European Central Bank, including low lending rates and large-scale purchases of securities, which have increased liquidity and boosted growth.[16]

In the United States, concern has shifted to possibly excessive expansionary policy. The budget deficit in the United States had risen to about 1 trillion by 2019 and is estimated to rise even more in coming years as a result of the Trump administration's large tax cuts and relatively expansionary spending policies.[17] In this situation, the roles of the different schools of economics seemed to be reversed: classically oriented economists praised the Trump tax cuts, while some Keynesians warned of excessive deficits at precisely the wrong time, just as the economy approached full employment.

The real world is the testing ground for economic theories. As events unfold, the economic argument will continue, and new policies and new data will be grist to the mill of continued economic debate.

Discussion Questions

1. What is the effect of expansionary fiscal and monetary policies in the classical model?
2. Which do you think gives a better description of economic realities: classical or Keynesian macroeconomic theory? Explain.

REVIEW QUESTIONS

1. What does the *AD* curve represent, and why does it slope downward?
2. What shifts the *AD* curve?
3. What does the *AS* curve represent, and why does it have the shape that it has?
4. What shifts the *AS* curve?
5. Describe, using the *AS/AD* model, a combination of events that might cause an economy to suffer from "stagflation."
6. Describe, using the *AS/AD* model, the impact of an adverse supply shock.

7. Describe, using the *AS/AD* model, how Federal Reserve policy might bring down inflation over time.

8. Describe, using the *AS/AD* model, the effects of a series of positive supply shocks.

9. What does the *AS* curve look like in the classical model, and why?

10. What underlying dynamic did Keynes believe is behind the business cycle? Illustrate with an *AS/AD* graph.

EXERCISES

1. For each of the following, indicate which curve in the *AS/AD* model shifts (initially), and in which direction(s):

   a. A beneficial supply shock

   b. An increase in government spending

   c. A monetary contraction designed to lower the long-run inflation rate

   d. An increase in taxes

   e. An adverse supply shock

   f. A fall in people's expectations of inflation

   g. A decrease in consumer confidence

2. Suppose the inflation rate in an economy is observed to be falling. Sketching an *AS/AD* model for each case, determine which of the following phenomena could be the cause. (There may be more than one.)

   a. The federal government gives households a substantial tax cut

   b. Agricultural harvests are particularly good this year

   c. Businesses are confident about the future and are buying more equipment

   d. The Fed is trying to move the economy toward a lower long-run inflation rate

3. Suppose that an economy is currently experiencing full employment and inflation is only slightly higher than had been expected.

   a. Draw and carefully label an *AS/AD* diagram that illustrates this case. Label the point representing the state of this economy $E_{(a)}$.

   b. Suppose that investors' confidence is actually only in the middle of an upswing. As investor confidence continues to rise, what happens to inflation and output? Add a new curve to your graph to illustrate this, as well as explaining in words. Label the point illustrating the new situation of the economy $E_{(b)}$.

   c. What sort of tax policy might a government enact to try to counteract an excessive upswing in investor confidence? Assuming this policy is effective, illustrate on your graph the effect of this policy, labeling the result $E_{(c)}$.

4. Suppose that an economy is in a deep recession.

   a. Draw and carefully label an *AS/AD* diagram that illustrates this case. Label the point representing the state of this economy E_0.

   b. If no policy action is taken, what will happen to the economy over time? Show on your graph, labeling some new possible equilibrium points E_1, E_2, and E_3. (Think about which curve shifts over time, and why, when the economy stagnates. Assume that no changes occur in investor or consumer confidence or in the economy's maximum capacity output level.)

403

c. Suppose that the changes you outlined in (b) occurred very rapidly and dramatically. Is government policy necessary to get the economy out of the recession?

d. Write a few sentences relating the previous analysis to the dispute between classical and Keynesian macroeconomists.

5. Check recent inflation rates in Figure 12.15 and at http://usinflation.org/us-inflation-rate/. What do you think explains the recent pattern of inflation? How does this relate to *AS/AD* analysis and to the debate among different schools of thought, as discussed in Box 12.2?

6. Empirical data on the macroeconomy can be found in the *Economic Report of the President*. Go to www.gpo.gov/fdsys/ and download statistical tables for the "civilian unemployment rate" and "price indexes for gross domestic product." Jot down data on the *seasonally adjusted* unemployment rate and the *percent change in the GDP implicit price deflator* for recent periods. Plot a few points on a graph to show how the economy has performed recently. (Sometimes data are presented for months or calendar quarters rather than for years. For the purposes of this exercise, you may simply average the numbers within a year to get a number for the year.)

7. Match each concept in Column A with a definition or example in Column B.

Column A	Column B
a. Aggregate supply	1. A rightward shift in the *AD* curve
b. Real wealth effect	2. A suggested relationship between inflation and unemployment
c. Increase in autonomous consumption	3. People's feelings about prices, based on experience or observation
d. Maximum capacity output	4. The economy's total production in relation to inflation
e. Beneficial supply shock	5. A sudden shortage of a key resource
f. Reduction in autonomous investment	6. A self-reinforcing tendency of wages and prices to rise
g. Aggregate demand	7. Increased (or decreased) spending as a result of feeling wealthier (or poorer)
h. Inflationary expectations	8. Government regulations to prevent wages and prices rising
i. Phillips curve	9. The economy's total production if all resources are fully utilized
j. Wage-price spiral	10. A burst of technological progress
k. Wage and price controls	11. Total spending on goods and services in an economy
l. Vertical *AS* curve	12. A leftward shift in the *AD* curve
m. Adverse supply shock	13. Represents the classical model of an economy at full employment

NOTES

1. Some versions of the *AD* curve use "price level" rather than inflation on the vertical axis. The authors of this text believe that using inflation better represents the reality of an economic system in which prices are rarely constant.

2. As defined in Chapter 9, net exports are exports minus imports and represent a net addition to aggregate demand and GDP levels.

3. The specific role of net exports will be discussed further in Chapter 14.

4. Note that the nominal rate of return is the sum of the inflation rate and the real rate of return.

5. Blinder, Alan S., and Mark Zandi. 2010. "How the Great Recession Was Brought to an End." www.economy.com/mark-zandi/documents/End-of-Great-Recession.pdf

    Congressional Budget Office (CBO). 2013. "Estimated Impact of the American Recovery and Reinvestment Act on Employment and Output from October 2012 through December 2012." February 21, 2013. https://www.cbo.gov/publication/43945

    Montgomery, Lori. 2012. "Congressional Budget Office Defends Stimulus." *The Washington Post*, June 6.

6. Paletta, Damian, and Heather Long. 2019. "Trump Insists Fed Should Cut Interest Rates, Even though Economists Say That's Usually a Sign of 'Economic Distress'." *The Washington Post*, July 19.

7. Horsley, Scott. 2019. "Fed Cuts Interest Rates to Prop Up the Slowing Economy." *National Public Radio*, September 18.

8. Davidson, Kate, and Catherine Lucey. 2019. "Trump Says Fed Should Cut Rates to 'Zero, or Less,' Attacks Jerome Powell Again." *The Wall Street Journal*, September 11.

9. An online Appendix also examines the use of income policies as alternative tool to control inflationary pressures.

10. Harvey, Morris. 2013. "Europe Urged to Make a U-Turn on Austerity." *International Herald Tribune*, April 10.

11. Blinder, Alan S., and Mark Zandi. 2010. "How the Great Recession Was Brought to an End." www.economy.com/mark-zandi/documents/End-of-Great-Recession.pdf

12. Krugman, Paul. 2011. "Keynes Was Right." *New York Times*, December 29.

13. Krugman, Paul. 2013. "Deficit Hawks Down." *New York Times*, January 25.

14. Meltzer, Allan H. 2011. "Four Reasons Keynesians Keep Getting It Wrong." *Wall Street Journal*, October 28.

15. Based on data from Eurostat, European Commission.

16. El-Erian, Mohamed A. 2017. "How to Build on Europe's Economic Recovery." Bloomberg View, November 20.

17. Robb, Greg. 2018. "U.S. February Budget Report Shows First Sign of Wider Deficits to Come." Market Watch, March 12.

Part IV

The Global Economy, Development, and Sustainability

Financial Instability and Economic Inequality

The financial crisis that originated in the United States in 2007 and quickly became global has been widely referred to as the "Great Recession." It is the most serious economic crisis experienced by the industrialized world since the Great Depression. The UN estimates that between 2007 and 2009, the number of unemployed globally rose by 27 million, to a total of more than 200 million. High-income countries were especially hard hit, as more than 14 million jobs were lost in the United States and the member states of the EU. Why did this happen? Why were the effects of the crisis so large and so widespread? What lessons can be learned for the future?

This chapter provides some insights into these questions. We begin by describing the 2007–2008 financial crisis and examining the causes of such crises in general. We then take a closer look at the growing inequality of wealth and income in the United States—a central aspect of the financial crisis and a major economic challenge of the current century. Finally, we suggest some measures for avoiding future crises and creating a more equitable and sustainable economic system.

1. THE 2007–2008 FINANCIAL CRISIS

In retrospect, it is not difficult to see that something "big" was going to happen. Economic conditions were unusual. Interest rates were at historic lows, housing prices were rising rapidly, and consumption and growth levels were increasing, even though real wages had remained stagnant for decades. At the same time, the financial sector was booming with the invention of complex financial instruments—most of which were poorly understood. Yet many economists missed the typical signs of a looming crisis: rapidly rising asset prices and economic growth driven by excessive borrowing.

1.1 Entering the Crisis

In 2001, in response to the collapse of the dot-com bubble, the Fed lowered the federal funds rate from 6 percent to 1.75 percent with the goal of promoting growth. In the summer of 2003, the rate was lowered still further to 1 percent—its lowest in 50 years. The low federal funds rate led to reductions across the board, including rates for loans and home mortgages.

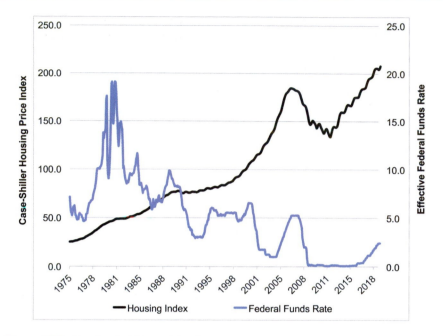

Figure 13.1 *Housing Bubble and Credit Access, 1975–2019*

Sources: Federal Reserve; Shiller dataset www.econ.yale.edu/~shiller/data.htm

The low interest rate was a boon to consumers who, amid stagnant wages, increasingly turned to the credit market to meet their consumption needs. The housing market, in particular, saw a boost as the demand for real estate increased, with mortgage rates falling to a 50-year low of just over 5 percent in 2003. This increased demand fueled a rise in home prices, which in turn fed a speculative frenzy where millions rushed to buy, believing that prices could only go in one direction—up! The buyers included not only would-be homeowners but also speculators who were buying simply with an interest in "flipping" the property (reselling at a higher price). During the mid-1990s, U.S. households borrowed an annual average of approximately $200 billion in mortgage loans. The figure rose abruptly to $500 billion for the period 1998–2002 and to $1 trillion from 2003 to 2006.

Housing prices—which had increased gradually for decades until the early 1990s—skyrocketed in the late 1990s and peaked in 2006. Many of the mortgages granted during this period were classified as "**subprime**"—indicating that the borrowers may have difficulty repaying loans due to high level of debt, relatively low income, or poor credit history. Historically, subprime borrowers were either charged higher interest rates to compensate for the increased lending risk or denied bank loans. During the housing bubble, however, they were allowed to borrow at low rates, often tied to risky conditions. Subprime mortgages increased from less than 10 percent of U.S. mortgages in 2002 to approximately 25 percent by 2005.

> **subprime mortgage:** a mortgage given to someone with high debt levels, relatively low income, or poor credit

While low interest rates are attractive to borrowers, they are decidedly unattractive to lenders. Why, then, were lenders willing to provide such high volumes of mortgages? First, financial institutions had a lot of funds to lend, as the low federal funds rate generated increased liquidity. Second, the lenders made a tremendous amount of income in the form of fees for originating and trading loans. An estimated $2 trillion was generated in such fees between 2003 and 2008.[1] Finally, financial innovation in the form of securitization motivated the lenders to increase the supply of loans.

Securitization is the process of pooling various kinds of loans (mortgages, auto loans, credit card debts, and commercial bank loans), slicing and sorting them according to their estimated risk levels, and repackaging them into new financial instruments. This process involves bundling high-risk loans with low-risk loans and selling them to investors as a single item. After making an initial loan, the lender could quickly sell the loan off to another financial intermediary (such as an investment bank) and receive an up front payment for it. The financial intermediaries would then securitize such loans into complex financial instruments and sell them off to other investors—which are often other financial institutions or foreign investors.

> **securitization:** the process of pooling various kinds of loans, slicing and sorting them according to their risk levels, and repackaging them into financial instruments

There were two direct benefits of securitization to the lenders. First, the ability to sell off the loans to other financial investors freed up capital to make new loans. Second—and perhaps more important—since the initial lenders could sell off the loans to other investors, they no longer carried the risks associated with the loans they made. Traditionally, home mortgages involved only the borrower on one side and the bank on the other. The banks generally continued to own the mortgages for their duration and carried the risk of default. The ability of lenders to transfer this risk to other financial institutions encouraged them to originate as many loans as possible without careful assessment of the risks. Lenders also had strong incentives to downplay the risks associated with the loans to make it easier to sell them to other financial institutions. The creation of such perverse incentives is what economists refer to as the **"moral hazard"** problem. In this case, the loan originators had no financial incentive to protect against the risk of default by ensuring the creditworthiness of the borrower.

> **moral hazard:** the creation of perverse incentives that encourage excessive risk-taking because of protections against losses from that risk

The investors buying the securitized loans obtain a share of mortgage payments, but they also take on the risks associated with these securities. Why weren't these investors worried about the creditworthiness of the borrowers? Unfortunately, most investors were not aware of the risks, partly because the sellers misrepresented the true risk. Additionally, securitization made these financial assets so complex that

Figure 13.2 (a) *Traditional Mortgage Lending Structure*

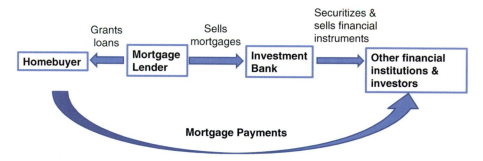

Figure 13.2 (b) *Basic Structure of Securitized Mortgage Lending System*

even sophisticated traders often did not understand what they were handling. Investment in these securities was mainly driven by the more attractive rates of return as compared to other types of bonds. Investors also depended heavily on the **credit rating agencies** (Standard and Poor's, Moody's, and Fitch Group) to evaluate the risks associated with these securities. Notably, these agencies mostly rated the financial securities as being very safe.

The failure of the rating agencies to evaluate the risks contained in the financial instruments is partly explained by the complex nature of these securities and the uncertain nature of the financial markets. There was also a moral hazard problem: the credit rating agencies were paid by the investment banks trying to sell these securities. Hence, the rating agencies had an incentive to understate the risks of default so as to not antagonize the investment banks who were their customers. The rating agencies also didn't face any consequences for inaccurate ratings, so they had little incentive to assess the risks more accurately.

credit rating agencies: companies that assign credit ratings by evaluating the risks of default associated with various loans and other financial instruments

Many investment banks—which were well placed to understand the high-risk nature of these financial securities—were actively creating, holding, and trading them. Why would they take such risks? This behavior is partly explained by their being "**too big to fail**," meaning the banks had become so large that their failure could spill over to the rest of the economy. If these banks reached the verge of failure, the government would have to rescue them. Presuming that the government would come to their rescue, large banks had little incentive to manage risks well, thus creating another moral hazard issue. This was what happened in 2008, when many large financial institutions were "bailed out" by federal regulators to avoid the catastrophic impacts that the failure of these institutions might have had on the economy.

> **"too big to fail":** when a company grows so large that its failure would cause widespread economic harm in terms of lost jobs and diminished asset values

1.2 The Collapse of the Housing Bubble and Impacts of the Crisis

As the economy moved from recession to boom in early 2000s, the Fed started increasing interest rates gradually, from about 1 percent in 2004 to just over 5 percent in 2006. This change, despite being gradual, caused a sharp increase in mortgage payments for many homeowners. By 2006, many borrowers began falling behind on their monthly payments, housing prices started declining, and some economists warned about the possibility of a large-scale crisis. The Fed, chaired by Ben Bernanke, started lowering interest rates in 2007, but the crisis was inevitable given the huge amount of risky loans made during the boom years.

As home values declined, the value of financial assets—derived from the value of mortgages—fell. First, the large mortgage companies, such as Countrywide and Washington Mutual, nearly collapsed. Securities firms and investment banks were next. In March 2008, the investment bank Bear Stearns took a huge loss. To prevent the crisis from spreading further, the Fed—which had essentially stayed out of the operations of investment banks—agreed to absorb $30 billion of Bear Stearns's liabilities, and Bear Stearns was bought by JP Morgan. The crisis, however, continued to worsen, with Lehman Brothers going bankrupt in September 2008, followed by Merrill Lynch selling itself to Bank of America and Wachovia selling itself to Wells Fargo. By the end of 2008, all the investment banks had reorganized themselves as bank holding companies to make themselves eligible for federal loans.[2]

With the failure of large financial firms, lenders became much less willing to give out new loans. This led to a "credit crunch" in which families and businesses were unable to obtain loans. With the tightening of credit, options for refinancing mortgages dwindled and default rates increased, further intensifying the crisis. Approximately 11 million homebuyers faced foreclosure from 2008 to mid-2012, accounting for about a quarter of the mortgages in the United States. Additionally, an immense amount of financial wealth disappeared as U.S. families lost $10.9 trillion in financial investments related to stocks and bonds from mid-2007 to early 2009.

The impacts of the crisis quickly spread from the financial sector to the real sector (the part of the economy that is concerned with producing goods and services, as opposed to the financial side, whose activities focus on trading in financial markets). During the housing boom, the real sector had experienced tremendous growth from home purchases, construction, and increased consumption of durable goods. When the crisis hit, consumers cut their spending drastically. Between 2008 and 2011, U.S. consumers on average reported spending $175 per month less than they would have in the absence of a recession. This decline in spending resulted in lower profits for businesses and rising unemployment. From 2007 to 2009, the United States economy lost nearly 9 million jobs. The official unemployment rate hit 10 percent in October 2009 and stayed above 7 percent through late 2013. Unemployment numbers, including marginally attached workers and those working part-time involuntarily, reached over 17 percent in late 2009. With rising unemployment, overall spending declined further. Hence the economy entered a vicious cycle of rising unemployment and declining demand (see Figure 13.3).

Income and wealth inequality, already severe before the crisis, only intensified after it. While the wealthiest members of society lost the most in dollar terms (although much of it was recovered by 2010), the lower and middle class, on average, lost a far greater share of their existing wealth. The value of retirement accounts plummeted during the crisis, wrecking the retirement plans of millions of middle-class families. From 2007 through 2010, the median household lost nearly 40 percent of their wealth, while the average household net worth of the poorest 25 percent fell to zero. The wealth of middle-income families increased by 68 percent (from $95,879 to $161,050) between 1983 and 2007, but most of this gain had disappeared by 2013, as their wealth levels had fallen to $98,000. At the same time, upper-income families saw their wealth more than double from 1983 to 2007 (from $323,402 to $729,930), and though they also faced losses during the recession, by 2013, their wealth had risen to $650,074.[3]

The impacts of the crisis spread to many other countries throughout the world (see Box 13.1). Global economic growth declined drastically as a result, becoming negative in 2009. This clearly demonstrated the dependence of the global economic system on a healthy financial sector and its vulnerability when that sector came close to collapse.

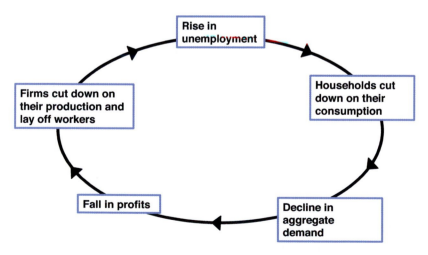

Figure 13.3 *Vicious Cycle of Unemployment*

BOX 13.1 GLOBAL IMPACTS OF THE 2008 FINANCIAL CRISIS

The financial crisis that started in the United States quickly spread to the rest of the world. World economic growth, which had remained relatively steady between 2004 and 2007, experienced a sharp decline of almost 3 percent in 2009. While high-income countries experienced the steepest decline, developing countries also suffered as their growth rates (while still positive) declined in 2008 and 2009 (Figure 13.4).[4]

There were several channels through which the crisis in the United States spread to these other countries. First, other advanced economies that had invested heavily in U.S. financial securities were severely hit. Globally, an estimated $50 trillion in financial wealth was wiped out during the crisis. Additionally, as U.S. banks faced liquidity pressures at home, they repatriated their funds from foreign banks. This caused a decline in lending activities of foreign institutions and an overall reduction in spending and growth.

Problems were especially severe in Europe, where some countries had accumulated high levels of debt. With the surfacing of the highly risky nature of the financial assets, investors started worrying about these debts and demanded higher interest rates. To meet these demands, governments cut down on their spending and increased taxes, lowering overall demand and exacerbating the crisis. As a result, the crisis in the U.S became a prelude to a second debt crisis in Europe, which led to further contraction in output and more job losses in countries such as Greece, Ireland, Portugal, Italy, and Spain.

The economic decline in the developed countries also affected oil-exporting nations in the Middle East and countries like China, Japan, and Mexico that have the United States and Europe as their major export markets. In 2009, exports from China fell by 17 percent.[5]

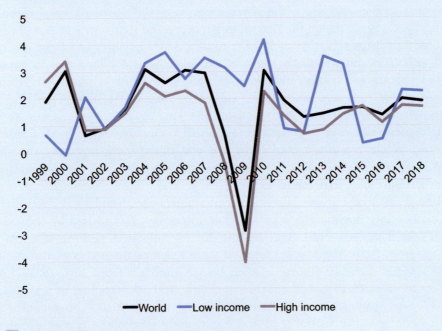

Figure 13.4 GDP per Capita Growth Rates, 1999–2018

Source: World Bank, World Development Indicators database.

Mexico's GDP—about a quarter of which is dependent on exports—declined by 6.6 percent as exports fell by over 17 percent in 2009.[6]

Other countries that did not have close economic ties with the United States were affected through indirect channels. For example, the decline in the Middle East economy from falling oil exports resulted in a rise in unemployment, especially for migrant workers from Asia and North Africa. This led to a fall in remittances sent home by these migrants, adversely affecting remittance-dependent economies such as the Philippines, Nepal, and Gambia. In the United States, the unemployment rate for immigrants from Mexico and Central America was higher (11.5 percent) than that for native-born Americans (9.5 percent, as of October 2009). Consequently, remittances received by these countries declined.[7] The crisis in the United States thus became truly global.

1.3 Policy Responses for Recovery

Recovery from the 2008 financial crisis involved active management of the economy, including regulatory reforms and expansionary fiscal and monetary policy. A decade later, it is possible to provide an evaluation of the impacts of these measures, though some issues, such as the appropriate extent and nature of financial regulation, remain controversial.

Fiscal and Monetary Responses

In response to the 2008 crisis, the government instituted a massive fiscal stimulus. Specifically, Congress passed the American Recovery and Reinvestment Act (ARRA) (discussed in Chapter 10). As of 2013, a total of $816.3 billion had been spent, of which $270.7 billion was in the form of tax relief; $264.4 billion was in benefits (unemployment, food stamps, and Medicare); and $261.2 billion was in job creation contracts, grants, and loans.[8] Independent analysts estimate that ARRA created between 1.5 million and 7.9 million new jobs from 2009 to 2012. Nevertheless, with the unemployment rate over 7 percent through 2013, employment growth remained lackluster. While economist Paul Krugman and others have criticized the fiscal stimulus as being not big enough,[9] others have expressed concern over its contribution to raising the government deficit.

While the federal bill was boosting spending, many state and local governments were cutting their spending due to a decline in tax revenues caused by the reduction in overall income levels. State budget deficits ballooned, peaking at a total of $191 billion in 2010. While states received some federal assistance as part of ARRA, it only covered about 40 percent of their budget shortfalls from 2009 to 2011. To make up the rest, 46 states had cut their spending, and 30 states had increased taxes by 2012. Such contractionary policies at the state level partially countervailed the recovery efforts at the federal level and significantly slowed the rate of economic recovery.[10]

The recovery efforts of the government also included a $700 billion Treasury bailout—known as the Troubled Asset Relief Program (TARP)—to make emergency loans to firms that were in critical condition. Major recipients of this bailout included large investment banks and financial corporations such as Citibank, JP Morgan Chase, Bank of America, Goldman Sachs, and insurance giant AIG. Even nonfinancial firms, such as General Motors and Chrysler, received billions of dollars in TARP loans, as they had invested heavily in financial assets. The goal was to keep the financial system from complete collapse (in which the bailout program was successful) and to get lending going again (which had much less

BOX 13.2 THE GREAT DEPRESSION AND THE GREAT RECESSION COMPARED

How does the "Great Recession" of 2007−2009 compare to the other "great" economic downturn of the past century, the Great Depression? Both downturns were preceded by a period of economic strength. Average annual growth during the 1920s is estimated to have been more than 4 percent, similar to the 4.4 percent average annual growth between 2005 and 2007. In the 1920s, people were feeling optimistic and spending, which drove asset prices up, comparable to the price bubble in the housing market in the 2008 crisis. In addition, inequality levels were at historically high levels preceding both of these crises.

In terms of possible explanations for each economic downturn, the two episodes may have been more similar than different. But in terms of economic consequences, the differences are noteworthy. For example, in the Great Recession, the U.S. economy moved into its recovery phase a mere year and a half after the financial collapse. During the Great Depression, it took almost four years, and the limited recovery was then interrupted by further downturns. Although inflation declined significantly in the 2008 crisis, there was no deflation, whereas a decline in prices of more than 25 percent took place during the Great Depression. In addition, over 5,000 banks and 85,000 businesses failed in the early years of the Great Depression, causing millions of depositors to lose their savings. GDP fell by 46 percent in the four years between 1929 and 1933. In contrast, far fewer banks failed in the 2008 recession, depositors' accounts were protected by the FDIC, and GDP fell by only about 3 percent between 2007 and 2009. The unemployment rate at the nadir of the Great Recession was about 10 percent, compared to the 25 percent unemployment during the Great Depression.

The principal reason for the difference in impacts of these two big economic downturns is explained by the existence of government regulation, automatic stabilizers, and discretionary fiscal and monetary policy in the recent crisis. During the Great Depression, the government was primarily focused on maintaining a balanced budget, while in the recent crisis, the government ran up huge deficits to help the economy recover. Unemployment benefits—which did not exist during the Great Depression—were extended to 99 weeks during the 2007−2009 recession and throughout much of the subsequent slow recovery. Such benefits helped many of those involuntarily jobless to spend on necessities, keeping consumption from collapsing too far and also averting the fears of deflation. The absence of such basic government support during the 1930s consigned millions to poverty and prolonged depression. After much discussion about deregulation and pressure to reduce social safety nets over the previous three decades, the financial crisis revealed the importance of these government activities in preventing a second Great Depression.

success). Although TARP loans were paid back to the government by 2014, there was widespread criticism of a policy that bailed out the banks that created the crisis rather than helping the middle- and low-income homeowners who suffered large losses during the crisis.

In the area of monetary policy, the Fed lowered the effective federal funds rate from over 5 percent to 0–0.25 percent and reduced the discount rate from 5.75 percent to 0.5 percent between August 2007 and December 2008. The Fed, through its quantitative easing program, purchased billions of dollars' worth of shaky financial assets that had lost the majority of their value. This increased the value of assets on the Fed's balance sheet from about $950 billion in 2007 to more than $2.5 trillion in 2008. These Fed purchases of "toxic assets" in danger of default helped to inject liquidity into the financial system and reduce the likelihood of systemic crisis.

Despite these efforts, the expansionary monetary policies had limited impact on economic recovery, since the increase in the flow of money did not alleviate the pessimism felt by consumers and businesses, who remained unwilling to start borrowing and spending. In addition, banks were not willing to increase their lending, both because they did not trust the creditworthiness of the borrowers and because they had just suffered huge capital losses.

The Dodd-Frank Bill

In the wake of the crisis, the political environment—which since the 1970s had increasingly been persuaded by the merits of deregulation—changed abruptly, and the need for regulating the financial sector to prevent future crisis became a priority. The principal response to the call for reform was the 2010 Dodd-Frank Wall Street Reform and Consumer Protection Act (Dodd-Frank), cosponsored by Senator Chris Dodd (D-CT) and Representative Barney Frank (D-MA). The key goals of the Dodd-Frank reform include:

- Protecting consumers: The Consumer Financial Protection Bureau was created to monitor lenders and protect vulnerable borrowers.
- Preventing predatory lending: Minimum criteria related to credit history, income, and debt levels were set to determine the eligibility of mortgages for prospective borrowers.
- Discouraging risky practices: Banks were required to hold at least 5 percent of the financial instruments they create in order to limit their incentives to make risky loans.
- Controlling executive pay: The act called for the Securities and Exchange Commission to ensure that corporate board members who determine CEO compensation do not have private interests in the company. It proposed allowing shareholders to have more say on corporate affairs with a non-binding vote on executive pay.
- Protecting investors: Rating agencies were required to disclose the method used to rate each security in order to increase transparency to investors.
- Ending "too big to fail": The act was designed to limit the amount of leverage (borrowing for investment) permitted to large financial firms and require them to

hold larger capital reserves. It imposed restrictions on the activities of financial companies with more than $50 billion in assets and forbade any merger that allowed a single firm to hold more than 10 percent of the liabilities of the entire financial sector.

■ Enforcing regulations: The act strengthened oversight and empowered regulators to aggressively pursue financial fraud, conflicts of interest, and manipulation of the system.

The financial sector was critical of the bill from the start, arguing that it would create significant costs to them and slow down job creation. Over time, the bill has been "watered down" to a great extent due to intense lobbying efforts from the financial sector. While the bill has been credited for making the financial sector safer and more resilient with higher capital and leverage requirements, it has also been criticized as being too complex and not sufficient to deal with some of the key problems in the financial sector.[11] For example, the bulk of derivatives (indirect forms of investment such as options to buy or sell stocks) are still traded directly by banks with little government supervision, and the rating agencies are still paid by the firms that they rate. Also, no regulators were fired and no big bankers subjected to criminal prosecution in the aftermath of the crisis, so there has been little incentive to change behavior in the financial sector. The basic structure, business model, and practices of large banks remain unaltered. In addition, the expansion of nonbank financial institutions has continued with little regulation, raising new dangers for financial stability. More recently, the Trump administration has focused on undoing most of the Dodd-Frank regulations. In 2018, legislation was passed to revise regulations pertaining to small and regional banks, to free midsize lenders from some of the strictest post-crisis oversight, and to weaken some accountability measures for larger banks.

Discussion Questions

1. Would you prefer interest rates in the economy to be high or low? On what does it depend? Who benefited from low interest rates during the housing bubble? How did the low interest rates create problems?
2. What do you think of the measures that were taken to recover from the 2008 crisis? Have we done enough to avoid similar problems in the future?

2. UNDERSTANDING FINANCIAL INSTABILITY

We now take a broader look at the financial system—discussing some of its key functions and transformations over the past century. We will then develop a theoretical model to understand the occurrence of financial crisis in general.

2.1 The Financial System

The principal function of the financial system is to *intermediate* the movement of funds between savers and investors. Households borrow from the financial sector to buy a car, or a house, or to pay for college. And businesses borrow from the financial sector to make investments needed to produce goods and services. Hence, the financial sector supports activities in the real economy.

The financial sector also facilitates "investment" in **financial assets**, which include stocks, bonds, foreign currencies, certificates of deposit, and money market accounts (specially designed savings accounts, which pay higher interest than normal savings accounts but generally place restrictions on withdrawals and set minimum deposit levels). Individuals can hold such financial assets as wealth or trade them in financial markets to make monetary gains. To an economist, "investment" in financial assets is not true investment in the sense that such investment does not directly add to the economy's stock of capital—it just transfers ownership of an existing financial asset from one person to another.

> **financial assets:** a variety of holdings in which wealth can be invested with an expectation of future return

Finance also supports speculation, that is, buying a financial asset in the hope of exploiting changes in its future price to achieve short-term financial gains. Speculative activity has the potential to influence the economy at a large scale, as we saw in the case of housing bubble created through excessive speculation in the 2008 crisis. Speculation is especially problematic when speculators use excessive **leverage**—investment based on borrowed funds—to finance risky ventures that have the potential to destabilize the entire financial system. Another possible problem occurs when lenders extend large lines of credit to borrowers who would not ordinarily satisfy minimum loan criteria.

> **leverage:** the use of debt to increase the potential rate of return of one's investment

There was a time when banks were responsible for most activities related to lending and investing in financial assets. However, over the past few decades, banks have been declining in importance relative to **nonbank financial institutions** (often referred to as the shadow banking system), which perform similar services as regular banks but are not licensed banks and not subject to banking regulations. Examples of nonbank financial institutions include hedge funds, pension funds, and insurance companies. Most savings today go through such institutions. Their proliferation relative to the much slower growth of traditional banks has raised concerns, since it effectively means that a greater share of "banking activity" is conducted by nonbank institutions that are not highly regulated.

> **nonbank financial institution:** a financial institution that performs a number of services similar to those offered by banks but that is not a licensed bank and is not subject to banking regulations

2.2 Deregulation and Financialization

The stock market crash of 1929, which triggered the Great Depression, brought about major changes in the financial sector. Most important were regulations set in place to minimize the risk-taking behavior of this sector. These included the Glass-Steagall Act, which separated investment banks from commercial banks, essentially preventing commercial banks from engaging in risky investments and investment banks from holding deposits. Also, interest was prohibited on checking accounts, and an interest rate ceiling was imposed on savings accounts (regulation Q). Most banking activity could not be conducted across state lines. In addition, several capital and leverage requirements were imposed on the financial sector, the Federal Deposit Insurance Corporation (FDIC) was set up to insure bank deposits, and the Securities and Exchange Commission (SEC) was established to maintain an orderly and efficient financial sector.

Until the 1960s, finance was mostly limited to facilitating the flow of funds through the economy and making investments in financial assets. However, the change in economic environment in the late 1960s and early 1970s (discussed in Chapters 9 and 12), partly due to the decline in business profits, resulted in the economic and political system becoming more responsive to the demands of businesses. This led to an era of deregulation starting in the 1980s, justified by the free-market mantra that banks and other financial institutions could be depended on to self-regulate, on the assumption that profit-seeking enterprises would voluntarily avoid risky practices that might cause them to fail.

The deregulation of the financial sector included policies for loosening restrictions on capital across borders, removing interest rate ceilings, allowing banks to measure the riskiness of their own products, permitting financial institutions to offer interest-bearing checking, and increasing the amount of leverage permitted to investment banks. In 1994, prohibitions on interstate banking were repealed, which resulted in a surge in bank mergers. Additionally, the separation between investment and commercial banks was gradually eroded through the 1980s and 1990s. In 1999, the Financial Services Modernization Act allowed large financial companies to engage in commercial and investment banking as well as in insurance activities. This act, perhaps more than any other piece of legislation, contributed to the increase in the number of "megabanks."

Supporters of large banks argued that large banks are more efficient and less vulnerable to risk than small banks, as they have a more diverse source of income and are able to lend to more geographically dispersed borrowers than smaller banks. Opponents argue that such benefits only encourage larger banks to take more risks. Empirical evidence generally supports the latter claim. In 2013, megabank JP Morgan Chase, for example, agreed to pay $13 billion in a settlement resulting from the bank's questionable mortgage practices.

Deregulation encouraged a proliferation of new kinds of financial institutions and instruments. Finance turned away from its traditional role of lending for consumption and investment, and most of the money got directed toward lending against existing assets such as housing, stocks and bonds—not creating new assets. From the 1940s to the 1970s, nonfinancial institutions received 15 to 20 percent of their funding for productive investment from the financial sector; this dropped to 7 to 10 percent after 1980. Most financial corporations started lending to each other instead of lending to nonfinancial corporations; such within-sector lending increased from 10 percent before 1970 to over 30 percent after 1980.[12] The operation of the financial sector has also expanded through the rise of the shadow banking system, which encouraged putting more money into high-yield financial schemes.

The frequency of bank mergers has increased steadily since the 1980s. From 1984 to 2019, the number of banks with more than $10 billion in assets increased from 28 to 141, and the share of banking sector assets held by these large banks increased from 28 to more than 84 percent (Figure 13.5). The consolidation continues to this day. In 2019, the nine largest financial institutions (with more than $250 billion in assets) held almost half of the total financial assets. From the 1980s to 2008, the financial sector took in a growing share of corporate profits. Its profit share collapsed during the 2008 crisis but has subsequently recovered, although not to the previous highs (Figure 13.6). Although finance only constituted about 7 percent of the economy and employed 5 percent of the workforce, it took over 20 percent of the corporate profits in 2014.

This process of increasing size and importance of the financial markets in the operation of the economy—with the financial sector accounting for a greater share of GDP and acquiring an increased ability to generate and circulate profits—is known as **financialization**.[13] Even nonfinancial corporations have become increasingly involved in investing in financial instruments rather than investing to expand

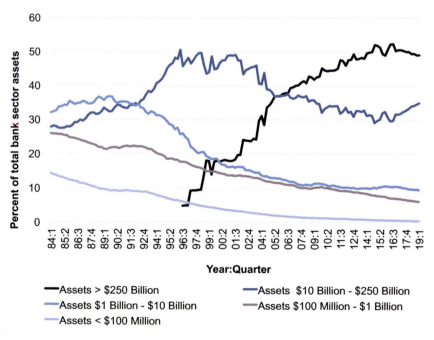

Figure 13.5 *Increasing Bank Size*

Source: Federal Deposit Insurance Corporation.

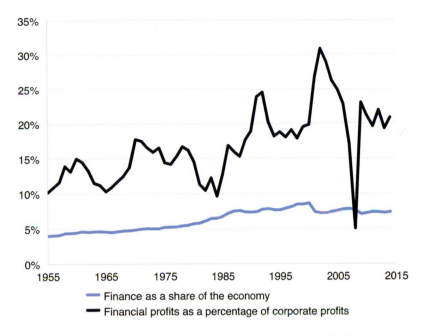

Figure 13.6 *Finance as a Share of the Economy and Financial Profits as a Percentage of Corporate Profits*

Source: U.S. Bureau of Economic Analysis, National Income and Product Accounts, Tables 6.2A-6.2D, and Thomas Piketty, Emmanuel Saez, and Gabriel Zucman. "Distributional National Accounts: Methods and Estimates for the United States," Appendix tables II: Distributional series, National Bureau of Economic Research Working Paper Series, Working Paper 22945, December 2016.

production of goods and services. For example, in 2000, Ford generated more income from selling loans than from selling cars, and GE Capital (GE's financial arm) generated approximately half of GE's total earnings.[14] Today American companies in every sector earn five times more revenue from financial activities, such as investing, hedging, and offering financial services, than they did before 1980.[15]

> **financialization:** a process of increasing size and importance of the financial markets in the operation of the economy—with the financial sector accounting for a greater share of GDP and acquiring an increased ability to generate and circulate profits

Households have also become increasingly dependent on the financial markets, relying more on loans to meet their expenses due to the stagnation of real wages. In 1980, for example, U.S. households held an average debt equal to about 60 percent of disposable income; this figure exceeded 130 percent in 2007. The financial crisis forced households to reduce debt to just below 100 percent of disposable income by 2017, still considerably higher than 1980 levels. In addition, the proliferation of mutual funds and their increased availability in employee accounts has caused a higher percentage of the population than ever before to have a stake in the financial

423

market. Today, the financial sector has expanded far beyond the provision of the financial intermediation services demanded by the economy; what has grown is not only the demand for credit but the overall volume of trading of financial securities, including speculative and risk-taking activities. This suggests a need for economic theory to account better for the role of finance in macroeconomics.

2.3 Theories of Financial Instability

The conventional theory of the financial market is based on the "efficient market hypothesis." This theory argues that the price of a financial asset at any moment reflects all the information available about its true value. As new information becomes available, market participants revalue the asset. The theory portrays the economy as consisting of rational individuals who live in a world of perfectly competitive markets and possess complete information about the price of assets. Elaborate logical and mathematical analysis, built on this assumption, concludes that markets are always self-correcting and that they always move to a stable equilibrium state in the absence of external interference. Based on these assumptions, the theory suggests that financial crises are caused by external shocks such as technological change, government action, or some unknowable force; hence, it is not possible to predict or foresee crises.

The key problem with this theory is not in its internal logic or mathematics but its foundational assumptions. In particular, it ignores how uncertainty and the expectations of market participants influence the value of assets. For example, if market participants expect the price of a certain asset to rise in the future, more people will buy it now, causing an increase in current prices. As current prices increase, many people expect prices to rise even further, thus fueling current demand, inflating prices, and creating a bubble. In such cases, the underlying value of an asset could be much lower than its market price. Theories of efficient markets lack an explanation for the creation of such bubbles and of their eventual collapse.

An alternative theory, which gained prominence in the aftermath of the 2008 crisis, is the "financial instability hypothesis" proposed by Hyman P. Minsky. Minsky's key argument is that unregulated markets will always produce instability and crisis. When an economy is just recovering from a crisis, investors will be cautious, since many of them will have been clobbered by the just-ended recession. Hence, they will keep large margins of safety, holding cash reserves as a cushion to protect against future crisis.

However, as the economy emerges from its slump and profits start rising, investors become more confident and willing to pursue risky ideas, and they let their safety margins and cash reserves dwindle. Bankers and financiers are also motivated to take greater risks when the economy is booming: they invent and reinvent new forms of money, substitutes for money, and innovative financing instruments that expand investment opportunities for capital gains and increased profit. Thus, during an economic expansion, the stance of financial firms tends to move from the safer financing to more risky financing practices. This weakens their financial strength and makes the economy more fragile and credit dependent.

Eventually, this expansion will cause the economy to go beyond a period of steady growth to one of speculative boom. This is unsustainable, and when some event triggers a fall in investment, the entire system falls apart. The complex structure of interlinked and overlapping cash commitments built during the boom era spreads the crisis widely, leading to a rapid collapse not only in finance but in the real economy.

In recovering from this state of disaster, firms reduce their debt burden, improve their liquidity positions, reduce their risk-taking behavior, and maintain large safety margins. Eventually, the financial system regains some strength and becomes less vulnerable. As economic conditions slowly start to improve, confidence builds up, and firms start narrowing their safety margins and taking more debt, thus eventually re-entering the phase of speculative boom. Based on these observations, Minsky argued that the seeds of instability are sowed while the economy is booming. Hence, stability is in effect destabilizing, since it is when market conditions are stable that there is a move toward deregulation and more risk-taking. For example, financial markets were regulated in the wake of the Great Depression, when banks were reeling from huge losses, investors were more cautious about taking risks, and the general market sentiment was focused on preventing future crisis. By the 1970s, much of the pain of the Great Depression was forgotten, allowing a movement toward relaxing regulations to gain momentum.

Minsky's theory is derived from Keynes's notion of "fundamental uncertainty," which argues that, since it is impossible to know the future, our actions are guided by our expectations, which are based on conventions that have been socially and historically created. Unlike the classical world, where things are in equilibrium until affected by some external event, expectations about the future, confidence levels, and risk-taking behavior all originate from within the economic system in the Keynesian world. During booms, optimistic expectations motivate agents to take more risks by borrowing and investing. This drives the boom forward, increases leverage, and brings capital gains. As the economy expands and agents take higher risks, their financial status becomes more fragile. Under these conditions, a fall in profit rates and a failure to meet expectations will have devastating effects on the economy, since investors rapidly adjust their expectation from optimistic to pessimistic, resulting in a "rush for the exits" as firms and individuals try to dump no-longer-profitable investments and in many cases are unable to cover their debts.

The Keynes-Minsky theory helps explain the occurrence of crisis as being inherent to the economic system. The numerous crises of the past few decades, including the stock market crash in 1987, savings and loans crisis in 1989, dot-com bubble of 2001, and the Great Recession of 2008, can be explained by the increasing risk-taking behavior in the financial industry during periods of boom. Both Keynes and Minsky argued that it is impossible to avoid wide fluctuations in a capitalist economy, because of the uncertain nature of market psychology based on expectations. They both advocated for government to play a larger role in creating regulations that can minimize fluctuations in investment and create a more stable financial system.

Minsky's theory is very helpful in understanding the roots of financial instability, but it does not shed much light on how problems in the real sector might contribute to financial instability or on the role of inequality in fueling a crisis. Given that rising inequality was an important factor in the 2008 financial crisis and is at the center of many current economic problems, we now turn to analyzing inequality.

Discussion Questions

1. Do you think changes in the value of "paper assets" such as stocks and bonds, or even homes, should have real economic effects? Why? Why do you think that employment suffered from the disappearance of so much financial wealth following the financial crisis?

2. Think about the ways in which uncertainty and expectations about the future may affect your current economic decisions, and give two examples of such decisions. What role does expectation about the future play in Minsky's theory of financial instability?

3. THE CREATION OF AN UNEQUAL SOCIETY

Over the last century, economists have for the most part converged on a consensus that overall economic growth is the most effective way to promote increased incomes and improve the quality of life. This appeared to be true throughout much of the post–World War II period, as fairly steady growth "lifted all boats" and led to improved living standards. In recent decades, however, rising inequality has meant that overall economic growth does not necessarily leave the majority of people better off.

In this section, we will look at the trends in income inequality and some of the causes of rising inequality in the United States. While we focus on the case of the United States, it is important to note that inequality has been increasing in most industrialized nations, as well as most of Asia, including India and China. And while inequality has generally been decreasing in Latin America and sub-Saharan Africa, these regions still have the highest overall levels of inequality.[16] We will discuss some trends in global inequality in Chapter 15.

Our analysis of inequality here is centered on inequality of income. But it is important to recognize that inequality extends beyond the realm of money. For example, vast inequalities exist in the quality of health care, which is reflected in differences in life expectancy and incidence of diseases across the world. There is also considerable imbalance in education—while children in developed countries can expect to receive an average of 17 years of education, the average for children in sub-Saharan countries of Niger, Mali, and Chad is less than eight years.[17]

3.1 Trends in Inequality

One of the most common ways to measure inequality is to measure the income share (percent of all income) held by various groups ordered by income from poorest to richest, such as the bottom 20 percent, the middle 20 percent, the top 1 percent, and so on. Table 13.1 presents the distribution of household income in the United States in 2018. The data are arranged in order of income, and the share of the total income "pie" that accrues to each twentieth percentile (or quintile) is in the second column. To understand what this table means, imagine dividing up U.S. households into five equal-sized groups, with the lowest-income households all in one group, the next lowest in the next group, and so on.

The lowest-income quintile, with household incomes below $25,600, received only 3.1 percent of all the household income in the country. The richest quintile, those with incomes of $130,000 or more, received 52 percent. In other words, more than half of all the income in the country was received by those in the top-income quintile.

Inequality levels are often expressed in terms of **Gini coefficient**—a measure of the distribution of income (or wealth) within a population represented by a number between 0 and 1. A Gini coefficient of 0 represents absolute equality, meaning each individual in the population gets the same amount of income. And a Gini coefficient of 1 represents absolute inequality, where all the income goes to a single individual. We see from Figure 13.7 that the Gini coefficient in the United States reached a

Table 13.1 Household Income Distribution in the United States, 2018

Group of Households	Share of Income (Percent)	Annual Income Range
Bottom 20%	3.1	Below $25,600
Second 20%	8.3	$25,601–$50,000
Third 20%	14.1	$50,001–$79,542
Fourth 20%	22.6	$79,543–$130,000
Top 20%	52.0	Above $130,000

Source: U.S. Census Bureau, Historical Income Tables: Households, Tables H-1 and H-2.

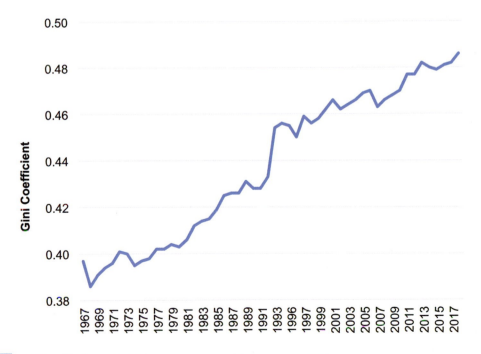

Figure 13.7 Gini Coefficient in the United States, 1967–2018

Source: U.S. Census Bureau, Historical Income Tables: Households, Table H-4.

record low of 0.386 in 1968. After that, the Gini coefficient increased in 39 of the next 50 years.

> **Gini coefficient:** a measure of inequality that goes from 0 (absolute equality) up to 1 (absolute inequality)

In the three decades before the 2008 crisis, the income gap between the rich and poor widened to levels not seen since the 1920s. During the last two decades of the twentieth century, rising income inequality was mostly due not to real income declines for the poor and middle classes but to relative gains for the wealthy. The low- and middle-income groups were gaining in absolute terms; the problem was merely to keep pace with the rich. But starting around 1999, the median U.S. household income began a real decline, signifying that the low and middle classes were now losing out in both absolute and relative terms.

In 1980, the bottom 50 percent of wage earners in the United States took home about 21 percent of the total income in the country—compared to 11 percent of the income being taken by the top 1 percent. In 2016, the bottom 50 percent only took home about 13 percent of the total income, while over 20 percent went to the top 1 percent.[18] We discuss some factors contributing to this shift subsequently.

Gini coefficients may also be calculated for the distribution of wealth rather than income. This distribution, which depends on what people own in assets, tends to be even more unequal than income distribution. Many lower-income people have almost no net wealth, and even people with middle-class income levels often have only a relatively small amount of wealth. It is even possible to have *negative* net wealth. This happens when the value of a person's debts (e.g., for a car, house, or credit cards) is higher than the value of her assets.

The distribution of wealth is, however, less frequently and less systematically recorded than the distribution of income—in part because wealth can be hard to measure. This is because wealth is usually held in the form of assets such as shares in a company; land; or commodities such as real estate, paintings, or antiques, whose values are realized only when they are sold. These caveats notwithstanding, the U.S. Gini coefficient for wealth is estimated to be in the neighborhood of 0.8, significantly higher than the income Gini coefficient of 0.48.[19] The top 10 percent by wealth own 77 percent of all wealth. The top 1 percent (those with more than $4 million in assets) own 42 percent of all wealth, much more than the bottom 90 percent combined.[20]

Note that income and wealth inequality in the United States is clearly related to race, age, and other demographic factors. For example, Figure 13.8 illustrates the difference in median household income and median household assets by race. We see that Asian households have the highest median annual income, about $87,000, while black households have the lowest at only $41,000. While white households' incomes are 62 percent higher than the incomes of black households, the assets of white households are more than 11 times higher than those of black households. Hispanic households also have little in assets, only about $12,000.

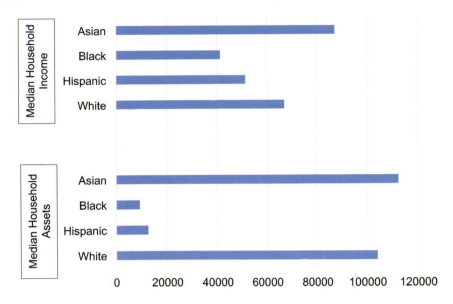

Figure 13.8 *Median Household Income (2018) and Median Value of Household Assets (2016) in the United States by Race*

Source: Proctor, Bernadette D., Jessica L. Semega, and Melissa A. Kollar. 2016. "Income and Poverty in the United States: 2015." Current Population Reports, U.S. Census Bureau, September 2016. Table 1; U.S. Census Bureau, 2019.

3.2 Causes of Rising Inequality

The question of why inequality has been increasing in the United States and many other countries is a source of much debate. We now consider several of the explanations, recognizing that rising inequality is something that cannot be attributed to a single cause.

Demographic Changes

Some of the increase in inequality in the United States and other industrialized nations is due to changing demographics. As people worldwide live longer on average, the proportion of the population that is elderly increases. Because elderly people tend to have relatively low incomes, this demographic trend pushes incomes down on the low end. The increase in the rate of single parenthood has also contributed to an increase in the share of the population with low incomes, as single-parent households are more likely to have low incomes.[21] A similar factor separating households is the increase in "assortive mating"—the tendency of people to marry partners who have a similar earning potential to themselves. For example, data show that men with undergraduate degrees are now about twice as likely to marry women with undergraduate degrees as they were in 1960. A 2014 study concludes that the U.S. Gini coefficient would be significantly lower (0.34 as opposed to 0.43) if people married randomly rather than selecting mates who are similar to themselves in terms of earnings potential.[22]

429

Decline in Wages as a Share of Total Income

Another factor explaining income inequality is the share of total income received by labor as compared to the share accruing to the owners of capital. As shown in Figure 13.9, between 1948 and 1979, wages grew faster than corporate profits. Since the 1980s, however, this trend has reversed, with annual growth in wages declining over time, while corporate profits increased rapidly. Between 2000 and 2007, corporate profits grew at over 5 percent annually, while growth in wages remained below 1 percent. Between 2007 and 2017, as the economy recovered from the financial crisis, profits grew at around 2.5 percent, while wages hardly increased at all.

One explanation for stagnant wages could be a reduction in labor productivity levels—but, as noted in Chapter 7 (Figure 7.10), labor productivity has actually been rising faster than wages. Indeed, the gap between productivity growth and real wage growth has been widening since the 1970s.[23] With wage increases not keeping up with productivity growth, a growing share of the gains from productivity growth has been going into expanding profits rather than raising wages. Some explanations for why wages have not kept up with productivity include:

1. **The decline of unions**: Decline in the bargaining power of unions in the United States is one obvious explanation for the widening gap between productivity and wages. Since the 1970s, government policy has become decidedly less supportive of unions and low-wage workers, and the rate of union participation has declined markedly. Labor union membership has also been falling recently in other wealthy

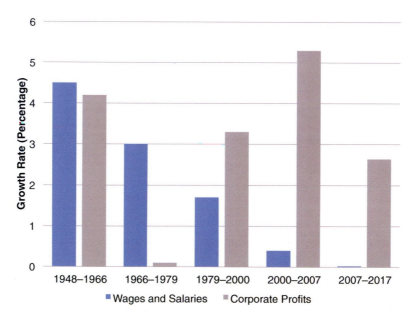

Figure 13.9 *Annual Growth Rates of Wages and Salaries and Corporate Profit*

Source: U.S. Bureau of Economic Analysis (2017) National Income and Product Accounts, Table 1.14, 1.1.4; Bureau of Labor Statistics (2017).

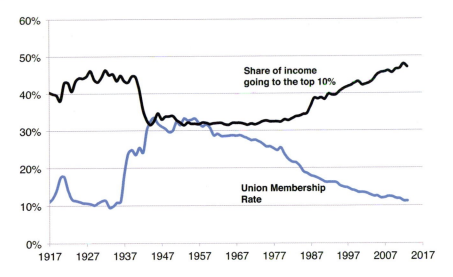

Figure 13.10 *Union Membership and Income Inequality, 1917–2017*

nations, including Germany, Japan, Sweden, Australia, and the United Kingdom.[24] Although the relation between union strength and income distribution is not simple, in general, it is likely that workers can push for higher wages when unions are stronger. It is also likely to be true that when inequality is high, the rich can have more influence over the political process and may be able to promote policies that weaken unions. Figure 13.10 illustrates that during periods with strong unions and high union membership, the share of income going to the rich was lower.

2. **Globalization and trade**: Globalization has also contributed to a decline in the bargaining power of workers. As employers have become accustomed to looking around the world for the lowest-cost workers, transnational corporations have shifted production facilities to developing countries, resulting in a loss of many middle-income jobs in the United States. Competition from cheaper imports from developing countries has compelled producers in developed countries to either lower their prices and wages or to simply leave the business. For example, many industrial jobs—in textiles and automobiles—that formerly fell in the middle of the U.S. wage distribution have been eliminated by competition from imports. Such impacts of increased trade and globalization have affected middle-income wages and eliminated middle-income jobs. When people who had worked in these middle-income jobs move to lower-income service and retail jobs, the "hollowing out of the middle" contributes to the increase in inequality.

3. **Technology**: Another factor driving the increase in inequality in developed nations is technological change.[25] New technologies related to computers, biotechnology, and other fields have become more important, increasing the income of skilled workers who understand and use the new techniques and equipment, while leaving behind the less-skilled workers who remain in low-technology occupations. Technological change has also, especially in the long run, led machines to replace human workers for certain types of jobs. It has contributed substantially to

431

polarization of the labor market into groups of "high-skill" jobs at one end and many more "low-skill" jobs at the other end. As technological unemployment creeps up the skill ladder, evidence suggests that fewer workers are experiencing a net benefit from technology in recent years. A 2012 paper notes:

> It is hard . . . to find the winners from technical change in the last ten years, as the wages of the bottom 70 per cent of college graduates have been flat or in decline. That would leave just 30 per cent of college graduates (6.6 per cent of the workforce) and the 11 per cent of workers with advanced degrees as the winners of technical change.[26]

Financialization and Inequality

The increase in inequality in the past few decades in the United States has occurred concurrently with the growth of the financial sector. A recent International Labor Organization (ILO) report examining the causes of inequality finds that about 46 percent of the rise in inequality can be attributed to financialization—much greater than the impacts of globalization (19 percent), technological change (10 percent), and other institutional factors (25 percent).[27] How does financialization contribute to inequality?

According to economist Gerald Epstein, as economies become more financialized, a greater share of income generated goes to the owners of financial assets, who tend to be in the upper income brackets in most countries. For instance, direct gains

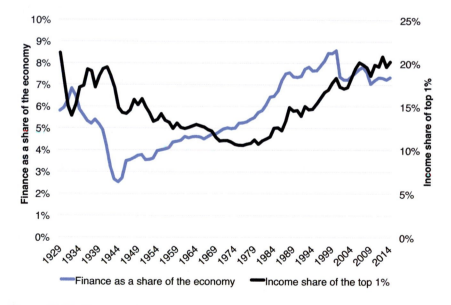

Figure 13.11 *Financialization and Inequality, 1929–2014*

Source: U.S. Bureau of Economic Analysis, National Income and Product Accounts, Tables 6.2A–6.2D, BEA; Thomas Piketty, Emmanuel Saez, and Gabriel Zucman. 2016. "Distributional National Accounts: Methods and Estimates for the United States." National Bureau of Economic Research Working Paper Series, Working Paper 22945, December 2016.

from rising stock prices go to those who own stocks—more than three-quarters of which in the United States are held by the wealthiest 10 percent.[28] Although higher stock prices also increase the value of retirement accounts, only about half of the country has retirement accounts. Access to stocks and bonds has increased in the last few decades, with about 51 percent of American families now owning stocks directly or through retirement accounts, but stock ownership is much lower among less affluent families.[29] This disparity in ownership of financial assets also explains why the economic gains during the recovery from the 2008 crisis went mostly to the rich.

One of the other major aspects of financialization that has affected inequality is the shift in focus of corporations from creating wealth by making productive investments to "maximizing shareholder value" by increasing stock prices, often by buying back their own stock. Between 2003 and 2012, S&P 500 firms spent 54 percent of their profits on stock buybacks.[30] Stock buybacks hit record values of over $753 billion in 2018 in the wake of the 2017 tax cuts.[31]

This focus on raising stock prices through buyback is partly motivated by the change in pay structure in large corporations. Until the 1990s, chief executive officers were generally paid a salary that would grow at a rate comparable to other employees. Since then, a larger proportion of executive pay has come in the form of stock options and bonuses, which has motivated executives to focus on raising stock prices, as they can gain personal benefits from it.

Domestic Policy Changes

The increase in inequality has also been explained in terms of policies that, intentionally or unintentionally, have led to higher inequality. In recent years, tax policies in the United States have become much less progressive than they used to be. There have, for example, been a series of tax cuts—during the 1980s under Ronald Reagan and during the 2000s under George W. Bush—that primarily reduced the tax burden on the wealthiest groups (though some of these tax cuts were reversed during the presidencies of Bill Clinton and Barack Obama). The 2017 tax cuts under President Trump follow the same pattern, with the largest benefits going to the higher-income earners.[32] Overall, the difference in effective tax rates paid by the rich and the poor has narrowed, with reductions in federal income tax rates on the highest income earners and declines in corporate taxes as a percentage of GDP, at the same time payroll taxes on the working class have increased.[33] As illustrated in Figure 13.12, since the 1960s, the total tax rate, combining federal, state, and local taxes, has declined for the top 0.1 percent by 2.1 points, while it has increased for the middle 40 percent by 3.8 points and for the bottom 50 percent by 4.3 points.

Starting in the 1990s, there has also been a reduction in support for low-income workers with the phasing out of programs such as Aid for Families with Dependent Children (AFDC). Government outlays on affordable housing and public infrastructure as a share of GDP have declined sharply, and the federal minimum wage ($7.25 as of 2019) has fallen significantly behind inflation. In addition to directly reducing such support, the diminished generosity of the welfare state also adversely affects workers' bargaining power, hence their wages. With less government benefits on

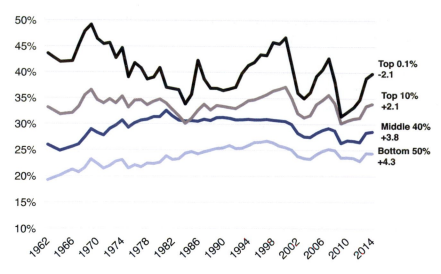

Figure 13.12 *Change in Tax Rates by Income Group*

Source: Thomas, Piketty, Emmanuel Saez, and Gabriel Zucman. 2016. "Distributional National Accounts: Methods and Estimates for the United States." National Bureau of Economic Research Working Paper Series, Working Paper 22945, December 2016.

which to rely, employees threatened with unemployment are more likely to accept a wage cut. Research has found that a strong public sector, particularly as a provider of public goods, can reduce income inequalities.[34]

3.3 Consequences of Inequality

Research on the impacts of inequality shows that economic inequalities often relate to inequalities in other aspects of human well-being and lead to various social problems. For example, richer Americans have a life expectancy 10–15 years higher than the poorest Americans. Low-income Americans are more likely to suffer from psychological problems such as anxiety, depression, and attention problems.[35] In their 2009 book *The Spirit Level*, Richard Wilkinson and Kate Pickett present data showing that rich countries with greater inequality tend to have lower life expectancy, higher rates of infant mortality, and higher rates of mental illness.[36]

Most economists tend to agree that excessive inequality can lead to reduced economic growth. A 2014 study published by the International Monetary Fund presents perhaps the most comprehensive analysis of the relationship between inequality and economic growth, based on data from 153 countries from 1960 to 2010.[37] The study found that high inequality can indeed result in reduced economic growth and that "it would be a mistake to focus on growth and let inequality take care of itself, not only because inequality may be ethically undesirable but also because the resulting growth may be low and unsustainable."[38]

Finally, excessive economic inequality often fosters concentration of political power and a weakening of democratic institutions. The 2012 book *Affluence and Influence*, by Princeton University professor Martin Gilens, analyzes the relationship between the policy preferences of Americans at different income levels and actual policy outcomes.[39] He concludes that:

> The American government does respond to the public's preferences, but that responsiveness is strongly tilted toward the most affluent citizens. Indeed, under most circumstances, the preferences of the vast majority of Americans appear to have essentially no impact on which policies the government does or doesn't adopt.[40]

Discussion Questions

1. In a 1963 speech, President John F. Kennedy stated, "A rising tide lifts all boats," implying that everyone benefits from economic growth. Is this statement still true? Have periods of economic growth been equally beneficial to people from different income groups?
2. If you could address one of the "causes" of inequality described previously, which one would you focus on? Why?

4. POLICIES TO PROMOTE FINANCIAL STABILITY AND GREATER EQUALITY

Restoring the economy from the damages of the Great Depression involved strong government intervention to increase growth and employment. This process emphasized infrastructural development, creation of the welfare state, redistributive taxation, regulation of businesses and financial activities, increase in provision of public goods, and strong trade unions; it took place in an environment of oligopolistic markets and weak foreign competition. From the 1940s to the 1970s, financial institutions were highly regulated, financial crises were relatively rare, and inequality levels declined. Since the 1970s, many of the earlier policies and regulations have been reversed. This has contributed to a rise in inequality and financial sector vulnerability. What kind of policies might help create a more stable financial system and promote equality?

Some economists argue that appropriate regulation could help with many of the current problems. However, given the changed economic landscape in the last few decades, with rising foreign competition, globalization, technological advances, and financialization, regulation alone may not be sufficient to resolve issues such as the wage-productivity gap and the shifts in corporate culture described previously. Structural changes as well as specific public policies to address such issues are essential to achieving a more equal distribution of income and wealth and a more stable economic system.

Other economists—mostly those following the free-market ideology—argue that further deregulation and smaller government are the path to prosperity, as the market is supposed to guide the economy toward equilibrium. There has, however, been little empirical evidence to support this view, especially as the rise of finance and increasing deregulation have been associated with rising inequality, more frequent economic crises, and a slower rate of economic growth compared to the earlier era of more regulated capitalism.

Regulating the Financial System

In the aftermath of the 2008 crisis, better oversight of the financial system and a new set of rules to discourage excessive risk-taking were seen as essential to reforming the system. The Dodd–Frank legislation was a step in this direction, but it has been under constant attack from the financial sector, and many of the problems it intended to address remain unresolved. Several suggestions have been made on regulating the financial system to make it more resilient, including:

- Giving the central bank greater oversight of the financial health of borrowing institutions. This could include requirements for large financial institutions to hold sufficient capital reserves to cover the risks associated with the financial instruments they create.
- Greater oversight and regulation of nonbank institutions in the shadow banking system.
- Reinstituting a version of the Glass-Steagall Act, separating banking and investment functions, promoting the role of smaller and regional banks, and possibly breaking up financial institutions in the "too big to fail" category.
- Blocking the revolving door between finance and politics by instituting requirements that individuals must wait a significant number of years between the time they leave a government position in which they can affect legislation on industry sectors and when they can begin work in those sectors.

Channeling Financial Resources to More Socially Useful Investments

One of the criticisms of the current financial system is that it directs too much effort and money toward short-term financial profit-making, while providing insufficient support for productive investment. Policies to reverse this bias might include:

- Promoting regional and community financial institutions, credit unions, and other smaller financial institutions whose main orientation is toward supporting local businesses and homebuyers.
- Instituting a small tax on financial transactions. Both Keynes and the Nobel laureate economist James Tobin supported such a tax as a way of discouraging short-term financial speculation. What has come to be known as a "Tobin tax" could be at a very low rate but would still raise substantial revenues due to the very large volume of financial transactions. In 2014, the European Commission adopted a tax on all stock, bond, and derivative trading in the European Union.
- Restricting companies from stock buybacks and rewarding them through the tax system for investing in their employees, linking executive pay to productive performance of the company instead of share prices, and adding worker representatives on corporate boards so their interests are represented when decisions are made.[41]

■ Encouraging the type of cooperative-based organizations discussed in Chapter 7 could also help create a stronger and more equitable economic system. Cooperatives have a motive to invest in the long-term viability of the company and improve the well-being of workers. Worker-owned companies, community development corporations, and credit unions tend to be locally oriented and resilient to economic fluctuations at the national level.

Policies to Reduce Inequality

Specific policies to mitigate inequality could include:

■ Fiscal policies, such as more progressive tax policies, expansion of transfer systems, and more public investment in areas with wide social benefit. Increased investment in social programs, such as career skills training, housing assistance, or health care, that enhance the well-being and productivity of workers could also mitigate inequality.

■ Raising minimum wages to improve the well-being of most low-wage workers and reduce poverty.[42] While some argue that increases in the minimum wage could result in increased unemployment, most real-world evidence indicates that smaller phased increases have little negative impact on overall employment.[43] Also, analysis based on Keynesian-type macroeconomic reasoning suggests that such wage increases can promote economic growth and employment.[44]

■ Investment in human capital through such programs as universal pre-kindergarten and more effective public schools systems, together with increased public financing to make public colleges more affordable and community colleges more accessible, can reduce inequality by strengthening workers' skills and their bargaining power. Increased investment in workers through training programs could increase their productivity and wage-earning potential.

■ Government policies that support the right to organize and the bargaining power of labor unions. Research by the International Monetary Fund (IMF) suggests that stronger labor unions may be able to reduce inequality.[45]

■ Reducing the gap in job protection between regular and temporary workers.[46] As discussed in Chapter 7, the increase in part-time and temporary workers, who tend to receive lower pay and benefits and have little job stability, has contributed to rising inequality. In Europe, more than half of all new jobs created since 2010 are based on temporary contracts.[47] Some countries, including Norway, France, and Sweden, have laws mandating that employers provide equal pay and benefits to temporary workers.[48]

■ Investment in infrastructure projects such as roads, water, and sewage systems; natural resource conservation; and other projects. Such investments can provide stable employment for people as well as general public benefits that improve the quality of life for all, including low-income workers. Even further, the government could serve as an "employer of last resort" to achieve full employment, directly hiring people to work on public projects.

- Direct income support for low-income workers. Expanding the current earned-income tax credit is one approach to providing direct income support. Another, more radical, proposal is to institute a guaranteed basic income, which involves providing a periodic cash payment unconditionally to all individuals to help cover their basic expenses. (See Box 15.3 in Chapter 15.) If set at a relatively low level, a guaranteed income for all could provide greater equity without removing incentive to undertake paid work.[49]
- Fiscal and monetary policies that promote full employment. Low-income and minority workers suffer most when unemployment rises. As we saw in Chapter 12, there is often a tradeoff between unemployment and inflation, but so long as inflation is not a major threat, placing a priority on maintaining low unemployment will promote a more equitable labor market.[50]

The economy of the future will be different from the economy of the past. But we can learn lessons from past experiences, both in the Great Depression and the Great Recession, about how to promote greater stability and equity and to avoid catastrophic crises. The policy solutions that we have discussed, together with other innovative approaches, will be required in the future in the effort to achieve the goal of an economy that works well for all.

Discussion Questions

1. Have you seen anything in the news in recent weeks about the regulation of banking and finance or changes in tax or wage policies? What do you think about the effectiveness of these policies in achieving greater financial stability and economic equality?
2. What do you think about a proposal to tax financial transactions? Would you prefer it to an income or a sales tax? Why or why not?

REVIEW QUESTIONS

1. What is "subprime" lending? How did it contribute to the housing bubble and the subsequent financial crisis?
2. How can a collapse of the U.S housing market and weakness in the banking system cause an economic recession?
3. What is securitization? How did it contribute to the problems leading to the financial crisis?
4. Explain "too big to fail" and why it is a potential economic problem in any economic setting. How is "too big to fail" related to moral hazard?
5. How did the 2008 financial crisis affect income and wealth inequalities?
6. What have been the principal fiscal and monetary responses to the recession to date? What have been the results thus far?
7. How is the recent economic downturn similar to the Great Depression? How is it different?
8. What is the purpose of the Dodd-Frank bill? What are its main provisions? Has it been favorably received?

9. What is the primary function of the financial sector? In what ways have these functions changed in recent decades?

10. What is financial deregulation? How important is it in explaining the financial crisis?

11. What do we mean by financialization? What are some of the ways in which it has supported or deterred growth in the real sector?

12. What is the "efficient market hypothesis"?

13. What is Minsky's theory of financial instability? How, according to Minsky, can we create a more stable financial system?

14. About what share of aggregate income does each quintile of households receive in the United States?

15. What is the Gini coefficient? What does a higher value of the coefficient signify?

16. How has income inequality in the United States changed in recent decades?

17. What are some of the factors that have contributed to a rise in wage inequality in the past few decades?

18. In what ways has globalization affected inequality?

19. How has the rise of financialization influenced the level of inequality in the economy?

20. What macroeconomic policies have contributed to the rise in inequality since the 1980s?

21. What are some consequences of inequality?

22. What are some of the ways in which we might address the problems of excessive risk taking in the financial market?

23. What is the Tobin tax? What would be its effect on financial transactions?

24. Discuss some policy measures that might help reduce inequality.

EXERCISES

1. How does the Great Recession compare to recent economic downturns? To explore this question in further detail, begin at the National Bureau of Economic Research Web site (www.nber.org).

   a. Select "Business Cycle Dates" from the "Data" tab at the NBER site and then record the starting dates (peaks) and ending dates (troughs) for the last four recessions. Assemble these dates in a table.

   b. Now gather some macroeconomic data. You can do this at the Federal Reserve Economic Database (http://research.stlouisfed.org/fred2/). Using the "National Income & Product Accounts" under the "National Accounts" tab within "Categories," locate Real Gross Domestic Product data for each peak and each trough in your table. Record these numbers in a new table. Calculate the percentage change in Real GDP from peak to trough for each of the last four recessions. Report these results in your new table.

   c. Return to the categories page at the FRED website. Select the "Current Population Survey (Household Survey)" link under the "Population, Employment, & Labor Markets" category. Select the "unemployment rate" series and record the numbers for each peak and each trough for each of the last four recessions. Organize these data in a table.

   d. Review your tables and calculations. Write a concise summary comparing the Great Recession to the previous three recessions. Make sure that you incorporate specific numbers into your summary.

2. The chapter identifies a series of contributing factors in its exploration of the underlying causes of the financial crisis. Identify the major factors and state which you think were most important.

3. What is the meaning of moral hazard? Give some examples of moral hazard, as discussed in the text, or others that you can think of.

4. Match each concept in Column A with a definition or example in Column B.

Column A	Column B
a. A Gini ratio close to 1	1. When a company grows so large that its failure would cause widespread economic harm in terms of lost jobs and diminished asset values
b. Securitization	2. Unregulated markets will always produce instability and crisis
c. Financialization	3. A would-be homebuyer whose credit-worthiness is suspect because he or she already has a high level of debt, and/or a low income, and/or a poor credit record
d. Subprime buyer	4. Increasing size and importance of the financial markets in the operation of the economy
e. Financial Instability Hypothesis	5. A very equal income distribution
f. Deregulation	6. The lack of any incentive to guard against a risk when you are protected against it
g. A Gini ratio close to 0	7. Process of pooling various kinds of loans and slicing, sorting, and repackaging them
h. Too big to fail	8. Increasing the amount of leverage permitted to banks and allowing them to measure the riskiness of their own products
i. Moral hazard	9. A very unequal income distribution

NOTES

1. Gapper, John. 2008. "The Fatal Banker's Fall." *Financial Times*, October 1.

2. Bank holding companies are companies that own or control banks. These companies are regulated by the Federal Reserve. Conversion of investment banks to bank holding companies imposes more regulations on them but also provides them with easier access to funding through the Fed.

3. Pew Research Center. 2015. "The American Middle Class Is Losing Ground." December 9.

4. Based on data from World Development Indicators, World Bank.

5. Li, Linyue, Thomas D. Willett, and Nan Zhang. 2012. "The Effects of the Global Financial Crisis on China's Financial Market and Macroeconomy." *Economics Research International*, Article ID 961694.

6. Villarreal, M. Angeles. 2010. "The Mexican Economy after the Global Financial Crisis." Congressional Research Service, September 16. (Note that almost 80 percent of Mexican exports are destined to the United States.)

7. Migration Policy Institute. 2009. "Top 10 of 2009: Issue #1: The Recession's Impact on Immigrants." December 2.

8. Amadeo, Kimberly. 2017. "What Was Obama's Stimulus Package?" *The Balance*, August 30.

9. Krugman, Paul. 2014. "The Stimulus Tragedy." *New York Times*, February 20.

10. Oliff, Phil, Chris Mai, and Vincent Palacios. 2012. "States Continue to Feel Recession's Impact." Center on Budget and Policy Priorities, June 27.

11. Montecino, Juan Antonia, and Gerald Epstein. 2015. "Banking From Financial Crisis to Dodd-Frank: Five Years on, How Much Has Changed?" Political Economy Research Institute, Working Paper, July 21.

12. Real World Macro. 2015. "From Boring Banking to Roaring Banking: How the Financial Sector Grew out of Control, and How We Can Change It." An Interview with Gerald Epstein, Real World Macro, July/August, Dollars and Sense.

13. Orhangazi, Ozgur. 2007. "Financialization and Capital Accumulation in the Non-Financial Corporate Sector: A Theoretical and Empirical Investigation of the U.S. Economy: 1973–2003." Political Economy and Research Institute, Working Paper Series Number 149.

14. Mukund, Gautam. 2014. "The Price of Wall Street's Power." *Harvard Business Review*, June.

15. Foroohar, Rana. 2016. "American Capitalism's Great Crisis." *Time*, May 12.

16. Dabla-Norris, Era, Kalpana Kochhar, Nujin Suphaphiphat Frantisek Ricka, and Evridiki Tsounta. 2015. "Causes and Consequences of Income Inequality: A Global Perspective." International Monetary Fund, IMF Staff Discussion Note 15/13, June 2015.

17. Data for 2017 from the United Nations Development Programme, Human Development Reports database.

18. Alvaredo, Facundo, Lucas Chancel, Thomas Piketty, Emmanuel Saez, and Gabriel Zucman (editors). 2018. *World Inequality Report*. World Inequality Lab, Paris School of Economics. https://wid.world/

19. Brandmeir, Kathrin, Michaela Grimm, Michael Heise, and Arne Holzhausen. 2016. *Allianz Global Wealth Report 2016*. Allianz. https://www.allianz.com/en/economic_research/publications/specials_fmo/agwr16e.html

20. Piketty, Thomas, Emmanuel Saez, and Gabriel Zucman. 2016. "Distributional National Accounts: Methods and Estimates for the United States." National Bureau of Economic Research Working Paper Series, Working Paper 22945, December.

21. Proctor, Bernadette D., Jessica L. Semega, and Melissa A. Kollar. 2016. "Income and Poverty in the United States: 2015." Current Population Reports, U.S. Census Bureau, September.

22. Greenwood, Jeremy, Nezih Guner, Georgi Kocharkov, and Cezar Santos. 2014. "Marry Your Like: Assortive Mating and Income Inequality." National Bureau of Economic Research, NBER Working Paper 19829, January.

23. International Monetary Fund. 2017. "World Economic Outlook: Gaining Momentum?" April.

24. OECD online statistics, trade union density.

25. Pavcnik, Nina. 2011. "Globalization and Within-Country Income Inequality." In Chapter 7 of *Making Globalization Socially Sustainable* (Marc Bacchetta and Marion Jansen, editors). World Trade Organization and International Labour Organization, Geneva.

26. Mishel, Lawrence, and Kar Gee. 2012. "Why Aren't Workers Benefiting from Labour Productivity Growth in the United States?" *International Productivity Monitor*, 23: 31–43.

27. International Labor Organization (ILO). 2012. "Global Wage Report 2012/13: Wages and Equitable Growth." http://piketty.pse.ens.fr/files/ILO2012(GlobalWageReport).pdf

28. Based on data from the Fed, Survey of Consumer Finances.

29. Egan, Matt. 2017. "Record Inequality: The Top 1% Controls 38.6% of America's Wealth." CNN Money, September 27.

30. Lazonick, William. 2014. "Profits Without Prosperity." *Harvard Business Review*, September Issue.

31. Brown, Courtenay. 2019. "Companies Prefer Buybacks in Wake of Trump Tax Cuts." *Axios*, March 5. www.axios.com/companies-buybacks-2017-tax-cuts-19d6cac4-4912-47da-bbff-038fd0d87b30.html

32. Tax Policy Center. 2017. "Distributional Analysis of the Conference Agreement for the Tax Cuts and Jobs Act." Urban Institute and Brookings Institution, December 18.

33. Piketty, Thomas, and Emmanuel Saez. 2007. "How Progressive Is the U.S. Federal Tax System? A Historical and International Perspective." *Journal of Economic Perspectives*, 21(1): 3–24.

34. Obst, Thomas. 2013. "Income Inequality and the Welfare State: How Redistributive Is the Public Sector?" Institute for International Political Economy Berlin, Berlin School of Economics and Law, Working Paper No. 29/2013.

35. Santiago, Catherine DeCarlo, Martha E. Wadsworth, and Jessica Stump. 2011. "Socioeconomic Status, Neighborhood Disadvantage, and Poverty-Related Stress: Prospective Effects on Psychological Syndromes among Diverse Low-Income Families." *Journal of Economic Psychology*, 32(2): 218–230.

36. Wilkinson, Richard, and Kate Pickett. 2009. *The Spirit Level: Why Greater Equality Makes Societies Stronger*. Bloomsbury Press, London.

37. Ostry, Jonathan D., Andrew Berg, and Charalambos G. Tsangarides. 2014. "Redistribution, Inequality, and Growth." IMF Staff Discussion Note 14/02, April.

38. Ibid., p. 25.

39. Gilens, Martin. 2012. *Affluence and Influence*. Princeton University Press, Princeton, NJ.

40. Ibid., p. 1.

41. Lazonick, William. 2012. "How American Corporations Transformed from Producers to Predators." *HuffPost*, April 3.

42. Dube, Arindrajit. 2017. "Minimum Wages and the Distribution of Family Incomes." Institute of Labor Economics, Discussion Paper Series.

43. Autor, David H., Alan Manning, and Christopher L. Smith. 2016. "The Contribution of the Minimum Wage to US Wage Inequality over Three Decades: A Reassessment." *American Economic Journal: Applied Economics*, 8(1): 58–99.

44. Lavoie, Marc, and Engelbert Stockhammer (editors). 2014. *Wage-Led Growth: An Equitable Strategy for Economic Recovery*. International Labour Organisation, Geneva.

45. Jaumotte, Florence, and Carolina Osorio Buitron. 2015. "Inequality and Labor Market Institutions." International Monetary Fund, IMF Discussion Note 15/14, July.

46. Organisation for Economic Co-Operation and Development (OECD). 2012. *Economic Policy Reforms: Going for Growth*. OECD Publishing, Paris.

47. Alderman, Liz. 2017. "Feeling 'Pressure All the Time' on Europe's Treadmill of Temporary Work." *New York Times*, February 9.

48. Grabell, Michael, and Lena Groeger. 2014. "Temp Worker Regulations around the World." *ProPublica*, February 24. https://projects.propublica.org/graphics/temps-around-the-world

49. Bregman, R. 2017. *Utopia for Realists*. Bloomsbury, London.

50. Matthews, Dylan. 2012. "Ten Ways to Reduce Inequality without Raising Tax Rates." *The Washington Post*, December 6.

Chapter 14

The Global Economy and Policy

Globalization and trade policies are hotly debated topics. Unfortunately, media discussions about global trade are often overly simplistic, pitting those who are "pro-trade" against those who are "anti-trade" rather than focusing on how to structure trade so that it enhances well-being by being efficient, fair, environmentally sustainable, and respectful of human rights. This chapter presents the core theories, evidence, and debates around trade and globalization.

1. TRADE, SPECIALIZATION, AND PRODUCTIVITY

In his 1776 book *An Inquiry Into the Nature and Causes of the Wealth of Nations*, Adam Smith argued that specialization (he called it "division of labor") would make people more efficient, producing more with a given amount of resources, because focusing our time on one task (or a few tasks) instead of many would make us learn it more quickly and become better at it. Smith then noted that the *extent* of the specialization achieved in a society would be limited by the size of the market. If, for example, the market for shoes were tiny, it would make no sense for you to allocate all your labor, or hire workers, or invest in capital for nothing but shoe production, as you would not make enough money in a small market to support yourself. If, however, the market were large, specialization would make sense.

The principle of economic specialization can be extended by expanding "the market" beyond a country's borders to include other countries. It is for this reason that Smith advocated not only a system of free markets but also **free trade** among countries, such that exchange in international markets is not regulated or restricted by the government. It seems reasonable to conclude that as markets expand to the whole globe, even more would be gained because of the maximized productive efficiency that results from maximum specialization.

> **free trade:** exchange in international markets that is not regulated or restricted by government actions

In Smith's view, specialization at the national level would lead each country to become so efficient in the production of some things that it would enjoy an "absolute advantage" over other countries in their production. An **absolute advantage** means an ability to produce something at lower per-unit costs than your competitor. Other countries would enjoy such an absolute advantage in the production of other goods, and because each country would produce more than it needed of the items in which it had exceptional capability, there would be ample opportunity for mutually beneficial trade between countries.

> **absolute advantage:** the ability to produce something at lower per-unit costs than one's competitors

Discussion Questions

1. Can you think of an instance where you have divided a job into specialized tasks by giving each task to a different person? If so, did it make a difference to your efficiency and productivity?
2. Are you currently "specializing" in a certain field? If not, what do you plan to do after college? Do you hope to develop knowledge or expertise in only one area or more than one? Why?

2. GAINS FROM TRADE

Suppose a particular country is so efficient that it has an absolute advantage over other countries in almost everything. Why would that country ever trade with other countries that have higher per-unit production costs when it could just make those same products domestically at a lower cost? David Ricardo answered this question in his 1817 book *On the Principles of Political Economy and Taxation*. Ricardo demonstrated that even if a country has an absolute advantage in *everything*, it can still benefit from trade provided that each country has different opportunity costs. Recall from Chapter 1 that **opportunity cost** is the value of the best alternative that is forgone when a choice is made. In this section, we present Ricardo's model, along with other arguments in favor of free trade.

> **opportunity cost:** the value of the best alternative that is forgone when a choice is made

2.1 Theory of Comparative Advantage

In Chapter 1, we discussed the production-possibilities frontier, which illustrates how a society might make tradeoffs between the production of two different goods, reaching higher output levels when it uses its resources efficiently. We showed how some points, which represent combinations of the two outputs (guns and butter), would be unattainable with current technology. Though points outside a societal PPF are unattainable in terms of *production* for the society, these points may be attained in terms of *consumption* when we consider the potential for international trade. The key to this is in the benefits that can arise from a system of exchange. Economists call these benefits the "gains from trade," and they are *efficiency* gains.

Ricardo presented his model using an example which included only two goods—wine and cloth—and two countries—Portugal and England. Like all economic models, it is a simplified story that includes relevant factors but omits many real-world complications. Here we give a simple version of his story, using PPFs, but the conclusion can be applied more broadly to the benefits of trade.

Suppose that, given its resources and technology, Portugal can produce a maximum of 200 cases of wine if it devotes all its resources to wine production, or 100 bolts of cloth (a unit of cloth is called a "bolt") if it devotes all of its resources to cloth production. In Figure 14.1, we have assumed constant opportunity costs, so the PPF is just a straight line.[1] Meanwhile, England can produce a maximum of 200 cases of wine if it devotes all its resources to wine production or 400 bolts of cloth if it devotes all its resources to cloth production, as illustrated in Figure 14.2.

Suppose that the Portuguese would like to be able to consume 100 cases of wine and 100 bolts of cloth, as represented by point A in Figure 14.1, and the English would like to be able to consume 100 cases of wine and 300 bolts of cloth,

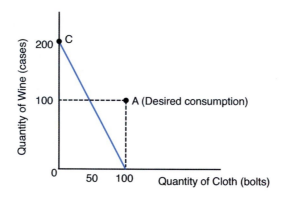

Figure 14.1 *Portugal's Production Possibilities Frontier*

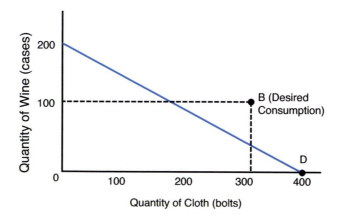

Figure 14.2 *England's Production Possibilities Frontier*

Table 14.1 Production, Exchange, and Consumption of Wine and Cloth

	Country	Wine (cases)	Cloth (bolts)
Production:	Portugal	200	0
	England	0	400
Total production:		200	400
Exchange:	Portugal	sell 100	buy 100
	England	buy 100	sell 100
Consumption:	Portugal	100	100
	England	100	300
Total consumption:		200	400

represented by point B in Figure 14.2. As we can see, if each relies only on its own production possibilities, points A and B are unachievable.

But suppose that Portugal produces only wine and England produces only cloth. In this case, Portugal produces 200 cases of wine (point C in Figure 14.1), and England produces 400 bolts of cloth (point D in Figure 14.2). This production combination is illustrated in the "Production" section of Table 14.1, with total production of 200 cases of wine and 400 bolts of cloth.

Portugal is producing only wine, but it desires to have some cloth. England is producing only cloth, but it wants some wine. Is an exchange possible that would clearly make both countries better off than if they didn't trade? Specifically, is it possible for Portugal to achieve total consumption of point A in Figure 14.1 while England achieves point B in Figure 14.2?

The answer is "yes." If Portugal trades 100 cases of wine to England in exchange for 100 bolts of cloth, as shown in the "Exchange" section of Table 14.1, Portugal and England can each *consume* the quantities listed in the "Consumption" section of the table. Note that their total consumption equals the total amount produced of each good (200 cases of wine and 400 bolts of cloth). Yet Portugal would consume at point A and England at point B—the desired points that neither country could reach on its own!

The "magic" behind this result is that Portugal and England differ in their opportunity costs of production. Note that we are only considering the *opportunity cost* of production, not the *monetary cost* of production. The monetary cost of production in each country does not matter in this simplified story. What matters is how much of one good must be given up in order to produce some of the other good.

To calculate the opportunity costs in this model, we undertake the following steps:

1. Locate the maximum production values on the y-axis and the x-axis. (Note that in order to produce the maximum quantity on the y-axis, the country must forego producing the maximum quantity on the x-axis, and to produce the maximum quantity on the x-axis, it must forego producing the maximum quantity on the y-axis.)

2. To calculate the opportunity cost of producing one unit of the good on the y-axis, divide the maximum quantity on the x-axis by the maximum quantity on the y-axis.

3. To calculate the opportunity cost of producing one unit of the good on the *x*-axis, divide the maximum quantity on the *y*-axis by the maximum quantity on the *x*-axis.

Let's calculate the opportunity cost to each country of producing a case of wine. Portugal's maximum production on the *y*-axis is 200 cases of wine and 100 bolts of cloth on the *x*-axis. This means that in order for Portugal to produce its maximum amount of wine (200 cases), it must forego producing 100 bolts of cloth. The opportunity cost to Portugal of producing wine is thus:

Portugal's opportunity cost of wine production = 100/200 = ½

This means that to produce one case of wine, Portugal must give up the production of ½ bolt of cloth. As Portugal's PPF is a straight line, its opportunity cost of wine production is constant along its entire PPF. England's opportunity cost of wine production is:

England's opportunity cost of wine production = 400/200 = 2

We see that Portugal can produce wine at a lower opportunity cost than England. We say that Portugal has a **comparative advantage** in wine production, because wine costs less in terms of the amount of the other good (cloth) that must be given up in Portugal compared to the amount that must be given up in England. In other words, Portugal has a lower opportunity cost associated with its wine production. Note that this determination of comparative advantage tells us nothing about whether either country has an absolute advantage in production of wine or cloth.

> **comparative advantage:** the ability to produce some good or service at a lower opportunity cost than other producers

The theory of comparative advantage says that a country should specialize in those goods and services for which it has a comparative advantage over its trading partners and trade for other goods and services. So in this case, Portugal should specialize in wine production because it has the lower opportunity cost of wine production and trade with England to obtain cloth. England should specialize in cloth production and trade to obtain wine.

We can also calculate each country's opportunity costs in terms of the wine it must give up in order to produce cloth. The opportunity cost of cloth production for the two countries is calculated as:

Portugal's opportunity cost of cloth production = 200/100 = 2
England's opportunity cost of cloth production = 200/400 = ½

So Portugal must give up producing 2 cases of wine for each bolt of cloth it wants to produce. Meanwhile, England's opportunity cost of cloth production is ½. So,

Table 14.2 Opportunity Cost and Comparative Advantage

Country	Opportunity cost of 1 bolt of cloth	Opportunity cost of 1 case of wine
Portugal	2 cases of wine	½ bolt of cloth
England	½ case of wine	2 bolts of cloth

England has the lower opportunity cost and should specialize in cloth production. Note that you should obtain the same answer regarding which country should specialize in which good whether you evaluate opportunity costs for the good on the x-axis or the good on the y-axis. The opportunity cost results are summarized in Table 14.2.

The outcome of Ricardo's example makes sense based on the circumstances of his time. England had energy resources (coal) that made it relatively good at industrial production such as spinning and weaving and a relatively cool climate that was not suitable for growing grapes. Portugal, by contrast, enjoyed a comparative advantage in production of wine, owing to its relatively warm climate—good for growing grapes—but lacked the necessary energy sources to produce cloth as efficiently as England.

The source of comparative advantage in the previous example is climate and other resource endowments, which differed between England and Portugal. It is not hard, by extension, to understand why, for example, bananas are currently exported by Ecuador, while Sweden finds it advantageous to import bananas. Comparative advantage can also be created by economic policies. Countries can become more efficient at producing particular goods by investing in the physical and human capital needed to produce them. Sometimes, technological advances or changes in the social organization of work can change the pattern of comparative advantage over time.

The most powerful implication of this model is that trading partners can both benefit through specialization and trade, even if one country has an absolute advantage in all goods and services. A country that is rather inefficient in its production processes, lacking an absolute advantage in any product, will still be able to produce some products at a comparative advantage relative to its trading partners.

Ricardo's example concerned trade between countries, but the principle of comparative advantage has also been used to show how other economic actors can reap gains from trade. Organizations seek gains from trade when they specialize in a particular area—say, production of training workshops—while contracting with other companies to provide support services—say, transportation or advertising design. You may reap gains from trade in your household if, instead of splitting all chores 50–50, the person who is more "efficient" at shopping takes charge of shopping and the person who is more efficient at cleaning takes charge of cleaning.

Even if some companies, or some people, are self-sufficient in producing everything they need, it is generally beneficial to engage in at least some trade, and this is what we usually observe in the real world. The story of specialization and gains from trade is a powerful one, though as we shall see, there also other dimensions of trade to consider.

2.2 Factor Price Equalization

Economists often make a distinction between countries that are thought to be more suited for **labor-intensive production** processes, such as stitching clothing or making handicrafts, and others that specialize in relatively **capital-intensive production**, such as the manufacture of airplanes or automobiles. The fact that the United States has more manufactured capital per worker than does Bangladesh, for example, is considered an explanation for Bangladeshi exports of clothing and U.S. exports of airplanes. Bangladesh presumably has a comparative advantage in relatively labor-intensive industries, while the United States has a comparative advantage in certain types of capital-intensive production.

> **labor-intensive production:** production using methods that involve a high ratio of labor to capital
>
> **capital-intensive production:** production using methods that involve a high ratio of capital to labor

The economic theory of **factor price equalization** predicts that free trade should tend to equalize the prices of different production inputs across countries over time. The most common application of this theory is to prices for labor (i.e., wages). Suppose that trade is initiated between the United States and Bangladesh. Initially, wages in Bangladesh are much lower than in the United States, leading Bangladesh to develop a comparative advantage in labor-intensive industries that require low-skilled workers. The low labor prices in Bangladesh will lead to an increase in U.S. demand for products imported from Bangladesh. Eventually, this increasing demand will put upward pressure on wages in Bangladesh. Trade has made low-skilled labor in Bangladesh a more valuable input.

The opposite effect on wages would be expected to occur in the United States. Trade with relatively low-wage countries means that the demand for relatively expensive low-skilled U.S. labor will decline. This will put downward pressure on low-skilled labor wages in the United States. Trade has in fact made low-skilled U.S. labor a less valuable input. Thus, the overall effect of trade is that wages for low-skilled workers in the United States and Bangladesh grow closer together over time.

> **factor price equalization:** the theory that trade should eliminate input price differences among trading partners over time

Of course, in the real world, wages in the United States are about 30 times higher than wages in Bangladesh. The theory of factor price equalization merely states that wages should *eventually* converge but says nothing about how long this process may take. Also, the theory requires that in order for factor prices to achieve equality, the prices of output goods must become the same in both countries—something that has not occurred yet between the United States and Bangladesh.

We find evidence of factor price equalization in some cases. For example, Japan (in the 1950s) and then South Korea were the first two Asian countries that spurred their economic growth by depending heavily on the export of goods made with very cheap labor. Wages in these two countries have risen to be essentially the same as in other industrialized countries (though government policies of industrial support played an important part in raising wages). Wages have also been rising in China; wages for Chinese factory workers increased by 64 percent between 2011 and 2016.[2] As a result, China is losing its comparative advantage in low-cost labor, and production for many products is shifting from China to countries such as Sri Lanka and Bangladesh, which still have very low wages.

Recall from Chapter 7 that wages are often "sticky" downward—they don't easily decline—so firms are likely to lay off some workers when demand falls instead of lowering wages. Thus, transfer of jobs to countries with cheaper labor may result in lower employment rather than wage declines in the United States. This dynamic suggests that trade between the United States and Bangladesh is expected to have a negative impact on low-skilled workers in the United States, though U.S. *consumers* will benefit from the lower prices of imports from Bangladesh. Trade's negative impact on low-skilled workers is often seen as contributing to the rise in inequality in the United States and other industrialized countries, as we discussed in the previous chapter.

2.3 Other Benefits of Free Trade

The Ricardian model demonstrates that trade allows each country to consume outside of its domestic PPF. By shifting production across countries to take advantage of low-cost resources, trade results in lower prices to consumers. Global trade enables production to shift relatively quickly in response to changing conditions. Suppose Portugal discovered that it could get more cloth by growing table grapes for Germany than by producing wine for England. It would be motivated to move resources into producing grapes for Germany. Trade gives producers an incentive to produce the goods that command the highest market value. Such an incentive has the potential to encourage competition and innovation, to the ultimate benefit of many consumers.

With trade, the volume of a country's production of a good can be substantially higher than its domestic market can use. Thus, firms can realize increasing "economies of scale," where the cost per unit of production falls as the volume of production rises. As Smith anticipated, a larger market means that goods can be produced more cheaply.

Trade can also encourage technology transfer across countries. Particularly when companies from technically advanced countries locate facilities in developing countries, new technologies can be introduced. For example, there is evidence that expansion of manufacturing exports in India has resulted in increased use of foreign technologies that have produced increases in productivity.[3]

Finally, some argue that trade forces countries to think in terms of their common interests, binding them together in a cooperative venture. If countries came to rely on each other for trade, they might think twice about engaging in a war with each other. After World War II, the United States provided significant aid for rebuilding the devastated countries of Europe, as U.S. policymakers realized that their own economy would not prosper unless the economies of its major trading partners prospered as well. Several studies in recent years support the theory that trade encourages peaceful relations among countries.[4]

Discussion Questions

1. Suppose that, in a one-hour period, you can buy six bags of groceries *or* clean three rooms. Your housemate, however, can buy only three bags of groceries or clean only one room in an hour. Does this mean you should do all the work?
2. Ricardo's model discusses benefits to countries at an aggregate level. But what if you were a Portuguese cloth maker or an English winemaker? Might you have a different view about the benefits of trade? Which factors might influence what you think about your country's trade policies?

3. DRAWBACKS OF FREE TRADE

David Ricardo's simple model neglects some political, social, and environmental issues that can partially or fully offset the efficiency gains from trade. The potential disadvantages of trade can include increased vulnerability, becoming locked into production patterns, abuse of power, environmental degradation, and increasing inequality.

3.1 Vulnerability and Lock-In

One obvious potential problem with specialization is that countries become more vulnerable to the actions of their trading partners. Supplies of commodities that you need, and markets for what you sell, could deteriorate or be cut off at any time. This is particularly serious when the goods in question are resources such as oil, minerals, food, or water, the lack of which would seriously weaken an economy. Vulnerability is also a serious issue for countries that rely heavily on sales of a single, or a few, export goods for much of their national income. The Ethiopian economy, for example, was heavily affected by the significant declines in coffee prices in 2015, since coffee accounts for about one-quarter of the country's exports.

Specialization may also lock a country into a production pattern that eventually becomes inefficient, making change difficult. It makes sense for Ethiopia to specialize in coffee production as long as it has a strong comparative advantage in coffee production, but there is a danger that Ethiopia may become "locked in" to a focus on coffee production even when better opportunities arise in the future. A country should not overspecialize in what it does well today if doing so prevents it from developing its future potential in other, more rewarding, pursuits. Hence, countries need to consider not only what their comparative advantage is today but what they would like it to be in the future. Although Ricardo's "gains from trade" argument is logically correct, the benefits of specialization must be weighed against the costs.

3.2 Power Differentials

Our simple story of England and Portugal also ignored the real-world political context of international trade. While trade is voluntary, that does not mean that all trading partners have equal power. Often, more powerful countries can exact terms on trade with less powerful countries that skew the benefits of trade toward the more powerful country. Such a power advantage may come from being the sole producer of a certain good, through military might, or through controlling important financial institutions and access to technology. Developing countries often argue that the rules of global trade have overly advantaged developed countries.

3.3 Trade and the Environment

Our simple model of trade did not consider environmental externalities, such as soil erosion and industrial pollution that result from increasing production for trade. When we include such externalities, the net benefits of trade can sometimes be much diminished or even negative.[5] For example, if trade with England greatly increases grape production in Portugal, producers may be motivated to engage in practices that raise productivity in the short run but with long-run negative effects such as severe soil erosion, wildlife habitat loss, and toxic chemical runoff. These damages may be so large that they offset the economic gains of trade to Portugal; however, they will be ignored if they are "external" to the market mechanisms perceived by individual producers or the government.

Another environmental concern is that countries involved in trade may become motivated to engage in a "**race to the bottom**," where each country lowers environmental, labor, or social standards to obtain a production cost advantage, setting off a vicious circle of lowering of standards. This "race to the bottom" can occur not only between countries but also between states or cities within countries.[6] Empirical evidence on the race to the bottom hypothesis is mixed. A 2006 paper looking at data from over 100 countries finds that firms that are heavily reliant on exports are more likely to adopt strict environmental standards. But other research, such as a 2015 paper, concludes that an increasing amount of toxic waste is being directed toward developing nations as a result of globalization.[7]

> **race to the bottom:** a situation in which countries, regions, or cities compete in providing low-cost business environments, resulting in deterioration in labor, environmental, or safety standards

Transportation of goods around the world by land, air, and sea also results in higher pollution than local production and consumption. According to the OECD, the most significant environmental impact of expanded global trade is higher emissions of carbon dioxide (CO_2), the main greenhouse gas. The OECD report notes that for the average country, a 1 percent increase in trade leads to a 0.6 percent increase in CO_2 emissions.[8]

453

More generally, global trade tends to shift the burden of pollution from developed to developing countries. This is often referred to as "**exporting pollution**," whereby a country reduces its domestic manufacturing and associated pollution, becoming more dependent on imports manufactured elsewhere (normally in poorer countries), resulting in pollution in those countries instead. For example, 400 million tons of CO_2 emitted in China each year is a result of demand in the United States for Chinese imports.

> **exporting pollution:** a situation in which a country reduces its domestic pollution but increases its imports of products that cause similar pollution in other countries

The transfer of developed country waste to developing countries has also been increasing in the past two decades.[9] In this case, polluting industries are based in developed countries, but the pollution is physically shipped to developing countries. A crucial problem with such waste transfers is that developing countries often do not have the technology or the regulatory supervision to process this waste in a way that protects their own citizens and the environment.

3.4 Inequality and Other Social Impacts of Trade

In our trade example, when Portugal specializes in producing wine and England specializes in producing cloth, there are benefits to consumers in both countries, as well as to the Portuguese wine industry and the English cloth industry. However, those working in Portugal's cloth industry and England's wine industry lose. This suggests it is important to consider both the efficiency gains *and* the redistributive impacts of freer trade. Trade economist Dani Rodrik has compared these two aspects of freer trade and found that:

> In an economy like the United States, where average tariffs are below 5 percent, a move to complete free trade would reshuffle more than $50 of income among different groups for each dollar of efficiency or "net" gain created. Read the last sentence again in case you went through it quickly: we are talking about $50 of redistribution for every $1 of aggregate gain.[10]

Rodrik suggests that global trade is more about redistribution than about efficiency gains. He argues that before recommending policies to expand trade, we must ask two important questions:

1. Are the net efficiency gains small compared to the magnitude of the losses, especially if those losses impact low-income or other disadvantaged groups?
2. Can the policy lead to actions that may violate social norms related to issues such as child labor, unionization rights, or environmental standards?

If the answer to one or both of these questions is yes, then such a policy may not improve human well-being even with an increase in economic efficiency. These issues are even more important when we consider that a race-to-the-bottom effect

BOX 14.1 THE 2013 RANA PLAZA COLLAPSE

On April 24, 2013, the eight-story Rana Plaza building in Bangladesh collapsed, killing over 1,100 people. The building housed five garment factories, which made clothes for companies such as Wal-Mart, Primark, and Benetton. Investigation after the collapse revealed that the building was overloaded with heavy equipment, constructed of substandard materials, and included three more floors than it was permitted to have.

As a result of the tragedy, the Apparel and Footwear Supply Chain Transparency Pledge has been drafted by human rights and labor groups to voluntarily commit retailers to disclose details about the factories where their products are made.[11] But as of 2017, only 17 of the 72 companies asked to join the pledge have done so. While Nike, Patagonia, Levi's, ASICS, and Adidas have committed fully to the pledge, Wal-Mart, Primark, Armani, Hugo Boss, and Urban Outfitters either declined participation or didn't respond to the request.

Since the Rana Plaza collapse, Bangladeshi workers have become more vocal in demanding better wages and working conditions. In late 2016, tens of thousands of workers walked off the job for a week in protest. In 2018, the Ministry for Labor and Employment announced the new monthly minimum wage of 8,000 taka (US $95) a month—a 51 percent increase from the existing minimum wage but much lower than the workers' demand for a minimum wage of 16,000 taka.[12]

from trade could weaken working conditions and increase inequality.[13] Box 14.1 demonstrates just how serious these problems are. A 2015 paper finds that many governments have been pursuing policies that lower the share of national income going to workers in favor of increasing exports.[14] Examples of such policies include limiting workers' rights to unionize and reducing corporate tax rates, both of which can increase economic inequality.

A final issue to consider is that international trade rules are often heavily influenced by international corporations. In fact, 93 percent of the external advisors to the U.S. Trade Representative represent business interests, and only a few advisors represent worker, environmental, or social interests.[15] Large and powerful corporations can exert inordinate amounts of influence in lobbying for trade rules that primarily benefit them. This diminishes the ability of citizens to make democratic decisions about the direction of their society.

Enumerating the possible problems with trade, as we have done here, does not invalidate the original theoretical insight about the mutual benefits from trade. Rather, it is a question of weighing the benefits, which are widespread and have driven a steady growth in global trade, against some of the problems in order to determine good trade policies.

Discussion Questions

1. Do you think it is better to buy products made in your own country? If so, why? Can you think of situations where it is better to buy foreign products?

2. What do you suppose Smith or Ricardo would have had to say about the disadvantages of free trade discussed in this chapter?

4. GLOBALIZATION AND POLICY

4.1 Patterns of Trade

International trade has expanded immensely in recent years. The sum of a country's imports and exports of goods and services, expressed as a percentage of GDP, is often used as a measure of an economy's "openness." Growth in trade according to this measure is shown for 1960–2017 in Figure 14.3. Although trade still remains relatively less important in the United States compared to many other countries, its importance has been increasing here as well.

A common misconception is that some countries are considered primarily exporting countries (e.g., China and India), while other countries are considered primarily importing countries (especially the United States). But the reality is that exports and imports are complements. Countries that import a lot, relative to their GDP, are also the countries that tend to export a lot. (See Figure 14.4.) For example, China currently does export more than it imports, but not by much. And while the United States is a net importer, the difference may not be as large as you expect from news stories. We might also expect that large countries such as China, India, and the United States are the countries with the greatest international trade integration, but, in fact, trade represents a relatively small percentage of their GDP compared to smaller countries such as Vietnam and Thailand.

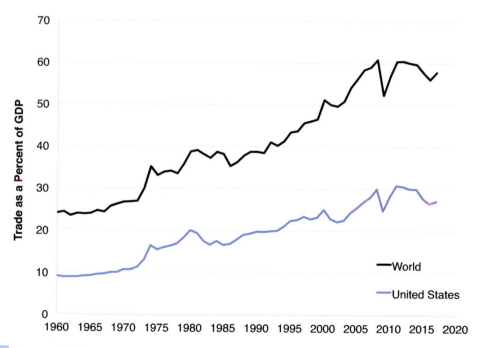

Figure 14.3 *Trade as a Percentage of Production, World and United States, 1960–2017*

Source: World Bank, World Development Indicators database, 2019.

Note: Since this measure includes both imports and exports, it does not mean that over 50 percent of all produced goods and services in the world are traded—it counts the same goods both as exports from one country and imports to another.

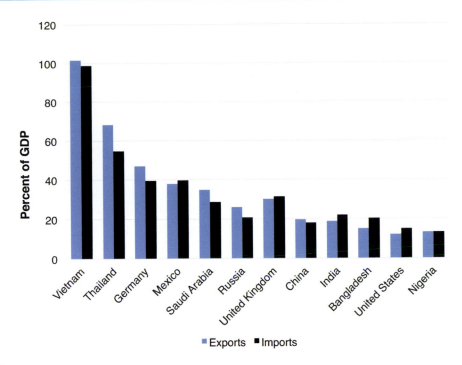

Figure 14.4 *Exports and Imports as a Percent of GDP, Select Countries, 2017*

Source: World Bank, World Development Indicators online database.

A final issue we consider here is the distinction between trade in goods and trade in services. About 43 percent of global trade is trade in services rather than manufactured goods, and developments in information technology make it likely that this will rise in the future. Examples of services that are traded across national borders include communication services, education, legal and accounting services, and tourism.

4.2 National Trade Policies

At a national level, countries can enact policies that either promote or limit trade. Fostering trade can be justified as an economic development strategy to increase incomes, employment, and access to foreign markets. For example, a country may set up a "free trade zone," defined as an area within a country (normally an airport or seaport) where goods and raw materials can be imported without tariffs or other fees. These imported materials are further processed or assembled in the free trade zone for eventual export elsewhere. Countries may want to restrict trade in order to limit some of the disadvantages we discussed previously. Perhaps most frequently, imports are restricted so that a country can protect its domestic industries.

Trade Protectionism

National governments frequently try to exert some control over trade flows into or out of their country. The use of such policies is referred to as **protectionism**, as it often has the goal of protecting domestic industries from foreign competition. In some cases, a country limits imports of certain goods and services so that these can instead be produced domestically for domestic consumption. This is referred to as **import substitution**. Another justification for protectionism is the **infant industry** argument, which states that emerging domestic industries may need to be temporarily protected from international competition to give them time to develop capabilities to better compete on world markets. Both these policies usually involve the government subsidizing domestic industry or placing trade barriers to discourage imports.

---

protectionism: the use of government policies to restrict trade with other countries and protect domestic industries from foreign competition

import substitution: the policy of subsidizing domestic producers or imposing protectionist measures to reduce reliance on imports and encourage domestic industry

infant industry: an industry that is relatively new to its region or country and thus may need to be protected from international competition by trade barriers until it can better compete on world markets

---

Many industrializing countries have engaged in both import substitution and infant industry policies in attempts to diversify their economies away from dependence on such sectors as agriculture or mining. Packages of industry-promoting policies are often referred to as "industrial policy" and can be thought of as an attempt to modify a country's comparative advantage.

Of course, a downside of deliberate industrial policy that restricts trade is that potential "gains from trade" are sacrificed. The potential upside is that, over the long run, the country might be able to increase its national productivity and competitiveness and thus avoid getting locked into a disadvantageous pattern of production and trade. We now consider four types of protectionist policies:

1. tariffs
2. quotas
3. trade–related subsidies
4. administrative obstacles

Tariffs

Perhaps the most common form of trade protectionism is a **tariff** (sometimes called a "duty"). Tariffs are taxes charged by national governments to importers of merchandise from other countries. They tend to reduce trade to some degree, because the tariff raises the price of the good sold in the importing country, thereby reducing the import quantity demanded. To the extent that domestically produced goods compete with imported goods, tariffs benefit domestic producers. Overall, tariffs tend to increase prices paid by consumers, just as any tax tends to result in higher prices. See Box 14.2 for an example of the Trump administration's effort to impose higher tariffs on Chinese goods, with the goal of protecting U.S. producers.

BOX 14.2 TRADE WAR BETWEEN THE UNITED STATES AND CHINA

Since the election of Donald Trump in 2016, trade tensions between the United States and China have escalated. At the time of writing, there are some signs of tensions easing, though there is considerable uncertainty as to whether that will occur. In mid-2019, President Trump imposed 25 percent tariffs on $250 billion of goods from China and threatened further hikes in tariffs. Trump defended his actions by accusing China of unfairly subsidizing its products and arguing that these subsidies have obstructed American companies from competing with low-cost Chinese imports and caused the loss of American jobs.

China responded by increasing its tariffs on $60 billion worth of U.S. goods and has also threatened to cease purchases of U.S. agricultural products and aircraft parts.[16] In 2018, U.S. exports to China were $179 billion, making China the third-largest market for U.S. exports (behind Canada and Mexico).[17] Several U.S. businesses have warned that further tariffs on Chinese goods would raise costs for consumers and disrupt supply chains and could result in business failures and job losses.[18]

Though it is still too early to understand the full impacts of the trade war, there has already been a decline in U.S. exports of agricultural products, electronics, and chemicals to China. California has taken the biggest hit, with exports from California declining by 13 percent in the first four months of 2019.[19] Furthermore, a trade war between the United States and China is expected to adversely affect the global economy. There has already been a slowdown in growth in Europe, Australia, and some other parts of the world, as rising trade tensions have led to a decline in business confidence and investment. Industrial production has fallen sharply in Germany following anxiety regarding whether the United States will impose tariffs on auto imports. Economists at the International Monetary Fund have estimated that if President Trump follows through on his threat to further restrict trade with China, tariffs added this year alone will subtract about 0.3 percent off global GDP in 2020.[20]

Tariffs also provide national governments with tax revenue. Historically, this has often been the primary motivation for tariffs. For example, in the 1800s, tariffs often provided 50–90 percent of federal revenues in the United States.[21] Today, tariffs provide more than 20 percent of all tax revenues for some developing countries, including the Philippines, Nepal, and Bangladesh.[22] Tariffs sometimes force foreign producers to lower their prices in order to remain competitive with domestic producers who do not pay the tariff.

tariffs: taxes (or duties) charged by national governments to the importers of goods from other countries

As a result of international trade agreements to promote trade, tariffs have generally been declining. According to the World Trade Organization, tariff rates declined by a global average of 15 percent over the past 20 years.[23] However, tariff rates vary significantly by country, and they tend to be higher in developing countries.

Another example of protectionism is a **trade quota**, which is a limit on the quantity of a good that can be imported from another country. By restricting supply, a quota generally has the effect of increasing the price of the good. Like a tariff, it helps domestic producers by shielding them from lower-price competition, and it hurts consumers by making them pay a higher price. Unlike tariffs, quotas generally do not provide monetary benefit to the government, except when the quotas are sold or auctioned to the importers. The effect on the exporting foreign country, however, is more ambiguous than with a tariff. The quota may hurt foreign producers because it limits their exports, but they may obtain some benefit from extra revenues from the artificially higher price. Which effect prevails depends on, among other things, the elasticity of demand (discussed in Chapter 3) for the imported good.

> **trade quota:** a nationally imposed restriction on the quantity of a particular good that can be imported from another country

One policy that has gained importance in recent decades is the **trade-related subsidy**, which, unlike a tariff or quota, may be used to either expand or contract trade (and therefore cannot always be regarded as "protectionist"). Trade expansion is facilitated through subsidies to exporters, since such payments reduce their production costs and help exporters price their goods more competitively in foreign markets. Such payments can also be granted to domestic producers to encourage the production of certain goods for domestic markets, with a goal of reducing the quantity of imports. This works when the demand for imports can be diverted to domestically produced products (i.e., import substitution). Trade subsidies can be used to support **dumping**, whereby a country temporarily exports products below their cost of production in order to drive out competition and build market share.

> **trade-related subsidy:** payments given by governments to producers to encourage more production, either for export or as a substitute for imports
> **dumping:** selling products at prices that are below the cost of production, normally in international trade

A final category of protectionism is the use of **administrative obstacles** such as regulations relating to the environment, consumer protection, and labor standards to block importation of goods from foreign countries. These are usually subtle and difficult to detect, because most of the time the pretext seems legitimate—and often it is. But in some cases, it is clear that the standard being upheld is nothing more than a form of protectionism. One example occurred in the 1980s when Japan sought to ban imports of European ski equipment on grounds that Japanese snow was "unique" and that only Japanese-manufactured equipment was suitable for skiing on it.

> **administrative obstacles:** use of environmental, health, or safety regulations to prevent imports from other countries under the pretext of upholding higher standards

4.3 International Trade Agreements

Historically, countries have seldom reduced their barriers to trade unilaterally. Starting in the 1940s, however, many countries became more interested in negotiating mutual reductions in tariffs and quotas. Some trade agreements are "bilateral," meaning that two countries negotiate directly with each other. Other agreements are "multilateral," involving a group of countries. The **World Trade Organization (WTO)**, currently made up of 164 member countries, is the main forum for multilateral trade negotiations. It sets out rules about trade and makes rulings on trade disputes between member countries. The announced goal of the WTO is to ensure that global trade is "fair" so that no country is able to display favoritism toward or discriminate against others.

> **World Trade Organization (WTO):** an international organization that conducts trade negotiations aimed at lowering trade barriers, creates rules to govern trade, and mediates trade disputes between countries

Some critics contend that the WTO's focus on trade alone is too narrow, sometimes undermining other social and environmental goals. For example, labor standards are currently not subject to the WTO's rules, meaning the WTO does nothing to promote the right to bargain collectively or to protect workers from workplace abuse (including forced labor and certain types of child labor).[24] Furthermore, the WTO currently has no specific agreement dealing with environmental protection.[25]

Questions of what will be ruled "fair" or "unfair" by the WTO—and whether such rulings can be enforced—come down to questions of power. Wealthy countries and corporations seek to tilt WTO rules to their favor, while it is harder for less powerful groups to have their voices heard. Many labor, environmental, and social justice groups, for example, charge that the WTO primarily serves the interests of powerful multinational corporations. They worry that WTO negotiations have served to speed up the "race to the bottom" and have also reduced national sovereignty.

Membership of the WTO is voluntary, and the WTO has no sovereignty over countries that wish to ignore its rulings. However, the WTO's rulings are generally followed, as they may otherwise authorize the injured country to retaliate against its adversary by imposing tariffs. This may then precipitate a trade war. Furthermore, not following a WTO ruling impinges on a country's international reputation.

Many countries have also entered into regional trade agreements with their neighbors. Leading examples of such attempts to integrate trade within a geographic area include the European Union (EU), the North American Free Trade Agreement (NAFTA), and Mercosur (Southern Cone Common Market) in South America. In addition, there are dozens of bilateral trade agreements between just two counties. Although each of these regional and bilateral agreements is unique regarding its specific policies, they all share a general commitment to reducing trade barriers such as tariffs or quotas.

There is some debate over whether such regional integration promotes "free trade" or retards it, because it promotes both trade *expansion* (within the region or countries) and trade *diversion* (away from trade with other regions or countries). So while regional and bilateral trade agreements have the explicit objective of lowering trade barriers, they also can implicitly promote trade discrimination against countries outside the membership of any particular trade agreement.

Another complication is that regional and bilateral trade agreements often conflict with WTO rules, as such agreements provide preferential treatment to specific countries. However, exceptions are permitted under WTO rules, normally for developing countries. Differences between developed and developing countries have stalled WTO trade negotiations in recent years, leading many countries to increasingly turn to bilateral and regional trade agreements.

Discussion Questions

1. What international trade issues have been in the news recently? What views are presented by different interest groups in trade debates? Are there any issues that particularly affect your community?
2. How aware are you of the debates between the advocates of "free trade" and the advocates of "protectionism"? Do you have more sympathy for one side over the other? What do you think you need to know more about—in terms of theories or real-world facts—to be able to decide with confidence whether increased world trade, in a specific situation, is a good idea?

5. GLOBALIZATION AND MACROECONOMICS

Globalization involves increasing international linkages through trade and income flows, as well as through flows of people, technological knowledge, cultural products, and the international sharing of common environmental resources. In this section, we provide an analysis of how international trade can affect aggregate demand. We also look at how international flows of money and finance affect a national economy.

> **globalization:** the extension and intensification of international linkages through trade and income flows, as well as flow of people, technology, and culture, and the international sharing of environmental resources, leading to expanded interconnections among different regions

5.1 The Trade Balance: Completing the Macroeconomic Picture

Consumers in the United States may have noticed that a large proportion of the goods they purchase are imported. Many U.S. jobs are in industries that depend on export markets. We often hear concern expressed about the **trade deficit**, which is the excess of imports *(IM)* over exports *(X)*. In 2018, the U.S. trade deficit in goods and services reached $621 billion, an increase of 12.5 percent from 2017.[26] This means that people in the United States were spending much more on foreign goods and services than the United States was selling to foreign buyers. In some other countries, the situation is reversed; China, for example, has a **trade surplus**, where its exports are higher than its imports.[27] How does trade affect the economy at the macroeconomic level?

> **trade deficit:** an excess of imports over exports, causing net exports to be negative
>
> **trade surplus:** an excess of exports over imports, causing net exports to be positive

Recall from the discussion on measuring GDP in Chapter 8 that net exports *(NX)*, which equals exports minus imports, is one of the components of GDP:

GDP = Consumption + Investment + Government Spending + Net Exports

Exports, like investment and government spending, represent a positive contribution to aggregate demand. More exports means more demand for domestically produced goods and services. Imports, however, represent a *leakage* from U.S. aggregate demand—a portion of income that is spent on foreign goods and services. Negative net exports [when *(X) < (IM)*] therefore represent a net subtraction from demand for U.S. output and a net leakage from the circular flow. In Chapters 9 and 10, we identified savings and net taxes as leakages from the circular flow; now we need to add imports as a third source of leakage. Imports are considered leakages because, like saving and taxes, they draw funds away from the domestic income-spending flow. We can also add exports to investment and government spending as a third source of *injection* into the circular flow, as exports add funds to the flow.

A decrease in exports (or an increase in imports) reduces the circular flow of domestic income, spending, and output. An *increase* in net exports, on the other hand, encourages a rise in GDP and employment. For example, an increase in U.S. purchases of foreign cars and a decrease in purchases of domestic cars would lower aggregate demand in the United States (and raise it in other car-exporting countries). But an increase in foreign sales by the U.S. computer software industry would raise U.S. aggregate demand and employment.

Adding exports and imports completes our basic macroeconomic model. We now have a slightly more complex model, with three leakages (saving, taxes, and imports) and three injections (intended investment, government spending, and exports). We can modify our original circular flow diagram to show all these flows (Figure 14.5). Macroeconomic equilibrium thus involves balancing the three types of leakage with the three types of injection.

The multiplier effect for an increase in exports is essentially the same as that for an increase in *I* or *G*. Using the same model as in Chapter 9 (with a multiplier of 5), an increase of exports (X) of $40 million, for example, leads to an increase of $200 million in economic equilibrium.

$$\Delta Y = mult\Delta X$$

We can use exactly the same logic for a lump-sum increase in imports—the effect on equilibrium income just goes in the opposite direction. An increase in imports

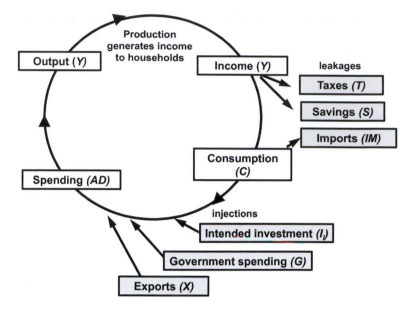

Figure 14.5 *Leakages and Injections in a Complete Macroeconomic Model*

of $40 million would lower the equilibrium level of income by $200 million, and a decrease in imports of $40 million would raise the equilibrium by $200 million.

In an open economy, a portion of any aggregate demand increase goes to stimulate *someone else's economy* via imports. Thus, U.S. consumers who buy imported goods from Canada are creating jobs and income in Canada, not the United States. Does this mean that imports are bad for the United States? Not necessarily. Two other factors are important to consider.

The first is that U.S. consumers and U.S. industry benefit from cheaper imported goods and services, raw materials, and other industrial inputs. The second is that at least some of the money spent on imports is likely to return to the United States either as demand for U.S. exports or as foreign investment in the United States; both of these are generally beneficial to the U.S. economy overall. More generally, the U.S. economy, and overall quality of life in the United States, improves when other countries have healthier economies and diminishes when other countries are suffering economic setbacks. A prosperous world is a happier world for all.

5.2 International Finance

In addition to trade in goods, countries are also linked through exchange of currencies, flows of income, and purchases and sales of real and financial assets across national borders. We introduce this area of international finance next.

Purchasing Power Parity

Purchasing power parity (PPP) refers to the notion that, under certain idealized conditions, the exchange rate between the currencies of two countries should be such that the purchasing power of currencies is equalized. When we cite the "**exchange rate**" for the dollar in terms of a foreign currency, what we mean is the number of units of the foreign currency that you can get in exchange for a dollar. Consider, for example, the exchange rate between U.S. dollars (US$) and euros (€). As of June 2019, US$1 was worth about €0.89. Equivalently, we could say that one euro was worth US$1.12. The two rates are inverses of one another.

> **purchasing power parity (PPP):** the theory that exchange rates should reflect differences in purchasing power among countries
>
> **exchange rate:** the number of units of one currency that can be exchanged for one unit of another currency

If currencies could be traded freely against one another, if goods were freely traded and identical across countries, and if transportation costs were zero, then there would be a strong logic to the theory of purchasing power parity. Suppose that a jacket costs US$200 in New York. If you lived in the United States and changed US$200 into euros, the theory of PPP says that the number of euros you would receive in exchange for your dollars should be exactly enough for you to buy the identical jacket in Paris. If the exchange rate were 0.89 euros per dollar and the jacket cost €178 (= US$200 × 0.89 euros per dollar) in Paris, PPP holds. If economies were as smoothly integrated as assumed in our idealized world, an item should cost the same, no matter where you are. This idea is sometimes referred to as the law of one price.

If this were *not* initially true, there would be considerable pressures leading toward change. For example, suppose that the jacket costs US$200 in New York and €178 in Paris, but the exchange rate is at €1: US$1. Why would anyone buy a jacket in New York, if by changing their money into euros, they could order it from Paris and save US$22? For jackets to be sold in both locations—in this idealized world—the price in New York would have to be bid down, or the price in Paris would have to be bid up, so that the jacket ends up being sold in both locations for the same price.

Of course, in the real world, national economies are not nearly as integrated as this theory assumes. Most obviously, transportation costs matter and are a key reason purchasing a good from overseas does not make always sense. Furthermore, there are many varieties of goods, and markets for goods and services do not work as quickly, smoothly, and rationally as the theory of PPP assumes. This means that converting monetary amounts from one country to another using the prevailing exchange rates may be misleading. Travelers often notice that a particular category of goods, such as books or clothing, are more expensive in one country than another; this could reflect real-world factors such as transportation costs, tariffs, and other imperfections in international markets.

Comparisons of international income levels are often expressed "in PPP terms." Rather than simply using current exchange rates to convert various income levels into a common currency, PPP adjustments try to take into account the fact that the cost of living varies among countries. For example, converting the Mexican average per capita income figure from pesos to dollars would probably understate

465

the living standard of the average Mexican. Even though the currency conversion using the exchange rate is "correct," many goods and services in Mexico are generally less expensive than in the United States. So the dollar equivalent of what the average Mexican earns each year goes much further in Mexico.

> **purchasing power parity (PPP) adjustments:** adjustments to international income statistics to take into account the differences in the cost of living across countries

Currency Exchange Rates

The supply-and-demand model explained in Chapter 3 can be applied to foreign exchange markets, as the exchange rate is really just another kind of price—a price for a national currency. Figure 14.6 shows an idealized foreign exchange market in which U.S. dollars are traded for euros. The quantity of dollars traded is shown on the horizontal axis, and the "price" of a dollar is given on the vertical axis in terms of the number of euros it takes to buy a dollar.

In a well-behaved foreign exchange market, U.S. domestic residents largely determine the supply curve of U.S. dollars, by deciding how many U.S. dollars they are willing to offer in order to buy foreign-produced goods and services and foreign assets. Because foreign-produced goods and services and foreign assets must be paid for in the currency of the country from which they will be purchased, U.S. dollars must first be traded for foreign currencies in the foreign exchange market. The more euros that U.S. residents can get for their dollars, the cheaper European items are to them and the more they will want to buy from Europe rather than from domestic producers. Thus, the higher the exchange rate, the more dollars they will offer on the market. Accordingly, the supply curve in Figure 14.6 slopes upward.

It is residents of other countries who largely determine the demand curve for dollars. They may want to buy goods and services from the United States or to invest in U.S. bonds or businesses. To make these purchases, they must first acquire dollars by selling their own currency. The more euros, or other currencies, they have to *pay* to purchase a dollar, the more likely they are to go somewhere other than the United States for the product that they want, and the lower will be the quantity of dollars that they demand. But if the U.S. dollar is relatively cheap in terms of euros, they will demand more dollars and purchase more U.S. goods and services. So the demand curve in Figure 14.6 slopes downward. Market equilibrium is established at point E.[28]

When the exchange rate falls, we say that the currency has **depreciated**. Suppose, for example, that a European technology firm comes out with a new device for listening to music that everyone wants to buy. In their desire to obtain euros to buy the good, people in the United States will offer more dollars on the foreign exchange market, shifting the supply curve to the right. Excess supply will, as in any other market, cause the price to fall, as shown in Figure 14.7. Commentators may say that the dollar is now "weaker" against the euro. (Conversely, of course, the euro is now "stronger" against the dollar.)

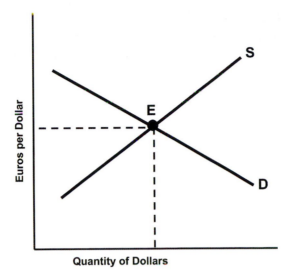

Figure 14.6 *A Foreign Exchange Market for Dollars*

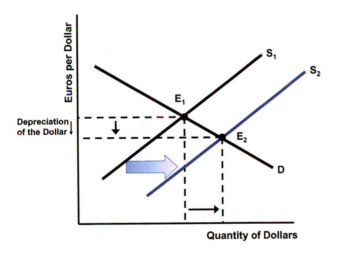

Figure 14.7 *A Supply Shift in a Foreign Exchange Market*

currency depreciation: when a currency becomes less valuable, for example, due to a decrease in demand for a country's exports or an increase in its demand for imports

But an increase in demand for U.S. products or assets would lead to an **appreciation** of the dollar. For example, if investors became eager to buy U.S. real estate, the demand curve for dollars would shift outward and the dollar would appreciate—that is, gain in value. A currency may appreciate or depreciate relative to a specific currency, or it may appreciate or depreciate generally—that is, in relation to all or most other currencies.

> **currency appreciation:** when a currency becomes more valuable—for example, when increased demand for a country's exports causes an increase in demand for its currency

The following four factors are most responsible for the depreciation or appreciation of a country's currency:

1. *Relative prices:* If prices in general rose more rapidly in the United States than in, say, Japan, the Japanese would be less interested in purchasing U.S. goods (so the demand for the dollar declines), and the Americans would be more interested in purchasing Japanese goods (so the supply of dollars increases as Americans exchange more dollars for yen). A rightward shift of supply coupled with a leftward shift of demand unambiguously lowers the yen "price" of dollars, meaning that the dollar depreciates relative to the yen, and the yen appreciates relative to the dollar.

2. *Relative difference in GDP growth rates between trading partners:* If the United States experienced rapid economic growth, Americans would spend more money on imports. If this extra spending on imports is not matched by an increase in U.S. exports, there would be a greater demand for foreign currencies (and a greater supply of dollars), which would cause the dollar to depreciate.

3. *Interest rates:* If the interest rate on, say, the six-month U.S. Treasury bill were higher than the rate on comparable investments in other countries, the United States might attract flows of money from foreign investors seeking to exploit the interest rate differential. Because Treasury bills are denominated in U.S. dollars, the foreign investors would have to exchange their currency for U.S. dollars, raising U.S. dollar demand. The result would be an appreciation in the value of the dollar. As a general rule, then, higher relative interest rates have a tendency to raise demand for the domestic currency and hence lead to a currency appreciation.

4. *Investment attractiveness:* Countries with more stable economies are likely to be more attractive to investors. For example, U.S. government bonds, as well as other investments in the United States such as real estate, are widely regarded as safe and desirable; hence, there is a steady flow of foreign demand for dollars to purchase these assets. This demand for U.S. dollars also causes appreciation of the U.S. dollar.

Note that while the United States has consistently imported more than it has exported, the dollar has *not* weakened. Indeed, it has remained one of most stable currencies. This is partly because of the more general foreign appetite for U.S. assets, such as government bonds, that has maintained a steady and reliable demand for dollars.

In addition to currency needs for trade and investment, many traders buy and sell currency for speculative reasons. Sometimes people buy something not because they need it but because they are betting that its price will go up or down in the future. Speculative buying and selling of currencies often plays a large, and sometimes destabilizing, role in foreign exchange markets, and some countries seek to limit it.

Many confuse domestic currency depreciation with inflation, since the latter is often (correctly) understood to be a decline in the "value" of the currency. But the "value" of a currency has two meanings. Price inflation refers to when a currency weakens in terms of *domestic purchasing power* (i.e., higher average prices mean that the currency is worth relatively less), while depreciation is the weakening of currency in relation to other currencies (a reduction of its *exchange rate*).

The relationship between domestic purchasing power and exchange rates can be analyzed by looking at the **real exchange rate** between currencies. As you may guess, the real exchange rate allows us to account for inflationary changes on exchange rate. For example, if a country experiences 10 percent inflation while its currency exchange rate is unchanged, the real exchange rate, which measures what foreign buyers can get for their money, is said to fall by 10 percent despite the fact the stated (nominal) exchange rate has not changed.

> **real exchange rate:** the exchange rate between two currencies, adjusted for inflation in each country

Most foreign exchange transactions are made in three currencies that are seen as relatively stable and secure: the U.S. dollar, the euro, and the Japanese yen. These currencies are often referred to as being **foreign exchange** due to their general acceptability.

> **foreign exchange:** the class of currencies (generally limited to the dollar, the euro, and the yen) that is broadly acceptable by foreigners in commercial or investment transactions

Our discussion so far has focused on the **flexible** or **floating exchange rate system**, where countries allow their exchange rates to be determined by the forces of supply and demand. However, flexible exchange rates can create significant uncertainties in an economy. A manufacturer may negotiate the future delivery of an imported good, for example, only to find that exchange rate changes make it much more expensive than expected to complete the deal. Foreign exchange markets can also be susceptible to wild swings from speculation. A mere rumor of political upheaval in a country, for example, can sometimes create a rush of capital outflows and cause a drop in the exchange rate.

> **flexible (floating) exchange rate system:** a system in which exchange rates are determined by the market forces of supply and demand

Weak, unstable economies are usually vulnerable to such large capital outflows and frequently suffer from what is known as **capital flight**, which occurs when investors fear investment losses and rush to move their assets to "safer" countries, such as the United States, Japan, or the member countries of the European Union.

Capital flight may represent international investors rushing to take their money out of a country that is temporarily weakened—as happened with South Korea, Indonesia, and the Philippines during the East Asian financial crisis of 1997—or wealthy elites seeking to take money out of their own countries. In many such cases, capital flight has the potential to destabilize economies by making foreign exchange scarce, and governments often go to great lengths to try to stop it.

> **capital flight:** rapid movement of capital assets out of a country

Since it can be hard to maintain normal economic activities when exchange rates fluctuate wildly, many countries have tried to control the value of their currencies in order to create a more predictable environment for foreign transactions. The strictest kind of control is a **fixed exchange rate** system, where a group of countries commits to keeping their currencies trading at fixed ratios over time. Starting in 1944, many countries, including the United States, had fixed exchange rates under what is known as the **Bretton Woods system**, where countries usually set a range around a "target rate" and allowed the "fixed" rate to fluctuate within this range.

> **fixed exchange rate system:** a system in which currencies are traded at fixed ratios
> **Bretton Woods system:** a system of fixed exchange rates established after World War II, lasting until 1972

Over the long term, the target rate can change, at the government's discretion. When a government lowers the level at which it fixes its exchange rate, what is called a **devaluation** occurs, and when it raises it, a **revaluation** takes place. But this system can be undermined if there are too many changes. The Bretton Woods system ended in 1972, when the U.S. dollar—the linchpin of the system—suffered large currency outflows when it was taken off the gold standard (discussed in Chapter 11) and allowed to float.

> **devaluation:** lowering an exchange rate within a fixed exchange rate system
> **revaluation:** raising an exchange rate within a fixed exchange rate system

After the Bretton Woods system ended, many countries moved to a "floating" system, while others tried to exert some management over their currencies by trying to maintain certain target exchange rates, by "pegging" the currency to a particular foreign currency or by letting it "float," but only within certain bounds.

Is devaluation of currency a bad thing? The answer to this question is complex. Devaluation is generally thought to be good for exporters, because it makes the country's goods cheaper abroad. But it also means that people in the country will find that imports are now more expensive. And sometimes devaluation is taken as a sign of instability or poor policy in a country, which can lead to rapid outflows of capital, forcing further devaluation. Countries will always prefer to *plan* a devaluation rather than be pressured into one by circumstances.

5.3 The Balance of Payments

The flows of foreign exchange payments into and out of a country are summed up in its **balance of payments (BOP) account**. Table 14.3 shows the BOP account for the United States in 2018. The top part of the table tallies the **current account**, which tracks flows arising from trade in goods and services, earnings, and transfers. The **trade account** refers exclusively to the portion of the current account related to exports and imports.

> **balance of payments (BOP) account:** the national account that tracks inflows and outflows arising from international trade, earnings, transfers, and transactions in assets
>
> **current account (in the BOP account):** the national account that tracks inflows and outflows arising from international trade, earnings, and transfers
>
> **trade account (part of the current account):** the portion of the current account that tracks inflows and outflows arising exclusively from international trade in goods and services

Table 14.3 U.S. Balance of Payments Account (2018, Billions of Dollars)

Current account

Inflows:	
Payments for exports of goods and services	2,501
Income receipts	1,084
Total	*3,585*
Outflows:	
Payments for imports of goods and services	−3,128
Income payments	−830
Net transfers	−117
Total	*−4,076*
Balance on current account (= inflows − outflows)	−491

Capital account

Outflows (e.g., U.S. lending, portfolio investment, or FDI abroad)	−306
Inflows (e.g., U.S. borrowing from abroad and portfolio investment or FDI into the United States)*	760
Balance on capital account (= inflows − outflows)	454
Official reserve account	−5
Statistical discrepancy	42
Balance of payments	0

Source: U.S. Bureau of Economic Analysis, U.S. International Transactions Accounts Data, table 1, with rearrangements and simplifications by authors.

*Also includes the net value of financial derivatives (financial instruments whose values are linked to an underlying asset, interest rate, or index, such as futures or options).

Various kinds of transactions lead to payments flowing into this country (and to a demand for dollars in the foreign exchange market). When we export goods and services (such as travel, financial services, or intellectual property), we receive payments. Incomes earned abroad (as profits or interest) by U.S. residents also bring in inflows. In 2018, inflows from exports of goods and services totaled $2.5 trillion, and incomes totaled more than $1 trillion, resulting in total inflows in current account of over $3.5 trillion.

Other transactions lead to payments going abroad (and to a supply of dollars to the foreign exchange market). When we import goods and services, we need to make payments to foreign residents. Foreign residents can take home incomes earned in the United States. The BOP account also includes a line for net transfers abroad. The account consists of monies paid out in government foreign aid programs as well as remittances—money sent home to families from the host country by foreign workers. All told, outflows of payments from the United States totaled over $4 trillion in 2018.

The balance on the current account is measured as inflows minus outflows. Because outflows exceeded inflows on the current account in 2018, the United States had a current account deficit. As you can see from Table 14.3, imports of goods exceeded exports, meaning that the United States had a trade deficit. Moreover, because income flows and transfers were relatively balanced, it was the trade deficit that largely accounted for the current account deficit of US$491 billion. In fact, the United States has had trade deficits fairly steadily since about 1980, with the gap between imports and exports widening to about 6 percent of GDP in some years but recently narrowing to about 3 percent (see Box 14.3).

BOX 14.3 U.S. TRADE DEFICIT WIDENS

The U.S. trade deficit for 2018 increased 12.5 percent to $621 billion, complicating efforts by President Trump to fulfill his vow to reduce the gap. Imports increased 7.5 percent to $3,121 billion, and exports increased by 6.3 percent to $2,500 billion. In percentage terms, however, the trade deficit was at a fairly moderate level of about 3 percent of GDP.[29]

In 2018, the United States imported more foreign-made cars, computers, and other consumer goods, much of which was produced in China. The trade deficit in goods with China widened by $44 billion and hit a record $419 billion in 2018. U.S. trade deficits in goods also increased with other major trading partners, including Mexico (by $11 billion) and the European Union (by $18 billion). Though China, Mexico, and the EU account for only about 54 percent of U.S. goods imports, they made up 86 percent of the increased trade deficits.[30]

Several factors explain this rise in trade deficits in 2018. Slowdowns in the economies of China and some European countries reduced demands for U.S. goods. Additionally, the dollar strengthened in the global currency markets, making it cheaper for Americans to buy foreign goods and more expensive for foreign customers to buy American goods. U.S. politicians have repeatedly hinted or stated outright that China unfairly intervenes in the foreign exchange market by keeping the value of its own currency artificially low. In 2018, China allowed its currency to fall by roughly 10 percent against the dollar, which also explains part of the increased trade deficit between the United States and China.[31]

How can a country steadily import more than it exports? If you, personally, wanted to buy something that costs more than you have the income to pay for, you might take out a loan or perhaps sell something that you own, such as your car. Likewise, countries can finance a trade deficit by borrowing or by selling assets; these sorts of transactions are listed in the **capital account**.

> **capital account (in the BOP account):** the account that tracks flows arising from international transactions in assets

To the extent the United States *lends* abroad (e.g., when the government extends loans to other countries, foreigners borrow from U.S. banks, or people in the United States buy foreign bonds), capital *outflows* are generated. This terminology may be confusing. Think about capital flows as going *in the direction of* the country that receives "the cash" or the power to purchase goods and *away from* the country that provides the cash or purchasing power. In the case of a loan, the borrower received "the cash," while the creditor receives a bond or other security representing a promise to repay; thus, a loan is an *outflow* from the lender and an *inflow* to the borrower. Similarly, if a U.S. firm engaged in investment in the stocks or bonds of a foreign country or company or in the purchase of all or part of business in another country (foreign direct investment), it is the people abroad who would end up with "the cash," while the U.S. company would receive the asset. This is also counted as an outflow from the United States. From Table 14.3, we can see that the United States had US$306 billion in capital outflows during 2018.

As we have noted, a country receives capital *inflows* when it borrows from foreigners or when foreigners purchase assets there. In the case of the United States, many people abroad buy U.S. government bonds and put funds into bank accounts. These are both capital *inflows*—the sellers of the U.S. securities and the U.S. banks receive "the cash." Likewise, if a foreign multinational bought an interest in a U.S. publishing company, it would be a capital *inflow*. Another large source of inflows is foreign investment in U.S. real estate. In 2018, the United States received just about US$760 billion in capital inflows.

As with the current account, the balance on the capital account is measured as inflows minus outflows. Thus, the United States had a US$454 billion capital account surplus in 2018. Therefore, it was the willingness of foreigners to buy U.S. securities (and other assets) that financed the deficit in the current account.

Many commentators worry that the United States is putting itself in a vulnerable position by relying on borrowing to "spend beyond its means" on imports. Notice that *present-day capital inflows* create the obligation to pay *future income outflows:* the interest due in the future on U.S. government bonds sold abroad this year, and future profits made by firms located in the United States that were bought by foreign parties this year, will become part of "income payments" in the outflows section of the current account in years to come.

Finally, we have what is known as the **official reserve account** in Table 14.3. It represents the foreign exchange market operations of the country's central bank. Consider a developing country, say, Indonesia, that needs to import some goods and services. In order to pay for its imports, it has to exchange its currency, the rupiah, to foreign exchange—that is, dollars, euros, or yen. This presents a problem for Indonesia, because it cannot produce its own dollars. It can, however, obtain them.

> **official reserve account:** the account reflecting the foreign exchange market operations of a country's central bank

For example, when Indonesia exports coffee, it can insist on being paid not in rupiah but in foreign exchange such as dollars. In this way, it has a strong currency available to pay for its imports. It works the same way with the capital account. If Indonesia has creditors to whom it owes interest that require payment in foreign exchange, it obtains this foreign exchange not only by exporting coffee and other products but also by attracting foreign capital, which it also insists should come in the form of foreign exchange.

Bank Indonesia, the country's central bank, holds reserves of foreign currency so that it can make up for a balance of payments deficit if necessary. Of course, it cannot do so indefinitely. If the central bank runs short of foreign exchange reserves, the country will have to cut back on imports. But in the short term, the central bank can supply foreign exchange to cover a balance of payments deficit or acquire foreign exchange if there is a balance of payments surplus. If the central bank supplies foreign exchange, it is recorded as a positive item in the official reserve accounts; if it acquires foreign exchange, it is recorded as a negative item.

In 2018, the United States reduced its official reserve account by about US$5 billion, which means that the Fed's holdings of these assets increased by this amount. If this is confusing, think of it as the negative sign signifying that the Fed removed US$5 billion in reserve assets (mostly foreign exchange) from the U.S. economy.

One additional caveat is the statistical discrepancy. It represents an inability of the BEA to make the accounts balance precisely, given problems in the quality of the data and some small items in the accounts that we do not get into here. Allowing for this discrepancy, the balances in the current account, the capital account, and the official reserve account *must* add up to zero (the "balance of payments"). The difference between the current and capital accounts *must* be "balanced" by a flow of foreign exchange to or from the central bank. Any gap can be fully attributed to measurement error, which is what the statistical discrepancy reflects.

Discussion Questions

1. Is it better for the United States to have a strong or weak dollar? What are the advantages and disadvantages of each?
2. Is a nation's balance of payments analogous to a company or household income statement? Is it necessarily a bad thing for a country's trade balance to be in deficit?

REVIEW QUESTIONS

1. How does specialization lead to greater productivity, according to Adam Smith? Why does a larger market promote specialization?
2. How is comparative advantage different from absolute advantage?
3. How do we determine the opportunity cost of producing something in the Ricardian model of trade?
4. How do we determine which country has the comparative advantage in the production of something in the Ricardian model of trade?
5. What is the theory of "factor price equalization"? Does the evidence tend to support it?
6. What are the potential benefits for a country in engaging in international trade?
7. What are some of the potential downsides that might occur by engaging in international trade?
8. What are some of the relationships between trade and the environment?
9. Explain the relationship between trade and redistribution.
10. What is globalization?
11. What are the different forms of "trade protectionism," and why do countries often utilize them?
12. What are some of the potential gains and costs of implementing industrial policies?
13. What does the World Trade Organization do?
14. What is the theory of "purchasing power parity"?
15. Who creates the supply of a currency on the foreign exchange market? Who creates the demand?
16. Draw a carefully labeled graph illustrating a depreciation of the dollar against the euro.
17. Distinguish between floating and fixed exchange rate systems.
18. What are the two accounts in the balance of payments account, and what do they reflect?
19. How and why is an imbalance (surplus or deficit) in the current account related to an imbalance in the capital account?

EXERCISES

1. Hereland and Thereland are two small countries. Each currently produces both milk and corn, and they do not trade. If Hereland puts all its resources into milk, it can produce 2 tanker truckloads, while if it puts all its resources in corn production, it can produce 8 tons. Thereland can produce either 2 loads of milk or 2 tons of corn. (Both can also produce any combination on a straight line in between.)

   a. Draw and label production-possibilities frontiers for Hereland and Thereland.
   b. Suppose that Hereland's citizens would like 1 truckload of milk and 6 tons of corn. Can Hereland produce this?
   c. Suppose that Thereland's citizens would like 1 load of milk and 2 tons of corn. Can Thereland produce this?
   d. Fill in the blank: "For each truckload of milk that Hereland makes, it must give up making ___ tons of corn."
   e. Fill in the blank: "For each truckload of milk that Thereland makes, it must give up making ___ tons of corn."
   f. Which country has a comparative advantage in producing milk?

g. Create a table similar to Table 14.1, showing how Hereland and Thereland could enter into a trading relationship in order to meet their citizens' consumption desires as described in (b) and (c).

h. Suppose that you are an analyst working for the government of Hereland. Write a few sentences, based on the previous analysis, advising your boss about whether to undertake trade negotiations with Thereland.

i. Would your advice change if you knew that unemployment in Hereland is high and that retraining corn farmers to be dairy farmers, or vice versa, is very difficult to do?

j. Would your advice change if Thereland insisted in trade negotiations that 1 truckload of milk be exchanged for exactly 4 tons of corn?

2. Continuing the Ricardian story from Section 2.1 of this chapter, suppose that England were, after a while, to put a tariff on imports of Portuguese wine. Since we only have wine and cloth in this story, we will have to (somewhat unrealistically) express this tax in terms of units of goods rather than units of currency. Say that England demands that Portugal "pay a tariff of 40 units of cloth" if it wants to sell 100 units of wine. Or, in other words, England now says that it will give Portugal only *60 units of cloth* instead of 100 in exchange for 100 units of wine.

a. With production unchanged, what would exchange and consumption be like under these modified terms of trade? (Create a table like Table 14.1.)

b. Does England benefit from instituting this tariff?

c. Would Portugal voluntarily agree to continue trading with these changed terms of trade? (Assume that Portugal has no power to change the terms of trade—it can only accept England's deal or go back to consuming within its own PPF.)

d. If trade is voluntary, does that mean it is *fair?* Discuss.

3. Suppose that, due to rising interest rates in the United States, the Japanese increase their purchases of U.S. securities.

a. Illustrate in a carefully labeled supply-and-demand diagram how this would affect the foreign exchange market and the exchange rate expressed in terms of yen per dollar.

b. Is this an appreciation or depreciation of the dollar?

c. Would we say that *the yen* is now "stronger"? Or "weaker"?

4. Determine, for each of the following, whether it would appear in the *current account* or *capital account* section of the U.S. balance of payments accounts and whether it would represent an *inflow* or an *outflow*.

a. Payments are received for U.S.-made airplanes sold to Thailand

b. A resident of Nigeria buys a U.S. government savings bond

c. A U.S. company invests in a branch in Australia

d. A Japanese company takes home its profits earned in the United States

e. The U.S. government pays interest to a bondholder in Canada

5. Match each concept in Column A with a definition or example in Column B.

Column A		Column B	
a.	Tariff	1.	Makes international incomes comparable by accounting for differences in the cost of living
b.	Import substitution	2.	When a region competes by providing a low-cost business environment, resulting in deterioration of labor or environmental or safety standards

c.	Purchasing power parity adjustment	3.	An organization charged with facilitating international trade
d.	Race to the bottom	4.	A rise in the value of a currency in a floating exchange rate system
e.	Dumping	5.	The theory that trade should eventually lead to input prices that are equal across countries
f.	Quota	6.	A tax levied on an internationally traded item
g.	Exporting pollution	7.	Occurs when a country reduces its own manufacturing and relies more on goods manufactured elsewhere
h.	WTO	8.	The use of environmental, health, or safety regulations to prevent imports from other countries under the pretext of upholding higher standards
i.	Factor price equalization	9.	The deliberate promotion of domestic good production to reduce reliance on imports
j.	Comparative advantage	10.	An industry that needs protection until it is able to compete
k.	Currency appreciation	11.	Selling goods abroad at a price that is below the cost of production
l.	Administrative obstacles	12.	Putting a quantity limit on imports or exports
m.	Revaluation	13.	Putting a tariff on orange juice imports to help Florida orange growers
n.	Protectionism	14.	A country is relatively more efficient in the production of some good(s)
o.	Infant industry	15.	A rise in the value of a currency under a fixed exchange rate system

NOTES

1. This means that, contrary to our earlier guns versus butter example, Portugal does *not* give up more and more of, say, wine as it increasingly specializes in the production of cloth. Here we are simplifying in order to more easily illustrate the advantage of trade.

2. Yan, Sophia. 2017. "'Made in China' Isn't So Cheap Anymore, and That Could Spell Headache for Beijing." cnbc.com, February 27. www.cnbc.com/2017/02/27/chinese-wages-rise-made-in-china-isnt-so-cheap-anymore.html

3. Mitra, Arup, Chandan Sharma, and Marie-Ange Véganzonès-Varoudakis. 2014. "Trade Liberalization, Technology Transfer, and Firms' Productive Performance: The Case of Indian Manufacturing." *Journal of Asian Economics*, 33: 1–15.

4. Polachek, Solomon W., and Carlos Seiglie. 2006. "Trade, Peace and Democracy: An Analysis of Dyadic Dispute." IZA Discussion Paper No. 2170, June.

5. Harris, Jonathan, and Brian Roach. 2017. *Environmental and Natural Resource Economics: A Contemporary Approach*, 4th edition. Routledge, London. Chapter 21.

6. New York Times Editorial. 2012. "Race to the Bottom." *New York Times*, December 5. www.nytimes.com/2012/12/06/opinion/race-to-the-bottom.html

7. Lucier, Cristina A., and Brian J. Gareau. 2015. "From Waste to Resources?" *Journal of World-Systems Research*, 21(2): 495–520.

8. Organisation for Economic Co-Operation and Development (OECD). 2010. "Globalisation, Transport and the Environment." OECD Publication Brief.

9. Kellenberg, D. 2015. "The Economics of the International Trade of Waste." *Annual Review of Resource Economics*, 7(1): 109–125.

10. Rodrik, Dani. 2011. *The Globalization Paradox*. W. W. Norton & Company, New York.

11. Westerman, Ashley. 2017. "4 Years after Rana Plaza Tragedy, What's Changed for Bangladeshi Garment Workers?" National Public Radio (NPR), April 30.

12. "Outrageous New Minimum Wage Announced in Bangladesh." Clean Clothes Campaign, September 21, 2018. https://archive.cleanclothes.org/news/2018/09/21/outrageous-new-minimum-wage-announced-in-bangladesh

13. European Parliament. 2014. "Workers' Conditions in the Textile and Clothing Sector: Just an Asian Affair?" Briefing, August.

14. Kiefer, David, and Codrina Rada. 2015. "Profit Maximising Goes Global: The Race to the Bottom." *Cambridge Journal of Economics*, 39(5): 1333–1350.

15. ActionAid. 2006. "Under the Influence." Johannesburg, South Africa. www.actionaid.org.uk/sites/default/files/doc_lib/174_6_under_the_influence_final.pdf

16. Lynch, David J., Taylor Telford, Damian Paletta, and Gerry Smith. "U.S. Prepares to Slap Tariffs on Remaining Chinese Imports, Which Could Add Levies on Roughly $300 Billion in Additional Goods." *The Washington Post*, May 13.

17. Bureau of Economic Analysis, Data on International Transactions, Table 2.2 and Table 3.2.

18. Swanson, Ana. "Businesses Plead to Stop More China Tariffs: They Expect to Be Ignored." *New York Times*, June 17.

19. Cohn, Scott. "How the Trade War with China Could Crush California's $2.7 Trillion Economy and Hurt Other States." CNBC, June 18.

20. Smialek, Jeanna, Jim Tankersley, and Jack Ewing. "Global Economic Growth Is Already Slowing: The U.S. Trade War Is Making It Worse." *New York Times*, June 18.

21. Data based on the Historical Statistics of the United States 1789–1945, U.S. Department of Commerce, Bureau of the Census. https://en.wikipedia.org/wiki/Tariffs_in_United_States_history

22. Data from World Bank, World Development Indicators database.

23. World Trade Organization (WTO). No date. *Trade and Tariffs*. www.wto.org/english/thewto_e/20y_e/wto_20_brochure_e.pdf

24. World Trade Organization. No date. *Press Brief*. www.wto.org/english/thewto_e/minist_e/min96_e/labstand.htm

25. The World Trade Organization. No date. *Trade and the Environment*. www.wto.org/english/tratop_e/envir_e/envir_e.htm

26. U.S. Census Bureau. 2019. "U.S. International Trade in Goods and Services, Exhibit 1." https://www.census.gov/foreign-trade/Press-Release/current_press_release/exh1.pdf

27. Based on data from World Integrated Trade Solution, 2019. World Bank.

28. For simplicity, this example ignores other sources of supply and demand for currencies, such as foreign lending and currency speculation.

29. Bureau of Economic Analysis. 2019. "U.S. International Transactions, 4th Quarter and Year 2018." March 27. www.bea.gov/news/2019/us-international-transactions-4th-quarter-and-year-2018

30. Kiernan, Paul, and Josh Zumbrun. 2019. "U.S. Posts Record Annual Trade Deficit." *The Wall Street Journal*, March 6.

31. Scott, Robert E. 2019. "Record U.S. Trade Deficit in 2018 Reflects Failure of Trump's Trade Policies." Working Economics Blog, Economic Policy Institute, March 7.

Chapter 15

How Economies Grow and Develop

The median income in the world today is about equal to that of the United States in the early 1900s. Although billions of people still live in severe poverty, some formerly poor countries such as South Korea have achieved high levels of economic development, and others such as China and India are now experiencing rapid growth. In this chapter, we evaluate how economies grow and why some countries are successful at promoting development, while others seem to be "stuck" at low levels of development. Our discussion here is mainly focused on developing countries, where there is a clear need for improving people's access to basic needs for food, shelter, health care, and education. But the term "development" can be used for *all* kinds of positive economic change and could be applied to developed countries. That is an issue to which we return in Chapter 16, where we will take a look at the changes that will be required both in wealthier countries and in rapidly developing countries if the global economy is to achieve a sustainable balance with its ecological context.

1. ECONOMIC GROWTH AND DEVELOPMENT

What do people mean by development? Standard economic models focus on GDP per capita as the key measure of economic progress. However, as we have discussed extensively in Chapter 8, focusing only on GDP values will leave us with a narrow measure of well-being, since it disregards important aspects like quality of health care, education, housing, and environmental considerations, as well as inequalities among genders, classes, and regions. Growth in GDP may be best seen as a means to achieve some improvements in human well-being, but it is not the ultimate goal in itself. Economists have increasingly recognized the need to pursue broad-based human development and to formulate development policies that balance the goal of GDP growth with promotion of human development.

Such an approach has been championed by Nobel laureate Amartya Sen, for whom the relevant concept is not *economic development* but *human development*. The **human development** approach (introduced in Chapter 8) is geared toward meeting basic needs and also encompassing other dimensions of a worthwhile life. Sen defines development as the process of enlarging people's choices, whatever it is that people have reason to value. He has proposed that one's **capabilities**—that is, the opportunities that people have to be well nourished, decently housed, have access to education, and live lives that they find worthwhile—are more important than a simple income measure. This requires a multidimensional approach that focuses on adequate access to clean water, nutrition, shelter, health care, and education, along with environmental sustainability, economic equality, and gender equality.

> **human development:** an approach to development that stresses the provision of basic needs such as food, shelter, and health care
> **capabilities:** the opportunities that people have to pursue important aspects of well-being, such as being healthy and having access to education

While we follow this multidimensional approach in our discussion of development, we begin by looking at two of the most commonly used indicators of economic progress—economic growth and poverty. At least during the earlier stages of development, rising production and income levels go hand in hand with improvements in quality of life. Also, measures of poverty can help us understand both how countries are doing in terms of general development and how effectively the benefits of development are being distributed.

1.1 Standard Economic Growth Theory

Recall from Chapter 8 that economic growth is defined as an increase in real GDP (i.e., GDP adjusted for inflation) and is mathematically expressed as the percentage change in real GDP from one year to the next. It is often more meaningful to focus on the growth rate of GDP *per capita*—that is, output *per person*—rather than simply on overall output, because the growth rate of GDP per capita indicates the actual increase in average income being experienced by the people of the country. Mathematically, GDP per capita is expressed as:

GDP per capita = GDP/population

The growth rates of GDP, population, and GDP per capita are related in the following way (where the sign ≈ means "approximately equals"):

Growth rate of GDP per capita ≈ Growth rate of GDP − growth rate of population

Thus, for example, an economy that has a GDP growth rate of 4 percent and a population growth rate of 2 percent would have a per capita GDP growth rate of approximately 2 percent. If a country had a 2 percent GDP growth rate but a 3 percent population growth rate, its per capita GDP growth rate would actually be negative, at −1 percent. The people would on average be getting poorer each year, even though the overall economy was growing. Thus, for people's incomes on average to increase over time, the GDP growth rate must exceed the rate of population growth.

In terms of the aggregate supply and demand model discussed in Chapter 12, economic growth can be shown as a rightward shift of the aggregate supply (*AS*), increasing the economy's maximum capacity (Figure 15.1). If the increase in

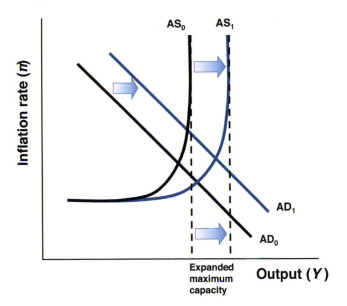

Figure 15.1 *Economic Growth in the AS/AD Model*

aggregate supply took place without any shift in aggregate demand (*AD*), its effects would include growth in output and a declining rate of inflation. In practice, however, economic growth is almost always accompanied by an increase in aggregate demand. Thus, a more typical pattern for economic growth would be for *both* the *AD* and *AS* curves to shift to the right, as shown in Figure 15.1. In this case, output clearly rises, but the effect on inflation is ambiguous.

1.2 Experiences of Economic Growth Around the World

Much of the economic development that has shaped the world we know today occurred during the twentieth century. As shown in Figure 15.2, gross world product has increased about fivefold since 1965 (in inflation-adjusted terms). This was accompanied by increases in energy use and food production, both by a factor of about 3.5. Even though world population more than doubled over the period 1965–2017, food production and living standards grew more rapidly than population, leading to a steady increase in per capita income.

This growth in income has been unevenly distributed among countries. Table 15.1 shows the per capita national incomes and rates of economic growth for selected countries and income category groups during 1990–2017. The table gives national income in purchasing power parity terms, which compare countries based on the relative buying power of incomes.[1]

We see that some countries achieved less than 1 percent annual per capita economic growth, and others achieved more than 4 percent, with China in the lead at a sizzling 8.7 percent. Some already poor countries, such as Haiti and Democratic Republic of Congo, are heading in the opposite direction and becoming even poorer. The average growth rate of the middle-income countries appears to be well above

481

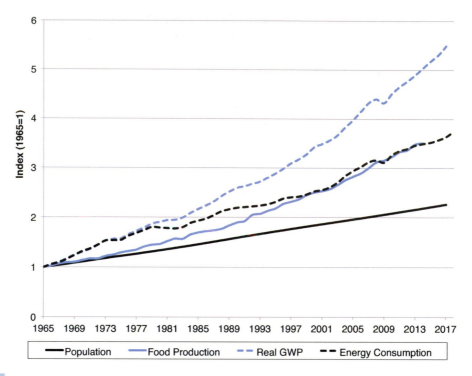

Figure 15.2 *Global Growth in Population, Food Production, Economic Production, and Energy Consumption, 1965–2017*

Sources: World Bank, World Development Indicators; BP, Statistical Review of World Energy 2018.

Notes: GWP is gross world product. Global food production index not available from 2015 to 2017.

Table 15.1 Income, Growth, and Population Comparisons, Selected Countries and Country Groups

Country or Category	GDP per capita, 2017 (PPP, 2011, International $)	Percent growth in GDP per capita (annual average, 1990–2017)	Percent of world population (2017)
High Income	*43,162*	*1.4*	*16.5*
United States	54,470	1.4	4.3
Japan	39,010	1.1	1.7
France	38,807	1.1	0.9
South Korea	35,938	4.5	0.7
Middle Income	*11,116*	*3.2*	*73.7*
Russia	24,790	0.7	1.9
Brazil	14,137	1.0	2.8
China	15,308	8.7	18.4
India	6,513	4.6	17.8
Low Income	*1,961*	*0.9*	*9.7*
Bangladesh	3,523	3.7	2.2
Haiti	1,653	−0.8	0.1
Ethiopia	1,729	3.7	1.4
Congo, DR	808	−2.1	1.1

Source: World Bank, World Development Indicators database, 2019.

that of either the high or low income. This is primarily a result of rapid growth in China and India, which together account for more than half of the population of all middle-income countries.

Traditionally, many economists have argued that the economies of low- and middle-income countries should grow faster than those of high-income countries. One line of reasoning for this view, among others, is that poorer countries should be able to take advantage of technologies and knowledge that have already been developed in wealthier countries and move toward the path of development. It is also argued that a given increase in the manufactured capital stock should lead to a greater increase in output in a country that is capital poor than in a country that is already capital rich. Therefore, as developing countries build up their capital stock, it is just a matter of time until they "catch up" with the more developed countries. This idea that poorer countries are on a path to "catch up" is often referred to as **convergence**.

> **convergence** (in economic growth): the idea that underlying economic forces will cause poorer countries and regions to "catch up" with richer ones

Some studies of GDP per capita growth rates, using data such as that in Table 15.1, emphasize that the low-income countries have grown more rapidly, on average, than the high-income ones. However, if we count each country equally, the average annual growth rate of real GDP per capita (PPP) in 1990–2017 was 0.9 percent in the low-income countries, 3.2 percent in the middle-income countries, and 1.4 percent in the high-income countries—suggesting convergence between currently middle- and high-income countries but further divergence between low-income countries and others.

With their recent high growth rates, China and India represent the "good news" side of the development story. Although many people in these two very populous countries remain very poor, at least the trend is going in the right direction, with a large number of people being lifted out of poverty in recent decades. The countries of sub-Saharan Africa, which have been hit particularly hard by war and depletion of natural resources, account for a substantial proportion of the very low and negative growth rates. This is the "bad news" side of the contemporary development, as some poor countries have become even poorer in recent decades.

1.3 Defining Poverty

One of the key goals of economic growth is eradicating poverty. The simplest way of defining poverty is according to average income, or GDP per capita, but averages tell nothing about the distribution of income. An average GDP per capita of US$9,000 could exist in a country where most people earn around US$9,000 as well as in a country where the majority of people live in dire poverty, and a small percentage are quite rich. We must therefore consider some other poverty measures to better understand where economic growth is most needed and what role it plays in development.

Headcount and Poverty Line

One common approach is to define poverty as the percentage of the population below what is known as the **poverty line**. One international poverty line that is often used as a minimum standard to escape extreme poverty is US$1.90 per day. According to this measure, many developing countries have succeeded in reducing the incidence of poverty. For example, from 1981 to 2017, Brazil had an average annual growth rate in per capita GDP of only 0.8 percent, yet this was sufficient to reduce its poverty rate from 21.4 to 4.8 percent (Table 15.2). Countries with higher growth rates, such as China and India, have experienced even larger declines in poverty rates. But growth in GDP per capita does not guarantee a decline in poverty rates. Of the countries shown, Rwanda experienced only a slight decline, and Nigeria actually saw an *increase* in poverty, despite the growth rates in both the countries averaging around 2 percent.

> **poverty line:** the income threshold below which members of a population are classified as poor

This comparison among countries is made relatively easy through use of a universal standard, such as the US$1.90-per-day threshold. Almost all countries also have their own (national) poverty line and calculate their national poverty rate based on it. The threshold for the United States, for example, is about US$25,000 per year for a family of four. According to the U.S. Census Bureau, an estimated 39.7 million (12.3 percent) Americans lived in poverty in 2017 (see Box 15.1).

Table 15.2 Growth Rates and Changes in Poverty Rates, Select Countries

	Period	Annual growth rate in per capita GDP, %	Poverty rate at beginning of period, %	Poverty rate at end of period, %
Bangladesh	1983–2016	3.1	29.9	14.8
Brazil	1981–2017	0.8	21.4	4.8
China	1990–2015	8.9	66.2	0.7
Egypt	1990–2015	2.3	7.4	1.3
Ethiopia	1995–2015	5.0	71.7	27.3
India	1983–2011	4.1	54.8	21.2
Indonesia	1984–2017	3.5	71.4	5.7
Mexico	1984–2016	0.8	8.1	2.5
Nigeria	1985–2009	2.1	53.3	53.5
Philippines	1985–2015	1.8	28.1	7.8
Rwanda	1984–2016	2.5	63	55.5
South Africa	1993–2014	1.5	31.7	18.9
Thailand	1981–2017	4.1	19.6	0

Source: World Bank, World Development Indicators database, 2019.

Note: The poverty rate is based on a poverty line of $1.90 per day (2011 PPP).

BOX 15.1 EXTREME POVERTY IN THE UNITED STATES

We often relate extreme poverty to countries in Africa and Asia where large numbers of people suffer from inadequate access to necessities of food, shelter, and clothing. But it is also true that a small proportion of the world's poorest live in high-income countries. Data from the World Bank show that about 3.2 million extremely poor people live in the United States and another 3.3 million people live in other rich countries like Italy, Japan, and Spain.

A 2017 report from the United Nations on the state of those living in extreme poverty in the United States gives an alarming picture, with accounts of unpayable debt and incarceration, as well as diseases and death resulting from lack of access to basic human services such as sanitation, shelter, and health care. The report shows that the United States has the highest infant mortality and highest prevalence of obesity among the OECD countries, and it ranks 35th out of the 37 OECD countries in terms of poverty and inequality.[2] Economist John Komlos writes:

> In 2017, a two-person household [in the U.S.] was considered poor if its total income was below $17,000 per annum. That meant that 45 million people were living in poverty, 15% of the population, as high a rate as in 1966, one year after Medicare began under the Johnson administration. . . . The poverty rate among U.S. children—19.6%—is about twice the mean rate prevailing in rich countries and seven times as high as in Denmark.[3]

In light of these findings, Nobel laureate Angus Deaton argues for the need to recognize America's poverty problem in the global context. He points out that the state of poverty in the United States looks even worse if we consider a need-based poverty line, based on the argument that the poor living in cold and urban regions in a developed country have more basic requirements than the poor in India, who may be able to survive on subsistence agriculture and less expenditure on clothing and shelter. Based on estimates from Oxford economist Robert Allen, a more realistic comparison would be to match the global poverty threshold of US$1.90 per day to $4 per day in the United States, which brings the number of poor living under this threshold in the United States to over 5.3 million.[4]

Why does extreme poverty exist in the United States, one of the richest, most powerful, and most technologically advanced countries in the world? The UN report on extreme poverty cites as some of the underlying causes of poverty issues such as physical or mental disabilities, family breakdown, illness, or job market discrimination, along with declining social mobility, where those born in poverty are trapped there because of their lack of access to opportunities.[5] To this we could add that the incidence of poverty is related to the quality of the social safety net, in particular, policy choices in regard to the level of unemployment benefits, subsidized health care, and housing.

Both national and universal poverty lines are typically referred to as "headcount" measures, since they simply require "counting" people who fall below the poverty line. But measuring poverty based exclusively on income reflects only a small part of the poverty picture. More broad-based measures of poverty include other aspects of life as well, and we will examine some of these next.

The Multidimensional Poverty Index

The multidimensional poverty index is based on Amartya Sen's capabilities approach. It was developed in 2010 by the Oxford Poverty and Human Development Initiative for the United Nations Development Programme's *Human Development Report*. The MPI considers ten elements that are critical for a decent life: years of schooling, school attendance, child mortality, nutrition, electricity, drinking water, sanitation, flooring, cooking fuel, and asset ownership. Although these 10 elements are not the only essentials, they are good proxies for essential categories of well-being; people who do not have these can reasonably be considered deprived, or poor.

According to a 2018 report from the Oxford Poverty and Human Development Initiative, a total of 1.3 billion people are living in multidimensional poverty. This is about 23 percent of the people living in the 105 countries surveyed. Multidimensional poverty is particularly acute in sub-Saharan Africa and South Asia—about 83 percent of all the multidimensionally poor live in these two regions.

In most cases, the percentage of population that is "MPI poor" is greater than the percentage of population that is income poor. Only 15 out of 110 countries, including Philippines, Lesotho, Maldives, and South Africa, had more people living under US$1.90 a day than those counted as being in multidimensional poverty. Some of the largest discrepancies between the levels of "income poor" and "MPI poor" were in African countries like Ethiopia, Niger, and Chad. Such

Table 15.3 Population in Multidimensional Poverty and Income Poverty

Country	Year	Population in multidimensional poverty (%)	Population living below income poverty line, PPP, $1.90 a day (%)
Bangladesh	2014	41.1	14.8
China	2014	4.0	1.4
Ethiopia	2016	83.8	26.7
Ghana	2014	28.9	12.0
Haiti	2012	47.6	23.5
India	2015/16	27.5	21.2
Mexico	2016	6.3	2.5
Nepal	2016	35.3	15.0
Niger	2012	90.6	44.5
Philippines	2013	7.4	8.3
Uganda	2016	56.8	35.9
Vietnam	2014	5.0	2.6

Source: Human Development Report, 2018.

discrepancies reveal the limitations of relying exclusively on income-based poverty measures.

All of this provides an overview of experiences of growth and poverty levels around the world. We will now look at different theories on development and use specific examples to explain the process of economic development.

Discussion Questions

1. How important to you are your income goals relative to your other goals? If you were asked whether each of the following goals was absolutely necessary, very important, somewhat important, not very important, or not at all important for you, how would you answer?

Earning a lot of money	Having an interesting job
Seeing a lot of the world	Helping other people who are in need
Becoming well educated	Living a long time
Having a good marriage	Having good friends
Having a good relationship with your children	Having strong religious faith

2. Do you think the categories in the multidimensional index of poverty do a good job of reflecting who is truly poor? If you were asked to add one item to this list, what would it be?

2. ECONOMIC DEVELOPMENT IN THE WORLD TODAY

As shown in Figure 15.2, the last 50 years have been a period of remarkable economic growth, worldwide. The United States and Europe had a head start in what is now known as development, as they had already benefited from many decades of economic growth by the middle of the 20th century. Hong Kong, Japan, and South Korea, whose growth took off after 1950, still had the advantage of being relatively early in the game; they were able to take advantage of a global trade regime that was highly advantageous for their combination of investment in manufactured and human capital. Other countries, mostly in sub-Saharan Africa, South Asia, and the Caribbean, on the other hand, continue to struggle with problems of poverty and low levels of development.

2.1 Early Experiences and Theories of Development

The idea of economic development only became formalized in the mid-twentieth century, as the world's colonial empires began to break down and the more industrialized countries gradually took on a changed set of attitudes toward the parts of the world that had not experienced industrialization.[6] During the period when European nations controlled colonies in the rest of the world—from the fifteenth century through the middle of the twentieth century—the economic relations between colonies and their rulers had been dominated by the desire of the ruling countries to enrich themselves. This was done first through extraction of raw materials and second through the creation of markets for goods that colonial countries wanted to export to their colonies. By the mid-twentieth century, resistance to imperial domination and strong movements for independence had made it impossible for the ruling countries to maintain their control. Some scholars argue, however, that the former colonial powers have continued to use political and economic power to maintain their dominant position.

As noted previously, some countries had a head start in development, as early as the eighteenth and nineteenth centuries. This early phase of development was largely driven by the **Industrial Revolution**, involving a dramatic transformation in the nature of economic production through a process of rapid social, technological, and economic change. The Industrial Revolution began in Britain in the late eighteenth century, and by the nineteenth and early twentieth centuries, it was well along in much of Western Europe and the "early industrializing" countries, such as the United States, Canada, and Australia.

> **Industrial Revolution:** a process of social, technological, and economic change, beginning in Western Europe in the eighteenth century, that developed and applied new methods of production and work organization, resulting in a great increase in output per worker

It is useful to understand the steps involved in creating the Industrial Revolution, taking Britain as the prime case and first mover. First, new agricultural techniques, along with new kinds of tools and machines, made agriculture more productive. Because farmers became more productive, fewer workers were needed to produce food, and many rural workers migrated to urban areas. Second, the invention and application of technologies using fossil-fuel energy (especially coal) contributed not only to the productivity gains in agriculture but also to growth in the number of factory jobs and the development of transportation networks. Third, Britain's increasing reliance on other countries, including its extensive network of colonies, for supplies of raw materials and as markets for its goods was critical in the development of its industrial sector. Britain imported cotton fiber from India, for example. It discouraged the further development of cotton manufacturing within India by putting high import tariffs on Indian-made cloth, while requiring that India allow British-made cloth to come in without tariffs.

With this history in mind, in the mid-twentieth century, the model for how development should proceed worldwide assumed an increase in production of goods and services achieved through rising productivity, technological advances, and globalization. Theories on economic development that emerged in the early 1950s focused on investment in manufacturing capital and technology as being central to the process of development.

The economic historian W. W. Rostow, for example, advanced the thesis that progress from "underdevelopment" to development invariably went through five stages. The first he referred to as "traditional, agrarian society," meaning an unchanging economy based on farming. In the second stage, the economy acquires the necessary "preconditions" (education and entrepreneurship) for growth. In the third stage of "takeoff," the country realizes its development potential by achieving a sufficiently high level of *savings* to finance the *investment* necessary for growth. From there, growth was expected to sustain itself, as the economy "drives to maturity" in the fourth stage. The final stage, characteristic of rich countries, is the "age of high mass consumption." The more mathematical Harrod-Domar model, named after the economists Roy Harrod and Evsey Domar, also emphasizes investment as being crucial to development.

Another theory, proposed by Sir Arthur Lewis (one of the earliest prominent black economists), describes development as a process of structural transformation from agriculture-based economy to industrialization. Lewis anticipated that the higher productivity in the industrial sector would gradually attract workers from agriculture without hurting agricultural productivity, because the agricultural sector had more labor than was actually needed. As happened in the Industrial Revolution, this flow of labor into the industrial sector allows firms to expand production, increasing their profits and incentivizing further investment in production. Hence, the economy moves toward self-sustaining development through the continuation of this process of labor flows and increased investment and production.

The development path taken by Russia, earlier in the century, could be interpreted as an extremely heartless version of such transformation from agriculture to industry. The number of Russian peasant deaths was appallingly high, as they were squeezed to transfer a hardly existing "surplus" labor into the nascent industrial economy. China followed Russia, with even less industrialization to show for it until the late 1970s, when China's agricultural policies changed to allow the flourishing of entrepreneurial spirit. At that point, much of what Lewis described did occur, as the agricultural sector quickly developed a capacity to send surplus labor and capital into the cities.

In contrast, post World War II, developing countries such as Hong Kong, Singapore, Taiwan, and South Korea (known as the Asian Tigers) adopted an export-oriented development strategy. They were less focused on substituting domestically produced high-value products for their own populations and more on policies designed to steer their industries away from exports of primary goods toward exports of manufactured goods. This model, involving protective tariffs and other supports to help develop key industries, has become increasingly hard for other countries to follow, especially as the high-income countries now increasingly insist that poor countries follow "free trade" rules. In fact, countries that are now wealthy typically used protectionism—tariffs and quotas to limit trade—to foster the early development of their domestic industries. Critics such as economist Ha-Joon Chang claim that such countries have "kicked away" the (protectionist) ladder that they themselves used to achieve higher living standards.

There is a danger in assuming that any one model of development can necessarily be transferred from a country where it has been successful to another set of circumstances. The history of colonization and the changing nature of the global economy suggest that the conditions faced by developing countries today are different from those faced by the early industrializing countries. Based on such arguments, **dependency theory** focuses on the interactions between developed and developing countries as being critical to the process of development.

489

> **dependency theory:** the theory that underdevelopment in developing countries is caused by unequal trade relations, where developing countries export primary goods that are much cheaper than the industrial goods they import from the developed nations

Dependency theory originated from developing countries (primarily Latin America) in the late 1950s. This theory locates the roots of underdevelopment in the dominance of developed countries and the unequal trade relations between the developed and developing countries. It notes that the poor countries mostly export primary goods—goods derived directly from agriculture or mining—that tend to be traded for much lower prices as compared to the industrialized goods exported by the developed countries. Thus, the value of what developing countries export to the world market is lower than the value of what they import, and trade is more beneficial to the rich countries. This theory argues that developing countries need to protect and promote their own domestic industries rather than importing manufactured goods.

Based on this view, Latin American countries as well as several Asian and African countries embarked on protectionist policies to promote import substitution and domestic industrialization. Some of these countries also created common markets and trading blocs with other similarly situated countries in hopes of securing greater advantages from their interactions with the developed world. Up to the 1970s, this model seemed to work, with real per capita income nearly doubling in many of these countries. But this approach ran into problems in the late 1970s, when many of the countries adopting protectionist policies in the 1960s and 70s suffered a debt crisis, as they had borrowed heavily from rich countries to fund their development projects.[7] The impact of the crisis was most severe in Latin American countries, where the total outstanding debt rose from US$29 billion at the end of 1979 to US$327 billion by 1982.[8] After this crisis, development strategies based on import substitution lost favor.

2.2 A Second Wave of Development Theory

By the 1980s, import-substitution industrialization policies, and any type of state-led development approach, fell out of fashion, and the neoliberal ideology—that promoted free trade, the abandonment of protectionist policies, and a reduced role for the state—gained support.[9] Developed countries and multilateral institutions such as the **International Monetary Fund** and the **World Bank** provided loans for development. But these lenders also insisted that *all* recipient governments undertake "structural reforms" that involved implementing a broad swath of neoliberal-inspired policy changes to qualify for further loans. The set of favored policies came to be known as the "Washington Consensus." The main principles of the **Washington Consensus** were:

- *Fiscal discipline.* Developing countries were urged to end fiscal deficits and balance government budgets by developing reliable sources of tax revenue and limiting spending, including social services, as well as subsidies for food or oil.

490

- *Market liberalization and privatization.* Countries were pushed to abolish government-controlled industries, price controls, and other forms of intervention in domestic markets, along with widespread deregulation.
- *Trade liberalization and openness to foreign investment.* Countries were pressured to remove tariffs and other barriers to trade, as well as capital controls and other restrictions on foreign investment flows.

International Monetary Fund (IMF): an international agency charged with overseeing international finance, including exchange rates, international payments, and balance of payments management

World Bank: an international agency charged with promoting economic development through loans and other programs

Washington Consensus: specific economic policy prescriptions used by the IMF and World Bank with the stated goal of helping developing countries to avoid crisis and maintain stability. They include openness to trade and investment (liberalization), privatization, budget austerity, and deregulation

---

A new element that arrived with the Washington Consensus was a set of limits on the autonomy of developing country governments. The implicit promise was that if these policies were followed, the conditions for rapid growth would be created as developing economies would attract foreign investment. During the 1980s and 1990s, the slogan "stabilize, privatize, and liberalize" governed the thinking of development policymakers. The presumption was that the same guidelines applied to every developing country and that each country's specific circumstances, history, capacities, and culture (i.e., its context) were irrelevant in determining development policies and outcomes.

Subsequent growth performances seriously call into question the validity of these policy prescriptions. (See Box 15.2 for an example.) The region of the world most influenced by the Washington Consensus has been Latin America. As can be seen in Table 15.4, average growth rates in most Latin American countries were much

Table 15.4 Average per Capita Annual Real GDP Growth, Select Latin American Countries, 1961–2018 (%)

Country or Region	1961–1980	1981–2018
Argentina	1.90	0.76
Brazil	4.52	0.93
Chile	1.72	3.03
Colombia	2.68	1.81
Ecuador	2.65	0.94
Mexico	3.53	0.88
Peru	1.60	1.68
Latin America and Caribbean	3.18	0.95
Middle Income	3.21	2.68

Source: World Bank, World Development Indicators database, 2019.

BOX 15.2 JAMAICA'S DEBT PROBLEM

Jamaica is one of the most highly indebted countries in the world. In 2016, the total government debt amounted to 121 percent of the country's GDP. This large debt burden has limited the country's ability to direct public spending to development programs and stagnated growth, as most Jamaicans continue to live amid poverty and unemployment.

Not long after the country became independent from Britain, in 1962, the Jamaican economy was hit by global economic problems that included rising import prices due to the oil price hikes of the 1970s. As the country's economy went into debt, it was forced to reluctantly sign its first agreement to borrow from the IMF in 1977. Interest rates hikes in the 1980s caused Jamaica's debts to soar. In an effort to stabilize its economy, the Jamaican government ended up signing on to billions of dollars in loans.

Why hasn't the country made significant economic gains, despite the large inflow of aid? Some blame the neoliberal policies of the IMF and World Bank, while others point to the high level of corruption in the government and its failure to implement policies effectively.[10] The imposition of Washington Consensus policies turned out to be a significant deterrent to growth, as lower tariffs on imports flooded the Jamaican markets with cheap foreign goods and destroyed the local businesses. The agricultural sector was especially hurt, as imports of fruits, vegetables, meat, and milk replaced locally produced food. In addition, the austerity measures imposed to maintain fiscal discipline led to steep declines in public expenditures on health, education, and housing and worsened the overall living standards.

Amid rising debt, without much improvement in economic conditions, the IMF forced a devaluation of the Jamaican currency with the claim that a depreciated currency would help the country achieve a more sustainable international investment position. The Jamaican dollar's worth has declined from being equal to the U.S. dollar in the 1970s to an exchange rate of 125 Jamaican dollars for each U.S. dollar as of 2018. The devaluation of currency has added to the country's debt burden, as more Jamaican dollars are now needed to pay the same debt.

According to a 2013 article in *The Guardian*, "Jamaica has repaid more money (US$19.8 billion) than it has been lent (US$18.5 billion), yet the government still 'owes' US$7.8 billion, as a result of huge interest payments."[11] The government currently spends twice as much on debt repayment as it does on education and health combined.[12] Such sustained underinvestment in basic necessities poses a severe problem for Jamaica's long-term development prospects.

higher between 1961 and 1980 than they have been since then. Since the 1980s, the average growth rates of Latin American countries compare rather unfavorably to the average growth rate for middle-income countries as a whole (with few exceptions, Latin American countries are in the "middle-income" category). The poor performance of this region of the world is, to date, the strongest indictment of the Washington Consensus.

Discussion Questions

1. Do you think that the economic challenges faced by developing countries today are similar to those faced by industrialized countries when they were starting out? If not, how are they different?

2. Discuss how the Washington Consensus affected the development of the countries in Latin America and the Caribbean since the 1980s.

3. TWENTY-FIRST CENTURY RECONSIDERATIONS OF THE SOURCES OF ECONOMIC GROWTH

Figure 15.3 illustrates the huge discrepancies in GDP per capita levels across countries. While countries such as the United States, Canada, Australia, and Japan, along with most of Europe, enjoy a per capita GDP of more than US$25,000, some of the poorest countries have income per capita below—sometimes much below—US$2,500. The countries whose economies continue to stagnate are mostly in sub-Saharan Africa, parts of Asia, and the Caribbean.

What are some of the ways in which poorer countries could achieve higher growth levels? In Chapter 1, we described five kinds of capital: natural, manufactured, human, social, and financial. Increase in these capital resources could push the production-possibility frontier out and increase the production level.

In addition to increasing the *quantity* of inputs, there can also be significant increases in their *quality*. Human and social capital, in particular, may be increased through education, better laws, or improvements in social norms of honesty or collaboration. Technological advances and efficiency gains may also make it possible to increase output without increasing physical quantities of inputs. The following observations summarize a range of possible sources of economic growth and development; their relevance varies from one situation to another.

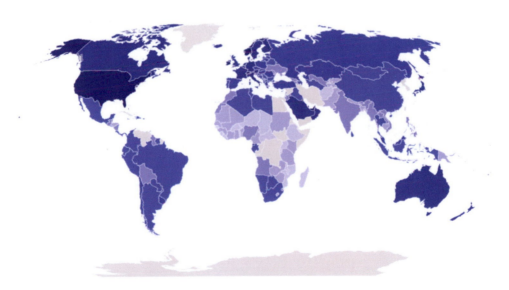

■ **$50,000 or more** ■ **$35,000-$50,000** ■ **$20,000-$35,000** ■ **$10,000-$20,000**
■ **$5,000-$10,000** ■ **$2,000-$5,000** ■ **<$2,000** ■ **Data unavailable**

Figure 15.3 GDP per Capita in 2017 (in Constant 2011 PPP $)

Source: World Bank, World Development Indicators database, 2019.

Urbanization

Development often results in people moving out of the countryside into urban industrial centers. Today over 55 percent of the world population lives in cities, versus 1960, when it was 33 percent. This proportion is expected to rise to 66 percent by 2050.[13] The United Nations has projected that nearly all global population growth from 2017 to 2030 will be absorbed by cities, bringing about 1.1 billion additional people into cities over the next 13 years.[14] One factor driving urbanization is the advances in agricultural productivity that have continually lowered the number of people who can profitably work at farming. One caveat to this is the possibility that, as soils continue to be exhausted by industrial agriculture techniques, there will be at least a slight rise in the demand for farm labor due to the adoption of regenerative agriculture techniques that require more workers per acre. Furthermore, recent studies argue that there are strong economic, social, and environmental benefits to maintaining small-scale farming rather than moving to industrial agricultural models.[15]

Natural Resources

The role of natural resources is also essential to development. Large expanses of arable land, rich mineral and energy resources, good natural port facilities, and a healthy climate may make it easier for a country to prosper, while a poor natural endowment, such as a climate that makes a country prone to malaria or drought, can be a serious drag on development. But the historical record includes some surprises. Hong Kong and Singapore are among several examples of countries that have developed prosperous trade-based economies even though they have scant domestic resources, with little land and few energy sources of their own.

In fact, the overexploitation of natural resources can lead both to environmental degradation and to economic and political distortion. Countries such as Nigeria have found that oil reserves, seemingly a source of wealth, can easily be misappropriated by elites, with very damaging effects on development. Misdirected oil revenues can lead to massive corruption and waste, or other sectors of the economy may be starved of investment as available resources go primarily toward oil production. And because oil is an exhaustible resource, the country can eventually run out of oil and find itself worse off than before. Nigeria's experience is symbolic of what many have referred to as the "resource curse" (the idea that countries endowed with abundant natural resources often do worse than countries with fewer resources).

Savings and Investment

Financial capital is essential for investment in manufactured capital and human capital to maintain and improve productivity levels. Starting in the mid-twentieth century, Japan and other "Asian Tigers" demonstrated a pattern of **virtuous cycles** in which high investment and savings lead to greater productivity, a competitive export industry, and growth of domestic industries. The resulting financial capital is then invested in machines, factories, and other equipment, as well as in education and health care systems that can further enhance productivity—and the cycle begins again. As the economy grows, more resources are available to invest in both human and manufactured capital. It sounds simple and obvious—yet many countries have had great difficulty in achieving such virtuous cycles.

> **virtuous cycles (in development):** self-reinforcing patterns of high savings, investment, productivity growth, and economic expansion

Additions to capital do not automatically lead to growth. Technologies that are highly automated or **"capital intensive"** may sometimes be inappropriate in countries with high unemployment. In such countries, more appropriate investments might be made in technologies that make greater use of abundant potential workers—in other words, technologies that are more **"labor intensive."** However, because goods produced by labor-intensive processes tend to be less sophisticated than goods produced through the use of higher technology, they usually result in less export revenue than high-tech products. Indeed, one of the conflicts regularly confronted by developing countries is the need to balance economic diversification (especially into "higher-end" products) with the need to provide employment opportunities. There may also be a significant tension between producing more sophisticated products for export versus producing goods for domestic use. Cheaper domestic products may be squeezed out by more capital-intensive exports that are more profitable but too expensive for the local population.

> **capital intensive:** a process or procedure that makes use of more capital relative to other inputs such as labor
> **labor intensive:** a process or procedure that makes use of more labor relative to other inputs such as capital

Allocation of Investment

According to market theory, investors should be attracted to the most profitable opportunities. But market allocation of investment may ignore externalities and social priorities and will not necessarily contribute much to the development of infrastructure (things like roads, railroads, and electronic networks). These and other important public goods such as education, environmental quality, and water supplies require a public role in directing investment.

In addition to investing in public goods, governments have often played a role in planning other industrial investments. Known as **industrial policy**, this approach can involve promoting particular industries, using tariffs, subsidies, and other economic tools as needed. Virtually all currently high-income countries used some type of industrial policies in earlier stages of their own development. A critical requirement for effective industrial policy is a government that is oriented toward the economic success of the country and that is capable of designing and implementing policies that will work well in its particular context.

> **industrial policy:** a set of government policies designed to enhance a country's ability to compete globally

Foreign Sources of Financial Capital

If a country is not able to finance the investments it needs for development out of its own domestic savings, it generally seeks grants, loans, or investments from abroad. The sources of foreign capital can be either public or private. Public aid for development can take the form of either bilateral or multilateral assistance. **Bilateral development assistance** consists of grants or loans made by a rich country's government to a poorer country. Many developing countries also receive **multilateral development assistance** from institutions such as the World Bank, International Monetary Fund, the Inter-American Development Bank, and UN agencies such as the United Nations Development Programme (UNDP). In 2018, the flow of development aid from 30 OECD member countries totaled US$149.3 billion—a decline of 2.7 percent from 2017. One especially concerning aspect of this decline is that less aid is flowing to the least-developed and African countries, where it is needed the most.[16]

> **bilateral development assistance:** aid or loans given by one country to another to promote development
> **multilateral development assistance:** aid or loans provided by the World Bank, regional development banks, or UN agencies with the announced intention of promoting development

Private foreign investment is carried out by private companies or individuals. Foreign direct investment (FDI) occurs when a company or individual acquires or creates assets for its own business operations in a foreign country (e.g., a German company building a television factory in Mexico). FDI may or may not increase the capital stock in the recipient country, because it can include acquisitions of existing capital structures. Private flows also include loans from private banks.

The empirical evidence concerning the contribution of public and private foreign capital to economic growth is mixed. While aid money has made important contributions to poverty reduction in some cases, there have also been instances of aid going to corrupt leaders who spent it on their own luxurious lifestyles rather than on benefits for their people. Some of today's poorest countries have also been the heaviest recipients of concessional aid (meaning loans given at below-market rates). Because most aid comes in the form of loans, rather than grants, many poor countries are now highly indebted and spend more on debt service (payment of principal and interest) than on improving well-being for their population. (See Box 15.2.)

Foreign investment can sometimes play an essential role in spurring development, but welcoming foreign businesses also can be culturally and politically disruptive. When a large, powerful transnational corporation moves into a developing country, it may "crowd out" local initiatives by competing with them for finance, inputs, or markets, sometimes in effect replacing a viable local business sector with an international corporation. Some of the most oppressive actions in development history (such as peasants being forced off their land or union organizers repressed with violence) have come about through alliances between large transnational corporations and corrupt governments.

Foreign Migration and Remittances

The high unemployment and poverty levels in developing countries have pushed many workers to pursue employment opportunities in other developed and developing countries. The remittances sent by these migrants to their families back home are an important source of livelihood for millions of poor households. In 2018, a total of US$529 billion in remittances was sent to low- and middle-income countries. Total remittances received by these countries were larger than official development assistance (ODA) and FDI flows.[17] Remittance flows are also more stable than FDI flows, so they have become an important source of financial capital for developing countries.[18]

Research on the impacts of remittances shows gains in income levels along with better human development outcomes in terms of education and health.[19] In addition, remittances can ease credit constraints for poor rural households, facilitate investment in assets and in income-generating capital resources, and help reduce poverty levels. However, some aspects of migration may impede development. In some cases, remittances could discourage the receiving household members from working and reduce domestic production. In addition, the loss of a portion of the active labor force along with the dependence on foreign nations for continued employment could pose serious challenges for the migrant-sending country's long-term development.[20]

Microfinance and Savings Groups

The poor often struggle to get loans because of their lack of assets for collateral, limited financial literacy, and the absence of financial services in rural areas. Both microfinance and savings groups programs are designed to address this issue by providing the poor with access to credit. Being able to take loans could help the poor meet their immediate consumption needs and also provide them with the financial capital to invest in some income-generating activity, such as starting a home-based enterprise or gaining skills to join the labor market.

A traditional microfinance program requires borrowers to form small groups; loans are provided to group members, in turns, with the borrowing ability of each member being dependent on the loan repayment history of all the group members. Hence, social collateral in the form of peer pressure, instead of physical collateral, is used to ensure credit discipline. In the past two decades, microfinance institutions have spread rapidly across the developing world.

497

Evaluations of the effectiveness of microfinance programs mostly show increases in household income; improvements in access to health care, education, and nutrition; and increased investment in small enterprises. However, microfinance programs are often less accessible to the poorest of the poor, as they might find it difficult to get accepted into borrowing circles. There has also been some evidence of borrowers getting even poorer from having to sell their assets to pay off the debts or getting trapped in vicious debt cycles from having to take new loans to pay off old ones.[21]

Savings groups, like microfinance programs, provide access to credit to the poor. The key difference between the two is that, instead of receiving loans from a bank or development agency, the funds for savings groups are generated by pooling the savings of group members, who normally create and run these programs in a truly grassroots manner. Savings groups are seen as an improvement over the microfinance model, as they are relatively easy to operate and extremely low cost and require minimal outside support or supervision. Most studies evaluating the ability of savings groups to address poverty find positive outcomes. For example, a 2016 study on three African countries (Ghana, Malawi, and Uganda) finds that promotion of savings groups has led to improvements in household incomes.[22]

Cash Transfer Programs

Cash transfer programs involve providing cash grants to the poor to help improve their standards of living. In general, there are two types of cash transfer programs—conditional and unconditional. In **conditional cash transfer (CCT)** programs, the recipients are required to make specific commitments, such as getting health check-ups or sending their children to school, to receive cash. **Unconditional cash transfer (UCT)** programs, on the other hand, involve a transfer of funds to individuals with no specific conditions on how the funds should be spent. (See Box 15.3 for an example.) Some such programs require the recipients to show some evidence of need; others are distributed to all individuals above a certain age or all households, regardless of need.

> **conditional cash transfer (CCT):** programs providing cash to the poor based on the condition that they commit to spending it on specific things, such as children's education, food, or health care
> **unconditional cash transfer (UCT):** programs providing cash to the poor with no specific conditions on how the funds should be spent

Evidence on the effectiveness of CCT programs shows that such transfers improve outcomes related to health, education, and nutrition. For example, recipients of PROGRESA—a CCT program in Mexico that required sending children to school and attending health clinics—are found to have greater school enrollment, lower incidence of illness in young children, and fewer sick days for adults.[23] Despite such achievements, CCT programs are often difficult to implement because of high administrative costs. Also, they may not be effective if local educational or health facilities are poor. Finally, CCT programs are sometimes viewed as being demeaning to the poor, as the government imposes conditions on how the poor should spend the funds, irrespective of their preferences.

The UCT programs address many of these criticisms. Because they don't have to monitor how the recipients use the cash inflow, administrative costs are much lower. UCT programs are based on the idea that people are the best judges of how to use their money. Evaluations of UCT programs mostly find positive outcomes. For example, a study led by Haushofer and Shapiro found that in Kenya, unconditional cash transfers had increased household assets, consumption, food security, and psychological well-being.[24] UCTs have often been shown to be more effective than some traditional development programs, and there is increasing research on identifying contexts where UCTs are the most appropriate intervention to make.[25]

BOX 15.3 GUARANTEED BASIC INCOME

A guaranteed or universal basic income (BI) is a specific form of unconditional cash transfer, where periodic cash payments are provided unconditionally to all individuals, without means-test or work requirements, so that people can at least cover basic expenses such as housing, food, and health care. Advocates of BI argue that such a program would not only mitigate issues of unemployment and poverty but also provide a basic social net and help relieve work-related stress. A BI system could also encourage innovation by providing individuals with freedom to explore their interests, and it could bring benefits, such as lower crime rates and reduced environmental damage from lower economic activities.

However, there are several challenges to instituting a BI system. First, would giving people unconditional income disincentivize them from seeking work? Research on a number of experiments shows mixed findings. For example, a pilot program implemented in the Namibian village of Omitara in 2008 and 2009 showed that the introduction of a basic income program increased the rate of those engaged in income-generating activities from 44 percent to 55 percent.[26] However, a two-year government experiment in Finland, making monthly cash payments of €560 (US$635) to 2,000 unemployed individuals, showed that individuals receiving BI were happier and healthier than those receiving unemployment benefits, but they were not more likely to work.[27]

Another concern relates to funding a BI program. In the United States, for example, giving every American $10,000 a year—a value below the poverty line—would cost at least $3 trillion, which is about eight times the current government spending on social service programs.[28] Other suggestions for funding BI programs include collecting fees from government-created monopolies (such as the broadcast spectrum and utilities), income from private uses of government land (currently leased out, in general, far below market rates), or income from taxing carbon emissions.

Various experimental trials of basic income policies have been implemented in parts of Canada (Ontario), Spain (Barcelona), and Netherlands, as well as in developing countries such as India, Namibia, Uganda, and Kenya. The most well-known BI experience in the United States is in the state of Alaska, where each individual gets an annual share of the state's fossil fuel income—$1,022 per person in 2016. Other recent trials include small-scale experiments in the cities of Oakland and Stockton in California.

Domestic Demand vs. Export Orientation

Businesses are unlikely to increase production if what is made cannot find a market. Indeed, they might even lower production if they are not confident they can sell what they produce. This suggests that the level of aggregate *demand* in an economy is also of great importance for growth (i.e., it is not just a matter of increasing the capacity to *supply* more good and services). One reason developing countries sometimes fail to achieve sustained growth is that, while production for export is emphasized, not enough is done to develop domestic markets. There are counterexamples to this statement: countries such as Japan and South Korea broke into the ranks of more advanced economies by developing powerful export industries, and China is now following this same path. But export dependence can become a trap that stifles economic development when countries depend on exporting products for which world demand is limited.

Financial, Legal, and Regulatory Institutions

Financial, legal, and regulatory institutions (which fit into the category of social capital) play an important role in encouraging—or discouraging—development. Very poor countries sometimes have banking and legal systems that do not reach the poor, especially in rural areas, making it difficult for small businesses and entrepreneurs to finance new or growing enterprises. The experience of Russia, where GDP fell more than 40 percent during its emergence from communism in the 1990s, highlighted the need for markets to be based in a good institutional framework.

Countries that have been successful in maintaining growth generally have effective systems of property rights, contract enforcement, and corporate and bank regulations, which allow entrepreneurs to benefit from their investments. However, in some cases, even countries that do not have strong property rights systems (such as China and Vietnam) have been able to attract significant amounts of investment and assure firms that they can operate profitably.

Some developing countries suffer from severe corruption, internal conflict, and other factors that make it difficult to establish effective institutions. Political instability leads to economic inefficiency, difficulty in attracting foreign investment, and slow or no growth. This, in turn, stifles future investment, reinforcing the problems. Breaking this vicious cycle is essential for development but can be very difficult to achieve.

Discussion Questions

1. Think of a poor country that you know something about. Considering the various sources of economic development, where would you propose starting to design a development plan for that country?

2. How would you balance the issue of human development with the issue of economic growth? What approaches do you think are best for promoting human development?

4. INEQUALITY AND DEVELOPMENT

In previous chapters, we have discussed trends in inequality, mainly in the United States, and examined some of its causes and consequences. We now present a more global overview on trends in inequality and analyze how inequality may affect development outcomes.

4.1 International Data on Inequality

The World Economic Forum has identified income inequality as one of the top global issues. According to the 2018 World Inequality Report, global inequality seems to have stabilized after widening for several decades, as the share of world's income captured by the richest 1 percent has shrunk slightly since its peak in 2007. However, inequalities between and within countries are still high. Between 1980 and 2016, the richest 1 percent of individuals in the world received 27 percent of the income growth, while the bottom 50 percent only got 12 percent. The actual level of global inequality would have been even higher had it not been for recent rapid growth in China, moving many people in China out of extreme poverty and toward "global middle class" status.

While there has been a general decline in global poverty levels, rising inequality remains a key challenge for both developed and developing countries. Figure 15.4 shows the range in income and wealth inequalities, based on Gini coefficients, for selected countries. South Africa, with a Gini coefficient of 0.58, has the highest degree of income inequality, while Iceland, with a Gini coefficient of 0.24, has the

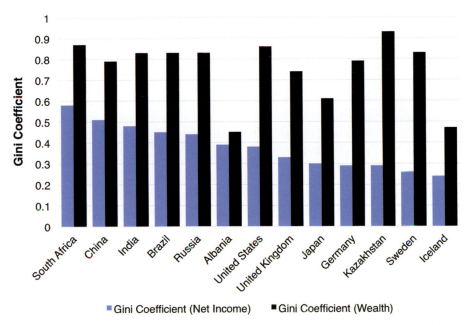

Figure 15.4 *Gini Coefficient for Income and Wealth, Select Countries, 2018*

Source: The World Economic Forum's Inclusive Development Index 2018.

lowest income inequality level. While many of the countries with the lowest income inequality are high-income countries, inequality is also relatively low in Ukraine, Hungary, Mali, and Pakistan, among others. The 2018 World Inequality Report notes that since 1980, income inequality has increased more rapidly in North America, China, India, and Russia than anywhere else in the world.[29]

Patterns across geographic regions are fairly consistent. Latin American countries, for example, tend to have relatively high degrees of inequality. Brazil, Mexico, Guatemala, Costa Rica, and Chile all have Gini coefficients above 0.44. Asian countries (except India, China, and a few others), in contrast, appear by this measure to be more economically equal, with Gini coefficients between 0.30 and 0.43. Sub-Saharan Africa appears to have the greatest variability, ranging from 0.32 (Burundi) to 0.58 (South Africa).

International comparisons on Gini coefficient for wealth (Figure 15.4) show that wealth is significantly more unequally distributed than income. Kazakhstan has the highest level of wealth inequality, with a Gini coefficient of 0.93, while Albania has the lowest wealth inequality level, with a Gini coefficient of 0.45. Though income inequality is relatively low in developed counties like Germany and Sweden, wealth distribution in these countries seem to be highly unequal, with a Gini coefficient of around 0.8. Wealth inequality is quite high all over the world, with the poorest half of the population controlling less than 10 percent of the wealth in most countries.[30]

4.2 Inequality and the Kuznets Hypothesis

In 1955, Simon Kuznets wrote a famous paper on the relationship between growth and inequality.[31] He proposed that during the initial stages of economic growth, inequality increases as investment opportunities create a wealthy class, while an influx of rural laborers into cities would keep wages low. Eventually, according to Kuznets, further industrialization leads to democratization, widespread increases in education, and safety-net policies that would lead to lower inequality. This **Kuznets curve hypothesis** suggests an inverted-U relationship between economic growth and inequality—inequality would first rise, then fall, with economic growth. Although Kuznets himself warned against drawing simple conclusions from this hypothesis, some economists have interpreted it to mean that, as long as we maintain growth, inequality will eventually decline.

> **Kuznets curve hypothesis:** the theory that economic inequality initially increases during the early stages of economic development but then eventually decreases with further economic development

The evidence does not always support the Kuznets hypothesis. Some countries, such as Brazil, have remained highly unequal even as their per capita incomes have increased. Further, in recent decades, inequality has been rising in some highly developed countries, contradicting the Kuznets hypothesis. Additionally, extreme inequality can retard growth or limit its benefits to a small rich class while the majority of the population remains excluded from the beneficial effects of development. When we broaden our scope to consider the well-being aspects of development, instead of just economic growth, the negative effects of inequality, and the need to address it more directly, become more apparent.

4.3 Inequality and Economic Well-Being

Why does inequality matter for development? As discussed previously, inequality is often seen as a drag on economic growth, since high inequality often undermines investment and productivity levels. Furthermore, high inequality encourages corruption, resource misallocation, and erosion of social trust. Often, inequality is a prime cause of political upheaval and civil conflicts. Hence, in addition to examining the relation between economic growth and inequality, we need to explore how inequality may affect broader well-being outcomes.

Countries with higher income inequality generally perform more poorly on many well-being indicators. Take, for example, the effect of inequality on the health of the population in a country. Figure 15.5 plots one proxy for health—average life expectancies—against GDP per capita, with spheres proportional to the population of the country represented. A curve is drawn to fit the general pattern made by the data points. We see that living in a very poor country, such as Nigeria, dramatically increases the chance that one will die prematurely, compared with living in a country with somewhat higher GDP per capita, such as India or China.

Moving from left to right, we see countries such as Mexico, which has achieved a life expectancy fairly close to that of the richest countries, even though its average

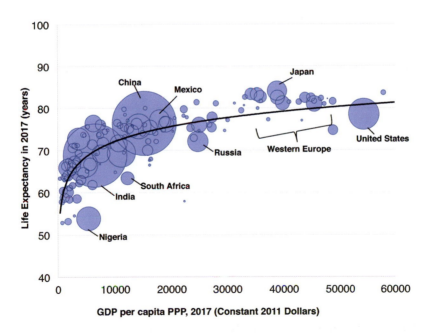

Figure 15.5 *The Relation Between Life Expectancy and Income, With Area Proportional to Population, 2017*

Source: World Bank, World Development Indicators database, 2019.

income per capita is not even half as high. But South Africa lies far below the line, reflecting a case in which high inequality makes it difficult to translate a moderate *average* level of income into well-being and longevity.

Looking at the spheres representing Western Europe, Japan, and the United States at the right-hand side of the figure, we see that the positive relationship between income and life expectancy essentially disappears. At high incomes, in fact, inequality within countries—not income per capita—may be a more important factor in determining health and life expectancy. For example, according to a 2010 study, despite the fact that the average U.S. citizen can expect to live about 77 years— which is considerably better than the global average of about 70 years—U.S. life expectancy is lower than that of most other industrialized countries (e.g., Japan and Western Europe), where life expectancy is in the 78- to 82-year range. Inequality is also positively associated with a range of negative social outcomes, including mental health and incidence of violence.[32]

5. RECENT PERSPECTIVES AND SUSTAINABLE DEVELOPMENT GOALS

In September 2000, the member states of the United Nations unanimously declared their intention to try to reach a set of development objectives called the **Millennium Development Goals** (MDGs) by 2015. The MDG initiative included eight objectives:

- eradicating extreme poverty and hunger
- achieving universal primary education
- promoting gender equality and empowering women
- reducing child mortality
- improving maternal health
- combating HIV/AIDS, malaria, and other diseases
- ensuring environmental sustainability
- developing a global partnership for development based on fair trade, debt relief, and access to health and information technologies

> **Millennium Development Goals (MDGs):** a set of goals declared by the United Nations in 2000, emphasizing eradication of extreme poverty; promotion of education, gender equity, and health; environmental sustainability; and partnership between rich and poor countries

Between 2000 and 2015, many dimensions of human development improved much more quickly than in the 15 years prior to 2000. According to the UN, the goal of halving the proportion of people living on less than US\$1.25 a day (the threshold in 2000) was met three years *before* the target date. By 2015, the global poverty rate had decreased from 47 percent to 14 percent, and the proportion of undernourished people in developing countries had dropped from 23.3 percent to 12.9 percent, though narrowly missing the target of cutting it by half. This progress has, however, been very uneven, with regions such as South and East Asia (especially China and India) having seen considerable gains, while conditions in parts of sub-Saharan Africa have deteriorated.

Despite these achievements, it is not clear that poor countries as a whole are moving closer to the levels of human development enjoyed in the industrialized world. Some scholars have criticized the MDGs, believing that the goals do not go far enough in addressing inequalities between rich and poor countries. A technological gulf persists between rich and poor countries, and little progress has been made in opening up rich countries' markets to the products of poorer countries.

In 2015 the United Nations initiated a follow-up to the Millennium Development Goals, called the **Sustainable Development Goals**. They have replaced the 8 MDGs with 17 "focus areas" (see Box 15.4), which are broader than the original

---

BOX 15.4 THE SUSTAINABLE DEVELOPMENT GOALS

1. End poverty in all its forms everywhere.
2. End hunger, achieve food security and improved nutrition, and promote sustainable agriculture.
3. Ensure healthy lives and promote well-being for all at all ages.
4. Ensure inclusive and equitable quality education and promote lifelong learning opportunities for all.
5. Achieve gender equality and empower all women and girls.
6. Ensure availability and sustainable management of water and sanitation for all.
7. Ensure access to affordable, reliable, sustainable, and modern energy for all.
8. Promote sustained, inclusive, and sustainable economic growth; full and productive employment; and decent work for all.
9. Build resilient infrastructure, promote inclusive and sustainable industrialization, and foster innovation.
10. Reduce inequality within and among countries.
11. Make cities and human settlements inclusive, safe, resilient, and sustainable.
12. Ensure sustainable consumption and production patterns.
13. Take urgent action to combat climate change and its impacts.
14. Conserve and sustainably use the oceans, seas, and marine resources for sustainable development.
15. Protect, restore, and promote sustainable use of terrestrial ecosystems; sustainably manage forests; combat desertification; halt and reverse land degradation; and halt biodiversity loss.
16. Promote peaceful and inclusive societies for sustainable development; provide access to justice for all; and build effective, accountable, and inclusive institutions at all levels.
17. Strengthen the means of implementation and revitalize the global partnership for sustainable development.

Source: United Nations, Sustainable Development Goals. https://sustainabledevelopment.un.org/

MDGs. For example, the SDGs not only address the conditions in developing countries but also living conditions in rich countries, including goals such as "reducing inequality" or promoting "just, peaceful and inclusive societies." The SDGs are further specified in targets, such as "by 2030, eradicate extreme poverty for all people everywhere."

> **Sustainable Development Goals (SDGs):** a set of goals set forth by the United Nations in 2015, building on and expanding the MDGs, including goals such as promoting inclusive growth and limiting climate change

While this widening in focus and ambition clearly addresses dimensions neglected in the MDGs, it also has its critics. Some commentators have pointed out that one of the MDGs' merits was the identification of clearly defined goals that could be effectively targeted by specific policy measures. In contrast, some of the SDGs' targets are formulated more vaguely, so that monitoring progress becomes difficult.

Discussion Questions

1. What does the mixed success in achieving the Millennium Development Goals say about current development policies?
2. Do you think the Sustainable Development Goals are realistic or achievable?

6. DIFFERENT KINDS OF ECONOMIES

One question that arises when discussing the importance of investment as a source of growth is: who decides what are the most important investments to make? Should investment decisions be left to private markets or controlled by the government, or some combination of the two? Historical experience offers a number of models. We can categorize economic organizations according to *forms of ownership*, making a basic distinction between capitalist vs. socialist economies and further subdividing each of these.

Capitalism is a system characterized by predominantly *private ownership* of productive assets by individuals or businesses. Under **laissez–faire capitalism**, the role of the state is supposed to be relatively small; at least in theory, it is confined to maintaining a legal-institutional environment conducive to corporate ownership and market exchange. The United States and the United Kingdom are countries that lie closest to this end of the spectrum. In contrast, **administrative capitalism** involves a more substantial amount of state activity alongside market-coordinated activity. Japan, France, and Scandinavian countries fit this description.

> **laissez–faire capitalism:** a national system characterized by private corporate ownership and a great reliance on exchange as a mode of coordination, with relatively little coordination by public administration

> **administrative capitalism:** a national system characterized by private corporate ownership and a substantial reliance on public administration (as well as exchange) as a mode of coordination

Socialism is a broad term that can encompass a diverse range of economic systems. A central feature of all socialist systems is a much heavier reliance on *collective ownership*, where the owners may be either government or various kinds of cooperatives (for example, worker-owned firms). The Soviet Union formerly and North Korea in the present exemplify **administrative socialism**, which centralizes a very large proportion of economic ownership and power in the government. In contrast, China and Vietnam have been experimenting with a hybrid—**market socialism**—that keeps *political* power centralized, with state ownership predominating, but releases a growing amount of *economic* decision-making power to market forces.

> **administrative socialism:** a national system in which state ownership predominates, and activity is coordinated primarily by public administration (command)
>
> **market socialism:** a national system in which either state ownership or worker ownership predominates, but much economic activity is coordinated through markets

Which of these systems is most conducive to development? To compare the success of various types of economies, review some of the data presented in Chapter 0. How do the laissez-faire economies of the United States and United Kingdom perform compared to the administrative capitalist economies of Japan, France, and the Scandinavian countries? Or to the market socialism of China or Vietnam? Consider the economic categories of growth rate of GDP per capita and the unemployment rate, as well as the more well-being-related categories of income inequality, educational performance, life expectancy, and CO_2 emissions per capita.

Clearly, there is not a single winner. The United States does relatively well in some areas such as GDP per capita growth but performs poorly on some other measures such as educational performance and inequality. If you look at the ranking of the countries whose economies are described as administrative capitalism (for example, Japan and the Scandinavian countries), you will find some appealing outcomes, such as greater equality and better health and educational measures.[33] And China, as an example of market socialism, is virtually in a class by itself. It has an extraordinarily high GDP growth rate, along with high income inequality, and is a major emitter of greenhouse gases. India, which has a form of administrative capitalism, is compared to China in Box 15.5.

BOX 15.5 COMPARING INDIA AND CHINA IN HUMAN DEVELOPMENT

Both India and China have experienced rapid economic growth since 2000, but a comparison of the human development indicators between India and China reveals that China is ahead of India in most aspects. For example, in 2015, life expectancy in China was 76.1 years compared to 68.3 years in India, infant mortality rate (per 1,000 live births) was 9.2 in China compared to 36.2 in India, and maternal mortality ratio (per 100,000 live births) was 27 in China compared to 174 in India.[34] Nobel Prize winner Amartya Sen comments that the most significant gap between China and India is in the provision of essential public services:

> Inequality is high in both countries, but China has done far more than India to raise life expectancy, expand general education, and secure health care for its people. India has elite schools of varying degrees of excellence for the privileged, but among all Indians 7 or older, nearly one in five males and one in every three females are illiterate. . . . The poor have to rely on low-quality—and sometimes exploitative—private medical care, because there isn't enough decent public care.[35]

Despite their lower achievements in health and education outcomes, most Indians strongly appreciate the democratic structure of the country with uncensored media, systematic free elections, and an independent judiciary—things that many other developing countries, including China, have failed to achieve. Much of the progress in India toward achieving equality and better access to education and nutrition has been influenced by public protests and court decisions. In China, by contrast, most decisions are made by leaders without much pressure from the public. Though Chinese leaders have placed a priority on improving the living standards of their population, there is little recourse or remedy if they decide to alter their goals or suppress their failures.[36]

The debate on development continues. As the experience of development over the last century reveals, there is nothing "automatic" about achieving sustained growth and high living standards. Undoubtedly, a combination of market and government-led policies will be used as countries continue to strive to develop. The unsettled questions are (1) how to determine the mix between government and market, (2) how to develop the supporting institutions that will work best for a particular country, and (3) how best to promote a combination of goals that include economic development and social well-being.

Discussion Questions

1. Which of the four economic systems discussed previously do you think might be most conducive to achieving sustainable growth and economic equality? Explain why.

2. How do China and India compare as models for development? What are some problems and drawbacks in each country?

REVIEW QUESTIONS

1. What is the capabilities approach to development? How is this approach different from the traditional approach of defining development based on GDP per capita growth?
2. How evenly has economic growth been distributed among different countries in recent decades?
3. What do we mean by convergence in economic growth?
4. How can economic growth be represented using the *AS/AD* graphs discussed in Chapter 12?
5. Define the headcount and multidimensional poverty measures.
6. What was the Industrial Revolution? What factors were essential in creating the Industrial Revolution?
7. What, according to Rostow, are the five "stages of growth" that countries must pass through to become developed?
8. What is the key argument of the dependency theory?
9. What are the main principles of the Washington Consensus?
10. What is the evidence regarding the performance of the Washington Consensus recommendations?
11. What factors are generally considered responsible for GDP growth in developed countries? Have the factors responsible for growth been the same in all developed countries?
12. How can investment promote economic development?
13. Is an abundance of natural capital a prerequisite for economic development?
14. How can export development both promote and threaten economic growth?
15. In what different methods can foreign capital be provided to promote economic development?
16. Describe how microfinance and savings groups programs could promote development.
17. Discuss the strengths and limitations of cash transfer programs as a tool for development.
18. What are Millennium Development Goals? What have the MDGs achieved?
19. What are Sustainable Development Goals? How do they differ from the Millennium Development Goals?
20. Discuss some common trends in income and wealth inequality across countries.
21. How does inequality affect development outcomes?
22. Describe the four kinds of economic systems discussed in the chapter.

EXERCISES

1. Suppose the growth rate of real GDP of Macroland from 2017 to 2018 is 4.5 percent, and the population growth rate for the same period is 2.3 percent. What is the growth rate of real GDP per capita in Macroland?
2. Using the data for each country in Table 15.1, create a graph similar to Figure 15.5 showing real GDP per capita in 2017 on the horizontal axis and the rate of real GDP per capita growth for 1990–2017 on the vertical axis (instead of life expectancy as shown in Figure 15.5). (You don't need to include the three country income groups.) Draw each data point as a sphere approximately equal to the population of the country. Does your graph support economic convergence? Explain.

3.   Match each concept in Column A with a definition or example in Column B:

Column A	Column B
a. Remittances	1. Underdevelopment in developing countries is caused by unequal trade relations between developing and developed countries
b. A country that has shown significant economic convergence in recent decades	2. A European company purchases a factory in an African country
c. Foreign direct investment	3. Development assistance from one country to another
d. Kuznets curve hypothesis	4. Singapore
e. Fiscal discipline	5. A characteristic of the Industrial Revolution
f. Dependency theory	6. Income inequality first increases, then decreases, with development
g. Conditional cash transfer program	7. Flows of money and goods sent by migrants to their families back home
h. The use of technologies employing fossil fuel energy, especially coal	8. A structural reform under the Washington Consensus
i. Bilateral development assistance	9. Poverty alleviation program that gives funds to the poorest if they meet certain conditions
j. A country that has grown despite a lack of natural resources	10. China

NOTES

1.   As discussed in Chapter 14, purchasing power parity accounts for differences in purchasing power across countries based on the cost of living.
2.   Alston, Philip. 2017. "Statement on Visit to the USA, by Professor Philip Alston, United Nations Special Rapporteur on Extreme Poverty and Human Rights." United Nations Human Rights, December 15.
3.   Komlos, John. 2018. "The Economic Roots of the Rise of Trumpism." CESifo Working Papers No. 6868, January.
4.   Deaton, Angus. 2018. "The U.S. Can No Longer Hide from Its Deep Poverty Problem." *The New York Times*, January 24.
5.   Alston, Philip 2017. "Statement on Visit to the USA, by Professor Philip Alston, United Nations Special Rapporteur on Extreme Poverty and Human Rights." United Nations Human Rights, December 15.
6.   In the first half of the twentieth century, a number of Western countries, including Britain, Germany, France, the Netherlands, Portugal, and Spain, were colonial powers, exerting control over many colonies in Africa, Asia, and South America. Japan was also a colonial power, ruling South Korea and, at various times, parts of China. Most of the colonies had become independent countries by the 1960s.
7.   Arias, Maria A., and Paulina Restrepo-Echavarria. 2015. "Sovereign Debt Crisis in Europe Recalls the Lost Decade in Latin America." *The Regional Economist*, The Federal Reserve Bank of St. Louis, January.

8. Federal Deposit Insurance Corporation (FDIC), and Division of Research Statistics. 1997. "The LDC Debt Crisis." In Chapter 5 of *History of the Eighties: Lessons for the Future, Volume I: An Examination of the Banking Crises of the 1980s and Early 1990s*. FDIC, Washington, DC.

9. "Neoliberal" here refers to market-oriented development theory. It is derived from an older sense of the word "liberal," meaning freeing markets from government controls. This can be confusing since "liberal" in U.S. politics today often means using government action to help the poor. For an explanation of ideologies and their evolution over time, see Heywood, Andrew. 2017. *Political Ideologies: An Introduction*. Macmillan, London.

10. Morais, Stephanie. 2014. "Jamaica: Skyrocketing Debt, Poverty and Even More Austerity." *The Upstream Journal*, May.

11. Dearden, Nick. 2013. "Jamaica's Decades of Debt Are Damaging Its Future." *The Guardian*, April 16.

12. Hall, Arthur, 2018. "$31B Cut in Budget-Security and Roads Get Top Priority after Debt Payments." *The Gleaner*, February 16.

13. United Nations. 2014. "World's Population Increasingly Urban with More Than Half Living in Urban Areas." *News Item*, July 10.

14. Cohen, Barney. 2015. "Urbanization, City Growth, and the New United Nations Development Agenda." *Cornerstone*, 3(2), June: 4–7.

15. Wise, T. 2018. *Eating Tomorrow: Agribusiness, Family Farmers, and the Battle for the Future of Food*. The New Press, New York.

16. Data from OECD database. www.oecd.org/development/development-aid-drops-in-2018-especially-to-neediest-countries.htm

17. Ratha, Dilip, et al. 2019. *Migration and Remittances: Recent Developments and Outlook*. Migration Development Brief 31, World Bank Group, Washington.

18. World Bank. 2017. "Migration and Remittances: Recent Developments and Outlook." Migration and Development Brief 27, World Bank, Washington, April.

19. Ratha, Dilip. 2013. "The Impact of Remittances on Economic Growth and Poverty Reduction." Policy Brief No. 8, Migration Policy Institute, September.

20. Amuendo-Dorantes, Catalina. 2014. "The Good and the Bad in Remittance Flows." *IZA World of Labor*, 2014: 97.

21. Westover, Jonathan. 2008. "The Record of Microfinance: The Effectiveness/Ineffectiveness of Microfinance Programs as a Means of Alleviating Poverty." *Electronic Journal of Sociology*. https://www.researchgate.net/publication/47706389_The_Record_of_Microfinance_The_EffectivenessIneffectiveness_of_Microfinance_Programs_as_a_Means_of_Alleviating_Poverty

22. Karlan, Dean, Beniamino Savonitto, Bram Thuysbaert, and Christopher Udry. 2017. "Impact of Savings Groups on the Lives of the Poor." *Proceedings of the National Academy of Sciences*, 114(12), March 21.

23. Gantner, Leigh. 2007. "PROGRESA: An Integrated Approach to Poverty Alleviation in Mexico." Case Study #5–1 of the Program "Food Policy for Developing Countries: The Role of Government in the Global Food System." Cornell University, Ithaca, New York.

24. Haushofer, Johannes, and Jeremy Shapiro. 2016. "The Short-Term Impact of Unconditional Cash Transfers to the Poor: Experimental Evidence from Kenya." *The Quarterly Journal of Economics*, 131(4): 1973–2042.

25. Hagen-Zanker, Jessica, Francesca Bastagli, Luke Harman, Valentina Barca, Georgina Sturge, and Tanja Schmidt. 2016. *Understanding the Impact of Cash Transfers: The Evidence*. Office of Development Assistance, London.

26. Claudia and Haarmann. 2014. *Basic Income Grant Coalition.* See: www.bignam.org/BIG_pilot. html

27. Reuters. 2019. "Finland's Basic Income Trial Boosts Happiness, But Not Employment." *New York Times*, February 9. www.nytimes.com/2019/02/09/world/europe/finland-basic-income. html

28. Goodman, Peter S. 2017. "Capitalism Has a Problem, Is Free Money the Answer?" *New York Times*, November 15.

29. Ventura, Luca. 2018. "Wealth Distribution and Income Inequality by Country 2018." *Global Finance*, November 26. Note that data on income and wealth inequality are based on the World Economic Forum's Inclusive Development Index. www.gfmag.com/global-data/economic-data/wealth-distribution-income-inequality

30. Ibid.

31. Kuznets, Simon. 1955. "Economic Growth and Income Inequality." *American Economic Review*, 45: 1–28.

32. Wilkinson, Richard, and Kate Pickett. 2010. *The Spirit Level*. Bloomsbury Press, New York.

33. If you want to look into this further, you can go to the Web site, http://www.bu.edu/eci/education-materials/textbooks/essentials-of-economics-in-context/ which provides figures for all countries for which there are reliable statistics, not just those that are presented in Chapter 0.

34. World Development Indicators database 2015, World Bank, New York.

35. Sen, Amartya. 2013. "Why India Trails China." *New York Times*, Op-Ed, June 19.

36. Sen, Amartya. 2011. "Quality of Life: India vs. China." *The New York Review of Books*, May 12.

Chapter 16

Economics of the Environment

As we have discussed at several points in this book, environmental quality is an important component of our well-being. Recent research shows, for example, that higher air pollution levels not only harm human and non-human health but also lower people's overall happiness.[1] Our contextual economics approach recognizes that all economic activity depends on a continual supply of natural resources, as well as ecological functions that break down our wastes and purify our air and water.

Environmental issues are clearly not separate from economics. As we saw in the last chapter, the UN's Sustainable Development Goals recognize the importance of the environment in fostering human development. Climate change, in particular, represents a threat to our economic well-being. A 2018 report by 13 U.S. government agencies concluded that without significant reductions in emissions, climate change would cause "substantial net damage to the U.S. economy."[2]

Some people see economics as the cause of many of our environmental problems. Global economic growth over the last few centuries has clearly been associated with increasing pollution, deforestation, species extinctions, and other negative impacts. But economics does not necessarily prioritize economic growth over the quality of the environment. In fact, Nobel prize–winning economist Paul Krugman has written that:

> economists are on average more pro-environment than other people of similar incomes and backgrounds. Why? Because standard economic theory automatically predisposes those who believe in it to favor strong environmental protection.[3]

In this final chapter, we explore how to use insights from economics to better manage our shared environment. We will find that environmental concerns often present a valid justification for government intervention in markets and that a healthy economy and a healthy environment can coexist. We will discuss the policies that economists have developed to address environmental problems. We will end with a focus on climate change, as it is widely recognized as the most important environmental issue of the twenty-first century. But first, we provide a summary of the current state of the world's environment.

1. OVERVIEW OF GLOBAL ENVIRONMENTAL ISSUES

Debate over the ability of the earth's resources to sustain human populations can be traced back to 1798, when British economist Thomas Malthus wrote *An Essay on the Principle of Population*. Malthus predicted that unchecked human population growth would eventually outpace the growth in agricultural production, leading to widespread food scarcity and a resulting population crash. Malthus's prediction turned out to be inaccurate, as technological advances during the Industrial Revolution increased food production at a greater rate than population growth.

In recent decades, there has been renewed debate over whether the planet's natural resources can adequately provide for a growing human population. For example, in 1972, the book *The Limits to Growth* predicted that without significant policy changes, resource scarcity and increasing pollution would lead to declines in global food production, GDP, and population starting around 2020.[4] Although none of these predictions have come to pass so far, global environmental problems including climate change have grown much more pressing, indicating that the kind of crisis predicted in *Limits to Growth* cannot simply be dismissed.[5]

Recall from our discussion in Chapter 15 (Figure 15.2) that global food production, economic activity, and energy production have all grown at a faster rate than population. Thus, it is reasonable to state that, on average, people are better fed and wealthier and have more access to energy than at any time in the past. However, such improvements in living standards have come at a cost of a degraded environment. In Figure 16.1, we graph global carbon dioxide emissions for the same time

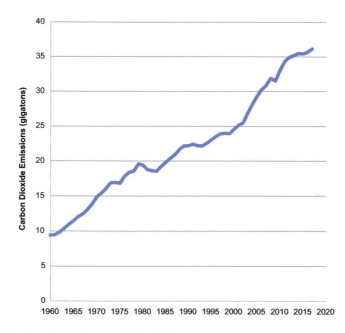

Figure 16.1 *Key Global Trends, 1961–2017*

Sources: World Bank, World Development Indicators; U.S. Energy Information Administration, International Energy Statistics; U.N. Food and Agriculture Organization, FAOSTAT; International Energy Agency, World Energy Balances; Organization of the Petroleum Exporting Countries, Annual Statistical Bulletin, 2018; BP, Statistical Review of World Energy, 2019.

period (1961 to 2017). We see that carbon dioxide (CO_2) emissions are now about four times higher than they were in 1961 and are continuing to grow. Nearly all scientists agree that CO_2 emissions are the most significant cause of human-induced **climate change**. The increasing trend of CO_2 emissions aligns with increases in other environmental impacts, such as water pollution, deforestation, and habitat degradation.

> **climate change:** long-term changes in global climate, including warmer temperatures, changing precipitation patterns, more extreme weather events, and rising sea levels

A central challenge of the twenty-first century is to transition to a more sustainable global economy—one that is more reliant on renewable energy, generates less waste, and respects ecological limits. We now turn to a summary of five key environmental issues that will need to be addressed if we are to make significant progress toward sustainability:

1. Global population
2. Nonrenewable resource availability
3. Renewable resources
4. Pollution and wastes
5. Climate change

1.1 Global Population

Economic and technological growth since the Industrial Revolution has fostered a dramatic increase in world population. In general, as population increases, so do negative environmental impacts. The global population has increased from approximately 1 billion in 1800 to 7.6 billion in 2019. According to the United Nations' "medium variant" population projection, global population will increase to nearly 10 billion by 2050 and to nearly 11 billion in 2100 (See Figure 16.2). The vast majority of population growth is expected to occur in developing countries, particularly in Africa.

Successfully predicting long-term population growth has proven to be difficult, as it depends on being able to accurately estimate how factors such as economic growth and women's education will affect fertility and mortality. This explains why the UN produces multiple forecasts. As Figure 16.2 illustrates, these forecasts are notably different from one another. In the "high variant" scenario, population grows to more than 15 billion in 2100, but in the "low variant" scenario, population peaks at just under 9 billion around 2055 and then starts to decline.

Obviously humanity's environmental impacts will be quite different in 2100 if only 7 billion humans are on the planet as opposed to 15 billion. Some demographers see the UN's high variant as a realistic scenario,[6] while others conclude that the low variant is the most likely outcome.[7] One thing that nearly everyone agrees on is that the most effective way to encourage declines in fertility is to enact

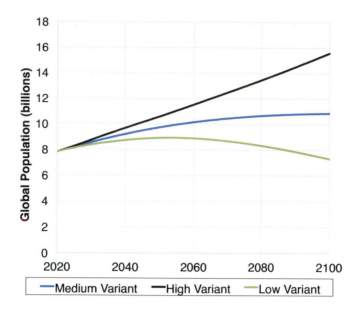

Figure 16.2 *United Nations Global Population Projections, 2020–2100*

Source: United Nations, World Population Prospects 2019.

policies that increase girls' education. Educated women are more likely to use contraception and desire fewer children because of higher opportunity costs if they leave the workforce to care for children.[8]

1.2 Nonrenewable Resources

Nonrenewable resources are those resources that do not regenerate through natural processes, at least on a human time scale, such as oil, coal, and mineral ores. While the global physical stock of a nonrenewable resource is a fixed quantity, known reserves fluctuate as some resources are extracted while new reserves are discovered. Also, changes in technology and prices can determine whether particular reserves are economically viable to exploit.

> **nonrenewable resources:** resources that do not regenerate through natural processes, at least on a human time scale, such as oil, coal, and mineral ores

Known global reserves of oil have actually been increasing in recent decades. Global reserves of many other important nonrenewable resources, including coal, natural gas, aluminum, copper, and lithium, are also sufficient to meet human needs for the foreseeable future. However, there are concerns about limited supplies of some nonrenewable resources. Some data suggest that about 90 percent of the world's supply of rare earth elements, used in many high-tech products such as cell phones and electric vehicles, may be running low.[9] Overall, the greatest concern with nonrenewable resources does not seem to be that we will run out in the foreseeable future but the negative environmental consequences of mining, consuming, and disposing of these resources. Policy solutions include increased recycling, effective mining regulations, and transitioning away from fossil fuels in favor of renewable energy.

1.3 Renewable Resources

Renewable resources such as forests, fisheries, freshwater, and soil are regenerated over time through natural and biological processes. If renewable resources are used by humans at rates below the natural rate of regeneration, then sustained availability is possible. Excessive rates of use, however, can lead to depletion or degradation of renewable resources. For example, overfishing can rapidly deplete fish stocks, possibly causing their complete collapse.

> **renewable resources:** resources that are regenerated over a short term through natural and biological processes, such as forests, fisheries, and freshwater

The health of many of the world's renewable resources is declining, including forests, fisheries, freshwater, agricultural soils, and biodiversity. While global deforestation rates have been declining, the world is still losing about 18 million acres of forests each year, shrinking wildlife habitats and contributing to climate change.[10] Nearly 90 percent of the world's fisheries are classified by the UN as either fully or overly exploited, leading to a call for policies such as catch limits and the elimination of harmful fishing subsidies.[11]

While freshwater is continually renewed through natural processes, only a limited amount is available for human use at any one time. Over 2 billion people live in countries experiencing water scarcity, with water stress expected to increase in the future as a result of climate change.[12] Another water challenge is excessive reliance on groundwater. India in particular is facing severe depletion of groundwater, mainly as a result of electricity subsidies that artificially lower the costs of pumping water.[13] In 2019, the World Economic Forum ranked water crises as the fourth most impactful global risk, behind only weapons of mass destruction, a failure to respond to climate change, and extreme weather events.[14]

According to the Food and Agriculture Organization of the United Nations, about a third of the world's soil has already been degraded. If population growth and current agricultural practices continue, the global amount of arable and productive land per person in 2050 will be only about a quarter of the level it was in 1960.[15] A 2019 UN report warns that one million species may be pushed to extinction in the coming years. The main threats to wild species are deforestation, overfishing, hunting, climate change, and pollution.[16]

1.4 Pollution and Wastes

As discussed in Chapter 8, damage from pollution is not reflected in traditional national accounting measures, even though it clearly reduces well-being. A 2017 study on the global health and economic costs of air, water, and soil pollution indicates that:

> Diseases caused by pollution were responsible for an estimated 9 million premature deaths in 2015—16% of all deaths worldwide—three times more deaths than from AIDS, tuberculosis, and malaria combined and 15 times more than from all wars and other forms of violence. . . . Pollution disproportionately kills the poor and the vulnerable. Nearly 92% of pollution-related deaths occur in low-income and middle-income countries and, in countries at every income level, disease caused by pollution is most prevalent among minorities and the marginalised.[17]

Of the 9 million deaths attributed to pollution, 6 million were linked to air pollution, 1.8 million to water pollution, and 0.8 million to workplace-related pollution. The global economic damage from pollution-related disease is estimated to be $4.6 trillion annually, or more than 6 percent of global economic output.

Pollution levels are generally declining in developed countries, producing significant economic benefits. For example, in the United States, aggregate emissions of the most common air pollutants have declined by 73 percent since the 1970s while providing about $30 in benefits for every dollar spent.[18] Meanwhile, air pollution in developing countries has typically increased. As we see in Figure 16.3, air

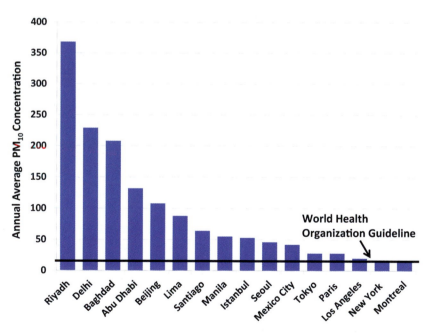

Figure 16.3 *Average Particulate Matter Concentration, Selected Major Cities*

Source: World Health Organization, Ambient Air Quality Database.

Notes: Particulate matter concentrations in μg/m³; data year varies by city, from 2012 to 2015.

pollution levels in most major cities in developing nations exceed the World Health Organization's recommended level of 20 micrograms per cubic meter ($\mu g/m^3$) of particulate matter (PM_{10}), composed of suspended particles of dust, ash, and other harmful material.

1.5 Climate Change: Science and Impacts

The vast majority of scientists have concluded that human activity is changing the planet's climate.[19] Emissions of various greenhouse gases, particularly CO_2 and methane from the extraction and burning of fossil fuels, trap heat near the earth's surface, leading not only to a general warming trend but to sea-level rise; ecological disruption; and an increase in severe weather events, such as hurricanes, floods, and droughts.

Climate change is already having an impact on both developed and developing countries. But the impact is more adverse in developing nations, as they tend to lack the resources to adapt to a changing climate and are located in tropical regions that will see the greatest impacts from extreme weather, rising seas, droughts, and disease spread. With increasing food scarcity, the number of people at risk of hunger is projected to increase up to 20 percent by 2050.[20] A 2019 paper finds that climate change is responsible for increased migration, not only directly due to crop failures, water scarcity, and extreme weather, but also indirectly as climate change increases the probability of armed conflicts.[21] According to another study, climate change "could fundamentally redraw the map of the planet, and where and how humans and other species can live."[22]

As we saw in Figure 16.1, global emissions of carbon dioxide have generally been increasing in recent decades. The wealthier OECD nations were responsible for the majority of global emissions up to 2003, but by 2016, the non-OECD nations emitted over 60 percent of the world's CO_2. China is currently the world's top emitter of carbon dioxide, followed by the United States, India, and Russia. While developing countries emit more total carbon than developed countries, emissions per capita are still much higher in richer nations. For example, annual CO_2 emissions per person are about 16 tons in the United States, 10 tons in Japan, 7.5 tons in China, 1.7 tons in India, and 0.5 tons in Ghana.[23]

At the 2015 international climate meeting in Paris, participating nations set a target of limiting the eventual global temperature increase to no more than 2° Celsius (3.6°F), relative to pre-industrial levels, and to pursue "efforts to limit the temperature increase to 1.5°C above pre-industrial levels, recognizing that this would significantly reduce the risks and impacts of climate change."[24] In order to meet these targets, global emissions of greenhouse gases will need to decline significantly. For example, the UN estimates that in order to limit warming to no more than 2°C, global emissions will need to fall about 25 percent by 2030 and to essentially zero by 2070.[25] But over time, global emissions instead continue to increase, lowering our chances of meeting these targets.

Dramatically reducing, or eliminating, carbon emission will require a transformation of how humans obtain energy. Currently the world economy obtains over 80 percent of its energy from fossil fuels, roughly equally split between coal, oil, and natural gas.[26] Research suggests that transitioning to a world that runs entirely on renewable energy by 2030 is technically feasible, and energy costs faced by users would be about the same as now.[27] Such a transition will require policy changes at the national and international level. We will explore climate change economics and policies in more detail in the final section.

Discussion Questions

1. Do you think policies are needed to reduce population growth rates? What specific policies, if any, would you recommend? Does your answer differ whether we are considering a developed or a developing nation?
2. Which resource and environmental problems, other than climate change, do you think are the most pressing? What kinds of policies might be appropriate in responding to these problems?

2. EXTERNALITIES

In Chapter 2, we introduced the concept of externalities. Recall that externalities are side effects, positive or negative, of an economic transaction that affect those not directly involved in the transaction. Pollution is the classic example of a negative externality. When a consumer buys a product, such as a T-shirt, he or she rarely considers the negative environmental impacts associated with its production. T-shirt producers generally do not consider these environmental impacts either. But these impacts clearly do occur, and society as a whole suffers damages from them. The externalities associated with producing T-shirts include the pesticides used to grow the cotton, the chemicals used to dye the shirts, the emissions from the fuels burned to transport the shirts to stores, and other costs.

2.1 Negative Externalities

We can analyze externalities using our standard supply-and-demand graph, as shown in Figure 16.4. In this hypothetical T-shirt market, we assume that neither consumers nor producers consider the negative externalities associated with T-shirts. Thus, the market equilibrium for T-shirts will be determined by the interaction of supply and demand, just as described in Chapter 3. In this market, the equilibrium price of T-shirts is $8, and the quantity sold is 25,000.

In order to include externalities in our model, we first need to think a little deeper about what a supply curve represents. Recall from Chapter 6 that a competitive firm maximizes its profits by producing as long as price is greater than or equal to its marginal production costs. So when we see in Figure 16.4 that firms are willing to supply a total of 25,000 T-shirts at a price of $8, we can conclude that each firm produces T-shirts up to the point where its marginal cost per shirt is $8. In other words, $8 is the highest marginal cost of T-shirts that firms are willing to supply at a price of $8. If the price rises to $8.10 per shirt, the quantity supplied

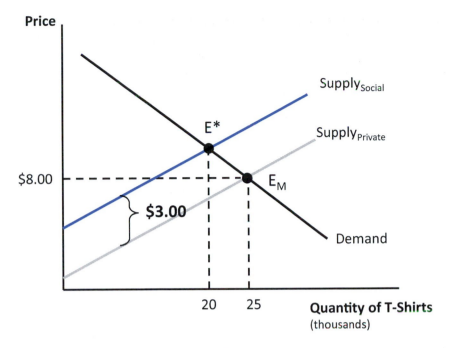

Figure 16.4 *Analysis of Negative Externality*

would be 25,100. We can then conclude two things about the marginal cost of producing these 100 additional T-shirts:

1. These 100 T-shirts all cost more than $8.00 to produce, because these 100 T-shirts were *not* produced when the price was only $8.00. In other words, these 100 T-shirts were not profitable when the price was only $8.00.
2. These 100 T-shirts all cost no more than $8.10 to produce, or else they wouldn't be profitable at a price of $8.10.

So we can conclude that at the higher price of $8.10 per T-shirt, the maximum marginal cost of T-shirts supplied to the market is $8.10. The point on the supply curve where price is $8.10 and quantity is 25,100 is actually telling us something about the marginal cost of production of the last few T-shirts. The important insight here is that points on a supply curve actually represent the marginal cost of the last few units supplied. Or, even more simply, a supply curve is actually an aggregate marginal cost curve!

We can now use this insight to incorporate externalities into our model. We label the market supply curve in Figure 16.4 *Supply*~Private~ because it is based solely on the marginal costs of private suppliers (i.e., T-shirt businesses). As previously stated, private suppliers do not consider externality costs. However, the true costs of supplying T-shirts not only include the private costs such as labor, materials, and transportation, but also the externality costs. So *Supply*~Private~ understates the true marginal costs of T-shirt production.

521

Economists have developed numerous techniques for estimating externality costs in monetary units, making inferences from market decisions and survey research. While we don't explore these techniques in this book, let's assume that the externality cost per T-shirt is $3. This $3 cost represents the damage from all the environmental impacts of T-shirt production, including pesticide runoff, air pollution, and so on.

The cost to society as a whole for each T-shirt produced is the sum of the private production cost and the external cost of $3. From the social perspective, the supply curve "should" be $Supply_{Social}$, not $Supply_{Private}$. Note that $Supply_{Social}$ is obtained by vertically adding $3 to each point on $Supply_{Private}$. Further, instead of the market equilibrium at E_M with 25,000 T-shirts being sold, the optimal social outcome is actually at $E*$ with only 20,000 T-shirts being sold. For each T-shirt sold above 20,000, *society is actually becoming worse off*, as the true social marginal costs (along $Supply_{Social}$) exceed the value consumers along the demand curve place on these T-shirts. In the presence of negative externalities, the unregulated market equilibrium will not be the best outcome from a social perspective—it is economically inefficient.

If the unregulated market outcome is inefficient, how can we shift to the optimal social outcome at $E*$? Economists tend to favor instituting a tax in a market with negative externalities. A tax that is levied in response to a negative externality is called a **Pigovian tax**, after British economist Arthur Pigou, who proposed the idea in the 1920s.

> **Pigovian tax:** a tax levied on a product to reduce or eliminate the negative externality associated with its production

Suppose that we impose a tax of $3 on each T-shirt, to be paid by producers. This tax increases the marginal cost of supplying each T-shirt by $3. Effectively, the Pigovian tax will shift $Supply_{Private}$ upward by $3 so that it overlaps $Supply_{Social}$. With the tax in place, the equilibrium will shift to $E*$—the economically efficient outcome considering society as a whole.

We say that the Pigovian tax has **"internalized the negative externality,"** because the external costs of $3 per T-shirt are now integrated into the market. While we indicated that producers paid the tax, you might think that the tax will simply be passed on to consumers, who will now pay $11 per shirt. But looking closely at our graph, we see that only some of the tax has been passed on to consumers. Note that the vertical distance between the two supply curves is always $3. At a quantity of 20,000 shirts, we see that price has increased from $8 by an amount smaller than the vertical distance between the two supply curves. So perhaps the price of T-shirts will rise from $8 to $9 or $10 as a result of the $3 tax.

> **internalizing negative externalities:** bringing external costs into the market (for example, by instituting a Pigovian tax at a level equal to the externality damage), thus making market participants pay the true social cost of their actions

The extent to which a Pigovian tax is passed on to consumers depends on the elasticity of demand. If demand for a product is relatively elastic, then producers won't be able to pass on much of the tax, because doing so will significantly reduce the quantity demanded. If demand is relatively inelastic, then producers can pass on most of the tax, because consumers won't significantly reduce their quantity demanded as price rises.

Note that a Pigovian tax internalizes, but doesn't eliminate, negative externalities. Externality damages are still $3 per shirt, but the quantity sold is now only 20,000 shirts. Also notice that the government now collects $60,000 in revenues from the tax. In principle, the government can use this revenue however it wants. Some economists suggest that the tax revenues should be used to lower other taxes, as we'll discuss later in the chapter.

Economists have estimated appropriate Pigovian taxes for various products, particularly gasoline and other fossil fuels. For example, two recent estimates of the Pigovian tax on gasoline in the United States are $1.60 and $3.80 per gallon, meaning that the price of gasoline should approximately double in order for its price to accurately reflect social costs.[28] For more on Pigovian taxes on fossil fuels, see Box 16.1.

BOX 16.1 PIGOVIAN TAXES ON FOSSIL FUELS

A 2015 analysis by the International Monetary Fund estimated Pigovian taxes on fossil fuels in 156 countries.[29] Taxes for coal, oil, and natural gas were calculated based on greenhouse gas emissions and local air pollutants. Taxes on motor fuels also included the externalities associated with accidents and road congestion.

The report found that energy prices in many countries "are set at levels that do not reflect environmental damage." The most significant externalities were associated with generating electricity using coal. As burning natural gas emits 40 percent less CO_2 per unit of energy than coal, suggested taxes on natural gas were more modest. For motor fuels, higher taxes were generally warranted due to the impacts of accidents and traffic congestion rather than emissions.

Appropriate Pigovian taxes varied considerably across countries. Recommended gasoline taxes were the equivalent of about $4.30/gallon in Japan, $4.00/gal. in Russia, $2.10/gal. in China, $1.60/gal. in the United States, and $0.80/gal. in Nigeria. The recommended coal tax was about 65 percent higher in China than in Germany due to fewer coal pollution regulations in China. The study found that coal taxes could significantly reduce air pollution deaths in many countries—by 66 percent in China, 63 percent in India, 47 percent in the United States, and 38 percent in the United Kingdom.

The report concludes that the results:

> suggest large and pervasive disparities between efficient fuel taxes and current practice in developed and developing countries alike, with much (in fact, a huge amount in many countries) at stake for fiscal, environmental, and health outcomes. The main challenge is how to get it done—how to build support for energy price reform.[30]

2.2 Positive Externalities

Externalities can also be positive, meaning that an economic transaction positively affects those outside the market. One example is a homeowner who installs solar panels on his or her house. Society as a whole benefits, because the solar panels reduce the need for generating electricity from fossil fuels, thus improving air quality and reducing other ecological damages.

We present a basic analysis of a positive externality in Figure 16.5. The demand for solar panels by homeowners is $Demand_{Private}$, assuming private consumers don't consider the social benefits of the panels. The market equilibrium is E_M, which is the normal intersection of supply and demand. The market price of solar panels would be P_M, and the quantity sold would be Q_M.

In addition to the demand for solar panels by homeowners, we need to add the benefits society as a whole receives from each panel. Similar to our addition to supply in the case of a negative externality, with a positive externality, we add the social benefit per panel to the demand curve. While the private demand curve represents how much consumers are willing to pay for solar panels, based on the perceived benefits to themselves, we also need to include the benefits to society as whole. This "social" demand curve is $Demand_{Social}$ in Figure 16.5. The social demand curve intersects the supply curve at $E*$, resulting in a higher quantity of $Q*$. From the social perspective, this is the "correct" or economically efficient level of solar panels.

In the case of a positive externality, the most common policy recommendation is to subsidize the product to encourage greater production. A **subsidy** is a per-unit payment to producers to offset, and thus lower, their production costs. This

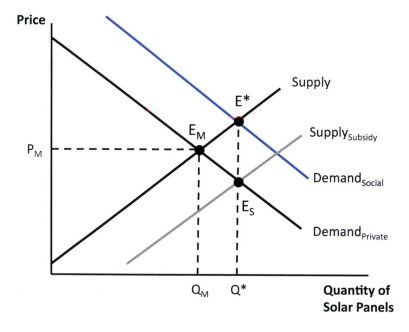

Figure 16.5 *Analysis of a Positive Externality*

effectively encourages greater production. We model a subsidy by shifting the supply curve downward, as it lowers the marginal production cost of each panel. With the appropriate subsidy in place, the new supply curve is $Supply_{Subsidy}$, and the new equilibrium point is E_S. The resulting level of solar panel sales, $Q*$, is the efficient level from the perspective of social welfare.

---

subsidy: a per-unit payment to producers to lower production costs and encourage greater production

---

Discussion Questions

1. What are some of the practical problems of internalizing negative externalities using Pigovian taxes? Can you think of situations where Pigovian taxes might not be the best policy?
2. Consider three different ways a Pigovian tax may be implemented on automobile use: a tax on gasoline, a tax on vehicle purchases, and a per-mile driving charge. Which one do you think would be the best approach for internalizing automobile externalities? Why?

3. MANAGING COMMON PROPERTY RESOURCES AND PUBLIC GOODS

3.1 Defining Common Property Resources and Public Goods

By implementing appropriate taxes and subsidies, governments can increase the social benefits we obtain from goods and services sold in private markets. But when we think about the range of environmental issues, we often need to go beyond the regulation of private goods to consider other types of goods.

Economists classify **private goods** as those that are excludable and rival. An **excludable good** is one whose consumption or use by others can be prevented by its owner. A **rival good** is one whose use by one person reduces the quantity or quality available to others. So your shirt would be considered a private good because, as the owner, you can legally prevent others from using your shirt. A shirt is also rival because two people can't wear the same shirt at the same time.

---

private good: a good that is excludable and rival
excludable good: a good whose consumption or use by others can be prevented by its owner(s)
rival good: a good whose use by one person reduces the quantity or quality available to others

---

Many environmental issues involve the management of goods that aren't private goods. Specifically, we will consider common property resources and public goods. Recall from our discussion in Chapter 2 that a **public good** is nonexcludable (goods whose benefits are freely available to all) and nonrival (goods whose use by some does not reduce the quantity or quality available to others). National defense is an example of a public good because no one in a country can be excluded from receiving the benefits of national defense, and the fact that I am "using" national defense does not reduce the quantity or quality of national defense available to others.

Common property resources are those that are nonexcludable and rival. An unregulated ocean fishery is an example of a common property resource because anyone can access the fishery. Note that a fishery is rival because excessive fishing pressure will lead to a reduction in the fishery stock.

> **public good:** a good that is nonexcludable and nonrival
> **common property resource:** a good or service that is nonexcludable and rival

Note that whether something is classified as a common property resource or a public good may depend on how heavily it is being used. A national park that is sparsely visited may be considered a public good if each additional visitor doesn't reduce the quality of the experience for others. But if the park gets quite crowded and each additional visitor reduces the quality of experience for others, then it would be considered a common property resource. We will now explore insights from economics about the management of common property resources and public goods.

3.2 Management of Common Property Resources

A common property resource is available to essentially anyone, but it cannot be used or enjoyed by multiple people at the same time, at least with the same level of quality. Overuse is often a problem with a common property resource, as when too many people fish the same fishery, want to play basketball on the same court, or withdraw groundwater from the same aquifer. We can use tools of economic analysis to examine how this problem arises and what policy solutions may be available.

One way to model a common property resource is to realize that eventually, every user of the resource essentially imposes a cost on other users. In the example of a fishery, if the number of fishing trips is relatively low, adding one more trip is unlikely to affect the catch of other fishers. But above a certain level, each additional fishing trip begins to harm the overall health of the fishery and thus reduce the catch of everyone else in the fishery. Each individual fisher will consider only whether he or she is making a profit. So the fact that others' profits have declined will not be taken into account by additional fishers. This is similar to the idea of a negative externality, but in this case, market participants are harming other market participants.

Figure 16.6 models a fishery as an example of a common property resource. The horizontal axis indicates the number of fishing trips taken in the fishery. Assume that it costs $15,000 to operate a fishing trip, considering labor costs, boat payments, fuel, and other costs. We also include the opportunity cost of fishing as part of the $15,000 total—by taking a fishing trip, one foregoes the opportunity to engage in the next best alternative, such as working a job as a teacher or electrician for a salary. The $15,000 cost represents the private cost of each fishing trip, as shown by

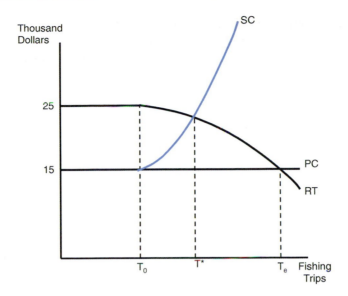

Figure 16.6 *Common Property Model of a Fishery*

the *PC* line in the graph. For simplicity, we assume that the cost to operate a fishing trip is constant, regardless of the number of trips taken.

Next, we need to consider the revenue obtained from each fishing trip. Obviously, this depends on the number of fish caught. For the first few trips, we assume that each fishing trip yields $25,000 in revenues (see curve *RT* in the graph). When we subtract operating costs, each fishing trip results in $10,000 in profits.

Initially, plenty of fish are available for all fishers, so each additional trip does not affect the catch of anyone else. Up to T_0, each fisher is able to obtain revenues of $25,000 per trip and profits of $10,000 per trip. But once the number of trips exceeds T_0, the revenue per trip begins to decline. The fishery is becoming crowded, and because more fishers are competing for limited fish stocks, it becomes more difficult to catch fish. Each fishing trip will still result in a profit, but, instead of making a $10,000 profit, the profit per trip will be smaller.

Each fisher will obviously be disappointed to have lower profits. But as long as profits are still positive (*RT* > *PC*), there is an incentive for more fishers to take trips to the area. In fact, as fishers begin to notice they are catching fewer fish per trip, they may be motivated to increase their fishing efforts in order to catch fish while they still have the opportunity. Note that even if profits per trip are quite small, as we've included opportunity costs in the $15,000 cost per trip, small profits are still better than the value of the next best alternative.

We can model the cost that additional fishers impose on others similarly to how we modeled a negative externality—it represents an additional cost above the private cost of operating a boat trip. Above T_0, each additional trip imposes a social cost as shown by curve SC, equal to the reduction in the profits of *all other fishers*. In other words, *SC* represents the total social cost of operating a boat trip above T_0, considering the private costs of $15,000 plus the external cost equal to the reduction in others' profits.

The socially efficient level of fishing trips is equal to $T*$. This is the level at which the profits from a new fishing trip are just enough to compensate for the loss of others' profits. Up to $T*$, total profits in the industry are increasing, but above $T*$, aggregate profits start to decline.

The problem is that in an unregulated fishery, there is no reason for fishers to stop at $T*$. So long as individual fishers can make a profit, the number of fishing trips will continue to increase until we reach T_c. At this point, the economic profit for each fishing trip falls to 0. There will then be no further incentive for additional fishing trips. But at such a high level of fishing effort, the health of the fishery is likely to decline. Over time, the stock of fish may become so depleted that the fishery crashes, leading to collapse of the local fishing industry. The collapse of a common property resource is often referred to as the "tragedy of the commons."

One solution to the problem of overuse of a common property resource is much like the implementation of a Pigovian tax. We could charge a fee for each fishing trip equal to the external cost imposed on others. If fishers had to pay this fee in addition to their out-of-pocket costs of $15,000, we could adjust the fee until we reached the efficient level of fishing trips, $T*$. This solution has the problem that in this industry, there are a few very large companies, but the far more numerous individuals who make their living by fishing are typically not well off; any tax is likely to have serious welfare consequences for them.

Another solution is to institute **individual transferable quotas** (ITQs). With this approach, an organization managing the resource (such as a government agency) sets the total allowable fishing level, such as the number of fishing trips or the total harvest per season. This level of effort is set low enough to maintain the ecological integrity of the resource. The ITQs can be distributed for free or auctioned off to the highest bidders. If they are auctioned, the proceeds can be used by the government to maintain the quality of the resource or as compensation for those who are forced out of the industry. Holders of ITQs may then use them to fish or offer them for sale to interested parties. The price of an ITQ is not set by the government but allowed to vary depending on supply and demand. ITQ programs for ocean fisheries have been established in several countries, including Australia, Canada, Iceland, and the United States. (For more on ITQs, see Box 16.2.)

> **individual transferable quota (ITQ):** tradable rights to access or harvest a common property resource, such as the right to harvest a particular quantity of fish

3.3 Management of Public Goods

Public goods are at the opposite end of the spectrum from private goods. For private goods, the ability to charge a price acts as way to exclude nonbuyers. But anyone can enjoy the benefits of a public good without paying, and each additional user does not affect the amount or quality of the good available to others. Hence, we can't rely on private markets to provide the efficient level of public goods. In fact,

BOX 16.2 COMMON PROPERTY RESOURCE MANAGEMENT IN PRACTICE: INDIVIDUAL TRANSFERABLE QUOTAS

Iceland has one of the most extensive systems of individual transferable quotas for its marine fisheries. In 1990, Iceland passed the Fisheries Management Act, which established ITQs for all fisheries, with permits allocated to each fishing vessel based on its proportional share of the national catch during a baseline period. Each year, the total allowable catch is determined based on the current scientific evidence regarding the health of each fishery. For example, the allowable cod catch each year is set equal to 20 percent of the "catchable biomass" of the stock. As the health of the cod fishery has improved, the allowable catch has increased—from 130,000 tons in 2007 to about 230,000 tons in 2015.[31]

The ITQs are fully tradable and even divisible into smaller shares if a fisher wishes to only transfer part of his or her total allocation. Iceland has also implemented regulations that prohibit one company from obtaining an excessive proportion of the permits for a fishery. For example, one company cannot have the rights to more than 12 percent of the national cod allowable catch or 20 percent of the halibut catch. A separate quota system is in place specifically for smaller boats to allow the coexistence of both small- and large-scale fishing operations.[32]

According to Sigurdur Ingi Johannsson, the minister of fisheries and agriculture, the ITQ system has been very successful, as the approach has both improved the health of Iceland's fisheries and led to an increase in fishery revenues. He said, "We need to use responsible, science-based analysis, but I would say it's a case of so far, so good. Cod, our most valuable fish-stock, is stronger than it has been for 50 years. We are also using fewer vessels, too, which is having less of an environmental impact."[33]

even though many people value the benefits of public goods, private markets normally fail to provide any public goods at all.

Consider again national defense as an example of a public good. Could we rely on a megacorporation to provide national defense in a market setting? Obviously not. No individual would have an incentive to pay because he or she could receive essentially the same level of benefits without paying. Thus the "equilibrium" quantity of public goods in a market setting is normally zero, as no company would want to produce something for which no one is willing to pay.

Perhaps we could rely on donations to supply public goods. This is done with some public goods, such as public radio and public television. Also, some environmental groups conserve habitats that, while privately owned, can be considered public goods because they are open for public enjoyment. Donations, however, generally are not sufficient for an efficient level of public goods since public goods are nonexcludable—although some people may be willing to donate money to public radio, many others simply listen to it without paying anything. Those who do not pay, but still receive benefits, are called **free riders**.

> **free riders:** those who obtain the benefits of a public good without paying anything for it

Although we cannot rely on private markets or voluntary donations to supply public goods, their adequate supply is of crucial interest to society. One potential source of funding public goods is through taxes collected by the government. Since we all pay taxes, the cost of providing public goods is shared by taxpayers. In democracies, decisions regarding the provision of public goods, such as the national defense or environmental public goods, are commonly decided in the political arena. In most countries, elected officials make these decisions for society as a whole. An alternative is to devise a participatory approach where people vote on proposals to increase or decrease the funding for specific projects. For example, town residents may vote on a proposal to increase funding for public schools or parks, which would require higher taxes if approved. Regardless of how the decision is made, some people will surely feel they are paying too much in taxes to support certain public goods. Debates regarding efficiency and fairness in the case of public goods are inevitably both political and economic in nature.

Discussion Questions

1. Suppose that you are living with three roommates in an apartment with a common area for living, dining, and cooking. Do you think that a "tragedy of the commons" outcome is a likely result without some rules regarding cleaning? What rules would you propose instituting?
2. Consider the provision levels of the following public goods in society: national defense, public education, environmental quality, and highways. Do you think that the current "supply" of each of these goods is too high, too low, or about right? What factors do you think determine the amount of resources that are allocated toward each of these goods? Do policies need to be changed to adjust the allocation?
3. How would individual transferable quotas affect people whose livelihood depends on fishing? Does this seem more or less fair than a tax on fish that are caught?

4. ECONOMIC GROWTH AND THE ENVIRONMENT

Economic growth has generally been associated with increasing environmental damage. But does further growth necessarily have to come at the expense of the environment? What would an economy that is environmentally sustainable look like, and how might we transition to it?

In this section, we explore the relationship between economic growth and the environment in three ways:

1. How does economic growth tend to affect environmental quality?
2. Does protecting the environment harm employment and economic growth?
3. How have economists envisioned the transition to a more sustainable economy?

4.1 The Environmental Kuznets Curve Hypothesis

Some researchers have suggested that, in the long run, economic development reduces environmental damages. The logic behind this assertion is that sufficient wealth and technology allow countries to adopt clean production methods and move to a more service-based economy.

The **environmental Kuznets curve (EKC) hypothesis** posits an inverted U-shaped relationship between economic development and environmental damages. It states that environmental damage per capita increases in the early stages of economic development as a country transitions away from an agricultural-based economy to an economy with more manufacturing, energy use, transportation, and so on. Eventually, however, damages reach a maximum and then diminish as a country attains even higher levels of income, allowing it to invest in cleaner production methods. If the evidence supports this hypothesis, it would imply that policies that foster economic growth will eventually promote a cleaner environment as well.

> **environmental Kuznets curve (EKC) hypothesis:** the theory that as a country develops economically environmental damages per capita initially increase, then peak and eventually decrease

The evidence indicates that the EKC relationship does seem to hold for some pollutants. Figure 16.7 shows the findings of a study that estimated the relationship between the average particulate matter (PM_{10}) concentration in a country and a country's per capita income. We see that at very low levels of income, PM_{10} concentration tends to rise quickly as a country develops economically. But the PM_{10}

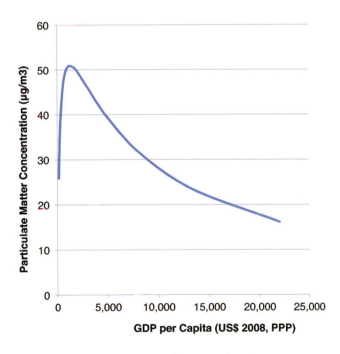

Figure 16.7 *Environmental Kuznets Curve for Particulate Matter*

Source: Mazurek, Jiří. 2011. "Environmental Kuznets Curve—A Tie Between Environmental Quality and Economic Prosperity." *Ekonomie a Management,* 14(4):22–31.

concentration peaks when a country reaches an average income of around $1,300 per person. Air pollution levels then fall steadily with further economic advancement. As noted earlier in the chapter, the World Health Organization has recommended that PM_{10} levels be below $20\mu g/m^3$. On average, countries achieve this standard when income per person rises above $17,000. Evidence supporting the EKC hypothesis has also been found for municipal solid waste and other air pollutants such as sulfur dioxide and carbon monoxide.[34]

However, the EKC relationship does not appear to hold for several other major environmental problems. Perhaps most importantly, CO_2 emissions show a continuous positive relationship with average income, as shown in Figure 16.8. A simple statistical test to fit an inverted-U curve through the data in Figure 16.8 finds that there is no turning point—per capita CO_2 emissions continue to rise as GDP per capita increases. A more sophisticated analysis in 2015 reached a similar conclusion, that "rising income is associated with an increase in [CO_2] emissions. No income turning points are found for the observed sample of countries." Thus, simply promoting economic growth does not appear to be an effective means to address the issue of global climate change.

The relationship between economic growth and the environment is, in reality, more complex than implied by the EKC hypothesis. As a 2014 paper concludes:

> it would be misleading to follow the policy of polluting first and cleaning later as espoused by proponents of EKC. It does not make much sense to "do nothing" and wait for the magic-wand of economic growth to cure environmental problems. Proactive policies and measures are required to mitigate the problem.[35]

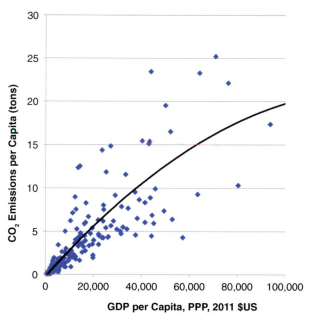

Figure 16.8 *Relationship Between Carbon Dioxide Emissions and GDP per Capita, 2014*

Source: World Bank, World Development Indicators database.

4.2 Does Protecting the Environment Harm Employment and Economic Growth?

Policies that increase environmental protections are sometimes criticized for causing decreases in employment or harming economic growth. What is the evidence on this subject?

Several research studies have explored the relationship between employment and environmental regulation. The overall conclusion is that while increased environmental spending leads to the loss of certain jobs, it creates other jobs. These effects may cancel out or actually result in a net gain of jobs. For example, a 2008 analysis of the U.S. economy tested the notion that environmental protection results in job losses. The study estimated the impact of environmental spending and regulation on employment in various industries and found that:

> contrary to conventional wisdom, [environmental protection (EP)], economic growth, and jobs creation are complementary and compatible: Investments in EP create jobs and displace jobs, but the net effect on employment is positive.[36]

A 2009 review of the literature on the relationship between environmental policies and employment concluded that strong environmental policies will change the distribution of jobs in society but have little effect on the overall level of employment.[37] Focused on Europe, the study found that well-designed environmental policies can sometimes result in net job gains. For example, the additional revenue from higher environmental taxes could be used to reduce the taxes on labor, thus reducing the cost of hiring workers and leading to higher overall employment.

A similar conclusion was reached by a 2016 analysis that estimated the employment impacts of various potential policies to reduce carbon emissions in the United States and found that job losses in "dirty" sectors such as coal mining would be offset by job gains in cleaner sectors such as renewable energy. They concluded that the "overall effects on unemployment should not be a substantial factor in the evaluation of environmental policy" because the net effects are likely to be quite small.[38]

According to a 2012 paper, public investments in clean energy in the United States create about three times as many jobs as similar spending on fossil fuel energy sources. The reasons are that clean energy sources tend to be more labor intensive, and the money invested is more likely to be spent domestically, as opposed to funding imports.

Another criticism of environmental protection is that environmental regulations reduce GDP growth rates. Some studies support this argument. For example, a comprehensive analysis of the Clean Air Act in the United States estimated that economic output in 1990 was about 1 percent lower than it would have been without the policy. The aggregate macroeconomic loss from the Act over the period 1973–1990 was estimated to be about $1 trillion.[39] However, such findings are contradicted by more recent analysis. For example, a 2017 OECD report argues that integrating measures to tackle climate change into regular economic policy will have a positive impact on economic growth over the medium and long term.[40]

In any case, any economic costs that might exist must be assessed against the benefits of the regulations. When an estimate of the Clean Air Act benefits was made, it was found that the central estimate of the 1973–1990 benefits was $22 trillion, or a benefit–cost ratio of 22:1. So while some studies find a slight negative impact of environmental regulation on economic growth as traditionally measured, we need a more complete analysis to determine its overall effect on social well-being. As we saw in Chapter 8, GDP was never intended to measure social well-being, and economists have developed alternative national accounting approaches to supplement or replace GDP. These alternatives offer a more comprehensive framework for fully assessing the impacts of environmental regulations on social well-being.

4.3 Economic Perspectives on the Transition to a Sustainable Economy

Let us now consider whether continued economic growth is compatible with environmental sustainability. Some economists believe that, at least for the foreseeable future, further economic growth is acceptable or desirable as we transition to a more sustainable economy. Other economists believe that we have already exceeded the planet's carrying capacity and advocate for a transition to a "no growth" economy, perhaps requiring a period of de-growth during that transition.

One proponent of the view that continued growth is desirable is the United Nations. The UN's Green Economy Initiative, launched in 2008, seeks to promote an economy that "results in improved human well-being and social equity, while significantly reducing environmental risks and ecological scarcities." The Initiative proposed an annual investment of 2 percent of global GDP over 2010–2050 to fund sustainable technologies and practices. The UN developed a macroeconomic model to estimate the short-term and long-term effects of this investment relative to a business–as–usual (BAU) scenario. Their results found that, while in the first few years, the additional investment reduced global GDP/capita by about 1 percent, by 2030, global GDP/capita would be 2 percent higher in the Green Economy scenario relative to BAU. And by 2050, global GDP/capita would be 14 percent higher as a result of sustainable investments.[41]

The Green Economy scenario resulted in dramatic reductions in predicted environmental impacts. Relative to the BAU scenario, by 2050, global energy demand is reduced by 40 percent, water demand is reduced by 22 percent, total forested land increases by 21 percent, and the global ecological footprint is reduced by 48 percent.

Economist Robert Pollin, in his 2015 book *Greening the Global Economy*, also advocates for an investment of 1.5 percent of global GDP in renewable energy and energy efficiency to fund a transition to a sustainable, low-carbon economy. His analysis concludes that green investments expand employment and economic growth, as jobs in renewable energy and energy efficiency tend to be more labor intensive than jobs in the fossil fuel sector, as shown in Figure 16.9. In each country, investments in green energy result in higher job creation, yielding 75–135 percent more jobs per dollar than fossil fuel investments. To assist displaced fossil fuel-industry workers, Pollin argues for job retraining programs and policies promoting full employment.[42]

534

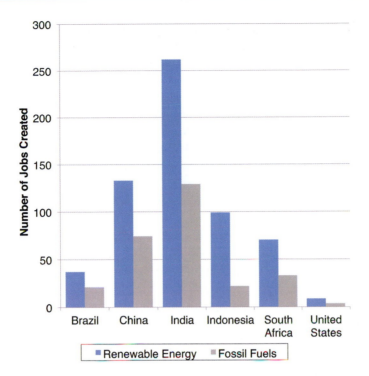

Figure 16.9 *Jobs Created by Investing $1 Million in Clean Energy Versus Fossil Fuels*

Source: Pollin, Robert. 2015. *Greening the Global Economy.* MIT Press, Cambridge, MA.

Analyses such as Pollin's book and the UN's Green Economy Initiative suggest that not only is sustainability compatible with economic growth, green investments can actually *increase* rates of economic growth. But other economists argue that continual economic growth is incompatible with long-term sustainability. Economist Herman Daly has noted that continual expansion of the macroeconomy within a finite biosphere is physically impossible. Since the 1970s, Daly has advocated for a transition to a **steady-state economy** in which population and the stock of physical capital are held constant.

> **steady-state economy:** an economy that holds constant population and the stock of physical capital

A steady-state economy would not hold human well-being constant, as things such as technology, information, fairness, and wisdom could continue to improve. Also, activities that do not involve resource consumption, and are environmentally neutral or environmentally friendly, could continue to grow. Such activities could include services, arts, communication, and education. Daly maintains that consumption levels should be kept "sufficient" but not extravagant. He distinguishes between growth and development—the steady-state economy "develops but does not grow, just as the planet earth, of which it is a subsystem, develops without growing."[43]

A similar viewpoint is espoused in Tim Jackson's book *Prosperity Without Growth*. Jackson calls for an ecological macroeconomics that maintains economic stability without a reliance on traditional growth. He proposes that macroeconomic interventions such as a transition toward service-based activities with limited environmental impacts, investments in ecological assets, and working time policies that maintain employment levels but lower economic production and hours worked are necessary to transition to a sustainable economy.[44]

Economist Peter Victor, in his book *Managing Without Growth: Slower by Design, not Disaster*, has developed a macroeconomic model to explore how a national economy would perform during a transition to a sustainable low- or zero-growth future.[45] Figure 16.10 shows Victor's model applied to the Canadian economy. In this scenario, the Canadian government is assumed to introduce a comprehensive program for lowering greenhouse gas (GHG) emissions by imposing a carbon price on GHG emissions, investing in GHG emissions reduction, and the electrification of road and rail transport. Such measures are predicted to reduce greenhouse gas emissions by 85 percent by the year 2067.

Victor's model for the Canadian economy shows that GDP per capita stabilizes after 2052, and the environmental burden index (which includes variables such as GHG emissions) decreases by 14 percent by the year 2067. Reduced working hours play a key role in preventing increases in unemployment. A range of government policies, including more spending on health care and education, is predicted to reduce the level of inequality by 56 percent by the year 2067. The Sustainable Prosperity Index, combining various economic, environmental, and social variables, is predicted to rise by 35 percent by 2067.

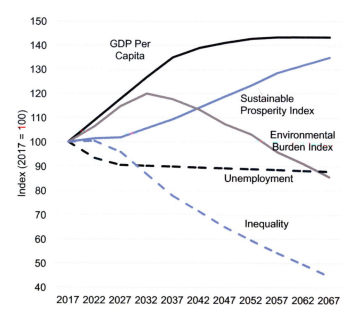

Figure 16.10 *A No-Growth Scenario for the Canadian Economy*

Source: Victor, Peter. 2019. *Managing Without Growth: Slower by Design, not Disaster.* Edward Elgar, Northampton, MA.

Discussion Questions

1. What is the principle of the environmental Kuznets curve (EKC)? In what areas does it seem applicable, and in what ways could it be inaccurate or misleading? What are some policy implications that can be drawn from an analysis of the evidence regarding the EKC?
2. The promotion of economic growth is often seen as a major policy goal. What do you think is the feasibility of a model that stresses alternative goals such as ecological sustainability and well-being? How would you compare the Green Economy and steady-state economy concepts?

5. POLICIES FOR SUSTAINABLE DEVELOPMENT

Regardless of whether we favor "green" growth or no growth, policy changes will be needed to achieve a more sustainable economy. In this section, we explore some of the environmental policies advocated by economists. But first, we need to define sustainability more precisely.

5.1 Defining Sustainability

While nearly everyone agrees that we should transition to a more sustainable economy, what exactly does this mean? Economists studying the environment have proposed two definitions of sustainability. One definition, referred to as **weak sustainability**, assumes that natural capital and other types of capital (produced, human, or social) are substitutes. Thus, weak sustainability asserts that natural capital depreciation is justified as long as it is compensated for with adequate increases in other types of capital. So, for example, the destruction of a wetland in order to construct a new highway could be justified if the economic and social benefits of the highway exceeded the lost ecological value of the wetland.

Strong sustainability takes the perspective that sustainability should be defined solely in terms of natural capital. Under strong sustainability, natural and other types of capital are not substitutes. Strong sustainability doesn't mean that natural capital can never be degraded, but it requires that any degradation of a particular type of natural capital (such as the cutting of a forest for timber) be compensated for with appropriate natural capital restoration (such as replanting trees or restoring a wetland).

---

weak sustainability: an analytical perspective suggesting that natural capital depreciation is justified as long as it is compensated for with adequate increases in other types of capital

strong sustainability: an analytical perspective suggesting that natural capital depreciation is justified only if it is compensated for with adequate restoration of other natural capital

---

Strong sustainability isn't necessarily "better" than weak sustainability, but it changes the metrics we would use to determine whether an economy is sustainable.

For weak sustainability, we could use a metric such as the Genuine Progress Indicator or the Better Life Index (discussed in Chapter 8), which combine economic, social, and environmental components. The value of both of these indicators could theoretically increase even if overall environmental quality declines, as long as other components increase sufficiently.

Meanwhile, if we wished to pursue strong sustainability, then we would only need data on natural capital. We could keep satellite accounts on all important natural capital variables, such as fishery stocks, forest area, greenhouse gas emissions, and mineral reserves. Satellite accounts can be maintained in physical units, such as tons of fish, board-feet of timber, and so on, or in monetary units. If the accounts are measured in physical units, then comparisons across different categories are difficult. For example, what would we conclude about natural capital overall if we lose 50 acres of wetlands and deplete fish stocks by 100 tons but gain 80 acres of forest? Measuring accounts in monetary units allows for direct comparisons, but converting all variables to monetary units is not straightforward and requires many assumptions. The Sarkozy Commission (mentioned in Chapter 8) recommended a "dashboard" approach to assessing environmental sustainability, relying on disaggregated physical indicators with a particular emphasis on monitoring variables related to climate change.

The ecological footprint measure, discussed in Chapter 4, provides another perspective on sustainability. Recall that, according to the ecological footprint results, humanity is already in a situation of unsustainable "overshoot." The most recent data suggest that humanity's global environmental impacts are equivalent to using 1.7 earths, considering all the resources we use and the wastes we generate.

Disaggregating the global ecological footprint provides some insight into how we can reach a sustainable level of impacts. In Figure 16.11, we see that about 60 percent of humanity's ecological footprint is attributed to its carbon emissions. In order to bring our overall impacts down to a sustainable level, global carbon emissions would need to decline by at least 70 percent, as strongly recommended by the vast majority

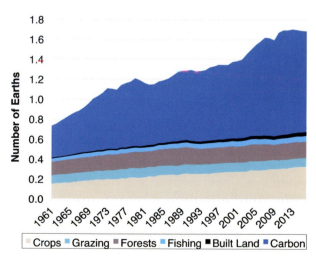

Figure 16.11 *Global Ecological Footprint, by Impact Type, 1961–2016*

Source: Global Footprint Network, NFA 2019 National Footprint and Biocapacity Accounts dataset.

of climate scientists. Of course, this doesn't necessarily mean we shouldn't reduce other negative impacts, such as deforestation and overfishing. But once again, we conclude that addressing climate change is our most critical environmental challenge.

5.2 Green Taxes and Subsidy Reform

As we've already seen, Pigovian taxes are justified by widely accepted economic theory. The policy implications of expanding environmental taxes are extensive. Virtually every product produced in modern markets results in *some* pollution and waste generation. Given that a Pigovian tax increases economic efficiency, should we tax *every* product based on its environmental impacts?

Few economists would support placing an environmental tax on every product. The first reason is that we must consider the administrative costs of collecting Pigovian taxes. For some products with relatively minor environmental impacts, the tax benefits are probably not worth the administrative costs. Second, the task of estimating the environmental damage of *every* product sold, in dollars, is clearly excessive.

Some economists have thus suggested a broad system of **upstream taxes** on the most environmentally damaging products, particularly on fossil fuels (coal, oil, and natural gas), as well as important minerals and key renewable resources. An upstream tax is placed as close as possible to the point where raw materials are extracted. In the case of coal, for example, an upstream tax might be instituted on each ton of coal extracted from coal mines. Upstream taxes on a handful of products are easier to implement than taxes on numerous final consumer goods.

Of course, the upstream taxes would ultimately lead to higher prices on final goods, such as gasoline, air travel, and electricity. In many countries, these cost increases would fall most heavily on lower-income people. In order to avoid an overall increase in economic inequality, complementary policies would be needed, such as increased funding for public transportation or direct rebates to lower-income households.

> **upstream taxes:** taxes instituted as close as possible in a production process to the extraction of raw materials

The main barrier to implementing Pigovian taxes is that few politicians are willing to support higher taxes. However, environmental taxes can be **revenue neutral** if any tax increases are offset by lowering other taxes so that the total taxes on an average household remain unchanged. Given that environmental taxes tend to be regressive, revenue neutrality could be achieved by reducing a regressive tax, such as social insurance taxes.

> **revenue-neutral (taxes):** offsetting any tax increases with decreases in other taxes such that overall tax collections remain constant

In addition to higher economic efficiency, a broad shift away from taxes on income and toward taxes on negative externalities provides people with more options to reduce their tax burden. If environmental taxes constituted a large portion of some-one's total tax burden, he or she could reduce this burden by using more efficient vehicles and appliances, relying more on public transportation, reducing energy use, and numerous other options (some of which, however, depend on whether social goods, such as public transportation, are actually available). Again, we would need to consider how such policies would affect people at different income levels. Higher-income households may be able to afford efficient appliances, electric vehicles, and other environmentally friendly products. But lower-income households will have fewer options for avoiding the impact of Pigovian taxes. As stated previously, comple-mentary policies would be necessary to avoid exacerbating existing inequalities.

As we saw earlier in the chapter, subsidies can be used to encourage people to pur-chase products that generate positive externalities, such as solar panels and electric vehicles. For example, Norway has the most extensive subsidies for electric vehicles. About one-third of all new vehicles sold in Norway were pure electric vehicles, compared to only about 1 percent of all new vehicles sold globally being battery powered.[46]

Unfortunately, subsidies currently in place in many countries instead *encourage* environmentally damaging behaviors. Agricultural and energy subsidies encourage the overuse of electricity, gasoline, fertilizer, pesticides, and irrigation water. Reducing or eliminating these subsidies would reduce government expenditures, and the money saved could be used to lower taxes or to promote more sustainable practices. The fossil fuel industry receives the largest share of these perverse subsidies. This mispric-ing of goods and services effectively permits producers to transfer the costs of environmental damage on to society. (See Box 16.3.)

BOX 16.3 FOSSIL FUEL SUBSIDIES

Fossil fuels are subsidized by governments around the world in numerous explicit and implicit ways. Beyond reducing suppliers' production costs through direct subsidies, implicit subsidies include the failure to institute appropriate Pigovian taxes on fossil fuels for air pollution and climate change damages. According to a comprehensive 2017 journal article, global fossil fuel subsidies were $5.3 trillion in 2015, equal to 6.5 percent of global GDP.[47]

About half of total subsidies were attributed to a failure to internalize the externalities associated with local air pollution. Another 22 percent of subsidies were related to global climate change externalities. The analysis found that coal subsidies were larger than oil and natural gas subsidies combined. Among countries, China's annual subsidy was the largest, at nearly $2 tril-lion, while the United States had the second largest subsidy, around $0.6 trillion.

The authors conclude that the economic and environmental benefits of eliminating perverse fossil fuel subsidies are significant:

> The gains for subsidy reform are substantial and diverse: getting energy prices right (i.e., replacing current energy prices with prices fully reflecting supply and envi-ronmental costs) would have reduced global carbon emissions in 2013 by 21% and fuel-related air pollution deaths by 55%, while raising extra revenue of 4% of global GDP and raising social welfare by 2.2% of global GDP.[48]

5.3 Green Macroeconomic Policies

Designing macroeconomic policies that are compatible with sustainability requires some fundamental rethinking about economic goals. The macroeconomic models we developed in earlier chapters have implicitly assumed that more employment, and thus more income, is better. There is no doubt that employment contributes to people's well-being. People's satisfaction with their jobs is an important predictor of their overall life satisfaction.[49] Thus, maintaining employment levels is important, but people also benefit from time that they spend away from paid employment to do unpaid work, including family care, and to pursue leisure activities.

Several European countries have instituted labor policies that mandate comparatively short working weeks for most employees. Both France and Germany have instituted a standard 35-hour working week. According to one study, policies to reduce annual work hours by just 0.5 percent per year for the remainder of this century could mitigate one-quarter to one-half of future global warming.[50]

As discussed in previous chapters, Keynesian economics focuses on using monetary and fiscal policy to spur aggregate demand during economic downturns. In response to the global financial crisis of 2007–2008, some economists proposed implementing Keynesian macroeconomic policies to both promote an economic recovery and meet sustainability objectives. In fact, stimulus packages passed in several countries in response to the crisis included significant public investment in green projects. For example, over 10 percent of the 2009 stimulus package passed in the United States (the American Recovery and Reinvestment Act) was directed toward investment in energy efficiency, renewable energy, and other green spending. Green stimulus government spending in China was even higher, at over $200 billion.[51]

Some critics have argued that there is a contradiction between the "green Keynesian" goals of economic growth and environmental protection.[52] But it is possible to direct policies toward different kinds of growth. Instead of just thinking of consumption (C), investment (I), and government spending (G), we can divide each of these terms into environmentally harmful and environmentally positive impacts. Thus, it should be possible to achieve growth in employment and well-being while reducing **throughput**—the flow of inputs into the economy and outputs of wastes and pollution. According to one "green Keynesian" analysis:

> we can distinguish between those macroeconomic aggregates that should be strictly limited—resource-intensive consumption and investment, and energy-intensive infrastructure—and those that can expand over time without negative environmental consequences. The latter would include large areas of health, education, cultural activity, and resource- and energy-conserving investment . . . there is plenty of scope for growth in economic activity concentrated in these categories, without growth in resource throughput, and with a significant decline in the most damaging throughput, that of carbon-intensive fuels.[53]

> **throughput:** the flow of raw materials and energy through the economy, leading to outputs of waste

Discussion Questions

1. What specific economic incentives and policies would you recommend for promoting sustainability? Have you heard of any policy examples from the news recently that you think were good ideas?
2. Can you identify areas in which "green Keynesian" economic growth would be desirable and areas in which economic growth is more destructive to the environment? In what ways would a "green" economy look different from our current economy?

6. CLIMATE CHANGE: ECONOMICS AND POLICY

Climate change is widely considered our greatest environmental challenge. Further, climate change ties together many of the issues we have discussed in this chapter and throughout the text. Emissions of greenhouse gases are clearly a negative externality. The earth's atmosphere is a global common property resource that is suffering from a tragedy of the commons problem. Critics of aggressive climate policies suggest that such policies would hamper economic growth and result in job losses.

Climate change raises important economic and human development questions. Will addressing climate change limit the economic aspirations of developing countries? How should the cost of climate policies be split between developed and developing countries? In this final section, we explore insights from economics about climate change.

6.1 Economic Analysis of Climate Change

Carbon dioxide emissions are clearly a negative externality, and thus the standard economic response is to tax them. This tax, reflecting the current and future environmental damages from emitting CO_2 (normally 1 ton), is referred to as the **social cost of carbon**. As far back as the 1990s, economists have widely recommended instituting carbon pricing as a policy response to climate change.[54] However, estimates of the social cost of carbon have varied considerably. A relatively low social cost of carbon would imply a modest policy response to climate change. A high social cost of carbon would mean that climate change demands more aggressive policies.

> **social cost of carbon:** a monetary estimate of the discounted long-term damages from emitting a ton of CO_2 in a given year

Most initial estimates of the social cost of carbon were quite low. For example, in 1992, William Nordhaus (who received the 2018 Nobel Memorial Prize in economics for his climate change analyses) estimated that the social cost of carbon should start at around $1 per ton of CO_2 and gradually rise to $5/ton in 2100.[55] For context, a carbon tax of $1/ton of CO_2 would raise the price of a gallon of gasoline by only about 1 cent and obviously have very little impact on the quantity of gas demanded or carbon emissions.

While Nordhaus has adjusted his social cost of carbon upward over time—in a 2017 paper, he calculated a value of \$31/ton of CO_2[56]—other economists conclude that the social cost of carbon should be even higher. The 2006 *Stern Review of the Economics of Climate Change*, written by economist Nicholas Stern, estimated a social cost of carbon of \$85 per ton of CO_2. A 2015 paper by researchers at Stanford University concluded that the social cost of carbon should be \$220/ton,[57] and a 2018 journal article obtained an even higher value of \$417/ton.[58] What accounts for these differences in the social cost of carbon?

One important factor in calculating the social cost of carbon is how to value future damages. Carbon emitted into the atmosphere persists for decades, so we need to economically value damages that will occur in the future. Economists do this by applying a **discount rate** to any future impact. A discount rate is expressed as a percentage, indicating how much future impacts are reduced for each year into the future that they occur. So, for example, if a damage of \$100 million occurs 50 years into the future, using a discount rate of 3 percent, we would value that future damage today at only about \$23 million [\$100 million/$(1.03)^{50}$]. Thus, in this scenario, economists would recommend not spending more than \$23 million today in order to avoid \$100 million in damages 50 years from now. Future damages are discounted more the higher the discount rate and the longer the time period.

> **discount rate:** the annual percentage rate at which future impacts are discounted relative to the present

Economists justify discounting for a couple of reasons. First, assuming real rates of economic growth remain positive, future generations will be richer than we are today. So, expressed as a percentage of total income, \$100 million in damages in 50 years is not as significant as a \$100 million damage today. Second, discounting reflects the general tendency for people to devalue the future relative to today. Young people frequently save very little for retirement because they simply don't concern themselves much about their future selves. From a policy perspective, discounting means that we place less weight on future generations relative to our present needs.

The discount rate used in an economic analysis of climate change can significantly influence the social cost of carbon and, consequently, the policy recommendations. William Nordhaus's models have used a discount rate of around 3 percent, concluding that relatively modest policies are needed (he has gradually reduced his discount rate over time). Meanwhile, Nicholas Stern's rate of 1.4 percent produces a recommendation for more aggressive climate policies. Stern makes an argument for a lower discount rate primarily based on an ethical argument—that future generations will clearly not consider themselves any less "valuable" than us today.

Under the Obama administration in 2017, the U.S. Environmental Protection Agency estimated the social cost of carbon at around \$40/ton using a discount rate of 3 percent.[59] In reviewing Obama-era climate policies, the Trump administration has lowered the social cost of carbon to as little as \$1/ton by only considering damages that occur in the United States but not elsewhere in the world. Even with a relatively modest social cost of carbon of \$30–40 per ton, economic analyses

543

conclude that a stronger policy response to climate change is warranted. While the costs of adequately addressing climate change are generally considered to be about 1–2 percent of the global economy, we must compare these to the costs of *inaction*.

The Stern Review estimated the most severe effects of climate change could be avoided at a cost of approximately 1 percent of gross world product. However, without such policies, Stern found that the damages from climate change in the twenty-first century would range from 5 to 20 percent of GWP. Thus, the report concludes that the benefits of immediate action to minimize climate change significantly exceed the costs and would prevent severe social and economic impacts:

> Our actions over the coming few decades could create risks of major disruption to economic and social activity, later in this century and in the next, on a scale similar to those associated with the great wars and the economic depression of the first half of the twentieth century. And it will be difficult or impossible to reverse these changes. Tackling climate change is the pro-growth strategy for the longer term, and it can be done in a way that does not cap the aspirations for growth of rich or poor countries.[60]

Thus, with few exceptions, economists recommend stronger climate policies than those currently in place. A 2015 study revealed that economists are much more concerned about the impacts of climate change than the American public.[61] For example, half of the surveyed economists indicated that "immediate and drastic action is necessary" compared to just 23 percent of the American public. The survey also found that a majority of economists (about 78 percent) feel that climate change will have significant negative effects on the economy. About 77 percent of the surveyed economists also indicated that the United States should commit to reducing its greenhouse gas emissions regardless of the actions of other countries.

6.2 Climate Change Policy

Carbon Taxes vs. Cap-and-Trade

As mentioned previously, one economic policy to address climate change is to tax carbon emissions. A carbon tax would charge large emitters of CO_2, such as electricity producers, gasoline refineries, and factories, a per-ton fee, effectively internalizing the externality. The individual emitters would choose their pollution level by comparing the tax against the cost of actions to reduce emissions. As long as it was cheaper to reduce emissions than pay the tax, companies would reduce their emissions. The tax would then, to some extent, get passed on to consumers in terms of higher prices. Revenues raised by such a tax could be used to fund the transition to renewable energy or to lower other taxes as part of a revenue-neutral tax shift, as discussed previously.

Note that the extent to which a carbon tax would lower emissions depends on how businesses and households respond to higher prices for products such as gasoline, electricity, and air travel. Thus, predicting how much emissions would decline requires information about the price elasticities of demand for these products. Unfortunately, estimates of elasticity can vary significantly, leading to uncertainty about how much emissions will decline. For example, the U.S. Department of Energy has estimated the elasticity of demand for gasoline to be as low as −0.02,[62] suggesting very little change in quantity demanded with higher gas prices, while other research finds the elasticity to be around −0.30.[63] If a carbon tax ends up not reducing emissions as much as expected, it may need to be significantly adjusted.

The main alternative to a carbon tax is a cap-and-trade approach. With this system, the government requires large CO_2 emitters to obtain permits for each ton they desire to emit, with the government capping total emissions by controlling the number of permits. These permits would either be auctioned to the highest bidders or freely distributed according to some criterion, such as historical emissions. Permits could then be traded among firms, with firms holding unneeded permits offering those for sale to other companies that find they need additional permits, with the permit price fluctuating based on market forces.

Permits would create many of the same incentives as taxes—encouraging businesses and consumers to shift away from fossil fuels, fostering investment in renewable energy, and even raising government revenue if the permits are auctioned. The main advantage of permits is that the government directly controls the overall level of emissions. However, a permit system creates uncertainty about the permit price, which may make it difficult for firms and households to determine whether energy-efficiency investments will prove worthwhile. With a carbon tax, such long-term investment planning is more clear. Another advantage of a cap-and-trade approach is that it avoids using the politically unpopular word "tax," even though the ultimate impact on businesses and consumers is essentially the same.

National and Regional Climate Policies

Both carbon taxes and permit systems have been used by a number of countries. Carbon taxes have been implemented in India, Japan, South Africa, Costa Rica, and in Quebec and British Columbia in Canada. India, the world's third-largest carbon emitter behind China and the United States, instituted a carbon tax in 2010. The tax is currently equivalent to about $6 per ton of CO_2 and generates $1 billion in revenues per year.[64] However, India also provides over $2 billion annually in subsidies to the coal industry, showing that carbon pricing needs to be combined with subsidy reform to be truly effective.[65]

The most extensive permit system is the European Union's Emissions Trading System, which has been in place since 2005. The system covers about 11,000 power stations and manufacturing plants, covering nearly half of all greenhouse gas emissions in the EU.[66] The price of permits in the EU system has varied significantly, ranging from more than €30/ton to less than €1/ton, depending on economic conditions and the allocation of permits. California has also instituted a carbon trading system and has partnered with Canadian provinces to expand the system. South Korea implemented a cap-and-trade system in 2015, initially freely allocating all permits but gradually increasing the share of permits that are auctioned.[67] In 2017, China initiated a nationwide carbon permit system, effectively doubling the proportion of the world's carbon that is subject to pricing.[68]

International Climate Policy

As climate change is a global problem, international cooperation is critical in mounting an adequate response. The first international treaty to address climate change, the 1997 Kyoto Protocol, specified emissions targets only for richer nations, with penalties planned for those that failed to meet their targets. When the treaty expired in 2012, some countries achieved their targets, while others did not (the United States never ratified the treaty), but no penalties were ever enforced.

In order to bring nearly all nations into the process, the 2015 Paris Climate Agreement let each country set their own targets on a voluntary basis, referred to as Nationally Determined Contributions (NDCs), without enforceable penalties. It is left to each country what national policies they will enact in order to meet their NDC, whether these policies be taxes, permits, or other regulations. As mentioned earlier, the goal of the Paris Climate Agreement is to limit warming to "well below" an increase of 2°C above pre-industrial levels and to pursue efforts to limit warming further to no more than a 1.5°C increase. As of 2019, 186 nations have ratified the treaty, out of 195 countries that signed it. While the United States announced its intention to withdraw from the agreement in June 2017, it cannot officially leave the agreement until November 2020.[69]

An overall evaluation of the Paris Climate Agreement is shown in Figure 16.12. Given scientific and policy uncertainties, each scenario is graphed, showing a range of expected annual global emissions. We see that without the agreement, national policies in place prior to the Paris Agreement would have resulted in global greenhouse gas emissions continuing to rise until at least the middle of the twenty-first century and an eventual temperature increase of 3.1 to 3.5°C relative to pre-industrial levels. The Paris NDCs collectively reduce the expected temperature increase to 2.7 to 3.0°C—still failing to meet the goal of limiting warming and allowing global emissions to increase for at least a couple of decades. In order to achieve the 2°C target, emissions need to begin declining essentially immediately and rapidly fall to around zero by about the end of the century. In order to achieve the more ambitious 1.5°C target, emissions need to decline even more quickly and actually become negative by the end of the century. Note that negative emissions can be achieved by more than offsetting any remaining emissions with efforts to draw carbon out of the atmosphere by expanding forests, changing the management of agricultural and grasslands, and protecting wetlands. Withdrawal of carbon from the atmosphere and storing it in plants and soils is increasingly recognized as an important companion to reducing emissions—not only in the future but right now. The dangers of climate change are sufficiently real that it is necessary to use both approaches: emit less and store more.

The Paris Climate Agreement resulted in nearly all nations committing to regulate their greenhouse gas emissions and a slight reduction in the expected degree of warming. But Figure 16.12 illustrates that a large gap still exists between projected emissions and the pathways needed to meet global climate targets. The organization Climate Action Tracker, which presents independent scientific analysis on climate issues, rated the NDCs of 30 nations and the European Union. They determined that only seven countries presented NDCs that were compatible with the 2°C target

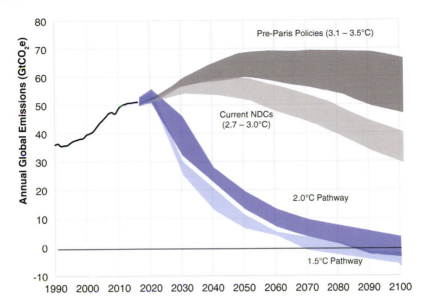

Figure 16.12 *Global Greenhouse Gas Emissions Under Alternative Scenarios*

Source: Climate Action Tracker, https://climateactiontracker.org/global/temperatures/

Note: $GtCO_2e$ is gigatons of CO_2 equivalent, with all non-CO_2 greenhouse gases converted to an equivalent amount of CO_2 warming.

or better. Meanwhile, the NDCs of 14 countries were rated as either "highly insufficient" or "critically insufficient," including China, Russia, and the United States.[70] Under the agreement, participating nations will convene every five years to review progress and hopefully offer more ambitious NDCs.

As with our discussion of various environmental issues in Section 1 of this chapter, the data on climate change reflect a mixture of good and bad news. While global CO_2 emissions were essentially constant from 2014 to 2016, global emissions rose by 1.6 percent in 2017 and 2.7 percent in 2018.[71] In the United States, greenhouse gas emissions fell by a total of 12 percent over 2007–2017, mainly as electricity production switched from coal to natural gas.[72] However, a preliminary analysis indicates that emissions in the United States also rose in 2018, by a significant 3.4 percent.[73]

Despite these recent increases in emissions, there are still several reasons for optimism:

1. Analysis of countries' actions since the Paris Agreement finds that several countries are "taking significant steps in the right direction," including Argentina, India, Costa Rica, and the European Union, and that if such progress is "extended and scaled, these combined efforts could begin to bend the global emissions curve."[74]
2. In recent years, energy investment has significantly shifted toward renewable sources. In 2017, global investment in renewables was $333 billion, compared to only $144 billion invested in fossil fuels and nuclear energy.[75]
3. Over the last decade, the cost of renewable energy has declined dramatically, with wind energy costs down 69 percent and solar costs down 88 percent. In fact,

renewable energy costs have declined so much that as of 2018, the two cheapest sources to generate electricity, considering global average costs, were wind turbines and photovoltaic solar panels, even without including subsidies.[76]

4. Economic analysis demonstrates that a global transition to 100 percent renewable energy is both technically and economically feasible. According to a 2017 study, a complete transition to renewables by 2050 would increase net global employment, reduce total energy costs, increase access to energy in developing countries, avoid over 3 million annual deaths from air pollution, and allow the ambitious 1.5°C Paris climate target to be met.[77]

Discussion Questions

1. What do you think should be done by the United States and other countries in response to global climate change? Can you think of specific policies that would reduce carbon emissions without resulting in significant economic disruption or that might be helpful economically?

2. The 2015 Paris Climate Agreement allows each country to set its own targets on a voluntary basis. One consequence of this has been that many countries have not done enough to meet the goals of limiting global warming to "well below" an increase of 2°C above pre-industrial levels. What are some of the challenges associated with imposing more strict conditions on all countries? Can you think of ways in which international agreements that require participation by countries facing different kinds of development challenges can be made more effective?

7. FINAL THOUGHTS

We started this book by saying that economics is essentially about improving people's well-being. Our contextual approach to economics has recognized that well-being is fundamentally multidimensional, as we saw in Chapter 0. In this book, we have addressed standard economic issues such as markets, consumer and business decisions, economic fluctuations, and global trade. But we have also shown that economic "success" means creating societies that provide fair opportunities for everyone, support quality-of-life goals, and are environmentally sustainable.

In many ways, insights from economics have clearly improved the well-being of billions of people over the last couple of centuries. More people than ever are able to develop their capabilities and achieve a comfortable living standard, although unacceptable levels of inequality, poverty, and discrimination persist and must be rectified. Society's economic goals are increasingly expanding beyond traditional goals such as fostering markets and increasing income and employment toward broader well-being goals such as human empowerment and environmental sustainability. As social goals transform, economics must also adapt and respond.

The idea that economics must evolve as conditions change is not new. During the Great Depression in the 1930s, the famous economist John Maynard Keynes looked into the future and tried to imagine a world of relative affluence, where humanity's true long-term problem might be to determine how to live "wisely and agreeably and well." (See Box 16.4.)

BOX 16.4 ECONOMIC POSSIBILITIES FOR OUR GRANDCHILDREN

Looking beyond the dire conditions during the Great Depression, John Maynard Keynes imagined what the world, and economics, might be like 100 years into the future (in 2030).[78] Considering what would be the "economic possibilities for our grandchildren," Keynes's main conclusion was that as people's needs and goals changed with further affluence, so should economics. Writing in 1930, Keynes suggested that:

> a point may soon be reached, much sooner perhaps than we are all of us aware of, when [basic] needs are satisfied in the sense that we prefer to devote our further energies to non-economic purposes. . . . I draw the conclusion that, assuming no important wars and no important increase in population, the economic problem may be solved, or be at least within sight of solution, within a hundred years. This means that the economic problem is not—if we look into the future—the permanent problem of the human race.
>
> Thus, for the first time since his creation man will be faced with his real, his permanent problem—how to use his freedom from pressing economic cares, how to occupy the leisure, which science and compound interest will have won for him, to live wisely and agreeably and well.

Keynes recognized that economics has been of critical importance in helping people meet their basic needs. But as people increasingly shift their energies to "non-economic purposes," our views on both policy issues and even morals must also shift:

> When the accumulation of wealth is no longer of high social importance, there will be great changes in the code of morals. . . . The love of money as a possession—as distinguished from the love of money as a means to the enjoyments and realities of life—will be recognized for what it is, a somewhat disgusting morbidity, one of those semi-criminal, semi-pathological propensities which one hands over with a shudder to the specialists in mental disease. All kinds of social customs and economic practices, affecting the distribution of wealth and of economic rewards and penalties, which we now maintain at all costs, however distasteful and unjust they may be in themselves, because they are tremendously useful in promoting the accumulation of capital, we shall then be free, at last, to discard.
>
> Of course there will still be many people with intense, unsatisfied purposiveness who will blindly pursue wealth—unless they can find some plausible substitute. But the rest of us will no longer be under any obligation to applaud and encourage them.

An economy that is stable, equitable, and sustainable is possible. As we have seen throughout this book, economists have developed numerous policy recommendations that can help us achieve our goals. Some of these ideas have been tested and proven effective, some haven't worked as expected, and others remain to be tried. We hope this book has helped you think more deeply about what policies are best in your various roles in life: as a consumer, as an employee or business owner, as a family member, and as a voter. We can't promise that economic decisions are always easy, but we hope the information from this book will help you approach these choices with an informed and open mind.

Discussion Questions

1. How can we reconcile the need for global economic development with the problems of environmental limits? In what ways will established models of economic development have to be modified to deal with new realities?
2. Do you agree with Keynes's belief that industrialized countries can reach a point where needs will be "satisfied in the sense that we prefer to devote our further energies to non-economic purposes"? Do you think that we are any closer to this point than in 1930, when Keynes wrote his essay? Do you see any evidence that this is starting to occur?

REVIEW QUESTIONS

1. Summarize some of the key trends in environmental and well-being indicators since the 1960s.
2. Are we currently in danger of running out of key nonrenewable resources?
3. How do air pollution levels differ in developed versus developing countries?
4. What temperature targets were set under the 2015 Paris Climate Agreement?
5. What is a negative externality?
6. How can we represent a negative externality in a supply-and-demand graph?
7. What is a Pigovian tax, and why do economists recommend this policy to respond to a negative externality?
8. What is a positive externality, and how can it be represented in a supply-and-demand graph?
9. What policy do economists recommend in the case of a positive externality? Why?
10. What two characteristics define a common property resource?
11. What two characteristics define a public good?
12. Why is an unregulated common property resource likely to be exploited? How can we represent this graphically?
13. How can a common property resource be regulated to achieve the socially efficient outcome?
14. Why are public goods not provided by private markets?
15. What is the environmental Kuznets curve hypothesis? Do the data tend to support it?
16. What is the consensus among economists about the relationship between environmental protection and the economy and jobs?
17. What are the different views among economists regarding the transition to a sustainable economy (i.e., green growth versus no growth)?
18. What is the difference between weak and strong sustainability?
19. What are the implications from the data on humanity's ecological footprint?
20. Why do economists tend to prefer Pigovian taxes that are upstream and revenue neutral?
21. What are some green macroeconomic policies?
22. What is a discount rate? Why is it important in determining the social cost of carbon?

23. What are the advantages and disadvantages of carbon taxes?

24. What are the advantages and disadvantages of a cap-and-trade system to regulate carbon?

25. Are the collective Nationally Determined Contributions under the Paris Climate Agreement sufficient to achieve stated temperature targets?

EXERCISES

1. Issues of environmental sustainability can sometimes be a bit abstract. This exercise is designed to bring them to an individual level. Start at www.footprintnetwork.org/ and familiarize yourself with the notion of "ecological footprints," then take the quiz to discover what your personal footprint looks like. What did you learn that was new information to you? What specifically can you do about this new information?

2. Go to https://data.footprintnetwork.org/ and access data for a number of different countries. For each country, answer the following questions:

   a. What was the per capita ecological footprint of consumption?

   b. What was the per capita biocapacity?

   c. Explain the meaning of the two numbers you just located. What are the implications?

3. Match each concept in Column A with a definition or example in Column B:

Column A		Column B	
a.	"Green" taxes	1.	The perspective that natural capital depreciation should be compensated for with restoration of other natural capital
b.	Tradable permit systems	2.	An inverted U-shaped relationship between economic development and environmental damages
c.	Strong sustainability	3.	A situation where population and the use of raw materials and energy have stabilized
d.	Throughput	4.	Based on the principle that a process of pollution reduction may be most efficiently achieved if businesses have choices
e.	Social discount rate	5.	Designed to discourage pollution and natural resource depletion by making them more expensive
f.	Environmental Kuznets curve	6.	Reflects social rather than market valuation of future costs and benefits
g.	Steady-state economy	7.	The flow of raw materials and energy into the economic system and the flow of wastes from the system

NOTES

1. Yuan, Liang, Kongjoo Shin, and Shunsuke Managi. 2018. "Subjective Well-Being and Environmental Quality: The Impact of Air Pollution and Green Coverage in China." *Ecological Economics*, 153: 124–138. Orru, Kati, Hans Orru, Marek Maasikmets, Reigo Hendrikson, and

Mare Ainsaar. 2016. "Well-Being and Environmental Quality: Does Pollution Affect Life Satisfaction?" *Quality of Life Research*, 25(3): 699–705.

2. U.S. Global Change Research Program. 2018. *Impacts, Risks, and Adaptation in the United States: Fourth National Climate Assessment*, Volume 2. U.S. Global Change Research Program (globalchange.gov), Washington, DC, p. 46.

3. Krugman, Paul. 1997. "Earth in the Balance Sheet." *Slate*. April 18. https://slate.com/business/1997/04/earth-in-the-balance-sheet.html

4. Meadows, Donella H., Dennis L. Meadows, Jørgen Randers, and William W. Behrens III. 1972. *The Limits to Growth: A Report for the Club of Rome's Project on the Predicament of Mankind*. Universe Books, New York.

5. Turner, Graham, and Cathy Alexander. 2014. "Limits to Growth Was Right." *The Guardian*, September 1.

6. Haub, Carl. 2011. "What If Experts Are Wrong on World Population Growth?" *Yale Environment 360*, September 19.

7. Bricker, Darrell. 2019. *Empty Planet: The Shock of Global Population Decline*. Signal, Oxford.

8. Kim, Jungho. 2016. "Female Education and Its Impact on Fertility." *IZA World of Labor*, February.

9. Schultz, Colin. 2012. "High-Tech's Crucial Rare Earth Elements Are Already Running Low." Smithsonian.com, June 22. www.smithsonianmag.com/smart-news/high-techs-crucial-rare-earth-elements-are-already-running-low-133603653/

10. Bradford, Alina. 2018. "Deforestation: Facts, Causes, and Effects." LiveScience, April 3. www.livescience.com/27692-deforestation.html

11. Kituyi, Mukhisa, and Peter Thomson. 2018. "90% of Fish Stocks Are Used Up: Fisheries Subsidies Must Stop." UN Conference on Trade and Development, July 13. https://unctad.org/en/pages/newsdetails.aspx?OriginalVersionID=1812

12. UN Water. 2019. *Water Scarcity*. www.unwater.org/water-facts/scarcity/

13. Jain, Neha. 2018. "India's Groundwater Crisis, Fueled by Intense Pumping, Needs Urgent Management." *Monogabay*, June 7.

14. World Economic Forum. 2019. *The Global Risks Report 2019*. Geneva, Switzerland. http://www3.weforum.org/docs/WEF_Global_Risks_Report_2019.pdf

15. Arsenault, Chris. 2014. "Only 60 Years of Farming Left if Soil Degradation Continues." *Scientific American*, December 5.

16. Leahy, Stephen. 2019. "One Million Species at Risk of Extinction, UN Report Warns." *National Geographic,* May 6.

17. Landrigan, Philip J., and 46 other authors. 2017. "The Lancet Commission on Pollution and Health." *The Lancet*, 391: 462–512.

18. Ibid. U.S. Environmental Protection Agency. 2017. *Our Nation's Air: Status and Trends through 2016*. U.S. Environmental Protection Agency, Washington, DC.

19. See, for example, "Scientific Consensus: Earth's Climate is Warming," Global Climate Change Vital Signs of the Planet, National Aeronautics and Space Administration. https://climate.nasa.gov/scientific-consensus/

20. World Food Programme. 2019. *Climate Action*. www1.wfp.org/climate-action

21. Abel, Guy J., Michael Brottrager, Jesus Creso Cuaresma, and Raya Muttarak. 2019. "Climate, Conflict, and Forced Migration." *Global Environmental Change*, 54: 239–249.

22. Vidal, John. 2013. "Climate Change Will Hit Poor Countries Hardest, Study Shows." *The Guardian*, September 27.

23. Data for 2014 from the World Bank, World Development Indicators.

24. United Nations. 2015. *Paris Agreement*. p. 3. https://unfccc.int/sites/default/files/english_paris_agreement.pdf

25. Masson-Delmotte, V., and 18 other authors. 2018. "Summary for Policymakers." In *Global Warming of 1.5°C*. IPCC, Geneva, Switzerland.

26. International Energy Agency. 2018. *World Energy Balances: Overview*. https://webstore.iea.org/world-energy-balances-2018-overview

27. Jacobson, Mark Z., and Mark A. Delucchi. 2011. "Providing All Global Energy with Wind, Water, and Solar Power, Part I: Technologies, Energy Resources, Quantities and Areas of Infrastructure, and Materials." *Energy Policy*, 39: 1154–1169.

28. Parry, Ian, Dirk Heine, Eliza Lis, and Shanjun Li. 2014. *Getting Energy Prices Right: From Principle to Practice*. International Monetary Fund, Washington, DC. Shindell, Drew T. 2015. "The Social Cost of Atmospheric Release." *Climatic Change*, 130(2): 313–326.

29. Parry, Ian, Dirk Heine, Eliza Lis, and Shanjun Li. 2014. *Getting Energy Prices Right: From Principle to Practice*. International Monetary Fund, Washington, DC.

30. Ibid., p. 8.

31. Davies, Ross. 2015. "Certification and Fish Stock Status Order of the Day at Iceland Responsible Fisheries Event." *Undercurrent News*, September 22.

32. Agnarsson, S., T. Matthiasson, and F. Giry. 2016. "Consolidation and Distribution of Quota Holdings." *Marine Policy*, 72: 263–270.

33. Davies, Ross. 2015. "Certification and Fish Stock Status Order of the Day at Iceland Responsible Fisheries Event." *Undercurrent News*, September 22.

34. Inchonose, Daisuke, Masashi Yamamoto, and Yuichiro Yoshida. 2015. "The Decoupling of Affluence and Waste Discharge under Spatial Correlation: Do Richer Communities Discharge More Waste?" *Environment and Development Economics*, 20: 161–184. Georgiev, Emil, and Emil Mihaylov. 2015. "Economic Growth and the Environment: Reassessing the Environmental Kuznets Curve for Air Pollution Emissions in OECD Countries." *Letters in Spatial and Resource Sciences*, 8(1): 29–47.

35. Akpan, Usenobong F., and Dominic E. Abang. 2014. "Environmental Quality and Economic Growth: A Panel Analysis of the 'U' in Kuznets." MPRA Paper, University Library of Munich, Germany, February. p. 16.

36. Bezdek, Roger H., Robert M. Wendling, and Paula DiPerna. 2008. "Environmental Protection, the Economy, and Jobs: National and Regional Analyses." *Journal of Environmental Management*, 86: 63–79.

37. Rayment, Matt, Elke Pirgmaier, Griet De Ceuster, Friedrich Hinterberger, Onno Kuik, Henry Leveson Gower, Christine Polzin, and Adarsh Varma. 2009. "The Economic Benefits of Environmental Policy." Report ENV.G.1/FRA/2006/007, Institute for Environmental Studies, Vrije University, The Netherlands, November.

38. Hafstead, Marc A. C., and Roberton C. Williams III. 2016. "Unemployment and Environmental Regulation in General Equilibrium." Resources for the Future, Discussion Paper 15–11, Washington, DC, May.

39. Commission of the European Communities. 2004. *The EU Economy: 2004 Review*. ECFIN (2004) REP 50455-EN, Brussels.

40. OECD. 2017. *Investing in Climate, Investing in Growth*. OECD Publishing, Paris.

41. UNEP. 2011. www.unenvironment.org/explore-topics/green-economy/why-does-green-economy-matter/what-inclusive-green-economy

42. Pollin, Robert. 2015. *Greening the Global Economy*. MIT Press, Cambridge, MA.

43. Daly, Herman. 1993. "The Steady-State Economy: Toward a Political Economy of Biophysical Equilibrium and Moral Growth." In Chapter 19 of *Valuing the Earth* (Herman Daly and Kenneth Townsend, editors). The MIT Press, Cambridge, MA. p. 330.

44. Jackson, Tim. 2011. *Prosperity without Growth*. Routledge, New York.

45. Victor, Peter. 2019. *Managing without Growth: Slower by Design, Not Disaster*. Edward Elgar, Northampton, MA.

46. Lambert, Fred. 2019. "Electric Car Sales Grew by 40% in Norway this Year." Electrek, January 2. https://electrek.co/2019/01/02/electric-car-sales-norway-2018/

47. Coady, David, Ian Parry, Louis Sears, and Baoping Shang. 2017. "How Large Are Global Fossil Fuel Subsidies?" *World Development*, 91: 11–27.

48. Ibid., p. 12.

49. Unanue, Wenceslao, Marcos E. Gómez, Diego Cortez, Juan C. Oyanedel, and Andrés Mendiburo-Seguel. 2017. "Revisiting the Link between Job Satisfaction and Life Satisfaction: The Role of Basic Psychological Needs." *Frontiers in Psychology*, 8: 1–17.

50. Rosnick, David. 2013. "Reduced Work Hours as a Means of Slowing Climate Change." Center for Economic and Policy Research, February.

51. Tienhaara, Kyla. 2018. *Green Keynesianism and the Global Financial Crisis*. Routledge, London.

52. Blackwater, Bill. 2012. "The Contradictions of Environmental Keynesianism." Climate & Capitalism, June 14. http://climateandcapitalism.com/2012/06/14/the-contradictions-of-environmental-keynesianism/

53. Harris, Jonathan. 2013. "Green Keynesianism: Beyond Standard Growth Paradigms." In *Building a Green Economy: Perspectives from Ecological Economics* (Robert B. Richardson, editor). Michigan State University Press, East Lansing, MI.

54. https://en.wikipedia.org/wiki/Economists%27_Statement_on_Climate_Change

55. Nordhaus, William D. 1992. "An Optimal Transition Path for Controlling Greenhouse Gases." *Science*, 258(5086): 1315–1319.

56. Nordhaus, William D. 2017. "Revisiting the Social Cost of Carbon." *Proceedings of the National Academy of Sciences (PNAS)*, 114(7): 1518–1523.

57. Moore, Frances C., and Delavane B. Diaz. 2015. "Temperature Impacts on Economic Growth Warrant Stringent Mitigation Policy." *Nature Climate Change*, 5, published online January 12.

58. Ricke, Katharine, Laurent Drouet, Ken Caeira, and Massimo Tavoni. 2018. "Country-Level Social Cost of Carbon." *Nature Climate Change*, 8: 895–900.

59. U.S. Environmental Protection Agency. 2017. "The Social Cost of Carbon: Estimating the Benefits of Reducing Greenhouse Gas Emissions." https://19january2017snapshot.epa.gov/climatechange/social-cost-carbon_.html

60. Stern, Nicholas. 2007. *The Economics of Climate Change: The Stern Review*. Cambridge University Press, Cambridge, UK. Executive Summary. p. 2.

61. Howard, Peter, and Derek Sylvan. 2015. "Expert Consensus on the Economics of Climate Change." Institute for Policy Integrity, New York University School of Law, December 2015.

62. U.S. Energy Information Administration. 2014. "Gasoline Prices Tend to have Little Effect on Demand for Car Travel." December 15. www.eia.gov/todayinenergy/detail.php?id=19191

63. Levin, Laurence, Matthew S. Lewis, and Frank A. Wolak. 2016. "High Frequency Evidence on the Demand for Gasoline." NBER Working Paper Series, Paper 22345, June.

64. https://en.wikipedia.org/wiki/Carbon_tax#India

65. Timperley, Jocelyn. 2019. "The Carbon Brief Profile: India." CarbonBrief, March 14. www.carbonbrief.org/the-carbon-brief-profile-india

66. European Commission. 2019. *EU-ETS Webpage.* https://ec.europa.eu/clima/policies/ets_en

67. Environmental Defense Fund. 2015. *Republic of Korea: An Emissions Trading Case Study.* https://ieta.wildapricot.org/resources/Resources/Case_Studies_Worlds_Carbon_Markets/republicofkorea_case%20study_june_2015.pdf

68. Harvey, Fiona. 2017. "China Aims to Drastically Cut Greenhouse Gas Emissions Through Trading Scheme." *The Guardian,* December 19.

69. United Nations Climate Change. Paris Agreement-Status of Ratification. https://unfccc.int/process/the-paris-agreement/status-of-ratification. Johnson, Keith. 2019. "Is the United States Really Leaving the Paris Climate Agreement?" *Foreign Policy,* November 5.

70. Climate Action Tracker. 2019. https://climateactiontracker.org/countries/

71. Carrington, Damian. 2018. "'Brutal News': Global Carbon Emissions Jump to All-Time High in 2018." *The Guardian,* December 5.

72. U.S. EPA. 2019. Inventory of U.S. Greenhouse Gas Emissions and Sinks. EPA 430-R-19-001.

73. Rhodium Group. 2019. "Preliminary U.S. Emissions Estimates for 2018." January 8. https://rhg.com/research/preliminary-us-emissions-estimates-for-2018/

74. Climate Action Tracker. 2018. "Some Progress since Paris, But Not Enough, as Governments Amble towards 3°C of Warming." December 11. https://climateactiontracker.org/publications/warming-projections-global-update-dec-2018/

75. Jackson, Felicia. 2018. "Renewables Investment Nudges out Fossil Fuel and Nuclear." *Forbes,* May 15. www.forbes.com/sites/feliciajackson/2018/05/15/renewables-investment-nudges-out-fossil-fuel-and-nuclear/#73c1a99c3752

76. Lazard. 2018. Lazard's Levelized Cost of Energy Analysis: Version 12.0. November 2018.

77. Jacobson, Mark Z., and 26 other authors. 2017. "100% Clean and Renewable Wind, Water, and Sunlight All-Sector Energy Roadmaps for 139 Countries of the World." *Joule,* 1: 108–121.

78. Keynes, John Maynard. 1930. "Economic Possibilities for Our Grandchildren." *Essays in Persuasion.* New York: Harcourt Brace, 1932, pp. 358–373.

Glossary

absolute advantage: the ability to produce something at lower per-unit costs than one's competitors (14)

absolute deprivation: severe deprivation of basic human needs (4)

abundance: resources are abundant to the extent that they exist in plentiful supply for meeting various goals (1)

accelerator principle: the idea that high GDP growth leads to increasing investment, and low or negative GDP growth leads to declining investment (11)

accommodative monetary policy: loose or expansionary monetary policy intended to counteract recessionary tendencies in the economy (11)

accounting costs: actual monetary costs paid by a producer as well as estimated reduction in the value of the producer's capital stock (5)

accounting profits: the difference between total revenues and accounting costs (6)

administrative capitalism: a national system characterized by private corporate ownership and a substantial reliance on public administration (as well as exchange) as a mode of coordination (15)

administrative obstacles: use of environmental, health, or safety regulations to prevent imports from other countries under the pretext of upholding higher standards (14)

administrative socialism: a national system in which state ownership predominates and activity is coordinated primarily by public administration (command) (15)

aggregate demand: the total demand for all goods and services in a national economy (9)

aggregate demand (AD) curve: graph showing the relationship between the rate of inflation and the total quantity of goods and services demanded by households, businesses, government, and the international sector (12)

aggregate supply (AS) curve: graph representing the relationship between the rate of inflation and the total goods and services producers are willing to supply, given the reality of capacity constraints (12)

altruism: actions focused on the well-being of others, without thought about oneself (4)

anchoring effect: overreliance on a piece of information that may or may not be relevant as a reference point when making a decision (4)

aspirational group: the group to which an individual aspires to belong (4)

austerity: policy of cutting public expenditures or raising taxes to balance the government's budget (10)

automatic stabilizers: tax and spending institutions that tend to increase government revenues and lower government spending during economic expansions but lower revenues and raise government spending during economic recessions (10)

availability heuristic: placing undue importance on particular information because it is readily available or vivid (4)

average cost (or average total cost): cost per unit of output, computed as total cost divided by the quantity of output produced (5)

backward-bending individual paid labor supply curve: a labor supply curve that arises because, beyond some level of wages, income effects outweigh substitution effects in determining individuals' decisions about how much to work (7)

balance of payments (BOP) account: the national account that tracks inflows and outflows arising from international trade, earnings, transfers, and transactions in assets (14)

balanced budget: situation in which the total government outlays is equal to the total government tax revenues (10)

balanced budget multiplier: the impact on equilibrium output of simultaneous increases of equal size in government spending and taxes (10)

bank reserves: funds not lent out or invested by a commercial bank but kept as vault cash or on deposit at the Federal Reserve (11)

bargaining: an activity in which a single buyer and a single seller negotiate the terms of their exchange (2)

barriers to entry: economic, legal, or deliberately created or maintained obstacles that keep new sellers from entering a market (6)

barter: exchange of goods, services, or assets directly for other goods, services, or assets, without the use of money (11)

base year (in the constant-dollar method of estimating GDP): the year whose prices are chosen for evaluating production in all years (8)

basic neoclassical model: a model that portrays the economy as a collection of profit-maximizing firms and utility-maximizing households interacting in perfectly competitive markets (2)

behavioral economics: a subfield of economics that uses insights from various social and biological sciences to explore how people make actual economic decisions (4)

Better Life Index (BLI): an index developed by the OECD to measure national welfare using 11 well-being dimensions (8)

bilateral development assistance: aid or loans given by one country to another to promote development (15)

bounded rationality: the hypothesis that people make choices among a somewhat arbitrary subset of all possible options due to limits on information, time, or cognitive abilities (4)

Bretton Woods system: a system of fixed exchange rates established after World War II, lasting until 1972 (14)

budget deficit: an excess of total government outlays over total government tax revenues (10)

budget line: a line showing the possible combinations of two goods that a consumer can purchase (4)

budget surplus: an excess of total government tax revenues over total government outlays (10)

Bureau of Economic Analysis (BEA): the agency in the United States in charge of compiling and publishing the national accounts (8)

Bureau of Labor Statistics (BLS): in the United States, the government agency that compiles and publishes employment and unemployment statistics (8)

business cycle: recurrent fluctuations in the level of national production, with alternating periods of recession and boom (1)

business sphere: firms that produce goods and services for profitable sale (2)

capabilities: the opportunities that people have to pursue important aspects of well-being, such as being healthy and having access to education (15)

capital: any resource that is valued for its potential economic contributions (1)

capital account (in the BOP account): the account that tracks flows arising from international transactions in assets (14)

capital flight: rapid movement of capital assets out of a country (14)

capital intensive: a process or procedure that makes use of more capital relative to other inputs such as labor (15)

capital-intensive production: production using methods that involve a high ratio of capital to labor (14)

ceteris paribus: a Latin phrase meaning "other things equal" or "all else constant" (2)

change in demand: a shift of the entire demand curve in response to something changing other than price (3)

change in supply: a shift of the entire supply curve in response to something changing other than price (3)

change in the quantity demanded: movement along a demand curve in response to a price change (3)

change in the quantity supplied: movement along a supply curve in response to a price change (3)

circular flow diagram: a graphical representation of the traditional view of an economy consisting of households and firms engaging in exchange (2)

civilian noninstitutional population (BLS definition): persons 16 years or older who do not live in institutions (for example, correctional facilities, nursing homes, or long-term care hospitals) and who are not on active military duty (8)

classical economics: the school of economics, originating in the eighteenth century, that stressed issues of growth and distribution, based on an image of smoothly functioning markets (9)

climate change: long-term changes in global climate, including warmer temperatures, changing precipitation patterns, more extreme weather events, and rising sea levels (16)

closed economy: an economy with no foreign sector (8)

collusion: cooperation among potential rivals to gain market power as a group (6)

commodity money: a good used as money that is also valuable in itself (11)

common good: the general well-being of society, including one's own well-being (4)

common property: ownership of assets by government or particular subsections of society (2)

common property resource: a good or service that is nonexcludable and rival (16)

comparative advantage: the ability to produce some good or service at a lower opportunity cost than other producers (14)

compensating wage differentials: the theory that, all else being equal, workers will be willing to accept lower wages for jobs with better characteristics and will demand higher wages for jobs with unappealing characteristics (7)

complementary good: a good that is used along with another good (3)

concentration ratio: the share of the market, based on revenues, output, or value added, attributed to the largest producers in an industry (6)

conditional cash transfer (CCT): programs providing cash to the poor based on the condition that they commit to spending it on specific things, such as children's education, food, or health care (15)

conscious consumption: being aware of the costs of consumption on others and on the planet and making consumption decisions responsibly to minimize waste and achieve a more sustainable lifestyle (1)

constant marginal costs: the situation in which the cost of producing one additional unit of output stays the same as more output is produced (5)

constant marginal returns: a situation in which each successive unit of a variable input produces an increasing marginal product (5)

constant returns to scale: situations in which the long-run average cost of production stays the same as the size of the enterprise increases (5)

consumer price index (CPI): an index measuring changes in the prices of goods and services bought by households (8)

consumer sovereignty: the idea that consumers' needs and wants determine the shape of all economic activities (4)

consumerism: having one's sense of identity and meaning significantly defined through the purchase and use of consumer goods and services (4)

consumption: the final use of good or service (1); purchases of goods and services by the households and institutions sector (8)

contextual economics: economic analysis that takes into account the social and environmental realities within which the economic system operates (1)

contractionary fiscal policy: reductions in government spending or transfer payments or increases in taxes, leading to a lower level of economic activity (10)

contractionary monetary policy: the use of monetary policy tools to limit the money supply, raise interest rates, and encourage a leveling off or reduction in economic activity and inflationary tendencies (11)

convergence (in economic growth): the idea that underlying economic forces will cause poorer countries and regions to "catch up" with richer ones (15)

core sphere: households, families, and informal community groups (2)

cost-benefit analysis: a technique to analyze a policy or project proposal in which all costs and benefits are converted to monetary estimates, if possible, to determine the net social value (5)

countercyclical policy: fiscal policy in which taxes are lowered and expenditure is raised when the economy is weak, and the opposite occurs when the economy is strong (10)

credit money: money that is transferable to another through credit and debit bookkeeping entries (11)

credit rating agencies: companies that assign credit ratings by evaluating the risks of default associated with various loans and other financial instruments (13)

credit rationing: when banks deny loans to some potential borrowers in the interest of maintaining their own profitability (11)

cross-sectional data: observations on a variable for different subjects at one point in time (0)

crowding in: the process in which government spending leads to more favorable expectations for the economy, thereby inducing greater private investment (10)

crowding out: a reduction in the availability of private capital resulting from federal government borrowing to finance budget deficits (10)

currency appreciation: when a currency becomes more valuable, for example, when increased demand for a country's exports causes an increase in demand for its currency (14)

currency depreciation: when a currency becomes less valuable, for example, due to a decrease in demand for a country's exports or an increase in its demand for imports (14)

current account (in the BOP account): the national account that tracks inflows and outflows arising from international trade, earnings, and transfers (14)

cyclical unemployment: unemployment caused by a decline in economic output (9)

debt ceiling: a congressionally mandated limit on the size of the gross federal debt (10)

debt held by the public: the gross federal debt minus the debt owed to other government accounts (10)

decreasing marginal costs: the situation in which the cost of producing one additional unit of output falls as more output is produced (5)

defensive expenditures: money spent to counteract economic activities that have caused harm to human or environmental health (8)

deficit ceiling: a congressionally mandated limit on the size of the federal budget deficit (10)

deflation: when the aggregate price level falls (9)

demand: the willingness and ability of purchasers to buy goods or services (3)

demand curve: a curve indicating the quantities that buyers are willing to purchase at various prices (3)

demand schedule: a table showing the relationship between price and quantity demanded (3)

dependency theory: the theory that underdevelopment in developing countries is caused by unequal trade relations, where developing countries export primary goods that are much cheaper than the industrial goods they import from the developed nations (15)

depreciation: a decrease in the quantity or quality of a stock of capital due to wear and tear or obsolescence (8)

devaluation: lowering an exchange rate within a fixed exchange rate system (14)

diminishing marginal returns: a situation in which each successive unit of a variable input produces a smaller marginal product (5)

diminishing marginal utility: the tendency for additional units of consumption to add less to utility than did previous units of consumption (4)

direct public provision: the supply of goods or services from government or nonprofit institutions (2)

discount rate: the annual percentage rate at which future impacts are discounted relative to the present (16)

discount rate (Federal Reserve Bank): the interest rate at which banks can borrow reserves at the Fed discount window (11)

discouraged workers: people who want employment but have given up looking because they believe that there are no jobs available for them (8)

discretionary fiscal policy: changes in government spending and taxation resulting from deliberate policy decisions (10)

diseconomies of scale: situations in which the long-run average cost of production rises as the size of the enterprise increases (5)

disinflation: a decline in the rate of inflation (12)

disposable income: income remaining for consumption or saving after subtracting taxes and adding transfer payments (10)

distribution: the sharing of products and resources among people (1)

division of labor: an approach to production in which a process is broken down into smaller tasks, with each worker assigned only one or a few tasks (9)

dual labor markets: a situation in which primary sector workers enjoy high wages, opportunities for advancement, and job security, while secondary sector workers are generally hired with low wages, no opportunities for advancement, and little job security (7)

dumping: selling products at prices that are below the cost of production, normally in international trade (14)

duopoly: a market with only two sellers (6)

ecolabeling: product labels that provide information about environmental impacts or indicate certification (4)

ecological footprint: a measure of the human impact on the environment, measured as the land area required to supply a society's resources and assimilate its waste and pollution (4)

economic cost: the total cost of production, including both accounting and opportunity costs (5)

economic profits: the difference between total revenues and economic costs (6)

economics: the study of how people manage their resources to meet their needs and enhance their well-being (1)

economies of scale: situations in which the long-run average cost of production falls as the size of the enterprise increases (5)

effective tax rate: one's taxes expressed as a percentage of total income (10)

efficiency: the use of resources, or inputs, such that they yield the highest possible value of output, or the production of a given output using the lowest possible value of inputs (1)

efficiency wage theory: the theory that an employer can motivate workers to put forth more effort by paying them somewhat more than they could get elsewhere (7)

elasticity: a measure of the responsiveness of an economic actor to changes in market factors, including price and income (3)

empirical investigation: analysis based on observation and recording of specific events, represented in words, images, or numerical data (2)

employed person (BLS definition): a person who did any work for pay or profit during the week before he or she is surveyed by the BLS or who worked for 15 hours or more in a family business (8)

environmental Kuznets curve (EKC) hypothesis: the theory that as a country develops economically, environmental damages per capita initially increase, then peak and eventually decrease (16)

equilibrium: a situation of rest, in which there are no forces that create change (3)

estate taxes: taxes on the transfers of large estates to beneficiaries (10)

excess reserves: the portion of bank reserves that banks are permitted to lend to their customers (11)

exchange: the trading of one thing for another (1)

exchange rate: the number of units of one currency that can be exchanged for one unit of another currency (14)

exchange value: value that corresponds to the value of goods or services for which the item can be exchanged (11)

excise tax: a per-unit tax on a good or service (10)

excludable good: a good whose consumption or use by others can be prevented by its owner(s) (16)

expansionary fiscal policy: the use of government spending, transfer payments, or tax cuts to stimulate a higher level of economic activity (10)

expansionary monetary policy: the use of monetary policy tools to increase the money supply, lower interest rates, and stimulate a higher level of economic activity (11)

exporting pollution: a situation in which a country reduces its domestic pollution but increases its imports of products that cause similar pollution in other countries (14)

externalities: side effects in which the market does not make economic actors feel the full consequences of their actions—consequences that, however, are felt by unrelated persons or entities (such as the environment) (2)

factor markets: markets for the services of land, labor, and capital (2)

factor price equalization: the theory that trade should eliminate input price differences among trading partners over time (14)

federal funds rate: the interest rate determined in the private market for overnight loans of reserves among banks (11)

Federal Open Market Committee (FOMC): the committee that oversees open market operations (11)

fiat money: a medium of exchange that is used as money because a government says it has value, and that is accepted by the people using it (11)

final goal: a goal that requires no further justification; it is an end in itself (1)

final good: a good that is ready for use, needing no further processing (8)

financial assets: a variety of holdings in which wealth can be invested with an expectation of future return (13)

financial capital: funds of purchasing power available to purchase goods and services or facilitate economic activity (1)

financial intermediary: an institution such as a bank, savings and loan association, or life insurance company that accepts funds from savers and makes loans to borrowers (11)

financialization: a process of increasing size and importance of the financial markets in the operation of the economy—with the financial sector accounting for a greater share of GDP and acquiring an increased ability to generate and circulate profits (13)

fiscal policy: government spending and tax policy (10)

fixed costs (sunk costs): production costs that cannot be adjusted quickly and that must be paid even if no production occurs (5)

fixed exchange rate system: a system in which currencies are traded at fixed ratios (14)

fixed input: a production input that is fixed in quantity, regardless of the level of production (5)

flexible (floating) exchange rate system: a system in which exchange rates are determined by the market forces of supply and demand (14)

flow: something whose quantity is measured over a period of time (1)

foreign exchange: the class of currencies (generally limited to the dollar, the euro, and the yen) that is broadly acceptable by foreigners in commercial or investment transactions (14)

fractional reserve system: a banking system in which banks are required to keep only a fraction of the total value of their deposits on reserve (11)

framing: changing the way a particular decision is presented to people in order to influence their behavior (4)

free riders: people who seek to enjoy the benefit of a public good without paying for it (2, 16)

free trade: exchange in international markets that is not regulated or restricted by government actions (14)

frictional unemployment: unemployment that arises as people are in transition between jobs (9)

full employment: a situation in which those who wish to work at the prevailing wages are able to find work readily (9)

full-employment output: a level of output that is assumed to correspond to a case of no excessive or burdensome unemployment but the likely existence of at least some transitory unemployment (9)

functional finance: the idea that a sovereign government should finance current needs and provide for adequate aggregate demand to maintain employment levels (10)

GDP deflator: price index for measuring the general level of prices and defined as the ratio of nominal GDP to real GDP (8)

gender wage gap: the difference in average wages between men and women; women are paid, on average, less than men (7)

gift taxes: taxes on the transfer of large gifts to beneficiaries (10)

Gini coefficient: a measure of inequality that goes from 0 (absolute equality) up to 1 (absolute inequality) (13)

globalization: the extension of international linkages through trade and income flows, as well as flow of people, technology, and culture, and the international sharing of environmental resources, leading to expanded interconnections among different regions (14)

gold standard: a monetary system in which the monetary unit is based on some fixed quantity of gold (11)

government bond: an interest-bearing security constituting a promise to pay at a specified future time (10)

government outlays: total government expenditures, including spending on goods and services and transfer payments (10)

government spending: the component of GDP that represents spending on goods and services by federal, state, and local governments (8, 10)

green consumerism: making consumption decisions at least partly on the basis of environmental criteria (4)

Green GDP: GDP less depreciation of both manufactured and natural capital (8)

gross domestic product (GDP) (BEA definition): a measure of the total market value of final goods and services newly produced within a country's borders over a period of time (usually one year) (1, 8)

gross federal debt: total amount owed by the federal government to all claimants, including foreigners, the public in the United States, and other government accounts (10)

gross investment: all flows into the capital stock over a period of time (8)

heuristic: a rule of thumb or mental shortcut that we use to make decisions (4)

historical investigation: study of past events (2)

human capital: people's capacity for engaging in productive activities and their individual knowledge and skills (1)

human development: an approach to development that stresses the provision of basic needs such as food, shelter, and health care (15)

Human Development Index (HDI): a national accounting measure developed by the United Nations, based on three factors: GNI per capita level, education, and life expectancy (8)

import substitution: the policy of subsidizing domestic producers or imposing protectionist measures to reduce reliance on imports and encourage domestic industry (14)

imputation: a procedure of assigning values for a category of products, usually based on the market values of related products or the cost of inputs (8)

inadequacy: a situation in which there is not enough of a good or service, provided at prices people can afford, to meet minimal requirements for human well-being (3)

income elasticity of demand: a measure of the responsiveness of demand to changes in income, holding price constant (3)

increasing marginal costs: the situation in which the cost of producing one additional unit of output rises as more output is produced (5)

increasing marginal returns: a situation in which each successive unit of a variable input produces a larger marginal product (5)

index number: a figure that measures the change in magnitude of a variable, such as a quantity or price, compared to another period (8)

individual demand: the amount demanded by one particular buyer (3)

individual supply: the amount supplied by one particular seller (3)

individual transferable quota (ITQ): tradable rights to access or harvest a common property resource, such as the right to harvest a particular quantity of fish (16)

industrial policy: a set of government policies designed to enhance a country's ability to compete globally (15)

Industrial Revolution: a process of social, technological, and economic change, beginning in Western Europe in the eighteenth century, that developed and applied new methods of production and work organization, resulting in a great increase in output per worker (15)

infant industry: an industry that is relatively new to its region or country and thus may need to be protected from international competition by trade barriers until it can better compete on world markets (14)

inferior goods: goods for which demand decreases when incomes rise and increases when incomes fall (3)

inflation: a rise in the general level of prices (8)

informal sphere: businesses, usually small in scale, operating outside government oversight and regulation (2)

in-kind transfers: transfers of goods or services (1)

input substitution: increasing the use of some inputs, and decreasing that of others, while producing the same good or service (5)

inputs: resources that go into production (1, 5)

institution: formal and informal rules that structure the relationship between individuals and groups (2)

intermediate goal: a goal that is primarily desirable because its achievement will bring you closer to your final goal(s) (1)

intermediate good: a good that will undergo further processing (8)

internalizing negative externalities: bringing external costs into the market (for example, by instituting a Pigovian tax at a level equal to the externality damage), thus making market participants pay the true social cost of their actions (16)

International Monetary Fund (IMF): an international agency charged with overseeing international finance, including exchange rates, international payments, and balance of payments management (15)

intrinsic value: value related to the tangible or physical properties of the object (11)

investment: an activity intended to increase the quantity or quality of a resource over time (1); spending by businesses undertaken to increase or maintain their productive capacity in order to produce final goods and services for sale (8)

Keynesian economics: the school of thought, named after John Maynard Keynes, that argues for an active government involvement in the economy to keep aggregate demand high and employment rates up through changes in government spending and taxation (9)

Kuznets curve hypothesis: the theory that economic inequality initially increases during the early stages of economic development but then eventually decreases with further economic development (15)

labor force (BLS definition): people who are employed or unemployed (8)

labor force participation rate: the percentage of the adult, noninstitutionalized population that is either working at a paid job or actively seeking paid work (7)

labor intensive: a process or procedure that makes use of more labor relative to other inputs such as capital (15)

labor-intensive production: production using methods that involve a high ratio of labor to capital (14)

labor market discrimination: a condition that exists when, among similarly qualified people, some are treated disadvantageously in employment on the basis of race, sex, age, sexual preference, physical appearance, or disability (7)

labor productivity: the level of output that can be produced per worker per hour (9)

labor unions: legally recognized organizations that collectively bargain for their members (workers) regarding wages, benefits, and working conditions (7)

laissez-faire capitalism: a national system characterized by private corporate ownership and a great reliance on exchange as a mode of coordination, with relatively little coordination by public administration (15)

laissez-faire economy: an economy with little government regulation (2, 9)

leverage: the use of debt to increase the potential rate of return of one's investment (13)

liability: anything that one economic actor owes to another (11)

libertarian paternalism: the policy approach advocated in the 2008 book *Nudge*, where people remain free to make their own choices but are nudged toward specific choices by the way policies are designed and choices are presented (4)

limiting factor: a fixed input that creates a constraint to increasing production (5)

liquidity: the ease of use of an asset as a medium of exchange (11)

liquidity trap: a situation in which interest rates are so low that the central bank finds it impossible to reduce them further (11)

local monopoly: a monopoly limited to a specific geographic area (6)

long run: (in terms of production processes) a period in which all production inputs can be varied in quantity (5)

long-run average cost: the cost of production per unit of output when all inputs can be varied in quantity (5)

M1: a measure of the money supply that includes currency, checkable deposits, and travelers checks (11)

M2: a measure of the money supply that includes all of M1 plus savings deposits, small certificates of deposit, and retail money market funds (11)

macroeconomics: the subfield of economics that focuses on how economic activities at all levels create a national (and global) economic environment (1)

manufactured capital: all physical assets that have been produced by humans using natural capital (1)

marginal analysis: analysis based on incremental changes, comparing marginal benefits to marginal costs (5)

marginal factor cost of labor (MFCL): the amount that a unit of additional labor adds to the firm's costs (7)

marginal product: the additional quantity of output produced by increasing the level of a variable input by one, holding all other inputs constant (5)

marginal propensity to consume: the number of additional dollars of consumption for every additional dollar of income (9)

marginal propensity to save: the number of additional dollars saved for each additional dollar of income (9)

marginal revenue: the additional revenue obtained by selling one more unit. In a perfectly competitive market, marginal revenue equals the market price (6)

marginal revenue product of labor (MRPL): the amount that a unit of additional labor contributes to the revenues of the firm (7)

marginal tax rate: the tax rate applicable to an additional dollar of income (10)

marginal utility: the change in a consumer's utility when consumption of something changes by one unit (4)

marginally attached workers: people who want employment and have looked for work in the past 12 months but not in the past 4 weeks (8)

market (first meaning): a physical place or Web location where there is a reasonable expectation of finding both buyers and sellers for the same product or service (2)

market (second meaning): the interaction of buyers and sellers defined within the bounds of broad product categories, such as the market for used cars or the real estate market (2)

market (third meaning): an economic system (a "market economy") that relies on markets to conduct many economic activities (2)

market clearing equilibrium: a situation in which the quantity supplied equals the quantity demanded, and thus there is no pressure for change in price or quantity bought or sold (3)

market (or aggregate) demand: the amount demanded by all buyers in a particular market (3)

market disequilibrium: a situation of either shortage or surplus (3)

market failure: situations in which markets yield inefficient or inappropriate outcomes (2)

market power: the ability to control, or at least affect, the terms and conditions of a market exchange (2, 6)

market price: the prevailing price for a specific good or service at a particular time in a given market (2, 3)

market quantity sold: the number of "units" of a specific good or service sold in a given market during a particular period (3)

market socialism: a national system in which either state ownership or worker ownership predominates, but much economic activity is coordinated through markets (15)

market (or aggregate) supply: the amount supplied by all sellers in a particular market (3)

market value: the maximum amount that economic actors are willing and able to pay for a good or service (i.e., effective demand) (3)

markup (or cost–plus) pricing: a method of setting prices in which the seller adds a fixed percentage amount to his or her costs of production (3)

maximum capacity output: the level of output an economy would produce if every resource in the economy were fully utilized (12)

maximum efficient scale: the largest size an enterprise can be and still benefit from low long-run average costs (5)

meliorating: starting from the present level of well-being and continuously attempting to do better (4)

microeconomics: the subfield of economics that focuses on activities that take place within and among individuals, households, businesses, and other groups at the subnational level (1)

Millennium Development Goals (MDGs): a set of goals declared by the United Nations in 2000, emphasizing eradication of extreme poverty; promotion of education, gender equity, and health; environmental sustainability; and partnership between rich and poor countries (15)

minimum efficient scale: the smallest size an enterprise can be and still benefit from low long-run average costs (5)

model: an analytical tool that highlights some aspects of reality while ignoring others (2)

modern monetary theory: the belief that fiscal expenditure and taxes determine output and price levels, while money is supplied or withheld merely in response to fiscal policy (11)

monetarism: a school of economic thought that argues that governments should aim for steadiness in the money supply rather than playing an active role (9, 11)

monetary base (or high-powered money): the sum of total currency plus bank reserves (11)

monetary neutrality: the idea that changes in the money supply may affect only prices while leaving output unchanged (11)

monetary policy: the use of policy tools controlled by a nation's central bank to influence interest rates, available credit, and the money supply (11)

money: a medium of exchange that is widely accepted, durable as a store of value, has minimal handling and storage costs, and serves as a unit of account (2)

money multiplier: the ratio of the money supply to the monetary base, indicating by how much the money supply will change for a given change in high-powered money (11)

money supply rule: committing to let the money supply grow at a fixed rate per year (11)

monopsony: a situation in which there is only one buyer but many sellers. This situation occurs in a labor market in which there are many potential workers but only one employer (7)

moral hazard: the creation of perverse incentives that encourage excessive risk-taking because of protections against losses from that risk (13)

multilateral development assistance: aid or loans provided by the World Bank, regional development banks, or UN agencies with the announced intention of promoting development (15)

National Income and Product Accounts (NIPA): a set of statistics compiled by the BEA concerning production, income, spending, prices, and employment (8)

natural capital: physical assets provided by nature (1)

natural monopoly: a monopoly that arises because the minimum efficient scale of the producing unit is large relative to the total market demand (6)

negative (or inverse) relationship: the relationship between two variables if an increase in one variable is associated with a decrease in the other variable (or vice versa) (2)

neoclassical model: a model that portrays the economy as composed of profit-maximizing firms and utility-maximizing households interacting through perfectly competitive markets (4)

net exports: the value of exports less the value of imports (8)

net investment: gross investment minus an adjustment for depreciation of the capital stock (8)

net taxes: taxes minus transfer payments (10)

network externality: (in production) a situation in which a particular technology or production process is more likely to be adopted because other economic actors have already adopted it (6)

neuroeconomics: the interdisciplinary field that studies the role our brains, physiology, and genetics play in how we make economic decisions (4)

nominal (current-dollar) GDP: the dollar value of all final goods and services produced in a year in that year's prices (8)

nonbank financial institution: a financial institution that performs a number of services similar to those offered by banks but that is not a licensed bank and is not subject to banking regulations (13)

non-excludable good: a good whose benefits are freely available to all (2)

non-price competition: competition through activities other than setting prices, such as advertising and location (6)

non-price determinants of demand: any factor that affects the quantity demanded, other than the price of the good or service being demanded (3)

non-price determinants of supply: any factor that affects the quantity supplied, other than the price of the good or service offered for sale (3)

non-renewable resources: resources that cannot be reproduced on a human time-scale, so that their stock diminishes with use, such as oil, coal, and mineral ores (16)

non-rival good: a good whose use by one person does not reduce the quantity or quality available to others (2)

normal goods: goods for which demand increases when incomes rise and decreases when incomes fall (3)

normative questions: questions about how things should be (1)

"not in the labor force" (BLS definition): the classification given to people who are neither "employed" nor "unemployed" (8)

occupational segregation: the tendency of men and women to be employed in different occupations (7)

official reserve account: the account reflecting the foreign exchange market operations of a country's central bank (14)

Okun's "law": an empirical inverse relationship between the unemployment rate and real GDP growth (9)

oligopsony: a situation in which there are only a few major buyers but many sellers. This situation occurs in a labor market when there are many potential workers but just a few large employers (7)

open economy: an economy with a foreign sector (8)

open market operations: sales or purchases of U.S. Treasury bonds by the Fed (11)

opportunity cost: the value of the best alternative that is forgone when a choice is made (1, 14)

outputs: the goods and services that result from production (1, 5)

paradox of thrift: the phenomenon that an increase in intended savings can lead, through a decline in equilibrium income, to lower total savings (9)

path dependence: the idea that the state of a system such as the economy is strongly shaped by its history (6)

perfect competition: a market for the exchange of identical units of a good or service, in which there are numerous small sellers and buyers, all of whom have perfect information (6)

perfectly competitive market: a market in which there are many buyers and sellers, all units of the good are identical, and there is free entry and exit and perfect information (3)

perfectly competitive market equilibrium: the market equilibrium in a perfectly competitive market in which the economic profits of each individual seller are zero and there is no incentive for entry or exit (6)

physical infrastructure: roads, ports, railroads, warehouses, and other tangible structures that provide the foundation for economic activity (2)

Pigovian tax: a tax levied on a product to reduce or eliminate the negative externality associated with its production (16)

positive (or direct) relationship: the relationship between two variables when an increase in one variable is associated with an increase in the other variable or a decrease in one variable is associated with a decrease in the other variable (2)

positive questions: questions about how things are (1)

posted prices: prices set by a seller (2)

poverty line: the income threshold below which members of a population are classified as poor (15)

predatory pricing: a powerful seller's temporary pricing of its goods or services below cost in order to drive weaker competitors out of business (6)

price discrimination: the practice of charging different customers different prices for the same good or service (6)

price-elastic demand: a relationship between price and quantity demanded characterized by relatively strong responses of buyers to price changes (3)

price-elastic demand (technical definition): the percentage change in the quantity demanded is larger than the percentage change in price. The elasticity value is more than 1 in absolute value (3)

price elasticity of demand: the responsiveness of the quantity demanded to a change in price (3)

price elasticity of supply: a measure of the responsiveness of quantity supplied to changes in price (3)

price fixing: a form of collusion in which a group of sellers implicitly agree to maintain a common price (6)

price-inelastic demand: a relationship between price and quantity demanded characterized by relatively weak responses of buyers to price changes (3)

price-inelastic demand (technical definition): the percentage change in the quantity demanded is smaller than the percentage change in price. The elasticity value is less than 1 in absolute value (3)

price leadership: a form of collusion in which many sellers follow the price changes instituted by one particular seller (6)

price maker: a seller that can set the selling price, constrained only by demand conditions (6)

price taker: a seller that has no market power to set price. Price is determined solely by the interaction of market supply and market demand (6)

private good: a good that is excludable and rival (16)

private property: ownership of assets by nongovernment economic actors (2)

procyclical policy: fiscal policy in which taxes are lowered and expenditure is raised when the economy is strong, and the opposite is done when the economy is weak (10)

product markets: markets for newly produced goods and services (2)

production: the conversion of resources into usable products, which may be either goods or services (1)

production function: an equation or graph that represents a relationship between types and quantities of inputs and the quantity of output (5)

production-possibilities frontier (PPF): a curve showing the maximum amounts of two outputs that society could produce from given resources over a given period (1)

profit maximization (under perfect competition): a seller should increase production up to the point where $MR = MC$. As $MR = P$ under perfect competition, we can also define the profit-maximizing solution by setting $P = MC$ (6)

profits: the difference between total revenues and total costs (6)

progressive tax: a tax in which the percentage of one's income paid in taxes tends to increase with increasing income levels (10)

proportional tax: a tax in which all taxpayers pay the same tax rate, regardless of income (10)

protectionism: the use of government policies to restrict trade with other countries and protect domestic industries from foreign competition (14)

public good: a good whose benefits are freely available to anyone and whose use by one person does not diminish its usefulness to others (2, 16)

public purpose sphere: governments and other local, national, and international organizations established for a public purpose beyond individual or family self-interest and not operating with the goal of making a profit (2)

purchasing power parity (PPP): the theory that exchange rates should reflect differences in purchasing power among countries (14)

purchasing power parity (PPP) adjustments: adjustments to international income statistics to take into account the differences in the cost of living across countries (14)

quantitative easing (QE): the purchase of financial assets, including long-term bonds, by the Fed, creating more monetary reserves and expanding the money supply (11)

quantity equation: $M \times V = P \times Y$, where M is the money supply, V is the velocity of money, P is the price level, and Y is real output (11)

quantity theory of money: the theory that money supply is directly related to nominal GDP, according to the equation $M \times \bar{V} = P \times Y$ (11)

race to the bottom: a situation in which countries, regions, or cities compete in providing low-cost business environments, resulting in deterioration in labor, environmental, or safety standards (14)

rationalist investigation: analysis based on abstract thought and the use of logic and reason (2)

real exchange rate: the exchange rate between two currencies, adjusted for inflation in each country (14)

real GDP: a measure of gross domestic product that seeks to reflect the actual value of goods and services produced by removing the effect of changes in prices over time (8)

real money supply: the nominal money supply divided by the general price level (as measured by a price index), expressed as M/P (12)

real wealth effect: the tendency of consumers to increase or decrease their consumption based on their perceived level of wealth (12)

recession: a downturn in economic activity, usually defined as lasting for two consecutive calendar quarters or more (9)

reference group: the group to which an individual compares himself or herself (4)

regressive tax: a tax in which the percentage of one's income paid in taxes tends to decrease with increasing income levels (10)

regulated monopoly: a monopoly run under government supervision (6)

regulation: setting standards or laws to govern behavior (2)

relative deprivation: the feeling of lack that comes from comparing oneself with someone who has more (4)

renewable resources: resources that are regenerated over a short term through natural and biological processes, such as forests, fisheries, and freshwater (16)

required reserves: the portion of bank reserves that banks must keep on reserve (11)

resource management: preserving or improving the resources that contribute to the enhancement of well-being, including natural, manufactured, human, and social resources (1)

restorative development: economic progress that restores economic, financial, social, or ecological systems that have been degraded and are no longer adequately supportive of human well-being in the present and the future (1)

revaluation: raising an exchange rate within a fixed exchange rate system (14)

revenue-neutral (taxes): offsetting any tax increases with decreases in other taxes such that overall tax collections remain constant (16)

rival good: a good whose use by one person reduces the quantity or quality available to others (16)

satellite accounts: additional accounting systems that provide measures of social and environmental factors in physical terms, without necessarily including monetary valuation (8)

satisfice: to choose an outcome that would be satisfactory and then seek an option that at least reaches that standard (4)

saving: refraining from consumption in the current period (1)

Say's law: the classical belief that "supply creates its own demand" (9)

scarcity: the concept that resources are not sufficient to allow all goals to be accomplished at once (1)

securitization: the process of pooling various kinds of loans, slicing and sorting them according to their risk levels, and repackaging them into financial instruments (13)

self-correcting market: a market that automatically adjusts to any imbalances between sellers and buyers (3)

shortage: a situation in which the quantity demanded at a particular price exceeds the quantity that sellers are willing to supply (3)

short run: (in terms of production processes) a period in which at least one production input has a fixed quantity (5)

social capital: the institutions and the stock of trust, mutual understanding, shared values, and socially held knowledge that facilitate the social coordination of economic activity (1)

social cost of carbon: a monetary estimate of the discounted long-term damages from emitting a ton of CO_2 in a given year (16)

social insurance taxes: taxes used to fund social insurance programs such as Social Security, Medicare, and Medicaid (10)

social value: the extent to which an outcome moves us toward our final goals (3)

specialization: in production, a system of organization in which each worker performs only one type of task (9)

stagflation: a combination of rising inflation and economic stagnation (12)

standard of living: the quality of people's diet; housing; medical care; education; working conditions; and access to transportation, communication, entertainment, and other amenities (1)

status quo bias: a cognitive bias in favor of that which is familiar, expected, or automatic (4)

steady-state economy: an economy that holds constant population and the stock of physical capital (16)

stock: the quantity of something at a particular point in time (1)

stock-flow diagram: an illustration of how stocks can be changed, over time, by flows (1)

strong sustainability: an analytical perspective suggesting that natural capital depreciation is justified only if it is compensated for with adequate restoration of other natural capital (16)

structural unemployment: unemployment that arises because people's skills, experience, education, or location do not match what employers need (9)

subjective well-being (SWB): a measure of welfare based on survey questions asking people about their own degree of life satisfaction (8)

subprime mortgage: a mortgage given to someone with high debt levels, relatively low income, or poor credit (13)

subsidy: a per-unit payment to producers to lower production costs and encourage greater production (16)

substitute good: a good that can be used in place of another good (3)

sunk cost: an expenditure that was incurred or committed to in the past and is irreversible in the short run (6)

supply: the willingness of producers and merchandisers to provide goods and services (3)

supply curve: a curve indicating the quantities that sellers are willing to supply at various prices (3)

supply schedule: a table showing the relationship between price and quantity supplied (3)

supply shock: a change in the productive capacity of an economy (12)

surplus: a situation in which the quantity that sellers are prepared to sell at a particular price exceeds the quantity that buyers are willing to buy at that price (3)

Sustainable Development Goals (SDGs): a set of goals set forth by the United Nations in 2015, building on and expanding the MDGs, including goals such as promoting inclusive growth and limiting climate change (15)

tacit collusion: collusion that takes place without creation of a cartel (6)

tariffs: taxes (or duties) charged by national governments to the importers of goods from other countries (14)

tax multiplier: the impact of a change in a lump sum tax on economic equilibrium, expressed mathematically as $\Delta Y / \Delta \overline{T}$ (10)

taxable income: the portion of one's income that is subject to taxation after deductions and exemptions (10)

technological progress: the development of new products and new, more efficient methods of production (1)

technological unemployment: unemployment caused by reduced demand for workers because technology has increased the productivity of those who have jobs (9)

theory of market adjustment: the theory that market forces will tend to make shortages and surpluses disappear (3)

throughput: the flow of raw materials and energy through the economy, leading to outputs of waste (16)

time discount rate: an economic concept describing the relative weighting of present benefits or costs compared to future benefits or costs (4)

time lags: the time that elapses between the formulation of an economic policy and its actual effects on the economy (10)

time-series data: observations of how a numerical variable changes over time (0, 1)

"too big to fail": when a company grows so large that its failure would cause widespread economic harm in terms of lost jobs and diminished asset values (13)

total cost: the sum of fixed and variable costs (5)

total cost curve: a graph showing the relationship between the total cost of production and the level of output (5)

total product curve: a curve showing the total amount of output produced with different levels of one variable input, holding all other inputs constant (5)

total revenues: the total amount of money received by a seller, equal to price times quantity sold (6)

trade account (part of the current account): the portion of the current account that tracks inflows and outflows arising exclusively from international trade in goods and services (14)

trade deficit: an excess of imports over exports, causing net exports to be negative (14)

trade quota: a nationally imposed restriction on the quantity of a particular good that can be imported from another country (14)

trade-related subsidy: payments given by governments to producers to encourage more production, either for export or as a substitute for imports (14)

trade surplus: an excess of exports over imports, causing net exports to be positive (14)

transaction costs: the costs of arranging economic activities (2)

transfer: the giving of something with nothing specific expected in return (1)

transfer payments (TR): payments by government to individuals or firms, including Social Security payments, unemployment compensation, interest payments, and subsidies (10)

triple bottom line: an assessment of the performance of a business according to social and environmental as well as financial performance (5)

unconditional cash transfer (UCT): programs providing cash to the poor with no specific conditions on how the funds should be spent (15)

underemployment: working fewer hours than desired or at a job that does not match one's skills (8)

unemployed person (BLS definition): a person who is not employed but who is actively seeking a job and is immediately available for work (8)

unemployment rate: the percentage of the labor force made up of people who do not have paid jobs but are immediately available and actively looking for paid jobs (8)

unit-elastic demand: the percentage change in the quantity demanded is exactly equal to the percentage change in price. The elasticity value is -1 (3)

upstream taxes: taxes instituted as close as possible in a production process to the extraction of raw materials (16)

utility: the level of usefulness or satisfaction gained from a particular activity, such as consumption of a good or service (2, 4)

utility function (or total utility curve): a curve showing the relation of utility levels to consumption levels (4)

variable costs: production costs that can be adjusted relatively quickly and that do not need to be incurred if no production occurs (5)

variable input: a production input whose quantity can be changed relatively quickly, resulting in changes in the level of production (5)

velocity of money: the number of times that a dollar would have to change hands during a year to support nominal GDP, calculated as $V = (P \times Y)/M$ (11)

virtuous cycles (in development): self-reinforcing patterns of high savings, investment, productivity growth, and economic expansion (15)

voluntary simplicity: a conscious decision to live with limited or reduced level of consumption in order to increase one's quality of life (4)

wage and price controls: government regulations setting limits on wages and prices or on the rates at which they are permitted to increase (12)

wage-price spiral: when upward pressure on wages creates upward pressure on prices and, as a result, further upward pressure on wages (12)

Washington Consensus: specific economic policy prescriptions used by the IMF and World Bank with a goal of helping developing countries to avoid crisis and maintain stability. They include openness to trade and investment (liberalization), privatization, budget austerity, and deregulation (15)

waste products: outputs that are not used either for consumption or in a further production process (1)

weak sustainability: an analytical perspective suggesting that natural capital depreciation is justified as long as it is compensated for with adequate increases in other types of capital (16)

well-being: a term used broadly to describe a good quality of life (1)

World Bank: an international agency charged with promoting economic development through loans and other programs (15)

World Trade Organization (WTO): an international organization that conducts trade negotiations aimed at lowering trade barriers, creates rules to govern trade, and mediates trade disputes between countries (14)

Index

Note: Page numbers in italics indicate figures; page numbers in bold indicate tables.

trade-related subsidy: definition of 460;
protectionism 460
trade surplus: definition of 463;
macroeconomic picture 463
trade war, United States and China 459
traditional goals: good living standards
27–28; stability and security 28–29;
sustainability 29–30
transaction costs: definition of 71; markets
70–71
transfer, definition of 33
transfer payments: definition of 311;
government budget 310–311; taxes and
321–323
Treasury bills (T–bills) 335
triple bottom line 148; definition of 148
Troubled Asset Relief Program (TARP)
416–418
Trump, Donald 459
Trump Administration 214, 314, 319–320,
368, 419, 433; interest rates 390; tax cuts
339; trade deficit of U.S. 472
trust, social institutions of 64–65
Turkey, percentage population living below
poverty line *17*

Uganda: percentage population living
below poverty line *17*; population in
multidimensional poverty and income
poverty **486**
Ukraine: income inequality (Gini coefficient)
16; percentage population living below
poverty line *17*
"Ultimatum Game" 125
unconditional cash transfer (UCT):
definition of 498; economic growth
498–499
underemployment, definition of 264
underground markets **67**
understanding: empiricism 46–49;
rationalism 49–50; theory and evidence
50–51
unemployed person 260; definition of 260
unemployment: cyclical 284; financial
crisis (2007–2008) 414; frictional 284;
Keynesian theory *301*; persistent, and
Keynesian labor market theory 300–302;
structural 285; technological 285–286;
vicious cycle of *414*
unemployment rate 4, 261–262; calculating
262; definition of 261; description of
6, 13; by groups **262**; Okun's law 282;
percent of labor force (2018) 13, *13*; real

GDP growth rate and **47**; United States
(1960–2018) *6*
Union Bank of Switzerland (UBS) 373
United Arab Emirates, trade balance on
goods and services (2017) *15*
United Kingdom: average annual hours
worked (2018) *231*; average inflation rate
(2009–2018) *14*; average PISA science
score (2015) *18*; Behavioral Insights Team
138–139; carbon dioxide emissions per
capita (2014) *20*; exports and imports as
percent of GDP (2017) *457*; GDP per
capita (2018) *12*; Gini coefficient for
income and wealth (2018) *501*; income
inequality (Gini coefficient) *16*; life
expectancy at birth (2017) *19*; time bank
66; UK Office of National Statistics 251;
unemployment rate (2018) *13*
United Nations: absolute deprivation
definition of 129; Food and Agriculture
Organization 517; global population
projections (2020–2100) *516*; Green
Economy Initiative 534–535; Human
Development Index (HDI) 274–275;
Millennium Development Goals (MDGs)
504–506; satellite accounts 280n11;
Sustainable Development Goals 505–506,
513; Sustainable Development Goals
(SDGs) 17, 40
United Nations Development Programme
(UNDP): financial capital 496; *Human
Development Report* 486
United States (U.S.): advertising regulations
140; annual growth rates of wages,
salaries, and corporate profit *430*; average
annual hours worked (2018) *231*; average
inflation rate (2009–2018) *14*; average
PISA science score (2015) *18*; balance
of payments (2018) account **471**; Better
Life Index (BLI) 273, *274*; carbon
dioxide emissions per capita (2014) *20*;
change in tax rates by income group
(1962–2014) *434*; climate policies 545;
concentration ratios for select industries
199; consumption taxation 140; corporate
taxes in 314; domestic and foreign
ownership of U.S. debt (1970–2018) *336*;
ecological footprint per capita (2016)
135; exports and imports as percent of
GDP (2017) *457*; extreme poverty in
485; federal outlays, receipts and surplus/
deficit (1980–2018) *317*; federal surplus
or deficit as percent of GDP (1930–2018)